The

ROLLS

RR

ROYCE

40/50hp

Sir Henry Royce with the prototype Phantom II at Le Lavandon in the South of France. The photograph was taken on 12th April 1930. (The car was code named S.S. or Super Sport. The chassis number was 18EX, later changed to EX-69GX). See Part II, Chapters 1, 2 and 3 *(photo M.H. Evans)*

The
ROLLS-ROYCE
40/50 hp

Ghosts, Phantoms and Spectres

W J Oldham

G T FOULIS

First published November 1974

ISBN 0 85429 162 8

Library of Congress Catalog Card Number 74-18751

Printed in England by J H Haynes and Company Limited
for the publishers

G T FOULIS & CO LTD
Sparkford Yeovil Somerset BA22 7JJ England

Bound by the Wigmore Bindery Poole Dorset England

Distributed in the USA by

MOTORBOOKS INTERNATIONAL
3501 Hennepin Avenue South
Minneaplois Minnesota 55408

CONTENTS

DEDICATION

This book is dedicated to the memory of the Honourable C S Rolls, Claude Goodman Johnson, Sir Henry Royce and Ernest A Claremont who were the original founders

FOREWORD

My object in this foreword, as an independent but sympathetic observer, is to indicate to the reader something of the purpose of the book and at the same time to introduce the Author and to say those things about him which modesty must otherwise have left unsaid.

It gives me real pleasure to be allowed to do these things.

I have of course known of John Oldham for many years as an Author and as a most dedicated enthusiast for the marque Rolls-Royce; we first met however in 1967 at that splendid hostelry, the Leicester Arms at Penshurst in Kent. John and I had arranged to meet so that I might see his Phantom II, 74GN, of which you will read the extraordinary history in Part II Chapter 8. At that time the car was still fitted with the enormous bus body which he had converted to a roomy and well designed caravan. The sheer enormity of the vehicle left one speechless but we spent some absorbing hours together, and from then on we have been in regular contact on matters Rolls-Royce. John has been a member of the Rolls-Royce Enthusiasts' Club for some years, having been introduced by Peter Baines when living in Cornwall.

Now resident in Jersey, he has been researching the Phantoms for several years, and we have frequently had long conversations, mostly on the telephone, as new information came to light and new sources were uncovered.

When, after much deliberation John told me that he proposed writing a book on the 40/50 cars, I was delighted because I knew what an authority he had become on this particular subject.

Few people can match the extent and depth of his knowledge in this field. His personal and family associations with Rolls-Royce cars, over so many years, comes out clearly in this book which represents a piece of powerful, sustained and detailed research, culminating in a factual and historically accurate story, for to John a fact is a fact only when it can properly be sustained by the evidence and yet he has kept the book eminently entertaining.

It was John Oldham who in his book 'The Hyphen in Rolls-Royce' first told the full story of Claude Johnson, without whom it is improbable that the Rolls-Royce Company would have survived.

John has motored many thousands of miles in Rolls-Royce cars. He uses his Phantom II Continental 101 SK; The Amsterdam Show and ex-Indian Trials car, regularly for long distance motoring; his 20/25 for shorter hauls, and a truly superb Phantom III, 3-AZ-146, for really exotic motoring.

This car, a Hooper Pullman enclosed drive limousine must be one of the finest of these great twelve cylinder cars existing anywhere. To be wafted along in a superbly maintained Phantom III is one of the most sophisticated and enjoyable experiences in motoring. Alas, all too many of these cars have died or are dying of poor maintenance and uninhibited corrosion. The good specimens therefore, are all the more valuable as a memorial to fine design and the highest standards of workmanship of their day.

The book traces the development of the 40/50 hp, from 1906 onwards. Wherever enthusiasts meet, stories are bandied about which have become established legend. Stories of the experimental cars, stories of the 'Continentals', snippets of fact heavily larded with myth.

Now, for the first time, the full story is told; the Springfield tale is told, and fabulous adventures across desert and mountain.

In so far as the evidence is still available, history has been coherently recorded in a polished and absorbing book, which will become a standard work on every discerning motorist's book shelf.

by Lt Col Eric B Barrass, O B E , T D
Secretary, Rolls-Royce Enthusiasts' Club

1

Publisher's Note about the photographs

To retain strict authenticity of photographic reproduction none of the photographs have been 'improved' in any way. Where the original, often the only photograph available, is poor, it will appear to be poor here.

G T Foulis & Co Ltd
November 1974

ACKNOWLEDGEMENTS

It would be impracticable to acknowledge by name everyone who assisted me in compiling this book but I cannot let the assistance given me by the following go unrecorded, for without their particular help it would have been impossible.

Ivan F Evernden, formerly a member of Royce's design team and responsible for the coachwork on all Experimental chassis, has given me unbounded assistance and I am more than grateful to him.

Michael Havryn Evans, formerly Historical Information Officer, Public Relations Dept, Rolls-Royce Ltd, Derby, and the Company's Official Historian, has shown enthusiasm and interest and has lent me many documents which I could not have seen but for his help and kindness.

I have been greatly assisted too by W A Robotham, formerly in charge of the Experimental Department; Dennis Miller-Williams, in charge of Public Relations at the London Showrooms, who always made me welcome at Conduit Street, and gave me the run of the building to look up old records; Ron Haynes, Service Promotions Department, Hythe Road, Willesden, who took endless trouble supplying the answers to many questions regarding production chassis.

H F Hamilton, or 'Hoppy' as he is usually known, who accompanied the Phantom III chassis No. 34 EX on its epic journey across the Sahara to Nairobi, read my typescript and took the trouble to come over to Jersey to tell me more about this journey.

Glen Dickson, formerly librarian at Derby, allowed me to search the files in his charge and gave me photographs of my Phantom II Continental, Chassis No. 101 SK, taken when the car was out in India.

Dr Robin Barnard, who checked facts for me in the back files of *The Autocar* and other motor journals published before World War I.

Francis W Hutton-Stott, well known collector of Lanchester cars. Derek and Carol Randall, the former editors of the Rolls-Royce Enthusiasts' Club magazine, *The Bulletin*. Captain Peter Baines, Assistant Secretary and Nigel Hughes, Technical Secretary of the Rolls-Royce Enthusiasts' Club. Anne Waddilove for typing the manuscript and my wife, Margaret, who has done all the proof reading.

There are also many trans-atlantic friends who gave me invaluable assistance with the American Springfield built cars. My thanks are especially due to Dr Mark Sheppard, who put me in touch with John McFarlane, the former editor of *The Flying Lady*, R D Shaffner of the Rolls-Royce Phantom III Technical Society, Horton Schoellkopf, Register-Editor of the Rolls-Royce Owners Club, Inc. and finally Arthur W Soutter, who has written me reams of fascinating letters in answer to my many questions about Springfield and the cars that were built there; he spent almost his entire working life at Springfield and has been kind enough to read and check my chapters which deal with this project, so ensuring a degree of knowledge and accuracy I could never have achieved without his help.

The following have been most helpful and tolerant in supplying me with any information they had and allowing me to photograph the individual cars I wanted to use as examples of their type:

Stanley E Sears, the owner of Chassis Numbers 1721, 76 TC, 31 GX, 3-AZ-38 and 3-DL-76.

John G Hampton, the owner of 120 EU.

Stuart J Skinner, the owner of 1298.

David Berry, the owner of 9GX.

Lady Freda Valentine, the owner of 1 OR.

Kenneth Jenner, the owner of 53 DC.

Douglas Fitzpatrick, the owner of 74 SC and 3-CM-181.

A Meredith-Owens, the owner of 10 EX and 188 PY.

Douglas Worrall, the owner of 26 EX.

F M Wilcock, the owner of 3-AZ-186

Finally, throughout the preparation and writing of this book, my friend Eric Barrass, Secretary of the Rolls-Royce Enthusiasts' Club, has given me enormous encouragement and advice and also willingly agreed to write a foreword.

PREFACE

This book tells the story of the Rolls-Royce 40/50 hp cars which were made in four types over a period of 33 years.

The first model which came to be known as 'The Silver Ghost', was made from 1906 to 1925; the 'New Phantom' from 1925 to 1929; the 'Phantom II' was introduced late in 1929 and was in production until May 1935. This model was superceded in October that year by the 'Phantom III' which remained current until the outbreak of war in 1939.

Today, almost 35 years after the last Phantom III left the Derby works, any 40/50 hp Rolls-Royce is a sought-after treasure and will command a high price even in poor condition.

Each model has its particular devotees and whilst those 'Silver Ghosts' which were built before the 1914 War are the most valued collectors' pieces, they are no longer practicable vehicles for everyday motoring. On the other hand, a Phantom II in good condition is a most serviceable car and a really good Phantom III, with its light steering, superb brakes, a top speed of nearly a hundred miles an hour, excellent acceleration and the smooth torque of its twelve cylinder engine, is still an outstanding vehicle, albeit very expensive to repair.

In this book, I have endeavoured to set the scene for the birth of these luxurious motor carriages, to sketch in a brief history of the Rolls-Royce Company and then to describe the four models in as much detail as possible, providing typical examples of individual cars and their achievements both in the hands of their original owners and, where possible, their present owners. I have been particularly fortunate in being able to unearth the individual histories of many of the prototype or 'Experimental' cars.

From a massive array of photographs I have tried to select those which tell us as much as possible about the cars, their coachwork and particularly the rear - end treatment which differs almost from car to car. I hope many of these photographs will be new even to members of the specialist Rolls-Royce clubs.

Finally, I have assembled for easy reference, in Appendix A, as much data about individual chassis (by number) as the records provide, and in Appendix B, a most welcome bonus from my researches, some enlightening comments by the great F H Royce himself.

INTRODUCTION *

In the 35 years since 1939 a new generation has grown up who now own and enjoy the pre-War Rolls-Royce motor cars about which this book has been written.

The pattern of life of the people for whom these lovely cars were built is inconceivable to those who were not able to experience it. It was a life of unbelievable opulence and luxury, a life which has, for better or worse, gone for ever. For those who might be interested I will try and re-call the memories of my youth and attempt to set the scene into which the Rolls-Royce Phantom II and 20/25 were introduced in September 1929.

My mother, governess, five indoor staff, my brother and I lived in a house in Eaton Place, London SW1.

This was the area known as Belgravia and was considered to be one of the most fashionable parts of London. The big terraced houses, which had been erected in the mid-19th century by that famous builder Thomas Cubitt (1788-1855), were still being run as private residences, staffed with butlers, footmen and several maidservants. Various retired staff have told me that, back in 1929, life as a domestic in one of these houses could be quite pleasant, given that the employer was reasonably kind and

*This introduction was written before the ITV Series *Upstairs, Downstairs* was screened

considerate. 'Below Stairs' was a community of its own with its own code and rules, the butler would be in charge, the front room in the basement (or 'area' as it was usually called) was generally the servants recreation room, known as 'the Servants' Hall'.

On winter evenings, my brother and I, with our governess, would walk home to Eaton Place from Hyde Park at Albert Gate through Lowndes Square, Lowndes Street, etc. and we would see these cosy rooms brilliantly illuminated by electric light, a bright fire burning in the grate and the entire staff of the household sitting round the table having their tea; the butler seated at the head of the table, the cook (usually his wife) at the opposite end, and various members of the staff along each side. I have never been able to discover the reason why at this time in the evenings the curtains were not drawn; but it was a favourite occupation with us boys to decide whom we considered were enjoying the best meal, incidentally the table was always well laden, and each room looked a secure and comfortable world of its own.

Each member of the household staff had their own duties to perform. People sometimes wonder what they all did; it must be remembered that there were very few modern conveniences in most of these houses at the time; there was no central heating, fires were lighted in the bedrooms each day in the winter and all the coals had to be carried upstairs. Most houses did not have basins with running hot and cold water in the bedrooms so the hot water also had to be carried up in cans from below stairs. The work was hard, with only half a day off per week allowed in most households, with every alternate Sunday, but the compensations, in a 'good place' were security more or less for life, good food and clothes and a sense of belonging. The senior servants, who had often started in the household straight from school, were treated with respect and had the privilege of being waited-on by the more junior members.

Today, few can afford to run these graceful houses, the majority of them having been converted into spacious flats, or become an embassy or offices; the roads are lined with modern family saloon cars, many of which are owned by commuters and are parked almost

bumper to bumper on both sides of the streets. It was a very different picture in 1929; apart from the introduction of the motorcar, Belgravia was still enjoying a leisurely existence. There was very little traffic, almost all the cars belonging to the occupants of the houses were chauffeur driven limousines and landaulettes (or, as the Americans would say 'Formal Town Cars'). Some would be accompanied by a footman who sat in front beside the chauffeur dressed in livery to match his, which in many cases was chosen to tone with the colour of the car in his charge. The mews behind the houses where in years gone by the carriages and horses were stabled and the coachmen and grooms lived, had been converted into garages, with the living quarters for the chauffeur and his family over the top.

In the morning, the streets would be almost empty, apart from a horse-drawn cart making deliveries of coal which were shot through the iron manholes in the middle of the pavement. Whilst occasionally a Harrods' electric van out on its rounds passed silently along, or a delivery man could be seen running down the area steps to the back door (to deliver anything to the front door of the houses was unthinkable). Sometimes a street musician would appear and collect a few pennies, but he would usually be moved on quietly by the police, as several houses in Eaton Place bore a rather pompous notice on the area railings which read 'street hawkers, musicians, and others, are forbidden to proclaim their wares near these premises'. It was in the evening when an 'At Home' was taking place or when it was time to set off to the theatre or a dinner party, that these great houses were a blaze of light, and scenes of great activity took place. It was a splendid sight to see a dignified chauffeur-driven car standing at the door, its interior lighted, with the footman holding open the door, as the owners came out of the house in full evening dress attended by the head of the household staff, carrying rugs and cushions, etc., then, with the interior lights of the car still on and the silk blind drawn down across the division so that the chauffeur did not have the reflection on his windscreen, the car would glide away.

In the side streets around Belgravia and

Mayfair there were various public houses, *The Antelope*, *The Running Footman* and *The Grenadier*, were some of the most popular, where the chauffeurs and butlers from these houses congregated in their off-duty moments. For years it had been an unwritten law that the butler, cook, coachman etc., had 'perks' from the firm which supplied his or her employer; with the advent of the motorcar, the chauffeur took the place of the coachman, and in many establishments, it was the chauffeur who advised his employer what make of car to purchase and the same applied to tyres, oil, etc.

One ex-employee of Messrs Barker and Co., the coachbuilders, told me that most of his business was done in these public houses by talking to the various chauffeurs, plying them with drinks and arranging suitable terms of commission on the type of car and coachwork which he would persuade his employer to buy.

Some owners took such a liking to the coachwork on their existing chassis that when they bought a new car the old body was transferred on to the new chassis. The Rolls-Royce 20 hp, chassis No. 58-S-1, which now belongs to Stanley E Sears, illustrates this - the landaulette body was built by Hamshaw of Leicester in 1910 for Lord Lonsdale and he had it transferred on to his new 20 hp chassis which he purchased in 1923.

An amusing story of the transfer of a body concerns a 1908 Lanchester 20 hp Landaulette which belonged to a Mrs Hayes-Jackson of Tunbridge Wells. She had bought this car new and used it every day until about 1937, when one day as the car was parked at the top of Mount Ephraim whilst the chauffeur was shopping; Mrs Hayes-Jackson was sitting in the back of the car, the hand-brake slipped and the car started to move. Fortunately a passer-by averted a possible disaster by jumping in and re-applying the hand-brake but Mrs Hayes-Jackson was so frightened she felt it was time to change to a more up-to-date vehicle. However, she could not bear to part with what had been 'part of the scenery' for so long, so she bought an Austin 16 hp chassis, brand new, and had the body transferred from the Lanchester onto the Austin 16, so that as she rode in the Austin she had the impression she was still in the Lanchester! It so

happened that just about this time Francis Hutton-Stott and the late Richard Shuttleworth were in Tunbridge Wells to see if they could find any old cars which had been the property of that great motoring pioneer, Sir David Salomans, of Broom Hill, Tunbridge Wells. Francis heard about Mrs Hayes-Jackson and promptly bought the Lanchester chassis at the same time he kept in touch with Dutton, the chauffeur, and one day during the War he received a somewhat ambiguous telegram. It read 'my mistress has passed away, body now for sale!'. Francis was delighted and immediately bought the body which after the War was re-united with the 1908 chassis.

Although the majority of people did not go to these lengths in having their old carriage work transferred on to a new chassis, at the same time, there was usually no question of a part-exchange; if the coachbuilder's representative could 'talk' the chauffeur into persuading his employer to buy a new car it was more than likely that the old one would be kept and simply relegated to the back of the garage.

About this time, early 1930s, my mother rented one of a pair of garages in Lower Belgrave Mews South, which, many years earlier had been stables, from Lady Cory who was a Rolls-Royce owner and in the other garage there were three Rolls-Royce 40/50 hps. They all carried Barker limousine coachwork; the one in daily use was a Phantom II but when this car went into the service station at Cricklewood, the 'New Phantom', which was about 1926, was put on the road. Standing in the back of the garage, jacked up and sheeted down with dustsheets, was an open-fronted limousine of about 1921 which I do not remember ever seeing on the road. Right down at the bottom of the mews, which was a cul-de-sac, Lord Carsons' Daimlers were garaged; this was a very large garage and there were at least six Daimlers in it, two of which were definitely pre - the 1914 War.

Unfortunately, the head chauffeur who worked for Lord Carson was a very 'touchy' person and he objected strongly to my brother and I going anywhere near his charges, so we were never able to see exactly what was in the garage. This area held an irresistible attraction for two small boys; we used to wander about around 10 am when there was a scene of great activity; all the chauffeurs busy working on and cleaning the cars, there was quite a spirit of rivalry amongst them in turning out the best car. Almost every luxury car that one can think of existed in Belgravia Mews South; Rolls-Royce, Daimler, Lanchester, Minerva, Packard, Lincoln, Cadillac, Delauney-Belleville, Panhard-Levassor, Bentley, Crossley, Armstrong-Siddeley and Humber in some form or other, but there were more Daimlers than any other make.

Some of the owners employed more than one chauffeur, normally a head chauffeur with a second chauffeur under him, but in busy times, such as the London Season or for the Grouse Shooting in Scotland, when all the cars would be in use at the same time there were people who employed special additional chauffeurs.

Life in Belgravia continued more or less without change up to September 1939; most of the cars were then either laid up in their garages or taken out of London to the owners' country house for safety.

When the bombs began to fall on London and I came home on leave from the R A F, all private motoring had ceased; my mother's two cars were both laid up in Belgrave Mews South and our chauffeur had gone to work in a munition factory, whilst my mother drove herself around London in a horse-drawn trap. After a particularly heavy raid one night my mother and I walked round the mews to have a look at the cars to see if they were alright; the doors to our garage were perfectly sound, but some of the others had been forced open by the blast from the bombs, and in the garage on the opposite side of the mews we were able to see three 20/25 Rolls-Royce Sedancas standing on blocks and sheeted down.

When the War was over in 1945, it was a very different life to which everyone came home. Though some chauffeurs returned to Belgrave Mews South it was never the same as it had been in pre-War days. None of the big closed cars which had stood in the back of the garages there were ever seen again. I have often wondered what happened to them as none of them have ever appeared in either the Veteran or Vintage Car Clubs. I have often discussed this with people and have come to the conclusion that these cars must have been given away by their owners to the Government for War service, but because they were old and extravagant on petrol they were simply scrapped for the material they had in them. Today Belgrave Mews South consists in the main of small expensive luxury houses, which have been made out of the garages which once housed some of the most magnificent cars that have ever been built.

Such, then, was the social background of the 40/50 hp Rolls-Royce and it is ironic to think that the present fashionable generation lives in the quarters that their grandparents would have considered as suitable only for domestic staff whilst many of them are seeking out their grandparents' chauffeur-driven Rolls-Royce limousines for the pleasure of driving them themselves.

W J Oldham
Jersey 1974

PART I CHAPTER 1

The background and early life of the three partners, the Hon Charles Stewart Rolls; Claude Goodman Johnson and Frederick Henry Royce, the story of how these three men evolved the Rolls-Royce car. The early models which were built by Royce prior to the first 40/50 h p car

For over six decades the Rolls-Royce motor car has been universally acknowledged as 'The Best Car in the World', a phrase coined by Lord Northcliffe in appreciation of the products of the three partners, the Hon Charles Stewart Rolls, Claude Goodman Johnson and Frederick Henry Royce, who were Lord Northcliffe's personal friends and who between them were responsible for the design, production and publicity which created this legendary motor car.

Each in his own sphere played one important part; the three men worked as a team in founding the Company which came to be known as 'Rolls-Royce Ltd'. The early history of the Company has been written so often that it is only necessary to give a very brief outline here - first, something about the three partners.

The Hon C S Rolls was third son and youngest child of Lord and Lady Llangattock of Monmouth; he was born at their London home, 35 Hill Street, Berkeley Square, Mayfair, on 27 August 1877.

The Llangattocks were immensely wealthy and, in addition to the town house, owned a vast estate known as 'The Hendre', just outside the County Town of Monmouth on the borders of Wales.

Charlie, as he was always known amongst his friends, was educated at a Preparatory School, Mortimer Vicarage School, in Berkshire; from there he went to Eton and then on to Cambridge, where he obtained a B A degree. His principle interest had always been in anything mechanical or technical and he demonstrated this by being the first undergraduate at Cambridge to have a motor car of his own. This was in 1896 and when, the following year, the Automobile Club of Great Britain and Ireland was founded, with Claude Johnson as the first Secretary, Charlie became one of the first members. His exploits with early cars were legion and there is no need to go into them here; sufficient to say that by 1903 Charlie Rolls, now aged 26, had decided that his future lay in the motor business and he opened premises in Brook Street, Mayfair, trading as C S Rolls and Company. Later he moved his showrooms to 14/15 Conduit Street, which are the London offices of Rolls-Royce Ltd to this day.

Not very long after C S Rolls started in business, Claude Johnson was becoming rather bored with his position as the Secretary of the Automobile Club of Great Britain and Ireland. He was one of the most brilliant organizers imaginable. He had arranged the first motor exhibition in London, which took place in the grounds of the Imperial Institute in 1896 and it was the tremendous success of this event that led CJ *(as he was always known later at Rolls-Royce Ltd) to be invited by the Club, who had premises at 4 Whitehall Court, London, S W 1 to be their first Secretary at a salary of £5 per week and ten shillings commission for every new member.

He took up this position in the November of 1897 when the membership stood at 163; when he resigned in June 1903, the membership had grown to over 2,000 and when he left his duties were taken over by three men! He had known Charlie Rolls for about 6 years and was delighted when Charlie suggested he became his partner in his business. C S Rolls concentrated on buying imported foreign cars, Panhard-Levassor and Minerva, which he sold

*Reference to senior management by their initials is traditional with Rolls-Royce: Royce himself was always known as 'R', Claud Johnson as 'CJ', Claremont as 'EAC', Sidgreaves as 'Sg', Hives as 'Hs', Robotham as 'Rm' and so on.

to English clients as he was not particularly impressed with the British cars that were available at this time.

The two men had completely different backgrounds - whereas C S Rolls came from wealthy aristocratic stock, CJ was born at Datchet, near Windsor, on 24 October 1864, the younger son of a family of 7 children, whose father had been a glover at one time, and who ended up as a clerk at the South Kensington Museum with a pittance of a salary. Johnson was some 13 years senior to Rolls, he was 39 when they embarked on this new enterprise together, the success of which was to exceed their wildest dreams.

At the time the partnership was being formed between Rolls and Johnson, Frederick Henry Royce was running an electrical manufacturing business in Manchester in partnership with his brother-in-law, Ernest A Claremont. This business, known as F H Royce & Co had been founded in 1884 and had proved most successful, but now, owing to foreign competition the partners found it difficult to expand. Royce had, for a few months, been running a Decauville, a French car which he had bought second-hand. Being an extremely competent engineer and a perfectionist he had pulled this car to pieces and corrected a good many of its faults. However the crudity of its design offended him, so he announced to his somewhat surprised partner that he intended to build three motor cars to his own design, based on the Decauville, but without any of its faults and providing much more refined running. The first of these three Royce cars, a 10 h p twin-cylinder, which had overhead inlet and side exhaust valves, with a bore and stroke of 95 mm x 127 mm, took to the road on 1 April 1904 and ran without incident on its maiden trial trip as far as Brae Cottage, Knutsford, where Royce lived.

Later, it was entered in some 'side slip' trials down in Kent where Massac Buist, a motoring correspondent, who knew Charlie Rolls very well indeed, having been a fellow undergraduate at Cambridge, had a ride in the little car and wrote most favourably about it in the Press.

C S Rolls read this report with interest and

as he had also been hearing about the work Henry Royce was doing in Manchester from a fellow member of the Automobile Club, Henry Edmunds, he decided he would like to meet this talented designer for himself.

Frederick Henry Royce was 42 at this time, he had been born on 27 March 1863, the son of a miller at Alwalton, a village which lies between Oundle and Peterborough in Huntingdonshire; his upbringing had been extremely hard, but as Royce's early struggles and privations have been recorded many times already, there is no need to repeat them. He had served part of his apprenticeship with the Great Northern Railway in their locomotive sheds and workshops and this had given him a really good grounding on the correct and skilful use of tools, but it was his own genius which marked him as an exceptional engineer.

Early in May 1904 Edmunds took Rolls up to Manchester expressly to meet Royce for the first time. The three men had lunch together at the Midland Hotel in Manchester; of course, Royce had heard of Rolls and all the trials and races in which he had distinguished himself, and although there was a good deal of difference in their ages he had a great respect for the younger man's achievements. This was soon to be heartily reciprocated when C S Rolls inspected and tried a Royce car. From his previous experience he had become very much in favour of cars having four cylinders; but when he rode in the little 2-cylinder Royce he was completely won over. He persuaded Royce to let him make arrangements for the car to be sent down to London by rail. He accompanied the car himself and arriving at midnight, he triumphantly drove round to Claude Johnson's flat and knocked him up, declaring excitedly, 'I have found the greatest engineer in the world'. He insisted on Claude Johnson dressing and then drove him round the deserted streets of London in the car. CJ was quite as impressed as Rolls had been.

It was not that there was anything revolutionary about the car, it was completely orthodox in its design, like all later Rolls-Royce cars, it was not what it did, but the way it did it which was so surprising; it was so silent and smooth for a twin-cylinder, quite unlike anything that either man had experienced before and it must be remembered that Rolls and Johnson were two of the most experienced motorists in Britain at the time. The secret was the tremendous care which Royce had used in assembling the car, particularly the attention he had paid to the working of the valves and timing wheels to ensure complete quietness of running.

The partners, equally enthusiastic, quickly prepared an agreement to the effect that the firm of C S Rolls and Co., would take every chassis that Royce Ltd† could supply as the sole agents and would arrange to have the coachwork fitted, and then sell the finished completed car as a Rolls-Royce.

There were several old established carriage makers in London at this time who were gradually changing over from building horse-drawn carriages to motor car bodies; one with an enviable reputation, going right back to the reign of Queen Anne, was Barker & Co. The principal of this firm was Mr Hodges, who was already well known to Claude Johnson as a member of the Automobile Club, so it was Barker's whom Johnson and his partner approached to build bodies for the new Rolls-Royce car.

Rolls could see a ready market for a more powerful car than the 10 h p so he discussed with Royce the possibility of building larger models. Royce agreed to this and drew up plans which utilized the same bore and stroke, so that cylinder blocks, pistons, connecting rods, *etc.* would be common to all types, which would be more economical. His plan was simply to add more cylinders as required for the extra power. The first he produced was a 3-cylinder 15 h p, of which only six were ever made. One, with closed coachwork, was supplied by C S Rolls & Co. to the Headmaster of Eton on his retirement. One example, chassis no. 26330, owned by MacGregor Dick, survives in Scotland.

The next to be marketed was a 20 h p 4-cylinder model which proved most successful; two were entered in the 1905 Isle of Man T T and Percy Northey drove one to second place. The following year, the Hon C S Rolls won the Isle of Man T T at the wheel of a 20 h p

4-cylinder car. (There are two known survivors, one belongs to that great enthusiast, Stanley E Sears, who, over a period of three years, painstakingly built up one car out of two which had been found derelict; this was done regardless of expense and is now chassis No. 26350.* There is one other example in America, but the chassis number of this one is unknown. Out of the 40 cars of this model built, these are the only two left.)

In addition to these two models there was a 30 h p 6-cylinder, made in two chassis lengths, the longer for large closed coachwork. Thirty seven of these were built and the sole survivor is a short chassis example, No. 26355. This car was discovered on a tomato farm in Australia, having been used as a farm trailer and was the subject of a major restoration, again carried out by Stanley E Sears, who had a 2-seater body built on it, and who still owns it.

The exploits with the 4-cylinder 20 h p were almost all undertaken by the Hon C S Rolls and those with the 30 h p 6-cylinder by Claude Johnson, who won the trial known as the 'Battle of the Cylinders' at the wheel of a 6-cylinder 30 h p in 1906.

At a party held at the Trocadero Restaurant in London to celebrate Percy Northey's performance in the Isle of Man T T, the Hon C S Rolls informed those present that there would very shortly be a new model emerging from the Manchester factory. It would be made in two types, both utilizing a revolutionary new type of V8 engine; the first would have the engine mounted in the front of the frame like other Rolls-Royce models, but it would be governed so that it could not exceed 20 mph, which was the speed limit at that time. It therefore became known as the 'Legalimit'. One example was made for Lord Northcliffe to try out. It was exhibited on the Motor Show Stand at Olympia in 1905, chassis No. 40518, but the idea never became popular and no more were made. The alternative variation, using the same V8 engine was pure Claude Johnson. Just prior to his going into partnership with the Hon C S Rolls he had been working with Paris Singer on the manufacture of an electric Brougham, which he thought were the ideal cars for town work as

*A Rolls-Royce car is always known throughout the Company by its 'Chassis Number' even when complete with coachwork.

† The name of the Manchester firm was changed from F.H. Royce & Co to Royce Ltd in 1894

they were quiet and smooth and gave off no exhaust or petrol fumes. His idea was to have the V8 engine slung amidships to conceal it, shorten the car to facilitate parking and turning in town and make the whole car look like a true horseless carriage. This model is shown in the Company's Catalogue as the 'Landaulette par Excellence'. Only three of these and part of a fourth are thought to have been made.

There was still a lot of horse-drawn traffic in those days and because of the horses droppings, when it rained, the roads, made of wooden blocks, could cause the most terrifying skids, known as 'Side Slips', which were not helped by the narrow section tyres of the period or by the cars only having rear wheel brakes. The Electric Brougham was easily controlled and many were driven by old ex-coachmen, but their range was very limited owing to the batteries, which needed continual recharging. The other alternative for silent running was the steam car, but this was more complicated for the ex-coachmen to master.

Some of these old coachmen, who had been brought up amongst horses all their lives, did the most extraordinary things with motor vehicles when the change-over to mechanical propulsion was taking place. A good example of this is the story told by my great-uncle, Howard Figgis, who lived on the top of Hampstead Heath. Returning from the West End of London in his carriage-and-pair meant driving up the long and well-known hill, Fitzjohn's Avenue, at the top of which, on Hampstead Heath, is the Leg of Mutton Pond. In order to cool the horses down after their long haul up the hill, the coachman invariably drove the carriage-and-pair straight through the Leg of Mutton Pond, so, when Howard Figgis bought his first Daimler Landaulette in about 1905, the coachman did precisely the same thing, with the result that they were stuck in the middle of the pond and had to be towed out with horses!

It was because of this complete lack of understanding and knowledge of motor cars demonstrated by erstwhile coachmen, that Claude Johnson decided it was imperative to give them some sort of tuition in the handling of their vehicles. This was how the Rolls-Royce School of Instruction came into existence, a complete course of mechanics and maintenance was and still is given to chauffeurs and owners of Rolls-Royce cars.

Claude Johnson felt certain he could break into the market of London Society with his new motor Brougham as it had all the advantages of an electric Brougham but being a petrol car the range was to be unlimited. However, before this scheme was really launched it was suggested by Montagu Grahame-White, an old friend of Claude Johnson, that the 30 h p 6-cylinder car would be very much better if the chassis could be lengthened, making it into a full 7-passenger with all persons facing forwards. CJ appreciated this idea but realized at once that the performance of the car was bound to suffer, owing to the bigger and heavier bodywork, and that a new and more powerful engine would have to be installed to maintain the performance as a long distance touring car.

It should be mentioned here that the association between the firm of C S Rolls & Co. and Royce Ltd (the latter had become Royce Ltd in 1894) was working out so well that in November 1905 Mr A H Briggs, a Yorkshire businessman, who was the owner of a 20 h p 4-cylinder, suggested that the two firms should amalgamate into one concern, which he was prepared to back. So, in March 1906, a new company was formed, which was registered as Rolls-Royce Ltd, with a capital of £60,000 and which had Rolls, Royce and Johnson as the principle directors, and Ernest A Claremont as Chairman.

The original little 10 h p 2-cylinder car had been phased out and today there are three examples of the 16 originally made, still surviving. These are chassis No. 20154, owned by Oliver Langton of Leeds; chassis No. 20162, which is in the Science Museum in London; and chassis No. 20163, which belongs to Rolls-Royce Ltd, and at the time of writing it is on loan to the Montagu Motor Museum at Beaulieu. None of the three original Royce cars have survived, but an engine has been preserved at Manchester University.

The ROLLS-ROYCE 40/50 hp

Of the range of models that Royce was building, the 6-cylinder 30 h p was in many ways the one which was causing most problems. It had a troublesome vibration period from the crankshaft; in fact the car that Stanley Sears now owns actually broke its crankshaft when it went out on test for the first time with Royce at the wheel, so, after thinking it over, Claude Johnson persuaded Royce to design a brand new 40/50 h p model. This new design was so brilliant that it completely eclipsed everything of its day and is probably even now the best loved car in the world. It was first shown to the public at the Motor Show in London in the autumn of 1906 and was spoken of highly in the Press, but for a while very little more was heard of it, although a number of orders were taken. Then Claude Johnson took the 13th chassis to be built, chassis No. 60551, and had a semi-Roides-Belges body mounted on it, built by Barker and finished in silver paint, carrying silver-plated fittings. He named this car 'The Silver Ghost' and set out in true Claude Johnson fashion to show the world what the car could achieve.

PART I CHAPTER 2

The 1906 London Motor Show. Details of early 40/50 chassis which the Company sold prior to 'The Silver Ghost' completing its trials in June, July 1907. The trials of 'The Silver Ghost' and sale of same

Great efforts were made to have the new model ready for its first public appearance at the 1906 London Motor Show. It was to be built with two different lengths of wheelbase, 135½ in. for the short type, and 143½ ins. for the long chassis.

Unfortunately, it has not been possible to find out which chassis actually appeared on the Olympia Show Stand, but it is definite that chassis No. 60540, bearing Index No. AX 192, which was in fact the second chassis to be erected at Manchester, was used as the Conduit Street 'Trials Car' and was available outside the Show to give prospective clients a demonstration run. It was fitted with a Roi-des-Belges type of body and created a very favourable impression on those who rode in it.

Incidentally this car appears with others, including 'The Silver Ghost' in the photograph taken at the top of the Cat and Fiddle, which has become very well-known to Rolls-Royce enthusiasts. It was also used for an advertisement which appears in *'The Autocar'* of 30th March 1907 when, production of their new model being well under way, the Company bought a lot of advertising space in the Motoring Press and gave their latest product wide publicity.

However, shortly after the 'Cat and Fiddle' photograph was taken, this car must have been rebodied. This is interesting as it shows that the practice of 'body-swapping' so prevalent today on pre-War Rolls-Royce chassis, is by no means a new idea and in fact occurs all through the years, from the time when the 40/50 hp model first arrived on the scene.

This is indicated by the details given on the 'Body Card'* when the car was sold, on 26

November 1907, to Mrs Gjers of Bornwood, Bournemouth, Hants for £750. It is recorded on the card that a lot of work had to be done on the 'landaulette body' before it was sold. Mrs Gjers ran it until 1915 when she sold it to Major The Right Hon Count Gurowski of Worthampton Park, Berkshire. It changed hands again in June 1926 when it was sold to H S Howard of The Corner House, Chobham, Surrey, and again in 1931 to H L Wilton of 3 Smeaton Avenue, Golders Green, London. Finally, in November 1932 the Company were informed by Messrs. Eastwood, Lewis Cement Ltd. that they had bought the car and removed the engine which they had installed in a 'tug'!

Some time during its life it lost its original index number, AX 192, as for many years this number has been on chassis No. 2013, which was once offered for sale by H F Welham of Surbiton, one of the oldest Renault Agents and a staunch veteran car enthusiast, who has taken part in the London-Brighton Veteran Car Run since well before the 1939 War.

This car, chassis No. 2013, which carries a Landaulette body by Joseph Lawton of Liverpool, has recently returned from America and was present at the 1972 Blenheim Meeting of the Rolls-Royce Enthusiasts' Club. I can only assume that at one time these two cars, chassis No. 60540 and No. 2013, were at one time owned by the same person who transferred the original number plate to the later chassis. However, someone may know what really happened and if so may be able to throw some light on this mystery.

Reverting to the very first 40/50 h p chassis to leave the Manchester Works - this was apparently a long wheelbase type, No. 60539,

---

*A 'Body Card', sometimes known as a 'Chassis Card' was prepared for every car sold and contained the date the chassis came off test and to whom it was sold, the name of the coachbuilder, type of body etc. See example on page 30. These cards have been kept at the Rolls-Royce London Showrooms in Conduit Street, London W.1. until quite recently.

which was fitted with a chauffeur-driven limousine body, with 'A' type steering.

It would be appropriate here to explain that Rolls-Royce 40/50 h p chassis, being supplied for many different types of coachwork, were available with purpose-made steering columns identified by initial letters stamped on top of the steering box according to their angle of rake. Thus a Silver Ghost chassis made for a chauffeur driven limousine would have a nearly vertical column to allow plenty of room for passengers sitting in the rear compartment and to accommodate face-forward occasional seats. On a chassis drawing produced March 1919, the angle of rake for 'A' type steering was 52½ degrees. 'B' type steering had a rake of 48½ degrees according to a drawing made in June 1923 and 'C' type had a rake of 42 degrees from a drawing made in August 1919.

As the cars became more modern and coachwork changed, so the rakes of steering altered, but 'D' type was the lowest rake available on the later type of the old 40/50; John Hampton's car chassis No. 120 EU is a case in point with 'D' type steering; but in December 1928 the 'New Phantom' was available with 'E' type, which was at an angle of 27 degrees 13 minutes.

When the Phantom II appeared it was available in long chassis form with the following rakes, 'C' type 34 degrees, 'D' type 30½ degrees, 'E' type 28½ degrees and after the Continental Phantom II became available, 'F' type 27 degrees 18 minutes. In the short chassis form the Phantom II was available with 'E' and 'F' type steering only.

For the Phantom III the whole lettering system was changed and 'C' type was 37 degrees, 'E' type 34 degrees 22 minutes and 'F' type 33 degrees 5 minutes.

Confusion sometimes arises in the case of cars which at some time during their life have been re-bodied, perhaps a hearse body has been fitted to a chassis which previously bore an owner-driver saloon or drophead foursome coupe'. In which case it may have been necessary to alter the rake of the steering and the letter stamped on the steering box would be misleading.

When Rolls had first announced production of the two V8 cylinder models, Johnson had been very enthusiastic, as he saw that his favourite idea of a town Brougham could now see fruition, so he had arranged with Mr Hodges of Barker's for some carriage-type bodies to be produced for the V8 cars. However, as we know, he had then persuaded Royce to design the 40/50 hp model and the Manchester Works had devoted all their energies to this project and had abandoned the V8 completely. So Barker's were left with several surplus bodies on their hands; these were adapted for the new 40/50 hp chassis and it was one of these which had been fitted to chassis No. 60539.

Although I spent a great deal of time searching the records in Conduit Street, a number of points are still not clear and owing to the very considerable passage of time since 1907, I am afraid that it is most unlikely that they will now ever be unearthed. However, I was able to establish that this first chassis was not in fact sold until 12 May 1908, when it was purchased for £1,050 for the complete vehicle by John Stephens, Esq., of Lynscott, Pampisford Road, South Croydon. It was finished in olive green and bore the index number R 529. He sold it to Barker & Co., who re-sold it to Thomas Gracey of The Constitutional Club, London. When he died, it was re-purchased by Barker & Co who kept it as one of their stock cars until 1919 when they sold it to Mrs E R Workman of 3 Seamore Place, Gothic Lodge, Hayling Island; this is the last known about this car. As this chassis was built some time in 1906 and not sold until 1908 it must be assumed that this first chassis was used for extensive trials.

Chassis No. 60541, the third 40/50 chassis to be built, was a long-type with 'A' type steering, seating 6 passengers. It was like 60539, also fitted with a body originally intended for a V8. This chassis formed part of the exhibit at Olympia in 1907 by Barker & Co. and was sold for £900 on 19 February 1909, to Robert J Foster, Esq., Stockeld Park, Wetherby, Yorkshire, who took delivery from Conduit Street on 16 April 1909, the index number was R 538 and in March 1920 the car was owned by A Shackleton, Esq., 51 Rutland Gate, Harrogate, Yorkshire.

It should be mentioned here that a common

misconception amongst many people is that this 40/50 hp model was named 'Silver Ghost', and often all 40/50 h p cars from 1906 onwards are referred to as 'Silver Ghosts'. This in fact is not the case. There were 12 chassis built originally, which were simply known as '40/50' hp. It was then, as already mentioned, Claude Johnson wishing to attract even more publicity and attention than had already been effected, decided to have a Roi-des-Belges side-entrance body fitted on to a 40/50 hp chassis, No. 60551. He called this car 'The Silver Ghost' and performed many feats of endurance and trials with it which will be given later in this chapter.

It was not until May 1925 when the 'New Phantom' was introduced that the Company began to refer to these earlier 40/50s as 'Silver Ghosts' in order to distinguish them from the later 40/50 hp 'New Phantom' model.

From the records at Conduit Street it can be seen that the very first 40/50 hp chassis to be sold was 60546, the actual date is recorded as 18 May 1906, when it was sold to H Moreland of Beverley House, The Park, Gloucester. It will be noted that this date of sale is long before any 40/50 h p chassis had been built, or any announcement had been made in the Press regarding this new model. So, Mr Moreland must in fact originally have ordered a 30 h p 6-cylinder on 18 May, when he paid a deposit of £400.

60546 was a short chassis and was fitted with a tulip tonneau body by Barker, finished in cream, and it was not until 26 April 1907 that Mr Moreland took delivery of his new car at Conduit Street.

It is interesting to note breakdown of the cost of producing this chassis:

Cost of Chassis	..	..	£439.	0.	0.
Testing	..	..	20.	0.	0.
Plating	..	..	4.	4.	0.
Tyres	..	..	36.	1.	10.
Striping Bonnet	..	..	2.	0.	0.
Body	..	..)	112.	0.	0.
Painting and Trimming	)				
Extras given in	..	..	10.	0.	0.
Carriage on crate, etc.	..		5.	0.	0.
			£628.	5.	10.

Note - Mr Moreland had previously owned the 6-cylinder 30 h p chassis No. 26371.

Mr Moreland sold chassis 60546 on 25 October 1914 to F H David, Esq., of Claverham Manor, Hinton Charterhouse, near Bath. There were three subsequent owners of this vehicle in the course of the next five years, as follows: Mr Russell of Messrs Smedleys Hydro, Matlock, Derby; then C E Peezenik, Esq., of 53 Portland Place, London W1, and lastly Captain H A Evans of Cromwell Hall, East Grinstead, in Sussex. Unfortunately, no dates are shown for these changes of ownership, but there is a note to say that in March 1919 the car was shipped to Australia.

The second chassis sold was No. 60544, on 29 October 1906; this also was a short chassis, the body was a 'Clayton-East' with modifications, built by Barker. It was known by this name because the original version had been supplied to Sir Gilbert Clayton-East, Bart, to his own requirements. It was supplied to William Arkwright Esq., of Sutton Scarsdale, Chesterfield, and the finished vehicle was delivered to him on 20 April 1907, at Conduit Street. This chassis was still on the road in January 1920, having had four subsequent owners.

On 16 November 1906, another chassis (short), No. 60545, carrying a double landaulette body was sold to the Midland Counties Garage of Granby Street, Leicester. Unfortunately, the name of the coachbuilder is not given, but the car was a 'Trials Car' for the Midland Counties Garage and again the production cost of this chassis, plus the sale price, is given as follows:

Cost of Chassis	..	..	£439.	0.	0.
Testing	..	..	20.	0.	0.
Polishing	..	..	2.	0.	0.
Tyres	..	..	36.	1.	10.
Brb.	..	..	2.	10.	0.
Extras - say ..	..	..	5.	0.	0.
Carriage on crates	..		5.	0.	0.
			£509.	11.	10.
Sale Price:			£807.	10.	0.

The chassis was delivered on 12 March 1907 at Manchester and went direct to the coach-builders.

It was sold to R D Thompson, Esq. The Pool House, Groby, Leicester, in November 1920, and later owned by a Mr Edgecombe, Wellington College, Berkshire. On 31 October 1922, the car was sold for hire work, and in August 1925 was bought by L C Russell Esq., Balliol College, Oxford.

On 26 November 1906, chassis No 60547, also a short type, was sold to Rippon Bros of Carriage Buildings, Huddersfield, for delivery on 30 March 1907. Unfortunately, apart from recording that the weight of the body was 6/7 cwt, there is no mention of the type fitted. The car was for Mr A H Briggs of Tyningham, Duchy Road, Harrogate, who had already done so much to assist Rolls-Royce Ltd and was an old and valued customer.

The second owner of this car is given as C Foulds, Esq., Woodbine, Keighley, Yorkshire, and in October 1927 it was owned by that great Austin enthusiast Sir Harry Launder, 16 Jermyn Street, Piccadilly, London (the well-known Scottish comedian and singer, who made famous the song 'Keep right on to the end of the road'). In December 1928 the car was owned by Mr H G Hutchinson, Ardmollen Motor Works, Edinburgh, and in March 1929 by William Taylor & Sons of 145 Abercrombie Street, Glasgow.

Ever since the Hon C S Rolls went to America in December 1906, taking with him one of the Isle of Man T T cars, which he had driven in various races there, the citizens of the United States have been some of the most loyal and enthusiastic supporters of the Rolls-Royce car; this love of the make has never varied, the proof of which is shown today by the Rolls-Royce Owners Club of America Inc., which is probably the biggest of all the clubs devoted to the preservation of old Rolls-Royce cars. So it is hardly surprising that early versions of the new 40/50 h p chassis were very soon exported to the United States. The first chassis to be sold for export was 60552, on 11 December 1906. It was another short type bearing the index number AX 204, with coachwork by Barker, a Phaeton de luxe with leather hood. The weight of the body was 7½ cwt, and the car was sold to Mr J Seligman of Mills Buildings, New York. It was delivered on 24 May 1907 at Conduit Street.

On 4 January 1907, chassis No. 60560 was the first of the long type sold and was built for Lord Northcliffe of 36 Berkeley Square, London, W1. It was fitted with an extra long Pullman limousine body by Barker, weighing 9½ cwt, and the price was £1,220.

It has often been rumoured that Lord Northcliffe was the owner of the one and only 'Legalimit' and the only known photograph of this car appears in my book *The Hyphen in Rolls-Royce* with Claude Johnson seated behind the wheel. This appears to be borne out by a note added to the Body Card of chassis No. 60560, which reads as follows:

Extra cost of making body specially large - £25. To be charged with 8-cylinder, 4 months and 7 days at £25 per month, £106.5.0d. Magneto ignition £32.10.0d. extra. Credit - £1,060.15.0d. for 8-cylinder. Returned.

So the rumour is correct, Lord Northcliffe did have a 'Legalimit' which was returned when he took delivery of chassis No. 60560. He was given the index number AX 203 for his new car, which was painted grey, and he kept it until he died in 1922 when it passed to his son, St John Harmsworth of 1 Queen Adelaide Mansions, and Highcliff Castle, Christchurch, Hants.

In January 1907 another chassis was sold to America, No. 60553. It was a short type fitted with a standard side-entrance open touring body by Barker & Co and it is interesting to note that the cost of the complete coachwork was £92.14.0d. It was supplied to W C Martin & Co of Broadway and 62nd Street, New York, with whom the Hon C S Rolls had arranged an agency whilst he was in America a short time previously. The car was delivered on 9 April 1907, at Conduit Street, and on the 13th of the month was shipped to New York from Liverpool aboard the White Star Line's cargo steamer S.S. *Bovic*, where it was immediately sold to Mr S B Stevens, 315 North Nashi Street, Rome, New York.

This chassis has survived, it was bought and fully restored by Millard Newman in 1962 and was present at the Goodwood Pageant in 1964.

*There will be a number of references to the Guarantee Books, like the 'Body Cards', they have been kept at the Conduit Street Showrooms ever since the Company was first formed and they contain brief particulars of each chassis sold. The Guarantee which normally lasted three years was dated from the day the chassis, complete with coachwork had been inspected by the Company's

(Top) Chassis 26350. The 4 cylinder 20 hp short type owned by Stanley E. Sears, who is at the wheel. This beautiful little car was painstakingly restored from scrap by the owner, who had the present coachwork built by Messrs Harrington of Hove as a replica of the Hon. C. S. Rolls Isle of Man TT car *(photo S. E. Sears)*

(Bottom) Chassis 26355. Stanley Sears 1906 30 hp 6 cylinder at Goodwood Pageant in May 1964

(*Top*) The well-known 'Cat and Fiddle' photograph taken in June 1907, when Claude Johnson was on his way to Glasgow to take part in the Scottish Reliability Trial driving 'The Silver Ghost', the car bearing index number AX192 is the London demonstrator. See Part I, Chapter 2

(*Bottom*) C. S. Rolls at the wheel of a 6 cylinder 30 hp Rolls-Royce of 1906. This car, chassis 60528, was exported to America as a Roi des Belges by Barker, painted green with red leather upholstery

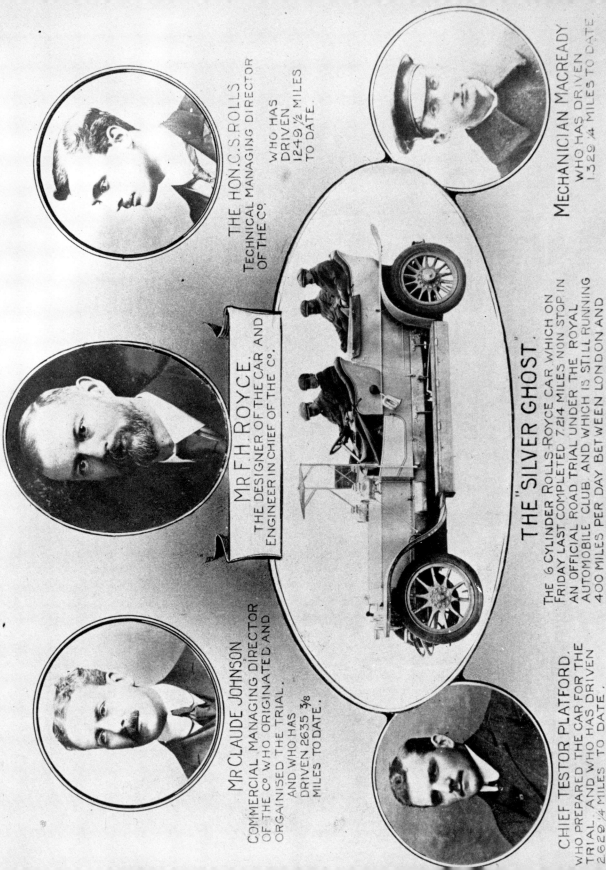

This photograph is copied from the original, which was presented to Reginald Macready. The original hung for many years in the Motor Traffic Office in St Helier, during the time that Reginald Macready's nephew was in charge of Traffic Control in Jersey. C.I. (*photo R. H. Mayne*)

(*Top and Bottom*) Chassis 60551. The Silver Ghost as the car is today. It was fully restored in 1948 under S. E. Sears' supervision for Rolls-Royce Ltd by H. E. Griffin of Haywards Heath who had so successfully restored chassis 1721 two years before. See Part I, Chapter 10 for further details

(Top) Chassis No 1100, index number R567, the first Silver Phantom
(Middle) The first Silver Phantom on trials in Scotland (chassis 1100)
(photo Johnson family)
(Bottom) Mr and Mrs Louis Bleriot with CSR after the first cross-channel
flight in 1909. The car could be chassis 60583, 'The Dreadnought'

(*Top*) The Works in 1908
(*Middle*) 'The Charmer', a 1908 Barker Double
Enclosed Limousine, chassis 1162, index number
R568 (*photo Johnson family*)
(*Bottom left*) 'White Knave' chassis 60726, in the
1908 Trials with Claude Johnson at the wheel
(*photo F. W. Hutton-Stott*)
(*Bottom right*) The second Silver Phantom with
Claude Johnson at the wheel (chassis 1106)

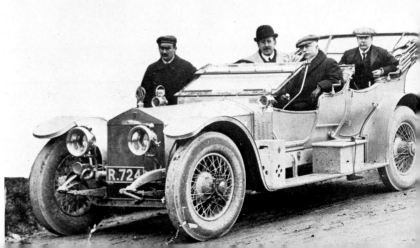

(Top) Index number R521 is 'White Knave' driven by Claude Johnson in the Scottish Reliability Trial. The car retired with a seized piston

(Middle) Rolls-Royce 40/50 production shop number one, July 1908. From left to right: Tommy Bell, chargehand in the Instrument Department; Walter Griffin, at the wheel, fitter (father of Albert Griffin) Billy Scott, fitter, on chassis

(Bottom) 'The Whisperer' chassis 1423, index number R1050 on 'French Trials'. It had a Double Limousine body by Labourdette (photo Johnson family)

(Top) Pig iron laid down on the test track at intervals for Hs to chassis test, 1912/13. Note the RR on the chimney stack entwined the wrong way round. Nothing could be done about it!

(Middle and below) A 40/50 on test at the Derby Works. Note CJ's sign on the wall

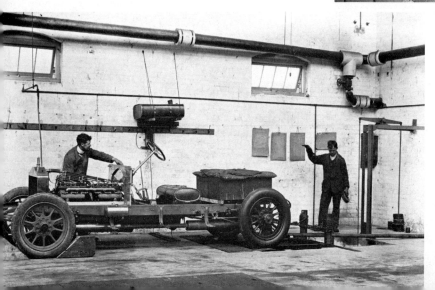

(For further details of this chassis see The Rolls-Royce Owners Club's bi-monthly magazine *The Flying Lady*, pages 602, 688, 700, 747).

On 26 January 1907, a third chassis, long type, No. 60555, carrying a landaulette body, was sold. It was destined for F G Bourne, Esq., 149 Broadway, New York City, and was shipped to New York aboard the Atlantic Transport Liner *Minnetonka* on 18 May 1907.

Chassis No. 60557 was also sold to America in January 1907, this was a chassis-only with 'B' type steering. It was shipped to W C Martin, Esq., the Rolls-Royce Agent, on board the Atlantic Transport Liner *Minneapolis* on 25 May 1907, and was subsequently fitted with a body by an American coachbuilder.

The following month, on 4 February 1907, chassis No. 60554 a short type, carrying a Roi-des-Belges body by Barker, which cost £115.14.0d., was sold to George Gillies. Esq., of 180 St. George Street, Toronto, Canada, and the car was shipped aboard the S.S. *Ontarian* on the 31 May 1907.

Four days later, on 8 February, another long type chassis was sold, No. 60556, index number LH 7588 the weight of the body was recorded as 9¼ cwt. The chassis was sold to James Gray, Esq., of Hatfield, Hertfordshire, and was delivered to his premises on 26 April 1907. Unfortunately, the Body Card does not give the type of coachwork fitted, nor the name of the builder, but in the Guarantee Book* this car is shown as a 2-seater with coachwork by Bridges Auto Carriage Co of Cirencester, which seems a little odd, considering it is a long chassis. There is a very old established garage in Hatfield on the original Great North Road called 'Gray' and it would appear to me that this car was supplied to them for Thomas Henry Day of Aberglaslyne, 93 Amhurst Park, North London, but there is no date given as to when Thomas Henry Day took delivery He later sold the car to C J Moyne, Esq., 89 Cromwell Road, South Kensington, and again no date is given, but in June 1913 the chassis changed hands once more, this time to E J Manual, Esq., Tanglewood, South Godstone, Surrey, and in July 1919 once again, this time to a titled gentleman who

was a K.C., V.C., whose name unfortunately is unreadable but who lived at 1 Airlie Gardens in London.

Exactly one month later, on 8 March 1907, chassis No. 60548 was sold for £1,252.10.0d. to H Moreland, Esq., Beverley House, The Park, Gloucestershire; it carried Pullman limousine coachwork by Barker, but unfortunately there is a discrepancy in the records between the Guarantee Book and the Body Card; the former gives this as a short chassis, the latter as a long type, but a long type is much more likely for a limousine body. Later this car was purchased by S Berkeley, Esq., of Bohum, Ross, near Hereford, who must be the same man who owned a 30 h p 6-cylinder, chassis No. 60525, in which he took Claude Johnson for a drive and frightened him to death (see *The Hyphen in Rolls-Royce*). Later, 60548 became the property of the Lady Charles Montagu, of Theobalds Park, Waltham Cross, and 18 Portland Square, but no date is given for either of these transactions.

On 12 April 1907, chassis No. 60549 was sold for £1,032.10.0d. to the Midland Counties Garage, Granby Street, Leicester, for R P Doxford & Son, Silksworth Hall, Sunderland. This was a long type, carrying a double landaulette body by Barker with no glass in the front windscreen, the car was finished in dark green with black mouldings and white line; it changed hands several times and was last heard of in October 1919 when Barkers advised that it was owned by W S Harris, Esq., 95 Harpendon Road, South Wanstead.

On 23 May 1907, chassis No. 60559 of the long type, carrying a Grahame-White limousine body by Barker, weighing 12 cwt, 3 qrs 11 lb with 'B' type steering, finished in green and upholstered in red, was sold for £1,300 to E W Husted, of 153 Queen Victoria Street, London, to be supplied to S F Barker, Esq., of Nutfield, Croxley Green, Hertfordshire. This chassis must have been subjected to a body change as there is a note to say that in July 1909, when it was sold to C J Sturdy, Esq., of Pax Hill Park, Lindfield, Sussex, it was carrying a large open touring body. It was then sold to Smith & Son of Camberley, but no date is given.

---

representative and satisfied him that the strict requirements of Rolls-Royce Limited had been adhered to, such as total weight, wheel arch clearances etc. Sometimes a chassis was sold without a guarantee because the purchaser had stipulated some fitting that did not comply with Rolls Royce specifications.

I have given the above cars in some detail to show that quite a number of chassis were sold before Claude Johnson was to make 'The Silver Ghost' so famous. This chassis, No 60551, index number AX 201, was, as has already been mentioned, fitted with a special body by Barker which cost £110.14.0d. It has been rumoured that it was the polished show chassis which appeared at Olympia in 1906, but it has not been possible to ascertain whether it is correct or not. When the car was completed, with green upholstery inside and gleaming silver everywhere else, it looked truly magnificent and Claude Johnson felt justifiably proud of the whole effect. He had wanted it to be striking and it certainly was - attracting attention wherever it went. The exact date it went on the road is not known, but the 'Trials' which Claude Johnson did with it can be divided into three parts. The first part comprised demonstrations to the Press, which consisted of carrying four passengers (6 ft guardsmen) up Netherhall Gardens, Hampstead; followed by further tests in Richmond Park, with later a drive to Old Bexhill Post Office and back to London, via Handcross Hill, without using a gear lower than third. The second part of this carefully calculated scheme to bring the car into the public eye was to take part in the 2,000-mile Scottish Trials from Glasgow, which took place in June 1907.

For this event 'The Silver Ghost', with Claude Johnson at the wheel, left the garage of The Royal Automobile Club in Brick Street, just off Down Street, near Piccadilly, carrying Mr Cairns, the R A C Observer. They were accompanied by the Hon C S Rolls, driving index number AX 205, and Mr Swindley of *The Autocar* driving the London 'Trials Car', chassis No. 60540, index number AX 192. All three cars had representatives of the Press riding in them and the route which they took to the Midland Hotel, at Derby, where they all stayed the night, was as follows: St. Albans, Northampton, Market Harborough, Leicester, Loughborough, Derby.

The following morning the cars left Derby for Glasgow going through Ashbourne, Buxton and over the 'Cat and Fiddle'. It was on this occasion that, arriving at the summit, the famous photograph was taken, showing the three cars in line with a fourth one, on trade number plates, which had come from Manchester to meet them; unfortunately it is not known who were the occupants of this car.

On arrival in Glasgow, 'The Silver Ghost', driven by Claude Johnson, prepared for the Scottish Trials. The car put up a magnificent performance which has been described so many times there is no need to tell it again, except to say that 'The Silver Ghost' won a Gold Medal, awarded for speed in hill-climbing, complete reliability and low fuel consumption. The route went from Glasgow through Dalmally, Perth, Stonehaven, Aberdeen, Grantown, Inverness, Kingussie, Pitlochry and Calendar, and so back to Glasgow. 'The Silver Ghost' returned to London on 1st July, having been driven by Claude Johnson the entire way. Almost immediately on their return they prepared to undergo the 15,000-mile Trial under R A C observation, the details and arrangements of which Claude Johnson had so carefully planned earlier in the year. This the third part of his publicity campaign was by far the most important; the organisation of this presented no problem to Claude Johnson. He had already arranged so many rallies and trials when he was Secretary of The Automobile Club that he found just planning for one car very simple. The one which had taken more work than any was the famous 1,000-mile Trial of 1900, when 65 vehicles had taken part and exhibitions of the motor cars were arranged in all the leading towns through which the competitors passed. This was a tremendous undertaking, which he had accomplished entirely on his own. It was this Trial which really put motoring on the map in the United Kingdom; the public were able to see how motor vehicles could be used in everyday life and realized that the motor car was not just a play-thing of the rich.

The route which he selected for 'The Silver Ghost' started from London. They left the R A C Garage (Brick Street, Down Street), through Park Lane, Portman Street, Wellington Road, Finchley Road, to Barnet, St Albans, Dunstable and Holyhead Road to Coventry, Stonebridge, Castle Bromwich, Erdington, Brownhills, Watling Street, Newport, Whitchurch, Tarporley, Northwich, Altrincham, Manchester (The Midland Garage, close to Midland Hotel, Gaythorn, Manchester), Oldham, Huddersfield, Bradford, Leeds, Wetherby, Boroughbridge, Leeming Lane, Darlington, Durham, Newcastle-on-Tyne, Morpeth, Alnwick, Berwick-on-Tweed, Dunbar, Haddington, Edinburgh, Bathgate, Airdrie, Glasgow (St Enoch's Hotel), and reverse. Note' London to Glasgow by this route, 512¾ miles.

The car covered this route 27 times. There were four drivers, Claude Johnson, the Hon C S Rolls, Eric Platford (the chief tester, who had prepared the car for all its Trials), and Reginald A Macready from Jersey in the Channel Islands. During the time that this Trial was taking place, the car carried four different official observers from The Royal Automobile Club, and on completion of the Trial the car returned to the R A C's Garage in Brick Street, where it was completely stripped and examined thoroughly; very little wear had taken place anywhere, and not long afterwards Rolls-Royce Ltd published *The Cost of Running and Repairing a Motor Car, now Certified for the first time by The Royal Automobile Club*.

This exploit of Claude Johnson's really put Rolls-Royce Ltd on the map. It must be borne in mind that the roads were nothing like they are today, and the outstanding performance which the car had given, together with the greatest possible publicity, had really brought the name Rolls-Royce to the fore in the motoring world. Not long after this it acquired the reputation of being 'The Best Car in the World'.

In September 1907 CJ took 'The Silver Ghost' to Cornwall on a short holiday, driving from London to Penzance in the day. Her days of glory were numbered, however, for on 14 July 1908, 'The Silver Ghost' was sold for £750, to the London Motor Cab Co of 82 Victoria Street, London, SW1, and was not heard of again until 1949, when the family of A M Hanbury (who must have been connected with the London Cab Co) generously returned the car to Rolls-Royce Ltd, who handed it over to Stanley Sears for a complete restoration to be carried out by Messrs H E Griffin of Haywards Heath, in Sussex, who had made such a good job of renovating the coachwork, etc. on chassis No. 1721 in 1946.

Today 'The Silver Ghost' spends most of its time on display in the Conduit Street showrooms; it is in perfect working order and was taken to America quite recently on board the *Queen Elizabeth 2* when that ship went on her maiden voyage from Southampton to New York.

PART I CHAPTER 3

Claude Johnson's exploits with 'The Silver Ghost' pay off, the Royal Family and their State Cars. Charles Knight's sleeve valve engine, which is adopted by the Daimler Co and other makers of luxury cars. 'The Silver Phantom', Claude Johnson's 'Heavenly Twins'; the Hon C S Rolls' 'Balloon Car'. The move to Derby. The death of the Hon C S Rolls, the illness of Royce and his visit to Le Canadel

By 1908 the Rolls-Royce 40/50 was becoming universally acknowledged as the world's finest automobile. The publicity Claude Johnson had achieved with 'The Silver Ghost' was paying off and owing to the incredible silence of the model, other companies felt that they would simply have to take counter measures. The one who was really worried was the Daimler Company, as, although the Royal Family ran their cars for general purposes and State Occasions, H M King Edward VII had also purchased one or two other makes for his personal use; amongst these was a Renault 14/20 landaulette with coachwork by Hooper, which he often used in the evenings when he was on a private visit and did not wish to be recognized. The chief objection to the Daimler was the noise it made, for which it was notorious, and the public were demanding something which ran very much more quietly.

In America, Charles Yale Knight from North Wisconsin and his partner, L B Kilbourne (a mechanic who had a great deal of experience with gas engines), had been working on an engine which employed a pair of reciprocating sleeves set between the piston and the cylinder wall and with ports cut in them, in place of the mushroom-headed valves installed in what is known as a poppet-valve engine.

Knight was convinced that the noise made by a conventional internal combustion engine emanated from the valve mechanism in the poppet-valve type. He felt that if another type of valve gear could be designed this noise problem could be overcome. His new design ran very much more quietly than the usual one

and he could see a great future in it; but when he tried to interest one or two of the leading American motor car manufacturers they were not at all impressed. He had started his experiments in August 1903, and by the summer of 1904 he was working on a 4-cylinder engine which in the October he had installed into a car which he and Kilbourne then drove many thousands of miles without any bother at all.

Early in 1906 Edward Manville, the Chairman of the Daimler Co, happened to meet a friend of Knight's who, in the course of conversation, told Manville what Knight and Kilbourne were doing in America and that they had now prepared an engine which ran extremely quietly. Naturally Manville was most interested and soon after this conversation, Knight was invited to come to England, bringing his car with him. He landed at Liverpool and drove to the Daimler Company's works at Coventry, and was met by the Managing Director, Percy Martin, who was also an American and who was the first to try out Knight's car. He was so impressed with its silent running that the Daimler Company asked Knight to adapt this type of engine to their own particular use.

Once the news leaked out of the experiments that were taking place at the Daimler Works, controversy began to rage; those who were in favour of the Knight double sleeve valve principle and those against it. There were many who saw lubrication of the sleeves as the great problem, both when starting cold and at speed on the open road; the arguments for and against became so heated in the motoring press that the Daimler Co decided that there was only one thing to do - that was to submit two engines to a very serious test which would be organized and run by The Royal Automobile Club.

The test which commenced on Monday, 22 March 1909, at the Daimler Works consisted of running two engines with sleeve valves for 132 hours continuously on the bench; the larger engine was a 4-cylinder with bore and stroke of 124 x 130 mm, which gives 6,281 cc or 38.1 R A C rated h p.

The smaller engine was also 4-cylinder, and the bore and stroke was 96 x 130 mm, which gives 3,764 cc or 22.8 R A C rated h p.

To appreciate more clearly the severity of the test, if the larger engine had been driving a car during the whole time, with the standard Daimler gear ratios, a distance of no less than 8,252 miles would have been covered at a mean speed of 43.45 mph while the smaller engine would have covered, similarly, a distance of 8,830 miles at 48.4 mph. The disparity in speed and distance between these results is, of course, attributable to the higher rate of revolutions of the smaller engine.

Both engines were then fitted into chassis with open touring coachwork and taken to Brooklands; the 38 h p car ran 1,930.5 miles at an average speed of 42.4 mph on the track, and the 22 h p car covered 1,914.1 miles at an average speed of 41.88 mph. Both vehicles ran non-stop, the cars were then driven back to Coventry from Weybridge, a distance of 112 miles each way, and the engines were subjected to a further bench test of 5 hours.

On dismantling the engines after this test the judges issued the necessary certificates and awarded the Daimler Co the coveted Dewar Award, adding the following rider to the certificate:

"The engines were completely dismantled, and no perceptible wear was noticeable on any of the fitted surfaces.

The cylinders and pistons were found to be notably clean. The ports of the valves showed no sign of burning or wear."

Naturally, after such an exceptionally severe test, especially for those times, the Daimler Co was elated and the public criticism of the sleeve valve engine was silenced. The Daimler Co were now so confident of this new type of engine that they deposited a cheque for £250 with the R A C as a challenge to any other motor manufacturer to see whether anyone could effect an improvement on these two engines, but there was no response to this challenge.

Claude Johnson was extremely worried about the performance of these two sleeve valve engines, and Rolls-Royce Ltd quickly bought a 38 h p Daimler which CJ took on an extended tour of the Continent with an RR 40/50, the Daimler running very well. He also talked to Royce about it, the latter said that he did not like the design, the whole object of a petrol engine was to conduct the heat away from the cylinder and into the water jacket as quickly as possible, but as the piston was surrounded by two reciprocating sleeves which operated between the piston and the cylinder wall, the heat had to be transferred through these sleeves first. Added to this Royce always felt that when designing a petrol engine it should be made so that the original could be continuously improved, but with the sleeve valve arrangement this could not be done; it meant scrapping the design and starting again from fresh each time.

Rolls-Royce Ltd subjected their 38 h p Daimler engine to the same tests as their own 40/50 h p engine underwent, and they were delighted to find that their own 40/50 was very greatly superior; this convinced Claude Johnson that Royce was on the right lines and that really there was nothing for them to worry about. From then on CJ loathed Daimlers, he sometimes referred to them as 'the unmentionable cars'. His attitude was that if Royce could design a silent valve gear using poppet valves why could not other motor manufacturers do the same thing, and that the sleeve valve arrangement was 'cheating'; it achieved the silence by a quick short-cut method

From 1909 until 1933 all Daimler engines in cars, buses, commercial vehicles and the first tanks of World War I were fitted with sleeve valve engines and during the years that followed from 1910 on, many of the builders of luxury cars used Knight's double sleeve valve arrangement.

It was never very satisfactory in an owner-driven car as most owner-drivers are impatient and wish to take their cars on the road immediately the engine is started; the great problem with the sleeve valve was lubrication when starting from cold. In order to overcome this the Daimler Co fitted two large cups on to the induction pipe, which had to be filled with engine oil and the moment the engine started, the taps on these had to be turned so that the oil was sucked into the engine ensuring that the sleeves received plenty of oil, with the result that a dense cloud of blue smoke came out of the exhaust pipe; at the same time the engine had to be allowed to warm up gently before the car was taken out on to the road, otherwise there was the possibility that one of the lugs attached to the bottom of the sleeves could break, so causing serious damage. This arrangement made the sleeve valve engine more suitable for a car to be chauffeur-driven, so that it could be warmed up quietly and then taken round to the door of the house, but on the other hand the silence of a sleeve valve was quite extraordinary and the engine would run for the most incredibly long period without any attention whatsoever; in fact the Daimler Co and others who used the sleeve valve engine claimed that it was 'the only type of engine in the world that actually improves with use.'

Many years later, in the mid-1920s, with the advent of steel sleeves, an oil primer worked in conjunction with the self-starter and mixture control on the steering wheel was fitted, this made cold starting much easier, but still great care had to be exercised in not racing the engine whilst it was still cold.

Today, the sleeve valve engine is no longer made and the poppet valve reigns supreme. With present day oils and fuels and high revolutions the interior of the engine remains clean so decarbonization, or as Rolls-Royce Ltd prefer to call it, 'top overhauling', is something that belongs to another era; but at the time that the sleeve valve was in its hey-day, the poppet valve engine was continually having to be pulled to pieces, decarbonized, the valves ground in and the tappets re-set. I can remember so clearly the period between the Wars, when it seemed that friends were always either just having the engine in their cars decarbonized, or this work had just been carried out; in fact some motor manufacturers in their handbooks recommended decarbonization taking place every 2,000 miles; this sounds fantastic today when many people cover over 2,000 miles in one month, but the oils used, as well as the petrol, and in many cases the actual materials used in the construction of the valve, were not up to the standard of those used today. A great deal of knowledge was gained during the last War when the internal combustion engine was relied upon by both sides for achieving a victory. One of the steels which is used in valves today to stop them burning out is known as 'K.E. 965', this material was unheard of before the 1939 War.

Other makes which used double sleeve valves of the Charles Knight pattern were Mercedes, Minerva, Panhard-Levassor, Voisin, Brewster, Stearns-Knight and Mors. Of course, apart from Daimler, Minerva of Belgium is probably the best remembered. Before the 1914 War a number of cars with sleeve valve engines took part in long distance trials on the Continent, and Minerva actually raced sleeve valve engines, but this type of engine was never really used for sporting and competitive events to any great extent, its chief use was amongst large chauffeur-driven 'motor carriages'.

There was also another type of sleeve valve engine, which consisted of a single sleeve which rotated as it went up and down between the piston and cylinder wall. It was known as the 'Burt McCallum' type and was used by Argyle, Arrol-Aster and the last big Vauxhall 25/70, made just before General Motors bought Vauxhall in 1927. The Burt McCallum single sleeve was also used in aero-engines and Royce once said that he had also considered this arrangement, before Burt McCallum came on the scene, but he did not proceed with it. However, when, years later, Rolls-Royce Ltd turned to building aero-engines, they made a range of single sleeve valves which included:

Exe - Air - and water-cooled 24-cylinder X.
Pennine - Aircooled 24-cylinder X.
Eagle 22 - Water cooled 24-cylinder flat H.
Crecy - Water cooled V-12 2-stroke.

But to revert to Rolls-Royce Ltd, in order to keep the model well before the public's eye, certain cars were built which have since become legendary; the first of these, chassis No. 1100, was an improved version of 'The Silver Ghost', with different gear ratios, and with Claude Johnson's mania for naming individual cars, this one was called 'The Silver Phantom'. As with the original 'Silver Ghost' the car carried at the bottom of the windscreen, a large solid silver engraved plaque, bearing the words 'The Silver Phantom' upon it. He took this car all over the Scottish Highlands, trying it out on the steepest hills he could find. There are many photographs of it, but most of them are just captioned 'Rolls-Royce 40/50' and many people think they are more photographs of 'The Silver Ghost', but, on looking closely, it can be seen that this is an entirely different car which carried the index number R 567. Chassis No. 1106 was another 'Silver Phantom'; there were also the two cars entered for the Scottish Reliability Trials, sometimes known as Claude Johnson's heavenly twins, 'Silver Rogue' and 'White Knave', both of which had special engines which gave 70 brake horse-power. Claude Johnson drove 'White Knave'; unfortunately he broke a piston and rather than let it be known that something had gone wrong with the car, he put himself to bed, called the doctor, and filled the bedroom with every conceivable sort of medicine so that it was given out that Claude Johnson could not continue with the Trial as he was in bed with a severe cold.

An engine of this type was also fitted into the Hon C S Rolls' well-known 'Balloon Car', known as 'The Cookie'. It was sold before the Hon C S Rolls' death in 1910, and was converted for some unknown reason to wooden artillery wheels with detachable rims. As the years went past and the 40/50 continued to gain popularity, Royce was proved to be right in his policy of producing something really good and then gradually improving on it. Claude Johnson was so delighted and confident in the model that he suggested that each chassis should be sold with a guarantee for life; this was, of course, completely unrealistic, especially as he also made the suggestion that each time one of

*The Three Year Guarantee became effective on June 1st 1909

the older models returned to the Works for overhaul it should be brought right up to date, free of charge. When he put this proposal before the Board it was turned down flatly, but then a compromise was reached; every chassis sold had a guarantee of three years* issued with it, provided that the carriage-work complied with the stipulations which the Company made in regard to weight, etc.

In 1908, a very significant year for Rolls-Royce Ltd, the Works were moved from Manchester to Derby; the new factory, designed by Royce, was opened on 9 July 1908. It is quite unbelievable how much was accomplished during these first few years of the Rolls-Royce Company's existence and how this, one of the newest and least known motor manufacturers in 1905, had come right to the fore of the whole industry. It is clear that a very great deal of this is due to the amazing amount of work that Royce put in to the various projects, spurred on, of course, by Claude Johnson and aided by his various publicity campaigns.

The following year another acquisition, which was to become well-known to most Rolls-Royce enthusiasts, entered into the life of CJ and eventually Royce and his staff as well. This was a tract of land at Le Canadel, in the South of France. Exactly when Claude Johnson came to buy this land is not known, but his neighbours were, on one side N Bleriot (who is famous for being the first man to fly the Channel), and on the other Clement-Bayard (an equally well-known French motor car manufacturer). Both these men were members of the Automobile Club de France of which CJ had also been a member for some years, so it is logical to presume that it was through one of these gentlemen that he heard of this delightful place. Anyway, the fact is that he bought a large piece of land in 1909 and in 1910 built himself a pleasant Villa there, which he named 'Villa Jaune'. It was whilst he was planning this venture that he and Royce received a terrible shock; the tragic death of their young partner and friend, Charlie Rolls, whilst taking part in a flying display at Bournemouth in July 1910.

He had become more and more interested in aeronautics ever since he had met the Wright brothers a few years previously. He had the true spirit of a pioneer, having had so much to do with the early years of motoring; now that it was a flourishing business, his enthusiasm was directed towards the new challenge of air-travel. He was only 31 when he died and was the first Englishman ever to be killed in an air disaster.

This bitter blow was partly responsible for the rapid deterioration in Royce's health. He had never looked after himself properly and would become so engrossed in his work that he would go for days without proper food or rest. Eventually his health collapsed completely and he underwent a major operation in 1911. When h e was recovering from this operation CJ suggested he should go, with a trained nurse in attendance, to convalesce at CJ's new Villa at Le Canadel. Royce fell in love with the place and the improvement in his health was marked. He benefitted so much from the climate and felt so much better and more relaxed that he declared it would be a splendid idea for him to have a villa there also where he could spend several months every year. So plans were drawn up by Royce himself for a villa, which he named at first 'Les Cypres', this name was changed in 1914 to 'Villa Mimosa'. There was also a drawing office for his team of designers, called Le Bureau and a smaller house where they lived named Le Rossignol'. When all this was completed Royce spent some months there every year with his design team and nurse, and the Experimental cars were sent down to him for approval. He never went to the Derby Works again except for one occasion, dividing his time between Le Canadel and West Wittering. (For more details of Le Canadel, see Part II, Chapter 3.)

PART I CHAPTER 4

The failure of a chassis component on a customer's car; Ernest Hives reproduces it and so evolves the Bump Test. Rolls-Royce cars for India for the Delhi Durbar. The London-Edinburgh Model and CJ's model 'The Mystery'. Three-quarter elliptic springs versus cantilever; the first chassis with twin rear wheels, later used on armoured cars

In 1911, a 40/50 hp car which had been involved in an accident was brought into the Works for repair, when it was discovered, much to everyone's consternation, that a component of the chassis had failed; though whether this was caused by the accident or not was impossible to say. However, the fact remained that a part manufactured by Rolls-Royce Ltd had failed, and as far as the Company was concerned this was a very serious matter. Although the damaged chassis was submitted to a very thorough examination, nobody could discover the cause of the trouble, and as a number of identical chassis had been sold a grave view was taken of the situation.

So it was left to Ernest Hives to see whether he could reproduce the same failure in another chassis. Shortly after the new Works had been opened at Derby a test circuit had been built for just this sort of occasion. It was designed like a miniature Brooklands and all new chassis were given a thorough trial round this track. Hives therefore had lumps of pig iron placed at intervals around the track and proceded to drive a chassis at high speed round and round the circuit until he finally induced the identical fault. He had such a terrible ride he decided there really must be an easier and less time consuming method of testing, rather than being shaken to pieces in this way - so he devised what has become known as the 'Bump Test', which incidentally is usually credited to Royce.

The trouble having been diagnosed was corrected, but the thing which really worried the Company and in particular Claude Johnson was those chassis which had already been sold.

It was obvious these must all be changed, but he wanted to avoid the owners knowing of the fault and was particularly anxious that no word of this should reach the Press, in case they were to give the Company bad publicity. So he decided the job must be done in the owners own garages. It was fairly easy to deal with the cars that were in the United Kingdom, but quite a number had been sold in America. However, as in England, all American owners knew that inspectors were sent regularly to see their cars as these stood in their own garages, so they were none of them unduly surprised when an inspector called to see their cars. The exception was Henry Ford, the maker of the famous Model-T, who expressed great astonishment and said that once he sold a car he never wanted to see or hear of it again and for Rolls-Royce Ltd to have sent a man all the way to America to inspect his car was something he just could not understand. The chassis he owned, No. 1972, is now in Australia. Finally, the modification was achieved and the faults rectified and nobody any the wiser.

In 1911 after the coronation the event of the year was the famous Delhi Durbar when King George V and Queen Mary travelled to India aboard the P & O Co's steamer *Medina*, which had been temporarily chartered as a Royal Yacht, sailing from Portsmouth on 11 November 1911 for the Durbar which took place on 12th December. Their Majesties visit to India and Coronation at Delhi as Emperor and Empress of India was an occasion of great pomp and splendour, attended by all the Indian Princes, in which motor vehicles played an important part.

The Rolls-Royce motor car had originally been introduced to India in 1908 by a Mr Norbury, whose car 'The Pearl of the East' did so much for the name of Rolls-Royce in India, and made it so popular with the Indian Princes. At the time of the Delhi Durbar the Viceroy of India was Lord Hardinge, but the previous Viceroy had been the Earl of Minto, who was a Rolls-Royce owner and this too had helped to popularize the make.

When the Durbar was being planned the Indian Government realized that a great many motor cars would be needed for this event, so they put out tenders to several motor manufacturers, who would be prepared to supply motor vehicles under contract, which, after the Durbar was over, could be sold to Rajahs and Maharajahs. One of the firms approached was Rolls-Royce Ltd who contracted to supply eight cars fitted with identical landaulette bodies built by Barker, Hooper, Windover and Thrupp & Maberly, the only difference between each being the interior fittings. Claude Johnson was very quick to seize on this as a piece of publicity, that His Majesty King George V was using Rolls-Royce cars in India. This was not strictly accurate, but Claude Johnson longed for Rolls-Royce cars to replace the State Daimler cars which King George V invariably used, so he became carried away with the thought of supplying the cars for the celebrations. In fact Lord Hardinge had two 50 h p 6-cylinder Wolseley Imperial limousines, which had been specially built for use in India; in addition he also had a 20/28 Wolseley. As officially the King and Queen were in some ways Guests of the Viceroy, one of the 50 h p Wolseleys was placed at the disposal of the King, whilst the smaller car was reserved for the Queen's exclusive use. So once again CJ's cherished dream of the King using a Rolls-Royce for a State Occasion was dashed.

The motor manufacturer who received far the biggest order for vehicles was the Standard Motor Co, who supplied no less than 17, one of which had a landaulette body specially built for His Majesty's use. In addition to these a further 30 were supplied to the order of the Viceroy to be used for a shooting expedition in Nepal.

The exploits of Ernest Hives in the 1911 London-Edinburgh car are too well known to need repeating; this model is today considered the absolute ultimate in sporting-type chassis built before the 1914 War, and many enthusiasts who have found a pre-War 40/50 chassis have had this rebuilt into a replica of the original London-Edinburgh car, which is known by this name for the Trials which it underwent between 6 September and 13 September 1911, when driven by Ernest Hives in top gear all the way between London and Edinburgh and back again in the R A C Trials with an R A C Observer travelling on the car. This Trial too is so well-known that nothing further need be written apart from mentioning that the car gave 24.3 miles to the gallon of petrol and was then taken to Brooklands without any change being made in it whatsoever, where it completed a lap at 78.26 mph. The following year another London-Edinburgh car was built; this was chassis No. 1826 E, and was for Claude Johnson's use in the London-Edinburgh Trials. This one he named 'The Mystery'.

From Body Card: C J London-Edinburgh Trials. 'The Mystery'.

Chassis No. 1826 E.   Received: 7.6.1912.
Tyres' 895 x 135 all round.
Car to be a duplicate of the 'London-Edinburgh Trials Car'.
R-R Mascot to be fitted to Radiator Cap.
Dunlop detachable wire wheels and one spare.
Brackets for Elliott Speedometer and Klaxon Horn.
Exhaust-cut-out.
Body: Duplicate of 'London-Edinburgh car'.
Maker: Holmes.
Colour: W Gibbs Grey, like the La Bourdette limousine.
Date of Sale: 6.7.1915, to Lieut Beardmore, Hotel Cecil, London.
Balance paid' £950. 7.7.1915.
Car delivered on: 6.7.1915, at 'S'.
Index No.: R 1265.
Side lamps: Lucas No. 626. Kit of tools with car, usual.
Tail lamp: Lucas electric. Horn and tubing Cobra.
Headlamps: Lucas self-contained.

Unfortunately, very little is known of this car which remained the property of the Company for just three years; the Guarantee Book then reads as follows:

1826 E.
Index No.: R 1265.
40/50 h p.
London-Edinburgh.
Body builder: Holmes of Derby.
London-Edinburgh Trials Car.
Mr Johnson's 'The Mystery'.
6 July 1915 - sold to Lt Beardmore, Hotel Cecil, London, WC.
Compensation Office, Canadian Headquarters, Shorncliffe, Major, Kent.
June 1917 - sold to Lt Hanslip, The Broadway House, Thorpe Bay, Essex, and 20 Warton Street, London, WC1, and 73 Cadogan Place.
May 1926 - C J Steen, Esq., Junior Constitutional Club, Piccadilly, London, W1.
Advised by PT, 1927 - Buckland, Australia.

These chassis were both fitted with cantilever rear suspension and it is worth noting that in all Rolls-Royce Ltd publicity handouts and instruction manuals of the time, from chassis No. 1700 to 2099, cars were supplied with three-quarter elliptic springing at the rear and that from chassis No. 2100 onwards cantilever rear suspension was a standard arrangement. However, my Grandfather's car, chassis No. 2445, was an exception to this rule as it had three-quarter elliptic rear suspension. If anyone can throw some light on this I shall not be the only one who will be very grateful.

In fact, there is very little information on chassis No. 2445. Richard Beaumont-Thomas was Chairman and Managing Director of Richard Thomas & Company, the steel and tin-plate manufacturers in South Wales (now known as Richard Thomas & Baldwins). He started motoring in 1903 and his first car was an open touring Crossley and later changed it for a more up-to-date model with landaulette coachwork. Some time about 1911 he was thinking of changing the Crossley landaulette for a 50 h p 6-cylinder Wolseley, which was an extremely good and very silent running car; he had decided on a Wolseley as they were made by Vickers, which was a company with which the firm of Richard Thomas & Co did a lot of business. However, his wife was insistent that if they were going to purchase a new car it must be a Rolls-Royce, she would not consider any other make after she had had a ride in her brother-in-law, Francis Treherne-Thomas' Rolls-Royce 40/50, Barker limousine. He was her husband's younger brother, and was in partnership with him. His car had one peculiar feature, it was fitted with twin-tyres to the rear wheels. Rolls-Royce Ltd were very much against this and withdrew any sort of guarantee when they supplied the chassis. Though Rolls-Royce Ltd had not had this request before, there was really nothing very unusual in it; Frank Treherne-Thomas intended to use the car for long distance Continental travel and tyres were one of the greatest problems at that time. Quite a number of the big Mercedes and Fiats which carried limousine coachwork and were used on the Continent were fitted with twin-tyres to the rear wheels. Treherne-Thomas said that twin-tyres at the rear on a heavy car loaded with a lot of luggage had far better braking, and in the event of a puncture or a tyre bursting there was always the second wheel which supported the weight and the car was far less likely to go out of control. He was determined that a guarantee should be issued to his chassis; therefore, he suggested that he would use the car extensively on the Continent and then return it to the Works at Derby, where he wished Royce personally to carry out an inspection of the chassis. When this was done the Guarantee was issued and Frank Treherne-Thomas was a Rolls-Royce owner until his death in 1932 and all his Rolls-Royce cars subsequently were fitted with twin-tyres to the rear wheels.

Unwittingly he had done Rolls-Royce Ltd a good turn as later, when the Great War broke out, and the 40/50 was used as an armoured car, owing to the tremendous weight, twin-tyres to the rear were essential, and the Company, having had the experience with Frank Treherne-Thomas, were able to go straight ahead with production.

Reverting to 2445, the details for this chassis are extremely scanty and below is a copy of the Body Card:

Chassis No. 2445. Complete Car Sale Price: £788.0.0d.
Tyres: Dimensions; Front - 895 x 135; Back - 895 x 135.
Makers: Dunlops, grooved front, S/S rear.
Date of Order: 17.6.13.

Sold to Barker & Co Ltd, 66 South Audley Street, London, W.
Deposit paid - £50.0.0d., 26.11.12. Balance paid - £739.6.9d., 8.7.13.
Car delivered on: 23.6.13. at Barkers.
Invoice: 9743 - 20th June 1913.
Brass.
Extra cost of Dunlops S/S rear.
Fit a set of Warland Rims - send direct to Barkers, o/2950. 2 spares.
Fit necessary part for C.A.V. dynamo. Charge C.A.V. direct. Their O/P.P. 5058, 5.5.13.

The car was fitted with a standard design of Barker & Co, a 'Torpedo Cabriolet', which is illustrated both open and closed in the Barker Catalogue of the time.

This car no longer exists, when Richard Beaumont-Thomas died in 1917 the car was used a short time afterwards on War work with the Green Cross. Then, at the end of the War, it was sold to Claude Grahame-White, who in turn sold it to the famous K C, Forbes Lancaster, who had the car for many years in the South of France. It returned to England, landing at Newhaven in 1931 and was later made into a shooting-brake; later still it became a breakdown car at a garage in Gerrards Cross and was unfortunately completely destroyed during the last War when incendiary bombs were dropped on the garage.

PART I CHAPTER 5

The Austrian Trial of 1913. The two chassis ordered by Czar Nicholas II. Sir John French's car, the Commander of the B E F. The difficulties of post-war production, a proposed merger with other companies. The new 20 h p car and a new small car based on a 10/15 Humber. Ivan Evernden's account of how he joins Rolls-Royce Ltd

By 1914 the prestige of the Rolls-Royce motor car was riding very high indeed, in the previous year at the Austrian Alpine Trials when competing against many other makes, the car had swept everything before it. There were four cars entered, of these three were entered by the Rolls-Royce Company, and were driven by Freiese, Austrian Agent, Car No. 1; Hives, Car No. 2; and Sinclair, Car No. 3. The 4th car to be entered was a private entry by James Radley. This was chassis No. 2260 E, and is owned now by W F Watson (who is Secretary and Hon Treasurer of the 20-Ghost Club and a past President). The route of this Trial was Vienna, Salzburg, Innsbruck, Rieva, Toblach, Trieste, Klagenfurt and so back to Vienna, a total distance of 1,654 miles. The average daily distance covered was 230 miles and the course included 19 Alpine Passes, rising to a maximum height of 7,382 ft above sea-level. On the second day of the Trial, when running from Salzburg to Innsbruck, the four Rolls-Royce cars were so fast that up the dreaded Katschberg they even overtook the official pace-making car which afterwards was unable to keep up with them, and they arrived in Innsbruck approximately one hour ahead of the official car!

Sixty years after this notable achievement in the Summer of 1973, the Rolls-Royce Enthusiasts' Club decided to commemorate the occasion by running a modified version of this same event. It was one of the most ambitious rallies which the R R E C have ever staged and models of all pre-war cars with the exception of the very early types and also the Phantom III were represented.

There were no less than 92 cars taking part, sixteen of which were Post World War II; but the old 40/50 was represented by twenty one cars built pre-1916 and twenty seven built between 1919-1926. Some of these had come from places as far away as America and Australia; in addition there were seven 'New Phantom', six Phantom II, five '20', seven 20/25, one 25/30 and one 'Wraith'.

However, the star attraction of this Rally was chassis No. 2260 E, the sole survivor of the original cars which participated in the 1913 event. On that occasion, James Radley drove her all the way and covered 500 miles from Paris to Turin in one day, a wonderful feat considering the state of the roads in those days; but this time, the present owner Fred Watson with his friend Skit Poulter wisely decided to take the car by rail from Ostend to Salzburg.

In spite of so many years having passed, 2260 E ran extremely well and the crew had only to contend with a small amount of boiling on the stiffer Alpine Passes (hardly to be wondered at after so many years), during which she had had a most chequered career including being used at one time as a breakdown car in a garage in Breconshire.

Although the 1913 Trial proved the superiority of Rolls-Royce cars the British Royal State cars remained Daimlers; however, the Rolls-Royce had found its way into the homes of other Royal persons, one of whom was the Dowager Empress Marie of Russia. Her son, the Czar Nicholas II, had had many Delauney-Bellevilles and a 15 h p Daimler 2-seater, but through the Paris Office he now ordered two Rolls-Royce 40/50 chassis; the first, 40 RB, was supplied in chassis-only form; the Czar took delivery of it and it was fitted with a limousine body and Franconia-type mudguards which he greatly favoured, but of its subsequent history nothing whatever is known. The second chassis, however, 57 PB, was never delivered. On 3rd September 1915 it was sold to Lady Wallace, 7, Chesterfield Gardens, London, and the next thing known is that by October 1933 it was owned by E Bagazacotia, of 2 Rue Street, Biarritz. Another Royal patron was the King of Egypt, who had chassis No. 12 YB.

When War broke out in 1914 the Rolls-Royce was the chassis most sought after by the Allied Command and Sir John French, Commander-in-Chief of the British Expeditionary Force used a Rolls-Royce limousine which has appeared many times in photographs; chassis No. 30 NA, index number R 1935, had actually been built as the 'Monte Carlo Trials Car', which was later to be sold to the War Office, the full details of which are below:

War Office - 30 NA
Chassis: Maker's No. 2741
Received: 6th January 1914.
Body: Limousine
Makers: Barkers
Order No. 747. Date: 31.12.13
Trimming & Painting
Green - with black mouldings.
Tyres
Front 895 x 135: Back 895 x 135
2 Dunlop Grooved
2 Dunlop S/Studded
Tyres supplied from Stores.
Sale Price: £1,400 complete
Date of Sale: 5th August 1914
Sold to: War Dept, per W H Young - Army Service Corps.
For delivery: 1st February without fail.
Car Order Form No. 1832 - Book 14 - Page 213.
Car delivered on 5.8.1914 at 'S'.
Invoice No. 13137/8
Barkers Spec. 15 December 1913.

Nickel
'B' Steering Column
London Edinburgh bonnet and dash
Lucas lighting dynamo and necessary parts, batteries, switchboard, headlights and brackets, side and tail lamps, roof and corner lights, dash lamp, inspection lamp and case of spare bulbs.
Change over switch to charge ignition batteries from dynamo

Instruments in scuttle board
One extra spare Dunlop wire wheel
Extra cost of Dunlop S/S rear
The two extra seats to be recessed in upholstery
Frameless glasses throughout
Headlight brackets
Registration No.: Yes (R 1935)
Number plates; Usual
Side Lamps: Lucas
Tail lamp: Lucas continental type
Horn and tubing: Cobra
Inflator: One
Jack: One
Repair outfit: One
Petrol funnel: One
Kit of tools given with car: Usual
Spare tyres or cover: One Dunlop S/S type
Cases for do: 2 black
Brackets to carry in: One set and well in slip. Barkers
Spare tubes: One Dunlop grooved type for 2nd spare
Headlights: Lucas
Brackets for head lights: One pair of for Lucas
Speaking Tube' One. Barkers
Inside Electric Lights: Lucas
Speedometer: Elliott
Clock: 8-day Elliott
Hood: Roll-up leather extension over driver's seat
Klaxonette - fitted to front - Lucas
Cigar lighter to interior - Lucas
Metal guards between steps and frame
Fibre mats to side footboards
Doran pattern dash lamp brackets
Aluminium treads to side footboards
Special pewter Cast India satin wood to doors and windows
Cominode handles to side pillars
Companions as selected at B. by Lord Portartington
Leather tool roll
Cabinet in inlaid satin wood to fore-end
Rugs for interior
Barker self lifting fittings to windows
Scuttle to be insulated from body by R-R method as in car 2703
Dome shaped steel wings and guards to front wings - Barkers
Scuttle ventilation
2 Elbow pieces for pressure gauges
One extra set of tyre brackets and well for carrying 2nd spare

At some time in the car's life its registration number was changed to LB 7535 and when the War was over General French took the car to Ireland with him, it was last heard of as belonging to Meller & Co, Torquay Road, Newton Abbott in Devon. General Joffre, famous as the French General who ordered reinforcements to be sent to the Battle of the Marne in Renault Taxi-cabs, which normally plied for hire on the streets of Paris, also had a Rolls-Royce for his use, chassis No. 10 ED, fitted with a cabriolet body and twin-tyres to the rear wheels. The contribution made to the Allied Forces Victory by Rolls-Royce cars and aero-engines is far too great to do justice to here. A great deal has already been written on this subject, but the reader is specially recommended to the reprinted book entitled *Rolls-Royce and the Great Victory*, which was originally published by Rolls-Royce Ltd, at the end of the Great War.

It is now necessary to go back to 1917 as, in the Spring of that year, it was quite clear that the end of the War in Europe, though still a long way off, was in sight and some plans for the future manufacture of motor vehicles had to be made; though the production of private cars had ceased in Britain and Europe, it had continued in America and on a vast scale as the figures for 1916 show:

Ford	734,811
Willys-Overland	140,111
Buick	124,834
Dodge	71,400
Maxwell	69,000
Studebaker	65,536
Chevrolet	62,898
Saxon	27,800
Hudson	25,772
Oakland	25,675
Reo	23,753
Chalmers	21,000
Chandler	20,000
Cadillac	16,323
Paige	12,456

These figures look phenomenal even to modern eyes, so it is hardly surprising that in April 1917 they were viewed with grave concern in Britain. The head of a well-known accountancy firm arranged to hold a meeting in London, with Edward Manville, Chairman of the Daimler Company and Claude Johnson, who represented Rolls-Royce Ltd. His proposal was to amalgamate all the leading motor manufacturers into one big combine which he felt would compete easily with any challenge presented by American and European Companies after the War.

In May a further meeting was held after the

following companies had been approached over this matter: Wolseley's (owned by Vickers), Arrol-Johnstone, Austin, Clement-Talbot, Crossley, Lanchester, Napier, Rover, Siddeley-Deasy, Sunbeam, Thorneycroft and Vauxhall. Of these companies the only one who had shown no interest at all was Napier. Claude Johnson was not very enthusiastic about the idea as he could forsee that all the secrets of Rolls-Royce Ltd, would have to be pooled into the 'Combine'. From his report at the next Board Meeting of Rolls-Royce Ltd, it is quite obvious that he hoped these proposals would not come to fruition and this hope now was shared by all the members of the Board. Royce wrote to his brother-in-law, Ernest Claremont, an extract from which shows the way his mind was working:

This is a very difficult subject. When I mentioned it to Mr Johnson some time ago, if I remember rightly, my ideas were that if we wanted to stay in government work and be in a strong aero position we ought to be associated with one of the bigger armament companies, preferably Armstrong Whitworths. Vickers have their motor car and aero engine departments. The only other combination of this type that I can call to mind with which we could associate ourselves would be John Brown's of Clydebank and Sheffield, which I believe includes Coventry ordinance. The Daimler Company are associated with or owned by B S A. This is one form of combination. Another form of combination would be to be associated with and control the manufacture of a comprehensive list of vehicles, such as our own luxury car, a small horse power utility chassis like a taxi and a motor lorry, which two latter would be made in separate factories and have a separate name, but would have the guarantee of being good because of being associated with Rolls-Royce. Such an amalgamation would have for its object economy of selling, manufacture and technical management.

It is difficult to see the position of the luxury car after the war. One has the impression that there will be somewhat limited use for such a car, probably much more limited than before the war. It is from this point of view perhaps that the advantages of amalgamation should have full consideration. We have always felt some effects of our isolation, and the effects of jealousy through success and I think that after the war it will be difficult to stand against it.

The amalgamation proposed by Sir William Peat appears, however, to be of a different character to what I had thought of, in which companies doing much the same work are to be amalgamated and specialized, and a point appears to be that if such an amalgamation were brought about, and we were the isolated successful Company, competition would be brought around us that would make it difficult to live.

From a personal point of view I prefer to be absolute boss over my own department (even if it was extremely small) rather than to be associated with a much larger technical department over which I had only joint control. This ought not to be considered. We would endeavour to work together.

An amalgamation of the kind mentioned has, of course, enormous economical possibilities, both commercial and manufacturing and could be represented in every civilized land, and would have a chance of competition with strong companies, or combinations of companies that will exist in America and Germany. I do not see any objection to giving the necessary figures for the proposed combination, so that we can go in or stay out, according to the character the amalgamation acquires.

I do not think the present way, that is the multitude of small companies doing a great variety of work, can possibly stand the competition after the war, and I am anxious that our own position shall not be equally weak. I feel that something must be done, otherwise the trade of motor manufacturing will leave England.

This very comprehensive summing up of the situation illustrates Royce's little mentioned grasp of the commercial world in which the Company had to operate (see Appendix B).

It is indeed fortunate that Sir William Peat's proposals never came to fruition as undoubtedly, if they had, the identity of the Rolls-Royce car would have been lost for ever.

On 11 November 1918 the Armistice was signed and many problems faced Rolls-Royce Ltd, the chief one being the enormous increase in cost of manufacture, owing to the rise in raw materials and wages.

In 1914, prior to the outbreak of war, the chassis price of a 40/50 was £985 and complete cars could be obtained for prices ranging between £1,200 and £1,400 approximately, depending upon the type of coachwork fitted, the Company had a large number of unfulfilled orders for chassis still on their order books and these clients were informed that their orders would be fulfilled as soon as possible, but there was the difficulty of a huge increase in manufacturing costs. Claude Johnson decided that the only way to deal with this and still keep on good terms with clients was to leave it to the purchaser of a chassis, in the hope that his conscience would make him voluntarily pay the price difference between 1914 conditions and those which prevailed after the War.

Owing to the all-out effort by Rolls-Royce Ltd, during the War, with Royce concentrating entirely on aero-engines, no real thought had been given to producing a new model on a return to peace-time, it was therefore decided to resume manufacture of the 1914 40/50 h p chassis, incorporating all the modifications which had been found necessary during the War.

For the first time, the chassis was to be fitted with an electric self-starter which was something Royce had been working on since before the outbreak of the War, but he had not been satisfied with his designs up until now.

In November 1913, Lord Northcliffe wrote to Rolls-Royce Ltd, urging them to fit a self-starter and Claude Johnson replied as follows:

We have long ago come to the conclusion that we should fit a self-starter, but other people may be in a position to fit self-starters, which are liable to go wrong, or which will not stand up against wear. We dare not fit anything which will ever go wrong, or which will wear badly, and we have not yet come across a self-starter which is good enough to fit a Rolls-Royce.

This letter shows clearly why in many ways Rolls-Royce Ltd, have always lagged a little behind their competitors in fitting one of the latest devices to their cars. They have often been criticized for this by members of the public, who know nothing of the problems involved, but they always refused to be rushed into premature and unsound designs.

In January 1919 a price of £1,350 was announced for the chassis of the post-war 40/50, in spite of Ernest Claremont's protests that it was far too little. Two months later it became £1,450, but by December it was essential to increase it again, this time to £1,850 and Claude Johnson did not look on the future of the 40/50 h p car with enthusiasm; especially when cancellations of orders for chassis began to arrive in Conduit Street. This was in some ways attributable to the fact that by the middle of 1919, Rolls-Royce cars which had been used in France under extremely arduous conditions at the Front, were returning home and being sold by the Government at public auction; these sales were conducted at the Agricultural Hall, Islington, and both Olympia and Earls Court in

London. These extremely well used 40/50, h p fitted with both closed and open coachwork were snapped up by a car hungry public and prices as high as 3,250 guineas were realized, on top of which most of these cars were returned to the Company for complete re-conditioning and in many cases new coachwork. Naturally after this spate of buying, orders for the 40/50 began to slow down.

Claude Johnson was most concerned about the rising production costs and he took a close look at his competitors. Below is a table which he compiled showing the increase in prices:

Make	Cylinders	HP	Pre-War price £	Post-War	% Increase
Daimler	6	45	925	1,300	40
		30	690	1,060	54
		30	690	1,000	45
Sunbeam	4	16	350	655	85
	6	24	585	965	65
Crossley	4	25/30	475	850	79
Vulcan	4	15/20	325	445	37
Humber	4	10	250	425	70
	4	14	395	600	52
Talbot	4	12	350	610	74
	4	25	425	850	100
	6	36	565	900	59
Wolseley	4	16/20	475	675	42
	6	24/30	695	875	26
	6	30/40	945	1,075	14
Swift	4	12	285	450	58
Vauxhall	—	25	480	875	82
Rolls Royce	6	40/50	985	1,450	47

Average increase – 57%

It can be seen from the above that the price increase in the case of the 40/50 was below the average general trend, so Claude Johnson considered very carefully the best course of action.

Prior to the outbreak of War, the Company had been building up a very fine export market, but this had been completely ruined by the War. The reviving of this overseas trade was not helped by European countries, in order to help their own manufacturers recover, they increased the duty payable on a foreign built car by a very great deal, in the case of France it was as high as 70%. In order to overcome this, Claude Johnson very seriously considered manufacturing the 40/50 in Europe and actually visited a works at St Dennis which was for sale. However, although he saw the possibilities, it was decided finally that the project was too expensive, though the Rolls-Royce 40/50 was in fact built at Springfield, Massachussetts, in the United States, but this is discussed in other chapters.

From time to time the potential of a smaller car had been discussed and immediately the Armistice was signed Royce started work upon a 20 h p car (known at the works as the 'Goshawk') which finally became available to the public in October 1922.

Meanwhile the cost of the 40/50 chassis had been rising so rapidly that Claude Johnson felt it was pricing itself right out of the market. It was now to receive a further blow from the Road Traffic Act 1921, as from this date all motor cars were to be taxed at a rate of £1.0.0d. per horse-power, R A C rating, and as the 40/50 is rated at 48.6 h p, this meant that in future owners would be forced to pay an annual duty of £49 per year road fund licence, which was exactly £28 more than the duty levied on a car of between 40 and 60 h p in pre-war days. A concession was made that 25% rebate could be claimed in the case of cars whose engines had been constructed prior to 1913, but this did not in any way assist Rolls-Royce Ltd, with the sale of a new chassis.

The more Claude Johnson thought about it the more he felt that the trend in world conditions would not continue to support the manufacture of the 40/50 h p chassis at an economic level, and at one stage he seriously considered an even smaller car than the 20 h p.

This was to be a 15 h p 4-cylinder, based on the designs of the 10/15 Humber, which was a car with an enviable reputation, but the Rolls-Royce version was to be built to a very much higher standard. It was given the name of 'Swallow', and was to sell for between £500 and £600, but when this idea was thoroughly costed it was realized that the car would cost appreciably more than this if manufactured to Rolls-Royce standards. It is interesting to note here that in 1922 the Austin Motor Co, brought out their famous 'Austin 12' with three alternative types of coachwork, and this car, excellent value though it was, did not compare in any way with anything that emerged from the Derby works but this model cost £550 in 1922.

One of Royce's design team at this time was Ivan Evernden, who has given me inestimable information and help in the course of my research.

In a lecture which he gave before the Derby Branch of the Royal Aeronautical Society in October 1956 he describes how he originally met the great man.

Early in 1916, I was directed to work for Rolls-Royce Ltd, by the Ministry of Munitions, having completed part of a Degree Course in Engineering at King's College, London, and being not fit for overseas service in the forces. I joined the Airship Design Office at Derby and soon learned of the mythical yet powerful personality bearing the name of Royce. The more I learned of his work, his ideals and his teaching, the more determined I was to meet him and eventually, if at all possible, to become a member of his select team.

My chance came when in the Summer of 1916, an acquaintance of mine went down to St Margarets Bay as his Secretary. I wasted no time in going down and arranged to be introduced to him.

I met him in the village, returning from a walk to collect pine cones for burning in the household grates to save coal. A tall and erect, genial man he was, like a country squire, with a soft voice and rather piercing eyes that seemed to look right inside one's mind and to read one's thoughts. So complete was the liaison between him and the Works, that, from his conversation, it was obvious that he was fully conversant with everything that they were doing and hoped to do. During the conversation I had the opportunity of conveying to him my wish to work with him some day.

This wish was realized when, in 1918, he was asked to join Royce's staff at 'Elmstead', West Wittering, where he quickly became the liaison between the Design Staff working under Royce, the Experimental Department at Derby with Ernest Hives in charge, and the Coachbuilders who were responsible for fitting the bodies on to the experimental chassis. It was in this last sphere that Ivan Evernden had to be extremely diplomatic and tactful in order to obtain from the coachbuilders the results required for a modern motor car chassis. From him I have obtained details of all the experimental cars.

PART I CHAPTER 6

The experimental 40/50 h p cars built at Derby in 1919, chassis Nos. 1 EX, 2 EX, 3 EX, 4 EX, 5 EX, and 6 EX. The first production 40/50 h p chassis in the 'X' series. The slump of 1921 hits 40/50 h p sales. The Emperor of Japan's two cars

1 EX

Chassis numbers 1 EX, 2 EX, 3 EX, 4 EX, 5 EX and 6 EX are all 40/50 h p of the 'Silver Ghost' type; the first of these, 1 EX, was on the road early in 1919. It was an open tourer with coachwork by Holmes Bros of Derby, finished in Royce's favourite colour, pale grey. Royce chose grey because it was practical, it did not show the dirt and could easily be 'touched in'. His attitude was that cars were made to be used and not just admired. In later years, the Sales Department, who were always naturally eager to see a new model and try out the latest developments, were overcome with chagrin when some fine new limousine, placed at their disposal, was finished completely in Royce's wretched grey paintwork. They, with their sights on the sales appeal, felt that the car looked absolutely nothing.

The first car to have a bulbous scuttle was 1 EX, which was used by the Experimental Department for testing and then, when they had finished with it, it was brought up to date to conform with the latest production model. All experimental pieces were removed and in many cases a new body was fitted before the car was handed over to Sales for disposal. I have no details of 1 EX whilst in the hands of the Experimental Department, but from the Body Card at Conduit Street, written up in 1923 when this chassis was to be sold, the details are as follows:

Chassis No. 1 EX	HP 40/50
Engine No. A 328	Type: Standard
Received: 28.2.1923	
Rear Axle: 16 x 52	
Sale Price: £1,100	
Date of Sale: 7.3.1923.	

Sold to: R S Arnell, Esq., 25 West End Lane, Hampstead, London. NW1.

For delivery: Immediate.
Dunlop Cord Tyres: 33 x 5, six in all.
Date of Order: 6.3.1923.
Deposit Paid: £100. Date: 23.1.1923.
Balance Paid: £1,000. Date: 7.3.1923.
Chassis delivered on 8 March 1923, to Park Ward & Co, Willesden, by 'S'.
Chassis drawing sent to Park Ward & Co on 24.2.1923.
Fittings: Nickel.
Steering: 'D'.
Levers: Body between.
Dunlop wire wheels and two spares all equipped Dunlop tyres.
Bonnet to be polished.
Locks to bonnet.
Second spare 33 x 5 straight side wire wheel.
Two spare 33 x 5 Dunlop straight side cord tyres to spare wheels.
Re-stove enamel wheels.
Complete tool kit.
Supply new battery.
'N' to supply new brake lever to standard 'set in' position.
The chassis is in second-hand condition.
Original Index number R3382.

2 EX

Unfortunately I have not been able to obtain any information from Ivan Evernden on chassis No. 2 EX, but from what I can discover from the records, this chassis was formerly number 2106, and was completed on 17 October 1912. The chassis was polished, obviously for exhibition purposes, but as nothing further was done with it until after the war, it was brought up to date and became the second experimental car, index number R3700. At one time this chassis carried a cabriolet body by Park Ward.

3 EX

Chassis No. 3 EX is the one that has frequently been referred to as the 'Hawke/Northcliffe'; Index number R4072. Apparently Lord Northcliffe, who had been a close friend of Claude Johnson since the days when CJ was Secretary of the Automobile Club of Great Britain, and who had always been a keen supporter of Rolls-Royce Ltd since the beginning and who had given advice and suggestions several times before, now had the idea of installing a Hawke aero-engine in a chassis. However, from the Company's point of view it was completely unacceptable; it was far too noisy. There was, of course, nothing original in installing an aero-engine in a motor car chassis; it had been done a number of times after the 1914 War by several firms; probably the best known of these were the famous 'Chitty Bang-Bang I, II and III' which were all powered by German aero-engines.

4 EX

There is not very much information available about 4 EX, but what there is is below taken from the Body Card:-

Chassis No.: 4 EX
Body: Second-hand, saloon limousine.
Drawing No.: 376.
Makers: Barker & Co Ltd.
Order No : 1001.
Date: 25.10.1919.
Upholstery: as fitted.
Steering: 'C'.
Body as ordered: £175.
Scuttle to be insulated from dash to break scheme.
New scuttle to rise gradually from bonnet, *i.e.* to be concave shape.
New screen to scuttle ventilation as drawing S.S.222.
Wells for two spare wheels - one each side of step or wing (tyre brackets already fitted to body).
Two bucket seats to be easily and entirely removable. To be fixed to floor boards which will come away with seats.
Standard levers set in.
Floor boards to permit easy access to chassis.
Division of screen to be 29 ins. high above top of compression cushions as on drawing S.S.221. Wrote to Barkers: 30.10.1919.
Registration No.: R 4099. Paint on petrol tank 22.6.1920. 10.0d.
Instrument board polished mahogany.
Preparing, supplying and fitting new fittings as per estimate dated 28.11.1919.
Order No.: 44297. 22.6.1920. £89.8.0d.

New lead coated steel mudguards between platform steps and chassis frame.
Order No.: 44297. 22.6.1920. Index number R4099. £8.10.0d.

Mention has been made briefly in the previous chapter about building 40/50 h p chassis in America, this will be fully recorded later, sufficient to say that by the time 4 EX was on the road, a factory had been purchased at Springfield and 4 EX was shipped out aboard the White Star Liner *Celtic*. The car was taken to America by Eric Platford, who was the Chief Tester at Derby, and on arrival at New York was driven straight to Springfield. Royce was in favour of the idea but wisely suggested that it was started in a small way and worked up gradually. Unfortunately, his excellent advice was not taken and initially the project was over-subscribed. Having served its purpose as a model to be copied 4 EX was later returned to England.

4 EX was later re-built before being sold, fitted with a new body. The details are as follows:

Chassis No.: 4 EX. (Card No. 2.)
Engine No.: 4 EX.
Body: limousine de ville.
Drawing No.: 5951.
Maker: Barker & Co Ltd.
Order No.: 1993. Date: 7.8.1924.
Chassis second-hand, sale price £1,175.
Date of Sale: 23.7.1924.
Sold to: A Spencer-Moore, Esq., 3 Cleveland Row, St James Street, London, SW1.
For delivery: 1st week October 1924.
Car order form No. 28, page 151.
Balance of chassis price paid £1,879.6.0d. Date: 12 November 1924.
Car delivered to customer on 12 November 1924, by 'S'.
2 on front seats.
2 on rear seats.
2 on extra seats.
Fittings: Nickel.
Steering: 'B'.
Levers: Standard.
Chassis sold as it stands in second-hand condition.
Body: £775.
Second spare wire wheel. Two spare 33 x 5 Dunlop tyres, £26.3.0d.
R-R Mascot, £4.0.0d.
Registration No.: XU 9989.
Number plate: Two Gransby.
Licence holder: Used.
Wind horn: Cobra.

Cases for spare tyres: Two Gertrite.
Brackets to carry in two seats.
Dictaphone in one companion.
Inside electric lights 2 and one switch.
Luggage grid at rear of approved type.
Ventilation, Spinney.
Instrument board polished.
Speedometer A.T. with R-R recording gear.
Clock, Switch.
Width of rear seat 42 ins., interior height 52 ins.
Lucas side lamps on wings.
Yale locks to rear doors.
Locks to bonnet. Folberth wiper to screen.
Windows behind driver to slide. Roper front screen.
Roll up extension over driver.
Customer to try upholstery before completion.
Four doors to open. Extra seats to face sideways and fold away flush.
Main seat to be at same angle as present Delauney-Belleville.
Silk rope pulls. Silk blinds to rear compartment.
Sorbo mats to front and rear.
Paraflor over rear seat boards.
Connect up lamps to chassis wiring. Hot-water bottle covered in pile carpet to match material used for upholstery.

This business of changing the body and up-dating the chassis to incorporate all the current features of a production model, then handing the vehicle over to the Sales Department for disposal, was standard practice with all experimental cars. The purchaser would be told little or nothing about the chassis which he was buy-ing, except that it was a second-hand car which had been used by the Company. What has been the ultimate fate of 4 EX is not known, but there is a note on the file to say that in 1946 this car was owned by Huntington's City Garage, Morton Street, Carlisle.

5 EX

The next experimental 40/50 of the 'Silver Ghost' type is 5 EX and this is undoubtedly the most interesting chassis of all in the first of the experimental series, as the car was fitted with a three-speed centre-change gearbox with the handbrake in the central position. This design was entirely Royce's idea; unfortunately it met with extremely fierce opposition from Claude Johnson, so much so that it is the one and only 40/50 h p chassis of the 'Silver Ghost' type ever to be built at Derby with a three-speed centre-change gearbox.

Royce had always maintained that a three-speed gearbox was sufficient for ordinary use, he felt that it was cheaper to manufacture and there was less weight to be carried. It was the failure of James Radley's London-Edinburgh car (which was fitted with three-speeds) when climbing the Katschberg in the 1912 Austrian Trials which had prejudiced CJ against the three-speed gearbox. (The 1972 edition of the A A Continental Handbook gives this Pass as being 5,384 ft high, 35 kilos in length and average gradient of (1 in 5½). Claude Johnson had driven previous models up just as severe if not even stiffer gradients in Scotland without any trouble at all, but the rarified atmosphere due to the altitude was undoubtedly what caused James Radley's car to fail in Austria, so that two passengers had to alight for the car to climb the hill. CJ was humiliated and was determined that such a thing would never happen again.

Though Royce was a perfectionist he was also a business man, he had already shown his capacities in this sphere in his electrical engineering company, long before he met Claude Johnson or the Rolls-Royce motor car was built, and he felt strongly that this was the design for the future. By 1920 many other makes had a centre-change gearbox. As the rule of the road had evolved in various countries with some driving on the left and some driving on the right, it was a fairly simple matter with a centre-change gearbox to put the steering on the opposite side, simply transferring the pedals and controls across, but Claude Johnson could not be convinced and so 5 EX was the only one to be made. Some time later 'The Silver Ghosts' which were built at Springfield had a centre-change gearbox and when the 20 h p became available in October 1922, Claude Johnson gave way and agreed that this model would have three speeds as it was not meant to compete with the 40/50 in any way, which was still THE car. Below are the details of 5 EX:

Card No. 1.
Chassis No.: 5 EX.
Body: Landaulette.
Drawing No.: 591.
Makers: Hooper & Co Ltd.
Order No.: 1213. Date: 29.6.1920.
Upholstery: Leather.
Body only, sale price £915.0.0d.

Sold to R-R Ltd, Derby.
Deposit paid £50 to Hoopers 14.4.21.
2 on front seat, 2 on main seat, 2 on extra seats.
Chassis drawing sent Hooper & Co 30.8.20. Later per spec. of 15.6.20.
Fittings: Nickel.
Steering: 'B'. Body as ordered £915.
Long type chassis. Central speed and brake levers.
2 ins. high radiator, bonnet and dash. Alterations to scuttle to suit.
2 ins. higher dash. Order No.: 47500. £5.10.0d.
Inside electric lights, 2 and switch. Speaking tube: None. Crests: None.
Luggage carrier to be supplied by 'W', Hoopers to fit.
Ventilation to top of scuttle.
Instrument board: Polished. Front doors to open. Both front doors equal size and position.
Extra seats to be reversible and detachable.
Tool box let into nearside step.
Front screen to slope back at top. Inside valances front wings to be carried well forward.
Spring blind to front body window only. No companion trays.
Patent window lifters of various approved patterns to windows.
Floor boards to be readily removable.
Rear seat to measure 44 in. wide.
Both doors to be fitted on American principle with Sears Cross locks.
Felt instead of rubber between scuttle and dash.
Patent window lifters - one each perfect - Tarnstedt, Two Jackson (one adjusted differently to other).
Electrical Device to be fitted if obtainable by Mr Berend.

5 EX remained a Company car right up until 1927 when it was more or less completely rebuilt and rebodied as the record shows:

Body Card No. 2.
Chassis No.: 5 EX.
Axle ratio: 15 x 52.
Tyres: Dunlop, S.S. 33 x 5.
Sale Price: £1,500.
Date of Sale: 28 February 1927.
Sold to: Major A C Abrahams, 'The Firs', Whitchurch, Nr. Aylesbury, Bucks.
For delivery: 14 March 1927.
Body: Enclosed limousine by Park Ward.
Colours: Dark blue and black.
Upholstery: Grey cloth and leather.
Deposit paid: £150. 1 March 1927.
Balance of price paid, £1,354.2.6d, 1 March 1927.
Steering column: 'B'.
Levers: Standard.
Fittings: Nickel.
Wheelbase: Standard.
Registration No.: YF 703.
Cocoa nut fibre mat to interior.

* Le C denoted Le Canadel Drawing

† Percy Northey

Altering rear squab fittings, 2 extra seats.)
Change colour to blue.   ) Not to be
Supplying luggage grid.   ) charged to
Supplying cocoa nut mat to rear.   ) customer.
Obtaining loose covers.   )
Park Ward's Estimate: £40.

The last recorded entry in the Service File for this chassis is on 30 March 1936, when it went in to Cricklewood for re-boring. On pages 45, 46 and 47 of that excellent book *Silver Ghost and Silver Dawn* by W A Robotham, he describes how he and Ernest Hives with two mechanics from the Derby works, neither of whom had ever been out of England before or could speak a word of French, took two cars, an open tourer and a landaulette, both fitted with different types of four-wheel braking systems, to the South of France for Royce's inspection, and what happened to the landaulette near Saulieu on the way home to England. I cannot help feeling that it was 5 EX which figures in this incident.

6 EX

The last experimental car of the 'Silver Ghost' type was 6 EX, details of which are laconically recorded by Ivan Evernden, as follows:

Open tourer. Pale grey. Sanderson & Holmes, Derby. Last Silver Ghost.

It was a brief summary to mark what was virtually the end of a motoring phenomenen - no other car before or since has ever raised such enthusiasm and loyalty.

And from the Body Card at Conduit Street the following information was obtained:

Makers No.: 6 EX.
Body: Open touring.
Drawing No.: LEC 1280.*
Makers: Park Ward & Co.
Order No.: 1570. Date: 11 November 1920.
Trimming and painting, grey as PN's † car. Wrote to Park Ward 5.8.1920.
Deposit of £50 paid to Park Ward 16.8.1920.
Chassis drawing sent to Park Ward 4.10.1920.
Fittings: Nickel.
Steering: 'D'.
Body as ordered: £575.
Tail lamp. 2 Lucas black finished, wing nut attachment.

Two spare wheels in wells.
Luggage carrier?
Two large vents in sides of scuttle.
Instrument board in polished teak.
Teak fillets round top of body.
Four doors to open, offside front door to be fitted with outside safety catch.
Black finish to screen.
Black fittings to hood, sticks to be polished teak.
Detachable foot rests to rear with partitions and padding to interior for tools.
Steps and front floor boards to be covered in India rubber.
Black carpet to rear of car.
Nearside front door to be 18 in. instead of 17 in.
Inclined front windscreen.
Space under front seat for one layer of tools.
Batteries in frame.
Coachbuilders to decide whether hood is to be covered in grey or black materials.
All above order dated 12.11.1920. Index number R4529.

Royce used this car up until 1925 when he took delivery of 7 EX, the first prototype experimental 'New Phantom' chassis (details of the sale of 6 EX are below), the last of the Silver Ghost' type experimental models.

Chassis No.: 6 EX.
Body: Open touring.
Sale price of car: £1,025.
Sold to Capt A M Hughes, Russet House, Tadworth, Surrey.
For delivery: Mid-June 1926.
Tyres: as fitted.
Balance of car price paid £1,120.12.9d, dated 16 June 1926. *
Car delivered 16.6.1926 to Capt Hughes by 'S' man.
Instruction book issued to customer: 24.2.1926.
Car sold as it stands with body, tyres and accessories as fitted, the whole in second-hand condition.
Duty on licence from 1st June to 31st December: £30.0.3d.
Repaint car Docker's Quaker Grey, No. 732, with black wings, petrol tank, luggage grid and chassis, and omitting red triangle on wing.
Beat out dents from wings and tie up wing stays.
Adjust the four doors.
Re-polish all polished woodwork.
Remove outside catch from o/s front door.)no charge
Repair and renovate upholstery.)   to customer
Stuff up driving squab and raise cushion.
Supply and fit new Calso Hood covered in leather cloth as selected.
Supply and fit new set of suitable side curtains, provide an envelope to match hood. Provide storage space for side curtains. £47.10.0d.
Make lower portion of windscreen to swing open. £8.10.0d.
Cover lid of battery box with India rubber and edge with angle plate 10.0d.

* Sales

Black enamel frame of rear screen. 7.6d.
Stove enamel six wire wheels. £7.0.0d.
Smith's wiper to front screen. Gill to fit. £4.10.0d.

The first 15 chassis that were built of the production series of this Silver Ghost marque were given the chassis number X; for some unknown reason this series does not appear in the usual lists at all, very little is known of them and the only details which I have as as follows:

1X. Sold to Brewster & Co, Long Island City, New York, July 1919. Shipped per White Star Liner *Belgic*. 'B' steering.
2X. Limousine Brougham. Park Ward. Sold 26 January 1922, to Reginald Mackenna, 36 Smith Square, Westminster. 'B' steering, originally sent to Paris, July 1919. Index number XK 1138.
3X. Enclosed cabriolet by Barker, in pearl grey. Ordered 28.7.1919. Sold 1920. 'C' steering. Index number R 3488.
4X. Chassis with no tyres. Sold 2.9.1919. 'D' steering, to R N Schuebe, 785 Fifth Avenue, New York.
5X. Open tourer. Kellner. 'D' steering. Sold Paris.
6X. Limousine by Barker. Sold September 1919 to Earl of Derby. 'A' steering.
7X. Barker Brougham. Show stand. 'B' steering. Index number R 4882.
8X. 3/4 Cabriolet by Barker. 'B' steering. Sold to R R Faber, 6 Berkeley Square, Mayfair.
9X. Open tourer by Hooper. 'C' steering. Sold 7.1.1921 to India by Neuralis.
10X. Barker Show Stand. Enclosed drive limousine. 'A' steering. Sold 21.11.1921.
11X. Cockshoot landaulette. Olympia. 'A' steering. Sold 10.11.1921. Col J E Groom, Dean's Green, Lymme, Kent.
12X. Barker enclosed cabriolet. 'C' steering. Ordered 11.8.1920. Index number XC 8874. Sold 25.2.1925 to Osward Faulk, Preston House, Basingstoke, Hants.
14X. Olympia Show Car. Saloon landaulette. 'C' steering. 2.12.1920. Invoice No. 24970. 20.9. 1921.
15X. Barker show 4-seater Torpedo 7½ cwt. 'C' steering. 14.5.1921.
16X. Open tourer. Mann Egerton Show. 'D' steering, 4-5 seats. Alpine Eagle type chassis. 8 September 1920.

16 X

The last of this series, 16 X, was supplied to the Soviet Government for the use of Comrade Lenin. It was later used for winter trials, with skis on the front and half-track drives at the rear and in this form it found its way into the Lenin Museum. In recent years it was removed and reconverted into the condition as used by

Lenin and given a most dedicated restoration by experts in the Likachev Motor Works.

Perhaps someone can throw more light on the remainder of these chassis in the X series. It should be noted that the number '13' was not used.

When the Slump of 1921 came, Rolls-Royce Ltd were by no means the only Company manufacturing motor cars which was seriously affected by the general trend in world trade. The Austin Motor Co, which prior to the outbreak of war in 1914 had been marketing several models including two luxury ones of 50 and 60 h p 6-cylinders, had introduced a new 20 h p 4-cylinder car built on American mass production lines. This, the Company's one and only model and which it was originally intended to sell at just over £400, had risen in price to £695 by September 1920, but by 1921 the Company was in the hands of the Receiver, in spite of the fact that the model sold in great numbers and was one of the most successful that the Austin Company ever made. Fortunately, with the introduction of the '12' in 1922 and later the famous '7', the Company recovered and never looked back.

At the time, the work people employed at Rolls-Royce Ltd in Derby who had almost doubled in number during the War when aero-engine production was at its height, were extremely skilled and efficient; the Company did not wish to lose them as they were hoping all the time that world trade would improve, so production of the 40/50 had continued, but at one stage things became so serious that there were some 300 unsold brand new 40/50 chassis stock-piled. No-one knew what to do with them. What was even worse, some 120 brand new chassis, smothered in grease, were standing in the open at Derby, under tarpaulins, as there was nowhere to put them.

Finally it was decided the only thing to do was to dismantle them and send all the parts down to the London Service Station. Those in charge in London were horrified when word reached them of this proposal; they were perfectly willing to take all small parts such as valves, guides, etc. and pieces which were fairly fast moving from the stores, but the idea of having gearbox cases, etc., appalled them; they

had never even been asked for one as a replacement; so these larger items were scrapped, or to use a Rolls-Royce expression 'reduced to produce'.

In the Guarantee Book in Conduit Street for the years 1920, 1921 and 1922, especially 1921, there are numbers of chassis with a brief note ' not erected' beside them, some of these are in the later 1920 'N' series, but the majority are in the 'O' series, commencing with 71 CE and ending with 212 MG.

It was, however, during this depressing state of affairs that an order was received for two identical cars from the Emperor of Japan; they were chassis numbers 21 UE and 38 UE the details from the Body Cards are as follows:

Chassis Nos. 21 UE - 38 UE.
H.P.: 40/50.
Engine No.: N.40 - N.86.
Type: Standard.
Received: 3.12.20 - 1.12.20.
Body: Limousine.
Drawing No.: 656.
Makers: Hooper & Co.
Order No.: 1111 & 1112.
Date: 29.10.1920.
Trimming & Painting:
Colours: Imperial red of Japan - gold line - mouldings, etc. black. (Wheels, body and bonnet painted red)
Upholstery: Light grey woollen cloth, red leather to match to front seat.
Tyres: Dunlop Magnum.
Dimensions: 895 x 135 x 150.
Front: 895 x 135.
Back: 895 x 135.
Date of Order: 30.9.1920.
No.: 46839.

Complete Car:
Sale Price: £2,100 (see letter 14.10.20).
Date of Sale: 19th June 1920.
Sold to: Emperor of Japan, thru: Tokio Gas & Electric Eng. Co Ltd, Automobile Department, Tokio, Japan.
Deposit Paid: £150.0.0d. Date: 19.6.20.
Balance of 1/3rd deposit paid: £450.0.0d. Date: 6.12.20.
Balance paid: £3,000. Date: 20.6.21.
Car delivered on 18.1.21 to Hooper & Co. by Rolls-Royce driver.
Shipped per S.S. *Inaba Maru*, 8 July 1921, from R A Docks by R Parks & Co.

Extras: Chassis drawing sent Hooper & Co on 25.10.20.
Fittings: Standard brass.
Column: 'A'.

(*Top*) A Ghost chassis on the bump rig. It is almost certainly an armoured car with twin rear wheels and possibly stronger springs, around 1915

(*Middle*) 'Le Bureau'. The drawing office at Le Canadel (*photo Johnson family*)

(*Bottom*) The 1912 40/50 hp polished show chassis number 2106

(*Top*) 1910/1912 Napier 45 hp taken in Jersey. Note the RAC badge on the radiator cap and the Frankonia mudguards. RAC rating 38.7 hp (*photo R. C. Queree*)

(*Bottom*) One of the two 1910 57 hp Sleeve-valve Daimlers of 9,422 - cc for HM George V. The Limousine coachwork is by Hooper. HM The King used these cars continuously until 1924. This photo should be compared with coloured one of chassis number 1721

(Top) Chassis 1298 as purchased by Jimmy Skinner in 1946. See Part I, Chapter 11 *(photo S. J. Skinner)*
(Middle) Chassis 1298 as she is today, restored by S. J. Skinner *(photo S. J. Skinner)*
(Bottom) James Radley's famous Alpine Eagle chassis 2206E as she is today owned and restored by W. F. Watson *(photo W. F. Watson)*

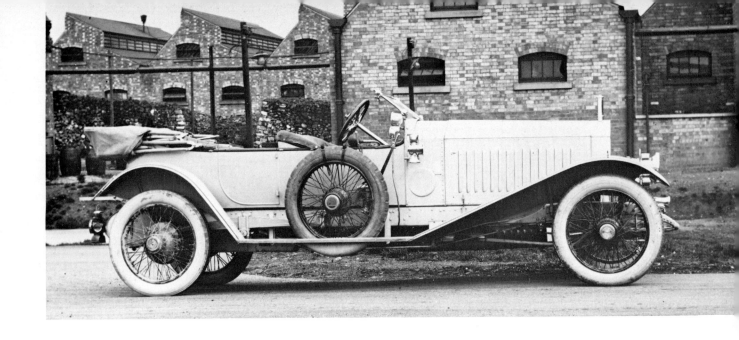

(*Top*) The 1913 Austrian Alpine works team car on the works test track. Radley's car had several different features including electric lights
(*Bottom*) The famous car used by Sir John French, Commander-in-Chief BEF 1914/18 war. Chassis 30NA is a Barker Limousine formerly the 'Monte Carlo Trials Car'

(*Top*) A special radiator experiment, about 1914

(*Bottom*) This photograph was taken in Jersey in 1934/36. It shows a pre-1914 40/50 hp car which had been modernised. It was used as a taxi between those years, however, an act was passed by the State of Jersey stating that all taxis must be closed cars. The car disappeared and nothing is known of its chassis number or its fate

(Top) November 22nd 1919. At Government Auction Sales prices of 950 to 3,000 guineas were paid for surplus Rolls-Royce cars both open and closed. This photograph, published in *The Autocar* shows some of the cars to be sold at Earl's Court. The cars in the row behind are Daimlers *(photo The Autocar)*
(Middle) *The Autocar* also published this photograph of five Rolls-Royce cars which had been used in France and were to be sold by public auction *(photo The Autocar)*
(Bottom) A Rolls-Royce with Barker body for the personal use of the Queen of Rumania *(photo The Autocar)*

(*Top*) Engine number 21664 in chassis S-266-PK built at Springfield in 1925, showing the difference between Springfield and Derby built chassis (*photo Ozzie Lyons*)

(*Bottom*) The left-hand side of engine number 21664 in chassis S-266-PK (*photo Ozzie Lyons*)

(*Top*) Chassis 9LW, a 1920 Barker Saloon Cabriolet owned by HRH Prince of Wales. He also owned the following 40/50 hp chassis: 58UG, 17TM and New Phantom 55MC (ex-81MC), all bodied by Barker (*photo The Autocar*)

(*Bottom*) Chassis 21UE and 38UE were two identical Hooper Limousines supplied to the Emperor of Japan. See Part I, Chapter 6 (*photo R-REC*)

Body: Standard chassis.
Levers: 'Set in'.
Dunlop wire wheels 895 x 135.
Springs for 6 seater limousine - weighing about 10¼ cwt.
Luggage light - usually carry 4-5 passengers.
Exhaust car heater (Dag. CB 5.10.20).
Three extra spare Dunlop wire wheels 895 x 135.
Instruction Book sent.
All accessories to be brass finished - cable 23.12.20.
Three-way switch - flush type - black finish.
Forging and fitting a pair of head lamp brackets.
Letting accumulator box into n/s step.
Forging and fitting stays for Cobra horn.
Apollo electric horn - brass finish.
Replating and treating Lucas lamps to match chassis finish.
Replating Cobra horn and Apollo horn to match chassis finish.
Two dash board lamps - black and brass finish.
Fitting Apollo horn to roof.
Pack ship and insure @ £3,200 by R Parks & Co.
Spare tail lamp - brass.
Wind Horn: Required - brass finish Cobra.
Inflator: Yes.
Jack: Yes.
Repair outfit: Yes.
Petrol funnel: Yes.
R-R Mascot: Yes.
Spare tyres or covers: Two - one x 135, one x 150 - complete tyres.
Cases for do.: Two.
Luggage carrier: Not required, see letter 14.10.20, (less allowance for luggage grid not shipped)
Spare cloth for re-upholstering, etc.
Ventilator: Spinny.
Instrument board: Polished mahogany.
Speedometer: Elliott, brass finish.
Clocks: Smith, brass finish.
Lucas lighting set (brass finish).
Leather wallet for chassis tools.
Locks to bonnet.
Carrier for extra spare wheel on nearside.
Roof ventilators
Lace and pile carpet - felt mat - two loose pile carpets for interior.

Lace armholders to rear seats.
Silk curtains on spring rollers to door and hind side 'lights'.
Front floorboards covered with rubber matting.
Drivers seat - red leather to match.
Platform steps covered in 1 in. rubber.
Tool box let into nearside step.
Canteen fitted with clock.
Cigar lighters.
Smokers tray - flower vase to interior.
Dome and reading lamp to interior.
Two step lights.
Spare material for carpets not worked upon.
Two yards of woollen cloth.
Carrier to offside for spare wheel.
Motor dictagraph to driver.
Two canopy lights - green - each with two lens.
Small supply of spare parts - bearings, piston rings, valves, etc.
Spare curtains in silk with curtain line.

In spite of the fact that Claude Johnson was delighted to receive such an order from a reigning monarch he was still deeply disturbed at the 40/50 market generally and was determined that no word of what was happening should reach the share-holders or the public. Later, when the old 40/50 was replaced with the 'New Phantom', he gave a statement to the Press which stated that during the whole 19 years the 40/50 car had been in production, there had always been such a demand for it that the Company had never been able to keep pace with the orders. It was a clever piece of publicity and the true story has never been told until now; the situation has no reflection on Rolls-Royce Ltd, it was simply a question of prevailing conditions in the world markets at the time and I cannot help wondering how other companies were faring during this extremely difficult period, made all the more so to a concern which was producing a luxury article like Rolls-Royce Ltd.

PART I CHAPTER 7

The Alcock & Brown flight. The unveiling of the Royce Statue at the Arboretum in Derby. Royce's life at West Wittering and Claude Johnson's at Villa Vita. The fitting of 4-wheel brakes to the 40/50 chassis, the plans for a replacement car. The American viewpoint on a luxury car and how the 40/50 h p sells in that country.

The problems in post-war production have already been mentioned. Royce loved his aero-engines and was never happier than when he was designing them, at one stage he remarked, 'We are in the aero-engine business to stay'.

After the war the production of aero-engines virtually ceased; there were only a very few people who had the vision to see the great potential of commercial flying and passenger-carrying aircraft; one of these was Lord North-cliffe, who offered a prize of £10,000 to anyone who attempted to fly the Atlantic. This was accomplished in 1919 by Alcock & Brown in a Vickers Vimy powered by two Rolls-Royce engines. The flight of Alcock & Brown was of tremendous value to the prestige of Rolls-Royce.

Lord Northcliffe had sent a telegram to Claude Johnson after this first transatlantic crossing by an aero-plane reading as follows: 'The superiority of the Rolls-Royce, both as a motor vehicle and as an aero-engine, is absolutely incontestable'.

Although civil companies in aviation accepted this fact and considered Rolls-Royce aero-engines the best for their aircraft, orders were not coming in fast enough for CJ. He wanted something more than this, he was determined to bring the great works at Derby to the notice of the British Authorities. So he organized a fund to which the shareholders were asked to subscribe, which was to be used for a statue of Royce to be made by Professor F Derwent Wood, R A. His idea was that the great man should receive public recognition for all the work that he had done for aero-engine design during the war. Claude Johnson himself had been offered a Knighthood, which he had declined, but Royce had only been awarded an O.B.E., which CJ felt was totally inadequate for

the man, who, to use his own words, 'was one of the greatest people alive and had undoubtedly done much to help win the war'.

The statue of Royce, when completed, was exhibited at the Royal Academy; arrangements were then made for it to be unveiled on a site in the Arboretum at Derby as a permanent memorial.

The astute CJ arranged for 250 invitations to be sent to the most prominent people in the land, especially those connected with aeronautics. Royce did not relish the tremendous publicity which he was receiving, he felt that it was most unusual to erect a statue to a living person, and his reaction to the idea was 'I am not dead yet!' However, he had tremendous respect for his partner's business acumen and he realized that this was a calculated method of attracting all the leading people in the aviation world to Derby; where they could be shown round the Works and see for themselves what tremendous care and precision went into building both Rolls-Royce aero-engines and motor car chassis. He hoped very much that the Government would place large contracts for aero-engines, thus enabling the Company to survive and continue to build 'The Best Car in the World'.

The actual unveiling ceremony was simply and briefly recorded by CJ in his Diary, thus: '27 June 1923, Wednesday. The Royce Celebration at Derby'.

It really is typical of the man that this should be the only entry. The whole organization of this affair was his and his alone, for which as usual, he would take no credit whatsoever; but it is a great pity that he has not left his impressions of the day's events.

The arrangements were that special reserved

carriages would be attached to the trains which ran from the leading cities to Derby; each guest was given a coloured flag to wear in his or her buttonhole, which corresponded with the colour of the label attached to the window of their reserved railway compartment. During the journey the guests were entertained with champagne, cigars, etc., and on arrival at the Midland Station, Derby, each party was met by a Rolls-Royce car complete with chauffeur and guide, all bearing the same coloured label as had been issued to the visitors. Each individual party consisted of no more than six persons, because CJ considered that this was an ample number for a guide to take round the Works and answer any questions efficiently.

The luncheon at the Assembly Rooms began at 1.15 p m, after which a speech was made by Lord Wargrave, Chairman of Rolls-Royce, and replied to by the Earl of Birkenhead, the principal guest.

Royce was not present at the gathering and Lord Wargrave read out to the assembled company the telegram it had been decided should be sent to him:

> Two hundred and eighty guests assembled here at a luncheon to meet Lord Birkenhead prior to the unveiling by the Under-Secretary for Air of your statue desire me to convey to you their deep appreciation of the work you have done for your Empire, and the hope that you may long enjoy health and vigour and continue your good services and to enjoy the happiness which you so richly deserve. They add hearty congratulations on air worthy certificate being granted by Air Ministry in respect of the Rolls-Royce 650 H P Condor. - Wargrave.

After this, the various parties, accompanied by their guides, were escorted to their respective waiting motor cars and taken to the Works, where they were conducted on a tour of inspection and were able to see aero-engines undergoing tests, also both the 40/50 and the 20 h p chassis.

In order that everyone present was able to examine the various departments in comfort, each party started its tour simultaneously from different points so that there would be no congestion.

The route that each party was to take was marked out by white lines and arrows (It has been said that this was the origin of the white lines now painted on so many roads.) As they entered a department, they found a table on which were cards explaining exactly what was taking place. By the end of the tour each guest had a complete memento of how Rolls-Royce aero-engines and motor chassis were made

There were many very distinguished people present, amongst whom were the following:

The Earl and Countess of Birkenhead.
The Duke of Sutherland.
Lord Montagu of Beaulieu.
Lord Herbert Scott.
Sir A Whitten Brown, K B E (who had accompanied the late Sir John Alcock in his flight across the Atlantic in June 1919 in an aeroplane fitted with Rolls-Royce engines).
The Mayor of Derby (Alderman Ling).
Mr F Derwent Wood (the Sculptor).
Viscount Curzon, M P, of Kedleston, Near Derby.
The Bishop of Derby.
Mr J H Thomas, M P.
Mr G H Oliver, M P.

The Duke of Sutherland was accompanied around the Works and throughout the whole proceedings by Mrs. Claude Johnson, whilst CJ remained completely in the background. So much so, in fact, that in his photograph album, which gives a complete picture of the day's proceedings, there is not a single photograph in which he appears, except a chance one which was taken when he was sitting in the stand erected at the Arboretum for the unveiling ceremony. This took place after the tour of the Works and was witnessed by a large crowd of people. He had foreseen this as he knew that, apart from the invited guests from other places, half Derby would be present as well. So, to give an indication of his attention to every minute detail he had ordered dozens of chamber-pots and arranged for them to be distributed in tents, placed at strategic points around the Arboretum.

What he had not foreseen was that one of the speakers would refer to him as the 'Chief Instigator of the House of Rolls-Royce'. At the mention of his name, the crowd cheered and applauded wildly. He was so overcome and embarrassed by this that he quietly left his seat and slipped away.

With the continual growing interest in aviation, Claude Johnson's plan worked and the Rolls-Royce aero-engines became more and more popular, with the result that the future began to look brighter; the 20 h p car was selling extremely well and it now only became necessary to continue with plans for a replacement to the 40/50 h p chassis.

By the time that his statue was unveiled in Derby. Royce's life had settled down to a more or less regular pattern. From December until April he lived at Villa Mimosa, in the South of France, invariably travelling by train both ways, and taking Nurse Aubin with him. From May until December he lived at 'Elmstead', West Wittering, near Chichester, in Sussex.

At the outbreak of the war, Claude Johnson and his family had been living near Burnham Beeches in Bucks, the famous beauty spot, in two cottages with adjoining gardens, one was the sleeping accommodation, the other the living; the property was known as the 'House at the End and the House Beyond'. However, when wartime travelling became difficult, he took a flat in Adelphi Terrace House, near the Savoy Hotel. In the flat above lived his friend James Barrie, the well-known playwright and author of 'Peter Pan'. It was in a central position and was very easy to travel from there to Conduit Street where his office was situated. He found it so convenient that he continued to use the flat after the war during the week but invariably spent the weekends at his own house near Dover.

For many years he had visited Lord Northcliffe at his home on the Kent coast and was never happier than when walking along the top of the cliffs between Deal and Dover, looking out over the Channel to France. It was not long before he realized his dream of owning a house there himself; the Earl of Granville had built a small shooting lodge in the Dutch style, for his grand-daughter, whose name was Vita Leuce, so he called the lodge 'Villa Vita'. When it was put on the market Claude Johnson seized the chance to buy it without delay.

In order to raise the necessary finance for this transaction, he sold the whole of the site at Le Canadel, to Rolls—Royce Ltd, and when the war was over a large wing was added to Villa Vita. So his life was divided between his flat at Adelphi Terrace, the house in Kent and Villa Jaune at Le Canadel for although it was now Company property, he still had the use of it whenever he so desired.

Early in 1920, the alterations to Villa Vita had been completed and it now made an extremely comfortable large country house where his second wife, whom he always called Mrs Wigs' resided with their daughter, known as 'Tink' (from 'Tinkerbelle' in James Barrie's play 'Peter Pan' her godmother was Pauline Chase, the original and most beloved of all Peter Pan actresses), and Claude Johnson's elder daughter, Betty, from a previous marriage. They were joined at the weekends by CJ himself, and also many of their friends from the artistic world came to stay. On these occasions Johnson arranged with the Railway Company to add a special coach to the train leaving Charing Cross Station on a Friday afternoon, especially for himself and his guests. This took place so many times that the coach became known as the 'Villa Vita Special'.

In his private life CJ was a patron of the arts, and any spare time which he had from his work in Rolls-Royce Ltd was spent in the Art Galleries in London. His hobby was discovering talent and Ambrose McEvoy, the painter, Marcel Dupre, the French organist, and Gustav Holst, the musician, were all financed and launched by Claude Johnson; it gave him great delight to help promote someone he considered talented and deserving. As his elder daughter wrote in the Forword to my book *The Hyphen in Rolls-Royce:*

His passion was pictures and music, especially Debussy and Bach (both representative of himself). He was both Romantic and Realist in the best sense of both, rare combination which must have spelt conflict.

Nothing beautiful or lovely went unnoticed by him or unworshipped - from the opening of a flower or leaf, a change of light on cloud or sea, to a masterpiece in painting or music. Beauty was his creed, as loving was. Self-glorification was an anathema to him - he would have none of it, neither praise nor honours. This was not modesty but realism. Everything he did he considered as a privilege, his brain or money had enabled him to put before the world a Good Thing, to be recognized as such - *he* simply did not come into it, to his way of thinking!

In sharp contrast to CJs extravagant way of life, Royce lived somewhat quietly, a remote figure cut off from Derby and alternating between West Wittering and Le Canadel in the South of France. During his life-time CJ built 'R' into a legend, which he did nothing to seek and in fact did not at all relish. CJs one thought, however, was to keep the Rolls-Royce car prominently in the public eye. Sometimes he travelled to Derby by rail from London and on these occasions always had a first-class carriage reserved in the name 'Rolls-Royce'; he invariably arrived at the station late, so the train would be held specially for him, so people would ask 'Why the delay?'. 'We are waiting for Mr Rolls-Royce' would come the reply, just one of the many ruses to make Rolls-Royce a household word.

'The Silver Ghost' model has been criticized for not having 4-wheel brakes fitted to it at an earlier date, but this is most unfair and is made without knowledge of the facts. In fact, almost immediately after the Armistice, Royce started working on 4-wheel brakes; many grave problems arose owing to the additional weight to the front axle, so Rowledge, who had joined the design staff from Napiers, was sent on a world tour to examine the various types being offered for sale, and if anyone cares to look in the back files of *The Autocar* they will see that the Company were fitting 4-wheel brakes late in 1923. In *The Autocar*, 2 November 1923, there is a whole article headed 'Rolls-Royce Adopt Front Wheel Brakes'. This was, of course, for the 1924 models and the system which Rolls-Royce fitted then was so efficient that it was carried on, even after this last war, on the 'Silver Wraith', etc.

At this time, few makers of luxury cars were fitting 4-wheel brakes as standard. For example, the Daimler Company were producing three basic large types as chauffeur-driven cars, the TJ 6/45, the TS 6/30 and TB 6/21; of these models front wheel brakes could only be obtained on the 6/45 and cost £50 extra. They were also making the following models for the owner-driver, C-type 35 h p, C-type 25 h p, C-type 20 h p, and D-type 16 h p, and of these only the 35 h p chassis was fitted with 4-wheel brakes. Armstrong-Siddeley would supply 4-wheel brakes on their big 30 h p car at an extra cost of £35, and it was not until the end of the following year, 1924, for the 1925 season that 4-wheel

brakes became very much more universal in use.

The cost of developing and fitting 4-wheel brakes to the 40/50 chassis was an extremely costly exercise, in fact over £70,000 was spent before Royce was satisfied with the design. Added to this a number of cars, which had already been sold, were returned to the Works to be fitted with front wheel brakes, which added something over £12,000 to the project, but this was a goodwill gesture at a very difficult financial time; it was however essential, as a motor manufacturer has to supply what the public demands.

In September 1922 it was decided that an entirely new 40/50 h p chassis should be designed to replace the old 'Silver Ghost' model; when the new car did appear however in May 1925, it was only the engine that had been changed and it emerged as the 'New Phantom'.

At the time that Royce was working on his designs for 4-wheel brakes and a replacement big car for the 40/50 chassis, Claude Johnson was heavily involved in the manufacture of Rolls-Royce cars at Springfield, Massachussetts, in the United States. The Springfield project, which was something entirely new to Rolls-Royce Ltd in manufacturing motor cars abroad, was almost like venturing into the unknown and it is fully discussed in subsequent chapters; sufficient to say here, that though the theory was excellent, to produce the cars in America, using the trained men already there, unfortunately in practice it did not work as well as he had visualized. Though the Rolls-Royce car had been used during the war both as an armoured car, and as a staff car, and had given magnificent service under the most arduous conditions, it must be remembered that Great Britain and her allies were making an all-out effort to win the war and no expense was spared to achieve this object. With Government backing, producing spare parts at Derby did not present a problem, and transporting them to Europe if required was also relatively easy as the distance was not great. However, America was an entirely different story, it was such a vast country and so far from Britain. Added to which the lack of roads and the varying climatic conditions of the different States produced all sorts of problems which had never been encountered before. The car now had to sell on its own merits and produce a profit for the Company. Excellent though the 40/50 model was, the problems of servicing a chassis which had been sold to a customer living possibly some 3,000 miles from Springfield made things very difficult and it soon became apparent that, in order to meet the conditions under which the 40/50 was being operated, some major changes would have to be made in the design.

To some wealthy Americans who prided themselves on buying the finest European automobile, the Springfield-built car was somehow not the same, and they still insisted on having a chassis direct from Derby, usually having English coachwork mounted on it. Many English enthusiasts who own Derby-built cars of the various models made pre the 1939-45 war, are inclined to dismiss the Springfield car as something inferior and point to the fact that Springfield finally closed its doors and built no more Rolls-Royce cars after 1931, to endorse this belief. In fact, nothing could be further from the truth, the Springfield cars were every bit as good as those built at Derby, only necessarily adapted to meet the peculiar requirements under which they were operated. It was not the car that caused the doors at Springfield to close, it was simply that an extremely expensive motor car was being manufactured there uneconomically, in small quantities, and there was nothing to underwrite it as the aero-engines did for the Derby works.

When I was researching into the Springfield car, I wrote to Dr Mark Sheppard of St Petersburg, Florida, who was kind enough to put me in touch with John W McFarlane, formerly Editor of the Rolls-Royce Owners Club of America Inc Magazine *The Flying Lady*, who in turn gave me the address of Arthur W Soutter, who worked at Springfield in several capacities from 1920 onwards, finishing up as Chief Engineer, having already been General Maintenance Manager. Mr Soutter gave me the most enormous assistance and was kind enough to read the typescript of all the chapters dealing with Springfield.

It must be remembered that the Rolls-Royce 40/50 chassis was not the only luxury and very expensive motor car being manufactured in America at this time. The Americans have never done anything by half measures and the wealthy American has always demanded the best and been prepared to pay for it; most English people regard the Packard, Cadillac and Lincoln as the only luxury American makes, with Buick and Chrysler in the middle price range and Ford and Chevrolet in the cheaper range. This is because these are the cars which were imported in considerably large quantities into Great Britain about this time and these Companies set up very good sales and service departments in England. There was a high customs duty imposed on the importation of any foreign car into Britain at this time, and this is the reason why many of the real luxury American chassis never reached these shores. Amongst these makes were the Dorris, the Cunningham, Locomobile and Brewster. All of these fell by the wayside in the 1920s as they were too expensive to produce and were manufactured in too small quantities to be a viable economic venture. It is therefore all the more to the credit of Springfield that in spite of all the difficulties and drawbacks the Rolls-Royce car was made there for so long.

PART I CHAPTER 8

How the American Works at Springfield came into being, with an account by Maurice Olley

Most people who have been associated with Rolls-Royce cars for any length of time know that the 40/50 h p chassis, both as 'The Silver Ghost' type and 'New Phantom', were built at Springfield, Massachussetts, in the United States of America. Various books which have already been published have mentioned the Springfield project, but until now no details have been given of how the idea arose of manufacturing Rolls-Royce cars in America.

In order to explain how this idea was formed it is necessary to go back to the year 1912, when a young man, named Maurice Olley, who had served an apprenticeship with H W Ward in Birmingham, became an employee of Rolls-Royce Ltd. Originally he had wanted to serve an apprenticeship with the Daimler Company in Coventry, but they had demanded a fairly stiff premium and a relative had advised, 'Put the boy into the machine tool trade, then at least he will know how to make the stuff'.

When Olley completed his apprenticeship, late in 1912, he answered an advertisement in the British edition of the *American Machinist* which only gave a box number; he was both surprised and pleased when he received a reply from Rolls-Royce Ltd at Derby.

At first he worked in Derby under Thomas Nadin, living in lodgings in Sale Street, not far from the Arboretum, and travelling by tram-car each morning to Osmaston Road, where the Rolls-Royce works were situated.

Early in 1913 he was sent by Nadin to Le Canadel and it was here that he met Royce for the first time and promptly became one of Royce's greatest admirers. He worked in the design team with the great man, but it was always understood from the commencement of Olley's employment by Rolls-Royce Ltd that he

would spend a certain amount of time each year in the United States of America, studying tooling and manufacturing out there, which was something that he particularly requested. However, in spite of the fact that this was agreed, owing to the outbreak of war in August 1914, he remained in England, working with Royce at St Margarets Bay in Kent, and later living in the Royal Norfolk Hotel at Bognor in Sussex whenever the design team was there. On one occasions he went down to Bournemouth to drive Royce home, but Royce thought so little of Olley's driving that he took the car over himself before they reached Southampton, and it was the first and last time that Olley ever drove him!

During all this time Olley was working on the designs of what was to become the first Rolls-Royce aero-engine, 'The Eagle'. This very important development, that of entering the field of aero-engines, came about in an interesting way.

One of the people to visit Royce at his house in Kent was James Radley, who had done so well in the Austrian Alpine Trials of 1913 with chassis No. 2260 E (now owned by W F Watson of the 20-Ghost Club).

He was at the time in charge of Navy 'Blimps' concerned with maintaining communications with the Dover Patrol, and in a letter dated 27 May 1965, written to Mike Evans, former Public Relations Officer and Rolls-Royce Historian, who has been such a help to me in compiling this book, Olley writes as follows:

> I recall Radley's visit very clearly. A very clear afternoon in the garden at St Margarets, with a light westerly breeze, and a Navy Blimp hanging apparently stationery over the Straits, facing our way. Two French rotary engines were driving the two propellers very slowly, and Radley was saying that they'd

probably run out of petrol before they reached the coast and have to ditch or be blown back over Belgium. Would R agree to let him have a couple of Silver Ghost engines which he could cut down and lighten in various ways, to provide some reliable power for his little airships? He described British production of aircraft engines as non-existent. The only thing even faintly resembling an aircraft engine made in Britain was the 4-cylinder, aircooled Vee engine made by J A Prestwich. This was really an adapted motorbike engine, lubricated with castor oil, which it spewed over the pilot (with predictable results!)

Also there were discussions in the British Press that motorcar builders were obviously not the ones to make reliable aircraft engines, since motorcar engines worked at full throttle for only a very small portion of their lives. Anyone like Gardner who built a good marine engine was far more likely to produce an airplane engine which would keep on running!

Radley thought this was all nonsense, and that valuable time was being wasted. And, although he didn't get his car engines, I think his visit led directly to the next act, which was the visit to Mervyn O'Gorman at the Royal Aircraft Factory at Farnborough.

This visit appeared at the time to be fruitless, since Mervyn O'G, and his ch. engineer Green, were interested only in aircooled engines. R. agreed that in the long run they might be right, but he understood that developing a successful aircooled cylinder was a lengthy process, and meanwhile both Mercedes and Austro Daimler were producing no engines of either sort. If he was required to get a lot of power out of a cylinder he would prefer to have it watercooled.

This about ended the discussion.

Meanwhile at Derby Claude Johnson's first reaction to the declaration of war was one of panic. He recommended that all employees join the Forces as he could see no likelihood of a Company which was building a luxury motor car being able to contribute to the War Effort, and it was actually Mr Biddulph, the night shift superintendent at Derby, who realized that it would be a war in which precision engineering would play a major part, and on his own initiative he negotiated a contract with the Government for manufacturing shells.

As a result of Royce's visit with CJ to the Royal Aircraft Factory at Farnborough, a contract was drawn up for Derby to produce Renault air-cooled aero-engines, which, as Olley has already mentioned, Royce did not like at all, as he said they were of unsound design and he much preferred a watercooled engine. For this purpose he chose a 60° V12 and work proceed-

ed rapidly, but when O'Gorman saw the designs Royce had produced, he still did not like them. The first real encouragement R-R received was from Comdr Briggs of the R N A S, who was living in the Russell Hotel in London. Within six months of starting to design the new aero-engines one was completed and was duly named the 'Eagle' by CJ, as he decided that aero-engines should be named after birds of prey. When it was run on test, which was supervised by Hives (later Lord Hives), it produced 25 brake horse-power more than the designers had intended. The earliest example delivered 225 b h p at 1,800 rev/min, and, as Royce's policy was always continuous improvement, by February 1918 the same engine, with modifications, was giving 360 b h p at 2,000 rev/min.

The Admiralty was now definitely interested and ordered 25 engines. In 1915, engines named the 'Hawk' and the 'Falcon' were produced.

In April 1917 the United States entered the war on the side of the Allies and there was a rumour that the American Government would contract to build Rolls-Royce 'Falcon' aero-engines. Olley was extremely interested in this as he still had thoughts of his promised yearly visit to America and, as he says in his letter to Mike Evans:

This was a time of uncertainty and finally R, looking over his spectacles with a wise and patient expression, said he would let me go for 8 months, but he had no doubts that, if I wanted to stay longer, I would find some good sounding excuse for doing so.

Maurice Olley sailed from Liverpool to New York aboard the Intermediate Cunard Liner *Andania* in July 1917, and had an eventful passage which lasted two weeks. Claude Johnson had gone to America a month before at the invitation of the United States Government, taking Thomas Nadin with him in order to sort out a projected contract for 1,000 Rolls-Royce aero-engines, but the Americans had designed an engine of their own which they named the 'Liberty', which had been designed by Major (later Col) Vincent of the Packard Motor Company. All the ramifications of the 'Liberty' engine and how Claude Johnson eventually succeeded in persuading the Americans to build Rolls-Royce aero-engines is such an involved story that there is no place for it here; sufficient to say that Maurice Olley remained in America and did not return home to

Britain until late in December 1918, when he sailed to Liverpool aboard the Cunard liner *Caronia*.

By the end of the war in Europe the future looked very uncertain; Great Britain was impoverished and at one time it was thought that all motor manufacturers would be asked to pool their resources and build a standard car to a set design. This was unthinkable to Claude Johnson who foresaw that there would be a ready market for the Rolls-Royce car in America as it had always sold well there, and a number of the best men in Rolls-Royce had now worked out there for some considerable time building aero-engines, and they had all the necessary contacts. Maurice Olley was one of the most outstanding of these. When he returned to England aboard *Caronia* he did not see Royce but he heard that Royce was agreeable to making 'The Silver Ghost' chassis in America if it could be started in a small way, and he describes what followed:

The Cleveland R-R office was still operating on the post-war clean-up, and Nadin was still in Cleveland. K K Mackenzie was interesting himself in finding a 'backer' for the car project and the matter of a factory and a location had to be settled. I think it must have been late February or early March 1919 that I started back for New York on the *New Amsterdam* of the Holland-America line, which had been in mothballs during the war. This was the old ship built in Belfast, a slow tub, but very comfortable. We lay two days or more in harbour at Brest, taking aboard a New York regiment which had been with British and Australian troops at the Hindenburg Line. They were enthusiastic in praise of the Australians, who had helped them when they first arrived in the line.

Arrived in New York, and almost immediately went with Kenneth Mackenzie to Charlotte, N Carolina, to see J B Duke, the 'Tobacco King', who was said to be interested in the car project. Duke must have been close to 70, but had the appearance and manner of an enormous boy. He declared he was not interested in the R-R proposal as it was outlined to him. Thought it should proceed very slowly indeed until after the post-war depression which was certain to come.

J B Duke's principal assistant was a Mr Patterson, who soon after called on us at the New York office and tried to hire me on a most interesting project. This was the design of a machine to make 'hand made' cigars! Machine made cigars are molded bundles of tobacco leaves covered with a single layer of hand wrapped outer leaves, whereas the real Cuban cigars are built up by wrapping the leaves from the centre outwards. Apparently this makes a real difference to the cigar smoker.

Patterson had a machine shop in Brooklyn where some Swedish toolmakers were experimenting with a machine which picked up individual leaves by vacuum cups and imitated the hand motions of 'the Cuban' cigar makers in building a cigar. He said it 'almost' worked.

Have heard nothing more of this machine and imagine that the increasing flood of cigarette smoking decreased interest in the cigar market.

Then J E Aldred appeared on the scene. He was the son of a Lancashire mill foreman. The father had been brought to New England when the first cotton mills were built. The son made his first money with a patent for printing wallpaper. Aldred and his associates became promoters of some very large hydro-electric projects in the U S and Canada, in the days when these could still be handled by private enterprise. They had a controlling interest in the Gillette Co, in Boston. They had money and enterprise, and, from their own point of view, showed great patience in handling such a very foreign project as the building of costly motorcars. But their ideas were quite at variance with Rs notion of a small and quiet beginning, and they were looking for adequate returns of the enterprise.

The summer of 1919 was spent, with a representative of a large New York real estate concern in looking for a suitable factory location. The line from Buffalo to Boston appeared at that time to cover the desirable area from the point of view of labour and material supply. Today the automobile has made the whole population nomadic, and skilled workmanship is available practically everywhere, but it was not so in the early twenties.

Finally the former American Wire Wheel plant in Springfield, Mass was found by far the most suitable, and was purchased and the R-R team assembled there. These were most of the W W I team from Cleveland with several additions, Ed Poole, Walter Hulley, John Southern, John Moon, Bob Burton, from Derby, and Ernest Caswell from New York, etc.

L J Belnap, who headed the enterprise, had been right hand man to Sir Henry Japp in the British Purchasing Commission, and stood very high with the R-R team. Kenneth Mackenzie was Secretary of the Company.

In November 1919, Maurice Olley married and the following month he and his wife arranged to take a sort of business honeymoon in England and they sailed aboard the big Hamburg-American liner *Imperator*, which later became the Cunard Company's *Berengaria* until she was scrapped in 1938. She had been taken over as a War Reparation at the close of hostilities and was being operated under her original name by the Cunard Steamship Company. This was her first return trip to Europe and Maurice Olley says that undoubtedly someone had lost the instruction book and the crew were unable to decipher the German instructions on all the controls; the result was the voyage lasted two weeks and they finally made Southampton with an appalling list!

The newly-weds visited Royce at West Wittering where he was 'exceedingly kind and hospitable. He still counselled a small and modest start at Springfield and of course he was right, but every external circumstance prevented it'.

When the Rolls-Royce works at Springfield opened, Maurice Olley was chief engineer; Thomas Nadin, general superintendent; George Bagnell, works manager; and Harry Purdon, chief inspector. The target rate was 350 chassis per year, a figure which unfortunately was never reached. As has already been mentioned in a previous chapter, chassis No. 4 EX, was sent out to Springfield to be used as a 'guinea-pig' and during 1920 the project was launched with 53 supervisors from Rolls-Royce Ltd at Derby to train the workers in the traditional Rolls-Royce methods and precision.

The first Springfield-built cars were identical in every way to their Derby counterparts, but it was soon discovered that, good as the Derby-built car was, a number of alterations would have to be made owing to the conditions under which the cars were being operated.

The servicing facilities which Rolls-Royce Ltd had always provided for their customers could not be bettered by any other company; during the war Rolls-Royce cars had played a very important part in practically every theatre of war. Now, however, the peacetime situation was different. Rolls-Royce Ltd were in business to make money, and the car, with no outside assistance, had to show a profit, so it was quite out of the question economically to set up a wide range of service stations throughout the length and breadth of America for a luxury car which was only going to sell in small numbers.

One of the snags quickly discovered was that the right-hand drive steering position was a major drawback from the sales point of view. No changes, however, could take place without the approval of Derby and this naturally took time to obtain, especially as Claude Johnson considered any alterations to what he thought was a perfect car was totally unnecessary.

Chassis numbers first used were Derby ones, 102 CE to 107 CE, 112 NE to 123 NE, then the following AG series cars, 7, 11, 15, 19, 22, 26, 30, 33, 36, 39, 42, 45, 48, 51, 53, 57, 60, 63, 66 and 69.

The first modification to appear was the substitution of the American Bosch Magneto which appeared on chassis No. 33 AG; also, the generator (or dynamo) on Derby-built cars was made by Lucas to Rolls-Royce specifications, and this was changed to a Bijur dynamo, commencing with chassis No. 95 MG. Then, beginning with chassis No. 147 JG, in addition a Bijur self-starter motor and a pilot jet (the well-known Royce starting carburettor) were fitted to the engine. On chassis No. 51 SG American Bosch single coil battery ignition was used, together with a Bosch horizontal coil. All these minor changes using American components facilitated servicing and replacement. The wire wheels were made by Dunlop, and with chassis No. 89 SG another change came in that the wheels were made in the U S A by an American firm.

Springfield managed to weather the slump fairly well, and, from a letter written to me by Arthur Soutter (who was employed by Rolls-Royce of America Inc throughout its entire existence, and without whose assistance this chapter could never have been written) the following is learned:

> During 1921, when a total of only 135 chassis had been built, it was necessary to curtail operations and reduce the working force, about mid-year, because the initial expenditure for plant and equipment, the tremendous cost of tooling, the commitments on purchase contracts, and the buildup of inventory had reduced the cash position of the company to a mere $45,696. To provide additional working capital to carry on it was necessary to issue 8% sinking fund Gold Notes in the amount of $2,000,000.
>
> During the year 1922, when 230 chassis were built, the operations netted a loss of $111,566, and the bonded debt had to be further increased by the issue of sinking fund Gold Bonds, of which $3,000,000 were authorized and $1,963,000 outstanding.

Although many British Rolls-Royce enthusiasts may dismiss the Springfield car as being an inferior article to the Derby-built one, nothing could be further from the truth. During the time that it was in production, there was a certain amount of competitive spirit at Springfield rather like the desire of a younger member of the family to do as well, if not better, than the elder brother. What is surprising, is that Springfield survived for so long, the cars were tremendously expensive and in the Sales List dated 25 November 1924, the price of the stripped chassis alone was $11,385, which was a sum very considerably in excess of the best American car available, complete with coachwork.

There were numbers of well-known coachbuilders in the United States, who specialized in building motor car bodies: Brewster, Locke, Willoughby, Dietrich, Judkins and Murphy, amongst others, were some of the most notable and in a letter on this subject, Arthur Soutter wrote to me as follows:

Coachwork was a problem, initially, principally because the customer had to be educated to accept a real change in his buying habits. Rather than to inspect and decide upon a completed car viewed on the sales-room floor, he bought a chassis, selected a body style from a series of pictures, discussed a lot of details and decided upon optional equipment, specifications for paint, upholstery, trim, etc, and then waited for the coachwork to be built and mounted. In the pre-lacquer days, when each of the 18-20 coats of paint and varnish required drying and rubbing time, this involved what the customer thought was a long, long time!

Fortunately, there were plenty of skilled craftsmen in the Springfield area who had experience in building fine coachwork for a couple of the pioneer automobiles which had been built locally - the Knox and the Stevens-Duryea. In 1922 we leased space in the old Knox building and set up a division to design and build Rolls-Royce coachwork. These were very satisfactory and many of our popular and better known body types were designed there.

The earliest list of Sales and Prices that I have is in the book *The Living Legend*, and Arthur Soutter says these were the lowest prices ever quoted and are for November 1923, and read as follows:

Rolls-Royce Chassis Complete Including Rolls-Royce Custom Coach Works

The Open Motor Carriages
The 'Pall Mall' 4 and 5
passenger Phaeton .. .. $10,900.

The 'Piccadilly' 2 and 3
passenger Roadster $11,400
The 'Oxford' 6 and 7
passenger Touring .. .. 11,450.

The Enclosed Motor Carriages
The 'Tilbury' Enclosed Drive
Cabriolet, permanent or collapsible .. $12,800.
The 'Windsor' Open Drive Limousine .. 12,850.
The 'Pickwick' 7 passenger Sedan .. 12,900.
The 'Canterbury' Surburban Limousine 12,900.

The Formal Motor Carriages
The 'Arlington' Limousine Brougham .. $13,050.
The 'Salamanca' Collapsible Cabriolet .. 13,500.
The 'Riviera' permanent three-quarter
Cabriolet with 15" side quarter windows 13,500.
The 'Mayfair' permanent full Cabriolet .. 13,800.

Regular Extra Equipment
Trunk Rack, Front Bumper, Radiator Shutters, Black (Allen), and Built-in Rear Shock Absorbers, all attached at Works, $150. F O B Springfield, Mass.

Standard Chassis Equipment Consisting of
Two Spare Detachable Wire Wheels
Two Spare Tires and Tubes
Five Lamps
Speedometer and Clock
Mascot
Klaxon Horn
Jack
Kit of Tools and Spares
(All Prices subject to change without notice)

WAR TAX EXTRA
(Extra equipment listed on inside pages).

Extra Equipment at Extra Charge
*Trunk Rack (Attached) $90.00.
Trunk Fitted with Three Suitcases 125.00.
Heater 75.00.
'Stop' Signal Light (Rolls-Royce design) 30.00.
*Front Bumper 25.00.
Rear Bumper 35.00.
*Radiator Shutter (Allen) Black 20.00.
Radiator Shutter (Allen) Nichel Silver 40.00.
*Built-in Rear Shock Absorbers 67.00.
J-H Tonneau Windshield (Nickel-plated
detachable) 185.00.
Menard Spring Gaiters, Set of 4 30.00.
Tire Cover (Tire only) 10.00.
Tire Cover (Entire Wheel) 15.00.
Fire Extinguisher (Pyrene Nickel Finish) 12.50.
Chains (Weed) 9.00.
Mirrorscope (Attached to spare tire) 30.00.
Mirrorscope (Windshield type - attached) 20.00.
Lucas Dimmer 17.50.
Automatic Windshield Wiper 20.00.
Searchlight without Mirror (Attached) 18.50.

Searchlight with Mirror (Attached)	20.00.
English Leather Upholstery (Open Cars)	150.00.
English Leather Upholstery (Closed Cars)	250.00.
Pull up Straps, Per Set	15.00.
Slip Covers (Roadster)	125.00.
Slip Covers (5 passenger Touring)	150.00.
Slip Covers (7 passenger Touring)	175.00.
Slip Covers (Limousine)	200.00.
Wood Wheels (If ordered before erection of chassis)	400.00.
Wood Wheels (If ordered after erection of chassis)	550.00.
Victoria Tops (Burbank)	125.00.

Victoria Tops (Patent Leather)   275.00.

NOTE - Charge for Victoria Top Covers extra charge when replacing Touring Tops.

*NOTE - Trunk Rack, Front Bumper, Radiator Shutter, Black (Allen), and Built-in Rear Shock Absorbers, $150, all attached at Works, if specified at time of original order.

All Prices Subject to Change Without Notice.
WAR TAX EXTRA.

PART I CHAPTER 9

The Springfield 40/50, and the alterations made to this model to make it more suitable for American conditions

Throughout the whole of the 1920s wooden spoked artillery wheels were extremely popular on all American cars. They had detachable rims and it will be noticed that they were available on the Springfield car at an extra charge Arthur Soutter tells me that he can only remember one car being supplied with them. He has been kind enough to give me a detailed list of the differences that were made between the Springfield car and the Derby original during the whole of the production run, and I cannot do better than quote from it here

During the years 1920 thru 1924 R H Drive were built (Chassis Nos. 1-1100).
Chassis 1-25 were identical with Derby in every respect.
26-90 American Bosch Magneto ZR6-ED19 replaced Watford Magneto C-6.
91-125 Bijur Generator replaced Lucas Generator
126-175 Bijur Starting Motor replaced R-R Starting Motor
176-210 American Bosch single Battery Ignition replaced R-R Battery Ignition
211-275 American Wire Wheels replaced Dunlop Wheels because of servicing difficulties.

All of the above changes were made because of wide-spread service facilities in this country for the items adopted, and the difficulty of servicing the items deleted.

276-625 Double row thrust bearings fitted to Torque Tube and rear axle; improved Fabric Coupling; oil fed automatically to Sphere, and trumpet retainers added. Changes deemed necessary by reason of experience.
626-700 Keyed tappets adopted incorporating Derby revision.
701-800 45 degree Engine Valves adopted per Derby revision.
801-1000 Changed from 12 volt to 6 volt electrical system, with Westinghouse Generator and Starting Motor. R-R was the only car in America with a 12 V system and service conditions necessitated the change. Metal Tool and Battery Boxes on Frame replaced Running Board Boxes as a styling change.
1001-1100 Torque Reaction Dampers and increased Foot Brake Leverage added to incorporate Derby revision.

Changing from R H to L H Drive was a rather extensive change which was found necessary to remove a definite deterrent to sales. All other cars manufactured in America had L H Drive. R H Drive was the distinctive mark of an European car and, while this appealed to a few prestige-minded people, the majority found the use of a car having R H Drive to be awkward and inconvenient in the American traffic pattern, and considered it unacceptable. The change was not, as rumoured, dictated by laws and regulations.

Making this change obviously affected the Steering Box, the Front Axle and the Pedal Mechanism. It also involved elimination of the Side Lever Mechanism and the introduction of a Central Gear-shift Mechanism. To accomplish this, a completely new Gearbox was designed which was made three speed instead of four-speed, three-speed being more popular at the time in America.

In moving the steering box to the L H side, it was necessary to avoid the radiant heat of the exhaust manifolds, which were on the same side This did not however, involve a major change. A one-piece manifold with a single downtake pipe at the front end replaced the two separate manifolds and two downtake pipes.

In addition to the changes essential to the change to L H Drive, the opportunity was taken to incorporate further changes as follows:-

Exhaust heated throttle body replaced the water heated, as standardized by Derby.

Cylinders revised and covers added to enclose Tappets and Valve Springs, to avoid tappet wear resulting from dust and dirt, and to avoid smell from escaping fumes.

A 5 in. Westinghouse Generator (engine driven) was mounted on the crankcase instead of being inaccessibly mounted on the gearbox and belt driven. A Wheelcase Generator Drive Brake was added to the wheelcase to avoid periodic vibrations being transmitted to the timing gears.

The Magneto was eliminated and a Double Battery Ignition added. This allowed synchronization of both ignitions at all speeds, a feature which was not obtainable with Magneto and Single Battery Ignition.

A receptacle under the Bonnet was added into which a special oil syringe could be conveniently coupled to lubricate the Clutch Throwout Bearing, the Engine Coupling, the Universal Joint and Sphere, and the Bevel Pinion in the Torque Tube. These lubrication points were previously rather inaccessible, and experience showed them to be neglected.

Improved Pilot Jet and Shutter Controls were mounted in a convenient location near the steering column, with notched levers to facilitate accurate setting.

The Radiator and Bonnet were made one inch higher as part of the overall styling change.

With the exception of the Exhaust Heated Throttle Body, all of the changes outlined were the result of Springfield design and development work. Complete arrangement and detail drawings were, of course, submitted to Derby for approval before being released for production. Subsequent developments of the L H Drive S G follows:

Chassis 1101—1250   Except for features outlined a b o v e, identical with last series of R H Drive S G.

1251—1360   Spring Gaiters of R-R design and make were substituted for purchased gaiters.

1361—1430   Radiator Tie Rod added to r e d u c e movement between radiator and bonnet. Serrated R o c k e r replaced Spring R o l l e r, Roller Pin, Roller Bushings, Shims, etc, and Serrated Rear Spring Plate replaced Rear Spring Plate, to a v o i d noise and periodic m a i n t e n a n c e. Tires were changed from 33 x 5 to 33 x 6.7 5 for improved riding quality.

1431—1510   Serrated Shackles adopted instead of plain shackles and bushings to avoid noise resulting from 'side shuck', and reduce maintenance. This feat u r e, otherwise known as 'T h r e a d e d Shackles', was developed by R-R of Am Inc. For a few years thereafter the use of this feature was quite

general in the automotive industry, and it is interesting that a fault in our Patent Application prevented important licensing income.

1511—1600   The Steering Worm and Nut were changed from three-start to two-start to improve the steering ratio for use with low pressure tires. Headlamps fitted with twin filament bulbs.

1601—1700   Special bolts added to wheel rims, with stacks of Bakelite and lead washers to provide a r e a d y means of balancing wheels; Standardization of a Vertical Slat Shutter of R-R design to replace purchased shutter. (This was a variation of the New Phanton shutter); standardization of a Fabric Engine Coupling (a variation of the New Phantom coupling); standardization of Tubular Bumpers of R-R design and make.

The above details reveal certain features incorporated in the Springfield L H Silver Ghost which were never available in the English Silver Ghosts. It is also true, however, that the latest series of English Silver Ghosts had important features, such as Front Wheel Brakes, which were never available in the Springfield Silver Ghosts. The essential time lag between the planning and the actual assembly of each series of chassis made it extremely difficult, if not impossible, to affect simultaneous Engineering changes at Springfield and Derby.'

I am frequently asked what happened to Springfield and why was the factory there closed down, and I wrote to Arthur Soutter concerning this, and in another letter discussing factors rumoured to be responsible for the failure of Rolls-Royce of America Inc, he wrote:

Now, I would like to submit, for your consideration, a further list of CERTAIN FACTORS WHICH HAD NOT BEEN TAKEN INTO ACCOUNT which history indicates to have been much more important:

1 Consideration of the wisdom of equipping a plant and tooling up for the 100% manufacture of a chassis, the design of which was already 14 years old, and which had steering unsuitable for use in America.
2 Comprehensive analysis of the cost of acquiring, equipping and tooling a plant for the complete manufacture of all components and units of the chassis.

3 Comprehensive analysis of the time lag between the start of a series of chassis components completion of chassis, completion of coachwork, and receipt of payment for a complete car, and the consequent build-up of inventory during that period.

He goes on to say, 'The Historical and Financial records indicate that the above three points were not properly considered.'

Maurice Olley recalls that when the first 20 h p Rolls-Royce arrived in Springfield with an Englishman driving it he had to apply for a driving licence. He drove the local police around the City and the car was so smooth and silent that they presented him with a licence for an electric vehicle and he had to show them the engine before they would believe that it was an orthodox petrol car! Quoting Arthur Soutter again, he says that he is often asked the question, 'Why did Rolls-Royce of America Inc not produce the 20 h p chassis?' His answer had been, 'Let's be charitable enough to call it good judgement rather than good luck. In any event, it certainly was fortunate! Since no part of this model could have been produced from existing tooling, it would have cost $750,000 to tool up. As it developed, the 20 h p model was available during the first two years, but only 35 were sold in America and Canada.'

In the meanwhile experiments were going on in Great Britain, the Continent and in the United States with the use of four-wheel brakes. How the Derby-built car acquired four-wheel brakes has already been explained in Part 1 Chapter 5, but Springfield was becoming concerned about four-wheel brakes which were appearing on other makes, so, on 18 June 1923 the following was circularized to the Sales Staff in the Sales Production Bulletin No. 8.

Several American manufacturers have incorporated front or four-wheel brakes in their design, one or two of which are now on the market, and at least another will be on the market, and advertised, within the next few months. These will doubtless be advertised as the most progressive step ever made in automobile design and something that is startlingly new and hot from the fires of inspired genius.

There is nothing very new about four-wheel brakes. This movement started in Europe in about 1910 ever since which time Rolls-Royce has followed it very closely with exhaustive test and experiment, with experimental cars, fitted with all types of four-wheel brakes driven, under careful inspection, over all kinds of roads. They have never been adopted by Rolls-Royce because of their showing such decidedly dangerous disadvantages that they are considered unsafe to put into the hands of the general public, and in this respect not nearly the equal of the powerful, efficient, lasting and easily equalized brake design now employed in our design.

Basically, the fault with front-wheel brakes lies in the danger of front-wheel skids, which are uncontrollable and consequently vastly more dangerous than a rear wheel skid.

It must be appreciated first of all, that for their ability to steer the car the front wheels depend on their rolling motion. When front wheels cease to roll they lose all power to steer the car, which slides straight ahead on a flat road, or into the ditch if on a crowned or cambered road. When the brakes are used in an emergency it is of primary importance that the direction of the car should be under control; that is, that the car can be steered from the time that the brakes are applied until it is brought to a complete stop. When an obstacle suddenly presents itself (as in night driving) the driver's instinct is to immediately apply the brakes as hard as possible; (a moment's consideration of one's state of mind in these circumstances will prove this to be true). If, under these conditions, the front wheels are suddenly locked, disaster may overtake the driver, through inability to control the car's direction even though it may stop before meeting the obstacle.

In traffic driving, the ability to dodge - to control the direction of the car - is of almost equal importance with the ability to stop. On a wet or sprinkled city street, granting that the front wheel brakes were perfectly equalized, the car would slide straight ahead, unable to take advantage of traffic conditions, either right or left. If the brakes were not perfectly equalized, immediately the pressure was applied, the front wheels would take on a skid, which would be uncontrollable, in whichever direction the equalization of the brakes was faulty.

In traffic driving, under most favourable conditions (perfectly equalized brakes and dry pavement) a sudden application of the brakes checks the car so precipitately that cars following have been known to crash into the car ahead, causing a rear end wreck through not having stopping room and time. It is, of course, obvious that front-wheel brakes present double the difficulty of keeping the brakes properly equalized.

Aside from the above apparent defects in front or four-wheel braking, there is the stiffening effect on the steering to take into consideration when the brakes are applied, and the drag on the steering unless the braking effects on both wheels is absolutely equalized. This, of itself, constitutes a serious disadvantage reflected in the handling of the car.

Also, there are extremely high stresses in the front springs due to the drag on the front wheels coupled with the leverage occasioned by the drop of the front axle.

Below we quote from a recent article by a well-known writer on automobile subjects:-

One year from now we may expect to see items in the newspapers like these: 'Mrs Jones was badly injured by being thrown over the windshield when her husband applied the brakes too suddenly. He had been accustomed to driving a car with the old, inefficient rear-wheel brakes and had not learned the dangers attendant upon the use of four-wheel brakes.

The car of John Williams, being equipped with four-wheel brakes, was stopped so suddenly that Mr Henderson, who was following a short distance behind in his car which is equipped with only rear wheel brakes, was unable to check his machine before it had crashed into the car ahead.

Young Williams, who has always tried to live up to his reputation as a fast, dare-devil driver, did not understand the action of the front-wheel brakes with which his new car is equipped. Consequently, in turning a slippery corner at high speed, his car started a front-wheel skid; Williams, thinking he could steer out of it, found himself unable to do so and went into the ditch.'

These are only a few of the things that are going to happen when the eight or ten companies rumoured as working on the front-wheel brakes proposition actually place cars on the market so equipped.

Undoubtedly, the movement on the part of these American manufacturers to experiment with front wheel brakes is due to the desire to avoid the burning out of brakes, and other defects to which the general type of brakes used in this country are susceptible. Much better than fitting with front wheel brakes would be a movement to first of all re-design the rear wheel brakes now fitted on the cars, to obtain adequate radiating and braking surface, rather than to multiply the number of brakes, with their difficulties, of the present design.

This was a fairly convincing and well worded argument in favour of only two wheel brakes, but in spite of it the general demand was for four wheel brakes. However, though the Derby-built car had them as a standard fitting from November 1923, they were never fitted to the Springfield Silver Ghost; in fact the first 'New Phantom' built at Springfield did not have them either. On reflection, the reason for this is obvious. It would have meant further costly tooling-up and modifying of the existing centre-change gearbox in order to fit the servo motor, etc, which operated the Rolls-Royce designed four wheel braking system.

Referring to the centre change gearbox Arthur Soutter writes as follows:-

The 3 speed gearbox used on the L H Silver Ghost was designed at Springfield. It was the year 1924 I was appointed Asst Chief Draftsman because of the additional load on the department caused by this design work, and I checked many of the original drawings. It was necessary, of course, to obtain approval of the design from R-R Ltd. This involved submitting a layout of the overall plan first. Then, after initial approval a complete set of detail drawings and super sheets had to be submitted for final approval before production was started. This, obviously, introduced a time lag and it was March 1925 before the first L H Drive chassis was finished. This fact, plus the additional time involved in planning and building a series, made it impossible to concurrently produce identical chassis at Springfield and at Derby. This accounts for the fact that our Silver Ghost never had Servo operated front brakes, and that Derby's Phantom I never had Centralized Chassis Lubrication, to name only two cases.

It will be noticed that nearly all the various types of bodies which were mounted carried English names, and when I wrote to Arthur Soutter concerning this, he replied as follows:

None of those who headed up the Sales Department were Englishmen, and I believe that it was after W E Hosac had been made Vice President in charge of Sales that the names were adopted. I would guess that he conceived the idea of using names of English places to accentuate the fact that this was, basically, an English car, and that he may have enlisted the aid of Tom Nadin, John Southern, Maurice Olley and/or others to select suitable names. Another conjecture - but the best I can offer. Incidentally, these names did not apply only to Brewster bodies. They were adopted to cover Rolls-Royce Coachwork built in Springfield prior to the acquisition of Brewster & Co.

The following Rolls-Royce Sales Promotion Bulletins published at Springfield are of interest:

No. 22. Re: Service Brakes

Rolls-Royce Service Brakes have proven to be almost indestructible and will wear indefinitely. In the past four years we have relined only 45 service brakes. This included pre-war cars, and 39 of these cars were eight years old or more.

As a result of this, we are able to announce that we will, should the customer require it, at any time within three years of purchase, replace the Service Brake lining, without charge.

It will be understood, of course, that the foregoing does not apply to our hand operated or emergency brakes, which are designed solely for the purpose of holding car stationary on the grades, which they do with equal certainty, both forward and reverse.

No. 23. Re: Smooth Driving and Demonstrating

The importance of smooth driving when demonstrating cannot be over-emphasized. There is a tendency among our drivers to speed up the car in third gear to 35 miles per hour before getting into top gear. This has the effect of making the car go screaming down the street, and is anything but pleasant to the prospective purchasers, or to anyone on the street who is a spectator, and the roughness of the acceleration is detrimental to the smooth performance of the car.

There should be a pride among our drivers in making the car operate smoothly. To accomplish this in starting the driver should get into top gear as soon as possible after the car has got under way. In ordinary driving conditions it is not necessary to use the gears at all except in starting. Only by smooth driving and operation may the car be displayed to the best advantage. At the Works efforts are expended to make the axles, gearboxes and engines quiet and smooth; all of this is of no value if the driver fails to present or display them in the best way.

Every driver should make it a point to give attention to his method of operation so his driving will be smooth and pleasing, and do full justice to the car.

No. 24. Re: Balloon Tires

At an extra cost of $350 list, f o b Works, Balloon Tires can now be fitted to cars coming through production. This price applies to cars and chassis on which front mudguards have not been fitted.

On cars or chassis which are already fitted with front mud guards, the additional charge will be $600 list. The reason for this is that mud guards will have to be taken off from such cars and entirely new ones supplied and completely repainted. This will, of course, delay delivery.

The tires will nominally be called 33 x 6.75 and under no circumstances must any other size of Balloon Tires or wheels be advocated or fitted. The wheels will be 21 in. in diameter with the face of the rim 5 in.

Branches and Service Stations must strictly adhere to this principle. The above prices are based upon Dunlop Full Balloon Tires and if other makes of tires are specified, there will be a still further additional charge.

Branches and Service Stations must under no circumstances take any responsibility for the fitting of Balloon Tires through any local dealer without the approval of the Works.

It is our desire to adhere strictly to the type of equipment with which our engineers have experimented and found to be best suited to our chassis. These experiments have now been going on for over a year.

All of the above applies to cars as we are now building them. The alteration to any cars which we have previously turned out on which are imported Dunlop wheels, special costs for fitting Balloon Tires must be obtained from the Works.

As can be seen tremendous care and trouble was taken to ensure that the Springfield model was kept up to the standard set by Derby, and it was not any inferiority of production that sealed the fate of Springfield. These reasons are set out by Aurhur Soutter as follows:-

The Key to the success or failure of either alternative was *VOLUME.*

Capital expenditure could be justified ONLY ON THE *VOLUME* OF CARS which could reasonably be produced and sold.

Avoiding import duty on completed chassis or complete cars was the idea upon which R-R of Am Inc was conceived with the hope, of course, that the sale price could be reduced accordingly, and that sales could be increased.

Quite apart from the large capital expenditures in getting started, it must have been apparent that manufacturing costs would exceed Derby costs by reason of labour rates alone. Furthermore, the transfer of 53 well paid executives and supervisors from Derby created a condition of 'too few Indians and too many Chiefs', and resulted in a big overhead. This was unfavourable from the financial point of view although it did assure the manufacturers of a quality product. The 'break even point' at which the rate of production and sales would produce earnings equivalent to the duty which might be saved was not, on the basis of American costs, established.

It requires no genius to analyse an operation in retrospect, when armed with historical and financial records. It is quite obvious, however, that the creation of R-R of Am Inc, as a manufacturing company, *was a mistake in conception and organization.* The *volume* did not exist, actually or in prospect, to produce earnings on the capitalization with the high tool cost *per car*, the high inventory *per car*, the high cost of changes *per car*, and the high cost of sales and advertising *per car*. What is more although the volume did not justify the operation of a second plant, its existence did detract from the number of Derby built cars which might have been exported to America, to the detriment of R-R Ltd.

PART I CHAPTER 10

Stanley E Sears 1911 Hooper limousine chassis No. 1721, originally built for King George V and found derelict in Oxfordshire; how this, the first pre-war 40/50 car was restored in 1946 to new condition

When the 'New Phantom' was announced in May 1925, production of the original 40/50 h p chassis ceased, and after this it was referred to as the 'Silver Ghost' type, (after the original car built in 1907), in order to distinguish it from the new 40/50 model. This was made known in an official announcement by the Company, made in the motoring press at the time for the 'New Phantom's' debut, and at the same time it was announced that those persons who still wished to have an original 40/50 could do so at no extra charge. This was comparatively easy, it was simply a question of installing the old side valve engine in place of the new overhead valve design, as otherwise the two chassis were almost identical. How many customers actually took advantage of this offer is not known but it is rumoured that Frank Treherne Thomas bought his last Rolls-Royce either late in 1926 or early in 1927 and that, as he had had such very satisfactory results with his previous cars, he insisted on having another of the 'Silver Ghost' type with, of course, Barker limousine coachwork and twin tyres to the rear wheels. 'The Silver Ghost' was also still being produced as an armoured car for the War Office and the Royal Air Force as late as 1928; these chassis were designated WO series.

At the present time the old Rolls-Royce 40/50 is probably the most sought after car in the world amongst collectors of antique automobiles and as much as £15,000 has been paid for one that was built in 1911; but there was a time when these cars could be bought for a few pounds and they were a great favourite with country garages who used them as breakdown vehicles; they were also put to all sorts of menial tasks, being used for such diverse jobs as hay-sweeps on farms, and light lorries. In fact, one in

Jersey in the Channel Islands, was actually used on the beach for collecting sea-weed, or vraic (pronounced 'rack') as it is known, which was spread on the land as fertilizer.

The preservation and restoration of old Rolls-Royce cars really came about through the Veteran Car Club of Great Britain, which had been formed in 1930 to preserve motor vehicles manufactured prior to 31 December 1904 which vehicles were then eligible for the annual London to Brighton Veteran Car Run, once known as the 'Old Crocks Run to Brighton'. However, after the 2nd World War the Veteran Car Club decided to expand and to take in motor vehicles that were manufactured prior to the 31 December 1916, and to call these 'Edwardians'.

Amongst the members of the Veteran Car Club was Stanley Edward Sears, whose enthusiasm for any well made piece of machinery was and is without limit; he had already been a Rolls-Royce owner of both the Phantom II and the Phantom III for many years, and also had a 1901 Mors and a 1903 Clement Talbot, both of which he had had since before the War. He was a regular participant in all the Veteran Car Club events and he was then serving as a Committee Member, he had found the Clement Talbot in 1936 and it was the first veteran car to undergo major restoration. When it made its first appearance at a meeting, other members were amazed when they saw it, as it looked like a brand new vehicle; until this time cars had been run in Veteran Car Club events exactly as they were found, the owners saying they were in original condition. However, Stanley Sears did not share this opinion; his point of view was that you restore a picture or a piece of antique furniture, so why not a car; he also pointed out that if the cars had still been with their original owners and been used regularly they would have been kept in proper order, and though some members looked rather askance at him, they began to follow suit.

When it was decided by the Veteran Car Club to take in 'Edwardians', Stanley Sears immediately saw the possibility of acquiring a Rolls-Royce car of the 40/50 h p type built pre-1914; but it was actually another enthusiast, Jimmy Skinner, proprietor of the Basingstoke Motor Company, who discovered chassis No. 1721, which is now owned by Stanley Sears.

Jimmy Skinner had been in the motor business nearly all his life, he already owned a Rolls-Royce 40/50 which he used as a breakdown vehicle and it was owing to the service that this car gave that he decided to insert an advertisement in *The Times,* asking for knowledge of a Rolls-Royce Silver Ghost, which was complete with coachwork, but built pre-1914.

He had a reply from the daughter of Lord Wavertree, who said that at Wallingford, near Oxford, her father's old car, a limousine, was stored in a barn. He was looking for a tourer, so was not interested in a closed car himself, but he contacted Stanley Sears and told him of his discovery, and the result was that they went over to Wallingford together to see chassis No. 1721.

Immediately Stanley saw the car he felt that it should be preserved. Although it had chickens roosting all over it, was in an incredibly dirty condition and the engine was seized solid, it was all complete, even to the lamps, so, after some bargaining, he arranged to buy it.

1721 has always been a bit of a mystery, and I have spent some time on research to try and verify the real facts; one rumour I had heard was that this chassis, which carries a Hooper limousine body, had originally been built for King George V. This has a certain ring of truth about it, as I was to discover later.

At the time of his Coronation in 1910, King George V took delivery of two 57 hp 6-cylinder sleeve-valve Daimlers, the engines of which had a bore and stroke of 124 x 130 mm, which gave them 9,421 cc. The limousine coachwork was built by Hooper & Co, who built all the bodies on the Royal Daimlers and the interior was finished in dark blue morocco leather.

The curious thing is that the coachwork fitted to 1721 is identical to that fitted to King George V's 57 h p Daimlers, apart from the door handles, which are of the straight pattern in 1721 and the 'sham-fall' type on the Royal Daimlers.

Also, from the records held at Conduit Street (which are in many ways contradictory) the original order for the car was placed on the 18 October 1911 with Messrs Hooper & Co. The car was to be finished in the Royal Colours namely claret and black, with red lines, and was to have dark blue morocco leather interior, with two large armchair-type occasional seats, which were of the type always used by His Majesty King George V and Queen Mary. So it does seem possible that it was intended for Royal use. However, this order was cancelled and, according to the Guarantee Card, the car was sold to Arthur Wagg Esq, 40, Bryanston Square, London W 1 on 4 June 1912, the Guarantee number being 934. This does not agree with the information on the original Body Card, which shows that the car was sold on 30 April 1912 to Hall Walker Esq, DL, MP, Sussex Lodge, Regents Park, and that the car was collected from Conduit Street by his chauffeur on 4 June 1912. On the Guarantee Card the second owner appears as Col Hall Walker, DL, MP, Sussex Lodge, Regents Park, London, NW 1, and the third owners as Lord and Lady Wavertree, Sandybrow, Tarporley, Cheshire, also of Sussex Lodge, Regents Park. This entry is dated January 1920. In fact, Col Hall Walker and Lord Wavertree are one and the same person, as he was elevated to the peerage in 1919.

William Hall Walker was born on 25 December 1856, he was most interested in all forms of sport in their seasons. He was a personal friend of Edward VII and a well known race horse owner and breeder; he bred King Edward VIIs horse 'Minoru' with which King Edward won the 1909 Derby, when the crowd went mad with joy that the King had won this famous race, even the policemen on duty hurled their helmets in the air and shouted 'good old Teddy! In 1916 Hall Walker gave all his race horses to the Nation to found a National Stud. He had no children of his own, but an adopted daughter, the Hon Rosemary Hall Walker.

Soon after 1721 was ordered in October 1911, King George V and Queen Mary set out for India and the Delhi Durbar on 11 November 1911, sailing in the *Medina,* a brand new ship built for the P & O Company. They left Bombay on 10 January 1912, in the *Medina,* for the return voyage to England and arrived at Portsmouth on 5 February.

There are two Body Cards for 1721, the second Card refers to when the car was sold to Col Hall Walker and there is a reference to the removal of two large revolving armchair seats, which were to be replaced by one occasional seat which folded flush against the division, and I can only think that on his return from India, King George decided not to take delivery of 1721 because there was not sufficient room in the rear compartment for these armchair seats, which he and Queen Mary so dearly liked. It is interesting to compare the interior dimensions of a Rolls-Royce 40/50 with a 57 h p 6-cylinder sleeve-valve Daimler. I find from my files that the length from dash to centre of back wheels on the 40/50 Rolls-Royce is 7 ft 8 in., as compared with 9 ft 2 in. on the Daimler; this gives some eighteen inches more space in the Daimler which makes a considerable difference.

It is perfectly possible that Col Hall Walker knew of these plans for 1721 and when the Royal order was cancelled the car was offered to him.

He ordered a new car from Hooper's in 1925, a limousine mounted on a 'New Phantom' chassis (No. 56 HC) which was to be finished in Lord Wavertree's own colours, dark blue with pale yellow lines, for delivery in September 1925. Incidentally, the same colours that 1721 carries to this day. Whether 1721 had been in the barn at Wallingford since the new car was delivered we do not know, but from the state it was in it had certainly been there for many years.

As soon as Stanley Sears completed the arrangements he towed 1721 behind his Morris farm van to Wallingford Station. There it was loaded into a closed box van and consigned to Haywards Heath Station, and from there it was

towed to the poultry farm at Bolney, which Stanley Sears had bought some years previously.

The first thing was to free the engine. This was achieved by removing the valve-caps and squirting a mixture of paraffin and engine oil liberally into the cylinders and valves and allowing it to stand. After about a fortnight the engine could be turned on the starting handle, then the oil in the engine was changed, a new set of plugs fitted, the carburetter, the coil and magneto all thoroughly cleaned and adjusted. 1721 was then started by being towed by the farm van. After the engine had warmed up the carburetter was adjusted and it soon became evident that there was a good deal of wear in the engine.

Stanley Sears was determined that the car should be restored to the condition it was in on the day it was delivered. He knew that it would be a very big undertaking and as this was the first Rolls-Royce he had ever restored, he went to see Roney Messervy, who was a great friend and head of the London Service Department at Hythe Road. Messervy told him that it was a very long time since the Service Department had had anything to do with such a very old 40/50. In the ordinary way they would not have undertaken it, but seeing whose car it was and knowing that they would be allowed carte blanche on the chassis, they were prepared to take it in and do whatever was required.

When they had the engine completely stripped down, Stanley went to see in detail what repairs were needed. The cylinder blocks were re-bored, the crankshaft re-ground, the valve seats re-cut and new valves, guides and springs fitted. Pistons and gudgeon pins were replaced, as well as the crankshaft bearings. The water passages in the cylinder blocks and the radiator were thoroughly cleaned out; the carburetter, magneto and coil ignition were also completely overhauled.

All the steering joints were adjusted and new kingpins and bushes fitted. The brakes were re-lined with Ferodo, in place of the old metal to metal, and the wheel bearings replaced where necessary. The clutch was re-lined and completely overhauled and the shackle-pins on the springs were all examined and renewed where necessary.

The total bill was extremely moderate (especially by today's standards) and Stanley Sears was so grateful and delighted that he said if the Company wished to put the car on show when it was completely finished, or have it in the Conduit Street showrooms, or in any other exhibition, they could do so. Now that the chassis was almost as good as the day it was made, he took the car to H E Griffin & Co, of Station Square, Haywards Heath in Sussex, about five miles from where he lived.

H E Griffin's garage was a very old established business, the men employed were real craftsmen of the old school, who took infinite pride in their work; on the first floor there was a paint-shop where Frank Elphick reigned supreme. The finish he put on a motor was as smooth as china, it was impossible to see a brushmark, it was to Frank Elphick that 1721 was entrusted for the restoration of the Hooper limousine body.

The car was completely stripped back to the original metal and wood framing and was re-painted from scratch. There was also a trimming department and here the front seats were re-upholstered in black leather to match the original. Fortunately, hardly any work was necessary on the blue morocco leather in the rear compartment, and this is still in original condition.

When completed, the car looked absolutely superb. Rolls-Royce Ltd, were delighted and had the use of it at all the Society of Motor Manufacturers' and Traders' Jubilee Cavalcades that year.

When I saw it at the London Cavalcade in May 1946 I considered that, without doubt, it was the finest car on show that day. It subsequently took part in the Manchester, Cardiff, Birmingham-Coventry and Edinburgh Cavalcades, in each instance shown by Rolls-Royce Ltd.

When 1721 was returned to Bolney after the Cavalcades, it was used in as many Veteran Car events as petrol rationing would allow, and it became quite well-known. After one of these events Stanley was approached by a film company who wanted to use it in a period film which they were making. They telephoned one day and said that they had heard that Stanley Sears had an old Rolls-Royce, which they would like to borrow in connection with a film. They proposed to send a lorry down to his home and asked him to arrange to have it loaded and *roped* on and they would deliver it back to him when they had finished making the film! Stanley was speechless at first, then told them they had no idea what they were talking about. If they really wished to use the car on a film set he would drive it up to them himself, and, providing they gave him a suit of chauffeur's livery, he would drive the car in the film himself, no one else was to drive it, and these were the only conditions under which he would consider letting them use it. The film Company agreed eventually and so 1721 set off to the film Company's studios.

When they arrived it was the turn of the film directors who had wanted to borrow the car to be astonished. Never in their wildest imagination had they expected to see anything like this, and they entirely agreed the car could not possibly have just been roped on a lorry and delivered!

1721 has been used in several films since then, including *The Winslow Boy* and *My Brother Jonathan*.

It is a long while now since 1721 was in regular use and only people who have either known Stanley Sears for a long time, or have visited his collection at Bolney, will remember seeing this superb vehicle. There are two reasons for this: firstly, since he had 1721 restored, Stanley has acquired other cars which he has used at rallies and meets, and secondly, there are now so many other 'Edwardian' 40/50 h p Rolls-Royce limousines and landaulettes in the Veteran Car Club of Great Britain, 20 Ghost Club, the Rolls-Royce Enthusiasts' Club, etc that he feels the novelty has worn off. But in the days about which I am talking, none of these Clubs, except the Veteran Car Club existed, and none of these other 40/50s had come to light, except for a few which Stanley had housed on his poultry farm at Bolney. I remember in the Summer of 1946 spending a most pleasant day with him at his home. In the garages I saw a collection of immaculate motor cars. Included were the 1901 Mors, 1903 Clement Talbot, 1721 herself, the 1929 'New Phantom' (chassis No. 109 WR) Barker-bodied open tourer, a 1933 Phantom II Continental chassis No. 7 MW close-coupled saloon with coachwork by Arthur Mulliner of Northampton, and a very nice Phantom III

Arthur Mulliner touring limousine 3-BU-118.

When we had examined each of these cars in turn, he took me to the poultry farm. There, in the condition in which he had bought them, was another collection. There was a 1909 40/50 (chassis No. 1009) which had been re-bodied with a limousine in 1919 (he told me that his intention was to restore this as a chassis), also a limousine by Joseph Lawton of Liverpool (chassis No. 1543) which he sold to his life-long friend W F Watson (Secretary and a Past President of the 20 Ghost Club) in 1949, who then had it restored by Messrs H E Griffin of Haywards Heath.

There was a 1914 Continental chassis, carrying a Barker landaulette de ville body which, to my astonishment, bore the registration number P6 (chassis No. 60 RB). This car had formerly belonged to a very great friend of my father, Stanley Shaw Bond, and in the early 1920s my father had toured all over Turkey in this car. This was also sold later. Then there was a 1923 20 h p (chassis No. 58-S-1) formerly owned by Lord Lonsdale and painted in Lonsdale yellow. This was unusual as the coachwork was much older than the chassis, for the body had origin-

ally been on a 1910 Napier. This one Stanley Sears decided to keep and have completely restored. Lastly, there was a 1925 Barker limousine with 4-wheel brakes, which had belonged to a timber merchant. It was suffering very badly indeed from moth in the upholstery and this was sold to a country hire firm in 1949.

It is difficult now, when beautifully restored old Rolls-Royce cars are a common-place sight, especially at rallies, etc, to realize the tremendous sensation that 1721 caused almost twenty-five years ago, when she was the only pre-1914 Rolls-Royce car of the 'Silver Ghost' type which had undergone a full restoration.

After the acclaim received by 1721, it is hardly surprising that three years later, when the Rolls-Royce Company acquired the original 'Silver Ghost' from the Hanbury family, it was Stanley Sears they entrusted with the arrangements for the restoration of the coachwork of this historic car. So once again, Stanley Sears felt that he could not do better than give the work to Messrs H E Griffin of Haywards Heath, and the same skilled team, who had so lovingly worked on 1721, under his eagle eye.

PART I CHAPTER 11

Jimmy Skinner's chassis No. 1298, how he found and restored this car which took part in both Anglo-American Rallies and was driven from Geneva to Bristol in one day. Chassis No. 149 AG which is still in the hands of its original owners. Chassis No. 77 AG 'The Ghost from Brownsea Island'. Arthur Soutter's Springfield 40/50 with 'Tilbury' coachwork by Brewster.

Reference has already been made to Stewart James Skinner and how he discovered Stanley Sears' chassis No. 1721.

It was towards the end of 1946 that Jimmy heard that a 1921 tourer was advertised for sale in North Wales for the sum of £150; although the advertisement had appeared some five months previously Jimmy felt that there was just a slight possibility that the car might be one of those rare ones which though advertised as 1921 was actually a pre-1914 vehicle. This was because of the 1921 Road Traffic Act and motor cars having then to be registered for the first time, so he decided to write to the address and he received a reply saying that the car was still available and that the chassis number was 1298. Of course, he knew instantly that it was a 1910 model and made arrangements to go up to Abergele in North Wales to meet the agent who was winding up the Estate for the Executors.

When Jimmy reached Abergele he found that the car had not been used for ten years owing to the ill-health of its owner and that the ignition leads and tyres had all perished; but the car was complete, so Jimmy made arrangements to purchase and for the local garage to put it in running order. He went up again to collect it in July 1947 and, leaving Abergele at noon, he arrived home at Basingstoke at 10 p m, the only trouble having been two burst tyres.

Unfortunately the whole story of the career of chassis No. 1298 cannot be told, as a great deal has been lost in the mists of time and over the years several modifications have been made to this chassis to bring it more up to date, as has always been the policy of the Company. I think

the chief alteration has been to the wheels, which on the original order were listed as wooden artillery with detachable rims; at some later date in the car's life these were changed to wire wheels. Below is a copy of the original Body Card for this chassis.*

Chassis No.: 1298   40/50 h p long wheel base.
Weight of body: 5 cwt - 4 - light.
Weight sent R-R Ltd: No. 133a - 7.4.1910.
Cost of chassis: £500.
Plating: £1.11.3d.
Tyres: 10.5d.
Sale Price: £788. £985 less 20%.
Date of Sale: 14 December 1909.
Sold to: Midland, Granby Street, Leicester, for delivery June 1910.
Tyres: 895 x 135.
Make: Dunlop grooved front, Palmer ribbed to rear.
Ordered from: 'W' ex-1277. Date of Order: 7.5.1910.
Car order form No.: 704.
Deposit: £20.0.0d. paid - 5.3.1910.
Balance: £768.0.0d. paid - 30.5.1910.
Car delivered on 4 June to Barker.
Invoice No.: 2467.

Extras
Nickel. Two padlocks and two keys to bonnet.
Extra cost of grooved Dunlop on account for use on front.
Extra cost of 6 in. Palmer including use.
Shrewsbury & Challiner Rims, and two spares.
Extra cost of Spencer Moulton tyres on front.
One spare Shrewsbury & Challiner Rim. C.7806.

I was able to find from the Guarantee Book at Conduit Street that chassis No. 1298 was sold on 10 July 1910 by the Midland Counties Garage, Leicester, to E H Broadhurst, Chelford, Chester, and the car bore a Cheshire registration number, M 2663. Later, though there is no date,

*This Body Card is obviously full of clerical errors, it is recorded exactly as the original. Tyres could never be obtained for 10.5d.

Mr Broadhurst moved to Roshley, Temple, near Leicester. Jimmy has been informed that the car was laid up with Barker's, the coachbuilders, whose premises were Olaf Street, Latimer Road, Ladbroke Grove, in London, during the 1914-18 War. In many ways I cannot help feeling that this is somewhat unlikely as Leicestershire is some distance from London and in May 1919 chassis number 1298 was sold to her second owner, Mr J A Maton, Lyndene, Stoney Gate Road, Leicester, so the car remained in the County where it was first supplied.

In November 1919 the car became the property of the Dunlop Rubber Company in Coventry and was used by them for testing tyres. Somewhere about this time the original Cheshire registration number was changed to that of a London number, LY 6407.

Later, but unfortunately we have no date, the car was sold to Mr H W Davey, Naesmyndam Hall, in Denbighshire, North Wales, where Jimmy found the car.

During the years, certain modernizations had been carried out to 1298 in order to make the car look more modern than it actually was, but fortunately nothing was done to the original bodywork and this most attractive Barker torpedo is still in its original form, and still has its Kolapso hood with no side-curtains, though after so many years this hood has naturally been re-covered. One of the reasons this particular chassis was chosen for inclusion in this book is that it is basically an original car.

At one stage in the car's career, Mr Davey sold it to the local colliery whose intention it was to remove the engine and use it for working pumps. The car was removed from Mr Davey's garage and put in a shed belonging to the colliery, but nothing more was done with it and Mr Davey evidently had a good deal of sentimental feeling towards the car as he decided to buy it back, and it was really by this lucky escape that the car remains intact and still in existence today. During the latter years of Mr Davey's life, the car was not licenced for use every year due to his ill-health. It was licenced on 30 September 1934 until the end of that year, when it appears that it passed into the hands of the colliery. It was licenced again 1 July 1937, presumably when Mr Davey had it back, and the last licence

in his name was taken out in June 1938.

As soon as Jimmy had this new treasure back in his own premises he decided that the only thing to do was to give the chassis a complete re-furbish as necessary. In order to carry out this work he removed the body completely from the chassis, at the same time removing and scrapping the later type front and rear wings and the discs on the wheels.

It is very much to his credit that he did practically all the work himself, unaided, with his own two hands.

The engine of this particular chassis has never, as far as it is known, had a complete major overhaul, crank re-grind, new bearings, etc; only the cylinder blocks have been removed, the bearings have never been touched and this must be one of the very, very few pre-war 40/50 chassis which apparently has never had a major overhaul. It is also one of the very few pre-war chassis which still has cast iron pistons, they are three-ring pistons with a raised head and the engine must have been re-bored some time before 1914. The engine still has unmodified connecting rods with 7/8th gudgeon pins. It is interesting to note that the pistons are all of different sizes and are as follows: 1 - 30: 2 - 30: 3 - 30: 4 - 25: 5 - 26: 6 - 26.

Jimmy spent literally thousands of hours working on this chassis which he decided should be painted ivory overall, with ivory coachwork lined in red with red upholstery, this finish gives a most attractive appearance.

When Jimmy had finished work on the chassis and had it running to his satisfaction, he attended the Veteran Car Club of Great Britain's Rally on 19 July 1948, at the Austin Motor Company's Longbridge Works, with the car in chassis form. This event took the form of a speed hill climb on the Austin Company's test track and the B B C were present and televised the event on their then weekly radio newsreel programme.

During the run from Basingstoke to the Austin Works at Longbridge and back Jimmy was able to see exactly how the chassis performed and he found that all his hard work was thoroughly justified, so he turned with satisfaction to the coachwork. In the course of his usual business of buying and selling pre-war

(Top) 42GO, a 1922 20 hp Barker Tourer now owned by John Fasal *(photo John Fasal)*

(Bottom) Bearing the personal mascot of HH The Maharaja of Udaipur in this photograph is 42GO. Notice the rounded edge to the radiator only used on early 20 hp cars *(photo John Fasal)*

(Top) Chassis No. 77AG 'The Ghost from Brownsea Island'. See Part I, Chapter 11
(Bottom) 149AG, a Barker open 5 Seater, the Southey sisters' car

(Top) 72MG, Engine number 0-406. Type AE. D type steering. Back axle ratio 16 x 52 (photo M. H. Evans)

(Middle) This chassis was sold to W. M. Broomhall of the Army and Navy Club. It was a very special order prepared by Harvey Baillie. All the fittings were silver plated, a CAV lighting set was installed in place of the normal Lucas. The original body was by Cunard who usually built coachwork on Napier chassis. Later the body was changed for a Barker Coupe Cabriolet and then later still the chassis converted to a hay truck to be used at Hawkhurst in Kent The car is now undergoing restoration, owned by M. H. Evans of Rolls-Royce Ltd (photo M. H. Evans)

(Bottom) This photograph shows a Barker Shooting Brake on a Rolls-Royce 40/50 hp long chassis supplied to HH The Nawab of Bahawalpur. Chassis number 41LK, steering type D. Supplied new in February 1924 the car was later returned to Barker & Co for this body to be fitted, The photo number suggests a date of 1933/4

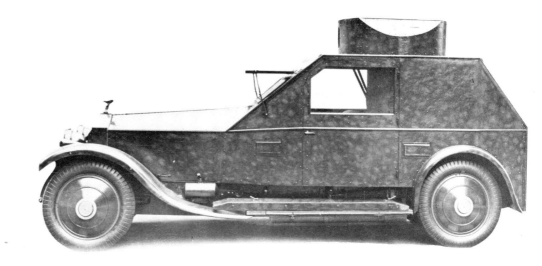

(Top) 54 EM. This is the first Weymann body to be
built on a R-R chassis by H. J. Mulliner. This car was
converted to four wheel brakes by R-R and radiator
shutters added (photo Hugh Keller)
(Bottom) Harry Fergusson-Wood with his chassis
number 40 UG Barker Cabriolet de Ville coachwork
(photo H. Fergusson-Wood)

(Top) A Silver Ghost type engine driving machinery in the Derby Works
(Bottom) The Derby Works about 1923 when 40/50 hp chassis were produced without front wheel brakes. The 20 hp line is shown on the left-ha[n]
side

(Top) HH The Maharajah of Bharatpur had no less than 25 cars including, 2 Daimlers, 5 Model T Fords, a Pierce-Arrow, an Isotta-Fraschini, several commercials and 7 Rolls-Royce. Exactly what the car is being used for here is unknown, but it shows that not all RRs in India were used for ceremonial purposes only. This photograph was brought back by a senior R-R representative Harry Madsen Snr *(photo M. H. Evans)*

(Middle) A 40/50 hp chassis being used as a compressor. Note the two radiators, something which would have caused CJ to raise his hands in horror. It does however confirm the hardiness of these chassis and engines *(photo H. Fergusson-Wood)*

(Bottom) The Motor House of the Maharajah of Mysore

(Top left, right and middle) The unveiling of the Royce Statue, 27 June 1923. Part of the line of cars and buses bringing the enormous crowd. The third photo shows, left to right: J. H. Thomas, MP for Derby, The Duke of Sutherland and Lord and Lady Birkenhead under the statue *(photo Johnson family)*
(Bottom) A Silver Ghost Armoured Car chassis. Note the New Phantom chassis to the right at the back of the photo

(*Top*) An interior view of the Gurney Nutting body on 97EU

(*Middle*) 97EU, engine number U185, long wheelbase, 'C' type steering. The chassis was sold to Griffiths Harrison & Co of 1 Albemarle Street W1 for Mrs P. D. C. Blake of Brooklands, Manchester. She would not accept delivery and the car was sold to Lord Torrington of 11 Clarges Street W1. The Pullman Limousine body is by Gurney Nutting. A second card then reads that 97EU was taken in part exchange, £480 allowed to a Miss McAdam for chassis GPS12, a 20/25, and 97EU was then sold to Clyde Automobiles of Glasgow for the same money. On an earlier order the chassis was then sold to Car Mart Ltd but a body order for an Enclosed Drive Cabriolet with an unknown builder was then cancelled

(*Bottom*) This extraordinary vehicle was originally supplied as a private car. It was bought by a firm who manufactured soft drinks and used in the form shown for advertisement purposes. The driver dressed as a cowboy rode the horse. Something else which would have horrified CJ, but Royce would have been intrigued and would have said, 'Let us have a smaller horse and make the linkages correctly'

Rolls-Royce cars, he had obtained another 1911 chassis. This still had its original front wings which Jimmy felt would be ideal to mount on 1298, as not only was the year about right, but they were completely in keeping with the Barker torpedo tourer coachwork, so, after shaping them to run parallel with the bonnet, these were fitted, and he designed a pair of rear wings to match which he had made up and fitted.

As I think most readers know, the majority of pre-war chassis carry the Derby registration letter 'R', and Jimmy Skinner's old breakdown vehicle, chassis No. 29 NA, carried the registration number R 1938, so he arranged with the Council to have this registration number transferred on to his new tourer.

When completed it looked magnificent, especially when fitted with a pair of Lucas paraffin side-lamps and rear lamp, and a pair of Lucas self-generating acetylene head-lamps, all of which are silver plated.

It was not long after this that Jimmy made his one modification to the chassis which concerns the exhaust pipe. On all chassis pre-1914 the exhaust gases are discharged from a small fish-tail which is situated just underneath the end of the silencer. However, Jimmy soon found that when the engine was started from cold, his beautifully painted ivory rear axle, springs, etc were deluged with soot and condensation, in the form of a nasty black liquid, which stuck like glue. So he decided to remove the fish-tail and replace it with an extension piece of copper which brought the exhaust fumes out clear of the petrol tank. He also used Ferodo lining on the rear brake shoes, to obviate the risk of cast iron dust running on to the wheels. Cast iron shoes were still used on the transmission brake as Ferodo would not stand up to it, literally catching fire on an emergency application of the foot brake.

By 1949 the car was completed and attended a full season of events. The only change that has been made since then is the registration number, because at a later date Jimmy had the opportunity of acquiring the index number R 1910, which he felt was most appropriate and which he promptly had fitted and re-registered. To enumerate all the events and journeys which Jimmy has undertaken with the car would make a book of its own, and much has been published already on 1298, which is probably the best known and most publicised pre-war Rolls-Royce 40/50, apart from the actual 'Silver Ghost', so I will just say now that the car has been in constant use and licenced every year except for the year 1969 when he, again with the help of his wife, Dulcie, removed the body to carry out the one hundred and one jobs that had accumulated over the past ten years and to re-paint the chassis and body by hand. Jimmy thinks that the total mileage which he has now covered with it is something in the region of 30,000 miles.

His most memorable drive was in July 1950 from Geneva to Dunkirk, in company with Francis Hutton-Stott, who was driving his 1913 38 h p Lanchester. They drove from Geneva to Dunkirk, 475 miles, in fifteen hours, 6.0 a m to 9.15 p m, in the most appalling weather, high wind and rain. They were so wet that they had to stop and change completely; then, when the weather cleared, they were driving into the setting sun and there can be few things more trying than this. The best time was 92 miles in two hours, remarkable considering the car was then 40 years old.

Having caught the night boat from Dunkirk they crossed to Dover, then had the long drive to Bristol to attend the Bristol Veteran Car Rally, which is held annually. Jimmy made straight for Basingstoke, changed the oil in the engine and pressed on to Bristol where they arrived at 1.30 pm, exhausted but mightily pleased with themselves.

In September 1954 the Anglo-American Rally was held. An invitation was extended to certain American enthusiasts to bring their cars over to England and compete in a Rally against the same number of English cars. Chassis No. 1298 was chosen as a representative Rolls-Royce to take part in this. The start was from London, making for Edinburgh, and on this first day competitors had the option of driving to Edinburgh or going on the train with their vehicles. Most people took their cars by rail but Jimmy and Dulcie drove all the way. Three years later, in April 1957, there was a return match of the Anglo-American Rally and this time competitors were invited to take their cars to America. So Jimmy drove from Horse Guards Parade in London to

Liverpool and sailed aboard the Cunard Liner *Parthia,* with the other competitors to New York. It is worth noting that chassis number 1298 was the only Edwardian car that did not drop a point on any road section in either of the Anglo-American Rallies, covering nearly 2,000 miles - good navigation by Dulcie! The car returned to England sailing from New York to Liverpool aboard the Cunard Company's *Scythia.*

Jimmy has taken 1298 abroad many times and on one occasion he was attending a Veteran Car Rally in France, which other members of the Veteran Car Club were also attending. This was in the days before a drive-on drive-off ferry was operating on the Newhaven-Dieppe service and the cars had to travel on a cargo boat, whilst their owners were expected to travel in the ordinary passenger steamer. This arrangement did not suit Jimmy at all; he had already, in filling in his insurance proposal form for taking a car abroad, caused great amusement because wherever they wanted to know the value of lamps, accessories, etc. Jimmy had written 'priceless', 'of irreplaceable value', etc! When he arrived at Newhaven and realized exactly what the shipping arrangements were, Jimmy said that under no circumstances was his car going to travel to France without him being there to look after it. The matter was finally resolved by Jimmy signing on as a member of the crew, as a responsible person in charge of the whole contingent; so, whilst he travelled in the cargo boat his wife went in the passenger steamer with all the other Club members. When word reached the French newspapers that Jimmy had travelled in the cargo boat as he would not permit his Rolls-Royce to travel unaccompanied, one of the newspapers reporting the arrival of the British contingent ran a headline which read something like 'Englishman prefers to sleep with his Rolls-Royce than with his wife!'

In June 1970 chassis number 1298, or 'Olwen', as she is called by her owner, had a special birthday party to celebrate her 60 years, and all those who had taken part in the Anglo-American Rallies with the car were invited to attend, together with many more of Jimmy's friends who are extremely well-known in the vintage motoring world.

Three years after this occasion, 'Olwen' set off again on another long journey, to take part in the 1973 Alpine Commemorative Trial and though the majority of the older 40/50 h p models were going by rail once across the Channel, Jimmy Skinner would not entertain this method of conveyance. He and his wife Dulcie elected to drive both ways, going out in convoy with some of the later cars.

No trouble at all was experienced on the outward run, but on the Trial itself some overheating was experienced, so Jimmy took a link out of the fan belt, which cured it. For the return journey to England the Skinners had such confidence in their beloved 'Olwen', that they came home by secondary roads entirely alone, using the car exactly as it would have been used when it was new in 1910. It behaved faultlessly and their only mishap of any description was one puncture.

It is now nearly 50 years since the last chassis of the 'Silver Ghost' type left the Derby works and most cars have changed hands not once but many times. However, there is one chassis, No. 149 AG, which has belonged to the same family ever since it was new, and which I have known for many years. It is fitted with an open touring 5-seater body, built by Barker, which has been in more or less continuous use since 26 October 1921. When the original owner died his three daughters continued to run the car and the youngest daughter drives it regularly and also does most of the servicing that is required, having received instruction from Rolls-Royce Ltd on the correct procedure.

The total mileage of this chassis is unknown, but, apart from the war years and when petrol rationing was in force during the Suez crisis, the car has been in regular use. It is still in original condition, and great credit is due to the three sisters for the way in which they have maintained it.

Each Rolls-Royce car seems to have a personality of its own, and in this book I have taken a selection of chassis with whose stories I am already familiar and most of them had covered considerable mileages in the hands of various owners long before any of the Clubs were formed, or there was any thought of preserving them; but 77 AG does not come in this category. This chassis, which was built and delivered to its first owner in 1922, was, incredibly, tucked away and never used until it suddenly came to light in the late 1950s.

It was supplied in chassis form to a Mrs Christie, who was enormously wealthy and lived in a large mansion near Frome, in Somerset. The two cars which she was using at this time were a Mercedes landaulette of 1912 and a Fiat limousine of 1913.

Not long after 77 AG was delivered to her in chassis form, her chauffeur gave notice and left her employment and she swore then that she would never go in another car, and she never did. About two years later she bought Brownsea Island, which is situated in the middle of Poole Harbour, near Sandbanks.

When Mrs Christie moved to Brownsea Island she simply closed the mansion near Frome and never returned there. It was so large that during the war it accommodated 1,000 troops quite easily, but by then everything was rotten and full of woodworm so that when the troops sat on the furniture it disintegrated beneath them. However, the cars were brought down to Poole and laid up in a large lock-up situated near the landing stage from Brownsea Island on the Sandbanks Road, and it was here that the three cars were to remain until 1957 when Mrs Christie suddenly decided to sell them.

The well-known racing driver, Rob Walker, lived at Nunney Court, near Frome, and knew both Mrs Christie's son and grandson. Knowing his interest in motor cars they told him that the two Edwardians and the Rolls-Royce chassis, 77 AG, were now for sale, and that Mrs Christie was open to offers for all three vehicles.

The bid which Rob Walker put in was the highest offer received, so Mrs Christie accepted it. At this time Rob Walker owned the Pippbrook Garage on the Dorking-Leatherhead By-pass and it was to this garage that 77 AG was taken after he had bought the chassis. He disposed of the Fiat but retained the Mercedes for some considerable time. 77 AG stood in the showroom of the Pippbrook Garage as a brand new chassis for which offers were invited. When he had collected it from Sandbanks, Rob Walker had re-wound the magneto and driven the chassis

up to Dorking. This mileage, and the original mileage run when it had been delivered to Mrs Christie, was the total it had run in 35 years.

It was not to remain long in the showroom at Dorking before Stanley Sears had word of its existence; as it was virtually a brand new chassis he was most anxious to try it out and invited me to accompany him on this expedition.

We made a close inspection of 77 AG and found the chassis exactly as it had left the Derby works, complete with the labels giving instructions to the coachbuilders as to how to fit wings, lamps, etc.

We were allowed to take the chassis out on a road trial and were most impressed. Stanley pronounced it in perfect running order but thought that there must be some rust in the gearbox, as, when running in neutral with the clutch held out, the engine ran remarkably silently; but when the clutch was in there was a slight whirring, which came from the gearbox. He said it was not in the least serious and that by using the car and changing the oil in the gearbox frequently this would undoubtedly disappear. He was so fascinated with it that he wanted to buy it with the intention of keeping it as an exhibition piece in chassis-only form, and made an offer for it then and there of £250, which was quite a sum at that time. However, this offer was refused and not long after this I had word that 77 AG had been sold to Roy Salvadori.

As the months passed by I more or less forgot about the existence of this chassis. Suddenly it was given tremendous publicity not only in the motoring press but also in the national press, as it had been purchased by Mr Jack Frost, a very well-known and most ardent antique automobile collector from America, who was arranging to have the chassis fitted with coachwork and, when completed, it was going out to America.

He obviously favoured an American body in preference to English coachwork and was able to obtain a Springfield chassis, No. 414 HH, which had been discovered in 1947 lying derelict in Tel Aviv by Major Charles Lambton. (Who incidentally, was later to own chassis No. 26 EX for a short time.) After purchasing the car and after doing a considerable amount of work on it Major Charles Lambton proceeded to drive it home to England via Egypt. For readers wishing to know more information about this trip there is an excellent article entitled 'Tel Aviv to Egypt in Silver Ghost 414 HH' by Major Charles Lambton, which appears in the Rolls-Royce Owners Club of America, Inc, Magazine *The Flying Lady*, April 1962, pages 572 - 5.

When Jack Frost had had the coachwork from this car transferred on to 77 AG it was inspected by Rolls-Royce Ltd, who then issued their normal three-year guarantee to this 35-year old chassis.

For any Company to issue a guarantee on such an old product must be unique and it shows what tremendous confidence Rolls-Royce Ltd had in their products.

In May 1967 the Rolls-Royce and Bentley Pageant took place at Goodwood and a contingent of cars was brought over aboard the Cunard White Star liner *Queen Elizabeth* by Members of the Rolls-Royce Owners Club of America to participate in this event. Several members of the 20 Ghost Club, including myself in my Phantom III, 3-AZ-146, motored down to Southampton to meet them and have lunch aboard the ship. I was most interested to see 77 AG again in her completed form and to be able to have a few words with her delighted owner.

Up to now I have described the careers of various Derby-built cars, but below, thanks to my correspondence with Arthur Soutter, I am able to give some details of a Springfield-built car, chassis No. S 288PL, about which Arthur Soutter writes as follows:

One of the Silver Ghosts which I owned was a Tilbury S 288PL. It was built in 1926, and in 1931 the second owner sent it to the Plant for extensive modernization. We installed booster operated front wheel brakes, fitted 7-20 tires and wheels, installed a radio, cut down the top by 4 inches, re-trimmed the interior, painted, and gave it a complete mechanical overhaul. Shortly thereafter, one of our travelling mechanics made a routine call at the owner's residence and, upon his return, advised me that this car was for sale. I wired an offer, which was accepted, and I acquired a very nice car with a mileage of approximately 30,000 miles. I used it for 11 years, but the gasoline rationing which was in effect during World War 2 made it impossible to obtain fuel to take cars of more than the Lincoln Zephyr I used daily, so the S.G. was temporarily laid up. In the meantime, the chap who had been our Maintenance Manager at Boston, who had phoned repeatedly to see if I wanted to sell it, called to see me. He explained that he had a customer who had a L H Drive Silver Ghost which had 260,000 miles on it and needed some repairs, and that he would like to get one like mine to replace it. He also pointed out that this customer had a R H Drive roadster blocked up in his garage which he kept polished just to look at. This seemed to be the type of home that was proper for the old car to go to, so I agreed to sell at a mileage of approximately 130,000. I have certainly regretted that decision!

About a year later, I received a letter from the new owner which was like one which might be received from a dear friend advising of the death of his wife or mother. He had been hit by a truck and damaged beyond what seemed to him to be feasible to repair, so he sold it to a junkyard.

Nearly five years later he again wrote bringing me up to date on the history of S 288PL as he knew it. After the junkyard had disposed of it, it changed hands six times, after which an Engineer acquired it and did a reasonably good job of repairing it. He drove it to the West Coast and used it in California for some time. He then put it on a boat and went to China, where he used it for a matter of two years, then returned to California. At this point its known history came to a close.

Several years later I was engaged in correspondence with a member of the R R O C when I, inadvertently knocked the Club Directory off my desk and, as I picked up the open book, here was the chassis number S 288PL staring me in the face! From this I learned that it was owned by a Club member in Victoria, B C. I wrote him and gave him the history of the car as I knew it, and, in return, I received a very long letter from him bringing the history up to date. He had bought it on a used car lot in Portland, Oregon, where it had been sitting for more than a year. It looked very bad, the frame was still bent, and the engine coupling was in bad shape due to running in the misaligned condition. He had the mechanical repairs carried out by a mechanic who had worked for me in Oregon, and later had the leather top replaced and the car painted. He told me of his delight with the car and of the trips he had taken with it, and sent a picture of it in its existing condition. This gentleman has since passed away but the car is still in use by his son who resides in New York State.

Thus, you will see, the history of this individual car can be traced over a period of 46 years!

PART I CHAPTER 12

John Hampton's chassis No. 120 EU, the last of the old 40/50 models, which was sold by the Company; its story up to the present time.

Chassis No. 120 EU is a most significant one in the 'Silver Ghost' series for not only does it possess all the improvements which were incorporated into the later type of this famous model but, although the chassis Nos. go up to 126 EU, for some reason 120 EU was the last one actually sold.

It was ordered on 19 December 1924 by John Henry Thomas and was to be his last car and his second 40/50 h p model. He had purchased the first one in 1909 and he had covered 307,000 miles in it, and, though he had been offered the later type of 'New Phantom' engine, whilst the chassis of 120 EU was in course of erection he had been so satisfied with his former car that he had decided to have the older type of power unit which he ran happily until his death.

Below are the details taken from the Body Card:

CHASSIS

Makers No.: 120 EU	h p: 40/50.
Engine No.: U 208.	
Off Test: 13.1.25.	Received: 16.1.25.
Axle Ratio: 14 x 52.	

TYRES

| Dunlop 33 x 5. | |
| Date of Order: 3.1.25. | No.: R.70865. |

BODY

Open Touring.	
Drawing No.: LD.7072 A.	
Makers: Barker	
Order No.: 2044	Date 7.1.25.
Copy of drawing to Sp on 13.2.25.	

TRIMMING & PAINTING

Colours: Grey, as selected at Messrs Barker's Showrooms
Upholstery: Green.

* 'S' means Sales

CHASSIS

Sale Price: £1,850.0.0d.
Date of Sale: 19.12.24.
Sold to: J Henry Thomas, Esq, Wedderburn House, Wedderburn Road, Hampstead, London. N W 6.
Car Order Form No. 4017, page 219, book 28. Drawing Book No. 1 AF, page 230.
Deposit paid: £190.0.0d. Date 19.12.24.
Balance of chassis price paid: £1,710.0.0d. Date 17.2.25.
Car delivered on 3.6.25 to Customer by 'S'.*
2/3 on rear }
2 on front } seats
Fittings: Nickel.
Column: D.
Cost of Body: £595.
Long wheel base
Second spare wheel
Two spare 33 x 5 Dunlop tyres
Locks to the bonnet
No cut-out
Battery leads to inside frame position
Change steering and springs
Side-lamps to be well forward on wings
Eural operator to Klaxon
Instruction book sent 20.1.25.
Registration No.: XY 6932
Number Plates: 2
Licence holder: Yes
Wind horn: Cobra and bracket
Fit customers R A C and A A badges
Leather flaps to lockers between interior emergency seats fitted with press-studs
Tool accommodation of approved type
Fitting up set of Brooks luggage trunks
Ventilator: Spinny
Instrument board: dull polish
Specdometer: AT
Clock. Smiths
Width of rear seats 48 in.
Lamps: Lucas - nickel
One gallon tin Price's Motorine C.
One gallon tin Price's Amber A.
No dimmer switch
Barker dipper to headlights
Triplex glass to front screen
Metal box for batteries in Frame
Four doors to open

Sorbo mats to front and rear
Tool accommodation must be adequate
Client to try upholstery
Front seat to slide and adjust
Two emergency seats behind driver
Stove-enamelled grid at rear tilted toward body to take customer's own trunks
Ventilator to each side of scuttle
Calso hood with black fittings and covered with twill
Flat reuter type handles
Screen to fold in half, *i.e.* upper part over lower part horizontal
Wheels only to be black
Second box under step for tools, no recesses.

John Hampton has long admired fine machinery and the best workmanship, his father had already owned two 20 h p models, chassis Nos. GNK 32 and GTM 28, and for many years prior to the Veteran Car Club admitting 'Edwardians' he had taken part in the *Kent Messenger* Old Car Run' with both a 1908 and a 1911 twin-cylinder Renault and, though he had other cars, including a 1912 12/16 Sunbeam and a 1904 Oldsmobile, he had never actually owned a Rolls-Royce himself and was thinking of buying a 20 h p with Coupe Cabriolet body and joining the 20 Ghost Club. When he told me of his idea, I suggested that if he was going to look for an old Rolls-Royce, one of the later type 40/50s which possessed 4 wheel brakes would be a very much better car in every way. Fortuitously, not long after this John's brother, Peter, attended the Bugatti Hill Climb which is run annually at Prescott. He took with him his little 1910 Bugatti, and decided to stay at the Rossleigh Manor Country Club at Andoversford, near Cheltenham.

In the morning, when he went to fetch his Bugatti from one of the lock up garages, he heard an interesting sound; that of a big engine running slowly. He decided to investigate, and to his astonishment found a magnificent, very late type 40/50 h p Rolls-Royce open tourer warming up, with a very old, bearded gentleman pottering lovingly around it.

Peter was soon relating this story to John, who was greatly interested, but it was not until the following year that he actually had the opportunity of seeing the car for himself.

John was absolutely charmed with Henry Thomas, whom he said was a fine old gentleman of the Victorian Era. He was Chairman of Tardery Thomas, Imitation Jewellers, with premises in Oxford Street.

He must have taken a great liking to John, because after this he frequently called at Hampton's in Pall Mall, where John was Managing Director, and they had a chat or a meal together.

When the old man died, John was approached by the Executors of Mr Thomas's Estate, who knew of his interest in the car. By 7 March 1954, everything had been satisfactorily arranged between them, and John delightedly took possession of 120 EU.

He went down to Cheltenham himself, accompanied by his cousin Evelyn Mawer and Fred Watson and drove 120 EU back to Guildford. He knew it had been laid up for 14½ years during its lifetime, but was still pleasantly surprised to find that it had only done 68,817 miles.

When he wrote to Rolls-Royce Ltd, for information about the car he was told that the official date of the car was 3 June 1925. This was the date from which the Guarantee was valid and would be the day on which the coachwork had been completed by Barkers and passed by the Rolls-Royce Company's Inspector.

I have driven the car many times myself and I must say that the brakes on 120 EU are quite fantastic. They are without doubt the best brakes of any pre-war Rolls-Royce car I have ever driven. In November the windscreen was altered from the two-piece, which had an unpleasant habit of leaking, into a one-piece windscreen, and at the same time small side screens were added which stopped a lot of the draught. The following month the car went to F H Melhuish of Camden Town to be completely re-upholstered in its present blue/grey leather. On the journey to London it ran from Merrow to St Martin-in-the-Fields Church in one hour dead and accomplished the total journey to Camden Town in one hour ten minutes, which is exceedingly good going. Two years later, on 12 February 1959, John took the car to the Rolls-Royce Service Station at Hythe Road. They re-bored the engine to 40 'thou' oversize and found that there was 14½ 'thou' wear on the cylinder bores, and also re-connected the extra oil supply and thermostat, which had been disconnected many years before. After this the car ran 530 miles on the 20 Ghost Club's Rolls-Royce Silver Ghost Jubilee Rally of 1957, travelling up and down the Derbyshire Hills around Buxton without faltering.

As can be seen from the Body Card, the original colour of the car was grey with green leather upholstery but, over the years, the varnish had become discoloured making the car a sort of coffee colour in appearance. The new upholstery made it appear even more shabby so, in January 1963, it went to Reddings of Portsmouth to be completely stripped and re-cellulosed in a very delicate shade of pale blue, with black mudguards and valences, after the style of the 'New Phantom' open tourer illustrated in the original 1925 Sales Catalogue. At the same time all nickel parts were chromium-plated, a set of Ace wheel discs were found with great difficulty and fitted to the wheels, and the luggage rack at the rear was removed.

Some purists may raise their hands in horror at not retaining the original nickel-plate and paint and varnish finish, but it must be remembered that when these cars were new, they were almost invariably looked after by a chauffeur who, when the car was not in use, spent hours and hours polishing, cleaning and oiling, etc. Those cars which have been restored exactly as they were turned out originally are usually only used once or twice a year now, probably to go to a Concours d'Elegance. John Hampton has always looked after his cars entirely himself, cleaning, washing, polishing, servicing and doing the general routine maintenance. It is only if some big job is required that he takes the car to an R-R retailer or the London service station, but at the same time he likes to use his car regularly, apart from attending rallies, and there are many occasions when the car is still used as everyday transport in place of his Bentley Continental R-type, his wife's Peugeot 304S or, the latest addition to his collection, a three-speed Silver Shadow with standard four-door coachwork. So to have kept 120 EU in the original paint and varnish with nickel-plating would have been impracticable and made running her a chore rather than a pleasure.

In May 1964 the car took part in one of the most ambitious tours ever organized by the 20 Ghost Club; this was sponsored by Gulf Oil, who very kindly agreed to supply free, all petrol used in Members' cars if they re-fuelled at Gulf Filling Stations in Belgium, Holland, Germany and Denmark.

120 EU and her owners crossed by drive-on drive-off ferry from Dover to Ostend on 6 June 1964, returning to the U K on 16 June 1964, by the new Motor Vessel *England*, sailing from Esbjerg at 5.30 p m to Harwich, where they arrived the following morning. 1,248 miles were covered on this trip during which the car used five pints of Castrol Grand Prix Oil in the engine, which equals 2,000 miles per gallon of oil. The weather was excellent and to their great relief it was never necessary for them to raise the hood. One great problem arose with 120 EU, which John surmounted as best he could in the circumstances. Most late model 40/50s and early type 'New Phantom' chassis were originally supplied with 33 x 5 straight-sided tyres, which had been unobtainable for many years as the Dunlop Co, who make tyres in other vintage sizes, no longer had the mould. In the mid-1920s, after the well base rim was invented, most of the leading tyre manufacturers were trying to discontinue the old beaded edge and straight sided tyres and concentrate on the new type, to achieve this they offered, free of charge, a later type of wheel to customers who still had the old type and supplied them with a new well base tyre to go with it. This, in a way, is what John Hampton now decided to do, he arranged for Dunlop's to rebuild the wheels to take 700 x 21 in. tyres, as this size was and is still readily available. This was done on 27 May 1965 when the car had done 85,488 miles from new.

120 EU was present at the last Goodwood Pageant, which took place in May 1967. (Incidentally, this car is illustrated on the cover of the Programme for this Event). She was again as she had been in the 1964 Pageant, entered in the multi-stable competition in conjunction with John's R-type Continental Bentley, and Ian Hallowes 3-AZ-112 but this time, as the third car, we used my Phantom III chassis No. 3-AZ-146, Hooper Pullman Limousine (for full details of 3-AZ-146 see Part III Chapter 8). Again, as she had done 3 years previously 120 EU and

her two stablemates took first prize in this competition.

Naturally, the car does not have the 'getaway' and performance of a modern one, but she cruises along in the most effortless way at any speed the driver wishes to take her, up to about 60 mph, and with her big 7½ litre engine climbs ordinary main road hills almost as if they were non-existent.

On 29 June 1968, I accompanied John to the 20 Ghost Club Rally at Oundle in Northamptonshire; he took 120 EU and I had my Continental Phantom II (chassis No. 101 SK).

Marion Hampton was accompanying me and John took the lead as I was not sure of the way. There was a fair amount of traffic about but John is a superb driver, religiously obeying all speed limits and never taking any sort of a risk and the way 120 EU settled down, whenever conditions allowed, to a steady 55 to 60 mph was really quite amazing. Of course, the Phantom II, especially a Continental is very much faster and I was able to keep up without the slightest difficulty, but when we reached Beaconsfield I took the lead and John followed me; this was because by now neither Marion nor I could tolerate any longer the awful smell of rich mixture that was coming from 120 EU! It is curious how all these big R-Rs suffer from this and later John said that the fumes we were putting out were simply ghastly, for which reason he kept about a quarter of a mile behind us! John did a good mileage that week-end, as it is 85 miles from Merrow to Oundle, and, when the Rally dispersed, he was making for Broadway in Worcestershire.

In 1969 John heard that Alan May had had great experience in working on the old 40/50, so in December he took the car over to Lingfield in Surrey where Alan May re-faced the inlet manifold, re-aligned and adjusted the exhaust layout, and converted the exhaust-heated carburration to water heating, which has given a much better tick-over, the total mileage was then 94,236.

On 14 December 1971, with the speedometer reading 96,963, John took the car to Alan May for a second time, on this occasion to his new premises at Battle in Sussex, where she remained until 4 March 1972, during which time the following work was carried out. The crankshaft was de-sludged and all new timing wheel ballraces were fitted, together with new ballraces in the ignition tower. New Phosphor-bronze valve guides were made, all big-ends were taken up 2 thou but No. 2 was replaced, and the stand-pipe in the sump was raised one inch so allowing the level to be increased to a capacity of two gallons.

John says that one of the best runs that 120 EU has ever done was coming home after the Turnbury Rally, 11-14 April 1973, on which the car had used 105 gallons of petrol for 1,089 miles and barely 5 pints of oil.

Motoring home down the M6 Motorway with his cousin, Evelyn Mawer, at the wheel John was seated comfortably in the rear of 120 EU, fully protected from the wind by the Auster rear screen. From 8 miles north of Lockerbie to the Welcome Hotel at Stratford-upon-Avon, including 278 miles on the M6 Motorway, 120 EU averaged 60 miles per hour, which is a fantastic performance for a 48 year old car.

Below is the annual mileage of the car since it has been in John Hampton's possession:

1954	2,465	1955	1,855	1956	1,191	1957	1,146
1958	940	1959	1,874	1960	725	1961	590
1962	597	1963	2,449	1964	2,839	1965	1,627
1966	2,388	1967	1,805	1968	1,907	1969	1,013
1970	645	1971	1,090	1972	1,009	1973	(to date) 1,785

The total mileage from new to 24th May 1973: 99,756.

The 'New Phantom'. Chateauroux in mid-France, the testing station for all experimental models. The experimental chassis Nos. 7 EX, (Royce's personal car), 8 EX, 9 EX and the Claude Johnson sports car, 10 EX, as described by Ivan Evernden

On Saturday, 2 May 1925, Claude Johnson made a cryptic entry in his diary: 'R-R Fire works, "New Phantom".'

This recorded the introduction of the much rumoured 'improved' version of the famous 40/50, which made its debut on that day in chassis form in the Conduit Street showrooms. The many members of the public who called in that summer morning to see the new model beheld a superbly polished, gleaming chassis, identical to the previous 'Silver Ghost' type model. The attention of the knowledgeable ones was drawn to the engine - this was an overhead valve 6-cylinder, operated by push rods. It stood much higher in the frame than the previous side-valve engine and was most beautifully finished in aluminium and stove-enamelling. The only other minor changes were that a set of vertical shutters had been added to the radiator, the horn button was on the top of the steering wheel, and an ignition switch had been added to the instrument panel; the really discerning noted that a much larger fish-tail had been fitted to the exhaust pipe.

This 'New Phantom' chassis was to be available in two lengths of wheelbase. 12'0" or 12'6½", for the sum of £1,850 for the shorter wheelbase and £1,900 for the longer type.

In announcing the 'New Phantom' Rolls-Royce Ltd stated:

Modern road conditions permit of rapid acceleration and the maintenance of a high average speed to an extent undreamt of before the war. The makers of the Best Car in the World, in the process of arriving at the type of perfection best suited to post-war conditions, have made exhaustive tests of so-called advances in the design of motor car engines. Thus, a 12-cylinder engine of the 'V' type, an engine with eight cylinders in line, and a 6-cylinder engine with overhead camshaft were all designed, made and tested. The supercharger was also tried and rejected on account of its noise, its complication and its extravagance.

After seven years of experiment and test, in the course of which no promising device had remained untried, the 40/50 h p 6-cylinder 'New Phantom' chassis has emerged, and is offered to the public as the most suitable type possible for a mechanically propelled carriage under present day conditions.

The maximum number of revolutions of the 'Silver Ghost' engine is 2,250 per minute. At the same number of revolutions the 'New Phantom' engine gives thirty-three percent greater horse-power, this being due to improvements in the form of the cylinder head, to a better disposition of the ignition plugs, etc. But the 'New Phantom' engine is capable of a maximum of 2,750 revolutions per minute; yet its annual tax is ten percent lower than that of the 'Silver Ghost'.

This great increase in power has been equalized, from the point of view of safety, by the application to the new chassis of the Rolls-Royce Six-Brake system, without which it would have been inadvisable to place so powerful a machine on the road.

The 'New Phantom' maintains the lead over all its contemporaries which its forerunner, the 'Silver Ghost' acquired 18 years ago.

The foregoing is taken from the Rolls-Royce Company's Sales Catalogue published at the time, exactly how much truth there is in it, it is impossible to say, but I must confess I find it extremely doubtful that the Company actually designed and built a V12 engine and also an 8-cylinder in line, as this would have been a very costly exercise indeed. We do know that a V12 Hawk engine was installed into a car, chassis No. 3 EX, which was called a 'Hawk-Northcliffe' and it is also an established fact that Rolls-Royce Ltd often purchased motor cars made by other manufacturers which particularly interested them, and subjected them to the same stringent tests as their own chassis had to undergo; therefore I cannot help feeling it is far more likely that both the V12 and the Straight-8 referred to were other people's designs and this was another example of clever publicity on the part of Claude Johnson.

In September 1922 it was decided to design a new model as a replacement for the old 40/50, but when the 'New Phantom' appeared it was really only the engine that had been changed; sales had been falling with the 40/50 model for some time as we have already seen and the replacement was becoming essential, so there was no time to design a completely new chassis.

Most of the testing of the 'New Phantom' or 'Eastern Armoured Car' as Hives, who was in charge of the experimental department at Derby, called the new model, usually known as E A C for short, was done in France. For a short while after the Armistice a testing headquarters was set up near Laval, in the Department of Mayenne, about 80 miles south-east of St Malo, and it was from here that Percy Northey carried out a lot of testing on the prototype 20 h p car, but Laval was only a temporary headquarters.

W A Robotham in his book *Silver Ghost to Silver Dawn* tells of his work in the experimental department at Derby with Ernest Hives and how he set up a permanent testing station at Chateauroux, just south of the Loire Valley, some short while before the 'New Phantom' appeared on the market.

There were several very important reasons why it was decided to go to the expense of having a permanent testing station in mid-France, these were as follows:

1   Though Derbyshire possesses excellent hills for testing and the adjoining Counties of Leicestershire and Nottinghamshire are comparatively flat with long straight roads, Leicestershire is the home of the 'hunting community' and as a result there was continual trouble with the police.

2   Public attention being drawn to what was going on at Derby was the last thing that Rolls-Royce Ltd desired.

3   If an experimental car was out on test anywhere near the Derby works and something

went wrong with it, there was always the tendency to return it to the experimental department and tear it to pieces, but with a set-up like Chateauroux, which was so far away, the difficulties had to be overcome on the spot.

Robotham chose Chateauroux as the ideal centre because from this town there were no less than six major roads and three secondary ones running out from the town in all directions of the compass, and each of them was more or less dead-straight for some considerable distance; it was therefore possible to test the cars at high speed without causing annoyance by driving the cars over the same road day after day.

The Hotel de France in Chateauroux became the headquarters, where the testing team lived. A large private garage in the Rue Hyacinthe, just behind the Hotel, was taken on a lease. The drivers worked in shifts, each shift covering 250 miles, so it was quite easy to quickly run the 10,000 miles of non-stop driving that was required for testing an experimental vehicle. The French roads at the time were in a very poor state of repair and the cars took tremendous punishment.

The first experimental 'New Phantom' was given the chassis number 7 EX; the coachwork, designed by Ivan Evernden for Royce's personal use, was a Beatonson All-weather cabriolet built by Barker & Co and finished in grey and black. This was the standard practice for a new model as Royce always wanted to test a model himself thoroughly in everyday use. Royce used 7 EX as his personal transport up until mid-1928; from the time that he took delivery of the car until he gave up using it, many modifications were made to the chassis to bring it up to date and into line with production chassis; I rather think that Royce used the car more during his time at Le Canadel than when he was at West Wittering, as when he was in Sussex the car would return to Derby to be fitted with new parts for Royce to try out when he returned to Le Canadel with the car for the winter.

From the Body Cards at Conduit Street it has been possible to piece together some of the story of the life of 7 EX.

Body Card No. 1

Chassis No.: 7 EX.
Body: All-Weather.
Maker: Barker & Co Ltd.
Colours: Dark blue and black.
Sale Price of Car: £1,700.
Date of Sale: 8.5.1928.
Sold to: Colin Campbell, 2 St Agnes Court, Porchester Terrace, Hyde Park, London, W.
Tyres as fitted.
Deposit paid: £250. Date: 30.4.1928.
Balance paid: £1,564.12.0d. Date: 17.5.1928.
Car delivered on 3.5.28 to Customer by 'S'.*
Instruction book sent to C.C on 7.5.1928.
The car for body, tyres and accessories sold as it stands - the whole in second-hand condition.

Barker discs to six wheels)
Polish aluminium bonnet) Included in selling price
Replate front screen)
Barker-type luggage grid)

Duty on licence from 1st May 1928, to
31st December 1928. —   £30. 16. 0d.
Nickel plate shutters to radiator) charge   4. 10. 0.
Nickel plate frames to windows) to cust-   12. 10. 0.
Two new spare tyres 33 x 6.75) omer   18. 0. 0.
Chassis repaired at Works - £71.17.9d.
Change colour of bonnet and body panels   26. 10. 0.
Set of two emergency seats   15. 0. 0.
Emblazon crest on main doors   3. 3. 0.
R-R Mascot   4. 0. 0.
Silver plate own mascot   12. 6.

When first on the road 7 EX would have been fitted with 33 x 5 straight-sided tyres, but it will be noticed that on being sold to Colin Campbell the tyre size had been changed to 33 x 6.75. This is the old method of measuring and is what is now known as a 7.00 x 21. Also the car had been repainted dark blue, in place of Royce's favourite grey.

Colin Campbell kept the car until 10 December 1936, when he part-exchanged it for 101 SK, a Phantom II Continental Barker sports saloon (see Part II Chapter 9).

The second Body Card held at Conduit Street reads as follows:

Body Card No. 2

Chassis No.: 7 EX.
Body: All-Weather.
Sale Price of Car: £80.0.0d.
Date of Sale: 10.12.1936.
Sold to: George Newman & Co, 369 Euston Road, London, N W 1.
Tyres as fitted.
Invoice No.: 7072. Date: 10.12.1936. £80.0.0d.

*'S' denotes 'Sales'

Car sold as it stands in used condition - £80.0.0d.
Registration Number: CH 5412.
Ex-Lt Comdr Colin Campbell, R N. £175 allowed in part-payment for 101 SK.

By 1936 7 EX would have been of an extremely old-fashioned design and though Colin Campbell always maintained his cars well the very appearance of a Barker cabriolet would make it exceptionally difficult to sell. So, as can be seen from Body Card No. 2, Rolls-Royce Ltd disposed of the chassis the best way they could for virtually a knock-down price, and George Newman sold it to the only possible buyer, a firm of Undertakers, who bought it for the chassis and removed the cabriolet body, replacing this with hearse coachwork.

Unfortunately, it has not been found possible to discover whether 7 EX is still in existence, but in 1950 the chassis was owned by Ashton Brothers, 369 Clapham Road, London, S W 9, who can give me no further details.

The details of both 8 EX and 9 EX are extremely scanty as unfortunately Ivan Evernden has few records of these, and all I have is as follows:

Chassis No.: 8 EX Limousine with proprietary body subframe.
Coachbuilder unknown. Grey. Unladen weight: 53 cwt 1 qtr.

From experimental records: 21.7.1925 - received from fitting shop.
5.7.25 - Hives to Sheringham and district (2269).
12.3.28 - 45,475 last recorded mileage.
Barker Limousine, Index number CH5239. Chassis No. changed to X103CL.

Chassis No.: 9 EX Cabriolet body by Barker. Grey and black. Unladen weight: 48 cwt 1 qtr.

The 'New Phantom' was never run in any sort of speed trial by Rolls-Royce Ltd, they had given up taking part in competitive events before the 1914 war, and the 'New Phantom' was primarily designed as a luxury motor carriage for long-distance touring, town work and all the social events which took place in the 1920s; but Claude Johnson had never despised speed for speed's sake and he was still interested to know what the car could do. He felt that there were a number of English peers and Indian princes who were sufficiently interested to buy an open touring 'New Phantom' which had a really outstanding performance.

When he put this suggestion to Royce, the latter was not particularly impressed and he is reported to have said 'You must remember we make cars for rich old ladies and if people are going to break their necks, let them do it in other people's cars and not ours'. In spite of this, CJ went ahead and the car, which became known as 'The Claude Johnson Special', was built. As with all experimental Rolls-Royce cars it was given a chassis number prefix, EX (this car, chassis No. 10 EX, is still in existence. Original Index number CH5877).

For a full description as to how this car came into being I cannot do better than quote from Ivan Evernden's article which appeared in *Early & Late*, December 1964, as he was given charge of the project.

The 'CJ' Sports Car - 10 EX.
The Prototype Continental Phantom I.

The London to Edinburgh car of about 1911, I seem to remember, did 78½ mph on Brooklands and now, with greater power, we only do 74 mph - the former must have been better for windage.' This letter, from Royce to Hives, his Chief Experimental Engineer at Derby, in November 1925, expressed the mood of the time. Earlier that year a modern overhead valved engine had replaced the side valve unit of the Silver Ghost, after 20 glorious years. There was disappointment that the enhanced power had not produced a proportional improvement in the car's performance. A special open sports Phantom I, chassis No. 10 EX, had been made by Barker & Co, coachbuilders, of London, the intention being to have a car to appeal to the small but influential fraternity of owners who would accept the discomforts of an open touring body in exchange for an increase in performance and particularly in maximum speed. In this category were certain Europeans who indulged in Continental touring and the Maharajas of India. This car, in spite of its special engine with a compression ratio of 5.2 to 1, proved to be little faster than the standard model, yet it had been hoped to be the reincarnation of the famous London to Edinburgh car and the Continental Silver Ghost.

The classic coachbuilder of the day, a craftsman whose ancestors had built carriages for the landed aristocracy, in some cases as far back as the reign of Charles I was an artist but certainly not a scientist or an engineer. His methods of body construction were still those evolved in the days of the horse-drawn carriage and were totally inadequate to cope with the stresses set up in the motor car capable of almost five times the speed. To cope with body cracking, more and more wrought iron was unscientifically introduced into the structure without an adequate reward in increase in strength. Consequently, since 1911, cars besides becoming materially bigger, had become disproportionately heavier. This fact, together with the advent of tyres of large section and lower pressure, caused an increase in the road rolling resistance. Even more important was the fact that the wind drag of the car had increased enormously due chiefly to the increase in the frontal projected area. The front wings had grown to envelop the wheels, the body was widened, headlamps had risen to add to the frontal area of the taller radiator and the higher bonnet and scuttle. Also there occurred little improvement in the aerodynamic form.

W.A.Robotham, assistant to Hives in Derby, had appreciated these facts and by a series of tests at Brooklands had demonstrated the cost in miles per hour of items of coachwork by the simple process of removing them in progression - the wings, side spare wheels, headlamps, etc. The removal of the front wings gave an increase in maximum speed of 6.4 miles per hour, by far the largest single item, but such features as the side spare wheel, the windscreen and the bonnet ventilation, in all were shown to account for 11.4 miles per hour. This, at first sight, may not look very impressive until it is known that with the exhaust system cut-out open 11 more horse power was available and only 2 miles per hour increase in speed was achieved.

At the time I was a Designer with Royce at West Wittering, Sussex. At his home, Elmstead, he had two or three designers whilst I was housed in a small studio in the village a quarter of a mile away. Royce lived at West Wittering all of the summer but from December to late April he moved to the South of France to his Villa at Le Canadel with one or more of his staff.

During the summer, almost fortnightly visits were made by Hives and members of the engineering staff to West Wittering for discussions which in fine weather, were held under the mulberry tree in his garden. As an extra duty I had been assigned the task of educating the coachbuilders by peaceful persuasion to improve the engineering of the body structure; an unenviable task since they had all the conservation of the craftsman, and the backing of a Worshipful Company in the City of London, founded years before the horseless carriage had been dreamt of. Also, for generations they had been coachbuilders to familes and, in consequence, they formed the core of the sales organization.

Royce became very impressed with these problems; for almost a year I was engaged in making designs of a new open touring car to reduce the windage drag and incorporating features which emerged from the Derby tests and the studies which had been made to the products of Continental competitors. It was not until the December of 1926 that ideas became crystalized and it was agreed to produce a car from the design I had made under the guidance of Royce.

As coachwork then was not the direct responsibility of the Company, there was some reluctance to spend money on a project of a completely new Phantom I experimental motor car and it was thought that the coachbuilder should share in the cost. I had the fortunate idea that the majority of the improvements required could be applied to 10 EX by cutting off the rear of the body at the back of the front seat and by making a new rear end to the car and also a new set of wings, a new windscreen and by lowering the steering wheel and front seat by 4 in. The original builders of 10 EX, Barker & Co. of London, finally agreed to do the work for £300. It was my happy day when Royce, who had been using 10 EX for a while, handed it over to me, to take to London to have the alterations put in hand.

The year had been a very memorable one for me, for, in the January I had married the youngest daughter of the Rector of the neighbouring parish of Itchenor, and had acquired a cottage on Itchenor Green.

Plate I (regrettably not reproduced) shows 10 EX outside my cottage complete with crates of Zeiss headlamps for the rejuvenated car ready for me to drive off to London. Having spent a year in deliberation, there was a frantic rush to get the work done. Royce went off as usual to winter at Le Canadel in the South of France.

I had great difficulty in getting the coachbuilders to comprehend the shape of the wings and the body required. These are difficult things to depict by a drawing using orthographic projection. Moreover the design was so ahead of its time that it was difficult to persuade the coachbuilders to depart so radically from the time honoured form associated with his name. Having obtained from Hives a slab of balsawood and some sheet aluminium, in Royce's workshop alongside his garage at Elmstead, I made a one eighth scale model of the car which is shown in Plate 2. I collected the modified car from the coachbuilders on 9 April 1927 - the car is shown in Plate 3.

Test driver George Radcliffe drove the car to Derby for work to be carried out on the chassis. After preliminary road tests Robotham reported, 'We consider that the performance of 10 EX at high speeds has been materially improved by the alterations to the body. It holds the road better and has a higher maximum speed'. In the last week of April of that year the car came to West Wittering for Royce to try. He was well pleased with it but many features he thought needed further design and development attention. Nothing was ever good enough for Royce. Subsequent improvements to the steering and suspension which were made on this car were eventually put into production of the standard model.

This car, 10 EX, was known domestically as the 'CJ' sports car. Claude Johnson the founding Managing Director of the Company had given the project his full backing, just as earlier he had sponsored the London to Edinburgh project. Unfortunately for all concerned, early in the year 1926, he died and his place was taken by his brother Basil who was less convinced of the wisdom of the project, fearing that we were falling under the spell of the monster of speed and power and would produce a rough and noisy car, typical of the sports car of the day.

Royce summed up his own intentions admirably in a letter which he wrote to Basil Johnson. '... We do not propose to make this car coarse as in the case of other sports cars or one that will not run in traffic in top gear. Otherwise we should simply have no special feature of merit. The object of preparing this chassis is that, if speed merchants, in the form of English peers or Indian Rajahs and others, doubt the capacity of the Rolls-Royce Phantom I, this specimen, which we should be able to repeat, can be tried by them. You want to bear in mind that we have no thought of making a freak machine or to depart from the smooth and silent model, but we do think that the owners of the smooth and silent models with their large bodies capable of 80 mph will be pleased to know that the same chassis and engine when fitted up as a touring car will be capable of 95 - 100 mph'.

After the car had received very considerable attention by Derby, in August it was sent to Frinton, where B J was staying on holiday, for him to try. After making a few comments on the mechanical features and the roadability of the car, his comments on its appearance were none too flattering of my styling, which obviously had taken a step forward far too big to be swallowed as one mouthful. He said, 'We realize that it is extremely difficult to carry the spare wheel, etc, behind the back seat, although it is necessary, and still to make the car look beautiful. We realize that the car is only an experiment and we are hopeful of being able to improve its appearance. The rest of the body in front of the great bulbous lump at the back gives an excellent impression of speed and is really attractive. Such a car standing about would always draw a crowd but their remarks would not always be complimentary.'

In the September of 1927 Robotham carried out a series of exhaustive tests on the car at Brooklands in comparison with the standard open touring car, chassis 46 PK. With the cut-out open the CJ Sports car showed an average maximum speed of 89.11 mph over the half-mile, as against 78.26 miles per hour put up by 46 PK; an improvement of approximately 11 miles per hour. By removing the front wings Robotham found that he could extract only another 3 mph.

These tests were conducted with the normal sixteen tooth axle pinion, when the engine power peaked well before the maximum road speed was reached. For the best maximum road speed obviously a seventeen tooth axle pinion was indicated. This could be fitted only at the expense of a reduction in the rate of acceleration, since no means were available to reduce the weight of the car at this stage. It turned the scales at 2 tons 6 cwt 1 qr and 20 lb, or 2.35 tons unladen. Actual tests at Brooklands in September 1927, under very adverse weather conditions and with the wind blowing up the railway straight, using a 17 tooth axle pinion a further 1.4 miles per hour was achieved. Under more favourable conditions this figure could have been 3 miles per hour, so putting the maximum speed, with the exhaust cut-out valve open, at 92 miles per hour.

Almost immediately it was decided to produce three entirely new cars based on the design of 10 EX, in which the coachwork weight would be reduced by 324 lb, thus making possible the use of the 17 tooth rear axle pinion, without loss of acceleration. The body construction was to depart from the heavy ash sills with wrought iron plating and to follow the aircraft principles of construction using vertical sills of sheet metal sandwiched between layers of plywood and the ironing was to consist of sheet metal gussets. The bodies were to be made by Hooper & Co, Barker & Co, and Jarvis of Wimbledon. The cars were called respectively 15 EX, 16 EX and 17 EX. A major advance in streamlining was to be achieved by having the rear compartment covered entirely by a metal tonneau cover which, when opened, would form the rear seat squab and a leg shield carrying the rear screen. The hood, made on a light duralumin tubular structure was made to be concealed in the body when folded down.

The first of these cars, 15 EX, was on the road early in the year 1928 and used for road testing on the Continent. Unfortunately it was involved in a serious accident and was damaged beyond repair. The second car, 16 EX, was shown on P.39 of E and L No. 24. The picture shows how the lines of the wings and the body had been improved in shape over those of 10 EX, and how the metal tonneau fares in the rear seat. This illustration should be compared with the picture of the 10 EX in this issue.

This car, which was completed in the September of 1928, was shown to H R H The Prince of Wales on the occasion of his visit to the works at Derby but no sale was effected.

A record card for the car indicates that 16 EX was sold later that month to a Mr A S Fuller of Ealing, London, but in the January of the following year it is recorded as being owned by Captain J F C Kruse of Sunningdale, Berks.

In November 1933, it was owned by Mr J Moore of London, and in September 1935 by a Mr W H M Ogilvie F R C S, of Harley Street, London. The latter is the last entry in the log.

The third car, 17 EX, was completed in the Autumn of 1928 and was sold in January of the next year, to H H The Maharaja Bahadur of Jammue and Kashmir. The last recorded owner is Mr V V Singh of Uttar Pradesh, India, in 1954.

I have no actual record of the selling price of these cars. The chassis price was £1,900. The total price would depend very much on the accessories to be included, but I believe that the basic price would be of

the order of £2,850 (from £8 - 10,000 of today's money!).

After being used for development test purposes, 10 EX remained the property of the Company, to be used by Mr W Lappin, Liaison Officer between the Company, the Air Ministry and the Royal Air Force. At airfields throughout the country this streamlined car aroused very considerable interest.

In 1932 it was sold to Mr T B Batchelor of Byfleet, Surrey, and in 1933 it is recorded as being owned by Mr J H R Smith of Hythe, Kent. There is a gap then until 1948 when it reappeared, in a very sorry state on a used car lot at Meriden, Warwickshire. From there it was acquired by Mr Laurence Mitchell of Edgbaston, Birmingham, who in 1951 sold it, still unrestored, to Mr A Meredith-Owens, Kings Sutton Manor, Banbury, Oxfordshire, who has spent the intervening years gradually bringing 10 EX back to its original specification. It was primarily his interest in this task which led me to record this history. I have no knowledge of any further cars of this design being built, although it is possible that some coachbuilders may have made and sold a few.

The efforts which had been made to revive the interest in the Sporting Open Rolls-Royce Car had failed for several reasons. Firstly, in the Autumn of 1929 the Phantom II chassis was introduced. This chassis had half-elliptic rear springs with a chassis frame extending backwards to the rear spring shackles, making it difficult, if not impossible, to provide an elegant tail to the body.

The second and by far the most important reason was the fact that the Sports Saloon had been invented. It was a fact that a saloon car could be made to have an aerodynamic drag no greater than that of the open bodied car. Its somewhat larger frontal projected area was more than compensated for by its better aerodynamic shape. Also, it was possible to build an enclosed body which would weigh no more than an open one and provide greater strength and rigidity because the former is a box like structure whilst the latter resembles a domestic bath with gashes cut into its sides.

The Sports Saloon had come to stay, and so Royce started me on a project design of the Continental Sports Phantom II, the Prototype of which, 26 EX, went on the road in 1930. Perhaps when this story is published, the whereabouts of 16 EX and 17 EX may be revealed.

Of the three cars, 10 EX is the one I would covet the most. To me it is the nostalgic symbol of those wonderful years I spent at West Wittering working for Royce and the romantic years of my early married life.

H I F E

Having quoted Ivan Evernden's excellent article on 10 EX and the later EX series 'New Phantom', it is necessary to return to 10 EX and leave the details of the other chassis until later.

The original registration number issued to 10 EX was CH 5877 and the car was finished in pale grey. It remained the property of the Company until 1931, when it was sold to its first owner and the registration number was changed to the one which it now bears, GK 5049, a London registration.

Chassis No.: 10 EX.
Body: Open streamline Sports Tourer.
Maker: Barker & Co Ltd.
Colours: Light blue and black.
Upholstery: Blue leather.
Tyres: as fitted.
Sale Price: £925.
Date of Sale: 2 March 1931.
Sold to: Messrs Howards Garage, West Byfleet, Surrey.
For: T B Batchelor, Esq, Hopwood, Dartnell Park.
For delivery: West Byfleet, Surrey.
Deposit: £90 paid. 3.3.1931.
Balance: £873.10.0d, paid 10.3.1931.
Instruction Book issued: 4.3.1931, to customer.
Levers: Standard.
Steering: 'D'.
Complete car sold in second-hand condition including chassis, body and extras, for the sum of £925.
Cost of licence duty from 1 March - 31 December -

£38.10.0d.

Weld cracks in body near doors	)	T.H. Gill & Sons
Eliminate rattles and squeaks	)	£8. 10. 0d.
New stays to undershield	)	£1. 10. 0d.

10 EX is now owned by Bill Meredith-Owens, who is a great enthusiast and has had the car for many years now and it was present at both the 1964 and 1967 Goodwood Pageants; it is interesting to note that in addition to 10 EX Bill Meredith-Owens is the owner of two other Rolls-Royce cars, both of which have covered incredibly small mileages of less than 10,000 during the whole of their lives, and that he purchased both of them when he was in India. The first is a 'New Phantom', chassis No. 71 DC, fitted with a Barker open touring torpedo body, finished overall in polished aluminium, the original owner was the Nawab of Dowla. The second car is a Phantom II, chassis No. 188 PY, this is also an open tourer, but is sometimes described as an All Weather Cabriolet, the coachwork is by Thrupp & Maberly Ltd, and the car is finished with polished aluminium bonnet and wings, Ace discs are fitted to the wheels. The body, which is still in its original cellulose, is finished in that very popular shade of brownish-yellow, which appears on modern Fiats, Minis, etc, and is sometimes called 'Burmese Yellow'.

PART I CHAPTER 14

The experimental chassis 11 EX, 12 EX, 14 EX, 15 EX, which was involved in an accident in France and later re-built as chassis No. 29 CL. 16 EX, including reports published on this chassis in the Rolls-Royce Enthusiasts' Club's magazine **The Bulletin** *in 1968; and 17 EX, the last experimental 'New Phantom'.*

I have very little information on 11 EX; unfortunately Ivan Evernden was unable to supply any information on this chassis, but from Conduit Street I was able to discover that the car was formerly a 'Silver Ghost' type, chassis No. 93 NK, and was fitted with an All Weather body by Park Ward in 1923, finished in rough grey and with no proper upholstery. The first Body Card reads as follows:

Chassis No.: 11 EX.
Engine No: YL 65.
Body: Weymann enclosed drive limousine.
Drawing No.: 2022.
Makers: H J Mulliner & Co.
Order No.: 2017 R. Date: 18.8.1925.
Colours: Blue and black.
Upholstery: Light cloth, black leather to front.
Coachbuilders instructed: 18.10.1925.
Fittings: Nickel.
Levers: Set in.
Steering: 'C'.
2 on front seats, 2 on rear seat, 2 extra seats.
Long wheelbase.
Body: £485.
Six 33 x 5 Dunlop tyres.
Second spare wheel.
Locks to Bonnet.
Two Dunlop 33 x 5 tubes.
Rubbolite tail lamp.
Registration No.: YM 2964.
Number plates: Two Gransby.
Licence holder: Usual.
Wind Horn: Cobra.
Lucas driving mirror.
Brackets to carry in; disc set and well.
Inside electric lights: 2 and 1 switch.
Luggage grid: To rear of approved type.
Ventilator: To top and each side of scuttle.
Instrument board: Polished.
Speedometer: Smith.
Smith mechanical wiper to screen.
Interior height: 51 in.

Number of doors to open: 4.
Windows to drop in door.
Windows to slide in division.
Floor covering front: rubber mat.
Floor covering rear: carpet.
Lamps: Lucas.
Fully floating scuttle.
Extra seats to face sideways and fold away flush.
Sorbo mat to front and rear.
Ample finger clearance between screen and steering wheel.
Wings, scuttle and bonnet to be treated with cellulose enamel.
Smith patent type Spot-light.
Fire frame Fire Extinguisher.
Special Lucas wing lamp with mirrors to be fitted to offside.
Bring blind to back light to be capable of operation from driving seat.
Two-tone Klaxon. Brooks Trunk, Headlamps to be fitted with Allan Leveridge dimming device.

It would appear to me that the reasons for the change of coachwork were as follows:

1. The Park Ward All Weather was of an old design.

2. Rolls-Royce Ltd have always been one of the first firms to try anything new and the Weymann body, the design of which originated in France, was becoming popular and there was no doubt it would become more so as time went by. It was fairly easy to construct, very much lighter than a coachbuilt body and did not suffer from requiring yearly varnishing, nor did it rattle to anything like the same extent as a coachbuilt one, and lastly, it was very much easier to clean.

So, taking all these things into account it is hardly surprising that Rolls-Royce Ltd would want to try out a Weymann body for themselves and see how it stood up to their own strenuous testing; it must have done this quite well, as when the car was sold it was still carrying the same coachwork; the details of the sale of 11 EX are as follows:

Chassis No.: 11 EX.
Body: Weymann enclosed limousine.
Maker: H J Mulliner.
Colour: Blue and black.
Upholstery: Cloth - black leather to front.
Sale Price of Car: £1,650.
Date of Sale: 4.1.1928.
Sold to: Joseph Tatton Esq, 'Lincroft', Carlisle Road, Eastbourne.
For delivery: Mid-January 1928.
Deposit paid: 6.1.1928 - £165.
Balance of car paid: £1,529 - 21.1.1928.
Car delivered to Mr Tatton - Percy Northey.
Instruction book issued to Mr Tatton - 13.1.1928.
Fittings: Nickel.
Levers: Set In.
Steering: 'C'.
Car with body, tyres and accessories sold as it stands, the whole in second hand condition for £1,650.
Duty on licence for year ending 31.12.1928 £44.0.0d.

After this there is no further record at all of 11 EX in the Company's files, so the later history of this chassis is a closed book at the moment.

The only information available on 12 EX from Ivan Evernden is that it was fitted with open touring coachwork by Bawker finished in grey bearing Index No CH 5886 and was returned to Derby from Chateauroux on about 19 December 1928. This latter information was gleaned from a letter written by G W Hancock in regard to the first prototype Phantom II, 18EX, which had just started to undergo its tests in France (see Part II, Chapter 1).

12 EX returned to England via Boulogne/Folkstone, the General Transport people dealing with it: 'Their agent, Mr Gillain, of 7 rue d'Artois, dealt with the car and all its papers. There were about 9 cars being shipped to England and Mr Gillain had to deal with 4 or 5 of them'.

12 EX was later to be made into a light lorry, or 'high speed truck', for transporting the Schneider Trophy Engines down to Gosport, but what happened to it after this is unknown.

The details which Ivan Evernden has given me on 14 EX are as follows:

Chassis No. 14 EX. Faux cabriolet by Barker. Grey and black.
Named E A C 7. (Eastern Armoured Car) when it was fitted with ½-elliptic springs and open propeller shaft. - Hotchkiss Control.

This was one of the chassis which were undoubtedly built to gain experience for the replacement model of the 'New Phantom', which was being planned; it is mentioned in that most interesting article 'Gearboxes: The Search for Perfection', written by S Harry Grylls, and published in three parts in *The 20 Ghost Club Record*, Vol. II, Nos. 2, 3 and 4, 1970, in which he says that he was assisting Robotham to test a gearbox on an experimental small horse power car, chassis No. 12-G-IV, which was fitted with the latest type of reverse gear. This they accomplished by towing 14 EX in second gear with the brakes on, by 12-G-IV, going in reverse at full throttle, along a straight piece of road for about ¾ mile. Harry Grylls had the task of driving 12-G-IV backwards and after about ½ mile 14 EX seized up, but freed itself when it cooled down again.

Frank Dodd, who was Royce's personal chauffeur for so many years, has a photograph of this chassis carrying coachwork built by James Young of Bromley, so some time in its life it must have been rebodied. Ian Rimmer, at Crewe, from whom I obtained most of these Index numbers as the book was going to press, told me that the Index number was CH6095 and that Rolls-Royce Records at Crewe give this car as being fitted with a Hooper Sedanca.

15 EX has already been mentioned in the previous chapter in Ivan Evernden's article and from him I was able to obtain the following additional information:

Chassis No. 15 EX. Decked sports body based on rebuilt 10 EX, made by Hooper & Co Ltd. This car was written off by Comdr Briggs when he wrapped it round a tree in France.
Special body construction by Ev. Pale blue.

This smash took place near Amiens, on 27 March 1928, and was caused through a tyre bursting.

On 20 January 1971, when searching through the files at Conduit Street, I found, much to my surprise, it appeared that 15 EX was not after all written off because of this accident, but was rebuilt and given a new chassis number, 29 CL, though it retained its original registration number of CH 7189. Later, when I went to spend an afternoon with Ivan and Sally Evernden at their home at West Wittering, I told them about 15 EX and Ivan was amazed to hear this, especially as when he had taken 29 CL to the Continent he had taken some photographs of the car and had absolutely no idea at all that he was driving his old 15 EX. After it had its new body it had nothing to do with the experimental division but was allocated to the Sales Department. It was based on 21 UF, which was the 'Riviera Trials Car', which is illustrated in colour in the Rolls-Royce Sales Catalogue 1928. The one difference between the two cars was that 21 UF had a side mounted spare wheel and 29 CL a rear mounted one. Incidentally, 29 CL is illustrated in the 1929 Sales Catalogue for the 'New Phantom', price complete £2,678.

The details of the rebuild are as follows:

Baden & Prague Propaganda Car.
Chassis 29 CL.
Reg. No. CH 7189.

Chassis No.: 29 CL.
Engine No.: 21 EX.
Works No.: 29 CL, ex-15 EX. 40/50.
Type: Long.
D I Issued: 29.6.1928.

Off Test: 3.7.1928.
Axle ratio: 15 x 52.
Chassis EX W and sent K & B direct to Barker.
Despatched: 4.7.1928.

Body: Torpedo.
Drawing No.: LD 7321 A.
Makers: Barker.
Order No.: 1441. Date: 14.6.1928.
Tyres: Dunlop, low pressure, silent tread. 33 x 6.75 all round.
Trimming & Painting: Cellulose (as 21 UF Riviera Trials).
Colours: Cream, fine green line. Polished aluminium top panels to bonnet, scuttle top, wings, chassis deck. etc.
Upholstery: Apple green leather. Hood: Twill pattern No. 725.
Car taken back from Cochran by R-R Ltd in part payment for 73 WJ, price to be taken as £500. *Note: this has been written over top on card and obviously added later.*
Sale Price: £1,850.
Baden & Prague Propaganda car, 20.8.1930.

* Works   † Nickel Plating

Sold to: G A Cochran, Guarantee Trust Co, Pall Mall, London SW1. (2.6.1931, owned by Count A Hochberg, Munich).
For delivery: chassis - end of June; car - end of July. Chassis delivered on 4.7.1928 to Barker by 'W'.*
Invoice: £2,761.19.3d. 15.8.1928.
20.9.1929 - car handed to Hms for sale second-hand.
Fittings: Nickel.
Levers: Standard (Set In).
Column: 'D'.
Special radiator, bonnet and dash, bonnet with standard shutters and with top panels polished, sides for painting.
Long wheelbase.
Springs for body as on 21 UF.
Passengers: 4-3. 8/9 cwt luggage, nil.
Springing for Continent generally - as 21 UF.
5 wheels, Dunlop 21 x 5 wire.
N P R-R Luggage grid and rear spare wheel carrier.†
N P R-R nearside spare wheel carrier.†
R-R Mascot and cap. Silver plated.
Locks to bonnet.
A T Speedometer in Kms.
North 8-day clock.
Instruments on dash to have venetian cream dials, black figures and black rims. Standard size, except smaller oil gauge and thermometer.
N P Cobra windhorn. †
2 N P Folberth wipers. †
Atlantic F W 13 stop-lamp.
Grebel spotlamp. 180 mms.
N P Lucas circular driving mirror. †
Pyrene Fire Extinguisher.
N P Licence Holder. †
2 Smiths N P Cigar lighters, 1 front, 1 rear.
Extra luggage straps (3 in all). Waterproof sheet 12 ft x 9 ft. Large dust sheet.
R A C badge, silver plated, supplied by C W B.
N P Lucas lighting set. †
P 100 headlamps. Chrysler type side lamps. Flexible tail-lamp. Barker semi-rotary dipping headlamps.
Barker Penny polished disc wheels. 5 wheels to be painted cream.

Two years later, with the Phantom II fully established, 29 CL became surplus to requirements and the car was sold to Hooper & Co Here is Body Card No. 2, giving full details as follows:

Chassis No.: 29 CL.
Second-hand, Hooper Co.
Index No.: CH 7189.
Torpedo body by Barker.
Sold to Hooper & Co, 54 St James Street, SW1 on 11.4.1930.
Ex Baden & Prague Propaganda Car.
Sale Price: £1,450.
Car delivered to Hooper & Co 11.4.1930 by Lille Hall.

Cellulose: Cream, fine green lines, polished aluminium top panel of bonnet, scuttle top, wings, deck.
Upholstery: Apple green. Hood: Twill.
Complete car sold as it stands, including chassis, body and accessories, the whole in second hand condition for the sum of £1,450.
Change dial of speedometer for one reading in miles.
Registration No.: CH 7189.

Somehow or other Rolls-Royce Ltd had 29 CL back to sell a second time; it can only be assumed that Hooper & Co sold the car to a client, who later bought another Rolls-Royce direct from Conduit Street, and they took 29 CL back on a part-exchange basis, for the third Body Card reads as follows:

Chassis No.: 29 CL.
Body: Torpedo.
Maker: Barker.
Colour: Black.
Sold to: T J O'Conner, KC.MP, 1 Temple Gardens, London, EC4.
Sold on: 5.8.1932.
Car delivered to customer by Lillie Hall* - 15.9.1932.
Price paid £700, allow for re-glazing front screen.
Complete car sold as it stands, the whole in second hand condition for the sum of £700. Allowance on old car, 18 JG, £50.
Convert speedometer to read in mph (A T & Co).
Ex Cochran. Taken over from Export Department, 27.1.1932.

After it was rebuilt, it was used as the Baden & Prague Propaganda Car, 29 CL, and then sent to Chateauroux on test for a short while before being sold to Hooper & Co for the first time. After the car was sold to T J O'Conner the changes of ownership read as follows:

March 1935	-	Barker & Co.
1937	-	Milber.
1940	-	Adelaide Garage.
1944	-	R o b e r t s, 115 Rocky Lane. Anfield, Liverpool.
1945	-	Jack Compton.
1950	-	Up to 1952 - Watsons of Liverpool.
1959	-	Harold H Jones. Crosville Motor Services, Crane Wharf, P O 15, Chester.

This car is still in existence as a Hooper Limousine. Meanwhile her sister car, 21 UF, was sold to Warwick Wright Ltd, who, on 13 March 1929 sold it to E A Wadsworth, Dairy Farm, Maresfield Park, near Uckfield, in Sussex. Then

there is a blank until 1937, when the car was with Jack Compton. In April 1940 it was owned by the Leicester Co-operative Society, and in 1948 had a complete overhaul at Crewe, which cost £930. In 1958 it was owned by the traffic department at Leicester and was last heard of in 1962 at James Howells Garage in Cardiff. Though I have been unable to check any further it would appear that both cars survive to this day.

16 EX has also already been mentioned in Ivan Evernden's article, the coachwork on this chassis was almost identical to that on 15 EX, but it was built by Barker, finished in blue and silver and possessed the following special features:

Compression ratio: 4.75.
Hartford shock absorbers all round in addition to hydraulics.
No tie rods.
Sideguards to streamline engine and gearbox.
Modified petrol tank.
Special rear wheel carrier.
Rubber engine mounting.
Cast dashboard.
Engine in further forward.
Modified position of pedals and steering column.
Battery in frame.

There is something of a mystery about the sale of 16 EX, it would appear from the Body Cards that the first intention in disposing of the chassis was to ship it to India, as Body Card No. 1 reads as follows:

Chassis No.: 16 EX.
Type: Short.
Body: Sports tourer.
Makers: Barker & Co Ltd.
Sale Price: £1,850, less 25% for chassis.
Date of Sale: -
Sold to R-R Ltd, Bombay, for Bombay stock.
KN, JP and JG advised 17.10.1928.
Fittings: Nickel.
Column: Special - see particulars in file.

A 40/50 h p normal wheelbase, chassis No 16 EX, complete with usual equipment as per specification, £1,850, less 15%.
A Barker special sports body, finished in blue cellulose with bonnet and wings of polished aluminium, £600.
A Lucas lighting set comprising P.100 headlamps and special type Chrysler wing lamps in lieu of standard wing lamps.

* Lillie Hall, Earl's Court, was the original service station of C S Rolls & Co; it became the despatch centre for new chassis and was used as a second hand sales department for used cars. It was sold by R-R Ltd a few years ago owing to re-development in the area. It is often written LH on the Body Cards

Extra for specially grouped instruments which include speedometer and a clock, £25.0.0d.
One spare Dunlop, 33 x 6.75 Balloon tyre, £9.1.6d.
N P Cobra horn, £6.6.0d.
R-R Mascot, £4.0.0d.
A set of 5 Barker 'Penny' polished aluminium wheel discs, £21.5.0d.
A Smiths wiper, £4.10.0d.
Collecting, packing and shipping London-Bombay.
Insurance to value of £ ? , @ ? .

However, it seems that whilst these arrangements were being made Capt Kruse heard that 16 EX was going to be sold. He was a great enthusiast who already had experience of running a 'New Phantom', as in 1925 he had purchased one with Barker coachwork, to which he had had a supercharger fitted.

The second Body Card for 16 EX reads as follows:

Chassis No.: 16 EX.
H P: 40/50.
Axle ratio: 16 x 52.
Tyres: Dunlop low pressure 33 x 6.75.
Chassis Sale Price: £1,900, less 15%.
Date of Sale: 7.9.1928.
Sold to : Barker & Co, 66-69 South Audley Street, W1.
For: Capt J F C Kruse.
Balance of chassis price paid: £1,663.8.10d, on 10.11.1928.
Steering column: Special rake.
Levers: Standard.
Fittings: Nickel.
Radiator shutters: White metal.
Springs for a touring sports with dickey weighing approximately 7½ cwt.
Seating: 4, usually 2. No luggage.
Extras for specially grouped instruments including speedometer and clock, £25.0.0d.
One pair of P 100 Lucas headlamps, £22.0.0d.
N P Cobra horn, £6.6.0d.
Smith windscreen wiper (supply only) £3.5.0d.
Locks to bonnet, £2.13.6d.
R-R Mascot, £4.0.0d.
One spare Dunlop tyre, £6.14.3d.

Later 16 EX changed hands and in 1933 Rolls-Royce Ltd took the car back again in part-exchange for a Phantom II, chassis No. 8 PY, and the third Body Card reads as follows:

Chassis No.: 16 EX.
Body: Sports open tourer.
Tyres: as fitted.
Date of Sale: 24 October 1933.
Sold to: Messrs Fleet Deliveries Ltd, 99 Caledonian Road, London, N1.

Colour: Blue with aluminium deck.
Deposit paid: £375, on 4 November 1933.
Car delivered: 4 November 1933 to Fleet Deliveries by Lille Hall.
Invoice No.: 3297. Date: 2.11.1933. £375.
Complete car sold as it stands, the whole in second hand condition for the sum of £375.
Ex - A S Fuller Esq. £575 allowance for part-payment on 8 PY (Phantom II).
Registration Number: XV 1771. (Original Index number CH7234).

To tell the whole story of the life of 16 EX is somewhat difficult, it would require almost a life-time to trace all the owners of this chassis, and I therefore cannot do better than quote the following letter which appears in the Rolls-Royce Enthusiasts' Club's Magazine *The Bulletin*, No. 49, July 1968:

I was intrigued by Ivan Evernden's article on the prototype Phantom I Continentals, reprinted in the Bulletin of March 1968, and somewhat perturbed by his last paragraph, from which it would appear that the ex-Sir Heneage-Ogilvie car 16 EX is no longer known to us.

The car was photographed 'in a Suffolk garden' in one of the last Rolls-Royce Bulletins sent to my late grandmother, in 1962 I think. But, more to the point of this letter, I had a good deal to do with this fine vehicle in 1950/51, when it was purchased by Mr Alfred Edmunds-Jones from the last owner recorded on the maker's service log, who by then was Surgeon Commander to the Royal Yacht Squadron, I believe. This may explain the presence of the jack-staff fitted to the rear deck!

I understand from Edmund-Jones that the car had for a time also been the property of Dorothy Paget, who used it for high-speed commuting between these shores and Cannes. Be that as it may, it certainly was, in 1950, a rapid machine - beautifully balanced under all conditions; I was allowed to drive it (very unofficially!) between Denham and my father's garage in Watford mostly, although there were two memorable late night runs to Bournemouth and back. The car left an indelible imprint on my memory, so much so that, if the present owner should read this, I will be very grateful if he could make it possible for me to see the Phantom once more at close quarters.

Believe it or not, when Edmund-Jones acquired it, the car had chromium-plated wheels, which just goes to show that there is nothing new under the sun, even among our American brethren! My father was commissioned to have them sand-blasted and stove-enamelled black, and also to have made a smaller hood, as the new owner did not anticipate carrying a full complement of passengers frequently and found the original vast, but beautifully contrived, equipment a sore trial to erect and stow. The fuel tank and feed system was overhauled after some years standing, and the cooling system flushed.

At this time the body side panels were in unpainted polished alloy, only the top surfaces and wings being black, and in my view the appearance was much enhanced by this scheme. The interior was almost faultless brown hide, and the lightweight bodywork had stood the test of time by not betraying a single sign of fatigue anywhere, truly a fine testimonial to the designer and to Barker's.

Of all the fine cars with which I have been acquainted I regret most of all losing touch with this one, for following a disastrous fire at Fulmer Chase, his home, Mr Edmund-Jones had to dispose of the Phantom, which luckily was not involved in the blaze. I have only once caught a glimpse of it since, climbing strongly over Hampstead. Of all the cars which left the factory prior to 1939, it was quite the easiest to drive as well as being by far the most entertaining, and my sincere hope is that it remains thus.

Incidentally, the factory gave me to understand that twelve of these were built, the greatest proportion of which went to owners in India; perhaps some light could be shed on this statement?

(A letter from Michael Doland, 33 Northumberland Avenue, Wanstead Park, London, E12).

In April 1959, the magazine *Road and Track* published an article entitled 'The New Phantom', written by the car's owner, Ian Graham, and re-printed in the Rolls-Royce Enthusiasts' Club Bulletin, No. 52, January 1969:

In October 1926 the 'New Phantom' was announced by Rolls-Royce, 19 years after its predecessor the Silver Ghost went into production. The overhead valve engine was entirely new and able to deliver perhaps 25% more power, while servo-assisted four-wheel brakes would match the higher speed. Yet the old Ghost was not laid; the new car steered with the same small, fat wheel covered in brownish hard rubber, the drive was still through a gigantic torque tube 'sewn' to the rear axle with innumerable bolts, and the body rested on this axle through cantilever springs.

Robust and powerful this car certainly was, yet it somewhat lacks the charm of the Ghost, and of its successor the Phantom II. Nevertheless a large number are still to be found in the U S (most of them produced at the Springfield, Mass, factory) while in England there must be at least a hundred in daily use as hearses.

The car featured here, which has also been in regular use throughout its life except during the war years, was not a production car, but one of those retained by the company as a test bed for new features. The chassis number is 16 EX, and the engine parts bear various experimental numbers.

The body, built by Barker but obviously derived from Delage and Voisin designs, might also appear to be experimental - a sort of stylist's dream, unhampered by tiresome considerations of luggage space, ease of entry, or of making tight the many hinged panels in the deck which conceal spare wheel, top and rear seats.

Apparently three cars were built, with bodies differing only in trifling details. An old photograph of one with side-ventilators (lacking in my car) appeared in *Road and Track* in August 1953.

With peacock blue sides, polished aluminium fenders, rear deck and hood top, and aluminium discs over the wire wheels, my car must have been a wonderful sight in the Twenties. It sped past other cars labouring along the highway with only the noise of air rushing into the carburettor (silent tires without cross-cuts were used).

During its first year with the Company it was taken to Venice for the Schneider Trophy races as a staff car, and was afterwards loaned to Lawrence of Arabia to tear about France in; this I learned when the car was spotted one day in the Rolls-Royce service department in London by the engineer who had taken it to Venice. Also during this period it was fitted with the aluminium head and recessed radiator shutters found on later production cars, as well as one or two excrescences which have no purpose now.

The first private owner was a Mr Kruse; next, in 1935, was Sir Heneage Ogilvie, the surgeon. Soon afterwards, Sir Heneage wrote me, a 'damned fool cyclist' made him take to the hedge, damaging the wheels, midship section and steering wheel, and, more important, one of the surgeon's hands. Some of the resulting $30,000 damages went into repairing the car, and it was at this time that it was painted black and acquired a Phantom II steering wheel and a jackstaff on the rear deck, for the owner was an enthusiastic sailor and liked to fly the burgee of whichever yacht club he was on his way to visit.

Bought after the war by Henry Peat, the car used to take him up to Scotland each year and to his office in London on most days, when it would be parked across the street from my apartment. It received many covetous glances from my direction, and then I heard he would sell it!

As I own no modern car, the odometer has been busy, particularly so on two trips we did together. One was through Germany to the south of Italy and back through France. Visiting the Daimler-Benz museum in Stuttgart on the way, I was invited by an official to bring my car up in the elevator. Then the director came in; he peered at the car, and all he said was, 'Oh, yes, Rolls-Royce; we know that make'.

In Italy the reception was tumultuous, and in trying to thread my way through Amalfi during their annual 'fiesta' I had a hard time repelling boarders. At one time there were 11 boys on running boards, fenders and tail, and the marks of their shoes remain on the paint to this day. Fortunately the aluminium was not dented. But in one respect the Italians were always disappointed; they would wait by the car to hear it start, and when it did, their faces fell: 'E bellissima, ma non si sente' - you can't hear it. This was the moment to open the cut-out.

The mechanical trouble on this tour amounted to a broken bolt in a door latch. I do not carry any spare parts; just a few tools and a kit of Araldite epoxy resin and hardener which is invaluable for small body-work repairs. I have used it very successfully to stop the leak from an oil line worn through by rubbing on something, and to fashion a new generator brush holder and repair the high tension slip-ring checks of the magneto when they were burned through by the sparks tracking along the dirty surface. This happened one night in upstate New York. There was a nasty smell, but no interruption of the journey. We continued on coil ignition alone.

My latest tour, 10,000 miles, wandering through the Eastern United States, down through Mexico City and then to Los Angeles, was completely free of mechanical trouble although I did have a fright one day after a picnic lunch in Louisiana, when horrid noises came from the engine on starting up. Putting my ear to the bonnet I could hear heavy pieces of metal clashing together. So this was the end of the trip, I thought, in an isolated part of the bayou country - but the noise was quickly traced to chattering gears in the generator drive, caused by a sticking brush. Once again, as with the magneto - poor maintenance on my part.

When I first had the car, oil consumption was very high until new compression rings and Duaflex scraper rings were installed. Now, 25,000 miles later, the consumption is still low, nearly 1,500 miles per quart.

More oil is consumed - and replaced with infinitely greater trouble - in the many chassis lubrication points, some of which are located with devilish ingenuity so as to be almost inaccessible. This is the great curse of this car. Yet one cannot really regret the many grimy hours spent with the oil gun; my car is a delight every morning, starting instantly in any weather, never temperamental, pulling quietly up Mexican mountains on 65-octane gas or sweeping past cars 30 years younger stalled at the roadside with vapor lock - or merely standing across the street like a big car at rest, full of the suggestion of power, and full of a beauty that has not dimmed for me after years of fond contemplation.

At the same time in *Road and Track*, April 1959, 16 EX was road-tested, the report of this was also re-printed in the Rolls-Royce Enthusiasts' Club Bulletin, No. 52 January 1969:

July 1959. It would be nice to say that Ian Graham's offer of his 1927 Rolls for test was the 'opportunity of a lifetime' but it wouldn't be quite true, because Phil Hill wanted us to do similarly with his magnificent 1931 Pierce-Arrow (*Road and Track*, April 1955). However, the opportunity to test drive a rare and unusual classic doesn't come every day - or even every year - and when the Barker bodied

torpedo phaeton pulled up in front of our offices, our test crew literally dropped everything and off we went.

In assessing the report on this car, readers should note both its age (32 years) and the mileage (in excess of 180,000 miles). Furthermore, the engine had not been specially tuned in any way, and it had just completed a tour to California from New York via Mexico City!

The internal body width of the torpedo is narrow by modern standards (though quite adequate for two) and even though this was considered a very low sporting-type body in its day, one certainly gets an impression of sitting quite high up. This gives an excellent view of the road and a feeling of great security. With right hand steering the right hand gear control lever is a boon for such as us, who are not ambidextrous. The clutch action is light, with a rather long pedal travel, and upward gear changes proved to be very simple, if a slight pause was allowed before a firm and positive gear lever movement was made. The gears, incidentally, are not as quiet as we had been led to hope for after reading R-R literature of that era.

You can feel 6 huge cylinders working under the hood, but for all that the powerplant is remarkably smooth and quiet. Most outstanding, it has tremendous torque at very low revolutions per minute. In fact, the gears are almost superfluous if you aren't in a hurry.

On the open road the engine feels very comfortable at a steady 60 mph (only 2180 rpm), but we were somewhat shocked at the amount of front-end flexing and moderate shake. Perhaps it is more noticeable because of the high seats and long expanse of automobile located out in front. Here again, we must stop and remember; in 1927 Rolls-Royce had used four-wheel brakes for only three years, the rear springs were still cantilever types, and independent suspension with an X-type frame was still 11 years away.

As for the actual performance tests, the famous R-R clutch is supposed to be extremely durable. The catalogue said 'indestructible even by continued slipping'. However, this one allowed us only one good standing ¼ mile check (also equivalent to 0 to 60 mph in 24.0 seconds), and on subsequent checks it slipped rather badly after each upshift (remember the 180,000 miles). Once the clutch was 'home', it held well enough for the Tapley readings and the high-speed runs. We rate the top speed potential as an honest 80; perhaps the car would do a little better than that when new. Our best time, as shown, was equivalent to 77.1 mph with the needle showing 78 mph.

We made no mileage checks, but 10 to 12 miles per gallon is the usual range in traffic and on the highway. Graham reported that he frequently achieved as much as 16 mpg on long trips by the expedient of accelerating to 65 mph, releasing the clutch, and coasting down to about 50 mph before repeating the process. This technique certainly takes advantage of the considerable inertia available (2.5 tons), but may also account for the clutch trouble we encountered.

In spite of rather harsh treatment for such a fine old lady, who came through none the worse for wear. Treated with proper respect, we believe she's good for another 31 years of faithful service.

Road and Track Classic Test - No. 27.
Rolls-Royce Phantom I.

Specifications

List price (1927)	$14,000
Curb weight	4730
Test weight	4950
distribution, %	47/53
Dimensions, length	191
width	72
height	60
Wheelbase	144
Tread, f and r	56
Tire size	7.00-21
Brake lining area	na
Steering, turns	2.5
turning circle	49
Engine type	6 cyl, ohv
Bore & stroke	4.25 x 5.50
Displacement, cu in.	467.7
cc	7668
Compression ratio	4.50
Bhp @ rpm (est)	107 @ 2750
equivalent mph	75.7
Torque, lb ft (est)	320 @ 1200
equivalent mph	33.0

Gear Ratios

O/d (n a), overall	
4th (1.00)	3.72
3rd (1.48)	5.52
2nd (2.21)	6.25
1st (3.40)	12.6

Calculated Data

Lb/hp (test wt)	46.3
Cu ft/ton mile	119
Mph/1000 rpm (4th)	27.5
Engine revs/mile	2180
Piston travel, ft/mile	2000
Rpm @ 2500 ft/min	2725
equivalent mph	75.0
R & T wear index	43.6

Performance

Top speed (4th), mph	80.0
best timed run	77.1
3rd (2750)	51
2nd (2750)	34
1st (2750)	22

Fuel Consumption

Normal range, mpg	10/12

Acceleration

0 - 30 mph, sec	6.5
0 - 40 mph	10.9
0 - 50 mph	16.8
0 - 60 mph	24.0
0 - 70 mph	35.8
0 - 80 mph	
0 - 90 mph	
0 - 100 mph	
Standing ¼ mile	24.0
speed at end, mph	60

Tapley Data

4th, lb/ton @ mph	185 @ 32
3rd	275 @ 23
2nd	375 @ 18
1st	450 @ 12
Total drag at 60 mph, lb	225

Speedometer Error

30 mph	actual 32.5
40 mph	40.0
50 mph	48.1
60 mph	57.2
70 mph	68.1
80 mph	
90 mph	
100 mph	

This chassis is now in America and is owned by Leon Clark of 1703 Laurel Street, South Pasadena, California, according to the Rolls-Royce Owners' Club of America, 1971-72 directory and register, though an asterisk appears against his name which signified that he is not a member of the Rolls-Royce Owners' Club of America.

The last experimental 'New Phantom' was 17 EX, with coachwork based on 15 EX but which was built by Jarvis & Co of Wimbledon (Jarvis & Co, whose premises were at the top of Wimbledon Hill, at the junction of The Ridgeway, were very old established Austin agents and were only in a small way in the coachbuilding business); it is interesting to note, however, that the 2-seater body which is now fitted on to Stanley Sears' 6-cylinder 30 h p was built by Jarvis in the early 1960s. 17 EX was finished in grey and below are the details of the car taken from the Body Card:

Chassis No.: 17 EX.
Engine No.: 25 EX
H P.: 40/50
Type: Short
Body: Jarvis sports
Colour: Blue, wheels black

Upholstery: Blue leather.
Sale price: £1,850 less 25%.
Sold to: R-R Ltd, Bombay.
For: H H The Maharajah of Kashmir.
Tyres: Dunlop well base 33 x 6.75.
Balance of car price paid: Rupees 42,000. 18.3.1929.
Car delivered on 22 December to Bombay via S S *Hatinura*.
Instruction Book sent to Bombay, 19.12.1928.
Fittings: Nickel.
Levers: Set in.
A normal 40/50 wheelbase Phantom Rolls-Royce chassis with usual kit of tools and spares.
Fitted with a Jarvis 4-seater sports body, painted light blue, trimmed with light blue leather.
Smith's screen wiper.
One pair of P.100 headlamps, N P.
Special dipping H/L brackets.
One pair of N P Chrysler wing lamps.
Red light let into rear portion of body.
Grouped instrument board comprising oil gauge, thermometer, speedometer, clock, ammeter, 2 instrument board lights, temperature warning light.
N P Cobra horn.
N P side ventilators in scuttle.
Case of bulbs.

Please invoice as described below:

Chassis   £1,850.0.0d.

A 4-seater sports body by Jarvis of London, painted blue, trimmed with blue leather and complete as per specification, including one pair Chrysler wing lamps.	600.	0. 0.
A Smith Wiper	4.	10. 0.
One pair P.100 Lucas headlamps, N.P.	22.	0. 0.
Case of spare bulbs		9. 0.
Cobra horn	6.	6. 0.
2 instrument board lamps	1.	10. 0.
Red lamp in rear of body	1.	0. 0.
Wiring up lighting set	4.	0. 0.
R-R Special dipping brackets	15.	0. 0.
A T Speedometer	11.	0. 0.
North Clock	5.	5. 0.
R-R Mascot and cap	4.	0. 0.

Collecting, packing and shipping London-Bombay.
Insurance to value of £2,750 @ 6/3d.%.
R-R Scheme. Order No. 96274.

This car has recently come to light in a derelict condition in India, the rear half of the body is missing; the present owner wrote to Rolls-Royce Ltd, and later to Peter Baines of the R R E C who passed the letter on to me. I have given what information I have on this chassis The original Index number was CH7763.

(Top) 120EU. As originally supplied to J. H. Thomas. See Part I, Chapter 12 (photo John Hampton)

(Middle) The engine in 120EU. See Part I, Chapter 12

(Bottom) A late type 40/50 hp Silver Ghost being used as a break-down truck, a purpose for which many of these cars were used during the 1930s

(*Top*) 39JG, a 1921 Springfield Silver Ghost (*photo John McFarlane*)
(*Bottom*) S-279-PL, a 1926 Springfield Silver Ghost (*photo John McFarlane*)

(Top/middle) Two photographs of 40/50 hp cars, which in later life were purchased for use as fire-engines by the Hong-Kong Fire Brigade. They were both specially prepared for this purpose by Dennis Bros of Guildford, manufacturers of commerical vehicles and motor lawn mower specialists (photo Dr Robin Barnard)

(Bottom) S-288-PL, another 1926 Springfield Silver Ghost. See Part I, Chapter 11 (photo Arthur Soutter)

(Top) An original publicity photograph of a left-hand drive Springfield Silver Ghost with a Piccadilly Roadster Body *(photo John McFarlane)*
(Bottom) Another original publicity photograph, this time of a Pall Mall bodied Springfield Silver Ghost with left-hand drive *(photo John McFarlane)*

(*Top left*) A Springfield Silver Ghost converted from right to left-hand drive with an altered gearchange gate, chassis number SG-39-AG (*photo John McFarlane*)

(*Top right*) A convertible sedan by Locke with a 'V' screen and 'V' shaped instrument panel. This design was not used by other coachbuilders (*photo John McFarlane*)

(*Bottom*) 1927 '20' Windover Limousine GXL-7. It has an upright steering column and seating for 6. It is a typical Windover Limousine body which was often mounted on other chassis such as Daimler 25/85, 20/70 and Lanchester 23

(Top) 1928 '20' Arthur Mulliner Limousine. The chassis for this coachwork was delivered by road. The car has seating for five instead of the usual seven and has Lucas black finish lamps throughout. The radiator, bonnet and dashboard were raised 1.4 inches and the steering column raked. This coachwork was often mounted on Daimler Minerva and Vauxhall chassis

(Middle) Daimler Double-six '30' Hooper Motor Brougham (Body number 7209) finished in the Royal colours with blue leather interior, this car which was for HM's personal use was supplied in July 1929 after the recovery from his illness at Bognor. The car is now at Sandringham in the collection of HM Queen Elizabeth II. HM Queen Mary took delivery of a very similar car (Body number 6861) finished in green with green morocco leather just prior to the King's illness and it was this car that they used whilst staying at Bognor Regis

(Bottom) 1928 Daimler 35/120 Barker Enclosed Drive Laudaulette See the photograph of the Barker New Phantom at the top of the penultimate page of the next photographic section

(Top) 7EX R's personal car. New Phantom Cabriolet by Barker at Le Canadel in 1928 with Royce and Sir James Percy. See Part I Chapter 13, and Part II, Chapter 1
(Middle) The CJ Special, 10EX at Brooklands. See Part I Chapter 13 (photo H. Meredith-Owens)
(Bottom) A drawing of the CJ Special 10EX. See Part I Chapter 13 (photo H. Meredith-Owens)

ROLLS-ROYCE "PHANTOM I"

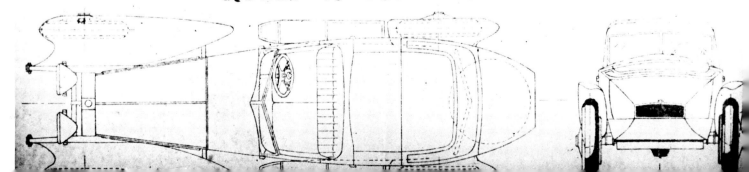

(*Top*) The underside of 10EX in the works

(*Middle*) 15EX, the Hooper Open Tourer which was involved in a serious accident in France

(*Bottom*) 17EX, the last experimental New Phantom with coachwork by Jarvis of Wimbledon. See Part I, Chapter 14

PART I   CHAPTER 15

The introduction of an aluminium cylinder head, problems with balloon tyres. Royce's dislike of disc wheels and as an alternative he recommends steel artillery. The Daimler Co introduce a steel sleeve valve and King George V orders a new 35/120. Royce's life at Le Canadel, and the death of Claude Johnson. The rival makes and the policy of the Daimler Co. The spare wheel arrangement is transferred to the rear on a 'New Phantom'. The proposed new motor speedway on the Wash

Having dealt with the experimental 'New Phantom' individually giving as much information on each one as there is available, we will now turn to the actual production chassis. With the announcement of the new model the demand for it immediately showed how highly it was regarded, as sales of the 40/50 h p greatly increased; in fact at one stage it surpassed that of the 20 h p car, which had already proved so successful.

The first 'New Phantom' had a cast iron cylinder head which was cast in one piece and had all 12 sparking plugs on the off-side of the engine, but it was found that if the car was driven really hard, when the engine was shut off there was a tendency for it to 'run on'. Another minor fault was that on accelerating hard on the petrol available in those days, the engine was prone to detonate or 'pink' unless the ignition was retarded. To overcome this, on all chassis after 1928, starting with 1 CL, the cylinder head was made of aluminium with six sparking plugs fitted on opposite sides of the head, the coil ignition being arranged on the off-side of the engine and the magneto ignition on the nearside.

Apart from this, in accordance with Rolls Royce's usual policy with a new model, a great many other changes and improvements were made in the 'New Phantom' during its production run. When it first became available a great many experiments were taking place with the road-holding and riding qualities of motor cars generally; 4-wheel brakes had become almost

universal by 1925 and the beaded edge tyre which had been popular for so many years was now distinctly out of favour. In 1923, on the previous model 40/50, unless a customer specially requested tyres of the beaded edge type, Dunlop straight sided cords were the standard fitting. This type of tyre had originated in America and had a tremendous advantage over the old beaded edge tyre because a different type of wheel was used which had a rim consisting of a flange which could be removed for tyre changing. Anyone who has an 'Edwardian' car fitted with beaded edge tyres will know how awkward beaded edge tyres are to change, unless they have Warland Dual rims fitted. A great advantage of the ones used by Rolls-Royce was that they had a wider tread which gave much better adhesion on wet roads. Another new idea on which many experiments were taking place was 'balloon' tyres, which ran at a very much lower pressure, and it was claimed in many quarters that, being so much softer and having a wider tread, they simply 'mopped up' the bumps on a bad road.

Rolls-Royce Ltd, however, would have nothing whatsoever to do with them, and in their Instruction Book the following words appear:

Balloon Tyres. - Balloon tyres should not be fitted to the front road wheels. The Company cannot be responsible for the proper running of cars so fitted.

I do not think that any other motor manufacturers have ever printed such an outspoken comment in one of their instruction books, in order to try and ensure that their customers were fully satisfied with the Company's products. After extensive testing they had decided that straight sided cords were the best type to use in all round service, and intended their owners should be in no doubt about it.

There were various types of wheels available at this time, most American cars were fitted with a wooden spoked artillery wheel with detachable rim, like the pre-war 40/50 models; in France, Michelin had produced a solid steel disc wheel which was immensely strong and very easy to keep clean, but which was extremely heavy to change and acted like a drum in transmitting all road noises up through the car. Royce disliked it intensely for use on a private car, though it was used for obvious reasons on 40/50 h p armoured car chassis. However, at least one owner, Mr Duckworth, of Hooton Grange near Chester, when he took delivery of chassis No. 24 NE, fitted with Hooper open touring body, insisted on Michelin steel disc wheels.

The wire wheel was the only type Royce really favoured, as it was light and immensely strong and he considered it looked elegant. However, it was unpopular with chauffeurs as it was difficult to clean, and discs which covered the spokes and therefore made this unpleasant task easier, became widespread.

Royce did not like this type of disc either, he said that the water from wet roads and from when the car was washed seeped in behind the discs and caused the wire spokes to rust. Mr Penny* of Barkers (who was later to invent what became known as the Barker 'Penny' disc, which made it possible to inflate the tyres through a trap in the side of the disc) decided that a way of overcoming this trouble was to insert a small piece of sponge soaked in oil into the wire spokes so that as the wheel revolved the sponge distributed oil over them. However, the surplus oil leaked out over the sides of the tyres which made a horrible mess and might also have caused the rubber to deteriorate. The result was exactly what Royce had forecasted. He also felt that wind pressure on the discs affected the steering.

So it was decided that in 1923 towards the end of the production run of the old 40/50, for those people who disliked wire wheels an alternative

*Works Manager of Barker & Co Ltd

90

would be offered in the form of a steel artillery wheel, for which an extra charge would be made; therefore, in the 1925 'New Phantom' Catalogue the following appears:

Steel Artillery Wheels
For those who object to wire wheels (on account of their appearance, or for any other reason), arrangements can be made for specially designed steel artillery wheels to be supplied at an extra charge. These have the advantage of being easy to clean; they are no heavier than wire wheels and are less expensive than discs. Rolls-Royce Limited deprecate the use of discs owing to their numerous disadvantages, such as the increase of tyre noises, etc.

Though some chassis were supplied fitted with steel artillery wheels, these were very much in the minority; the extra charge for the different type of hub put many people off and some disliked their appearance, especially as this type of wheel was standard fitting on so many cheaper cars, such as Austin, Humber, etc!

Claude Johnson was very pleased with the 'New Phantom', he felt that it was absolutely right up to date and way ahead of most, if not all the rival makes, for quietness, economy, acceleration, maximum speeds, reliability and general all round use; in fact he had such confidence in the car that he suggested to Royce that it would be good publicity to present one to His Majesty King George V, but Royce turned the suggestion down. The King was still using Daimlers fitted with cast iron sleeves; but in the meanwhile the Daimler Company, who were so loyal to the sleeve valve engine, had been conducting their own experiments at Coventry and, two months after the announcement of the 'New Phantom', they announced their new models. They had perfected a new type of steel sleeve which was extremely light and strong, faced with white metal and having large rectangular ports. The compression had been raised and new-type aluminium pistons which had spring expanded split skirts were used, in place of the old cast iron pistons.

These new models were known as 16/55, 20/70, 25/85 and 35/120, the last figure denoting the brake horse power which the engine developed. In September 1925 *The Autocar*, having completed a trial of 6 days on the new type 20/70 model, reported as follows:

> It is now not a case of changing down on ordinary hills, but of how fast one desires to take them. A mere whiff of gas is sufficient for a 30 mph gait (1,073 rpm); 45 mph entails no exertion, and the acceleration even from this speed is something to marvel at. At 60 mph the engine revs are 3,476.
>
> Those who may cherish old ideas that sleeve valve engines are sluggish and win approval merely on their silence, must needs modernize their ideas, or they will be rudely shocked. The liveliness and nippiness of the steel sleeve engine with its rectangular port openings are not merely a fraction better, but streets ahead, so to speak of its prototype. The engine is a positive glutton for hills, and its light reciprocating parts and 7 bearing crankshaft contribute to a smoothness of operation hitherto unknown. The nuisance of smoking, too, has disappeared with the introduction of new pistons and a force feed lubrication system.

Needless to say not long after this, King George V ordered a new 35/120, with a Hooper open fronted limousine body. His Majesty was extremely conservative in his ideas for a motor car; to the on-looker this new car could easily have passed for 1910 instead of 1925, it was upholstered throughout in blue buttoned morocco leather and, as with his previous Daimlers, the radiator and lamps were finished in black, the latter with brass rims to match the door handles, wheel centres and windscreen surround, whilst the bodywork was finished in the usual Royal Colours. Claude Johnson realized now that the opportunity for the Royal State cars to be Rolls-Royce was lost once again. However, the Prince of Wales, later to become H.R.H. Duke of Windsor, was a most ardent 'New Phantom' enthusiast and had several. He took great interest in the type of body fitted and each was built to his own special requirements; one was a sedanca de ville by Barker, of a type which later became known as a 'Prince of Wales Cabriolet', and, in 1928 His Royal Highness took delivery of another 'New Phantom', which carried special Weymann coachwork built by Gurney Nutting, chassis No. 14 RF.

At the time that the 'New Phantom' was announced, the lives of both Royce and Claude Johnson had settled down to a regular pattern. Royce left West Wittering in December and went down to Le Canadel in the south of France, taking Nurse Aubin and various members of his design team with him; he invariably travelled by train and a car would be sent down from Derby (usually 7 EX) for his use whilst in the south of France.

One who has told me a little about life at Le Canadel is Miss Florence Caswell, who was the first secretary employed by the Hon C S Rolls when he first started his motor business of C S Rolls & Co. Later, when Rolls was killed at Bournemouth, 'Cassie', as she was known, worked for a time as Claude Johnson's secretary, then for a period she went as companion to Lady Llangottock, but returned to work with Claude Johnson at Conduit Street. It was during this latter period that she made several journeys down to Le Canadel to stay with Royce whilst he was living there.

She told me that one of Royce's favourite past-times was to picnic on the beach; however, he liked to keep everyone busy, so, on reaching the beach, his party was detailed to look for fir cones and drift wood, etc with which to build a fire to boil the kettle. Royce personally supervised the building of the fire and made the tea when the water was boiling. 'Cassie' loathed this business of searching about the beach for fuel and, being rather outspoken, one day she said to Royce, 'Why can't you make tea like anyone else, it would be so simple either to bring it down in thermos flasks or have a primus stove.'

'Oh', he replied, 'you're just one of the la-di-dahs from Conduit Street.'

'Maybe I am', she answered, 'but I sell your old motor cars for you!'

In spite of Miss Caswell's objections Royce continued to have everyone scouring the beach for him, so that he could build his fire and make the tea.

He liked young people around him so that he could instil his own ideas and methods into them whilst imparting his own experience and knowledge. One of his faults was that he quickly tired of people, and Ivan Evernden says that for this reason he was very glad that he was never down at Le Canadel for long and that whenever he was there he always stayed at the Grand Hotel. It was difficult to find domestic staff to keep Le Rossignol permanently open for the design team, when they were available they were invariably Spanish, so for most of the time the draughtsmen lived in the Grand Hotel.

Although Villa Jaune was always available for Claude Johnson's use, after he purchased Villa Vita, he seldom visited Le Canadel; his life too had now taken on a definite pattern. He would spend the week in his flat at Adelphi Terrace House and weekends at Villa Vita; he had always been enthusiastic about boats and at one time he had had an electric launch on the River Thames. Now, living at Kingsdown he first had a motor cruiser, *Non-non,* which he kept in Dover Harbour. However, this cruiser was not very satisfactory and in February 1925 he gave an order to John I Thorneycroft of Hampton-on-Thames for a new motor boat. This fine, new craft was 48 ft in length with a beam of 9 ft, with Thames measurement of 17 tons. CJ decided that her motive power should be a Rolls-Royce 40/50 engine ('Silver Ghost' type). By modern standards she would be considered far too narrow in the beam, which no doubt caused her to roll uncomfortably when out in a beam-sea, but apart from this and trouble with the exhaust pipe becoming uncomfortably hot, which was cured by lagging, the new yacht was most successful and the family had many, many happy hours aboard her.

Vita would reach 11 knots with just over 1,000 revs on the engine and she was frequently used for going up and down the Thames; during the winter months she was laid up, but in March 1926 Claude Johnson was using her again as his Diary for Tuesday, 30 March 1926 records:

CJ left London on New Phantom 12.50. Arrived Gravesend 1.50. Boarded *Vita* and departed 2 o'clock. On flood to mouth of Medway 3.30. Against ebb up Medway to Chatham, arrived 5.5. Left Chatham on New Phantom 5.15. Arrived Canterbury 6.0. Five miles short of Sandwich 6.15. Villa Vita 6.45. Driven by Crawford, never once over 50 mph.

Easter was spent as usual at 'Villa Vita' and the last entry in the Diary is:

5 April 1926, Easter Monday. The wind is North. The glass is up. A rainbow month of March. The programme is that Mrs Wigs takes the kids to Smeeth point-to-point.
The two Cobbles, the two Ramages, and CJ drive in R-R to Chatham, and then on *Vita* to London.

*Elijah was the name given by CJ to his secretary Miss Elias

They were all back at Adelphi Terrace House on the evening of Tuesday, 6 April; on the following day CJ went as usual to his office in Conduit Street; he did not feel well and looked 'rotten', so much so, that his secretary 'Elijah'* persuaded him to go home. He had not been feeling well for some time and had lost a lot of weight, a fact which several of his friends had noticed.

Unfortunately, the following day, 8 April, was the day his brother Basil's daughter, Eroica, was to be married. The wedding was taking place at Gerrard's Cross. In spite of his illness CJ was determined to be present and insisted on motoring down with his elder daughter, Betty. At the reception he felt so ill that he was not able to join in the festivities but sat in another room with the blinds drawn. Finally, Betty was able to leave and drove him home as fast as she could. In the car returning to London he told her that he would not pull through this and it would be the end. He was quite calm and told her exactly what he wanted arranged for his funeral; there must be no fuss and no flowers. He did not wish any members of the family to attend as he could not bear them to go through the ordeal of a funeral on his behalf.

As soon as they got back to Adelphi Terrace House he went to bed and sent for the doctor. A nurse was brought, but it was too late. The chill had turned to pneumonia and although the King's physician was also consulted, there was nothing more that could be done and on Sunday 11 April 1926, he died.

Wireless was still an innovation and those who possessed wireless sets, as such, were few indeed; but those who listened to the news that Sunday night heard the announcement that Claude Johnson was dead.

He was cremated at Golders Green on Tuesday, 18 April 1926, and his ashes were scattered in the Garden of Remembrance there. His family respected his wishes, there were no flowers and only his brother, Basil, attended the funeral.

The papers were full of his death and carried the headline:

'CLAUDE JOHNSON DIES — HEAD OF ROLLS—ROYCE DEAD.

When Royce heard the news that his friend and colleague of so many years was dead he remarked sadly, 'He was the Captain. We were only the crew'.

Claude Johnson's position in Rolls-Royce Ltd was taken by his brother, Basil Johnson. This did not work out as well as everyone had hoped, Basil lacked the drive and initiative of his brother, he was not in favour of the later model EX chassis 'New Phantoms' which were being built for performance, nor was he particularly interested in Royce's work on aero-engines, and finally he was dismissed by Royce personally.

It was given out at the time that Basil Johnson retired owing to ill-health and the truth was not generally known. The question of who should succeed him posed a problem. There were two possible candidates for the position of Managing Director, one was Arthur Sidgreaves, who was a close friend of Basil Johnson and the other was Billy Cowan, who had started work as a page-boy under Claude Johnson at the Automobile Club in Whitehall Court when Johnson became the first secretary in 1897; so he had spent his entire life working under Claude Johnson, for when CJ left the Automobile Club and went into partnership with the Hon C S Rolls, he took Billy Cowan with him.

Eventually it was decided that Arthur Sidgreaves should be the Managing Director of Rolls-Royce Ltd; he had joined the Company in 1920 and had previously held the position of Export Manager. Later he was to become Sir Arthur Sidgreaves, and held the position of Managing Director right through the war years, 1939-45, but, tragically, he finally committed suicide by throwing himself in front of a London Underground Train.

In 1929, when Sidgreaves took up his new position, there were several makes which were in competition with Rolls-Royce:

Lanchester were still producing their 40 h p car but in addition they had just produced a 30 h p straight-8, as a replacement for the 40, which was beginning to be considered old-fashioned, in spite of the fact that His Royal Highness the Duke of York, (later King George VI), had a 40 h p with the Company's own ¾-landaulette body, supplied to him in 1929.

Napier, at one time a serious rival, had given up building a luxury car in 1924 and now concentrated entirely on aero-engines.

Just at the end of the 1914 war it was announced that Leyland, who made extremely fine commercial vehicles, were to enter the luxury field of motoring with a straight-8 Leyland car, designed by John Parry-Thomas, who was then chief designer to Leyland Motors, but this also disappeared about 1923, whilst the old Rolls-Royce 40/50 was still in production.

From Belgium there was the big Minerva fitted with a sleeve-valve engine, it was cheaper than the Rolls-Royce and carried coachwork made by specialist coachbuilders, usually by Vanden Plas of Brussels; this was a very fine car indeed, having excellent springing and a good turn of speed.

From France there was the Hispano-Suiza which has always been considered one of the world's greats, most beautifully made with excellent road holding characteristics and a very fine turn of speed though the engine, however, was not as quiet or refined as the big Rolls-Royce.

From Italy there was the Isotta-Fraschini, another big straight-8 which, though it must be conceded that these were some of the most handsome vehicles ever made were very heavy and tiring to drive, so that they almost invariably required a chauffeur.

From across the Atlantic there was quite a wide choice, the Americans have never done anything by half measures, Pierce-Arrow, Locomobile, Stearns-Knight, Packard and Lincoln were, just to mention a few, popular at this time. Of these only Packard and Lincoln found their way to Great Britain in any number, owing to the customs and import duties imposed on foreign cars, and the lack of servicing facilities.

There remains, of course, Daimler, still supreme as the Royal car. Percy Martin, the most charming of Managing Directors of the Daimler Co was very well pleased with the new type of steel sleeve-valve engine, and, as the demand for the Daimler car increased, during the year 1926 and for the following years, he embarked on a policy of producing models which let the customer have exactly what he wanted, that could almost be likened to living in 'cloud cuckoo land'.

To compete with these various makes, Rolls-Royce Ltd were producing two models, the 'New Phantom' (in the form of a short chassis 11 ft 11¼ in., and a long chassis of 12 ft 6½ in.), together with the 20 h p on a wheelbase of 10 ft 9 in. On these three chassis there was a wide choice of steering rakes and different spring ratings suitable for the type of coachwork to be fitted to each individual chassis. However, the Daimler Company's policy of tailoring each car to the customer's exact requirements went even further and each of their three models, the 35/120, 25/85 and 20/70 could be obtained in no less than five alternative types in each horse power range, these were again sub-divided as to whether the customer wanted a high or low frame.

Taking the 35/120 as an example, as the nearest equivalent to the 'New Phantom', this became available as a standard bonnet model in the following type:

'N' with 13 ft 0 in. wheelbase;
'R' with 12 ft 4 in. wheelbase;
'T' with 12 ft 4 in. wheelbase, but a narrower track; and
'S' with an 11 ft 10 in. wheelbase.

This gives four models, but in addition to these the car could be obtained with high bonnet as 'P' with a wheelbase of 13 ft, and as 'V' with a wheelbase of 12 ft 4 in. but again with the track at 4 ft 8 in. in place of the 5 ft track of the bigger models.

The 'V' and 'T' types were meant for the owner-driver and as such would exceed 80 mph, but very few were sold as most people who wanted an owner-driver car did not want sleeve valves. So the reputation of the sleeve-valve engines for being sluggish continued; as the large chassis 35/120 sold in very large numbers. They were colossal cars, far larger than a long chassis 'New Phantom' and the great appeal of the 35/120 was the immense amount of room in the body with full 7-seats, of which the revolving occasional ones were really armchairs.

A great many of the leading coachbuilders mounted their bodies on Daimler chassis, but the Company also built its own coachwork and a full 7-seater enclosed drive landaulette could be obtained for £2,000 which was considerably cheaper than a 'New Phantom' when fitted with similar coachwork. Added to this, the annual tax of £35 per year was less than the £44 payable on the 'New Phantom', these gigantic 35/120 Daimlers sold well, but they did not make a profit. The economic target of all models for the Daimler Company was 10,000 units per year, but this figure was never reached and though the cars were ideal chauffeur-driven carriages, throughout the whole range spares were a problem, owing to the complexity of the models offered, which had different wheel sizes, different axle ratios and other modifications. The car side of the Daimler Company's business was largely underwritten by the contracts made with the British Government by the parent company, the Birmingham Small-Arms Company, though the commercial side of the Daimler Company was doing well with the 35/120 h p engine being installed in motor coaches, omnibuses and even an extremely luxurious motor horse box.

Daimler coachwork was ageless, but the curious thing is that, considering it was so popular, as far as I know there are no survivors; the few sleeve valve models that have survived all have specialized bodies.

Respecting the comfort which a big Daimler afforded its occupants, Royce was the first to admit that, as a town car and for touring in England, the Daimler gave a superior ride, but Rolls-Royce Ltd had always taken the line that clients who bought their products would almost invariably use them for continental touring; in fact it is probably safe to say that no other British car has been used on the roads of Europe in such large numbers as the Rolls-Royce.

It was for this reason that, long before the Great War of 1914, Claude Johnson had personally visited most of the capitals of Europe, where he set up a chain of first-class service stations with ample spare part facilities and a trained Rolls-Royce mechanic in attendance. The principal servicing and sales department on the continent was in Paris and most cars that were sold abroad were supplied through this office; unfortunately the records have not survived, they were destroyed during the last war when the Germans entered Paris. The Daimler Company on the other hand had an entirely different sales policy: at the end of the 1914 war it was no longer possible to purchase a car direct from the Daimler Company, all chassis were supplied through their sole agents, Stratton-Instone, who had premises at 27 Pall Mall, London, SW1. Ernest Instone had served with the Daimler Company for 24 years and U Stratton had originally been the Company's London Manager in charge of sales. When Instone died, the name was changed to 'Stratstone', this concern is still in existence with a Daimler showroom in Berkeley Street and a service station in North London.

It would seem that Stratton-Instone concentrated entirely on selling cars to the home market except for those exported to foreign reigning monarchs and Indian princes and no proper servicing facilities were set-up on the Continent.

Ivan Evernden says that the springing on Daimler cars did Rolls-Royce Ltd a very good turn as though Daimler springing was superior on English roads to that of a Rolls-Royce, once a Daimler owner took his car across the Channel the ride was horrible owing to the different wave-lengths of undulations and many Daimler owners, who suffered from frightful car sickness, swore that they would never take their car abroad again and immediately on returning home visited the Conduit Street showrooms with the idea of purchasing a Rolls-Royce for continental use and keeping the Daimler as a town car.

Springing has always been one of the most difficult problems that all motor manufacturers have had to cope with, what is suitable under certain conditions is quite unsuitable for other occasions; a 7-passenger limousine might ride well when fully loaded, but with only one or two occupants in the rear seat over certain roads an extremely bumpy ride could be experienced. It was partly to overcome this that, commencing with chassis No. 1 CL, the rear of the chassis of the 'New Phantom' was extended beyond the petrol tank and the spare wheel was mounted at the rear of the car, which gave additional weight and helped to hold the back of the car down on the road. The arrangement for mounting the spare wheel was modelled on the 20 h p which meant, when using the luggage grid, it was necessary to change the spare wheel on to the side carrier bracket on the running board.

On 20 October 1928, Royce personally wrote a memo. which reads as follows:

'In no case do we recommend a side wheel carrier. We now consider that weight carried here is bad and the appearance ugly. Sgn. 'R'.'

Consequently, when the Phantom II appeared on the scene, Royce asked Ivan Evernden to design an entirely new rear mounted spare wheel carrier and luggage grid which made it unnecessary to transfer the spare wheel as described (See Part II, Chapter 1).

As the 'New Phantom' was ending production and tests were being carried out on its successor, the Phantom II, a number of men whose names were well-known in the motor racing world, such as the Earl Howe, the Earl of Scarborough, the Earl of Cottenham, Lord Ebery, Col the Master of Semphill, Capt (later Sir) Malcolm Campbell, Capt Woolf Barnato, had come to the conclusion that Brooklands Track at Weybridge in Surrey was totally inadequate for the speeds that racing cars were now capable of reaching. They decided it was time that a new race track was built which could be used by the entire motor industry for testing new models.

If this scheme had reached fruition there is no doubt that the testing at Chateauroux of all pre-war 40/50 h p models, as well as the 'small horse power' cars manufactured by Rolls-Royce Ltd would have terminated; the Company, together with other motor manufacturers, were most interested and enthusiastic about it. The idea of building a new motor speedway in Britain had first been thought of as early as 1924, after the death of Parry-Thomas in 'Babs' on Pendine Sands, when the R A C would not give permission for any attempts on a speed record at Pendine, which was the only stretch of sand in Britain where such high speeds could be attained.

A society was formed which was known as the Automobile Racing Association Air-Land-Water, which devised a scheme to build a new British sports centre on the Wash between Boston and Skegness, as being the most suitable site.

Capt Malcolm Campbell had the following to say about this project:

For many years I have been searching all over this country, over the Continent of Europe and elsewhere, to find a suitable track, and the great trouble with tracks that might be available is the fact that they are not permanent speedways. I decided that beaches were the only available places where a straight run of five or six miles could be obtained, and curiously enough I can state that not only in this country but on the Continent of Europe there are no suitable stretches of sand in existence of a greater length than six miles. This was all right until a few years ago but as the speeds increased so it became more important that other stretches of land should be found. I followed Sir Henry Segrave to Daytona but so far as that track is concerned there are great difficulties to be faced. The surface varies from day to day according to tide and wind, and you can never rely upon what is going to happen. When there is no wind it is very rough, when there is a wind it flattens it out, and it is dangerous to drive in a high wind. That proves that beach racing, as far as records go, has great limitations. I agree that at the present time there is no ideal track in the world. I am quite satisfied, as far as this beach is concerned, as to its suitability and its practicability as regards the motor standpoint.

And Capt Woolf Barnato wrote as follows:

In my opinion the value of this track to industry would be national, and would be very much welcomed. I think to a certain extent British manufacturers would support the scheme finanically if it were floated. The motor industry is flourishing at the moment and from their point of view it would be a sound investment.

Briefly, the scheme was to consist of the following:

A Motor Speedway, 15 miles in length, 200 yards wide, dead straight and flat, prepared for speeds greater than at present accomplished

A Grandstand, 4 miles in length, capable of accommodating 150,000 people

A 12-Mile Road Racing Track

A Motor Boat Speedway

An Aerodrome

A Racecourse-Stadium

A Clubhouse, pavilions, restaurants, hostels, bungalows and a large camping and caravan ground. Ample garages, and parking accommodation for, if necessary, 50,000 cars

If it had materialized there is no doubt that it would have been of enormous benefit to the entire British motor industry as not only would our own manufacturers have used it, but there would have been nothing like it anywhere else in the world and undoubtedly many European manufacturers would have brought their cars over for testing on it. Unfortunately, this imaginative plan for a British Speedway and Sports area never progressed beyond the planning stage, as in 1931 came the Slump and Britain went off the gold standard, when such expensive ideas had to be shelved, in this case never to be revived.

PART I CHAPTER 16

The American-built Springfield 'New Phantom' and the American automobile salons.

In spite of the fact that the 'New Phantom' was available from the Derby works in May 1925, it was not until 1926 that the new model became available at Springfield. This was chiefly because it was a mammoth job to convert the new overhead valve engine to make it suitable for a left-hand drive chassis. The old type 40/50 had been relatively easy to modify and the last ones produced at Springfield had all been supplied with left-hand drive. However, it was decided that the only successful method with the new engine was to completely reverse the whole thing. This was achieved entirely at Springfield, but all drawings and designs had to be sent to Derby and approved by the parent company before tooling-up for the 'New Phantom' chassis took place, so it is remarkable really that all this work was carried out in so short a space of time.

The first 66 chassis of 'New Phantoms' to leave Springfield did not have 4-wheel brakes, but from chassis No. S-66-PM the Derby arrangement of servo assisted 4-wheel brakes was fitted; eventually, all the original 66 cars were recalled to have servo operated front wheel brakes fitted.

There was one refinement, however, fitted to the 'New Phantom' Springfield chassis which was never fitted to the Derby-built car, this was a centralized chassis lubrication system.

The year 1926 is a very important one in the story of Springfield as, in addition to the afore-mentioned new model, the Company acquired the very old and well-known coach-building business of Brewster & Company, whose premises were situated at Long Island, New York. The firm had been founded by James Brewster at New Haven, Connecticut, in

1810, where he had built excellent carriages.

In 1874 they opened a factory and show-room in New York City and built their first motor car body in 1905 on a Delaunay-Belleville chassis; the first Rolls-Royce to receive Brewster coachwork was a landaulette for Mrs Harry S Brown in 1908. William Brewster realized that the motor car would quickly replace the carriage-and-pair, so, in 1910 the business was moved to a new site, Queensboro Plaza, Long Island, New York, where the demand for top quality coachwork on motor chassis continued to grow, though a few horse-drawn carriages were still being built in 1911.

At the beginning of 1914 the firm of Brewster & Company became agents for Rolls-Royce cars and by the end of 1916 46 Rolls-Royce chassis had been fitted with Brewster-built coachwork.

In 1915 Brewster decided to build a car of their own in the Long Island factory, this Brewster car was built exclusively for the 'carriage trade'. The power unit was a 4-cylinder sleeve valve engine with a bore and stroke of 4 x 5½ in., and was rated at 25.6 h p. The wheelbase was 10 ft 5 in., there were three forward speeds, cone clutch, magneto ignition, cantilever rear suspension and a 12-volt lighting system.

By 1924 there were five alternative types of coachwork available, these were as follows:

Double enclosed drive
Glass quarter brougham
Town brougham
Limousine
Town landaulette

The price of each type complete was $7,500, it was essentially a town car to be driven by a chauffeur and was slightly smaller than a 20 h p Rolls-Royce.

It was a most expensive production, beautifully made, but small volume quality production, however well made, has never really been a paying proposition and cannot survive unless there is something else to underwrite it.

Brewster & Company were also fitting coachwork on most American luxury chassis and at the same time, in 1924, rival makes, such as Pierce-Arrow (regarded by many as the 'R-R' of America), were offering a 6-cylinder 38.4 h p on an 11 ft 6 in. wheelbase with a wide variety of coachwork, for just about the same price of $7,000 for complete vehicle.

Also about this time, the most highly esteemed American firm The Packard Motor Co, were producing a 36 h p straight-8 on a wheelbase of 12 ft 0 in. with a very wide variety of standard Packard coachwork for just under $5,000, though a Packard could also be obtained as a chassis and fitted with any specialized coachwork built by leading American coachbuilders.

In addition to the above, there were numbers of small firms in America which concentrated on building a luxurious and extremely expensive chassis; amongst these were Cole, Cunningham, Daniels, Dorris and Locomobile. However, by 1929 all these makes had disappeared with the exception of Cunningham and Locomobile; it was the same story over again, a small volume of luxury chassis unsupported by some other venture.

Cadillac, the General Motors prestige car, and Lincoln, built by the Ford Motor Company, were still in production as both Cadillac and Lincoln had the cheaper models like Chevrolet and Oldsmobile, in the case of General Motors, on which to rely for their profits whilst the sales of the Ford Motor Company's Model 'T' and later Model 'A' were simply enormous.

It is therefore all the more to the credit of Rolls-Royce Inc at Springfield that, in view of the competition which the cars were receiving from other American makes, they managed to sell so many during the years that the 'New Phantom' was being built in the United States.

The main reason for Rolls-Royce taking over Brewster's was because the majority of American prospective Rolls-Royce owners liked a ready made product and could not be bothered to wait for a body to be built to their own requirements. So it was felt that if Rolls-Royce owned their own coachbuilding facilities they could supply standard models ready for immediate use. Arthur Soutter tells below how this was accomplished:

In January 1926 R-R of Am Inc acquired Brewster & Co for an investment of $202,500 and a guarantee of principal and interest of $400,000 in 10 year 7% notes and $1,400,000 outstanding in 5% bonds. The Brewster Building, located in Long Island City, New York, was a 5-storey structure with 70,000 sq ft on each floor. In addition to the Brewster coachbuilding plant, it housed the R-R Long Island Maintenance Depot and the General Sales Offices.

The American chassis was fitted as Standard with wire wheels and, although artillery wooden spoked wheels were offered as an optional choice, these were not popular and there was not a single 'New Phantom' sold with wooden wheels. Plain disc covers, arranged for mounting on wire wheels, were sold as an accessory and proved to be rather popular because they were so much easier to clean than the wire wheels.

Once Brewster & Company became part of Rolls-Royce Inc a whole set of designs for coachwork were produced (see illustrations which are reproduced by courtesy of The Flying Lady), most of which were named after well known places in England, thus giving the cars an authentic British ring.

The wealthy American of the time demanded the finest that money could buy and the best that expert craftsmen could produce, so in many ways it is hardly surprising that the most exclusive of all Motor Shows should take place in America.

These were called 'The Automobile Salons' and should not be confused with the annual motor show held in New York, at which all makes were exhibited. The Automobile Salons started in 1905, usually in the ballroom of a well-known Hotel. They were primarily a coachbuilders' exhibition, designed to display the finest craftsmanship available for coachwork on the most exclusive American chassis, provided they were fitted with specialized coachwork. From 1919 until the last Salon was held there in 1931, they were held in the Hotel Commodore in New York. Previously, however, other Salons had been held elsewhere, one in the Drake Hotel, Chicago in 1916, and also, soon after this, one was held at the Palace Hotel in San Francisco and another at the Biltmore Hotel in Los Angeles.

The New York Salon lasted a week; it was one of the 'high spots' of the social season, taking place in December of each year, and the opening night can only be described as being like the premiere of an opera. One day was set aside especially for chauffeurs but otherwise it was attended exclusively by the cream of American Society by invitation only.

The person in charge of the whole operation was John R Eustis, who was employed on the sales side of Rolls-Royce of America Inc. The exhibitors were also only there by invitation and, if selected, they had to pay $500 for the privilege of displaying each exhibit. They were then issued with a certain number of engraved invitations to distribute to their favoured clients.

Each day that the Salon was open a different type of function took place, a day was set aside for manufacturers who supplied paint, leather, upholstery, and such fittings as window winders, door handles, etc, and in the evening a banquet was held for the suppliers and exhibitors. One day was also kept for the motor manufacturing trade in general, and from here they often gleaned new ideas which they put into mass production.

The chauffeurs' day was a very important one and they were treated like real V I Ps; it was well-known that what a chauffeur advised would in many cases be accepted as the last word by his or her employer. It was customary for a chauffeur to receive commission on any deal that was made at the Salon.

Naturally Rolls-Royce of America was represented at each Salon, not only carrying Brewster coachwork, but also bodies by other American coachbuilders. A representative list of exhibitors of chassis shown reads as follows:

Cadillac, Chrysler, Cord, Cunningham, Duesenberg, Du Pont, Franklyn, Hupmobile, Isotta Fraschini, La Salle, Lincoln, Marmon, Minerva, Packard, Pierce-Arrow, Rolls-Royce, Stutz.

It will be noticed that apart from Rolls-Royce there are only two European manufacturers in this list, Isotta Fraschini from Italy and Minerva from Belgium. I do not believe that the Daimler Company ever exhibited at an American Salon. The exhibitors of coachwork were as follows:

Brewster, Brunn, Derham, Dietrich, Fisher, Fleetwood, Judkins, La Grande, Le Baron, Locke, Merrimac, Murphy, Rollston, Walker, Waterhouse, Willoughby.

For the 1930 Salon Brewster built a Super Sport Coupe with most unusual staggered lines, based on a Victoria 5-seat coupe; it was a most flamboyant type of body and was built in the Brewster factory under great secrecy; it had been proposed to mount this body on a new Derby-built left-hand drive Phantom II chassis, but unfortunately at the last moment there was no left-hand drive Phantom II chassis available, so a Springfield 'New Phantom' chassis, No. S132PR, suitably modified, was used instead.

In December 1931 the last of these wonderful Salons was held and this time one of the new Derby-built left-hand drive Phantom II chassis No. 248 AJS, was used as the basis of the Rolls-Royce exhibit. The success of the Super Sport Coupe on the 'New Phantom' chassis at the 1930 Salon decided the management of Rolls-Royce to build another coupe. Charles Wilmore, who had been a Brewster salesman for a long time, thought of a 'Tear Drop' design, the car was finished in oyster grey with black mudguards with discs fitted to the wheels and, as with the previous 'Super Sport' it received much favourable comment in the Press. Both these cars are still in existence in the Rolls-Royce Owners' Club of America.

Throughout the whole of the run of the 'New Phantom' produced at Springfield, close relationship was maintained between Derby and Springfield, any improvements that were incorporated in the Derby-built car appeared shortly afterwards in the Springfield version. Soon after the Derby chassis was extended for the mounting of the spare wheel, Springfield followed suit but in their case the spare was never actually mounted at the rear. This arrangement, used on the Derby-built chassis 1 CL, was first used on Springfield chassis 2501, but the altered frame was utilized to mount a rear bumper and a new and improved type of luggage grid.

The highest annual production figure reached at Springfield was 400 units, but in 1929 this fell to 200 and in 1930 to 100; the latter figure is perhaps partly due to the fact that the Derby Phantom II was available with left-hand drive and suitable for use in America, but it was also because of the world slump. In a letter to me written by Arthur Soutter, dated 20 September 1972, one paragraph reads:

> We built 700 Phantom I chassis with cast iron cylinder heads before changing to the aluminium cylinder head, which was the first major change to the Phantom I. Ours was available approximately one year later than Derby's. On the other hand, Springfield designed and developed a centralized chassis lubrication system to lubricate 40 chassis points by pulling a handle at the driver's seat, and introduced it on the first Springfield Phantom I. This was never available on the English Phantom I, but was later introduced on the Phantom II. We also introduced an engine oil filter on the first Springfield Phantom I, and this was not available on English cars until the Phantom II.

Whilst Springfield was still fully operational, many of the older models that had been built there were returned to the works for modernization, being fitted with low pressure tyres, four-wheel brakes and new coachwork, so that when completed the cars had a very much more up-to-date appearance.

It was inevitable that production of the Rolls-Royce car at Springfield would come to an end when Derby produced a completely new model. The change from the 'Silver Ghost' to the 'New Phantom' involved major changes to the engine, gearbox, steering, front axle and brake system, and this had been a fairly costly exercise as regards tooling, etc, but the Phantom II was a completely new design and the cost of tooling-up for this would have been prohibitive. Experience had already shown that, for the small number of 'Silver Ghosts' and 'New Phantoms' sold each year, the amount of money needed was simply not worth while, so very wisely, albeit reluctantly, it was decided to cease production at Springfield. There was no question of bad management, every effort had been made to maintain the reputation of Rolls-Royce and the sales staff had worked hard to make it a success. However, the prevailing economic factors, not only in America but throughout the world, had proved too great an obstacle. Although Rolls-Royce of America Inc ceased to exist, servicing facilities were maintained and the Brewster town car was evolved; this was actually a Ford V8 chassis fitted with Brewster coachwork, with radiator styling which was so completely altered that it bore no resemblance whatsoever to an ordinary Ford V8.

Eventually, all plant necessary for servicing and repairs was taken to the Long Island depot and Springfield was finally closed down. Maurice Olley, who had originally founded the Springfield Works in 1919, transferred to General Motors, where he undertook research on springing, and the first independently sprung chassis produced by General Motors were made to Maurice Olley's design. Though he worked for General Motors for many years he kept in close touch with his former colleagues in Rolls-Royce Ltd, sending them long letters written in his neat script-like writing. He recalls that on one occasion he was actually asked whether he was working for General Motors or if he was still employed by Rolls-Royce Ltd!

PART I CHAPTER 17

The decline in value of the 'New Phantom' on the second-hand car market, and the introduction of Rolls-Royce replicas. Douglas Fitzpatrick's Supercharged 'New Phantom' chassis No. 74 SC and Kenneth Jenner's chassis No. 53 DC.

Although naturally, as with all old cars, the value of a 'New Phantom' depreciated over the years, it was never used in the same way as the earlier 'Silver Ghost' type 40/50 had been used, for menial jobs such as a hay wagon, breakdown lorry, etc. This was because most 'New Phantoms' were fitted with limousine or landaulette coachwork and were therefore eminently suitable for Hire Car Firms to use for weddings, funerals, etc. They were very popular for this work and those that had open touring bodies or sedanca-de-ville coachwork were rebuilt into hearses. As they had usually originally been sold to wealthy people who changed their car every few years, they were generally in excellent condition and gave many years service with little or no expense.

During the years between the wars owning vintage cars as a hobby had not become popular, people who owned and ran an old car were considered rather eccentric. However, there were many people who wanted and admired a Rolls-Royce, who could not afford to buy a new one, but who nevertheless did not want to have one with an old-fashioned appearance. To fill this need Jack Compton bought old 'New Phantom' cars whose chassis were in good condition and rebodied them with a more up-to-date coachwork. Usually a late-type Phantom II sports saloon body was chosen and they were then sold and enjoyed a further lease of life in this way. Actually the most popular model for this type of conversion was the 20 h p owing to its lower rate of taxation and cheaper running costs. There are still a number of these cars about, known as 'Rolls-Royce Replicas' which are rather looked down on by the genuine enthusiast. How-

ever, it says a great deal for the durability and reputation of the cars that a firm was able to make a profitable business of bringing an old car up to date.

In 1957 a group of people who loved and appreciated these pre-war cars formed the Rolls-Royce Enthusiasts' Club which grew rapidly into the thriving body it is today, and the demand for pre-war Rolls-Royce cars increased accordingly. The pre-1914 40/50 model had already been certain of a secure future in the Veteran Car Club of Great Britain, but now the future looked brighter for the post-1914-war cars as well. Of the big model 40/50s, the one that immediately became the most popular was the Phantom II; a great many had survived, some having most attractive coachwork. Owing to its corrosion problems, overheating troubles and the vast cost of engine overhauls, many people were too frightened to tackle a Phantom III, so enthusiasts turned to the only other model left, namely, the 'New Phantom'.

In the late 1940s and early 1950s a good 'New Phantom' could be purchased for £150, many collectors then dismissing it as a sort of transitionary car and preferring to pay a much higher figure for a Phantom II, but now the 'New Phantom' has come right into its own and prices reaching £5,000 have been paid for this model. In fact, chassis which had already been rebodied as a hearse have been rebuilt again with open touring coachwork. There are now several firms specializing in building this type of body, probably the best known of which is Messrs I Wilkinson Ltd, of Strafford Street, Derby, who have built many replica bodies of the Barker torpedo touring type, which was so popular in the early and mid 1920s, though they have rebodied one hearse chassis with a Brougham de ville, most beautifully executed and a typical example of this type which was most popular as a formal chauffeur driven town car in the 1920s.

To the enthusiast who is prepared to do the regular routine maintenance with the oil-gun all round the chassis, the 'New Phantom' is still a perfectly practical car to use; the brakes are up to modern standards, the car will cruise all day at 60 mph very comfortably and return something in the region of 14 miles to the gallon on commercial fuel. The regular servicing necessary is the greatest drawback, as the British model lacks the one-shot lubrication system of the Phantom II, though the American-built Springfield cars were fitted with this refinement from the earliest chassis No. S/400/FL built in 1926.

I have been told on good authority that a very late type 'New Phantom' built at Springfield is one of the most desirable of all the pre-war 40/50 chassis to possess and that one of the best examples is the one which belongs to John McFarlane (for many years Editor of the Rolls-Royce Owners' Club Magazine *The Flying Lady*), so I have included some details of this car with the four 'New Phantom' chassis which were built at Derby.

The first of these is chassis No. 74 SC, which, during the last war, was the subject of an article published in *The Autocar* under 'Talking of Sports Cars', which appeared late in 1941; the car was also the subject of an article in *Motor Sport*, July 1939, and again in November 1942, when its present owner, Douglas Fitzpatrick, rebuilt it and supercharged it with considerable success, after which the performance it gave was astonishing.

Douglas Fitzpatrick has always been interested in fine cars with a good performance, he has been a member of the Veteran Car Club of Great Britain for many years and takes part annually in the R A Cs London-Brighton Veteran Car Run with his 1903 Achilles; in addition he has a 1906 Wolseley Siddeley and a 1907 Metallurgique which is powered with a 1910 6-cylinder 21-litre Maybach engine. He

also has a 20 h p Rolls-Royce of 1927, a Riley 9 and a Rolls-Royce Phantom III, chassis No. 3-CM-181 which is a most delightful Park Ward owner-driver saloon.

He was serving in the Royal Air Force in 1931 when he purchased 74 SC; the car belonged to the wife of his Commanding Officer (Flight-Lt, now Group-Captain Day), who had been the widow of a Mr Johnson who had originally bought the car, the details of which are as follows:

Chassis No.: 74 SC.
Engine No.: AN 85.
Off Test: 10.3.1926.
Axle Ratio: 15 x 52.
Straight side tyres: 33 x 5.
Chassis sold: 9.10.1925.
To: George Heath Ltd of Birmingham, for Hanley Garage.
Steering Column: 'D'.
By road to Hooper & Co Ltd from Lillie Hall 18.3.1926.
Springs for 5-seater semi-sporting tourer.
Extra spare wheel.
Mascot, Atlantic spot-light with driving mirror.
Polished bonnet, Barker dipper to head lamps.

As can be seen, 74 SC started life as an open tourer but when Victor Johnson died, his widow, who disliked an open car intensely, had Sanderson & Holmes of Derby build a top on to it to convert it into a closed car, the effect was somewhat peculiar, but unfortunately there are no photographs available of the car as it was when Douglas purchased it.

It was quite obvious to him that, though 74 SC was only six years old, it had not received the treatment which it deserved, so he decided it needed a major overhaul which involved a re-bore, two new connecting rods, new bearings in the gearbox and rear axle, also a complete new exhaust system. After this attention the car glided away once more, just as it had done from Derby when it was new.

Douglas decided that the chassis was now deserving of a better body, so he went to Cooper Motor Bodies of Putney, that extraordinary firm where it was possible not only to have a body built to one's own requirements for a very reasonable sum, but where it was possible to purchase second-hand more or less any type of body in extremely good order which had been removed, for one reason or another, from all sorts of makes of motor cars.

I remember once visiting Cooper's years before the war and seeing the vast collection of bodies available, from a first-class limousine, removed from a Daimler or Rolls-Royce, through saloons, coupes, 2-seaters, tourers, etc, down to the body from an Austin 7 Chummy! Prices ranged from £200 down to £10.

Douglas favoured what could be described as a drop-head foursome coupe, very popular on many chassis in pre-war days, with large luggage boot and rear mounted spare wheel.

When the car was completed it was almost impossible for anyone except an expert to detect that 74 SC was a 1926 model; it looked a thoroughly up-to-date vehicle and passed as a current Phantom II model. It was specially built for him and was considerably lighter than the original body and several inches lower, so he was hoping for very much better performance; to assist this the cylinder head was removed and aluminiumised, 1/32nd of an inch taken off and the ignition was slightly advanced, also the wheels were rebuilt from 33 x 5 straight-side to 7.00 x 19, which is late-type Phantom II size. This slightly lowered the axle ratio, but the car would cruise comfortably and quietly at 55 to 60 mph, the top gear acceleration was slightly improved and it was possible to reach 80 mph quite easily. The only snag was that it now needed new sparking plugs about every thousand miles, so a sports-type plug was tried which would run 4,000 miles if cleaned every 700 miles.

Douglas Fitzpatrick continues with the story as follows:

In 1938 I had the idea of fitting a supercharger as an interesting experience. I hoped to get some 'hot' performance while not having to buy a different car. As the Rolls was by then twelve years old I felt it had passed the stage when I could be accused of vandalism.

I approached Centric Superchargers, who fitted a replica of that fitted to Major Gardner's record-breaking M G. It is of 9 litres capacity, blowing at a maximum of 9 lb per sq in., and is driven by twin belts from an extension of the fan drive, being fitted with twin Solex carburetters.

Supercharging an 8-litre engine is a bit more complicated than fitting a blower to a baby Fiat, and the stresses on the engine are proportionately much greater, so it is not surprising that at first it was not quite a success. I have vivid memories of my first long drive after taking delivery, which, unfortunately, happened to be in the South of France and which was a continuous nightmare of loud explosions, burnt-out plugs and exhaust pipes, water boiling in the radiator, petrol boiling in the Autovac, and a night by the roadside after a particularly loud explosion, which blew off the intake pipe. However, none of these troubles was fundamental, and the causes were one by one traced and eliminated, and the return journey was made in more conventional manner.

Even so, the performance was not up to expectations, and I came to the conclusion that the carburetters were not suitable. I tried all sorts of chokes and jet sizes. Even so, it was great fun to drive, and, having found the best all-round setting, I left it at that for about three months.

At this stage the engine made a protest against its very considerably increased output. On a run up to London a continuous metallic tinkling noise started, and the engine became rather 'woofly' and all over the place at low speeds. On arrival I took the car to McKenzie's Garages, where it was discovered that an exhaust valve had broken and fallen into the cylinder; parts of it had gone out through the inlet valve and down into the next cylinder. The damage to the cylinders was very slight, and a rebore removed all trace.

It was also found that in any case calamity was on its way, because, apart from the thimble-head effect given by the valve parts dancing up and down for 40 miles on the two piston crowns concerned, the heads of all six were being squashed down over the rings with the high explosion force now generated with the 9 lb blower. (This can be understood. No other part of the engine or chassis has, after some thousands of miles, shown any sign of not being able to stand up to these conditions, for which they were not designed.)

What at first seemed to be a disaster turned out to be a blessing in disguise, for it was possible to modify the engine to suit the blower. Mr McKenzie made me some of his very light and very tough alloy pistons (the same type, actually, as in a certain very well-known 8-litre Bentley) and some special heat-resisting valves. The compression was again raised, in spite of the blower, and two oversize S U carburetters replaced the Solexes. Also, a modification was carried out which allowed the supercharger to blow almost directly into the inlet pipe instead of through several feet of piping as before.

The performance on the road was now really satisfactory. Rolls-Royce had shortly before this fitted me a special and only specimen of experimental crown wheel they had, giving a top gear of 3.2 to 1 (the highest gear possible to fit within the confines of the axle). With this gear the acceleration became better than on the previous lower ratio, and continuous right up the range; whether on the level or uphill seems to make no difference, in spite of a weight of just over 50 cwt. The car could with advantage take a much higher gear without loss of liveliness, and when the war came and stopped all ideas in those directions for the time being, I was endeavouring to take steps to fit one of 2.7 to 1, which would bring the maximum speed well up into three figures, while keeping the revs to a normal maximum of below 3,000.

A question I have often been asked is: 'Is it very noisy?' It is obviously not as dead silent as formerly, but, judged by any other than Rolls-Royce standards, it is still a very quiet car. When ticking over, the engine makes a certain amount of quiet blower rumble, which only draws attention because the car is a Rolls; from 20 to 40 mph the gears driving the blower vanes become audible from inside the car, making almost identically the sound produced by a very quiet 'silent third'. This disappears at 40, and from then on the car makes no more noise than a standard car, except, of course, on full throttle acceleration, when one gets the typical exhilerating supercharger 'growl' and an exhaust note like high pressure steam escaping.

The foregoing was published in *The Autocar* of 23 January 1942, under a series 'Talking of Sports Cars', so all the above took place over 30 years ago. After the war Douglas continued to use 74 SC and improved it considerably. He had a new radiator of larger capacity specially made for it, on the lines of a late-type Phantom II radiator and the wings and bonnet were altered to a more modern design, which greatly improved the appearance of the car; the performance was now such that the car would hold its own with the very much later Phantom III, though it still remained extremely docile and Douglas entered it in a number of rallies and trials in which he did very well.

One of these was the Firle Hill Climb, near Lewes in Sussex; he had taken 74 SC down to Firle some time before the actual event was to take place and he found that top gear was too high for climbing at speed whilst at the same time the engine was revving too high in third speed, so, after making some calculations, he had a pair of Rolls-Royce wheels rebuilt to just the correct diameter, with the result that on the day of the Hill Climb 74 SC went up like a rocket in top gear all the way and gave a wonderful performance. When he told me this he added, 'Fancy anyone going to the expense of rebuilding wheels for a hill climb, but things were so much cheaper then'.

Finally, about 15 years ago, tragedy overtook 74 SC. The car had been into Norwich for various work to be done, both mechanically and bodily; Douglas had collected the car and was driving home to Sheringham; for some reason the car seemed to lack power, when suddenly he realized it was on fire. Unfortunately he had no fire extinguisher, and although he rushed to the nearest house to telephone for the Fire Brigade, by the time they arrived there was virtually no hope of controlling the flames. 74 SC was so badly damaged that the Insurance Company paid out in full on the loss.

It seemed a monumental task to completely rebuild again, so instead Douglas bought a very fine Phantom III, chassis No. 3-CM-181. The forelorn chassis, engine and gearbox, etc, of 74 SC are in the garage at Sheringham Hall, and although over the years he has thought of rebuilding the car and putting it back to a 'New Phantom' of 1926 with an open touring body and has obtained the correct radiator and a set of the correct wheels, in view of the enormous cost, this project has not proceeded very far, but now Douglas informs me that he intends to rebuild the car next year to its original specification.

The next car is included here because it is typical of the big Rolls-Royce chauffeur-driven limousine so popular at the time the car was new, and also because of the restoration which the owner has carried out, a great deal of which he has done himself and for which great credit is due.

This is 53 DC, an extremely dignified Hooper limousine de ville which belongs to Kenneth Jenner, who lives and farms in Kent and frequently appears at Rolls-Royce Enthusiasts' Club events. Details, taken from the Body Card of this chassis, are as follows:

Chassis No.: 53 DC.
H P: 40/50.
Engine No.: AT 15.
Off Test: 29.4.26. D I Issued: 29.4.26.
Axle ratio: 15 x 52.
Tyres: Dunlop Straight sided.
Front: 33 x 5.
Date of Order: 25.3.26. No.: 79104 W.
Sale Price: £1,850. Less 15%.
Date of Sale: 8.10.25.
Sold to Hooper & Co Ltd, 54 St James Street, London, SW1. for Hillier Holt, Esq, 20 Avenue Road, Regents Park, London, NW8.
Balance of chassis price paid: £1,627.10.2d. on 17.5.26.

Chassis delivered 4.5.26 to Hoopers by road, ex L H.
Invoice No. 662. Dated 29.4.26. Total £1,627.10.2d.
(1925/6 Rebate 8230).
Erection particulars dated 18.2.26 from Hoopers,
Sheet No. 4990.
Instruction Book sent Hoopers on 20.5.26.
Steering Column: 'B'. Levers: Standard. Fittings:
Nickel.
Wheelbase: Long. Radiator Shutters: White.
Springs for an enclosed limousine or landaulette
weighing approximately 13 cwt.
Seating 6, usually 3-4. Max luggage 2 cwt, average 1
cwt.
One extra spare wire wheel without excluder. Side
lamps on wings.
A T Speedometer. Battery wiring to inside frame
position.

On the death of Mr Holt in March 1930, the
car became the property of his widow,
Mrs Florence Sarah Holt, who used it up until
1935, when it passed to Messrs Woodall &
Nicholson of Halifax, a firm which has always
dealt in the large chauffeur-driven type of car,
supplying mainly to Hire Car Firms, especially
Austins, Daimlers, Humbers, Lanchesters, Rolls-
Royce and Sunbeams, and they have built many
hearse bodies on chassis they have bought if
they did not consider the original coachwork
suitable for resale; but in the case of 53 DC the
car was sold complete and in March 1935
became the property of Mr Frederick Scobey,
Sycamore Garages, Bootham, York.

Mr Scobey was a 'hackney carriage proprietor'
and 53 DC was his pride and joy, he was also a
Councillor and a J P on the local bench, so it is
hardly surprising that when a large and impressive chauffeur driven limousine was needed for
the opening of the York Assizes, 53 DC was
used and continued this duty for over 20 years,
from 1937 to 1959 or thereabouts.

When King George VI, with Queen Elizabeth
and Princess Margaret, went to York to
Sledmore House, 53 DC was the Official Car
which the Royal Family used and Fred Scobey
acted as chauffeur.

By 1961 though still exceedingly well kept
and in good order 53 DC was looking distinctly
old-fashioned and it was felt that a replacement
vehicle was essential, so the car was sold to its
fourth owner, James Edward Robinson, of
Elmbank Club, The Mount, York, for £60. When
the car was sold, one of Scobey's drivers had

such an affection for the old car which he had
driven for so many years that he cried!

After this came the worst years for 53 DC.
She suffered a rapid change of owners, each of
whom neglected her. Mr Robinson moved to the
New Green Inn, Avon, near Christchurch, in
Hampshire, taking 53 DC with him, but in
February 1962 he sold her to Robin John
Hussey of 40 Wandle Road, Christchurch, who
three months later sold her to Alexander
Thomas Fraser of 30 Arundel Road, Cheam, in
Surrey.

Two years later, in June 1964, Kenneth
Jenner, saw her advertised for sale in *Motor
Sport*, and went to see the car which was kept in
a winchhouse near the quarry, at Reigate in
Surrey. By now she was in an appalling state,
though Fraser had done a lot of work on the
engine, which the previous owner had allowed to
freeze up doing irreparable damage to the
cylinder blocks, so much so that Fraser had
cannibalized the cylinder blocks from another
'New Phantom' he had, which carried hearse
coachwork.

Kenneth Jenner, who was already the owner
of a very fine Alvis Sedanca de ville,
immediately saw the possibilities the remains of
such a fine car promised if restored, and bought it
on the spot. Then came the difficulty. How to
move it from Reigate in Surrey to Marden in
Kent, a distance of some 50 miles, it was neither
taxed nor insured. However, this did not deter
the vendor who said he would drive it! The
exhaust system was so badly corroded it was
almost non-existent, so, with 53 DC sounding
like an aircraft, they set off in convoy from
Reigate to Marden; on approaching Oxted they
saw a police car stopped on a lay-by, both
policemen put their hands to their ears and
grinned broadly as the big limousine roared past!

Once back at Marden, Kenneth was able to
examine his new acquisition at his leisure, apart
from the engine needing a proper overhaul and
the exhaust system being rebuilt, the worst
features of the car were the wings, which were in
a shocking state because the judgement of one
of the former owners was obviously lacking and
he had continuously run into things!

The engine was tackled first by a friend
named Silver, who was conversant with Rolls-

Royce cars, the cylinder blocks were rebored plus 20 thou and new pistons fitted. The front compartment and the de ville head were restored professionally in Tunbridge Wells, the front seats being re-upholstered in black leather. 53 DC was all black when Kenneth Jenner bought her, but he chose an ideal contrasting colour scheme of black wings and uppers with pale primrose to the lower panels, which makes an attractive combination and gives the car a striking but dignified appearance. The wings and the re-cellulosing were done on the farm by local labour at weekends. Ken received great assistance with the restoration from his friend Beeman Howess.

The car now restored to her former glory, has run some 7,000 miles and given great satisfaction to her owner; one of her first outings was to the Rolls-Royce and Bentley Pageant at Goodwood in May 1967 and it was here that I saw it for the first time and thought what a handsome carriage it was.

In June 1972 when making researches for this book I was delighted to have a ride in the car which Kenneth Jenner and his brother had painstakingly re-upholstered themselves, a job which I would not care to tackle, especially as no short cuts were used in doing this work. The rear is in cloth executed in the original style, only the rollers to the blinds on the windows are missing. If a set of the original type rollers can be found these will vastly improve the interior. It looks a little sparse without them as all big closed cars of that period had them.

I rode both in the front of the car and the rear for a few miles through the Kent country-side, from both vantage points the vision is incredible, putting present day cars to shame. From the front seat the whole width of the car can be seen and the driver can place 53 DC exactly where he likes; riding in the rear is typical of any big limousine of the period and can only be likened to first-class travel on the railway.

PART I CHAPTER 18

Stanley E Sears' chassis No. 76 TC, and Lady Freda Valentine's chassis No. 1 OR, and finally John McFarlane's Springfield-built chassis No. 5154

Rolls-Royce cars have always been fitted with a wide variety of coachwork built to the exacting standards of their owners but probably the most unusual 'New Phantom' ever built is 76 TC, which is now owned by Stanley E Sears, whose name as a connoisseur has already been mentioned several times.

76 TC has appeared in illustrations in many books and magazines but until now the full story behind this chassis has never been told.

In 1952 Stanley E Sears saw an advertisement in *The Motor* which had been inserted by a firm trading under the name of Metcalfe & Munday, who had premises at Earls Court, which began - 'The Most Amazing Rolls-Royce of all Time', and then went on to give a description of the car which was undoubtedly a 'New Phantom'. Always interested in anything unusual Stanley contacted Metcalfe & Munday and went to see the car. Mr Metcalfe was a great Bentley enthusiast, especially for the model which had been designed by W O Bentley and built at Cricklewood, and did not often deal in Rolls-Royce. At this time Stanley did not have a 'New Phantom' in the motor houses at Bolney; the 'New Phantom' which he had been running, chassis No. 109 WR, built for J Pierpoint Morgan, Jnr, the American financier, he had sold shortly before to his sister, Mrs Crossley-Meates, so he was looking for a 'New Phantom' to replace it and complete his collection.

The coachwork on 76 TC was so unusual he felt he simply must have it, so he bought it on the spot. The details from the Body Card are as follows:

Chassis No. 76 TC
Engine No. RT 25.
Off Test: 11.6.1926.
Sold: 20.3.1926 to George Heath for Charles Clark Ltd.
Straight side 33 x 5.
'C' Steering.
21.6.1926 to Charles Clark by their man from W.
Coupe de ville
Seating: 6 - usually 3-4.
Luggage grid with-drawn.
One extra spare wheel.

And from the Guarantee Book at Conduit Street the details are given as follows:

Chassis No.: 76 TC.
Chassis sold to Charles Clark & Son, 10.4.1927.
Guarantee sent to owner, 21.4.1927.
C W Gasque Esq, Victory House, Kingsway, London, and The Elms, Spaniards Road, Hampstead Heath.

Mr Gasque was Secretary of Woolworths at the time he had the car built. It was ordered as a present for his wife and he was determined to make it something special. For some obscure reason he had the body built by the little-known coachbuilders, Clark of Wolverhampton. This is rather strange as Hooper's or Barker's would have been so much more convenient for him. However, Clark's did a very good job on this unusual order - Mr Gasque was a great admirer of Louis XIV style furniture and decided he would like the rear compartment of the car to resemble a Louis XIV salon in miniature. The effect is quite unique. Rumour has it that he obtained some Louis XIV furniture from Heal's in London and had it cut down and fitted into the car. However, for a full description there follows an extract from Stanley Sears' own book *A Collection of Interesting Cars*:

> The back seat is designed as a sofa, the small auxiliary seats are concealed in the special bow front cabinet, which also holds decanters for sherry and brandy, containers for biscuits and cigarettes. together with a small silver tray and glasses. The whole of the upholstery is carried out in 'Petit Point' needlework which was commissioned at Aubusson in France. It took nine months to make, and cost over £600. A French artist was specially brought over to paint the ceiling and door panels, etc. The curtains are of drawn thread work, and the companions on either side of the seat contain fittings of genuine Battersea enamel. All the external bright parts are silver plated; and the interior metal fittings gilded.

The exterior of the car was finished in all black and Mr Gasque stipulated white wall tyres, which were unobtainable in the standard 33 x 5 size and it was only possible to procure them in 7.00 x 20, so the wheels were cut down and rebuilt, which gives an odd impression, and Stanley tells me that the maximum speed is only 70 mph: as the car was built exclusively for town work (not even the luggage carrier was required) this is of no concern, in fact it makes 76 TC even more tractable in heavy traffic.

It also possesses another interesting feature, a Thermorad, which warms the interior and works off the exhaust system, this type of heater was frequently used prior to the present day method of hot-water system.

76 TC was used until 1937, when it was laid up somewhere in North London in the Finsbury Park area; the total mileage was just over 47,000 and it was not until 1948 that anything was known about this car at all. It was then offered for sale for the ridiculous price of £47.10.0d, but at that time no-one was the least interested in purchasing a 'New Phantom'; the meagre petrol ration of 7 gallons per month and the large annual road fund licence all assisted in making people uninterested in this model, which was simply looked upon as a very old Rolls-Royce and no longer a practical proposition to use; however, the car was finally sold and it then went all round the motor trade. Of course, everyone who actually saw the very unusual coachwork immediately realized that it was a true collector's piece, but it was not until later that Stanley saw the advertisement and bought it.

My wife and I were invited over to Bolney to see the car, soon after Stanley acquired it and he told me that he felt it resembled a funeral car, and he intended to put basket-work panelling on it to see if he could lighten the rather sombre effect.

The work of renovation was carried out by Frank Elphick in Messrs H E Griffin's Garage in Haywards Heath, who had previously worked on both 1721 and the original 'Silver Ghost'.

76 TC was used for the wedding of his younger son, Eric, and has appeared at a few rallies; it was present at the 1964 Rolls-Royce and Bentley Goodwood Pageant, where it won the stable competition; its companions being the 6-cylinder 30 h p chassis No. 26355 and the Phantom III, chassis No. 3-DL-76.

Stanley says that the trouble with the car is that it cannot be left anywhere unattended for one minute, it draws such a crowd of people round it, more so than any of his other cars, so that in a number of ways he is a little frightened of taking it out.

The last example of surviving 'New Phantom' chassis to be included here is No. 1 OR. This car, well-known to members of the 20 Ghost Club as a frequent entrant at their rallies, is owned by Lady Freda Valentine in whose ownership the car has been since 31 August 1934.

The coachwork is an H J Mulliner 4-light touring limousine of Weymann construction. The Weymann type of body, which has a light wooden frame covered with imitation leather in place of sheet metal panels, was extremely popular in the late 1920s as it was much lighter than a coachbuilt body of the period; it also was not nearly so liable to rattling and drumming, and it did not require the care that had to be taken with a car that was finished in paint and varnish. But by 1932 the vogue was over, gleaming cellulose paintwork had become the thing and on the cheaper type of car the pressed steel body was coming into its own; so the Weymann body, which had originated in France, virtually disappeared overnight.

The Body Card for 1 OR reads as follows:

Chassis No.: 1 OR.
Engine No.: 1 W.25.
Axle Ratio: 14 x 52.
Despatched: 1.6.29.
Date of Sale: 30.4.29.
Jack Barclay Ltd, for J P Glass, Meadcroft, Horley, Surrey.
Type of steering: 'E'.
To H J Mulliner - 5.6.29. - by road - Ex L H. *
Long chassis.
Weymann limousine weighing 10 cwt.
Seating: 6, - usually 3.
2 cwt luggage, usually ½ cwt.
Extra spare wheel.
Luggage grid.
Locks to bonnet.
No mascot.
Two spare wheel carriers.

While the Body Card states that 1 OR has two spare wheel carriers, this chassis actually has three, the third being at the rear. Mention has already been made of how the 'New Phantom' chassis was extended so that it was possible to carry the spare wheel at the rear of the car, a place greatly favoured by Royce, partly to meet complaints of cars giving an uncomfortable ride when only carrying one passenger on the rear seat.

1 OR is the only surviving example I know of a 'New Phantom' chassis which has this arrangement which has not been altered, but is as it left the Works in 1929.

1 OR was originally supplied to Mrs Edith Mary Glass in July 1929 by Jack Barclay Ltd; she kept the car until 20 November 1931, when it was sold to John Owen McNaught Turnbull of Golden Grove, near Whitby, Yorks, who moved on 6 March 1934 to 9 Broomfield Terrace, Whitby, Yorkshire.

Lady Freda had long admired Rolls-Royces but, on previous occasions, test runs in a softly sprung Rolls-Royce limousine made her feel ill. However, she knew that it was perfectly possible to find one with a fairly hard spring-rating in which she could ride happily.

When she married, her husband had a Lagonda with a folding top; this car had been built for four young men to use for golfing trips. As a family car it was less appropriate; even whilst on their honeymoon, the top blew off! After her elder son was born, the Lagonda had become quite unsuitable for use as a family

* Lillie Hall

car with a small boy, chauffeur and nurse, to say nothing of five dogs.

Lady Freda's husband went to the 1933 Motor Show to examine cars, which he felt were within his price range. On his return from the Show, he informed his wife that the most suitable car for their requirements was a large Armstrong-Siddeley. Accordingly, Lady Freda accompanied her husband to the Armstrong-Siddeley showrooms, 10 Old Bond Street, where they were able to examine at their leisure, examples of the model which he had picked out at the Motor Show. However, on attempting to sit in one displayed in the showroom, Lady Freda tore her stockings and her husband cut his hand when testing the hood, and that, was the end of the Armstrong-Siddeley! Not long after this they found 1 OR which was offered for sale at the Black Cat Garage, near Cavendish Square. It satisfied their requirements perfectly, and after a trial run they arranged to part-exchange the Lagonda, plus £600, for 1 OR.

The family took delivery of 1 OR on 31 August 1934. Their chauffeur, Hillier, had started his working life with carriages and horses, so the mysteries of effecting silent gearchanges with sliding straight-cut gears did not come easily to him. So Lady Freda arranged for Mr Bellringer (the head of the London Rolls-Royce Service Station at Cricklewood, whom she had met during her earlier trials of used Rolls-Royce cars) to give Hillier tuition on how to change gear. The car was used from then until 1939, when it was laid up in a garage improvised in a disused malthouse at Kings Sutton, near Banbury, until after the war. By this time her two sons were growing up and the younger, James (who must have travelled in 1 OR before he was born), became extremely interested in 1 OR, so the car was put back on the road. Later, as the result of taking the car to the 1967 Goodwood Pageant, he and his mother were invited to join the 20 Ghost Club.

The total mileage is now just over 109,000. Apart from an engine overhaul, very little work has needed to be done to this chassis; recently, however, as the Weymann body was rather shabby, James made arrangements for it to be re-covered, which has been very well done in blue fabric for the lower panels and black leather for the uppers; the bonnet, wings and wheels are finished in black cellulose.

When the *QE2* sailed on her maiden voyage to America, a contingent of 20 Ghost Club members sailed in the liner for New York, taking their cars with them, to be entertained in America by members of the Rolls-Royce Owners' Club Inc. It was a memorable occasion, being the very first time it was possible to drive on and off an Atlantic liner.

Lady Freda and her son travelled second-class in the *QE2* and fared at least as well as the majority of 20 Ghost Club members who went first-class.

The vehicles taking part were:
Four 40/50s, including 'The Silver Ghost' driven by D Miller Williams.
Three 'New Phantoms'.
Two Phantom IIs.
Two Phantom IIIs.
Three 'Twenties'.
Three 20/25s.
One 25/30.

In July 1972 I spent a very pleasant day with Lady Freda and her son, James, inspecting 1 OR. I had met Lady Freda at her London flat in Albany and we motored down to King's Sutton in my 20/25, chassis No. GGP 28.

It was an interesting experience to be driven through the Northamptonshire lanes in 1 OR having, only a few days before, been in Kenneth Jenner's 53 DC. It is quite unbelievable the difference there is in the two cars from a passenger's point of view considering there is only three years between them. Riding in 1 OR (or 'Auntie' as Lady Freda calls her) is comparable to travelling in an early Phantom II rather than a late-type 'New Phantom', it does not feel like a motor carriage but like a big luxury car;

the engine is the later type of 'New Phantom', fitted with an aluminium cylinder head and is very silent and smooth.

In a letter received from John McFarlane I have obtained the following details of his Springfield 'New Phantom':-

History of Springfield P I, 5154 FR

Engine No.: 21548 (The 2 and 8 shows the engine was built in 1928)
Coachmakers: Brewster - 'Derby' sports phaeton.
Body No.: 5609.
Test date - 1929.
Total weight: 5350 lb.
Original price - $17,840.

First owner - Samuel J Aronsohn, businessman, New York City. Undoubtedly ordered sometime in 1929 (before Wall Street slump).
Delivered May 31, 1930 from J S Inskip, N Y C.
Colour scheme - Yellow body, green fenders and undercarriage, green leather upholstery.

Second owner - Charles Howson Abbe, architect, N Y C.
Bought April 25, 1946, again from Inskip's.

Third owner - John W McFarlane, publication editor, Eastman Kodak Co.
Bought from Inskip's, January 7, 1950. (As of January 1973 retired from E K Co but still owns the car). Car had received a poor black paint job. Mileage 55,000+. Good condition mechanically, except aluminium cylinder head. Received new top and paint. New Connolly red leather upholstery, done by wife - Engine 'majored' at 75,000 miles, new cylinder head, pistons, main bearings, etc. Present mileage (January 1973) is 140,000+.

Has received 'Best of Class' in several clubs, 'Best Personal Restoration' in R R O C (1958), etc, etc.

Own name for this car - 'Lady Brewster'.

Sgn: John W McFarlane, Feb.13/73.

PART II CHAPTER 1

The announcement of the Phantom II; the first prototype chassis, No. 18 EX, and how this model came to be built; the testing of it at Chateauroux in France.

The announcement of the 'New Phantom' in May 1925 gave Royce the breathing space and time to produce a new and up-to-date 40/50 for which Claude Johnson had been pressing him for some time, (but sadly CJ died three years before the Phantom II appeared).

The drawings for the new model were all completed by March 1928 and the new chassis was a simpler version of the 40/50: it was Royce's last 'big six' and his last design. It made a tremendous impact on the public when it was first announced in *The Autocar* on 20 September 1929, and later when it first appeared at the Olympia Motor Show in October. It has always held a special place with connoisseurs and has been referred to as 'the greatest car of all time'. In many respects the Phantom II chassis followed the lines of the very successful '20', on a very much larger scale, whilst the engine was a greatly improved version of the 'New Phantom' with a higher compression of 4.75 : 1.

The whole appearance of the car was revolutionized by entirely re-designing the chassis and springing, using half elliptics all round in place of cantilever at the rear and a much lower frame, so that when carrying closed coachwork, the overall height of the car was reduced by some 9 in. or more giving the Phantom II a wonderfully modern low-slung look, which made a 'New Phantom' look archaic.

The original Sales brochure released at the time read as follows:

> Rolls-Royce Limited announce that after prolonged tests they can now demonstrate and accept orders for a new 40/50 h p Rolls-Royce chassis.
>
> The original chassis of this type was the famous 'Silver Ghost' and in 1925 the 'Phantom' was introduced. This new chassis will be known as 'Phantom II'.
>
> Like the 'Phantom' it is equipped with a 6-cylinder engine having a bore of 4¼ inches, and a stroke of 5½ inches, with a total cylinder volume of 7,668 cubic centimetres. The R A C rating is 43.3 h p and the annual tax is £44.
>
> The effect of these new features is to provide a car of reduced height and lower centre of gravity, improved appearance, greatly improved suspension at all speeds, steering control giving greater selectivity and ease of operation, lighter weight, increased acceleration and maximum speed, time and trouble-saving method of lubrication and still greater refinement throughout the chassis.
>
> The Company desires to state that this new chassis will retain all the characteristic features which have gained for their car the accepted title 'The Best Car in the World'.
>
> 'Phantom II' is not intended to compete with racing or ultra-sporting types of cars, nevertheless it will more than maintain the position the 'Phantom' has achieved amongst its owners of being the fastest genuine touring car in the world.
>
> Orders for 'Phantom II' chassis will be executed in strict rotation, which will be determined by the time of despatch of a telegram or by the date of receipt of a letter containing an order.

The following is a Table of Comparisons of the 'Phantom II' and 'Phantom' chassis:

	'PHANTOM II'	*'PHANTOM'*
Chassis Price	Short chassis - £1,850 Long chassis - £1,900 (These prices include the same equipment as given with the Phantom chassis and in addition, instrument board, speedometer, clock, spare tyre for spare wheel and locks to bonnet).	Short chassis - £1,850 Long chassis - £1,900
Engine and Gear Box	Unit Construction	Separate Units
Springing	Rear: Semi-elliptic Front: Semi-elliptic (Forced lubrication to spring leaves	Rear: Cantilever Front: Semi-elliptic
Lubrication of Chassis	Centralized system	By oil gun to each part
Electric Engine Starter	By sequence starter, operated by push switch on instrument board	By chain through gear operated by foot switch
Body Mounting	On separate subframe eliminating body distortions	Direct on chassis frame
Steering	Larger diameter wheel having smaller rim. Modifications giving greater selectivity and ease of operation	18 in. steering wheel
Back Axle	Of special design enabling height of chassis generally to be reduced	Spiral bevel
Propeller Shaft	Open, of lighter construction	Enclosed in torque tube
Petrol Gauge	On instrument Board	On tank
Petrol Feed	Autovac with engine-driven vacuum pump	Autovac operated by induction
Induction system	Water heated	Exhaust heated
Ignition	Battery, Magneto of improved design with wider range of synchronization between battery and magneto	Battery and magneto. Automatic and positively synchronized advance and retard

(*Top left*) The nearside view of a New Phantom engine
(*Top right*) The offside of the same engine
(*Middle*) 21UF, the Riviera Trials Car. After the accident in France 15EX was rebuilt to this design, except for a rear-mounted spare-wheel. The Chassis number was changed to 29CL
(*Bottom*) A later photo of 29CL (ex 15EX), showing the car carrying its third coachwork a Hooper Limousine. (Note the 'modernised' wings, a popular treatment, which looks so ghastly and done during the mid-1930s when it was unfashionable to run an old car). See Part I, Chapter 14

(*Top left*) Springfield New Phantom, Engine number 20807 in chassis number S-380-FM, offside (*photo Les Reggel*)
(*Top right*) Springfield New Phantom, engine number 20807 in chassis number S-380-FM, nearside (*photo Les Reggel*)
(*Middle*) A New Phantom engine on test in the Derby works
(*Bottom*) A pre-CL series New Phantom chassis

(Top left) 74SC, Douglas Fitzpatrick's super-charged New Phantom after he had had the car rebodied. See Part I, Chapter 17 (photo Douglas Fitzpatrick)

(Top right) Showing the supercharger on 74SC New Phantom. See Part I, Chapter 17 (photo Douglas Fitzpatrick)

(Middle) The Derby works chassis production. The 20 hp cars are on the left whilst the New Phantoms are in the centre and to the right

(Bottom) 1925 New Phantom with coachwork by Connaught. This is 82RC, engine number EM65 with 'C' type steering built for Cecil A. Joll, FRCS of 64 Harley Street, W1

(*Top*) 36DC, 1926 New Phantom with Paddon Brothers designed body built for J. Lucas Scudamore by H. J. Mulliner. Every bright part on the chassis and body was silver-plated (*photo Hugh Keller*)

(*Middle*) An African chief from one of the 'Cocoa States' with his gold threaded umbrella came to York to inspect the Rowntree factory and used 53DC in the 1930s for his visit. Scoby, the owner, acted as chauffeur and is on the right. See Part I, Chapter 17 (*photo Kenneth Jenner*)

(*Bottom*) A *Kent Messenger* photograph of 53DC at the Penshurst Pageant after the car had been restored by Kenneth Jenner. See Part I, Chapter 17 (*photo Kenneth Jenner*)

(*Top*) Barker photograph number 1693G. Name of owner A. McIlwraith Esq. Chassis make; Rolls-Royce type long HP 40/50. Chassis number 14NC. Column 'B'. Barker body number 5865. Barker drawing number L6670. Type of body, Pullman Laudaulette. Colour of body, blue

(*Upper middle*) The Prince of Wales took delivery of 14RF, a Gurney Nutting Weymann in 1928. He sold the car two years later to Mrs Fry of Hamble, Hampshire

(*Lower middle*) The post CL series extended frame chassis on test at the Derby works

(*Bottom*) 1926 New Phantom Brougham de Ville by Clark of Wolverhampton, chassis number 76TC, built for Gasque, secretary of Woolworths, now owned by S. E. Sears. See Part I, Chapter 18

(*Top*) A New Phantom chassis showing extension to the frame for the rear mounted spare wheel
(*Middle*) 94RF. A Windovers Limousine supplied to the Maharajah of Jodhpur (*photo John Fasal*)
(*Bottom left*) The interior of the Maharajah of Jodhpur's Windovers Limousine 94RF (*photo John Fasal*)
(*Bottom right*) The drawing for the end of the chassis frame showing the extension for the rear mounted spare wheel carrier

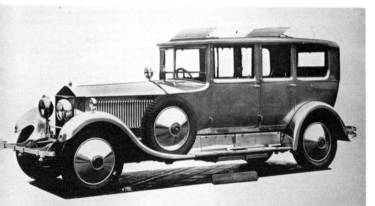

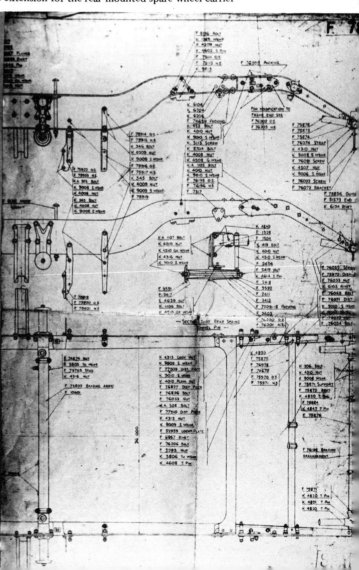

(Top) 1928 New Phantom Barker Landaulette

(Middle left) The Olympia Motor Show 1928 New Phantom with enclosed limousine coachwork by Arthur Mulliner Ltd of Northampton. Chassis number 22CL, engine number IU35, long type chassis fitted with 'C' type steering. A duplicate of this car was supplied to the Maharajah of Patiala on chassis number 74WR

(Middle right) 1928-29 Barker Pullman Limousine on the New Phantom chassis. (This photograph was damaged by water when found amongst series of photos which were being disposed of) (photo S.J. Skinner)

(Bottom) 81CL New Phantom Hooper Sedanca de Ville finished in blue and black built for the Vienna Show 1929. Long chassis, type 'C' steering

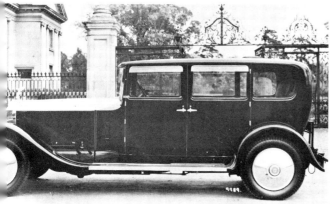

(Top) 1930 American Salon Car. This Brewster body was built for a Phantom II but no chassis was available with LHD, therefore the body was altered for a Springfield Phantom I. The photograph was taken on the roof of the Brewster building for secrecy. Chassis number S-132-PR

(Middle left) 10R, a H. J. Mulliner Weymann Touring Limousine New Phantom belonging to Lady Valentine, showing the rear mounted spare wheel in position. See Part I, Chapter 18

(Middle right) 248AJS Rolls-Royce Phantom II. This car is known as the 'Tear Drop Fast Back' and was specially built for the 1931 American Salon. It was the only Phantom II to be exhibited at a Salon. See Part I, Chapter 16

(Bottom) This photograph shows a Barker Pullman Limousine de Ville on chassis number 45WR with 'C' type steering. Extra seats facing forward were fitted and the car was supplied to HH The Nawab of Bahawalphur. The Body Cards for this chassis, however, do not agree with the Barker photograph. According to the cards this chassis was built for the Cairo Motor Show and fitted with a Thrupp and Maberly Open Tourer finished in ivory and Nile blue. It was then purchased by the Nawab and sent to Bombay late in 1929. The car *could* have had a body change before going to India (photo S. J. Skinner)

40/50 H P CHASSIS NOW ANNOUNCED
'PHANTOM II'

The first prototype Phantom II chassis was known as 18 EX. It was fitted with coachwork by Barker of a type known as a 'close coupled sports' saloon. It had flared mudguards and the spare wheel was mounted at the rear behind the luggage trunk and was an entirely new type of body to be mounted on a Rolls-Royce chassis. It was finished in grey and black and had a definitely 'sporty' look about it.

In 1927 the Riley Company had brought out their now famous 9 h p 'Monaco Saloon' and the story goes that one of Royce's friends had bought one of these cars and driven down to Le Canadel to see him. Royce was most interested in the little car, he was always intrigued to know what other designers were doing and was not above adopting and improving other peoples ideas if he admired them. He particularly liked the seating arrangement in the Riley in which everyone sat within the wheelbase, so that the occupants of the rear seat were not sitting right over the back axle, but had a much more comfortable ride, at the same time being able to carry on a conversation without effort with those in the front seats.

At this time Royce was using a 'New Phantom' chassis No. 7 EX with a Barker Cabriolet body and he told Ivan Evernden, who was one of his closest disciples and who was responsible for carrying out experiments with coachwork, that most of his journeys were taken with only Nurse Aubin as a passenger in the car, therefore he could not see the object of having a car with so much floor space in the rear compartment 'that it resembled a dance hall'. So he decided the type of body he had seen on the Riley 9 was just what he wanted for his new Phantom II.

18 EX was running on the roads late in 1928, the total unladen weight of the car was 44 cwt 2 qtrs 22 lb. Not very long after this, a replica was built which was known as 19 EX with coachwork by Barker finished in French grey and black. Very curiously this car was not a success, Ivan Evernden tells me that although 18 EX was free from shake, 19 EX 'was a pig!' In spite of the fact that the bodies on the two cars were exchanged the mystery of this 'shake' was never solved, both chassis were on the long wheel base of 12 ft 6 in.

Ivan Evernden was entirely responsible for all coachwork on EX chassis; the part he played in the story of the Rolls-Royce motor car is a very important one and I do not think that he has ever been given enough credit for all the work that he has done for the Company. When the designs for the Phantom II were being drawn Royce had noticed that instrument panels had been greatly improved and that many American cars now had an arrangement of neatly grouped instruments, instead of having them scattered all over the instrument panel; so, for the new model Royce asked Evernden to design a new panel with all the instruments together under one glass, where, in the event of one failing, it could easily be replaced. At this time most of the luggage grids were made by the coachbuilders of wrought iron and there was no standard design. There had been complaints from some clients who had lost their luggage from the rear of their car, especially on a long journey across France; so Royce asked Evernden to design for the new model a much better rear wheel carrier and a standard type of luggage grid, which when closed would look very neat, but at the same time would be immensely strong and on which the luggage would be safe.

Chromium plate was becoming popular in America and Royce wanted to see how it stood up to everyday use, so 18 EX was given a chromium plated radiator and the coachwork was finished in cellulose, which again was becoming popular in America, but was not being used to any great extent in Britain. Probably the largest English motor manufacturers who were using it at this time were the Austin Motor Company at Longbridge, who had changed to this method in the previous year, 1927.

Ivan Evernden had a terrible time with Barker & Co, over building the body on 18 EX, they had a habit of adding fittings which he had not specified and which he knew perfectly well Royce simply would not have. It was a difficult and delicate situation as Barker had only the drawings from which to build the body, the chassis of 18 EX was at Derby, Evernden did not like to say too much as he did not want to attract attention to the new model. The coachworks of Barker & Co, were in Latimer Road,

Ladbroke Grove, off Notting Hill and they were building a great many bodies for customers, not only on Rolls-Royce chassis but on other makes, such as Daimler, Minerva, Armstrong-Siddeley, Lincoln, etc. Many clients would come to the Works to see how the coachwork on their own particular car was proceeding; but they were almost invariably shown all round the Works and the one thing that Rolls-Royce Ltd did not want was for anyone to see that there was an entirely new type of Rolls-Royce chassis, as they knew only too well that this could upset Sales of present models. In many cases with these experimental chassis when the body was completed it was removed by motor lorry to the Experimental Department at Derby, where it was fitted on to the chassis by Sanderson and Holmes of Derby. In the case of 18 EX, in order to preserve secrecy the chassis was sent to Latimer Road, where it was hidden away and the work of mounting the body was done at night.

At the time when the chassis was laid down, 19 EX, 20 EX, 21 EX, and 22 EX were also laid down, each of which was to have a different type of coachwork; but work on these did not progress very quickly, as it was essential to discover how 18 EX performed on the road first, and it was ready for the first trial by late November 1928.

The Team who had designed the chassis consisted of:

Engine	Elliott (E), living in New Forest, July 1965. Jenner, now deceased.
Chassis	W (Bill) Hardy, responsible for gearbox, propeller-shaft and rear axle
	B (Bernard) Day, responsible for front axle, steering, brakes, shock absorbers and springing. (Now deceased) He came from Sheffield Simplex; CJ had wooed him away, from Sheffield Simplex in 1913.
Coachwork	H I (Ivan) F Evernden, responsible for coachwork.

All the original designing was done at Elmstead in a studio called 'Camacha'. The whole team worked under 'R's' supervision.

Below is the provisional programme for 'Super Sports' chassis drawn up at the time:

First chassis ready first week in December - 18 EX
Second chassis ready third week in December - 19 EX
Third and Fourth chassis ready before the end of January - 20 and 21 EX
Fifth and Sixth chassis ready early February - 22 and 23 EX

The Phantom II has been criticized as having a 'heavy' feeling when driving it; it is true that some Phantom IIs, depending on coachwork, are probably the heaviest of Royce's designs. This is because when this model was first discussed, the Company introduced the idea of having a chassis sub-frame. It was claimed that by using a sub-frame, the coachwork was insulated from the chassis and so was less likely to have to withstand the poundings that it would otherwise receive on a bad road. It became an integral part of the coachwork, effectively preventing distortion, the Daimler Company had been using a sub-frame for years and there is no doubt that Rolls-Royce Ltd, also decided to use this method in order to hasten delivery of models as, once the Phantom II came on to the market, it was such a magnificent chassis that the demand for it was very high indeed and orders poured in. Using this means of construction, as soon as a chassis was ordered, the sub-frame could be despatched to the coachbuilder and work on building the body could commence, whilst the chassis was still being erected and tested at Derby; then, when the chassis finally reached the coachbuilder, the body already built on to the sub-frame could be mounted straight on to the chassis.

The following chassis series were supplied with a sub-frame:

Phantom II

Chassis Series			
	J 2	1	- 200
	K 2	201	- 400
	L 2	401	- 600
	M 2	601	- 800

After M 2 series the sub-frame was done away with and the Company reverted to their original arrangement of supplying simply the chassis to the coachbuilder.

There are arguments for and against having a

sub-frame, it certainly does help to protect the coachwork with its insulation against road shocks, but on the other hand it adds considerably to the weight of a completed car and naturally if the coachwork is heavy the performance suffers.

On 12 December 1928, 18 EX (or 'S S' codename for 'Super Sports'), left Derby at 8.0 am for West Wittering, there was great urgency over this as Royce had to inspect and approve the car before it was sent to France and he himself was leaving for his winter quarters at Le Canadel the very next day. Immediately Royce had seen and approved 18 EX, arrangements were made to ship the car to France so that it could go through a 10,000 mile test at Chateauroux.

At this time George Hancock (known as 'Georgie') was in charge of operations at Chateauroux, he was a most conscientious man, prone to very strong language if provoked, and a strict disciplinarian. He worked extremely hard himself and was quite determined that his team at Chateauroux should do likewise and therefore expected everyone to be in bed at 9.0 pm and not out enjoying the sort of cafe life, which was so prevalent in French provincial towns at that time, there being no cinemas or television, or for that matter any other entertainment whatsoever.

The Company was most anxious to get 18 EX to France as unobtrusively as possible, so it was decided to send the car over on a night service cargo boat crossing Southampton-Le Havre. Hancock collected the car from the Experimental Department in Derby and in order to overcome customs restrictions, took the car to France as his own property.

The 10,000 mile test was scheduled as follows:

December 16th - Le Havre to Chateauroux - 280 miles
December 17th - Testers to report to police, garage to be prepared (this means the premises where the R-Rs were kept at Chareauroux) Car starts at noon.
December 18th - 24th - 600 miles daily equals 4,480 miles plus 280 miles from Le Havre.
December 25th - Christmas Day.
December 26th - Car inspected.
December 27th - January 4th - 600 miles daily, equals 9,880 miles.
January 5th-6th - For contingencies.

It was also arranged that various members of

the sales staff would go down to Chateauroux, they were allowed to ride in the car whilst the testers were putting it through its paces, but in no circumstances whatsoever were they to be permitted to drive it. When the car had been through its tests, then the sales people could take it out on their own and criticize it. The reason for this was because some years previously there had been a very bad accident when an experimental chassis, was being driven by one of the sales staff, and a most valued tester had lost his life. The Company felt very strongly that this risk must never be taken again.

Hancock wrote to the Experimental Department in Derby to say that the car ran very well on the run down from Le Havre to Chateauroux, apart from the 'jellying' of the steering at certain speeds; but it seemed to him that the maximum speed was a little disappointing, 80 mph with the cut-out open, and 75 mph with the cut-out closed, which was not as fast as the latest type 'New Phantom'. The reason was that in prototype form the engine in the 'S S' did not 'breathe' quite so well; however this was very quickly altered and the 'S S' then proved very much faster than the 'New Phantom'. He went on to say that at 70 mph the car rode beautifully and the steering was perfect.

Every day he was sending a lengthy written report on the car's performance and what troubles arose, however minor.

On 19th December, he was writing to Hives, who was in charge of the Experimental Department in Derby, to say that 12 EX was being sent home, she was being shipped from Boulogne, all organized by the General Transport people. The letter explains that they were running the car (18 EX) over one route only, as all the roads round Chateauroux were so bad they would break the car up. As this meant running the car over the same course at least three times every day, Hancock had instructed the drivers to use every consideration towards members of the public, especially when driving through towns and villages.

The buffeting which 18 EX was receiving at these continual high speeds, soon began to show up faults, but there were surprisingly few considering 18 EX was a brand new and untried model. The first thing to give trouble was the exhaust system, it was so big and so heavy and there was so much of it, built to withstand tremendous heat, that it very soon tore itself from its mounting brackets and they had to make modifications.

As the car was being run day and night it quickly became evident that the starter was not strong enough and that the dynamo which only generated 6 amps, did not put enough charge into the battery to keep the headlamps full on all night so, in the morning, when the car returned to the garage, the battery was nearly flat; in fact some of the tests were completed using side-lights only.

The petrol obtainable in France was not very clean and the testers were constantly hampered by the filter which lies between the carburetter and the autovac becoming blocked and having to strip it down and clean it. This was originally made of glass, but they broke so many that Hancock suggested a metal bowl be used instead; this is the reason why the standard production cars are fitted with a metal bowl.

Another difficulty they had was that when the petrol ran low in the tank, or ran out completely, it was discovered that turning the engine over on the starter, even with the throttle closed, did not give sufficient suction to draw the petrol up to the autovac as the starter turned the engine so slowly. The only way they were able to re-start the engine was to take the top off the carburetter, fill it with petrol, start the engine and the autovac would then begin to suck fuel from the main tank.

Hancock considered this problem carefully and finally suggested that the solution was to prevent the autovac from running right out of petrol, so that if the main tank was empty there would still be enough petrol left in the autovac which, by turning a tap to reserve, would then flow down to the carburetter and so allow the engine to be re-started.

This excellent arrangement, which was fitted on all production models, is described in the Handbook as follows:

> This reserve is not intended to be used for running the car but solely for enabling the engine to be run for re-priming the vacuum tank after the latter has been accidentally emptied down to the stand-pipe.
>
> The dial plate of the tap is marked OFF, MAIN, and RESERVE, and, normally, the tap should stand at MAIN. It can only be turned to RESERVE by depressing a catch. the object of which is to ensure that when turning on the petrol the tap shall not inadvertently be moved through the MAIN position over to RESERVE. The catch is arranged to be self-restoring when the tap is moved in the reverse direction.

The last complaint which Hancock mentioned concerned the 'jellying'. He wrote to Hives saying that the front of the car was riding very well but that they had experienced 'jellying' at speeds as low as 40 mph upwards, depending on the road surface, and he reminds Hives that on the journey down he found that the car ran sweetest at 70 mph; but on the whole he was very pleased with 18 EX and two days later he wrote as follows:

Extract of letter written to Hives from Hancock:

'Taking the car generally, its behaviour over here is truly wonderful compared to our previous Phantom'.

PART II CHAPTER 2

18 EX on test at Chateauroux

When 18 EX had run 5,000 miles at Chateauroux, Hancock took the car off the road for a most thorough examination and he compiled a nine page report on the car with the conclusions he had reached, divided into twelve separate items. Beginning with the engine, No. 75, he reported that the performance had been extremely good and that there was very little detonation or 'pinking', provided that the ignition lever was not left fully advanced during acceleration from low speeds, but he complained that, after a long run, the engine kept running after it was switched off. The valve clearances at the start of the test had been set to an easy 5 thou with the engine cold. When checked they were as follows:

1	2	3	4	5
.004 in.	.002 in.	.006 in.	.010 in.	.007 in.

6	7	8	9	10
.004 in.	.006 in.	.007 in.	.003 in.	.001 in.

11	12
.007 in.	.001 in.

There had been a period of valve noise at approximately 30 mph, No. 12 was the worst. The clearance of this valve had been decreased on the road to overcome the noise. His report continues: 'The lubrication appears to be ample. There is very little sign of exhaust smoke after running the engine slow for ten minutes. The warming up period does not appear too pronounced for tappet noise as with the present Phantom. [This refers to the then current 'New Phantom'.] There was very little fluff or dirt on the filter in the base chamber of the crankcase when the oil was drained.'

Hancock recommended a different type of Lodge plug as he said that there were distinct signs of those fitted overheating, but there was very little carbon deposit and no plug showed any sign of oiling up. He also mentioned that the timing gears were distinctly noisy at the start of the test when the engine was first started.

During the test this had improved and he was now quite satisfied with them. He then went on to complain about the autovac and said it was impossible for it to suck the last gallon of petrol out of the tank or for it to suck petrol up after the car was allowed to run out of fuel (a complaint already mentioned in the previous chapter). He then turned to the carburation and reported that the engine was very susceptible to the water temperature. Starting from cold it was impossible to open up the engine until a temperature of 60º had been obtained. It was also very noticeable on the road; if the temperature was allowed to drop the engine immediately showed signs of fluttering, but with the water and engine hot, carburation and distribution was usually good. Generally speaking he did not think that there was any serious fault, but thought the throttle control spring on the quadrant made too much difference to the slow running of the engine. He then mentioned the water pump and complained that the water pump gland nut was in a very inaccessible position, only two fingers could be used for tightening the gland nut and it did not seem possible to put sufficient load on the nut to make it remain in position. Although the nut had worked loose, no water leakage had occurred in the gland and the drive appeared to be satisfactory.

Hancock then made his report on the exhaust

manifold, which he says had been a complete failure, where the two outer pipes converged into one at the bottom they had burnt right through. He writes:

'It would appear that the pipe gets exceedingly hot at this point and it would appear to be advisable that the portion should be made as a casting, and should not be lagged'. He went on 'We have fitted a new manifold sent out which had been treated with aluminium by the Schoop method. This has been lagged the same as the first manifold and further running will verify whether it is a failure or otherwise'.

Commenting on the rocker cover he suggested that it should stand out more than on the present car, so that after it had settled down there was no possible chance of the metal coming into contact with the cylinder head flange. He continued 'The present rocker cover leaks oil at the front end due to the felt having become compressed too much, consequences being the metal of the cover is now resting on the cylinder head flange. We think it would also be advisable to fit three, if not four, holding down nuts; the two do not seem sufficient to get an even pressure for the length of the cover.

The four rubber engine mountings from an outside examination appear to be quite okay. We have had one bolt on the nearside front work loose, this bolt, or rather stud, is very difficult to get out, and in this case one of the nuts had unscrewed itself right off, the locking plate apparently not having been securely turned over. In case any of these bolts break, it is impossible to replace them without having to dismantle the engine foot from the frame'.

Hancock had already complained of the exhaust system and in his 5,000 mile report he wrote as follows:

'This pipe has distorted very badly and this causes the sliding joint to come right out of the silencer causing almost an open exhaust. The distortion of the pipe is at the first bend, this bend has quite straightened out, the result being the pipe being held at the other end of the silencer it had caused the straight portion of the pipe to become bow-shaped, and instead of the pipe lying horizontally to the frame, it is now approximately 2 in. lower in the centre. This has caused the pipe to shorten itself by approx-

imately 2 in. bringing the inner silencer pipe with it. The new inner silencer pipe sent out with an extra band on the front and to allow for a bigger expansion of the sliding joint is not satisfactory. If you will look at the drawing you will see that when this inner pipe is drawn out with the silencer, approximately 2 in., the rear end leaves its housing. This housing should be increased in length to take care for the increased movement of the sliding at the front, otherwise as happened in our case, the inner tube became detached at the rear end. Referring back to the exhaust pipe, we are of the opinion that a stay should be placed to support the pipe somewhere about the centre of the straight portion, as there is no stay between the manifold and the middle of the silencer. It does not appear that lagging this pipe would be very successful, as now we have the full exhaust gas going through this one pipe, which in our case has started to make the pipe scale very badly. To stop the distortion and scaling of the pipe as much as possible we have taken the lagging off, unfortunately this causes more exhaust noise, but it does keep the pipe much cooler'.

He said that the tail pipe with swan neck was perfectly satisfactory, then went on to report on the exhaust cut-out as follows:

'The exhaust cut-out functions quite O.K. and is mechanically in good condition. On the open roads over here we have found that the cut-out open gives us approximately 5 mph more. The noise from the cut-out is very definitely more pronounced. It has a very bad effect inside a closed body up to a speed of 50 mph. This has a very bad booming effect and is most irritating. Above this speed it has a very pleasant tone and is not at all objectionable. With cut-out closed there is a very bad retired boom from the exhaust, the exhaust noise is generally more pronounced than on the present Phantom. When starting up from cold the exhaust noise is very tinny'.

Loss of coolant from the radiator had been a problem and he wrote as follows:

'During the first portion of the mileage, we lost 2 gallons of water for every 200 miles run. We found this to be due to the overflow pipes coming in a direct line with the outflow of water of the top inlet pipe in the radiator. We have bent these pipes clear of the water flow, the result being that fairly little water is now lost. On an average approximately 1 - 2 gallons of water is needed for the 600 miles trip. We are of the opinion that the cast aluminium outlet which is fastened to the bottom of the radiator is hardly sufficient in area to take the water flow. Tests could be taken at Works to ascertain whether this is so or otherwise. The drain cock fitted to this portion is not in a very accessible position and requires a screwdriver to operate it. Our experience would tend to point that a handle would be far preferable to operate the tap'.

He went on to report that the radiator shutters had operated satisfactorily, but complained that the control knob for the shutters should be better marked, indicating the direction for open and close, because the present markings were very difficult to see from the driver's seat. He then stated that to keep the water temperature at 80° during the test runs, the shutters had been opened approximately one-quarter of the control.

To illustrate how detailed was his report he even mentioned that there was no problem with the bonnet catches, but that the first section of the top hinge nearest the radiator had broken away and that the corners of the fabric had worn allowing the bonnet to come into contact with the brass flange. He thought that the starting handle appeared to be very satisfactory for starting the engine by hand, but went on to complain that owing to its length it was very difficult to stow away in the compartment which was available for tools etc.

NOTE: This is especially interesting as on 101 SK and 3-AZ-146 the handle comes to pieces, which makes it comparatively easy to stow in with the tools. This was obviously an improvement implemented as a result of Hancock's observations.

The next item he examined was the oil pump for the engine lubrication. He says it became noisy and could be heard from the driver's seat. He goes on to say that there had been no failure of the oil supply but that it varied considerably after the brakes had been applied.

NOTE: This is also particularly interesting as I have noticed that with a sudden application of

the brakes on 74 GN, 101 SK and especially my 20/25, GGP 28, this failing occurs, and that great care has to be taken to drive on a very light throttle until the oil pressure has returned to normal. There is an article in the Rolls-Royce Enthusiasts' Club's Technical Manual 1967, which deals with this problem - it reads as follows:

A snag with the '20' and early 20/25 is that if brakes are applied sharply, oil surge occurs in the sump, and the input pipe to the oil pump may momentarily be above oil level. This causes a total loss of oil pressure, which can be overcome by running the engine light at a fast idle for a few seconds, but if it is not noticed and the engine is operated on heavy load, damage would occur. The following article describes how one member overcame the oil surge problem by modifying the sump of his engine.

The sump capacity of the 20/25 is given as 1¼ gallons, but the float indicator in the 1933 sump (GTZ 4) that I am now using reads to 1½ gallons. Perhaps this is intended as an increase in the capacity on later models to resolve the loss of oil pressure following hard braking?

The sump was blanked off at the front and one gallon of water added to resemble the oil when hot, thin and in need of topping up. The sump was secured in place of the passenger's seat in a Mini so that the behaviour of the liquid under hard braking could be observed. From 50 mph to a standstill it was possible to make the liquid surge forward to an angle of 30°, starving the centre take-off; about 80% of it occupying the front compartment. The two upper holes in the baffle could be blanked off as although they assist the oil in its forward rush, when it also flows over the top of the baffle, they play no part in the slower return, which takes place entirely through the centre hole at the bottom.

Reducing the size of the centre hole delayed the surge slightly, but it was soon obvious that only complete blanking off could be guaranteed to keep sufficient oil in the centre compartment. Some sort of flap valve would do this but difficulties arise because of the take-off pipe to the pump passes through the hole. The problem was solved by fitting two swing doors which fit round the pipe when closed by the rush of oil, or as a friend termed, "lock gates". These gates were hinged on long 3/16 in. diameter spindles to reduce wear and enable a fairly small clearance to be maintained between them and at the base.

The gates were mounted on a thin plate fitted against the baffle, which incorporated a sloping roof projecting 2½ in. back from the baffle to prevent oil passing over the top or going through the two top holes. This makes one unit easily fitted to the front baffle by two bolts through the existing holes in the baffle. The plate was stiffened by a 3/16 in. thick mild steel strip which was tapped to take the bolts thus avoiding the use of nuts. The bolt heads were drilled and wired and ¼ in. mild steel strips used to span the baffle holes were fitted with small riveted pegs to locate the whole thing in the correct position and prevent it rising towards the big-ends.

In use it has proved to be as satisfactory as the experiments suggested and fortunately the lock gates make no audible noise when suddenly caused to close.

The rest of Hancock's painstaking report is so informative that I have quoted it here in full:

'Front Axle and Brakes

There does not appear to be any faults with the front axle. We have had trouble with the lubrication of the o/s brake shaft. The Bijur lubricator had not been passing any oil. This was taken out and a new one fitted which passed 4 drops per minute. The brake drums were found to be fouling the anchorage bolts of the brake shoes. These had been rubbing hard on the inside of the drum. We found that it was possible to reduce the length of the bolt by .0625 in. which gave us clearance. The condition of the brakes showed that they had been doing considerable work and inside the drums were covered with black powder. There was no sign of any water having entered the drum. The lubrication of the toggle shafts appeared to be quite O.K. It was necessary to adjust the brakes one notch of the mechanical adjustment. We could not discern any wear in the pivot bearings. These appeared to be in good condition. There was ample lubrication, the oil showing top and bottom of the bearings.

Front Springs and Fittings

Upon examination there was no fracture discernable on any of the leaves of the springs. The lubrication of shackles was O.K.

Front Axle Control Dampers

The loading of the front axle dampers is quite satisfactory for conditions over here. The front of the car has ridden very steady. There has been no occasion of the buffers hitting the axle hard. We have had the casing of the two front dampers break. This was fully expected before leaving Derby, and new dampers were promised as soon as the manufacture of these could be made in a different alloy. The anchorage bearings of the n/s shock damper has given considerable trouble, the bearings having worn very much which caused bad knocking at this point. The lubrication of this has not been good, the Bijur lubricator not passing sufficient oil. This has had to be attended to. There is also no oil getting to the ball ends on n/s and o/s. The oiling scheme for these ball ends does not appear to be good, they rely upon the oil escaping from the anchorage bearing going up the tube to the ball ends. This is almost impossible with the present design. We should strongly advocate returning to the oiling of the ball ends by a pipe leading along the damper arm, as was used on 12 EX. We found that the Bijur lubricating pipe, where attached to the banjo supplying the n/s pivot, the soldered joint had broken away.

Steering Column and Box 'E' Type

There do not appear to be any faults with the design of this. We have had no loss of oil from the box. Steering has been free and no tightening up has been noticed. We had on one occasion, approximately half way through the test, the pendulum lever work loose to the extent of ¾ of a turn of the nut. This has not since showed any further sign of becoming loose. The lubrication of the pendulum lever bearing and ball end appears to be ample. It was necessary to adjust the thrust of the steering column once during the mileage. The increased size of the steering wheel and the less diameter of the rim is a distinct improvement. The controls, klaxon button, have been free from any rattles. The anchorage of the steering column to the dashboard appears to be satisfactory. The column is kept very steady.

Flywheel and Clutch

We had considerable trouble with the clutch when the car was first run over here. The clutch would not disengage freely and it was very difficult to change gears. This was dismantled, the cause found to be due to the inner sliding housing of the Hoff No. 4224 ball bearing having picked up. This was made free and clutch re-assembled. We have had no further trouble with the clutch not stopping. The pick-up of the clutch we consider to be equal to the present

Phantom. There are signs of jaggering. There has been considerable wear in the pins and shackles connecting the clutch pedal to the clutch lever. These do not appear to have sufficient surface area. The slack that has developed caused a very objectionable noise when driving the car along. As these joints are not included in the Bijur lubrication they are apt to be overlooked. We should strongly recommend these joints to be covered with well oiled felt. This would exclude all dirt and keep the joints in a good lubricated condition. The lubrication of the thrust housing appears to be O.K. The failing of the starter motor to engage during part of the test burred up the teeth of the gear ring on the flywheel. These had to be attended to. The clutch brake has not been very effective owing to oil getting on to the brake surfaces. The oil has escaped from the rear bearing of the engine and has been flung by the flywheel all over the inside of the case. This should not happen when the oil leak has been stopped. The rubber fabric coupling from the clutch to the gearbox is a failure. A different method of holding the spiders will have to be obtained. At these positions the holes have become elongated to over twice the diameter of the bolt. This has been caused by the engine torque and the over-run torque.

Gear Box and Actuating Gear

Generally speaking, there has been no trouble with the gear box. The 3rd gear, although an entirely different noise from the present Phantom, is in our opinion quite agreeable, and we should say a very good gear. The other gears are quite passable, but slightly uneven. The reverse gear at times is very difficult to engage. We understand this has been made right at the Works since we left. Our chief trouble with the gearbox here is oil leaks from the speedometer drive housing, covers over change speed mechanism, and from the selector shaft housing. The top end cover of the change speed mechanism on the gear box should, we think be attached by bolts to the main cover. This is a joint entirely void of bolts, and a considerable leak of oil has taken place from this joint. The rear suspension of the gear box has not showed any signs of failure and is apparently satisfactory. The servo cams at one period became

dry, making the working of the servo jerky. The oil feeding of this does not appear to be entirely satisfactory, and we have found that a drop of oil occasionally on the cam faces is necessary. The linkage has operated satisfactorily, and up to the present has not showed any faults. When rear brakes are in a satisfactory condition, the pedal pressure required is light, the increased pedal pressure required as reported was due to the ineffectiveness of the rear brakes and the dry state of the cams as previously mentioned.

Propellor Shaft and Universal Joints

We have had no trouble whatsoever with this shaft. We cannot detect any play or wear in the mechanic's joints. Loss of oil from the joints after 5,000 miles was 2/3rd in the rear joint, 1/3rd in the front joint. At 9,000 miles the loss was 1/3rd in the rear, 1/3rd in the front. As far as we can ascertain, the oil escapes from the inside of the joints, there is no sign of any oil leaks from the outer surfaces of the joints.

Rear Axle

The front housing of the rear axle showed lateral play when examined. No end play was discernible. The brake actuating shafts have worked satisfactorily and are well lubricated. There has been a considerable oil leak through the o/s tube. This collected in the brake housing, fortunately not getting on to the brakes. On the n/s there was no sign of any oil leak. The rear axle casing and tubes are quite satisfactory.

Rear Brakes

The brakes when examined were in a very poor condition. The brake drum shields are ineffective for keeping water out of the drums. The shoes and inside the drums were covered with water and sludge, making the brakes ineffective. There is insufficient clearance between these covers and the bodywork. On the compression of the rear springs, the wing stay belts have fouled the shields to such an extent that the shields at this point have been torn. We cleared the bolts of the wing stays as much as possible, but they still foul. During our second examination the brakes and inside the drums were in the same condition.

Rear Brake Equalizing Mechanism

These appear to be satisfactory, and lubrication appears to be O.K.

Rear Springs and Fittings

We have examined the springs and cannot detect any flaws. The anchorage of the springs as far as we can ascertain shows no sign of wear. Lubrication is satisfactory. The rear spring clips have been examined twice to observe if any stretching had taken place. On both occasions they were quite O.K.

Rear Hydraulic Shock Dampers

There is a slight knock from the n/s rear damper. We have not observed any other faults and the poundage up to this mileage has remained as first set. The connection links have remained in a very good condition, and have not once required any attention during the mileage.

Rear Spare Wheel Carrier

There has been no sign of any weakness of the design, and on no occasion has there been any sign of the wheels becoming loose. We presume there is a design for a distance piece to replace one spare wheel if the occasion arises.

Petrol Tank

We have had no petrol leaks from the tank. The anchorage when examined was O.K. We have lost one filler cap during the mileage, and should advocate some method for preventing this. The suction does not allow us to use the last 1 to 1¼ gallons. We found that when we had this amount of petrol in the tank, we were sucking air instead of petrol. From what we can observe, the angle of the tube at the bottom is too acute, thus allowing air to enter the pipe instead of petrol. This can be easily remedied. We have not had any main or reserve working, as this mechanism was not finished when we left Derby. The rear luggage case is quite O.K.

Hand Brake Equalizing Mechanism

The equalizing shafts have operated satisfactorily. The bearing for the hand brake lever lubrication has not been satisfactory, the Bijur lubricator having become choked. This had to be attended to. The hand brake, when in good condition, *i.e.* dry, is effective.

Body Subframe

As already reported, the second spring clip of the front end of the rear springs fouled the subframe upon compression of the rear springs. This bent the under side of the subframe to approximately .500 in. To prevent any further damage this spring clip was taken off. This was fully reported to you in our previous report. The anchorage of the subframe to the main chassis frame has given no trouble, and appears to be quite satisfactory. There has been a slight settling down which has caused the two rear doors of the body dropping slightly, making them bind slightly when closing.

Electrical Equipment of the Car

The electrical equipment was not in the first place a success, the dynamo output was low and would not maintain sufficient charge for all-night driving. The head lamps are very good, but the bulb connections are not sufficiently robust to take the heavy current needed for those bulbs. We had the n/s centre contact entirely fail, this becoming so hot that the springs in the plunger became useless, which caused excessive heat and ruined the holder. We have had to fit temporarily a makeshift holder for this lamp. It should be pointed out to Lucas that the plungers and springs are not satisfactory for the heavy current used. The arrangement of the spot light in conjunction with the head lamps using the Bosch switch is very good. The Grebel spot lamp needs attention, the ball end for swivelling is too tight for the other part of the fittings. The inside fitting is too poor a job and unscrews itself, allowing the lamp to swing about in the socket. The Lucas side lamps are a neat design, but are not weatherproof. As far as we can judge, water enters through the front screwed cap. We have, during the test, found the inside of these lamps covered with dirty water. The starter motor was changed during the test. The new one fitted was considerably better, but on most occasions the button had to be pressed two or three times before an engagement was obtained. The return thump from the starter motor will have to be attended to. The battery box and fittings have not given any trouble. The magneto earth switch on several occasions gave the driver a shock when operating same. This was reported and it transpired that the handle of the switch was not on the earth side. This has since been corrected, a new switch being fitted. The green lamp is not functioning correctly. Before alterations to the wiring, it lit up under any conditions, it now lights up when battery is charged, but cannot be switched off. The cut-out points for controlling the dynamo and the green light cut-out points are in good condition. The spot lamp mounted on the o/s of the bodywork was very erratic in action. This was found to be due to there being no earth from the body to the frame. This should be observed and noted for any electrical fittings which require an earth when fitted to a body mounted on a subframe. A general examination at the end of 9,000 miles has not shown up any other serious faults. A final examination will be made when the car returns here after completing the last 1,000 miles with the Sales Officials.

The body work generally has stood up well. It should, however, be noted that Cellulose painting is useless for the under portion of the wings. On this car dirt and water thrown by the wheels has completely sand blasted the cellulose paint off the wings, leaving the bare metal. The front wings show distinct signs on the outer side where small stones, etc, have hit on the under side. The Bosch windscreen wipers have not given any trouble. They have been extensively used, and from our experience are so far the best we know of windscreen wipers.

Total Mileage of Car: 9,000
Average Petrol Consumption during the test: 10.58 m p g.
Total weight of the car complete with body (no passengers): 2 tons, 4 cwt 2 qrs Dunlop Buttress tyres 32 x 6.75 fitted. Tyre pressures: 40 lb front, 35 lb rear.
Average life of tyres during test: Front 9,500, Rear 8,000.'

PART II CHAPTER 3

The tests on 18 EX are completed and 19 EX is taken to Chateauroux for testing. 18 EX is delivered to Royce at Le Canadel, a description of Le Canadel and the set up there. 18 EX after Royce took delivery of this car. 19 EX on test at Chateauroux

As can be seen from the foregoing report made at the end of a strenuous 5,000 mile trial and inspection, the results were extraordinarily satisfactory, especially when it is borne in mind that this was a brand new and untried model and when the Experimental Department at Derby received it, they were delighted, as also were Royce and his team, as they knew that they were on the right lines and that all their hard work had not been in vain.

In the meantime 19 EX had arrived at Le Canadel for Royce's inspection and approval, it was driven straight to Villa Mimosa and arrived there on 5 January 1929. As was mentioned in the previous chapter the chassis was an exact replica of 18 EX but it suffered very badly from 'shake'; even transposing the whole of 18 EX on to 19 EX chassis did not cure this trouble. On the other hand, 18 EX was still perfectly satisfactory when the exchange was effected and Evernden says that he can only think that this was what the Works called a 'rogue' chassis.

There is something very odd in the record of this car, the Body Card at Conduit Street shows this chassis as carrying Sedanca de Ville coach-work supposedly ordered by Ivan Evernden from Hooper & Co, on 12 November 1928. I have also closely questioned Robotham about this car and he says that Hives would have gone mad if it had been suggested that any sort of Sedanca was to be put through a 10,000 mile test at Chateauroux; the bodies took a tremendous pounding and Hives did not like even a Landaulette body being sent on test. In fact, after a comparatively short time all four doors were screwed up and the testers had to climb into the car through one of the windows or, in the case of a saloon, they used the sunshine roof. This does sound quite incredible, but both Evernden and Robotham have explained to me that they did not dare risk losing a valuable car in an accident, which could quite easily have happened if one of the doors had suddenly flown open on the road whilst the car was being driven at high speed.

The second part of the 10,000 mile test of 18 EX proved to be extremely satisfactory, so much so that Hancock decided the only way to really discover any possible defects, was to take the body off the chassis, removing the wings and all running gear, etc, and then go through it with a fine tooth comb. On 26th January he wrote to Hives to say that 'everything has gone back very nicely and the appearance of the car is as new', but they had not yet tried the car on the road again, they were so satisfied with 18 EX that the sole modifications which they recommended should be made on subsequent EX chassis were to the engine mountings and the exhaust system, with slight modifications to the starter motor, and the shock absorber casings.

On 15 January 1929, Hives wrote to Hancock saying that it had now been agreed that the new 'Super Sports' model was to be put into production and material ordered immediately. Also that it was proposed to prepare a list of the work, one showing on which part it was absolutely safe to proceed, a second which would give what parts were to be proceeded with slowly and a third list detailing which parts should be held up until further research had been accomplished.

This is really quite amazing, the 'Super Sports' had only gone on the road in December

1928 and now, about one month later, and with only two chassis, 18 and 19 EX, on the road, though the former had been subjected to extremely severe testing, the Company took the enormous decision to go ahead with production of this new model. It only goes to show how very well pleased they were with it and what tremendous confidence they were given by its behaviour under strenuous testing.

In this letter dated 15 January 1929, Hives also wrote as follows: 'When you have got 18 EX complete again, we should like you to arrange to have some photographs taken as we have no record of this car here and it is likely to be in France for some time. We want some good photographs taken in various positions'. It will be recalled that there had been a good deal of difficulty with the completion of the car by the coachbuilders, with the result that there was no opportunity for the usual coachbuilders' photographs to be taken. Hancock made the necessary arrangements with a local photographer, the prints came out very well and Hives, who was pleased with them, wrote and suggested that the plates should be left with the photographer, thinking they could always order any more prints they needed.

This, as it has turned out all these years later, proved a most unfortunate decision, as the set of prints of 18 EX sent to the Experimental Department at Derby have long since disappeared and amongst the Rolls-Royce Company's vast photographic file there is no photograph of 18 EX, except the one taken at Hyere showing the late Sir Henry Royce standing beside the car, captioned 'Sir Henry drives in the South of France'. Unfortunately, this photograph does not show the registration number of the car and as Derby always used chassis numbers for reference purposes, it seems to be quite impossible to find out exactly what has happened to this car. Since the above was written, after much difficulty two photographs of 18 EX have come to light, both of which are included in this Book.

On 24 January 1929, Hives wrote to Royce, sending copies of the letter to Basil Johnson,* Sidgreaves† and Wormald, part of which reads as follows: 'We have now six of these "S.S" chassis completed. 18 EX and 19 EX are in France. 20 EX is being used for test at Derby. This car is fitted with a Hooper limousine body.

21 EX, 22 EX and 23 EX are still chassis. They have been held up for Hypoid bevels for the rear axle. We have now received six more sets of Hypoid gears so that these chassis will all be available for road test at the end of this week. The bodies for these cars are practically ready.

We are endeavouring to complete 21 EX with all the modifications which have been instructed, which we hope will make this car a model of the first cars the Works will produce. As soon as the car is ready it will be tried by the various officials in England and sent to Le Canadel, afterwards going to Chateauroux for road test. We expect to have this car in France about the second week in February.'

This letter gives the position at this time of the way the production of the model, which was later to be known as the Phantom II, was proceeding; but in the meantime we will revert once again to 18 EX; the extract of 1 February 1929, taken from the experimental file of this chassis shows that the car set off to Villa Mimosa at Le Canadel with Hancock at the wheel and was handed over to Royce with a speedometer reading of 12,419 miles. Royce employed a chauffeur, Frank Dodds, who was therefore the one who drove the car most of the time. Royce was delighted with 18 EX and on 6 February 1929, he wrote to Hives, sending copies of the letter to Elliott, Sidgreaves, Day, Wormald, Cowan, Harvey Bailey, Percy Northey and Commdr Briggs, an extract from which reads as follows:

'18 EX. This is the car that has done 10,000 miles in France and altogether some few thousand more.

It has a Barker close coupled 4-seater body with leather top and it is the finest car that I have ever been in. For my use it is the best type of body.

The engine and whole chassis has improved with running and one hardly feels the engine, it is remarkably silent (car standing) or at speed.

We are running the car every day for a few hours in the mountains, but for the secrecy would let it be seen on the Riviera, because it

*Basil Johnson or BJ retired from Managing Director January 31st 1929
†Sidgreaves or Sg became Managing Director of R-R Ltd on January 14th 1929

cannot help but attract much admiration.

I compliment Mr Evernden especially on the coachwork and Mr Nutt.*

Signed 'R'.'

Le Canadel lies on the N 559 some 12 miles west of St Tropez and about 75 miles west of Cannes; the nearest small town, Le Lavandou, is about 6 miles west of Le Canadel and is the principal shopping centre for this district, it has always been a great favourite with yachtsmen and there is now a large marina there.

At the time of writing Le Canadel itself is rapidly expanding and small residential villas are being built up the hillside overlooking the sea. These are designed in the old Provencal style, and will blend in quite well when the scars of development have healed.

Everywhere there are signs proclaiming that there are villas and land for sale; there is one general store, a small recently built church and two Hotels. The main road through the centre has been widened since 'R's day', but there is still a small and secluded unspoilt beach with good bathing and a stretch of sand. The views are magnificent and at the time that Royce lived at Villa Mimosa, it must have been a delightful and remote place, with just the beach and the fragrant hillside, covered with cork trees, olive bushes and wild mimosa, with rosemary and thyme everywhere.

The tract of land which Claude Johnson bought in 1909 has not been developed in any way and is just as it was in 1910.

On approaching Le Canadel from Cannes, almost at the end of the village there is a turn to the right which curves steeply back on its tracks and is called 'The Avenue de la Corniche'. It is signposted 'La Mole' road No. D 27. Having rounded the bend on the D 27 the first house on the right hand side is still called 'Le Rossignol' where Royce's staff lived, a little further up on the left hand side of the road the outlines of the drawing office 'Le Bureau' can just be discerned through the trees, (this building is actually in the grounds of Royce's villa) which is just beyond it on the left. There is a sharp left-handed turn into 'R's' Villa Mimosa, which is now called 'Sans Peyre' and is partly screened from the road

*Mr Nutt was the Managing Director of Barker & Co Ltd

with blue shutters the same as 'Le Bureau'; both are owned by the same person and kept in good repair. Continuing up the Avenue de la Corniche for a short distance, another drive-way is to be seen on the left, this leads to 'Villa Jaune', the first of the villas to be built there.

This house is far and away one of the most palatial at Le Canadel and has a good deal of land; unfortunately it is in the most shocking state of disrepair, nearly all the wooden verandahs are rotten, and in fact one has completely collapsed, it has been empty for ten years and has been for sale all this time. It is sad to see it all so derelict as it must have been a delightful place with a lovely view over the Bay.

The road, which is very narrow, steep and winding, continues past where the old Grand Hotel was situated before it was burnt prior to the 1939 War, (there is now a block of flats on the site) and climbs for about four miles over the Col du Canadel with many acute hair-pin bends, the scenery is magnificent and miles of coastline can be seen from the top. The road descends tortuously down the mountain through a forest of cork, oak and olive trees until finally it reaches a flat, plain and the small town of La Mole. It is possible also from the top of the Pass to go to the left, instead of straight on to La Mole, there the road meanders about the mountain and eventually comes down to the coast near Le Lavandou.

These are obviously the mountains to which 'R' refers in his letter; in his day no doubt the road was not tarred and it would be quite a trial taking a big car over this route, today the whole is tarmacadam but the drop is sheer and the road unfenced, so care is needed when passing another car. Once over the top of the Col and making the descent, it is ideal for a sheltered picnic, when the wind is blowing strongly from the Mediterranean, and it is easy to imagine the party from Le Canadel enjoying the country in this way.

It is interesting to note that at the time of the Normandy invasion by allied troops, landings also took place at Le Canadel. These were North African troops and on the beach where 'R' was so fond of picnicing there are monuments to commemorate this event, and there is a small Cemetery by the main road, N 559 ('For those who gave their lives that the World would be free from the Nazi menace').

When Claude Johnson bought the land in 1909 the road, N 559, cut through the lower extremity of his property and on the opposite side of the road from the Avenue de la Corniche facing on to the road, with its back to the sea, is the garage where the cars were kept, now converted into a private dwelling house. It was here that the electric light engine and batteries which supplied the lighting for all the villas were installed.

It was in these surroundings that 18 EX underwent stringent tests and when Royce returned to West Wittering in the spring, Dodds took the car back to Derby on 17 May 1929, when the speedometer was showing 17,757 miles. It would appear that whilst Royce was at West Wittering he had other cars at his disposal, as 18 EX remained at Derby all summer until it returned to Le Canadel on 10 December 1929, showing 27,130 miles, so it must have been used by the Experimental Department. The mileage recorded was 38,267 when the car arrived back at West Wittering with Royce on 15 May 1930, so whilst at Villa Mimosa the car was again used extensively. Having been up at Derby for checking, 18 EX returned to West Wittering on 6 June 1930 with the speedometer reading 40,462 miles; it was back at Derby later in the year and on 29 November 1930, the speedometer was showing 40,711 miles when the car went direct from Derby to Southampton. On 13 January 1931, at Le Canadel, the speedometer recorded 41,448, and it returned to Derby on 9 April 1931, showing 48,761, the last entry made is for 14 September 1931, when the speedometer showed 53,210 miles. So it would appear that the car, only spent two winters with 'R' in the South of France. The radiator had been changed to one of Staybrite steel in 1930 and all parts, both exterior and interior, gear lever, hand brake, steering column, 'E' type, were chromium plated. The engine had also been changed in 1930 for Royce to try, to Unit No. 17, which was of a slightly different type with heavier crankshaft.

What exactly happened to 18 EX after this date is not known, there are people in the Sales Department at Conduit Street who can remember the car clearly, but unfortunately no-one can remember the registration number or to whom the car was sold. There is however one further entry in Bill Trimming's records at Crewe, it reads as follows: 'August 30th 1937 - new steering wheel fitted'.

I am most grateful to Ian Rimmer for the information that the Index number was CH7980 and that the chassis No. on being handed over to Sales, was changed to EX-69 GX.

There the story of 18 EX must rest, unless someone can come forward to provide further information and complete the story.

19 EX

From all the reports it would appear that 19 EX spent its entire life as an experimental car, all sorts of modifications were made to it over the years, but unfortunately there is no mention of the coachwork and whether this was changed or not I am afraid I have not been able to discover. On 5 February 1929, Hancock was writing to Hives saying that 19 EX had manifested the same symptoms as 18 EX, a very rough period at 70 mph upwards, and he remarks that generally speaking 18 EX is the better car. By 10 February 1929, 19 EX had completed 5,000 miles and Hancock was recalled to Derby as the chassis was being re-erected and the weather became appalling, as the following letter shows.

To Mr Hancock. Since you left Chateauroux the weather has been all against road testing and the job is practically at a standstill. There is about a foot of snow on the ground and everywhere is frozen up. For instance, when I noticed such a change in the weather I immediately ran the water off the engine (this was on Monday night). Tuesday morning, when we turned in at the garage the wash-tap was frozen up. It is still the same now. There was 25º of frost in the garage and it has been the same each day. No sign of the weather becoming warmer. I have not ventured to run the car since Monday - not even to fill the radiator in case of damage to engine. Tonight the roads are a mass of frozen snow and ice and looks likely to be for some time.

With expecting you turning up every day since Tuesday made me hang on - had I not received your note yesterday, would have wired you as I was getting very anxious about matters - as you understand, me being strange on this job makes things a little difficult to know exactly how to carry on.

We have completed the work on gear-box, servo

and brakes as far as possible and have done most of the lubrication investigations. At present I have both rear hubs and rear brake shafts out, tomorrow will erect these. Have we to dismantle water pump, starter motor, clutch trunion and brake equalizing shafts? All the rest is done. As regards bijur drip tests - this is altogether out of the question at present. The oil is so thick and in a congealed condition owing to the low temperature. All the bijur drip valves tested on the one shot only pass one drop of oil in four to six minutes. I have no information as to the correct amount each bijur valve should pass per minute - also is it necessary to open out bijur where necessary. Will you wire instructions, as you will note the job is practically at a standstill, what to do. It will be Monday before you get this and by the time we get a reply by post, a week will be passed by. Please reply and let me know more definite instructions.

I am making up a report on the work completed and will send it on to you. We have cured oil leaks from gear-box by felting baffle plate on lid and 1 and 2 gears - remaking all face joints and most important fit a vent on box. By fitting a vent cured oil from entering servo. The oil entered the servo by way of the shaft in the gear-box, the oil being pumped out caused by pressure in box.

It's been hell working in the garage this week - the stove comes in very useful in the way of warming spanners and tools. Will dry up now before I say something rude. Hope you are well. All your staff here have colds.

Yours faithfully,

J McStay.

Three years later on 24 March 1932, 19 EX had been rebuilt in accordance with current trends. In order to make the car easier to drive and to give it better acceleration with more power it was fitted with:

1 Synchromesh gear-box
2 R-R expanding carburetter
3 Crankshaft with balance weights and larger journals
4 Higher compression ratio
5 New camshafts
6 Cast iron brake drums
7 Flexible shackles

and one month later, on 22 April 1932, having been tested in Derbyshire, the car had been taken to Brooklands and Hives was writing to Royce as follows:

'This car was tested yesterday at Brooklands by Sidgreaves, Percy Northey, Robotham and myself.

There was a high wind which made it unsatisfactory for recording accurate speeds. The best laps speed on 19 EX was 84.8 mph, the best speed over the half mile in favourable wind was 91.5 mph. The car was certainly faster than the standard production Continental as we had one of these on the track at the same time. It was much too early to give any definite figures as regards increased performance obtained by the use of R-R semi-expanding carburetter. So far the results are not as good as with the S U but this is no more than what we would expect from the time this carburetter has been on test.

The engine was remarkably smooth at all speeds. The steering and the brakes were very good.

The following is a specification of this car:

Frame This has the following modifications compared with the modern standard one. 1. stiffners from frame to dash to suit spare wheel carriers. 2. road springs. These are the high-rating continental type. 3. pedals. Cantilever support for pedals. 4. petrol tank. Smith electric petrol gauge. Control for reserve from dashboard. 5. hydraulic dampers. Present standard type with split piston. Set to high pressure at 115 lb. Low pressure 90 lb front and rear.
6. Lucas Buzzer type horn fitted under front apron.
7. Exhaust fittings. Exhaust manifold made of chrome iron.
8. Radiator. Copper hexagon tubes.
9. Bonnet. Rivetless bonnet overhanging dashboard 6 in.
10. Bonnet fasteners. These have been bought out. There has been a certain amount of discussion on the cost of our present fasteners. The price we have been given is £3.10.6d. per set fitted. The price we paid for the four fasteners on 19 EX was 6.4d. per set. It is not proposed to standardise these fasteners, the object is to gain some experience with them.
11. Flexible spring shackle.
12. Brakes. Cast iron brake drums front and rear, Lake and Elliot material. Anti-squeak brake shoes front and rear.
13. Rear Axle. 12/41 ratio instead of standard 11/41.
14. Road wheels. 19 in. rims in place of 20 in. rims with two rose of spokes (cheaper construction.
15. Gearbox. Synchromesh 10° angle cones.

Engine Unit
Larger diameter crankshaft 2.8 in. diameter journals 2.37 in.
Crankshaft balanced 6/8 scheme.
Standard crankcase bored out.
Pistons standard.
Connectings Rods Standard except to suit larger

crankpins. Cylinder head, modified to give compression ratio 5.25 to 1.
Carburetter R-R semi-expanding.
Petrol pump to Le Canadel, 2961.

Electrical section

A separate report has been sent on this. Instrument Parch. The instrument patch fitted to 19 EX has been made from Pressings instead of aluminium die-castings. The chief object of this is to reduce cost. The instruments except the ammeter have been supplied by Messrs Smith. It is proposed to adopt these instruments on the 25 h p and so far nothing has been decided on the Phantom II. The saving with the sheet metal patch and Smiths instruments is approximately £10 per car.

This car is fitted with permanent D W S jacks. We have an insistent demand from customers which is becoming more and more definite, that they require something much better than the ordinary jack which we supply.

After trying several different schemes, those fitted to 19 EX are the best we can try. It is not proposed to standardize them, but we want to gain experience so that we are in a position to recommend them.

It is expected that it will be necessary to order more Phantom II material in about 6 weeks time. Therefore it will be necessary for 19 EX to complete a 10,000 miles Test as soon as possible in order that these improvements can be incorporated in future production.

By 14 July 1932, 19 EX had completed a further 5,000 mile test at Chateauroux, the car was accompanied by 60 JS together with chassis 28 MS, the latter was being used by Mr Pass of Pass & Joyce and all three cars were sent on an extended tour of the Alps, the Experimental Department wished to know how 19 EX performed on this test against two standard production Continental Type chassis, unfortunately, the report on this trip is not on the file.

On 14 February 1933, 19 EX was on test again at Chateauroux, the engine had been changed, an AC petrol pump had been fitted and thermostatic radiator shutters, a fully automatic lubrication system had also been installed and another rating of Continental type springing, so that the car bore no resemblance whatsoever to the chassis which had originally been taken down to Le Canadel for Royce's inspection four years previously on 5 January 1929.

On 26 EX and other Continental type chassis, which were being used for continuous high speed across France, the ordinary standard Rolls-Royce shock absorbers were used, in conjunction with a set of Hartfords which could be screwed up hard, to make the springs really taut for high speeds on the long straight roads; but now it was intended to dispense with the Hartfords and fit a variable controlled shock damper, the poundages of which could be altered by a small lever on top of the steering column. The Experimental Department at Derby had already had trouble with this type of shock absorber as several had burst owing to the very high pressures, but they felt that they had at last overcome this, so 19 EX was sent to Chateauroux with a note, part of which reads: 'We should like to have a report from you comparing 19 EX having Governor shock dampers and no Hartfords, *i.e.* 19 EX when you had it previously in France having the old type dampers and Hartfords'.

Unfortunately, whilst being tested, a back tyre burst which threw the car all over the road it went out of control and was involved in a very bad accident, which made it a write-off. It was consigned back to Derby by rail and there 'reduced to produce'. This was very bad luck, as work experimenting with shock dampers for Continental springing was just becoming interesting and the Experimental Department had a number of new pieces they wished to try out on 19 EX, but this was the end of the car's career and another chassis No. 85 JS, a production one, had to carry on with the work.

PART II CHAPTER 4

The experimental Phantom II chassis Nos. 20 EX, 21 EX, 22 EX and 23 EX. With the closing down of Springfield two further experimental chassis are built especially for the American market 24 EX and 25 EX. Hives takes 25 EX to America, the sale of this chassis and the re-building of it

20 EX

The third experimental Phantom II chassis 20 EX, carried an Enclosed Limousine body by Hooper & Co, and was representative of the big chauffeur-driven carriage with which the Company intended to replace the 'New Phantom'. It was fitted with 'C' type steering and finished in dark blue and black, with dark blue vaumol leather throughout the interior, the headlamps, wing lamps and tail lamps all had a black finish so as to save cleaning.

This car was on test at Derby in June 1929, it had a long chassis with sub-frame, and the total unladen weight was 47 cwt, 3 qrs, - lb. It spent its entire life shuttling between Derby and Chateauroux on test and on 12 September 1934, Hives wrote to Cowan of the sales department as follows:

'Proposed getting rid of 20 EX, the car has a very old fashioned type of body, there are several experimental pieces on it which should be taken off. We have had an offer of £400 for it from a local undertaker. Repair depot have given us a price of £30 to standardize it. Let me know as soon as possible if you are interested'.

On 21 September 1934, Hives was writing to say that the undertakers felt the price was too high and it was decided to do up the Hooper Limousine body and dispose of the car in London. The experimental pieces to be removed were as follows:

1 Gear box experimental. Silent second jumps out of gear.
2 Shock absorber system.
3 Front axle and brakes complete.
4 Flywheel with thin flange.
5 AC type petrol pump and timing case.
6 Cylinder head and valves.
7 Petrol piping autovac required.
8 Exhaust swan neck.
9 Check spring drive damping load.

The last recorded speedometer reading in the Log Book of the Experimental Department, taken on 22 September 1934, shows a reading of 55,787; it is interesting to note that, just six months before, on 19 March 1934, this chassis was completing its thirty sixth test for a new type of exhaust silencer. The Index number was CH8034. Again, as in the case of 19 EX, unfortunately this is where my present knowledge of the car finishes.

21 EX

Chassis 21 EX was also completed as a big chauffeur-driven car, which had a long wheelbase with a body sub-frame but which carried an Enclosed Drive Limousine by Barker & Co, finished in grey and black, with cloth upholstery throughout, and 'D' type steering. The coachbuilders had received their instructions from Ivan Evernden on 29 December 1928, and the complete vehicle weighed 48 cwt 2 qrs. It also had black Lucas lamps, but was fitted with a black F W B stoplight set; the registration number was CH 8147. It was received by the Experimental Department on 21 January 1929, and was one of the earliest experimental Phantom II chassis which they quickly finished testing. On 21 December 1929 when the car had run 16,094 miles it was sent to Lillie Hall to be disposed of and subsequently became a School of Instruction car and was last heard of in 1954 as the property of J Pennington, Esq, 1, Knighton Road, Richard Kelly Drive, Liverpool, so what happened to it after it was released by the School of Instruction and where it is now is a matter of conjecture.

22 EX

Like its two predecessors, 22 EX was a long chassis with body sub-frame, initially fitted with a Hooper Enclosed Landaulette, finished in grey and black with cloth to the rear interior and black leather to the front; the coachbuilders received their instructions for this body from Ivan Evernden on 29 December 1928. It had 'C' type steering and was fitted with black lamps throughout as these had proved practical on the previous cars, but in this case the Lucas P 100 headlamps had bi-focal dipping. The finished body cost £875. Index number CH8189.

On 2 May 1929, the car had completed 10,000 miles in France and Hancock was complaining that the springing of the car was too light, being insufficiently dampened, which caused violent bumping at the rear and consequently made the steering unstable. The riding quality was improved by altering the shock absorbers at the rear. The K S Telegauge was unreliable after the first day's run and was soon completely useless, which they discovered was due to the failure of cement at the top of the glass tube. The front brakes became too fierce during the test and made braking at medium and high speeds dangerous, and the starter motor failed to function after the first five day's run and failed altogether after ten days.

The steering very quickly became stiff and, after five days running, almost seized up completely on the ball ends of the cross steering tube; drastic alterations to the amount of oil supplied to these parts proved successful during the remainder of the test.

The propeller shaft caused periods of uneven running through loss of oil in the joints and until it was possible to make some oil change, the vibration still remained and could be felt through the rear floorboards.

The headlamps gave considerable trouble from the start. Hancock thought that the dimming arrangement, by use of two filaments, was not as good as a centre spot light, also he found the bulbs unreliable. One night four bulbs gave out and he had to finish the test on one dimmed headlight.

His summing up of this car was that the general running was noisier and had not the smooth gliding qualities of previous Phantoms, which he felt was due to dry ball races. He found the engine roughness ceased at over 60 mph but was still not as he would like it to be. He discovered that the shutters jammed on the radiator after 1,500 miles, due to dirt and dust in the bearings - he remarks that they had not had this trouble before, but after thorough cleaning the trouble did not recur. He was pleased with the gears, saying they were particularly good for tone, and also found the clutch smooth but prone to slip after the universal joints had been oiled.

This chassis had one rear mounted spare wheel with the new type of carrier designed by Evernden at Royce's special request, but Hancock observed that one spare wheel was no good for Continental touring as they had had two punctures in one day! Finally he criticized the bodywork, saying that that type of body quickly became full of rattles in the joints, etc, for letting the rear portion of the head down, and so made it unsuitable for touring purposes. He also complained bitterly about the quick signalling window, which was a Hooper patent and which they fitted on many cars carrying their coachwork for several years. This entailed the lower quarter of the driver's window being in a frame of its own, which could be lowered independently of the main glass, and would give just sufficient aperture above the wood fillet on the door to allow the driver to put his hand out. The object of this arrangement was that in bad weather the driver was able to give hand signals whilst the window on the driver's door was fully closed to prevent draughts. It must be remebered that this idea was before mechanical direction indicators were invented.

It is quite obvious that this Hooper Landaulette body was not able to stand up to the poundings it received at Chateauroux, as, in February 1933, it was removed from the chassis of 22 EX and a Park Ward limousine, which had formerly been mounted on 25 EX, was fitted in its place; with this body, the car continued to run in the hands of the Experimental Department until April 1935, when it was put back to standard design and sold to Jack Barclay Ltd, by Lillie Hall for £1,325. An interesting point is that the car was re-registered when sold and that the two years guarantee issued with it was from the date of delivery to Jack Barclay's customer. The Body Card reads: 'Complete car sold as it stands, the whole in second-hand condition for £1,325'. As far as the chassis was concerned it would have been brought right up to the latest specification for Phantom IIs, unfortunately neither its original registration number nor the number under which it was re-registered are known, so it is not possible to know whether 22 EX is still in existence or not.

23 EX

Like the others, 23 EX had a long wheelbase and sub-frame, it was completed as an Open Tourer by the Carlton Carriage Co, and finished in French grey, although originally it was to have been buff and black. The steering position was noted as 'special' and the lamps were finished in nickel which was an innovation as all the others had black lamps. Ivan Evernden originally gave instructions to the coachbuilder on 28 December 1928. After various tests had been carried out nearly a year later, on 29 November 1929, this chassis was sent for a 10,000 mile test at Chateauroux, with the following improvements incorporated in it.

1 Larger diameter crankshaft.
2 Improved Low Inertia slipper wheel.
3 Radiator with automatic shutters. Filter in top of radiator.
4 Extra oiling for starting.
5 Improved clutch.
6 Exhaust heat to carburetter.
7 New exhaust system.
8 20 in. wheels, 7 in. diameter tyres.
9 Staybrite and chromium finish.
10 Spare wheel and luggage carrier.
11 Radiator filter. It had been suggested that it would be better to have a filter to clean than let the matrix act as a filter.
12 Central lubrication.
13 Modified shape of radiator and fittings.
14 Shock absorbers.

Trouble had been experienced with loss of water and the blocking of radiators, hence the filter, and from this, on analysis, the water in the radiator was found to contain as follows:

Disintegrated rubber	50%
Aluminium turnings	25%
Aluminium Oxide (hydrated)	20%
Iron oxide	5%
Copper and Zinc oxide	5%

It was decided finally to do away with the filter, as it was not really very satisfactory, and the radiator was still choking.

On 11 May 1930, Hancock drove 23 EX from Paris to Chateauroux and he said that he considered that 24 EX was 50% a better car than 23 EX. The following year, 1931, on 14 May, 23 EX returned to the U K, she gave no more coolant problems but it was decided that, as the car had so many advanced features, it could not be sold, but was to be stored. Two days later, however, there was a change of plan. It was decided 23 EX would be re-bodied as a closed car and then sold, the open touring body by the Carlton Carriage Co, would then be sold separately.

So the chassis was rebuilt as a standard production model and came off test on 10 August 1931, the new coachwork was a Sedanca de Ville by Thrupp & Maberly, finished in black with horizontal mouldings, fine lined in cream, with cream wire wheels; the interior was soft brown leather to the driver's compartment, and cloth for the rear. All fittings were untarnishable and the steering position was 'E'. The new body cost £795 and the car was bought by Jack Barclay Ltd, on 12 May 1932, for £1,650. It was last heard of in the hands of Messrs Woodall, Nicholson of Halifax in 1950, this is the firm who specialize in building hearse bodies on Rolls-Royce chassis.

24 EX

As far as coachwork was concerned, 24 EX was a replica of 18 EX in that it was originally a Barker Close Coupled Sports saloon mounted on the long wheel base chassis and finished in two shades of grey, but there was one significant difference; this chassis was left-hand drive with centre-change and hand brake — there is an illustration of this car in *The Autocar* showing the centre-change gearbox.

This chassis and the succeeding one, 25 EX, were built expressly for the American market. In Part I it has already been seen what had happened at Springfield, the cost of tooling-up for the Phantom II to be manufactured there, which owing to the small volume of sales had not been worth while. So the same practice was carried out at Derby with the left-hand drive Phantom II as had been used at Springfield with the 'New Phantom'. The new car was not just a left-hand drive Phantom II with a centre change gearbox, everything was changed over just as it had been with the 'New Phantom' that had been manufactured at Springfield, (incidentally when in production the 'Silver Ghost' type had been known as the 40/50 at Springfield and when the Phantom I first appeared there, it was known as the 40/65 to distinguish it from the previous model).

On 27 April 1930, Hancock was writing from Chateauroux to say that they were again having problems with the radiator and that it had been necessary to take it off, tip it upside down and back flush it thoroughly. 24 EX had a different type of radiator and it would appear that this was not so satisfactory as the radiator on 21 EX, which had become standard production for the Phantom II. A month later, on 16 May 1930, Hancock wrote to Hives with reference to the springing on 23 EX and 24 EX as follows:

There is as much difference, as the saying goes, between chalk and cheese, in the springing of these two cars and the steadiness of the front. It has been forcibly brought to our notice, after making the alterations, to the radiator mountings on 24 EX.

Taking the two cars over the same route, whilst the radiator on 24 EX is more perfectly steady, the wingss and headlamps are joggling considerably. In fact, the movement is extremely bad and is not a production job. Taking 23 EX at exactly the same speed and on the same road, the radiator is 99% steady, as also are the wings and headlamps, etc.

There is an entire difference between the steadiness and the riding of the front between the two cars, as, against this, the general comfort both in the front and rear seats is 50% better in 24 EX than in 23 EX. 24 EX gives you the soft silky riding. At the same time, the car is holding the road quite O.K.

On the other hand, 23 EX is 50% harsher riding both in the front and in the rear and until we brought the poundage of the S/A up did not hold the road. The back would at the slightest provocation jazz straight across the road when running on a poor surface. We never knew when to expect this, it does not do this with the shock absorbers loads increased.

The impression given on 23 EX is that the springs have lost their silkiness through the leather becoming rusty and not being lubricated. That is the impression, but the real difference is in the two types of springing. We hope you can appreciate the difference we have endeavoured to give you.

Two months later 24 EX was taken to Montlhery Track for tests of water temperature, loss of coolant, etc. The car was driven flat out, with bonnet shutters open and closed, the thermostat removed, the ignition in various positions and with various grades of petrol. In all, 18 tests were made with the car. The temperature of the water in the top and bottom of the radiator was taken, together with temperature of oil and temperature of atmosphere, and the car proved satisfactory in all these.

The following year the car was rebuilt to be used as a Paris 'Trials Car', with a new Sedanca de Ville body by Carrosserie Fernandez.

Having been completely rebuilt as a standard production Phantom II, the chassis passed off test on 29 August 1931, and on 1 September 1931, was shipped from London to Boulogne aboard the S.S. *Silver Thorn* for permanent entry to France. It was still left-hand drive with 'E' type steering position. The chassis fittings were untarnishable throughout, and an R-R mascot in chromium plate was added, but there was no luggage carrier fitted. The Sedanca de Ville body was finished in deep crimson lake below the waist, with black mouldings, head, wings and petrol tank. The cloth interior in the rear of the car was the same as that in Sidgreave's personal car, 58 GN, and the driver's compartment was in red leather to match the crimson lake. The vehicle was completed one week before the Paris Show, which opened in October 1931. The chassis had been sold for the price of £900, which had been agreed by Sidgreaves and it became the property of Mr Blackman, Hotel Plaza Athene, Paris. It would appear that the car survived the German Occupation of France, as a letter which I received from Ron Haynes, dated 29 January 1970, states that spares were needed for this chassis in Paris in 1948.

25 EX

The second experimental Phantom II chassis which was given left-hand drive with a centre change gearbox was 25 EX, this one still survives in America, though very considerable changes have been made in it. It was built specially for Hives to take out to America to try alongside the current model 'New Phantom' which was still being manufactured at the Springfield Works in Massachussetts.

25 EX was completed in July 1930 as an Enclosed Drive Limousine by Park Ward, finished in black with an ivory white line and upholstered throughout in brown furniture hide, the steering position was 'E' and all exterior fittings were chromium plated and the interior fittings were finished in satin silver, there was an absolute minimum of woodwork, laminated glass was used throughout and extra tool boxes were specially requested. The price of the body was £800. There was no body sub-frame and no exhaust cut-out. As originally built, the car was mounted on 700 x 19 tyres, but these did not give good results and so the wheels were changed to ones of 20 in. The car was first licensed July 1930 and given the Derby registration number CH 9378.

As soon as 25 EX had done some preliminary running around Derbyshire to make certain everything was in order, Hives was anxious to take the car out to America by the first available boat. This was the famous old record breaking *Mauretania,* which had held the Blue Riband of the Atlantic from 1907 to 1929. The *Mauretania* was then operating the Cunard Steamship Company's express service to New York in conjunction with the *Aquitania* and *Berengaria* from Southampton, but unfortunately it was discovered that the apertures of the holds aboard the *Mauretania* did not allow access for such a large car as a Phantom II. Incidentally, it is interesting to note that *Mauretania* and her sister ship *Lusitania,* were both built in 1907, just before the time when wealthy people travelling across the Atlantic wished to take their motor cars with them, so, the White Star Liners *Olympic* and *Titanic* built in 1911 were the first Atlantic liners to incorporate special accomodation for the carriage of motor cars.

Hives very quickly discovered that the White Star Liner *Homeric* (ex-*Columbus*, an ex-German vessel taken over as war reparation) was capable of carrying the car, so he and 25 EX sailed from Southampton aboard her on 28 October 1930 bound for New York.

After a very pleasant crossing he landed at New York and drove straight up to Springfield.

The springing of the car had been very good in England, but the wavelength of the corrugations of the roads in the United States was quite different and he was disappointed in the way the car rode. He was very surprised too to find that, when tried out against a current Springfield 'New Phantom' carrying limousine coachwork, the latter had much better acceleration and rode far better, though 25 EX was actually faster on maximum speeds. At the same time he was interested to see how many women drove their own cars and it seemed to him that there would be a big sale in America for the 20/25 as it would provide an ideal high-class car for a lady, as though so many women drove, they did not like driving cars as large as a 40/50 with the parking problems in towns. Unfortunately though, when the matter was thoroughly examined and discussed, Hives' excellent idea of a good market for the 20/25 was completely squashed by the freight, customs and import duty charges on the smaller model. When Hives returned to England he brought 25 EX with him and on 19 May 1931, fitted with an AC petrol pump the car was sent to Chateauroux for her first 10,000 mile test in France.

By 2 January 1933, the chassis had run 60,597 miles and it was decided to remove the Park Ward Limousine body and to transfer it on to 22 EX which had formerly carried a Hooper Landaulette.

On 4 May 1933, having been made into a standard production Phantom II, but retaining left-hand drive the chassis passed its final test and was sold to Messrs Barker & Co, Ltd, the coachbuilders, who in turn sold the chassis to a Mr J Eskdale Fishburn, an American, who was living at 142, Piccadilly, London W1. It would appear that Fishburn wanted the car completed with a sporting open touring body before Easter, but as Messrs Barker & Co, had so much work on hand at this time, they found it was quite impossible to do this, so another coachbuilder had to be found to build the new bodywork, and the chassis was delivered to Messrs Whittingham & Mitchell in the King Road, Chelsea, London SW3.

This firm, then a comparatively new one, specialized in building drop-head coupes and open tourers of a sporting nature on such chassis as Wolseley Hornet, the small Vauxhall 12/6, Singer, Rover, Talbot, etc, for the man who wanted something different; this firm was not one of the leading coachbuilders by any means, but just one of the many firms which came into existence owing to the demand for specialized coachwork between the Wars; they exhibited at the London Motor Shows 1934, 1935, 1936, 1937 and 1938, but, when the War came in 1939, like so many others, they just disappeared.

Fishburn asked that the new coachwork should be as light as possible, he was keen on high speed and Continental touring, at the same time he was something of a sportsman, so the car was given extremely thick running-boards, which could be utilized for carrying his fishing tackle in one side and his guns in the other. The illustration shows the car as completed by Whittingham & Mitchell and delivered to him in 1933; he took the car back to America with him and later it passed into the hands of Ronald Blackway, who was kind enough to send me the photographs of the car as it is today; it will be seen that the wings have been changed and the car now looks very American, this was done before Blackway owned the car, but, the actual date of the rebuild is not known.

PART II   CHAPTER 5

The first prototype Continental Phantom II, 26 EX. The story how this car came to be built and its subsequent career

After 25 EX there was a break in the production of experimental chassis, the Company had all they needed to carry out experiments to continually improve the basic model of the Phantom II, which was now being offered for sale to the public. As can be seen by anyone who reads these pages, Royce and everyone else connected with the designs of the Company's products were extremely critical of themselves, (however they appeared to the outside world) and they were always striving for something better.

Royce had always been interested in speed and performance, though he did not like out and out sports cars and he always used to say 'if people are going to break their necks let them do it in other peoples cars and not ours!'

As we have already seen he was delighted with the running of 18 EX, but decided that with the assistance of his friend and colleague, Ivan Evernden, the performance and handling of 18 EX could be improved upon still further. In 1930 he told the sales people in London that he had an idea to build what could almost be termed 'a tuned-up' version of 18 EX: Using a short wheelbase of 12 ft and continental-type springing (which has 5 thick leaves instead of 9 thin ones to allow for continuous high speed on the Continent), he intended to install a higher back axle ratio and a specially tuned engine and have coachwork similar to that fitted to 18 EX, but the steering was to have a specially low rake of 'F' position. Strangely, the Sales Department were not in the least interested, so Royce decided to go ahead on his own with Ivan Evernden assisting him, but, before starting on the designs for it, he decided he would like to have a Riley Monaco saloon of his own, so he asked Ivan Evernden to purchase a car for him from the Riley agents in Guildford, in Evernden's name and not mention Royce at all.

Ivan did exactly as Royce requested, and returned from Guildford with a Riley 9 Monaco saloon bearing the registration number GW 3226; they had a lot of fun with this car pulling it to pieces and thoroughly examining the chassis and seating accommodation. The result of these activities was 26 EX, which is still in existence and is owned at the moment by Douglas Worrall, who lives near Chichester in Sussex.

Ivan Evernden has a very great affection for 26 EX, which he regards, quite rightly, as his 'baby'; he has written a number of articles about this car and I cannot do better than let him tell the story of how this car came into being in his own words.

The First Continental Phantom II, Rolls-Royce 26 EX

During the era of the Silver Ghost and that of the Phantom I, a very high percentage of Rolls-Royce cars were chauffeur driven limousines and cabriolets.

The owner-driven Rolls-Royce, and the open tourer with a cape cart hood eventually acquired side curtains and became an All Weather in order to provide protection against the 'elements' comparable with that afforded by the closed car. In this respect, it failed miserably, and so an owner-driven type of enclosed body was evolved, called in Great Britain, a 'saloon' and in the U S A a 'sedan'. In most cases this body utilized the whole body base of the chassis, like the enclosed limousine, with its glass division and extra seats. These items being deleted to make the saloon, left a useless area of floor space, as the rear seat was still perched above the rear axle.

(*Top*) A fleet of bullion vans run by Johnson, Matthey which were built on second hand chassis by the Express Body and Motor Works Ltd. They were a subsidiary of the carriers Carter, Patterson. The bullion vans were painted brown. They were often employed by the Bank of England, but were gradually withdrawn from service during the 1939/45 War

(*Bottom*) S-154-FR, a Springfield Phantom I fitted with a Brewster built Derby Sport Phaeton. See Part I, Chapter 18 (*photo John McFarlane*)

Chassis number 1721, the first pre-war 40/50 hp ever to be restored. Owned by Stanley Sears. See Part I, Chapter 10

Phantom II chassis number 18GX a Park Ward Limousine specially built for Mrs Churchill-Wylie is one of the most expensive productions ever built by Park Ward

Left to right The author's cars 74GN Phantom II, 3-AZ-146 Phantom III, 101SK Continental Phantom II and GGP28 20/25.

This car was formerly owned by Lord Pirrie, the Chairman of Harland and Wolfe, who talked Bruce Ismay, Chairman of the White Star Line into building *Olympic* and *Titanic*. The original coachwork was by Morgan of Longacre. On Lord Pirrie's death it became the property of his brother-in-law, the Honourable Alexander Montgomery Carlisle who was the designer of *Olympic* and *Titanic*. On his death the car was sold for £35. It was used for varying purposes amongst these as a prime mover for a set of gang-mowers on a golf course. It was for sale for £7.10s in a breaker's yard on the main London-Maidstone road in 1950.

It was sold to become a breakdown truck, later it was purchased by Jack Barclay and completely restored by Fergusson-Wood who designed and had the all-steel body built on the chassis. *(photo Fergusson-Wood)*

A series of special drawings of the Brewster coachwork fitted to the Phantom I chassis. Each one is described individually, showing the very wide choice of coachwork offered by Brewster and Company to their clients

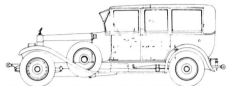

ARUNDEL--7-pass. double enclosed drive body. No's WC1576-1614 ''C'' 143 1/2'' w.b., 5775 lb. 51 1/4'' hd. rm. Photo p.183. Permanent roof, 2-pc. sliding division.

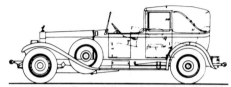

SALAMANCA--7-pass. full open front fully collapsible town car. Division drops, posts fold in over division. 143 1/2'' w.b., 50'' hd. rm. No's WC1786-1794. Aux. seats exp. side facing. 5350 lbs.
SALAMANCA PERMANENT--7-pass. full open front town car. No's WC1685, 1682, 1697, 1743, 1746, 1747. RR 1905, 1907-1920, 1921-1934 ''C'' 146 1/2''. 5580 lb. As Salamanca except permanent roof. 2-pc. sliding div.

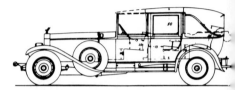

ST. STEPHEN--7-pass. semi-open drive town car with collapsible rear quarter. ''C.'' 2-pc. sliding div. No's 5028-5030, 5052-5061, 5164-5173 had 146 1/2'' 50'' hd. rm., forward facing exposed auxiliary seats No's 5190-5199, 5244-5248 same exc. 49'' hd. rm. No's 5440-5449 had 144 3/4'' w.b., 48 1/2'' hd. rm. slanted windshield, and flush type aux. seats, all bodies 5700 lb.

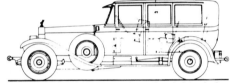

BERWICK--7-passenger single enclosed drive body. No's 1617-1624, 1837-1843 ''C'' 143 1/2'', 5625 lb., 49'' hd. rm. Permanent roof, no division. Photo p. 183.
PICKWICK--7-passenger double enclosed drive body. No's 1718-1741, 1832-1836, 1844-1846. 5700 lb. Single dropping division, otherwise like Berwick.

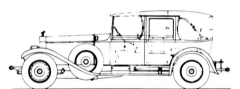

SALAMANCA DE VILLE--like Sal. Permanent except has semi-open front and curves in vertical moldings around rear door No's 5224-5240, 48'' hd. rm. No's 5241-43, 5293-97, 5650 lbs.

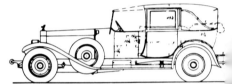

CHATSWORTH--7-pass. full open drive town car with collapsible rear quarter. ''C'' 146 1/2'' w.b., 49 1/2'' h.r. Two-piece sliding division. Exposed aux. seats 5550 lbs. No's 5038-5042.

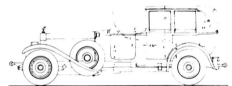

MAYFAIR--full open front town car. 1801-1831 ''C'' 143 1/2'' w.b., 5570 lb. 50'' hd. rm. 2-pc. sliding division. Landau irons behind rear quarter windows. Exposed auxiliary seats.

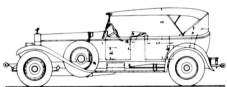

PALL MALL--5-pass. touring, one man top, storage cabinet back of front seat. 146 1/2'' w.b. 49'' h.r. ''D''. Body no's 1864-1880, 1884-1890.

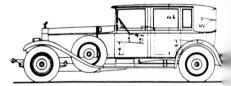

WARWICK--5- or 6-passenger double enclosed dri drop glass division, permanent roof, 1 aux. seat o 146 1/2'' w.b., 48'' h.r., 5600 lb. No's 5081-5095.
NORWICK--as Warwick except skeleton trim. Bo no's 5071-5080 h.r. 48''; 5273-5277 46 3/4''.
HARWICK--as Warwick exc. no div., bucket frt. sea no aux. seats. 5278-5282, 46 3/4'' h.r. 5096-5100, 4

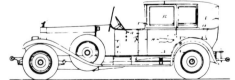

BREWSTER MAYFAIR--full open front town car. No landau irons. 146 1/2'' w.b. ''C'' 5600 lbs. 2-pc. sliding div. No's 5066-5070 have 50'' hd. rm., exp. aux. seats. Bodies 5341-5345 have 48 1/2'' hd. rm., flush aux. seats.

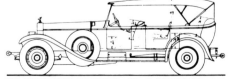

SIX PASSENGER PHAETON--like Pall Mall but longer. Flush type forward facing auxiliary seats, 146 1/2'' 5350 lbs. Body no's 1881-1883.

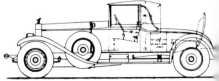

STRATFORD--2-pass. conv. coupe. ''D.'' No's 52 5262, 5450 lbs., 46'' hd. rm., 146 1/2'' w.b.

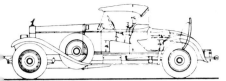

PICCADILLY--2-pass. roadster, with rumble seat. "D." Body no's 5321-5330, 5363-5368. 5306 lbs.

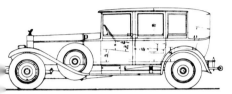

LONSDALE--7-pass. dbl. encl. dr. 2-pc. sliding div. exposed aux. seats, "C." 146 1/2" w.b., 5700 lbs. " hd. rm. (No's 5122-5141), 48" (No's 5142-5157).
LNSDALE--As Lonsdale, except painted skeleton trim unless otherwise specified. No's 5118-5121.
OVEDALE--As Lonsdale, except no division. No's 08-5112.
OWSDALE--As Lonsdale except single dropping division, flush aux. seats. Body no's 5113-5117.

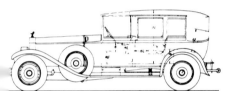

. ALBAN--7-pass. semi-open drive. 2-pc. sliding . Exp. aux. seats. No's 5174-5183, 146 1/2" w.b., " h.r., 5700 lbs. No's 5450-5454 and 5463-5477 have nt windshield, 144 3/4" w.b., 48 1/2" hd. rm.

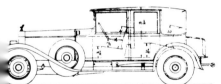

NILWORTH--4-5 pass. dbl. encl. dr. sport body. p div. Trim: natural skeleton. "D." 146 1/2" w.b. /4" h.r. No's 5301-5305, 5310-5319, 5372-5376.

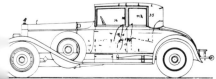

IBLEDON--four-pass. Victoria coupe. Rawlings ow lifts. "D." 144 3/4" w.b., 49 3/4" head room. lbs. Body no's 5346 to 5350, 5529 to 5533.

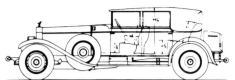

NEWMARKET--four pass. conv. sedan. Trunk extra. "D." Straight windshield, 44 1/4" hd. rm. and 146 1/2 w.b. on no's 5351-5355 and 5358-5362. Slant windshield 45 1/2" hd. rm., 144 3/4" w.b. on 5707-5726. 5590 lbs.

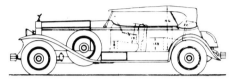

ASCOT--four-pass. phaeton. 5414-5418, 5570-5594, (drum lamps, tubular bumpers) 7156-7180 (revised as shown above). 144 3/4" w.b. "E." 5350 lb. 46" h.r. Leather trunk with cover of top material, no suitcases.

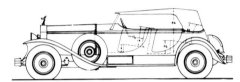

DERBY--four-passenger speedster. 5419-5423, (drum lamps, tubular bumpers). 5551-5555, 5595-5609 (revised as shown). 144 3/4" w.b. "E." 5350 lb. 46" h.r. Same trunk as Ascot. Early version, "Brewster Speedster" had high rear fenders.

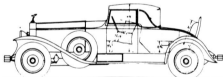

REGENT--2-pass. convertible coupe, with 2-pass. rumble seat. 7131-7155 "D." 144 3/4" w.b. 5450 lb. 44" h.r. Top bows painted to match trim.

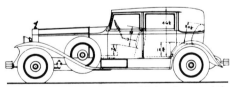

AVON--four-passenger enclosed drive close coupled. 7076-7130 "D." 144 3/4" w.b. 5625 lb. 46 1/2" h.r. Permanent roof, no division.

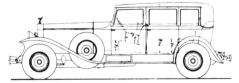

DOVER--five passenger enclosed drive. 5257-7281 "D." 144 3/4" w.b. 5650 lb. (?) 46 1/2" h.r. Permanent roof, no division.
HUNTINGTON -- seven - passenger double enclosed drive. Similar to Dover, but longer with double sliding division and 2 auxiliary seats facing forward. 7001-

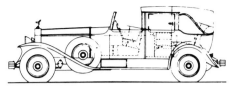

TROUVILLE--seven-pass. Semi-open drive, permanent rear quarter. Body no's 5541-45, 5631-45. "D." 144 3/4" w.b., 48 3/4" hd. rm. 2 side facing flush aux. seats. Single dropping division. 5750 lbs.

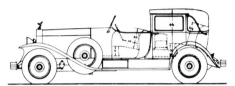

RIVIERA--six-pass. full open drive town car. Permanent or folding rear roof. Body no's 5694-5703. Walnut marquetry panels. "E." 144 3/4 w.b., 46" hd. rm. 2 side facing flush aux. seats. 2-pc. sliding division. 5450 lbs.

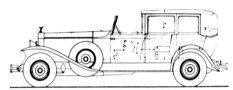

ST. ANDREW--7-pass. Semi-open drive body with permanent rear quarter lights. 7181-7210 "D" 144 3/4" w.b., 5700 lb., 47 1/2" h.r., permanent rear roof. 2 facing forward aux. seats. 2-pc. sliding div.

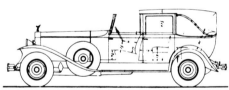

ST. REGIS--7-pass. Semi-open drive body with permanent leather rear quarters. 7211-7230 "D" 144 3/4 w.b., 5700 lb., 47 1/2" h.r. Double sliding glass division. 2 facing forward aux. seats.

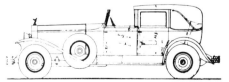

ST. MARTIN--7-pass. Semi-open drive. 5232-7256 "D" 144 3/4" w.b., 5600 lb., 46 1/2" h.r. Permanent rear roof. Dropping glass division. Full trim. 2 side-facing aux. seats.

101SK, the author's Continental Phantom II in Jersey

New Phantom chassis number 15TC is fitted with a Thrupp and Maberly Cabriolet de Ville with steel artillery wheels which were an extra charge

New Phantom chassis number 20AL carries a Windovers Limousine which was formerly owned by Rudyard Kipling. This car has been rebodied

Phantom III chassis no 3-CM-92 a Barker Touring Saloon owned by R. D. Shaffner, the chairman of the Phantom III Technical Society

(Top) Royce, Nurse Aubin and Arthur Sidgreaves are standing beside 18EX at Le Lavandou in the South of France 1930. The photograph was taken by Royce's chauffeur Frank Dodd. See Part II, Chapter 1,2 and 3

(Bottom) 19EX, the second experimental Phantom II fitted with a Barker Close Coupled Saloon. This photograph was taken by the late W.O. Bentley when testing the car after he joined Rolls-Royce Ltd

(*Top*) 21EX, a Barker Limousine. See Part II, Chapter 4
(*Middle*) 24EX, the first left hand drive Phantom II with
Nurse Aubin, Royce, Hs and Elliott in the South of France
The body is a Barker Close Coupled Saloon. See Part II,
Chapter 4
(*Bottom*) 25EX, a Park Ward Limousine, the second
Phantom II with left hand drive and centre gearchange.
See Part II, Chapter 4. Further photographs of this car
appear overleaf

(Top) 25EX as the car appeared in 1933 after it had been modernised and rebodied by Whittingham and Mitchell. See Part II, Chapter 4 *(photo The Autocar)* *(Middle)* 25EX as the car appears today with Packard type mudguards. See Part II, Chapter 4 *(photo R. Blackway)* *(Bottom)* 27EX as built. Later the car had independent front suspension and hydraulic tappets. See Part II, Chapter 6 *(photo H. J. Mulliner/Park Ward)*

(*Top left*) 31GX, the last experimental Phantom II with Park Ward coachwork. Owned in 1932 by S. E. Sears, it was his first Rolls-Royce. It now carries Hearse coachwork. See Part II, Chapter 6 (*photo S. E. Sears*)
(*Top right*) 29EX, the 'Vulture'. This is a 20/25 hp chassis with a Phantom II engine bored out to 8 litres. See Part II, Chapter 6 (*photo Ivan Evernden*)
(*Bottom*) An early type Phantom II chassis with water heated carburetter

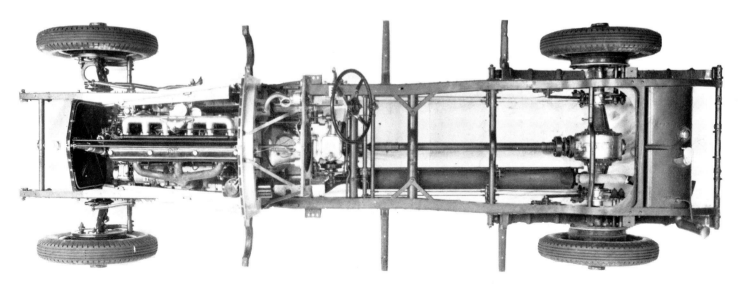

(*Top left and right*) A Phantom II engine
(*Middle*) The production line. 20/25 chassis on
the left with Phantom II on the right
(*Bottom*) A Phantom II engine on test

(Top) 1WJ. This was the first production Phantom II laid down as 24EX. An identical car 14WJ was exhibited at the 1929 Olympia Motor Show but it had its wheels painted cream to match the lower panels of the body (photo Hugh Keller)

(Middle) An early Phantom II chassis

(Bottom) 5WJ, a long chassis, 'D' type steering, Barker Sedanca de Ville. This car was on the Paris Salon Show stand in 1929

(Top) 15WJ, a long chassis, 'C' type steering, Hooper Enclosed Limousine for the 1929 Olympia Show finished in mulberry and black
(Bottom) 33WJ with coachwork by Weymann of Paris for the 1929 Paris Salon Show. The car was purchased by Ernest Hemingway

(*Top*) 128XJ, a long chassis, 'D' type steering 6 Light Owner Driver Saloon by Hoyal Body Corporation of Weybridge with a Pytcheley sliding roof and two spare wheels. The car was ordered by Sir Leonard Lyle of Canford Cliffs, Bournemouth. (The Hoyal Body Corporation built many bodies on the smaller Daimler 20/70, Buick, Chrysler and Hupmobile chassis but is unusual on a Rolls-Royce)

(*Bottom left*) 23GN, a Hooper Open Tourer for Sir Julian Cahn, Bart, ordered about the same time at 74GN. See Part II, Chapter 8 (*photo Jack Mackinlay*)

(*Bottom right*) 63GN, a Freestone and Webb Sedanca de Ville built for R. Beaumont-Thomas. This was the first Phantom II in which the author rode as a schoolboy. See Part II, Chapter 7

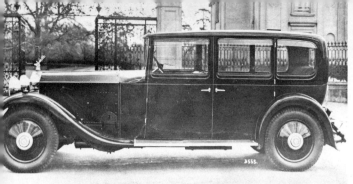

74GN in the desert on the route to and from Timbuktu

(Top left) 74GN as supplied to Sir Julian Cahn, Bart. May 10th 1930
(Top right) Loading up at Hotel Cote d'Or, Saulieu. December 17th 1933
(Upper middle left) A muddy road dig-out just south of Mecheria
(Upper middle right) A muddy road dig-out just south of Mecheria.
December 23rd 1933
(Lower middle) Buying petrol at Neni-Ounif at 7.15 am. It took us ½ hour
to get it. December 24th 1933
(Bottom left) Christmas Day lunch between Beni-Ounif and Ardrar
The menu: figs, dates, biscuits and pudding
(Bottom right) Le Camp Antoine. 'Staff' commandered by Wrighton to fill
up with petrol. Christmas Day 1933

In 1929, Early Phantom II saloon bodies had the rear seat moved forward and the body space released was often used to house a separate luggage box. About this time the smaller European cars, in order to accommodate four people in comfort, had developed the close-coupled body in which the rear floor was lower than that at the front. The feet of the occupants of the rear seat were in a 'well' in the floor under the front seats. The most outstanding British example of this type of motor car, at the time, was the 'Riley 9'.

Mr Royce, who had been using a Phantom I 'All Weather', having become tired of driving about in a car having a huge body, became impressed by the intelligent thought which had led to the design of the new close-coupled body.

Ever since the year 1912, when he suffered a major abdominal operation, his health had been the Company's serious concern, and he was never again allowed to work at the plant in Derby. At the time in question, he was living in an old country farmhouse in the village of West Wittering, on the English Channel, almost opposite the Isle of Wight. With him, he had a very select team of six designers, and this small but efficient organization, by working very hard, for long hours carried out the major design projects of the Company. I was fortunate to have got myself into this team.

Having failed to get enthusiastic support from the Sales Department in London, for making a small personal high performance car, he decided in 1930 that he himself would have such a motor car, particularly for the Winter when he would, as usual, move to his Winter quarters at the 'Villa Mimosa' in Le Canadal, on the French Riviera. I was asked to make a design investigation into the modification needed to the Phantom II chassis, and to style a close-coupled body.

It was obvious that the chassis wheelbase could be reduced to 144 inches and that certain chassis cross-members would need to be altered to enable the rear floor to be lowered, whilst, in order to preserve an adequate loading of the rear wheels, the two spare wheels, normally carried at each side of the bonnet, would have to be placed at the rear. From a close study of the body of the 'Riley 9' it became obvious that, even with the shortened chassis, there was no need to adopt such a high degree of close-coupling!

In the design of the body, I incorporated several features which at that time were novel, at least to Rolls-Royce cars. The flared, birdlike front wings, exposing their undersides, had the right appearance for this class of car, and had proven themselves to be very effective on a car some years previous in preventing mud from being thrown up on the windscreen and the body sides if the wide mud lip was tilted downwards at about 30° to line vertical.

In deference to the diehards, those votaries of the open tourer and the 'Allweather', the body was fitted with a 'sunshine roof', a device which recently had been invented. The design of revolving roof panel was evolved by Hooper & Co, Coachbuilders, of St James Street, London.

Having produced the designs and also a water colour sketch of the car, Barker & Co, Coachbuilders, in London - whose history went back to the days of King Charles and the Stage Coach - were entrusted with the construction of the body. I spent a busy spring supervising this work, and making the necessary designs which the plant at Derby would need to produce the modified chassis.

The conservatism of the British manifests itself in many ways, and not least in the colour of their cars. The majority of Rolls-Royce cars, the body style and colour scheme of which was always the customer's choice, in those days were finished in black, dark maroon, or dark blue, so dark indeed as to be indistinguishable from black.

It is indicative of the progressive mind of Royce, that he disliked these black monsters and was a votary of pale grey. He gave me considerable freedom of choice in selecting the colour scheme for this, the first continental Phantom II - 26 EX. The body and wings were finished in pale saxe-blue, over which was applied a coat of artificial pearl lacquer. This coating was produced by mixing finely ground herring scales, with a clear lacquer, which when applied to suitably tinted glass beads was the current means of making artificial pearls. The saxe-blue under-coat gleamed through the lacquer to give an oyster shell finish having a pale blue hue of great delicacy.

The interior was trimmed in very soft calf-hide, especially imported from France and pale saxe-blue in colour, with a headcloth of lighter shade. The interior woodwork was in sycamore wood, tinted faintly with blue.

By August that year the car was completed, barely four months after the drawings were issued, which today seems phenomonal. After the car had been tested at Derby, Mr Hives, and several of his assistants drove it to West Wittering for Royce to see. It was a beautiful summer's day, with blue sky, blue sea, and the pearl blue car to match them.

Royce had a quaint old Labrador dog, 'Rajah' of whom he was very fond. Of course he had to go with his master to try the new car. Unfortunately a stretch of road where they had halted had been sprayed with tar, on returning to Elmstead there were tar spots on the door panels and wings, and what was even more alarming, 'Rajah' had put his big feet in the tar, and it was all over the cushions of the car. As the sun was setting that evening there was a dejected body of important men - Royce, Hives and his colleagues, each with a saucer of olive oil, and a pad of cotton wool, removing the tar spots.

To this day, I do not believe Royce ever intended to use this car personally, but he had said so, just to get it made.

A great friend of the Company, and of Royce, was the Rolls-Royce agent in Madrid, Don Carlos de Salamanca, a relative of King Alphonso. In those days, the grandees of Spain ranked among our best customers. As the car failed to arouse any interest from the Sales Department in London, Royce contacted Salamanca and told him that I would take the car to him at his Villa Anglet at Biarritz.

One September morning, in company with an experienced continental driver by the name of Amster, I proudly headed the first Continental Phantom II for Folkstone and the Continent. Fortunately I was accustomed to taking a car to France, for the car was filled with spare parts and equipment, which I did not wish the 'douaniers' to unpack and leave me to put back.

At Boulogne, Amster and I took the Chief Douanier to a bar on the Quay where we plied him with brandy, while his assistant was supposed to be dealing with the customs clearance and the Carnet for the car. We sat imbibing for so long that the next ferry had arrived before we finally emerged. The young douanier tried to tell his chief that he had done nothing because I had left all the car doors locked, but his chief was too merry to listen to him. Kissing me on both cheeks, he hurried us off the quay calling 'Bon Voyage'. Some days later, this episode was destined to appear not so happy and amusing.

We reached Paris that evening, for the car had a good turn of speed and would cruise comfortably at 60-70 mph. It is the criterion of a good car that one can drive it the whole day long and at the end feel fresh and relaxed, to enjoy dinner. This we did alfresco at a café in the Place Pigalle in Montmartre, overshadowed by the great L'Eglise de Sacré Coeur.

French food and wine I enjoy but it gave me a disturbed night, which was responsible for our late start the next day. However, we reached Chartres for lunch and, after a quick tour of the famous cathedral, we started the long trek through Central France, to Poiters, Angouleme and Bayonne to Bordeaux, where we arrived at about midnight.

As we were due to reach Biarritz the next morning, in time to have the car washed before the Concours d'Elegance in the afternoon, there had been no time to stop for dinner. We had no hôtel reservation so, after fixing up at a lodging house down behind the old jail, we went to the docks and ate at a café frequented by stevedores on night shift. Before noon the next day we were at the Bar Basque in Biarritz drinking sherry, and reviving our thirst by nibbling Pamplona Sausage and forking mussels steeped in sherry, from a large tureen provided gratis at the bar.

The 'Continental' which was parked outside in the square caused a great sensation, for it was the height of the Autumn Season and this pearl of the Bay of Biscay was packed with wealthy visitors.

Don Carlos was enchanted with the car and could scarcely wait to have lunch before going down to the elysian bathing beach, poetically called Le Chambre d'Amour and to enter the car for the 'Concours'. It was apparent on arrival that, although the car was a great attraction and much admired, it caused a mild flutter in the dove-côte, for there was an array of large cars in the arena, Rolls-Royce, Isotta-Fraschini, Hispano-Suiza and the like, and owners had already decided how the judging would go, I sensed that I, the intruder, was not at all welcome.

My premonition was confirmed when Don Carlos left me to drive the car into the arena. An official, knowing that the car was British, and hoping that my knowledge of French might fail me, directed me to the park marked 'Hors de Concours' instead of that marked 'Au Concours'. I refused to be deceived.

It is a rule at a French Concours d'Elégance that the car shall be driven by a beautiful woman. Don Carlos met this requirement adequately by arranging that his relative, the Pomposa de Escandon, daughter of the Marquis de Villavieja, should drive the car, accompanied by the Arch Duchess Margarita.

Each car in turn has to be driven round the arena and halted before the panel of judges. When it was the turn of our Continental to arrive on the scene, imagine my consternation at the sight of steam issuing from the base of the radiator. The coolant was about to boil. I suspected that Pomposa had been running the engine rather fast in the queue of cars waiting to pass before the judges dais, and that the thermostat controlling the radiator shutters was sluggish in opening. Open it did eventually, for the whiff of steam subsided.

Great was our jubilation when the prize winners were announced and we learned that the Continental had won the Grand Prix d'Honneur. People crowded then to congratulate us, and to learn more about the car.

It was a beautiful September afternoon. There, on the beach, in the blazing sunshine, we sat, sipping cooling drinks at tables shaded by umbrellas, surrounded by beautiful women. That evening, at a dinner and dance, the prizes were presented. Pomposa received a large glass vase, about 4 ft tall, and I kept the plâque recording the award of the trophy.

We stayed several days with Don Carlos in Biarritz, calling on friends and new acquaintances, some of whom borrowed the car for a day. Each morning, I called up London and reported orders and enquiries, which indeed were not few.

An amusing incident occurred at the Concours. I had a long conversation about the car with a man who was obviously not English. We spoke French. So ensued a long chat, at the end of which he said shortly he would be in London and order a car. On exchanging cards, I discovered that he was Mr Brocow of New York! He had thought that I was a Spaniard!

Soon after came the time for Don Carlos and I to go to Madrid. I looked forward to this trip as I had never been to Spain. The frontier at Hendaye is not far from Biarritz, the road passing that gem of watering places, St Jean de Luz. The trip was not to have an uneventful start, for, at the frontier post, thanks to the episode at Boulogne, the car's papers showed it still to be in England and, to make matters worse, my passport was still in Biarritz.

Don Carlos persuaded the French authorities to let us pass, for an adequate sum in francs, and to join us at the Spanish customs at Irun, on the other side of the bridge over the river Bidassoa which marks the frontier. Eventually, it was agreed that if we arrived back on the same day a week later before midnight, we would find the same French and Spanish guards on duty, and would be allowed to re-enter France. All that week I prayed that none of the officials would fall ill. Otherwise, we would certainly be in serious trouble. In the meantime, the car's papers were returned to Boulogne for correction.

The Basque Provinces lying at the foot of the Pyrenees are most intriguing. After San Sebastian, the Royal seaside resort, the road goes inland to Vittoria, the capital of the Basque provinces, and on to Burgos, where we had lunch in a hôtel opposite the cathedral.

In those days, the main roads of Spain were good. The tarred surfaces which melted in the sun, had to be continually covered with sand by roadmen. King Alphonso was a great motorist, and a votary of Hispano-Suiza, who, largely because of him, had a plant in Spain. His Chief Minister, Primo der Reviera, built these great trunk roads leading out of Madrid. Very modern they were for their time, for often they crossed wide valleys by viaduct.

The road from Burgos to Madrid lay across the great Castillian Plateau, about 4,000 feet above sea level. The scenery was reminiscent of the pictures found often in old family bibles - men riding asses loaded with panniers, women flayling corn, and beasts turning a mill to pump water.

At times there was to be seen a striking contrast between the ancient and the modern, like the petrol filling station just outside the little town of Oranda. The building was of stone with no windows and an earth floor, yet, outside there were the electric petrol pumps and the whole scene was lit by electric lamps. In a field a tractor droned, whilst a little further on men were erecting the arena for a travelling bullfight.

Central Spain was in the throes of a heat wave. In spite of all the altitude and the high ambient temperature, the coolant never boiled, although the red light on the facia board on occasion gave a warning glow.

It was dark when we approached Madrid. An orange glow from the city lights could be seen in the sky over thirty miles away, like a flame on a desert horizon. I was cruising along at 70 mph through this barren land when the huge P100 headlamps picked up a group of people on the roadside waving their arms, and a white bundle resembling a woman lying in the path of the car. I was braking hard when Don Carlos, who had been dozing, woke up with a start and cried 'don't stop, and go on as fast as you can!' Apparently thieves had the habit of coming out of the city at night and used this trick to stop cars and rob their occupants.

At Madrid I stayed with Don Carlos in a wing of the Royal Residence. Little of Old Madrid remained, except those buildings of historic interest. Wide 'avenidas' such as the Puerta del Sol ran through the city. At intervals miniature skyscrapers rose to 24 storeys, the new post office for one. Madrid was an oasis of commercial wealth set in a land of poverty stricken peasantry. An uneasy tension reigned, and armed guards were everywhere.

The Continental was shown to many wealthy merchants, tobacco importers and cattle dealers. The many enquiries received I phoned to London during my morning bath and breakfast.

The grandees of Spain owned vast areas of land on which cattle were reared. In one instance I was asked to accept a Bill of Sale on a herd of cattle, to fall due at Christmas. This seemed to be very good security, but such Latin barter was very foreign to the business methods of our London Office. The nobility of Spain had, for many years, been customers of ours and their interest in the Continental was phenomenal.

For a visitor to Madrid, a trip to El Escorial, the Royal Mausoleum some 70 miles west of the city is a must. This huge stone Cathedral is set among the Guadaramma Mountains which rise some 3,000 ft above the plateau to a height of 7,000 ft. Seen from the distance, it looks small due to an optical illusion perpetrated by the architect, by giving the building a very large window and a huge main door. This became apparent on close scrutiny, for one saw people, the size of ants, entering through a small hole at the base of the door. The remains of the Kings are kept in a vault in large glazed earthenware vessels like soup tureens with lids, resting in niches around the walls. It was perhaps a little significant that the guide should have told us that only one empty niche remained.

Because of the altitude we had taken no chances with the Continental. We had removed the large undershield below the engine and gearbox, which restricted the egress of air from under the bonnet. Consequently, although we encountered many cars stopped at the roadside with steaming radiators, we reached La Granja without 'loss of marks'.

The heatwave had given way to torrential rain and storm on the day that Don Carlos and I were bound to return to Biarritz. So bad was the weather that, although we had allowed ample time to reach the frontier before midnight to meet the particular guards who would accept us with documents, we were hard pressed to make the rendezvous in time. On some stretches we were clocking well over 100 km in the hour.

It was a sad farewell to a fond child when I left the Continental in Biarritz to carry on its publicity tour of Europe and I entrained for home. The next week when I went up to London from West Wittering, I found that the Sales Department had produced a very attractive brochure giving details and a price for the car, and including also pictures of the Continental which were taken at the Concours d'Elegance.

My Rolls-Royce Continental Phantom II at last was a reality.

(H I F E, June 1960)

A legend has grown up around 26 EX that this car was built for Royce's own personal use, this however is incorrect. Royce was determined to have this car built, the interest in it was enormous and from its inception came a steady demand for the Continental Phantom II which is considered by many to be the finest model Rolls-Royce Ltd ever made. Royce was delighted with it and all the care and thought that Ivan Evernden put into its construction was fully justified, but apart from actually approving it, Royce never used it. After Evernden had done his trip across Europe with the car, it went to Chateauroux for the usual testing, when it returned as it was such a striking design, and as the Experimental Department had all the chassis which they needed, it was decided to remove the experimental parts in the engine, put the car back to standard and hand it over to Sales for disposal.

A Mr Tanner, who was Manager of the Westminster Bank in St Helier, and who lived at Corbiere in Jersey, Channel Islands, was a great admirer of Rolls-Royce cars and had been running a '20' h p for some years. When he felt he would like a change, he took this car back to the mainland and exchanged it for 26 EX.

All work on Mr Tanner's Rolls-Royce was done for him by Jones' Garage, at Five Oaks, on the outskirts of St Helier. The present owner of this garage is the son of the original proprietor, who told me he will never forget being taken down to St Helier docks by Mr Tanner to see his latest acquisition. The car was lying in the hold of the steamer. The sight of this magnificent car with its long bonnet took his breath away, he had never seen such a big Rolls-Royce before and it made a lasting impression on him.

Jones' Garage looked after 26 EX from the day of its arrival in Jersey until the outbreak of War in 1939, when Mr Tanner and his family went to live in Bournemouth and Jones' Garage laid up 26 EX in a lock-up garage behind the Grand Hotel in St Helier, hiding the car behind stacks of potato boxes. The Germans opened the garage once, saw the potato boxes and closed the door again. The car remained there undisturbed until 1945, when, upon the death of Mr Tanner in Bournemouth, his widow decided to dispose of the car, so Bill Jones put 26 EX

back on the road; the garage was a dry one and very little deterioration had taken place during the period of storage. After some preliminary tuning he took it out on test up Victoria Avenue and found it was still possible to exceed 90 mph with it, (this was before the days of the Island's blanket speed limit of 40 mph).

Mrs Tanner sold the car to a Mr Mitchley of Birmingham for £500. It then passed to a Mr Baker of Teignmouth and in 1957 it changed hands again, when it was bought by Major C W Lambton, who joined the 20 Ghost Club with it. Later he had the chassis and coachwork overhauled by Paddon Bros and in 1959 took the car to New York for three months. It changed hands again and became the property of a Major O R H Chichester, who entered the car in the first of the Sotheby Sales to be held at Earls Court in London on Friday, 5 November 1965. It was sold under the hammer to Douglas Worrall for £3,000, who attended the sale with the express purpose of purchasing 26 EX.

Douglas is a great enthusiast for fine cars, he was already the owner of an extremely fine 8 litre Bentley Limousine, with coachwork by Freestone & Webb, which he had purchased at a second Sword Sale of the John Sword collection held at East Belgray Farm, Ayrshire, on Friday, 12 March 1965. Incidentally, the Bentley is an interesting car, it was built to the order of Jack Barclay Ltd, and was to have been exhibited on the coachbuilding stand of Freestone & Webb at the 1931 Olympia Motor Show, together with another 8 litre, an exceedingly pretty sports saloon, which had been built specially for my uncle, R A Beaumont-Thomas, who at the time was Managing Director of Freestone & Webb; but, unfortunately owing to the fact that Bentley Motors had gone into liquidation earlier in the year, neither of these cars could be exhibited.

I spent an extremely pleasant day with Douglas Worrall and his wife at their charming house at Bosham, near Chichester, in April 1970 and was taken out in both the 8 litre Bentley limousine, which is a most impressive vehicle, and also in 26 EX. Douglas told me that 26 EX was in an extremely neglected state when he bought her, but is gradually restoring her into the condition which such a fine car merits. I was particularly interested to go out in

26 EX for two reasons, first, I know Ivan Evernden very well indeed and he has told me such a lot about this car, and secondly because I also have a Continental Phantom II in the form of chassis number 101 SK, though this is a very much later car and really the difference between them could almost be likened to the difference between chalk and cheese.

The amount of room in the body of 26 EX is very small and the body is obviously one of Barker's lighter efforts as the chassis is very lively, and not only is the acceleration brisk, but a high cruising speed is easily maintained, the springing at low speeds is somewhat on the harsh side, but cruising at 75-80 mph the car holds the road very well indeed and it can only be said that it is a good thing that such a fine car is now in the hands of someone who will appreciate it and look after it.

PART II CHAPTER 6

More experimental Phantom IIs, chassis 27 EX, which is later fitted with hydraulic tappets and independent front suspension. Ivan Evernden finds that Park Ward & Co, are more co-operative than Barker & Co, Ltd, so Park Ward build most of the coachwork for experimental chassis from now on. 28 EX and 29 EX known as 'The Vulture' and finally the last experimental Phantom II 31 GX.

27 EX

27 EX was basically the same design as 26 EX, in that it had a short wheelbase with a body sub-frame and the coachwork was very similar but built by Park Ward instead of Barker. For some time past Evernden had been becoming exasperated with Barker & Co, whose coachbuilding foreman was so dyed in the wool in the old tradition of building carriages that he simply could not and would not move with the times. Barker bodies had always been noted for being beautifully constructed but very heavy and over the years, whenever Evernden complained that something had broken when the cars were on test at Chateauroux, the invariable reply that Mr Munday, the chief body maker, gave was 'Well, we didn't make it strong enough and we must increase the dimensions of the wooden pillars' or whatever it was that had broken. This, of course, added to the weight, in consequence the performance of the car suffered. This was a serious matter as, with the public's demand for better acceleration and a higher top speed, other manufacturers were continually improving the performance of their models.

Finally it was over the 20 h p model that things came to a head. With this model the problem of additional weight showed up very much and Royce was insistent that the maximum weight he had laid down was not to be exceeded, as the whole chassis was designed for a light type of body. He felt so strongly about this that when the 20 h p was first announced in October 1922, a set of designs for standard coachwork had been drawn up by Ivan Evernden

and, as the model sold in a much more competitive market than the 40/50, in order to keep the price down the Company had been ordering in bulk and, for the first time, Rolls-Royce Ltd had been selling completed cars, carrying coachwork approved by Royce.

However, not all clients of enclosed cars would accept these designs, which were open-fronted limousines and landaulettes; other makers in this field were fitting enclosed drive bodies and in some cases they were cheaper, for instance, Austin, Crossley, Daimler, Humber, Sunbeam, to mention a few. When a heavier body was fitted to the 20 h p Rolls-Royce the performance suffered accordingly and consequently was known by some as the 'Gutless Wonder'!

Finally Royce said another coachbuilder must be found and by coincidence not long after this he had to go to Conduit Street, something which he did not do very often. He travelled by rail from Chichester to Victoria where his own car met him and took him to Conduit Street. When he was ready to leave he discovered that his own car was not available. Brushing aside the apologies he made for a strange car with an unfamiliar body, which his eagle eye had spotted outside. He was most intrigued with the coachwork and gave it a close examination. He liked the lightness of the doors and the way they closed and was impressed with the extra thin pillars incorporated in the design, which he said made for good visibility.

He was told that this particular coachwork

was by Park Ward, a small firm at Willesden and the car had been taken in part exchange.

As soon as Royce arrived home at West Wittering, he told Ivan Evernden to put on his hat and coat and catch a train to go and see Park Ward, (of whom Ivan had never heard at that time) but who had a factory at Willesden where in fact it still is. His visit came at a most propitious time for them as they were on the verge of bankruptcy and were eventually bought by Rolls-Royce Ltd in 1939.

This firm had been founded by William H Park and Charlie W Ward in 1919. The following year they built their first body on a Rolls-Royce chassis and in 1924 they founded the firm of Park Ward & Co, as a limited company; their standard of work has always been of the very highest quality and it is said that Charlie Ward was extremely exacting. On one occasion, when a car was being prepared for Olympia, the valance behind the running board did not meet with his approval, so he picked up the heaviest sledge-hammer he could find and hit it a resounding blow; turning to the people who were working on completing the car he said; 'Now, do it properly' and with that he walked away.

This was the beginning of Rolls-Royce Ltd, using Park Ward for coachwork on the experimental cars, 27 EX was the first but others were to follow. It was Ivan Evernden who evolved with Park Ward the use of steel door pillars instead of wooden ones which had always been used up till then. Steel was very much stronger and therefore the pillars could be much thinner in construction, which had the added advantage of giving the driver very much better visibility.

By 1932 the co-operation between Rolls-Royce Ltd and Park Ward had become so close that it was decided to extend the idea, tried out on the '20' h p model, of having standard bodies designed, so for the first time in the history of Rolls-Royce Ltd, it was possible to purchase direct from the Company complete cars of any model, fitted with Park Ward coachwork. In the case of the Phantom II there was a long wheelbase 7-passenger limousine or a short Continental owner-driver touring saloon, and on the 20/25 there was the choice of a limousine or

a 4-light owner-driver saloon, the latter could be had with a glass division if the purchaser so desired. This new arrangement was found to work extremely well as not only was a would-be purchaser able to take immediate delivery of a new car, but they also knew exactly how much he, or she, was going to have to pay for the new model.

But to revert to 27 EX, which bore the index number CH 9656; this chassis was used to pave the way for the coming of the Phantom III, the first and last V-12 cylinder car engine Rolls-Royce ever made, and the first Rolls-Royce ever to be fitted with independent front suspension.

It was early in 1934 that 27 EX was fitted with a new type of cylinder head, which had hydraulic tappets after the type evolved by General Motors on their Cadillac, at the same time it was fitted with an experimental front wheel independent suspension. At this stage the car, which had formerly been painted grey and black, was re-painted all black. On 27 August 1934, the Cadillac-type cylinder head was removed and transferred on to Sidgreaves' personal car, 104 MY. On 17 December 1934, the car was involved in an accident on the Mansfield-Newark road when it crashed into a ditch, where it remained for two hours until a breakdown vehicle could come and tow it out. It was driveable but the wings, lamps and radiator were damaged. It was not long after this that it was re-built and given a new chassis number, 85 JS; it was last heard of as being owned by R R L Young, Sougham, Kenya, 1951-55.

28 EX

28 EX was also with coachwork by Park Ward. This was an Enclosed Drive Limousine and in April 1934, whilst on a 10,000 mile test at Chateauroux this car was fitted with what was known as a vulture-type cylinder head which gave a compression ratio of 6.875 : 1. This was the last type of cylinder head to be tried on the Phantom II; it was never sold to the general public as the great increase in compression caused the engine to become extremely rough and the Company felt that it was so unlike the gliding qualities which had always been

associated with a Rolls-Royce car that it was unacceptable.

The speedometer showed a reading of 49,806 miles when the Experimental Department decided to dispose of the car on 5 December 1935, and 5 days later it was handed over to the repair depot and made into a standard production Phantom II, then sold. The chassis No. was changed to 203 TA. It was last heard of as belonging to John Walker in 1955.

29 EX

29 EX was also a close coupled saloon with coachwork by Park Ward, finished in all black, the registration number was RC 1681. This is a most interesting specimen and it is a great pity that so little is known about it. The engine was a bored-out Phantom II giving total capacity of over 8 litres; the chassis was a prototype 25/30, which had the code name of 'Japan 3'; the gearbox, rear axle and suspension were all those of the prototype 25/30.

'The car was made to discover how much too heavy it could be, in fact except for a strengthening of the gears failures were few.' This quote is an extract from a letter by Ivan Everndon.

No doubt the performance of this chassis, which was known as 'The Vulture' was quite extraordinary. According to the Log Book held at the experimental garage in Crewe, the car was still being tested by the Experimental Department as late as 10 July 1937. On its last entry, the speedometer showed a reading of 34,661 miles. A conversation I had in Conduit Street abouts this car with one person there who remembered it told me that it was involved in a very bad accident near Great Missenden, after it had been down to Brooklands Track for test at high speed. I was told that after this unfortunate occurrence it was written off.

31 GX

The last experimental Phantom II to be built was for some unknown reason given the chassis number 31 GX. It was a Continental touring saloon mounted on the short wheelbase with coachwork by Park Ward. The body had been made as light as possible, only weighing 7 cwt 3

qrs 16 lb, even window winders had been eliminated, and the windows slid to and fro in channels, which made ventilation in hot weather a serious problem. When this chassis was built in 1931 the Continental Phantom II was already available to the public. The original prototype 26 EX, which we have already discussed in a previous chapter, was the first to be sold but the following chassis numbers had been manufactured as true Continentals:

82 GY;   104 GY;   6 GX;   28 GX.

A great deal has been written about the Rolls-Royce Continental Phantom II, which has no doubt added to the glamour and attraction of what is without question a very fine car indeed, but unfortunately most of what has been said about it is incorrect. Briefly then, the following are the features which go to make a Continental Phantom II, of which some 375 were made in all. The steering column has a specially low rake at 'F' type, as the model was built for the enthusiastic owner-driver who liked speed and performance, so his comfort was chiefly borne in mind. The springs consist of 5 thick leaves of a specially flattened type instead of 9 thin ones in the front suspension, to allow for continuous high speeds on the long straight roads across France, which at the time did not have as good a surface as they have today. The rear axle ratio is 12 x 41, in place of the standard 11 x 41, so as to give a higher cruising speed with less revolutions of the engine. On early model Continentals, in addition to the standard Rolls-Royce shock dampers, a set of tele-control Hartfords were fitted, which could be screwed up by hand control from the driver's seat to make the suspension really rigid when traversing a bad road at high speed; but these friction shock absorbers were deleted from the specifications when Royce designed the controllable shock damper, which is operated from a small lever on the top of the steering column, replacing the mixture control which was fitted on all early Phantom II chassis. This innovation was first incorporated on 160 PY in 1933 (this chassis left the factory at Derby as a true Continental Phantom II) and then became a standard fitting on all Phantom II chassis.

The policy of Rolls-Royce Ltd, over the years had always been one of continuous improvement, so gradually more power was extracted from the engine of the Phantom II. This was done by raising the compression, fitting a higher lift camshaft and bigger valves with heavier valve springs. This arrangement became standard practice on all models commencing with chassis number 102 MY in 1933 - in other words the engine of a Continental Phantom II is exactly the same as that fitted in a standard Phantom II and the special engine about which so much has been written is a myth. Not all Continental Phantom IIs were the short wheelbase model, in fact chassis numbers 89 RY, 128 SK, 190 SK and 97 TA all had the long chassis and though the model was built primarily as an owner-driver car, quite a number were sold with coachwork to be chauffeur-driven, and Barker produced a very elegant Sedanca de Ville especially for the Continental chassis as one of their standard designs.

The order for the coachwork of 31 GX was given to Park Ward on 9 April 1931, the body, described as a metal panel Weymann-type saloon, was finished in black cellulose and the head covered with fawn leather with the interior in blue leather. The tools were fitted in the top of the luggage box which was mounted at the rear, after the style of 26 EX, but only one rear mounted spare wheel was fitted, and there was no sub-frame. This car carried a London registration number, GP 2449. The Company did not keep this car in the Experimental Department for very long; on 19 January 1932, it was sold to James Grose Ltd, of Northampton, who supplied it to Stanley E Sears of Collingtree. This was his first Rolls-Royce car and he was so delighted with it that it began his long association with Rolls-Royce Ltd.

Wishing to know all about his new car and be able to maintain it in perfect condition, Stanley Sears attended the Rolls-Royce School of Instruction at Cricklewood, motoring there daily from his home in Northampton. He found this chassis extremely lively, in fact he has told me that it is the most lively Phantom II he has ever driven and that when he took the car on the Continent he was able to reach 100 mph with it.

However, he found it had one very serious defect; on hot days, and particularly in the South of France, it became like a furnace in the front compartment, the sliding glass windows did not help to alleviate this situation as the ventilation through them was most inadequate. Stanley Sears has told me that he purchased the car through James Grose Ltd, from Rolls-Royce Ltd, in Conduit Street when it had covered about 15,000 miles from new; the policy of the Company at that time was never to discuss a car's previous history with the purchaser and all he was told was that it was their demonstrator. It was not until last year that he discovered that the car was their last experimental Phantom II and he was most interested when I told him this. He says that it would pull 275 lb per ton on the Tapley performance meter at 40 mph, which is exceptional, and that it would run up to 70 mph in third gear and do 95 mph in top gear at any time. In 1933 he had it repainted in nigger brown, with fine orange lining, and the blue leather upholstery, which was somewhat worn, was changed to brown leather; ace discs were fitted to the wheels.

He says that the car was extremely reliable and gave no trouble at all, but he found that the rear springs were a little soft, that they bottomed at high speeds on Continental roads, so these were changed to ones of a higher rating.

He motored over 50,000 miles with 31 GX, but then began to find the ventilation problem insurmountable. 'One was absolutely roasted alive in the summer' he says. Also, owing to its very light construction, the body was beginning to rattle on rough roads. So in 1934 he took delivery of one of the new 3½-litre Bentleys, with coachwork designed by himself and built to his special order by Salmons of Newport Pagnell.

Some time during the next few years 31 GX was owned by Madelaine Carroll, the famous film star, and eventually, just before the 1939 War, it was bought by a firm of undertakers, George Cullen Bros of 38, Carholme Road, Lincoln, and after using it as a following car for a while it was converted into a hearse, a far cry from its original sporting start in life. However, Cullen Brothers were delighted with it and still own it today, although they have not actually run it since 1961.

PART II CHAPTER 7

The first production chassis Phantom II in the WJ series. The impression of an 11 year old schoolboy and his first run in the Phantom II chassis No. 63 GN and later in 167 GN.

When the Phantom II was first announced in September 1929, it created enormous interest, which is hardly surprising as it was the first completely new design by Royce of a 40/50 h p model since 1906. Unfortunately it coincided with a crisis on Wall Street, and a general slump in the world economic situation, therefore the Company did not receive anything like the number of orders for the new model they had envisaged and in fact did not quite reach the number of orders which had been accepted for the 'New Phantom' in 1925.

The first chassis series was WJ, often stated by people in the various Clubs today to be a 1929 model Phantom II, which is not strictly correct. It is true that both WJ and early XJ series were erected at Derby in 1929, but they are really 1930 models, as it was customary at that time to bring out new models prior to the Annual Motor Show. Actually in the later 1930s, when Austins had entered the cheaper market with Morris, there was such rivalry between the two to announce their new models first, that at one stage they were being brought out in June!

Once Rolls-Royce Ltd, had decided to bring out a new model, the first cars of the series were invariably built for the Company's use as 'Trials Cars'. The first production chassis Phantom II, chassis No. 1 WJ was already in the early stages of erection; it was to have been 24 EX, another experimental car, but the Company were so satisfied with the previous models tested at Chateauroux that they felt sufficiently confident to produce the new car without further trials.

The details of Chassis No. 1 WJ are as follows:-

Chassis No. 1 WJ
Engine No. VK 75
Steering position 'E'
Fittings nickel. Levers standard
Long wheelbase
Second spare wheel. Locks to bonnet. RR mascot.
Carrier at rear for both spare wheels
4 black grid locks (Harrison & Sons). Trunk by Harrison as supplied to 18 EX
Closed coupled saloon by Barker & Co Ltd, finished in cellulose Old Ivory and Havana Brown. Brown leather upholstery as in front of Sg's car
Body was laid down for Chassis No. 24 EX
Body price £825
Coachbuilders instructed 31.7.1929
Index No. UU 8045
Mr Northey to try seats and settle position of instrument board as soon as possible
Ventilator to top of scuttle. Side ventilators to scuttle
No arm-rests to front seats
Front seat control to back-light blind
Baffle plates to wings
Rear ivory fittings to interior
Painted asbestos lined metal shield to part of petrol tank
Main cushion in two, detachable arm-rest to fit between cushions of rear seat
Companion with ashtray recessed into each quarter. Type to be selected
Smith wireless type lighter to front instrument board and to nearside of main seat
Pockets to all doors except offside front door
Window winder on offside front door must be clear of driver's arm
Driving mirror to offside
Lucas P 100 headlights. Central lamp foot operated two way switch
C.A.V. type wing lamps. Triplex glass throughout

In addition to this type of Barker body being mounted on 1 WJ, another was built for 14 WJ, so in all this coachwork appeared on five 40/50 hp chassis of the Phantom II type, 18 EX, 19 EX, 24 EX with left hand drive, 1 WJ and 14 WJ.

1 WJ remained a Company car being used as a 'Trials Car' until 23 March 1931 when the car was sold to Sir William H Peat, KBE, of 11, Ironmonger Lane, EC2 for £1,850 — 'Car sold as it stands with body, tyres and accessories, the whole in secondhand condition'.

An allowance of £1,275 was made against 20/25 Chassis No. GGP 70 which the Company took in part exchange.

During the time that 1 WJ was in use as a 'Trials Car', it was taken to Spain by the present Marquis of Ailesbury,* who now lives in Jersey and who at the time was a well-known motoring journalist. After the completion of this trip he wrote an article which appeared in three parts in the *Autocar* for the weeks of July 11th, 18th and 25th 1930, entitled 'A Hurricane Tour' by Vagrant.

The Marquis of Ailesbury remembers this trip quite clearly, he had a representative of the sales department with him, who, on going through a town at about 30 mph said, 'Either drive very slowly and let everyone see the car or really impress them by going at 60 mph'.

Rolls-Royce Ltd were to sell this car no less than three times, as, on 15 April 1932, Sir William H Peat did another part exchange with the company. This time he took delivery of Chassis No. 49 GX, a Continental Phantom II, and the Company sold 1 WJ to Jack Barclay Ltd for £1,100.

1 WJ has not been heard of for many years, the last known of this chassis is that it was out in India.

A Hooper enclosed drive limousine had been laid down as the original body for chassis No. 26 EX. Now it will be recalled that 26 EX was the prototype Continental Phantom II with coachwork designed by Ivan Evernden and now owned by Douglas Worrall (see Part II, Chapter 5). This shows quite clearly that there was a break in building experimental chassis, as this body was then allocated to 2 WJ. The details therefore of 2 WJ are as follows:-
Chassis No. 2 WJ. Engine No. XI 15. Coach-work - enclosed drive limousine by Hooper.

Finished in Bergers platinum grey cellulose and black.
Cloth to rear compartment, black vaumol leather to front. Interior wood-work laurel French polish.
This chassis had 'C' type steering and the cost of the body was £875. It had the latest type folding luggage grid at the rear, designed by Ivan Evernden, and the latest pattern rear mounted spare wheel; there was a second spare wheel on the nearside front wing, a special cover was provided to cover the well when the wheel was not being carried. The index number of 2 WJ was UU 8046, and the car remained the property of the Company until it was sold as a second-hand car to Jack Barclay Ltd, on 24 October 1931, for £1,530.

3 WJ carried an open touring body by Barker, originally laid down for 25 EX, which it will be recalled had started life as a Park Ward limousine, left-hand drive with centre-change gearbox. It had been taken out to America by Ernest Hives aboard the White Star Liner *Homeric* and later the body had been removed and fitted to 22 EX. The chassis was sold and rebuilt as an open tourer by Whittingham & Mitchell and 25 EX survives to this day in the Rolls-Royce Owners Club of America (for full details see Part II, Chapter 4).

The details of 3 WJ therefore are as follows:-
Chassis No. 3 WJ. Engine No. VK 35. Axle ratio 11 x 41. Open touring body by Barker. Finished in cream and olive green, with olive green leather interior and hood. Steering column 'E'. Two spare wheels mounted at the rear vertically (as on 18 EX and 1 WJ). Long wheelbase.

This chassis was a 'Trials Car' until 3 November 1930, when it was sold for £2,000 as a second-hand car to Henry Palethorpe, Esq, Palethorpe Ltd, (a well-known food manufacturer) Tipton, Staffs. The registration number was UU 8047.

4 WJ was built to be exhibited at the Paris Salon, 3 - 13 October 1929 and the details are as follows:-
Chassis No. 4 WJ. Engine No. VK 25. Axle ratio 11 x 41. Long chassis. Saloon limousine by Hooper. Finished in body panels, top of bonnet, scuttle and wheels in Bergers

*It is regretted that the Marquis of Ailesbury has died since this was written

platinum grey. Mouldings along bonnet side and uppers in Ford grey. Head leather, wings and valences in azure blue. Seats and squabs in striped cloth. 'E' type steering.

This coachwork must have been after the style of 18 EX and 1 WJ as there was a fitted luggage trunk at the rear with no luggage grid, and two spare wheels mounted vertically at the rear of the car. It was exhibited on the Paris Show stand, having been shipped over to France aboard the General Tramp Company's steamer *Whitstable* from Folkestone to Boulogne. After being exhibited at the Paris Motor Show, it was taken to the Prague Motor Show, the 23 - 31 October 1929. It was then sold to a Mr Herbert Warden of 34, St James Street, London.

5 WJ. Engine XI 25. Long chassis. Axle ratio 11 x 41. Sedanca de Ville coachwork by Barker. Finished in cellulose yellow with black wings, chassis valance and petrol tank. Interior brown vaumol leather in front, sand stone cloth in rear, (as on chassis No. 43 KR - Sidgreaves car). 'B' type steering. Rear mounted spare (1) with the new type luggage grid.

This chassis was also to be exhibited on the Rolls-Royce stand at the Paris Motor Show. It was shipped over to Boulogne via Folkestone on the Southern Railway Company's 11.0 am service and was sold after the Show to Messrs Emilio F Vagner of Edificio Wiese, Lima, Peru, for the use of Mr Augusto N Wiese.

Production of the 'New Phantom' ceased at Derby with the introduction of the Phantom II and those clients who already had a 'New Phantom' on order took delivery of a Phantom II.

The first time that I personally knew that Rolls-Royce Ltd, had introduced a new model in the form of a Phantom II, was when my mother's younger brother, Reginald Beaumont-Thomas, arrived quite unexpectedly one late afternoon with a beautiful, red covered Rolls-Royce Sales Catalogue, (which I still possess) in his hand; he had come to see my mother to tell her about the new car he had ordered that very afternoon, and he gave me the Sales Catalogue to keep.

The following year in August 1930, whilst we were staying at Canford Cliffs near Bournemouth my uncle came down to stay for a few days at the Royal Bath Hotel and he had with him his new Phantom II chassis No. 63 GN, which was carrying Sedanca de Ville coachwork by Freestone & Webb, he had taken delivery of the car earlier in the year and was very pleased with it.

I still remember vividly my first run in a Phantom II, it was from Canford Cliffs to Corfe Castle and the Purbeck Hills, via Poole and Wareham; even as a boy I was struck by the extraordinary silence of the car, coupled with the fantastic acceleration and superb springing.

It is difficult now, over four decades later, for the younger generation to realize the tremendous impression the Phantom II made in 1930, as there has been such a tremendous improvement over the years in the acceleration, suspension and general handling of all mass produced cars, so much so Rolls-Royce Ltd, have found it difficult to keep ahead in this way, especially during the post-war years. Nevertheless, old as it is now the Phantom II is still a most impressive car and this is borne out most strongly by the reaction of present day motorists when they ride in one for the first time.

As soon as she saw her son's 63 GN, my grandmother, Norah Beaumont-Thomas, (who was running chassis No. 85 AU with an enclosed drive limousine body by Connaught), immediately ordered a Phantom II, chassis No. 167 GN for herself and arranged for Freestone & Webb to build the body for her. She ordered an enclosed drive limousine de ville, most elaborately fitted with a specially woven blue Bedford Cord to the rear compartment, facing sideways occasional seats, a dropping division and between the occasional seats a cocktail cabinet, all the woodwork was figured walnut and all the exterior and interior fittings silver plated, the window winders and interior door handles had real tortoise-shell back plates to them.

167 GN was in constant use from the day the car was delivered in July 1930, until 1939, and during this time a total mileage of something over 75,000 miles was covered, including one trip to the Continent to Baden-Baden. Naturally over the years I made innumerable journeys in this car.

When the War came it was laid up in the garage at Brighton and on the death of Mrs Beaumont-Thomas, in January 1944, was included in the sale of her Estate held on the premises, and was bought by Philip Turner, (who traded as Philip Turner Ltd, in St James Street, Piccadilly, and who dealt in second-hand cars of exotic design which were low mileage). He purchased it for re-sale and it passed to a firm of Wedding and Funeral Furnishers at Southsea.

They ran 167 GN until 1955 by which time it was more economical to purchase another second-hand Rolls-Royce for their business than to give 167 GN a complete overhaul and, much to my regret now, the car was scrapped, but I was able to retrieve its original mascot which I have on chassis No. 101 SK.

My uncle did not keep his cars very long, but he used 63 GN for several Concours d'Elégance and won a number of cups with it. He also entered the car in the 1930 Monte Carlo Rally, but unfortunately, owing to family reasons he had to cancel at the last moment. He decided he would like another body built by Freestone & Webb, this time on an 8-litre Bentley chassis, so 63 GN was sold, also to Philip Turner whose stock must have been somewhat slow moving as several advertisements appeared for 63 GN in the second-hand columns of *The Autocar* and *The Motor*, worded as follows:-

£2,100 very latest Phantom II with Freestone & Webb sports saloon with division, specially built for Managing Director, winner of several Concours d'Elégance, cost with extras £3,000 tax paid until end of year, and insurance for six months, in every respect a new car.

This advertisement appeared in May and June 1931. When the car was finally sold it was shipped out to India where somewhat bizarrely it was sat on by an elephant, and it came home to Freestone & Webb for repairs long before the War. After the work was completed it went back to India, and the last known owner of it was a Mrs Desaray of Mysore, in 1953, and I have often wondered what has become of it.

It is interesting to recall that in the foreword to the original sales catalogue for the Phantom II, Wilfred Gordon Aston, one of the motoring critics of the time concludes as follows:-

Finally, my impression of this wonderful new 'Phantom II' Rolls-Royce is that it is unequalled, much less surpassed, in its peculiarly well balanced combination of all the qualities which should be found in the highest expression of automobile engineering. It is as appropriate to long-distance high-speed touring as to the congestion of Bond Street, as fitted for the Alps as for the English by-lane. In all conditions it is the quintessence of tractability, of implicit obedience to control. With its broader scope of performance and with its heightened standard of refinement, the introduction of this 'Phantom II' Rolls-Royce may be truthfully said to mark a new epoch in the world's automobile history, and, in particular it will be the pride, as it will be the envy, of every Briton.

PART II CHAPTER 8

The strange story of 74 GN built for Sir Julian Cahn, Bart. The car changes hands and is owned by Mrs Bower Ismay and crosses the Sahara on a trip to Timbuktu in December 1933, later it is made into a bus and laid up for 24 years, it becomes a caravan, then is re-bodied as a 'Victoria' 5 seat Coupé

The expression 'once a Rolls, always a Rolls' is often used when describing the effect which owning a Rolls-Royce has on people. This is borne out by looking through the original Guarantee Books, a fascinating past-time, the same names appear, again and again, which illustrates how satisfied customers have been over the years.

The name Sir Julian Cahn appears many times; he lived at Stanford Hall, (a large Estate on the B5324 between Loughbrough and Melton Mowbray, now a Co-operative Training College); and was famous as the enthusiast who ran his own private cricket team. He was also a most ardent admirer of Rolls-Royce and between 1929, and his death in the early 1940s, he owned the following chassis:

93 WJ - ordered 11 July 1929, landaulette by Hooper.

23 GN - ordered 18 October 1929, open tourer by Hooper.

74 GN - ordered 29 October 1929, Arthur Mulliner limousine.

77 MW - ordered 26 May 1933, sports limousine by Arthur Mulliner.

85 MW - ordered 16 June 1933, limousine by Hooper.

50 SK - ordered 25 May 1934, coupe by Woolley.

In addition to the above mentioned Phantom II chassis he also had two Phantom III chassis, 3-AX-15, a sports saloon limousine by J S Woolley (a Nottingham coachbuilder), and 3-AX-37, an enclosed limousine by the same firm.

As can be seen, he never kept his cars long and, early in 1932, chassis No. 74 GN was back in Northampton at Arthur Mulliner's for sale. It was offered as a second-hand vehicle carrying the unexpired portion of the guarantee and was bought by Mrs Bower Ismay of Haselbech Hall, Northampton, who had been running a 1926 Daimler 35/120 'R' type, fitted with a landaulette body built by Arthur Mulliner of Bridge Street, Northampton, in which she had toured all over Europe, including such countries as Yugoslavia. It was invariably driven by Billy Wrighton, who must have been an outstanding chauffeur and who had been employed by Mrs Ismay for some years.

Mrs Bower Ismay was an American by birth, and a widow. She had long been fascinated by the mysterious East and the way of life of the Arabs, and had even learned to speak Arabic by attending classes in London. So it was not surprising that she conceived the idea of journeying to Timbuktu by car, knowing that she had not only a first class chauffeur, but 'The Best Car in the World'. She was aware it would not be an easy journey, but, judging from the extent of the preparations, it would seem doubtful whether she had any real appreciation of the privations she and her entourage would suffer.

The name Timbuktu has a romantic ring about it and for years had drawn motorists and other hardy adventurous types to attempt the crossing of the Sahara Desert in order to reach their goal. The crossing is possible only during December, January and February, and it was December that Mrs Ismay chose for her attempt. Permission for the crossing was sought from the French Government, who laid down strict rules that were necessary to ensure survival in the event of a mishap. Mrs Ismay always had the roof of her cars reinforced with wooden battens and a luggage rail fitted, to accommodate the many items of personal luggage she always carried. The reinforcement made the roof strong enough to support the weight of a man stowing luggage.

The journey commenced on Tuesday, 12 December 1933. Mrs Ismay set out from Haselbech Hall, with Wrighton driving 74 GN. She was accompanied by her great friend, Dora Smee, and her personal maid, Edna. Their destination that day was Mrs Ismay's London flat, in Brook Street.

The following day Edna was sent to cash a cheque for the money needed on the journey, an event that caused quite a sensation because the Bank clerk did not believe Timbuktu existed in reality. Perhaps this was an omen, for the journey started badly and got worse as it progressed. On the morning of 14 December, which was the day when they had planned to motor to Dover and cross the English Channel, the weather was exceptionally bad. A telephone call to the A A revealed there was no hope of crossing the channel that day, but because 74 GN was already partially loaded, they decided to proceed to Dover as planned and spend the night at the Lord Warden Hotel. By 1.00 p m the following day they had embarked, arriving in Calais at 2.15 p m after a rough crossing. They were met by the French Agent for the A.A. who knew both Mrs Ismay and Wrighton quite well as a result of their previous trips to the Continent. It was very cold in Calais and they endured a chilly drive to Amiens where they arrived at the Hotel de Univers just after 9.00 p m. Fortunately the hotel was both warm and comfortable, for France was in the grip of the coldest winter for 26 years.

On Saturday, 16 December, the party left Amiens at 8.50 a m and travelled along snow covered roads as far as Versailles, en route for Saulieu. Hot water bottles, which were refilled at the Juvisy-sur-Orge lunch stop, helped keep them warm until they arrived at their destination, the Coq d'Or Hotel. Although the hotel was not as warm as that at Amiens, a hot bath compensated for the cold drive.

The morning of Sunday, 17 December,

proved exceptionally cold, with a piercing wind and ice in abundance. Wrighton had found frost in the radiator, even though he had drained it, and all the other cars garaged at the hotel needed hot water before they would start. There had been 14 degrees of frost (Centigrade) that night. Mrs Ismay's party left at 9.00 a m, again on snow covered roads, comforted by their hot water bottles. A good lunch at Villefranche-sur-Saone and the thought that they had only a short distance to cover before they embarked on the steamer for Algiers helped ease their anxiety. It was during the afternoon run to Marseilles that they encountered the most dangerous part of the journey so far: a long ice-covered hill littered with abandoned vehicles. It was here that Wrighton displayed some of his driving skill, and they arrived safely in Marseilles without further incident.

The crossing from Marseilles to Algiers proved exceptionally rough, and both Dora Smee and Edna were soon prostrate in their cabins, the latter completely oblivious of Mrs Ismay's four huge suitcases which lurched about her cabin. The general situation is best summed up by Mrs Ismay's pronouncement when she knocked on Edna's cabin door to enquire about her well-being. 'Miss Smee is flat out in her cabin, half the crew are ill, the crockery has smashed and Wrighton has gone to bed with his boots on!' With this, she disappeared.

When the party disembarked at Algiers, none was in good shape, apart from Mrs Ismay, who was a good sailor and in consequence felt fine. All luggage was deposited at an hotel, whilst they made the necessary preparations for the four-day journey across the Sahara. The authorities advised that it was not a dangerous undertaking if the rules were observed. It was essential to carry plenty of food and water and to understand that if they lost the road or struck trouble, they must remain where they were until help arrived. A deposit was paid to the French Consul to cover this latter eventuality; at the same time they also obtained additional supplies of petrol, which were carried in bidons, on the luggage grid of 74 GN. The petrol tank held only 20 gallons, hopelessly inadequate for the now heavily loaded car. A strange addition to the luggage was 400 candles; Mrs Ismay had a fear of the dark and read late into the night.

They reached Mascara on the first day without incident and it was not until the second day, South of Mecheria, that they encountered the first of many hazards. Snow and rain had turned the track into a morass of mud and 74 GN was soon hopelessly bogged down in an area of complete desolation. Wrighton managed to dig the car out, aided by Dora Smee and Edna, who helped push. Eventually they reached Beni-Ounif on 23 December, when they had covered the most unbelievable distance of 310 miles.

It was their practice to set off each day, soon after it was light, in order to reach the next Fort before darkness fell. The first Fort would telegraph ahead to the next Fort on the route and advise them to expect the car at a time of arrival which they could estimate. If they happened to meet another car they stopped, as requested by the authorities, and exchanged details so that they could report the time at which they had passed each other. This simple precaution made it possible to check when a car was last seen and its approximate location in the event of it being overdue at its destination.

Mrs Ismay's party carried no firearms and it is indeed fortunate that Wrighton paid no heed to her requests to offer a lift to every Arab she saw walking along the road. Throughout the journey, Mrs Ismay sat in the back of the car, either reading a book or occasionally looking at the drab scenery. She also had a typewriter, with which she recorded the highlights of the day's events, and a camera with a great number of films. These two last acquisitions enabled her to make a complete record of the journey, which was subsequently translated into three extremely large photograph albums.

As may be expected, the hotels in which they stayed were primitive in the extreme. Lighting was often provided by means of a hand-turned dynamo; the lights dimmed and eventually extinguished when the Arab turning the handle grew tired. One of Edna's first duties on reaching an hotel was to place candles around Mrs Ismay's bedroom, so that if she woke in the night, she could read in comfort. One hotelier's wife, who could speak a little English, likened this performance to a funeral!

The hotels or Forts at which they had stayed provided a packed luncheon and to supplement this, figs, dates, biscuits, raisins and chocolate were also carried. On one memorable occasion the screwdriver and pliers from 74 GN's toolkit were used to dissect a chicken, the hotel having forgotten to include either knives or forks! Worse still, they later found the chicken had been cooked without first being drawn. It was full of eggs, which Mrs Ismay had first thought to be a very novel form of stuffing!

Christmas Day was spent driving between Beni Abbes and Adrar. When they stopped for lunch they found the hotel had forgotten to pack any meal at all, so they ate figs, dates and biscuits, followed by a Christmas pudding. It was fortuitous that Dora Smee's students* had presented her with the pudding as a joke, 'to prolong her life in the desert!' In her notes that day, Mrs Ismay recorded that they had covered no less than 284 miles, over roads so rough and stony that she expected it would break one of the springs.

Adrar was reached at 6.30 p m, where a good meal and good accommodation helped offset the rigours of the day. On 26 December they had a short run to Reggane, over a flat track that passed by several oases. At Reggane, they were faced with a barren, waterless crossing but were comforted by a young French Lieutenant who volunteered to accompany them with his men and lorries as he would be travelling in the same direction the following morning.

Mrs Ismay's party started early, leaving the Lieutenant and his men to follow. The lorries were too slow and would have curtailed progress. On this occasion they started in the dark, an unwise move since they had extreme difficulty in keeping to a track which was anything but well marked. The only consolation was the extreme hardness of the road, which permitted speeds of up to 70 mph, and the placing of metal boxes every 6¼ miles that acted as markers also for aircraft using the road as a navigational aid. They managed to cover 330 miles that day, to a remote spot known as 'Bidon Cinq'.

At Bidon Cinq, the hotel comprised two old motor bus bodies standing back to back, with a space between them in the shelter of which a table was placed. All meals were served at this

*Dora Smee was a doctor of geography at Bedford College for women in Regents Park, London until her retirement

table; the interiors of the bus bodies contained a series of bunks on which the travellers slept, protected only by sacking that hung across the windows to replace the broken glass. The establishment was run by one Berber, who also had responsibility for a petrol pump, used to replenish traveller's cars. Supplies were brought to Bidon Cinq every fortnight and the Berber usually took in more provisions than was necessary so that he could cope with emergencies. As luck would have it, the supplies were overdue on the occasion of 74 GN's arrival and although there was food, no petrol was available. Somehow Wrighton managed to explain that petrol was essential to their progress and the Berber led them to a place a half-mile away where the Foreign Legion had buried petrol for their own use. In due course 74 GN's main tank was refilled and also the bidons carried on the luggage grid. They had just completed refuelling when a column of dust announced the approach of the Foreign Legion. With great presence of mind, Mrs Ismay typed a letter in fluent French to the Capitaine-in-Charge, explaining that she was travelling to Timbuktu in her chauffeur-driven Rolls-Royce with her companion and maid and that they were stranded without petrol. 'So', she wrote 'we have stolen yours. We are quite prepared to pay for it but we are not prepared to return it'. The Berber delivered her letter and reappeared with a most courteous reply, in which the Capitaine stated he quite understood the reason for taking the petrol and would be grateful if the whole party would join him for dinner that evening. Thus sprang up a pen friendship between Mrs Ismay and the gallant Capitaine that continued for many years after the journey. Returning to the dubious comforts of the old buses late that night, the party experienced one of the most miserable nights they had spent whilst in North Africa. The temperature plunged downwards and even though they wore every available garment, supplemented by rugs and hot water bottles, the inadequacies of the sacking over the broken windows and the frailness of the old bus bodies offered little protection from the intense cold.

When they set out the following morning, 28 December 1933, they were still 250 miles away from their destination. All went well at first, but

then the track began to climb steadily towards the distant horizon. Without warning, 74 GN sank into soft sand and no matter what he did, Wrighton succeeded only in making it settle more deeply. In the heat of the Sahara sun he had no option other than to unload the car completely, then place under the rear tyres some sheets of corrugated iron he had picked up en route and had stowed on the luggage grid. When everyone pushed, the car would drive the length of the corrugated iron sheets, only to bury itself in the soft sand once more. In desperation, he deflated the rear tyres in an endeavour to obtain better grip, a task made difficult because it was first necessary to remove the wheel discs to reach the valves. They toiled for 5½ hours in this fashion and eventually succeeded in extricating the car. Wrighton then inspected the road ahead to Timbuktu which was just as soft and Mrs Ismay then realized with disappointment that they would have to turn back. The hill stretched ahead interminably and it would clearly have been impossible to reach the summit in the heat of the sun if the car bogged down every few yards. Mrs Ismay's decision was undoubtedly wise, although it was an acute disappointment to have been so close to their objective. They did not retrace the same route on their return and instead stayed overnight at Tabankor. They had travelled only 110 miles that day, and were in a state of almost complete exhaustion. The following day, 29 December, they set off for Reggane, some 330 miles away. On arrival, they were dismayed to learn that a heavy snowfall in the Atlas Mountains had made their intended route impassable. So they made a detour from Reggane to El Golea and from there to Laghauot, arriving back in Algiers on 3 January 1934. They had covered 1,490 miles in six days, a quite remarkable feat when it is remembered that Wrighton was the only member of the party qualified to drive. 74 GN had acquitted itself well too, for it had received tremendous punishment throughout the journey. Dora Smee boarded the boat to Marseilles and travelled across France by train, in order to return to Bedford College for the start of term.

Mrs Ismay decided she would like to see

more of North Africa and on 6th January, only three days after her return to Algiers, she was joined by John Churchill (a relation of Sir Winston Churchill) for a journey to Fez. They departed for Tlemcen on the first day, covering 368 miles, and on the following day continued on to Fez, a further 292 miles. Profiting from his earlier experiences, Wrighton now carried shovels on the car and they were used to good effect when the car encountered a landslide that would otherwise have stopped them. Aided by John Churchill, a passage was cleared just wide enough for 74 GN to negotiate. Wrighton took the car through on his own, no mean feat since the car leaned at an angle of some 30º in places. From Fez they returned to Algiers, stopping in Oran for the night after covering another 386 miles. The following day they were back in Algiers, having covered the remaining 292 miles.

Three days later, on 12th January, Mrs Ismay and her party left Algiers to travel westward to Constantine, a distance of 94 miles, and then to Le Kef, 342 miles further on. The next day they reached Tunis, covering a further 192 miles, where they spent a whole day sightseeing. On 16th January they motored from Tunis to Philippeville, a distance of 114 miles on an alternative route back to Algiers. From Philippeville

they travelled a further 270 miles to Biskra and whilst staying there overnight learned that the Arues were worth a visit. This is a range of mountains 120 miles from Biskra, reached by a picturesque route. They made a day's excursion as a result, a round trip of 262 miles in total. The following day was spent sight-seeing in Biskra before they returned to Algiers on 20th January, a distance of only 150 miles, easily achieved when compared with the many miles 74 GN had already undertaken. Three days later they embarked for Marseilles, the first stage of their return journey across France. They arrived in Calais on 26 January 1934.

On 27th January, 74 GN arrived back at Haselbach Hall, the long adventure successfully accomplished. The car was still smothered in sand, especially on the underside where it adhered to oil from the one-shot lubrication system. It took a whole day to restore the car to her former pristine appearance, as a prelude to a complete check-over two days later at the Rolls-Royce Service Station at Cricklewood.

It is sad that Wrighton died many years ago, as I would so much like to have had this personal view of this journey and his opinion of how 74 GN stood up to the conditions.

The Mileage and Route taken by Mrs Bower Ismay in her Rolls-Royce Phantom II, chassis No 74 GN, December 14th, 1933 - January 27th, 1934

1933					Miles
Dec	15	Calais to Amiens	:	:	90
	16	Amiens to Saulieu	:	:	280
	17	Saulieu to Avignon	:	:	290
	18	Avignon to Marseilles	:	:	90
	22	Marseilles to Mascara	:	:	255
	23	Mascara to Beni-Ounif	:	:	310
	24	Beni-Ounif to Beni Abbes	:	:	210
	25	Beni Abbes to Adrar	:	:	248
	26	Adrar to Reggan	:	:	98
	27	Reggan to Bidon Cinq	:	:	330
	28	Bidon Cinq to Tabankor	:	:	110
	29	Tabankor to Reggan	:	:	330
	30	Reggan to Timimoun	:	:	210
	31	Timimoun to El Golea	:	:	265

1934	1	El Golea to Ghardaia	:	:	205
Jan	2	Ghardaia to Laghouat	:	:	130
	3	Laghouat to Algiers	:	:	350
	6	Algiers to Tlemcen	:	:	368
	7	Tlemcen to Fez	:	:	292
	8	Fez to Oran	:	:	386
	9	Oran to Algiers	:	:	292
	12	Algiers to Constantine	:	:	94
	13	Constantine to Le Kef	:	:	342
	14	Le Kef to Tunis	:	:	192
	16	Tunis to Philippeville	:	:	114
	17	Philippeville to Biskra	:	:	270
	18	Day's Excursion in The Arues	:	:	262
	20	Biskra to Algiers	:	:	150
	24	Marseilles to Montelimar	:	:	126
	25	Montelimar to Troyes	:	:	325
	26	Troyes to Calais	:	:	283
					7,297

Ron Haynes gave me the following details, from the Service Files which are appended here. These show what a very big mileage 74 GN covered between Mrs Ismay first having the car in 1932 until the spring of 1939, when she purchased 3-AZ-146. It also shows what extraordinarily good service the car gave during this time, it is very unfortunate that it is not known exactly how many miles 74 GN had covered before Mrs Ismay bought the car nor is it known when the engine was re-bored and the main bearings of the crankshaft re-ground; there is nothing about either of these items on the File at Hythe Road, so it can only be assumed that this work was carried out before Mrs Ismay bought the car.

Extract from Service File at Hythe Road

First Job Card: 30.8.1933. Front brakes and servo re-lined, dynamo overhauled. Tune up engine. Lubricate chassis.

29.1.1934. Mrs Ismay. 67,207 miles. Top decarbonisation. Rear S/A reset. Skim brake drums. Re-line front and rear. Fit new front silencer. Modify rear silencer. Job Card endorsed: Repair underneath of chassis after a Tour of the Desert. Car finished 9.2.1934.

8.3.1935. Mrs Ismay. 84,718. Fit new exhaust swan neck and telegauge.

25.6.1935. Mrs Ismay. 90,604. Fit replacement water pump.

18.5.1936. Mrs Ismay. 105,205. Fit new Hardy Clutch coupling.

7.2.1939. Mrs Ismay. 125.012. Top decarbonisation. Renew water pump gland. Adjust clutch toggle. Re-line servo. Car Completed 14.2.1939.

Note: In April 1939 Mrs Bower Ismay bought Phantom III, chassis 3-AZ-146, and later 74 GN became an estate bus, and was laid up from 1939 to 1964 at Haselbech Hall.

I first met Mrs Bower Ismay in March 1958 and from then until her death in February 1963 I was fortunate enough to come to know her very well indeed, also her chauffeur Kenneth Hunnisett and the two Rolls-Royce cars, which he always kept in the most impeccable order. When Mrs Ismay died she left both cars to Hunnisett, who had been in her employ for 38 years and after her Will was proved I purchased them from him (for details of Phantom III 3-AZ-146 see Part III Chapter 8).

When Mrs Ismay acquired 3-AZ-146 to replace 74 GN, the original Arthur Mulliner limousine was removed from the latter which chassis was rebuilt into a sixteen seater bus. The coachwork was by James Grose of Northampton; the idea was to use it as a general utility vehicle about the Estate and to take the staff on outings, but War broke out before the new body was completed, so 74 GN returned to

Haselbech and was laid up, where it was to remain until March 1964 when I collected it and drove the car down to Cornwall. It had not been on the road for twenty four years and, apart from some boiling owing to the radiator being partially choked, it ran superbly, cruising effortlessly at 60 mph.

We found a first class coachbuilder near Penzance, who removed the interior and rebuilt it as a fully motorized caravan to sleep four persons, complete with sink, cooker etc. The cost of this interior conversion was approximately £375 and later in the year we toured all over Scotland, living in the car for a whole month. During this trip the car climbed the famous 'Pass of the Cattle' and the Tornapress to Applecross with plenty of power in hand and no signs of over-heating, though it was necessary to reverse twice on each hair-pin bend, which has a gradient of 1 in 3. The reception that 74 GN received in Scotland was one of mild curiosity and time and time again we were asked if it was an old ambulance, as the outside paint-work was very similar to that used on ambulances in Scotland.

In spite of an overall weight of 58 cwt on the open road 74 GN would cruise comfortably at 60 - 65 mph and would return 14 mpg on commercial fuel, but great care had to be exercised in cornering, owing to the height which was 8 ft 8 in. over the luggage rail, the overall length was 21 ft 5 in. The combination of these made steering, in cross-winds or badly cambered roads, something which required extreme caution, apart from this however the car provided very comfortable transport and mobile home. We never went into a caravan site, but always found a friendly farmer and obtained permission to park in a field or wood for the night. Level ground was essential as otherwise we found ourselves rolling out of our bunks all night!

Three years later we took the car to Ireland, using the Holyhead-Dun Loaghaire drive-on ferry and spent a month touring Southern Ireland. The reception which the car received in Ireland was if anything more amusing than it had been in Scotland three years before; on one occasion whilst parked at the roadside in Bray, a

crowd gathered around and finally a priest said in a rich brogue 'Glory be to God but it is a hearse you are riding in!' Later motoring towards Killarney, a Morris Minor containing two priests approached and as the two cars passed both priests removed their hats and crossed themselves.

The car ran so well that I felt it was worthy of a very much better body, so in December 1967 after the 'bus body' was removed in Sussex I drove the car in chassis form to Messrs I Wilkinson & Son Ltd, of Stafford Street, Derby, who were to build a 'Victoria 5 seat Coupe' body for me. They gave an estimate of £2,500 and the work took 11 months to complete. This style of coachwork is American and forms an ideal body for the person who does not wish to carry a large number of passengers, it is very compact and gives the impression that the car is considerably smaller than it actually is, though it requires a long wheelbase in order to have it correctly proportioned. It has never been very popular with English people, though Sir Harold Bowden of Raleigh Cycle fame had this style of coachwork built by the Carlton Carriage Company on chassis No. 55 GN and the complete vehicle was supplied to him by Jack Barclay Ltd. Also a similar body was built by Windovers Ltd, on a Daimler Double-Six '50' chassis for Joseph A Mackle, one of the Directors of the Daimler Company, this latter car won a great many prizes in Concours d'Elegance.

A great problem arose over the steering on 74 GN. This had originally been 'C' type, which was quite unsuitable for an owner-driver car, so it had to be lowered to 'E' position, and at the same time the poundage of the rear springs had to be drastically altered, as they had been set up to carry the heavy bus body and were far too stiff for the new coachwork.

I shall always be extremely grateful to Ron Haynes of Hythe Road for the tremendous interest and help which he gave me when trying to make the car ride properly with its new coachwork. He suggested that when the body was completed it should be weighed off the chassis and then asked me how many passengers I intended to carry in the car and what would be the maximum amount of luggage which would be carried when touring. From the figures I gave him of 4 persons and 2 cwt of luggage he worked out the necessary spring poundage.

When I collected 74 GN from Wilkinson's on 6 December 1968, the steering was still 'C' type and the top of the rim of the wheel was over ¾ way up to the top of the windscreen and the rear luggage boot was ballasted with concrete blocks in order to hold the rear springs down.

Arrangements had been made for Jack Compton to have the car immediately to lower the steering and the poundage on the rear springs. The car now rides extremely well, in fact, Ivan Evernden says it is one of the best riding Phantom IIs that he has ever been in, and even the ultra critical, Jimmy Skinner, says that he can find no fault with the way the 74 GN rides.

Since the new coachwork was built, 74 GN has toured France, Switzerland and the Isle of Man, and the total mileage is now 160,360. Immediately prior to visiting France and Switzerland the radiator was back-flushed and though the car went over some of the highest passes no overheating occurred. The car is now in Jersey, where it came after a complete engine overhaul during the winter of 1971, which was carried out by Jack Compton, the engine was taken right out of the car, the crankshaft de-sludged, the engine re-bored and sleeved and a new set of standard size pistons fitted, also a new cylinder head was fitted. There was extremely little wear in the engine and the only ball race which had to be renewed was the one in the ignition tower as this was rusty, obviously due to the very long time that the car was out of use at Haselbech Hall.

When I took over 74 GN, on 19 March 1964, the speedometer was showing 129,720 miles and since that date the annual mileage has been as follows:

1964	6,338
1965	579
1966	279
1967	3,351

Making a grand total of 10,275 as a Bus, Caravan and in chassis form.

1968	396
1969	5,759
1970	5,103
1971	4,891
1972	2,665
1973	1,053 to date.

Which give a total of 19,876 since the car was re-built as a 'Victoria 5 seat Coupe'.

PART II CHAPTER 9

The Amsterdam Show Car and Indian 'Trials Car', chassis No. 101 SK, the running of this car from October 1954 up to the present time by the same owner. Chassis No. 9 GX and the owner's impressions of it

During the years before the War of 1939, Rolls-Royce Ltd had a number of chassis fitted with coachwork built to their own special requirements, these cars were used for a wide variety of exhibition purposes throughout the World, one of which is chassis No. 101 SK.

It is a short Continental Phantom II with a Barker Sports saloon body designed by Ivan Evernden, and incorporating a sunshine roof. It was a very attractive design which was also built for chassis No. 70 SK (the 1934 London Show Car) 96 SK, 138 SK and 188 SK. It is probable that there were others also, but if so it has not been possible to trace them.

Chassis No. 101 SK was exhibited at the Amsterdam Show in January 1935, it was the 'Piéce de Resistance' of that show and the car is fully described in *The Autocar* of January for that year. It was finished in two shades of green with emerald green upholstery and steering wheel to match, and must have formed a striking exhibit.

When the Show was over, the car was shipped out to India for the use of the late Raymond Chandler, who was the Rolls-Royce representative in India.

When the Phantom III came into production, 101 SK returned to England and a Phantom III was sent out as a 'Trials Car' replacement.

On arrival back in Britain, 101 SK was put into the Conduit Street Showroom for sale as a used car, the total mileage was very small and the whole condition of the car was as new; in November 1936 it was seen by Lieutenant Commdr Colin Campbell R N, who had been running chassis No. 7 EX (see Part 1 Chapter 13).

He liked the car on sight, but could not stand the colour and would only purchase the car on condition that it was re-painted black throughout, the green steering wheel removed, a front bumper fitted and Ace discs to the wheels. Rolls-Royce Ltd, agreed to all this and the car was delivered to its new owner on 23 November 1936, bearing the index number DGT 365.

Colin Campbell invariably drove the car himself and it was looked after entirely by the Rolls-Royce London Servicing Department. He ran it with great satisfaction until the Munich crisis in September 1938. He knew that inevitably there would be a major European War and that he would be re-called to Active Service with the Navy, and he also felt that, as in the 1914 - 18 War, petrol rationing would almost certainly be introduced. In view of these factors he reluctantly decided to sell 101 SK, which he did sometime in 1939 to H R Owen Ltd, in part-exchange for a new Rover 12 Sports Saloon.

In *The Autocar* just prior to the outbreak of War, in the second-hand columns under 'Rolls-Royce' the following advertisement appeared for several weeks.

H R Owen Ltd, 17, Berkeley Street, London, W1.
40/50 h p Phantom II (last of the series, first registered November 1936), four-door, sports saloon with boot and concealed folding luggage carrier by Barker, painted black with green leather upholstery, mileage 24,000, almost as new. £575.

Of course, the advertisement is not correct, the car is not the last of the series by any means, as the SK series was followed by TA and finally

UK. The price makes interesting reading today, but even at the figure quoted, H R Owen Ltd, were unable to sell the car, the future was too uncertain.

By the end of 1939 H R Owen realized that the car was virtually unsaleable at the present time, so it was moved to the country, where it was laid up until 1945, and was eventually sold on 8 June, to Geoffrey Spence Davis, of Aberfoyle, Barnt Green, Worcestershire, who had a supplementary petrol ration for the car. However, he did not keep it very long and on 14 October 1945, it was sold to a Frank Reginald Ford of Blythe Bridge, Stoke-on-Trent, Staffordshire, who also obtained supplementary petrol for the car, to the tune of 116 gallons per month. It was not licensed again after 1947 until 8 April 1950, when it was licensed until the end of June, and another supplementary petrol ration was obtained for it. During this time 101 SK obviously did not receive the care and attention which a Rolls-Royce car deserves, and some time during the 3 months in 1950 it was offered for sale in the Car Auctions at Measham. It must have looked in a sorry state, as the highest bid was £200 when it was bought by Coachcraft of Evesham, who stored it locally until I bought it.

I had been looking for a second-hand Rolls-Royce for sometime as at the price which I could afford I would not consider a modern car and a Rolls-Royce seemed the best alternative. I had been looking at 20/25, but it was Jimmy Skinner who advised me strongly to buy a Phantom II, I shall always recall the conversation, 'Don't be silly Jimmy its 10 mpg'. 'I know it is', he replied, 'but they are very consistent performers, after all it is not as if it is to be your only car, 5,000 miles a year will cost you £100 in petrol, surely you can afford that, and you will have a car that will last you for the rest of your life'.

Not long after this 101 SK was advertised in *The Motor* and, acting on Jimmy's advice we went immediately to Evesham and bought the car for £450, a decision which I have never regretted. The speedometer reading was 39,733 when we first saw the car.

Ever since that day in October 1954, the car has been in regular use (apart from the time of the Suez crisis when petrol rationing was introduced), and at the time of writing, September 1973, the car has run approximately 82,000 miles in almost 19 years, the total mileage now recorded is 122,603.

Immediately I had the car, I took it into H E Griffin of Haywards Heath for their mechanic, Ernie Pike, (who re-built the 1905 4-cylinder 20 h p and the 1906 6-cylinder 30 h p for Stanley Sears), to give it a complete check-over and change all the oils throughout. The exhaust system was found to be in a very bad way indeed, so a new silencer and tail-pipe with fish-tail were supplied by Rolls-Royce Ltd, and fitted at the same time.

Ernie gave the car an exceedingly good report otherwise and we proceeded to use it regularly as a big family car principally for touring. In fact we have toured all over England, Scotland, Wales and Southern Ireland in 101 SK, and on the Continent Belgium, Holland, Germany and Denmark. It has never ceased to give great satisfaction and has done some exceedingly long runs, e.g., from Kent to Helensburgh, 508 miles in the day, also from London to Perth, 450 miles very easily in one day, which journey has been done several times.

Having run a Phantom II over such a large mileage and almost two decades, it might be helpful to give in some detail the various problems which can be encountered with a Phantom II, and the methods used to overcome them.

From the reports on the running of the Experimental Phantom II chassis, made at Chateauroux, it can be seen that Rolls-Royce Ltd, did their utmost to improve their product, but there is no doubt that, superb as a Phantom II is, it was designed with certain faults, which in use are bound to show up. The perfect machine has not yet been built and probably never will be, if Rolls-Royce Ltd had been determined to go on experimenting until all faults were eliminated the Company would probably have gone bankrupt in the process, and the Phantom II would never have seen the light of day at all.

The following are some of the points in a Phantom II which can cause trouble to an owner:

Camshaft

When I bought 101 SK the engine ran quietly, though it was never as silent as I remembered the engine in chassis Nos. 63 GN and 167 GN, it lacked the sweetness and silence of the two earlier cars and had a very much more 'beefy' sound to it, but after some 8,000 miles the engine became very noisy with all sorts of alarming knocks and bangs which sounded rather like a diesel engine! It was soon quite

evident that this noise was coming from the camshaft and bottom tappets as it could be stopped temporarily by removing the rocker-box cover and pouring a heavy gear oil down the valve guides. This was because during the time that the Phantom II was in production, more and more power was extracted from the engine in order to keep the model abreast of its rivals. So, commencing with chassis No. 2 MY, a higher compression cylinder head, together with bigger and heavier valves and stronger valve springs had been fitted; these allowed the engine to 'rev' more highly on the gears which gave better acceleration, but the loading on the camshaft and cam followers was such that they could not survive. Within 8 - 10,000 miles the cam followers had torn themselves to pieces, in fact Rolls-Royce Ltd, had so much trouble with the high lift camshaft that commencing with chassis No. 101 TA, the Company had reverted to the low lift camshaft for the remainder of the Phantom II series.

We had moved to Kent when this trouble first appeared and I had been strongly recommended to take the car to Jack Compton, the well known Rolls-Royce specialist who had premises at Norwood in those days; it was really too far to go all the way to H E Griffin in Haywards Heath.

As soon as I met Jack he told me that the only way of dealing with this problem was to change the camshaft to a low lift and added that he had changed several of them and could guarantee that the engine would remain quiet for the rest of its life. He gave me a quotation of £150 for doing the work, plus the cost of the new camshaft which would be £26.13.4d.

Arrangements were accordingly made for him to have the car, which he said he would require for at least a month, as it meant removing all the trays around the engine, dropping the sump and removing the pistons and connecting rods; the cylinder head had to come off, also the cylinder blocks, as it was quite impossible to remove the cam followers with the cylinder blocks still in place; in addition to this the radiator had to be removed so that all the timing wheels and the slipper drive could be checked and adjusted. The camshaft, which runs on seven bearings, has to be removed from the front of the engine.

The cylinder head was removed and sent away to Hythe Road for examination and testing and pronounced perfect; there was not all that amount of wear on the cylinder bores and it was decided that new piston rings would suffice. When I collected the car it was completely transformed and well worth every penny that had been spent on it, when Jack Compton and I took the car on a road test I could hardly believe it was the same one. I proceeded to run the engine in most carefully, at speeds not exceeding 40 mph, using plenty of Redex to allow the new piston rings to bed in, and doing long journeys especially for this purpose, and from the time that the camshaft was changed the engine has remained silent. It has been taken down twice since this work was done, the first time in February 1961 when the total mileage was 89,725. Compton had the car again and re-bored it and the cam followers were then examined and found to be in perfect condition. It was necessary to strip the engine again in August 1969 when the total mileage was 116,715, this was done by the Rolls-Royce mechanic employed at the time by St Helier Garages in Jersey. The car was running most beautifully at the time, but a very bad external water leak* had developed from the cylinder head in between the cylinder blocks, the cylinder head was most reluctant to come off and unfortunately some damage was done to the blocks in removing it, with the result that the cylinder blocks had to be sent to Hythe Road for refacing. Whilst the cylinder blocks were away the opportunity was taken of examining the camshaft and cam followers, which were still showing no signs of wear at all.

*This was simply due to a leaking cylinder head gasket

GN in the desert on the route to and from Timbuktu
(Top left) Dora works. Filling up 74GN with petrol from a 50 litre
[ti]n. Christmas Day 1933
(Top right) 'Where we found rest'. At Bidon Cinq. 27 December 1933
(Upper middle left) 'We raid the dump'. Bidon Cinq. 27 December 1933
(Upper middle right) Stuck in the sand south of Bidon Cinq. 28
[Dec]ember 1933

(Lower middle left) Deflating the tyres. 'Will sheets of tin help us move?'
(Lower middle right) 5½ hours later. 74GN completely unloaded to
lighten her, Dora Smee and Wrighton dig, whilst Edna looks on
(Bottom left) Hotel Transatlantique, Tlemcen. Ready to start again.
7 January 1934
(Bottom right) Returning to Fez from Sidi-Haraza over a land-slide.
Wrighton would permit no one to ride in the car, which heeled over to
30 degrees, but he took it across on his own. 8 January 1934

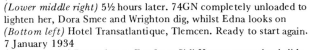

(Top left) 74GN as a bus with coach-work by James Grose of Northampton. This photograph was taken 31 years after the preceding ones, in March 1964 after the car had just completed a 280 mile run to Cornwall not having been on the road for 24 years

(Top right) 74GN with the bus body removed en route to Derby to Messrs I. Wilkinson Ltd for its third body. The metal box over the rear axle contains 10 cwt of concrete to keep the rear wheels on the road. November 1967

(Middle) 74GN as the car is today, carrying its third body, a 'Victoria 5 Seat Coupe'. This photograph was taken at Pontalier, the frontier between France and Switzerland. 17 September 1970

(Bottom) A Van Ryswyk body on an unknown chassis (photo Hugh Keller)

(*Top left*) 9GX, a Barker Saloon owned by David Berry (*photo D. Berry*)
(*Top right*) Chassis number 6JS being used as a hotel bus in Interlaken in Switzerland (*photo H. Fergusson-Wood*)
(*Middle*) Phantom II, chassis 9JS, the car from the film *The Yellow Rolls-Royce*
(*Bottom*) 11JS, a Phantom II Continental chassis carrying a Hooper Saloon Limousine body, built for the Olympia Motor Show of 1931

(Top) A left-hand drive Phantom II with American coach-work on an unknown chassis
(Middle) The interior of a left-hand drive Phantom II
(Bottom left) The offside of the same engine, number R45E, in chassis number 204AJS
(Bottom right) AMS and AJS series Phantom II engine. Left-hand drive was used for America and other overseas markets. Chassis number 204AJS, engine number R45E, showing near-side

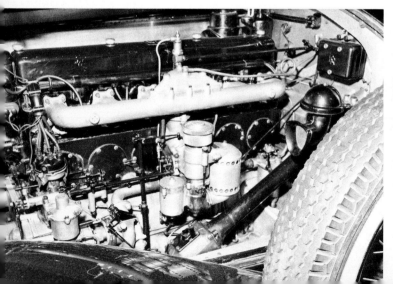

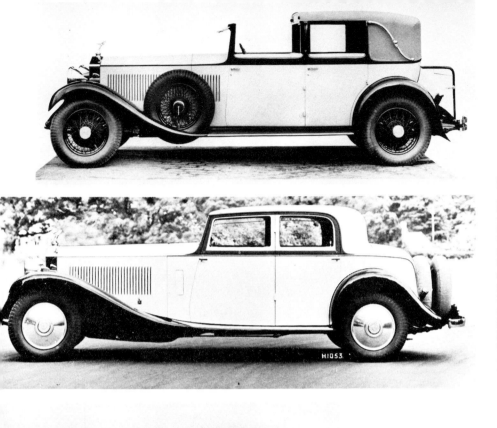

(Top) 29JS, an Enclosed Cabriolet de Ville by Park Ward (photo Hugh Keller)

(Upper middle) Chassis number 6MY, Hooper Owner Driver Saloon built for Major Delap

(Lower middle left) Built for the 1933 Paris Show this Barker Tourer Phantom II Continental chassis number 4PY with 'F' type steering had special instruments with white faces and black figures and a plated border to the instrument panel

(Lower middle right) This photograph shows a Barker Sunshine Saloon on chassis number 8PY ('F' type steering). It was built for the Olympia Show of 1933 finished in grey and blue with blue leather upholstery. The body cost £731, although the complete car cost £2489.1s.4d.

(Bottom) Hooper coachwork specially prepared for use in India. The chassis number is unknown

(*Top*) 152PY, ('C' type steering) fitted with a Barker Pullman Laudaulette body with extra seats supplied to Mrs J. Clark
(*Middle left*) 180PY, ('F' type steering) with a Barker Sunshine Foursome Coupe Continental supplied to HH The Nawab of Bahawalpur (*photo S. J. Skinner*)
(*Bottom*) A Barker Sedanca de Ville on chassis number 105RY with 'E' type steering supplied to Mrs Peel

(Top) A Barker Drophead Foursome Cabriolet de Ville on chassis number 189RY with 'F' type steering supplied to The Hon Mrs E. Harmsworth

(Middle) The production lines at Derby, note the Bentleys in the centre with the Phantom II chassis to the right

(Bottom left) Chassis number 101 SK formerly the 1935 Amsterdam Show Car, but this photograph was taken during 1935 when the car was being used by the late Raymond Chandler in India as a 'Trials Car'

(Bottom right) Chassis number 101 SK Barker Continental Sport Saloon in October 1954 just after the author purchased the car and was touring Devonshire with it. See Part II, Chapter 9

(Top) Continental Barker Sports Saloon, chassis number 188 SK, this car was originally built as another 'Trials Car'. It later became the property of Craven Ellis, MP and after his death was shipped to America. It has recently returned to the UK, having been purchased by Michael Campbell, whose maternal grandfather was Craven Ellis and strangely his paternal grandfather was Colin Campbell, who purchased an almost identical car, chassis number 101 SK from Rolls-Royce Ltd, when 101 SK came back to the UK from India in 1936. For 101 SK see previous page

(Middle) Chassis number 169TA, a Barker Enclosed Pullman Limousine de Ville with 'D' type steering and extra seats facing forwards built for and supplied to Don Juan March

(Bottom) The last Phantom II ever made supplied to the Dowager Lady Fox. The chassis number is 84UK with a Barker Enclosed Limousine Body, 'C' type steering and extra forward facing seats. This car is now in Tom Mason's collection in Kent

It is interesting to note that 74 GN has the low-lift camshaft, lower compression head with the smaller valves and lighter valve springs, and when Jack Compton had that car in the autumn of 1971 to give the engine a complete overhaul, which meant removing it right out of the chassis, the camshaft and cam followers were in perfect condition, in spite of the fact that the car had covered almost 150,000 miles from new.

I personally cannot help feeling that one of the faults in the design of the Phantom II camshaft is lack of lubrication when the engine is idling at low speed, it is for this reason that I use Castrol GTX oil in the engine to which I add 3 tins of STP every time the oil is changed, and I never allow the engine to idle really slowly for any length of time.

Radiator

If the owner of a Phantom II is going to motor happily on long journeys at a fairly high average speed, it is absolutely essential that the radiator is back-flushed at least once every twelve months. The tubes of the radiator in a Rolls-Royce car are so fine that the cars will not run satisfactorily with a partially blocked radiator. Flushing the radiator through the filler spout is really a waste of time, what is required is a really good pressure of water from the bottom hose connection with a long hose added to the top radiator connection to take the surplus water away. To obtain the best results in back-flushing, first remove the filler cap, a Bars Radiator Flushing Gun, which costs approximately £1.25p should be inserted into the bottom hose connection, when the water has been turned on from the hose and the matrix is full, compressed air can be introduced into the matrix through the Bars Flushing Gun. It is quite amazing how much sediment will be forced out. This method makes an awful mess over the front of the car, but it is well worth it as it can quickly be washed off. This treatment is also beneficial if used on all other pre-war models, with the exception of the Phantom III which should have filters fitted to both water up-takes to the radiator.

In order to assist in preserving the cylinder head and cooling system generally I use Prestone Anti-Freeze and inhibitor specially made for aluminium engines, at the rate of 25% Prestone. Drain, back-flush and refill with fresh coolant, once a year.

Cylinder Head

Mention has already been made of the fact that all 40/50 h p models, commencing with chassis No. 1 CL in the 'New Phantom' series, right through the Phantom II to the end of the Phantom III have aluminium cylinder heads, and it is essential that an inhibitor is used in the coolant, but the problems can still occur with corrosion between the aluminium head and the holding down bolts, which cause the head to bind on the studs making it extremely difficult to remove. This was the trouble with 101 SK when the car was in St Helier Garages, it took almost a month to remove the head. When carrying out this operation it is wise to use nothing but wooden wedges.

The cylinder head on a Phantom II should always be watched most carefully for any signs of corrosion on the exterior. If the car is standing for long periods in the garage out of use, and the level of the coolant in the matrix appears to drop, but there is no sign of any leaks on the garage floor, it is more than probable that there is a leak from one of the studs, which is allowing the coolant to go down into the crankcase. If this is suspected on no account start the engine, but drain the oil out of the base chamber when it can immediately be seen if this is contaminated with coolant. If this is the case there is no alternative but to remove the cylinder head and send it away to a specialist.

Springing

Many people complain that their car gives a hard ride; the ride which pre-war models give (with the exception of the Phantom III and 'Wraith', as these have independent front suspension), does vary from car to car, as it depends so much on what spring rating was specified by the original owner when the car was new, but Rolls-Royce cars do not ride 'hard' if the springs are properly lubricated. The springs receive their lubricant from the one shot lubrication tank under the bonnet. Care has to be exercised in using this as otherwise it is quite possible to get oil on the front brakes rendering them in-operative.

When I took 101 SK on the Continent, I was most bitterly disappointed with the way in which the car rode, it is a Continental chassis and I had heard how the Phantom II Continental glided effortlessly over the most appalling road surfaces at speeds of 60 and 70 mph. 101 SK did nothing of the kind; on the famous Belgium Pave, we crept along at speeds of 20 - 25 mph with the whole car quivering like a jelly, suddenly it dawned on me what was wrong. The lubrication to the springs was totally inadequate. As soon as I had the car back home in Cornwall I removed all four spring gaiters and fitted Enots Oilers to them, two to each rear gaiter and one to each front one. I found the springs were in perfect condition all were Cadnium plated, but bone dry. After smothering them with Molyslip grease, I replaced the gaiters and then, using the Enots Oil Gun filled with Castrol XL, I oiled the springs until it ran out on the newspapers I had spread on the garage floor.

On taking the car out on the road, I found the springing transformed and estimated the improvement as being about 75%.

Carburetter Heater

All Phantom II chassis up to 120 GN are fitted with a water heated carburetter and this should never give any trouble. A change was made on 120 GN and all subsequent chassis to an exhaust heated carburetter; the reason for the change was to accelerate the warming-up process, especially as when the cars were new a great many of them were only used for town work.

The exhaust heated type carburetter can be troublesome, the centre section through which

the exhaust gases flow was usually known at the Works as the 'Dogs Body', over the years a build up of carbon forms inside it, which is extremely difficult, if not impossible to clean out, if it is left without attention the build up of carbon will be such that it will cause the aluminium casting to crack. The simplest method was to remove it, throw it away and fit a new one, before it reaches this stage, but unfortunately no more new ones are obtainable, therefore the 'Dogs Body' should be carefully watched and removed periodically. The best method of cleaning it out, though even this is not one hundred per cent satisfactory, is to fill the 'Dogs Body' with thinners and allow it to soak for some hours, then to apply an acetylene torch to it and make it thoroughly hot, the carbon on the interior will burn, then by tapping it gently all over, a good deal of the surplus carbon will drop out, but unfortunately some of the passages are so fine it is impossible to completely clear them. The exhaust pipe from the 'Dogs Body' to the small silencer on the off side of the chassis suffers from a great deal of condensation and this is liable to corrode through, particularly on the elbows and to date 101 SK has had these pipes renewed no less than 3 times.

One Shot Lubrication System

This requires checking at least twice a year to make certain that oil is reaching every part of the chassis, and that a pipe has not become blocked. The off side rear spring shackle is one point where if a blockage occurs, a shortage of oil will be felt; for this reason on the rear spring shackle there is a small plug fitted which can be removed, then the spring shackle can be lubricated by means of a force-feed oil can.

To clear the line to the spring shackle is not a particularly easy exercise, if the diagram of the lubrication system in the Instruction Book is studied it can be seen that the pipe line runs along inside the channel of the rear chassis side member; the rear of the chassis side member on the car is boxed in with a small plate which runs along the length of it and disappears behind the petrol tank. In order to clear this line it is necessary to remove the petrol tank, then this side plate can be disconnected and the offending pipe line dealt with by unscrewing from the rear shackle spring end.

Apart from these items mentioned above, if the car is properly looked after it will give years of service and be a constant delight to its owner.

The policy of Rolls-Royce Ltd, has always been one of continuous improvement and the difference between an early Phantom II and that of a late one shows very forcibly how this policy was carried out; the difference between 74 GN and 101 SK is very marked indeed. 74 GN handles and feels like a vintage car, the engine is extremely silky and very quiet indeed but it lacks the punch of 101 SK. To drive one car, then the other immediately afterwards really marks the difference. 101 SK feels more like a modern car with much superior acceleration although there is very little difference in maximum speed, as both cars will exceed 90 mph, the synchromesh gearbox in 101 SK is one of the most beautiful gearboxes ever made. 74 GN has the Royce type carburetter and will return 14 mpg on a long run, whilst 101 SK has the latest type carburetter to be fitted to a Phantom II, it is designed to give 10 mpg, and I have never been able to do better than 11¾ mpg.

A great deal has been written about the Continental Phantom II and I cannot help thinking that some writers have over-rated it, it is without doubt one of the worlds 'great cars' and, with the springs properly lubricated and the ride control set over into the hard position, it is possible to maintain a high speed on long straight roads which have a bad surface, this is not possible with a Phantom II with ordinary springing, but at low speeds and pottering on a winding road with a bad surface, the Phantom II with ordinary springs gives a greatly superior ride.

As a car for use for everyday transport the Phantom II is still a perfectly practical proposition, even though it was made so many years ago, providing, that is, that the owner can afford the somewhat fierce thirst for fuel!* It must be admitted that by modern standards, specially at low speed, turning in awkward places, it is very heavy, particularly compared with a modern light car, or one fitted with power operated steering. Also the parking of a Phantom II can present problems in town, in fact there is only

*The above was written before the present world oil crisis

one thing to do, which is to adjust one's life accordingly and put it straight into a multistorey or convenient car park and 'hoof it'!

On the open road the model will hold its own with modern traffic without the slightest difficulty, cruising effortlessly mile after mile at 60 - 65 mph, which gives an ample reserve for overtaking quickly when the need arises. The car has so much power that on a long hill, when the road is clear, it will sweep past all other modern conveyances, and it is to the everlasting credit of Royce and his design team that the car is so good so many years after it left the Derby Works.

Personally I very much regret the remark which Dr Llewellyn Smith, who was the Chairman of the car division, made on his retirement, when he was interviewed by a member of the Motoring Press. He said something to the effect that the Phantom II was 'like an electric eel, of which the front part was not on speaking terms with the rear half'. For this to appear in a motoring magazine for people to read who have possibly never been in a Rolls-Royce car of any sort, I think is a great pity, and gives the average modern car owner a completely wrong conception of a Phantom II. It is perfectly true that on a rough winding road a Phantom II can take quite a lot of handling, after all it is a very big car, but it is not fair to compare it in this respect with any sort of modern car. It must be compared with its contemporaries of a similar size (which is difficult now, because practically all of them have been consigned to the scrap heap years ago), then it would immediately be seen how outstanding the handling of a Phantom II was when it was new in comparison with other makes.

On 4 August 1933, The Autocar published a road test of a Phantom II Continental, which was headed as follows: 'Speed, Silence, Tractability, a Wonderful Top Gear Performance and Unsurpassed Controls'. The following year, on 20 March 1934, The Motor carried out a road test and their report is headed 'A Car of Outstanding Performance and Refinement'.

Naturally, in nearly 40 years, some sort of progress has been made and the Phantom II cannot in any way be compared with the modern Phantom VI, let alone a Shadow or Corniche, but in its day it was supreme.

Below for quick reference is recorded the annual mileage of 101 SK since the car came into my possession:-

1954	4,323
1955	9,564
1956	7,881
1957	4,295
1958	8,904
1959	6,709
1960	7,078
1961	7,807
1962	869
1963	3,191
1964	5,390
1965	1,288
1966	645
1967	1,024
1968	7,574
1969	1,324
1970	1,303
1971	635
1972	882
1973 todate	814

There is another Phantom II I would like to mention which belongs to David Berry, who is the owner of chassis No. 9 GX, and a great enthusiast. Not only does he keep this car superbly, but in addition he carries out the repair work on it himself in his own garage at home. It must be added that he is not in the motor trade, he is simply possessed of a flair for mechanical work and he tells me that once you begin to carry out major repair work on a Rolls-Royce car, it is not difficult to understand at all; all that is needed is great patience and care in putting things back together, and no force at all must be used. He finds it is a great relaxation to work on 9 GX to the accompaniment of Beethoven! He has had the car for a long time now and driven many miles in it. I asked him to record his impressions of the car for me, which are printed below.

The Early Phantom II Today
Some Impressions of 9 GX on the Road

I was excited and nervous when John Oldham asked me if I would record my impressions of 9 GX on the road; excited because the car is always this to drive, and nervous at the responsibility of doing justice to the car and her designers in the knowledge that my words may well be read by those of them who are fortunately still with us!

The guarantee for 9 GX became effective on 22 June 1931, the chassis having been tested on 17 April, and sent to Barker & Co, on 7 May for the fitting of 'Saloon Limousine' coachwork on a 'long dropped' sub-frame. The chassis is a standard one (12 ft 6 in. wheelbase) with 'E' type steering column and 11 x 41 axle ratio. The body weight is given as 12 cwt on the chassis record card, maximum seating 5, usually 2, with 2 cwt maximum luggage. The original (and existing) specification included twin type No. 3 wheel carrier at the rear, and second spare wheel, and speedometer to register in k p h as well as m p h.

I acquired the car in January 1959 when the mileage was 95,000. It is now 145,000 and I have driven all but a small fraction of this 50,000 miles myself over all sorts of roads in England, Wales, Scotland, France and Spain. In the 5 years immediately prior to taking over 9 GX, I was the owner of 1927 '20' h p chassis No. GAJ 7, and 1932 20/25 h p GFT 33, which I drove on two European expeditions to France, Italy and Spain. Before the War my father had owned 1929 '20' h p GKM 74 and 1933 20/25 h p GSY 76. I was therefore 'weaned on the breed!'

First impressions are always interesting, and for a car of forceful character like the Phantom II quite revealing. Luckily, soon after I bought 9 GX in 1959, I recorded my views in *Early and Late* (The Bulletin of the Rolls-Royce Section of the Vintage Sports Car Club) for December 1960, and I quote it undiluted by the passage of time:

'My wife and I went 225 miles to collect our new acquisition on a bleak, freezing cold January Saturday, with frozen snow and ice covering quite a few roads, including the A1.

Not to be daunted, and leaving quite a lot to faith, in "the marque", we set off for home, popping, banging and on battery ignition only! As I had anticipated, the autovac mechanism gummed up before we had gone very far; I soon got over this with the syringe and bottle of petrol I had brought in my brief case for just such an emergency. As the wireless was telling everybody that road conditions were very treacherous, 9 GX was very nearly the only vehicle on the Great North Road and we eventually arrived home at midnight, frozen stiff but I was pleased to note, not at all fatigued in spite of the conditions. I was most impressed with the precise handling, acceleration, and general overall stability of the chassis on the road.

At the time of writing (1960) I had covered some 8,500 miles - all of them fast, very enjoyable and somewhat thirsty! The car is really luxuriously comfortable, and I am particularly pleased with the absence of road fatigue, even after long (say 300 miles) journeys. The car is not effortless to drive, however - in fact, I find it quite good exercise! At very low speeds you have got to put your weight behind the wheel to get it round. At speed, however, the steering characteristics are, I think, beautiful -

perfect balance and very positive and light reaction, with the feeling of being in touch with the road all the time.

The gearbox is, in my view, difficult and I can well understand the pressure for synchromesh in 1932. The engine is really too quiet to judge its speed easily; the clutch pedal requires a heavy foot pressure to depress it, and must travel right to the floor boards to disengage the floating ring, free the first motion shaft fully and bring the clutch stop into operation. Once, however, you have got the knack of this, the change itself can be effected with one finger on the lever! I can now do fairly sporty changes down for really quick acceleration up steep hills, of which there are plenty in my part of the world.

I find the performance very adequate for literally any situation, and more than one of my friends used only to modern medium powered cars, have expressed absolute amazement at its apparently superior acceleration, braking power, road holding and flexibility. I think the Phantom likes to be driven fast, and mine seems happy on the M1 at a continuous genuine 60/65 mph which it reaches with no sense of 'pushing' whatever. The third gear is also most useful and one can do anything in it from starting to accelerating at 50 mph up a steep hill for overtaking purposes.

After a year or so's driving, I have no doubt that the Phantom II is by far the finest Rolls-Royce I have owned. It is not, however, a large version of the 20/25 and all its driving characteristics are different. Its massive engine does not run like a sewing machine, but turns over in a way which reminds one of an express steam engine at speed! The car itself is large and demands clear, masterful control from the driver if it is not to get the better of him - rather like some of the more difficult classical piano pieces.'

And now 10 years on, in 1969, what did I think about the handling and performance of the car on the mountain passes of the Pyrenees, and on the long straight roads of France? This:-

'We made the Col du Pourtalet (1,792 m) with one stop for road improvement work and two 'muffed' hairpins on the Spanish side. These required one reverse, but would have presented no problem to a 'Ghost' with its better lock, or possibly a short chassis Phantom II.

We then cruised down to Gabas in complete silence in top gear on a closed governor and shutters (the effect of the controls is really appreciated under these conditions). We climbed in third gear, with second for some of the hairpins.

A tour of this sort seems to be ideal for a 40/50 h p car and the flexibility of the engine produces a feeling of limitless power on long ascents. Going down, the engine gives effective retardation (much more so than modern cars) on a closed governor, even in top gear, leaving the braking system free for control or emergency use. I have never had any 'fading' symptoms, or apparent overheating.

The undulations in the straight roads of France illustrated that the over-riding Hartford shock dampers which were fitted to the front axle of early 'Continentals' in the GX and JS series, and the subsequent overall ride control, were worth while refinements to reduce 'see-sawing' and some 'bounce' at the front. However, I have not experienced on 9 GX the 'jellying' which was, I believe, never cured on the later series.

On the Col d'Aubisque (1710 m) our water temperature rose to 90°, so after the descent I strengthened the 85 octane Spanish petrol in the tank with 'super' and this reduced it to 80/85° on the other ascents. Some water was lost through the overflow pipes on expansion (some people say this was because I had the level too high in the first place) and on the descents which seemed to indicate a need for a pressure cap as fitted to later models, or an expansion reservoir as on the Alpine Eagle Silver Ghosts. Vital statistics for this tour were:

Car mileage 1,729
Average fuel consumption (85/91 octane) 11 mpg
Oil consumption 20/50 multigrade. 2300 mpg
Repairs or stoppages - None
Load - driver and three passengers, plus luggage complement and boot rack.

To come to the present, how does the car behave in modern traffic?

I find her docile, precise, and responsive, even on, say the London North Circular Road, which must be the nearest thing to a race track in England! The power of the braking system is limitless and quite able to hold its own. The stopping power is superior to a Singer Gazelle, Austin 1300, and Morris 1000, to quote but three examples, and my present everyday car - an Austin 1800 - is the first I have owned with braking performance superior to the Phantom II. It is, of course, servo assisted.

And what about Motorways? The M1 was opened soon after I bought 9 GX, and I have driven her many miles on them - as needs must if I am to reach a rally at, say Sandhurst, 225 miles from my home, by 11.30 a m! I drive hard, and the car averages 60/65 mph, effortlessly in the sense that there is no sign of strain anywhere. Incidentally the dynamics of the Barker body are such that there is far less wind noise at this speed than on modern cars up to the 2 litre range! There is no noise from the engine, only regular vibration, and I have always felt that under these conditions the car would be happier with an overdrive. If ones speed is taken up to, say 70/75 mph and the clutch disengaged and the engine left to idle, the chassis is quite silent and 'floats' - I am less conscious of the road than in my 1800.'

Why do I like the early Phantom II? In my opinion this car represents Sir Henry Royce's ultimate masterpiece - the last and the best of the "Big Sixes". It is a true grand touring car with a long stride which eats up the miles without effort - helped in the case of 9 GX by Messrs Barker & Co's superbly comfortable and well designed owner driver coachwork.

The car is representative of an era of motoring forever gone - the stuff of dreams and pictures only - and a mobile example of the best of many different crafts now being swallowed up under the tide of modern economic conditions.

In conclusion I would like to paint you a true picture of an incident of my 1969 Pyrenean tour; of 9 GX, fully-laden and 39 years old, overtaking in top gear, a new Mercedes Benz on one of the long mountain ascents, and to see the consternation and disbelief on the face of its German driver. He overtook us later on the way down, due to his superior road holding on corners, and possibly my caution.

It is with this image that the Phantom II deserves to pass into history. A motor car which was, and still is, 'adequate for the purpose for which it was designed', that purpose being a grand touring car of character, comfort, grace and elegance.

David Berry.

PART II   CHAPTER 10

The rival Makes which were in production during the time the Phantom II was available to the public. A new small Rolls-Royce the 'Peregrine' is built and tested. Rolls-Royce Ltd purchase the assets of Bentley Motors and later the 'Silent Sports Car' is born. The last production chassis Phantom II in the U K series

When the Phantom II was first announced in September 1929 and was hailed by the public as a great advance over the 'New Phantom', it was selling in a highly competitive market. The Daimler Company were still producing their 35/120 in various lengths of wheelbase, but in addition they were now offering a smaller Double-Six in the form of a 30 h p. The engine of this car was in fact two 16/55 cylinder blocks joined together in a 'V' and mounted on a common crankcase, with bore and stroke of 65 x 94 mm, they were sleeve valve, of course, and made an exceptionally smooth and silent running motor. Exactly the same policy was used as with the other models, the Double-Six 30 could be obtained in 'O', 'V', 'M' and 'Q' types.

The 'O' had a wheelbase of 12 ft 1 in. and was capable of carrying unusually commodious coachwork, and, with landaulette body built by the Daimler Co, sold for £2,180. It made a good town car, but the performance was somewhat flat on the open road. At the other end of the scale there were the 'M' with a wheelbase of 11 ft 9 in. and the 'Q' with a wheelbase of 10 ft 11 in.; these were primarily for the owner-driver and the performance was not at all bad for 1929, a light bodied 'Q' type would just exceed 80 mph.

The Double-Six 30 had first appeared in 1928 and was being continued through the 1929 and 1930 seasons; in some ways it was a rival to Rolls-Royce, being cheaper to purchase and operate and carrying such roomy coachwork, but what constituted a much more formidable rival to the newly announced Phantom II was the 8-litre Bentley, which was to prove a serious rival indeed.

Bentley Motors began manufacturing motor cars in 1919, with Walter Owen Bentley as the chief designer. The engine of their first model, a 3-litre, was designed and built in New Street Mews, off Baker Street, but shortly afterwards a factory site was acquired at Cricklewood.

Like Royce, W O Bentley had served his apprenticeship in a locomotive works, since when he had been involved chiefly with the sporting variety of motor cars, notably the D F P, a French car.

The 3-litre Bentley was a brilliant design and it quickly attained the reputation of being the ultimate in sports cars; all the exploits of Bentley Motors in the competition and racing field cannot be recorded here, sufficient to say that the car attained tremendous popularity. Soon clients began to ask for closed coachwork on the 3-litre chassis, which would have the performance of the touring car, but inevitably heavier coachwork killed the performance. Also, being a big long stroke 4-cylinder engine, the car not only lost its performance but became somewhat noisy, so for the 1925 Season W O Bentley designed a 6½-litre and from this the 8-litre Bentley was developed and first appeared in 1930. It was made in two lengths of wheelbase, 12 ft and 13 ft, making a luxury car for the 'carriage trade', which carried full enclosed limousine coachwork capable of seating 7 passengers, and exceeding 100 mph. The shorter 12 ft wheelbase was built for the wealthy connoisseur who wished to drive himself, and was usually fitted with a sports saloon body.

Like Rolls-Royce, the Bentley Company only built the chassis and the leading coachbuilders fitted the most elegant designs which they could produce on these two chassis; the price of which was £1,850. The 8-litre Bentley was not only considerably faster than the Phantom II but it also had far better acceleration. Personally I do not think that it handles as nicely as the Phantom II nor was it quite as refined, but this is simply my own opinion; many other motorists have assured me that it was a very much better car, and there is no doubt about it that many former Rolls-Royce owners bought one of these new 8-litres instead.

Unfortunately, for Bentley Motors production of this model was ill timed, as it was released just before the World Slump in 1930 with the sad result that by 1931 Bentley Motors were in the hands of the Receiver.

W O Bentley says in his book, *An Illustrated History of the Bentley Car,* that it was the most profitable model that his old company produced, exactly 100 8-litres Bentley chassis were made and sold before the Company collapsed and this model was held in such high esteem that approximately 80% of them are still on the road today, and if one should come on the market it usually changes hands in the region of £15,000.

There is no doubt that the 8-litre Bentley worried Rolls-Royce Ltd greatly, they were determined to stop any further production of it at all costs, so at the Bankruptcy Court they anonymously purchased, over the heads of Napiers, the assets of the Bentley Motor Company, which naturally included the design of the 8-litre, and in fact the services of W O himself.

The whole sad story is so well-known and has been written by W O Bentley in his Autobiography *W O,* that it need not be repeated here; sufficient to say that this outstanding car was never produced again. However, the Bentley car had a world wide reputation and Rolls-Royce did not intend to miss the opportunity of exploiting the sports car market and decided to produce their own designs which would be marketed under the Bentley name. Ivan Evernden was sent out by Royce to buy an Alvis, which was taken to West Wittering where it was thoroughly tried and pulled to pieces, so that Royce was able to glean ideas for the evolution of a new sports model.

A little while before the collapse and acquisition of Bentley Motors, owing to world trade conditions generally, Rolls-Royce Ltd had thought of producing a very much smaller car than either the Phantom II or the 20/25.

The idea behind this project was to produce a car that was exclusively for the owner-driver; more and more people were driving themselves and it was felt that if this car could be reasonably priced and produced in fairly large quantities, the profits made from it would enable the Phantom II to remain in production as 'The Best Car in the World'.

In prototype form this new model was given the name 'Peregrine', it was a 6-cylinder, having a bore and stroke of 2.725 in. and 4.25 in., which gave a total cubic capacity of 2,364 cc. The engine was rated at 17.7 h p, R A C rating, the wheelbase was 10 ft and the track 4 ft 8 in., so the complete vehicle was considerably smaller than the 20/25 which had a wheelbase of 11 ft.

The completed vehicle with 4-door 4-light saloon body by Park Ward looked exactly like a 20/25 in miniature and the car went on test in England where it performed very well; but when one was sent to Chateauroux in mid-1931 it was a different story. One of the troubles was that the cylinder head gasket kept blowing and Ivan Evernden tells me this was because the water passages around the cylinder blocks were inadequate for sustained high speed on the Continent. It was at this stage that the whole cost of tooling-up to produce the 'Peregrine' was examined and it was found that to make the car to Rolls-Royce standards it would be almost, if not equally as expensive to manufacture as the 20/25 and that sales would simply encroach on those of the 20/25 model. This was undoubtedly because the Company generally had no idea how to produce a cheaper car and would not contemplate lowering the tremendously high standard of precision and workmanship. The whole idea was therefore abandoned.

There is an almost complete parallel to the story of the 'Peregrine' and the policy adopted by Rolls-Royce Ltd but with a different conclusion.

At the same time as the 'Peregrine' was under discussion, the Packard Motor Company were beginning to run into difficulties. Sales of their big luxury car were falling and they also decided the only thing to do was to produce a very much smaller model which could be made in quantity and sold cheaply. This was called the model '900 light 8', it was a complete failure in that it was just as expensive to manufacture as the Standard-8 and sold for considerably less money. Packard quickly realized that they did not know how to manufacture a cheap car, so decided the only way to go about this was to recruit a new design team familiar with the manufacture of what has been described as 'Detroit Iron' who were trained in low cost mass production. From this team the Packard 120 emerged which was given tremendous publicity when it was announced on 6 January 1935 in the Lawrence Tibbett radio show, though a publicity drive had already been mounted from the end of 1934 with the result that by the end of January 1935 Packard had taken $ 10,000,000 in cash from customers who had never even seen the new car, and by the end of the year 24,995 Packard '120s' had been sold.

As the Phantom II continued in production, its old rivals were disappearing. The Lanchester Motor Company had replaced their '40' chassis with a Straight-8, which was a much lighter design and had a very much better performance, it was also very much cheaper to manufacture as many of the parts that were used in it were identical to those used in their smaller car, the '21'; indeed, Lanchester's had seen 'the writing on the wall' just as clearly as Rolls-Royce had, but they had no aero-engine division on which to rely. George Lanchester had designed a very much smaller car for the owner-driver, which he had tried to persuade his co-directors to market, but they would not agree to this and finally, in 1931, the Lanchester Motor Company was also in the hands of the Public Receiver, and was taken over by its old rival, the Daimler Company, who actually were owned by the Birmingham Small Arms Company (itself founded in 1861), whose interests were widespread, as the following list of its other subsidiaries shows:

In Birmingham:

B S A Cycles Ltd: Designers and manufacturers of motor cycles and pedal cycles

B S A Tools Ltd: Manufacturers of engineers' tools and specialists in the design of production equipment.

B S A Guns Ltd: Designers and manufacturers of sporting and military small arms.

In Sheffield:

Wm Jessop & Sons Ltd: Sepcialists in the production of high-grade steels for tools and constructional purposes.

J S Saville & Co, Ltd: Associated with Messrs Wm Jessop & Sons Ltd, in steel production.

British Abrasive Wheel Co, Ltd: Manufacturers of abrasive wheels.

In London:

Daimler Hire Ltd: This Company operates the largest fleet of private hire cars in the world.

Burton Griffiths & Co, Ltd: Forming part of the sales organisation of B S A Tools Ltd.

The absorption of the Lanchester Motor Company into the Daimler Company was a tragedy, as the Lanchester car was reduced to a sort of small cheap Daimler with Lanchester written on the radiator. However, the Daimler Company did produce the small model George Lanchester had designed, though it was modified and fitted with the fluid flywheel and self-changing gearbox; this car was known as the 15/18.

By 1935, as production of the Phantom II was coming to an end, the Daimler Company had almost totally abandoned Knight's Double sleeve valve arrangement, except on the two big V12, or Double-Six, chassis. A new model Straight-8, using push-rod overhead valves replaced the 25 and 35 h p models, but this was not really a competitor to the Phantom II.

Although the cost of a complete car was approximately £1,000 less than the Phantom II, the steering was very heavy and it was principally intended for a chauffeur to drive. The fluid flywheel transmission and self-changing gear took some of the strain out of driving for town work, but the car was extremely ponderous, and the top speed was only about 70 mph.

By 1935 the big 6-cylinder engine was the chief criticism levelled at the Phantom II. It was no longer as smooth as the engines that were now being fitted to other makes, in fact the improvements which had been made to it, such as raising the compression, fitting bigger valves and heavier valve springs, made the engine very much more 'beefy' than in the earlier model Phantom IIs. In all chassis, the high-lift camshaft, as fitted to the Continental, had been used, but this had caused so much trouble with the cam-followers, that from chassis No. 101 TA to the last Phantom II which was built, chassis No. 84 UK, the Company had reverted to the low-lift camshaft. In all, 95 units were built incorporating all the final engine modifications, including synchromesh second gear. However, the era of the multi-cylinder engine was dawning both in America and in Europe, and behind the scenes in the Experimental Department at Derby, under great secrecy, a new V12-cylinder engine was being developed and tested to replace the Phantom II.

PART III - CHAPTER 1

The increasing popularity of the V12-cylinder and the V16-cylinder engine in America, the Daimler Double-Six '50', Rolls-Royce Ltd decide to replace the Phantom II with a V12, code name 'Spectre'. Royce's last work and his death. The first three 'Spectre' chassis 30 EX, 31 EX and 32 EX on test in France

The designers and manufacturers of motor cars can never sit back feeling they have produced the ultimate, but must always be looking ahead and keeping an eye on their competitors, whilst at the same time satisfying the demand of the public, if they are going to be able to maintain their sales. By 1932 the Phantom II was thoroughly established with a great reputation; there was virtually no other big British luxury car still being manufactured which compared with it for general all-round use; the only comparable one was the Daimler Double-Six '50', which was fitted with a V12 sleeve valve engine and fluid flywheel transmission, but it was bought by an entirely different type of customer. It was if anything even more suitable than the Phantom II for the carriage trade and town work, having an enormous wheelbase of 13 ft 1 in. and therefore capable of carrying extremely commodious coachwork. There was also an owner-driver version on a short wheelbase of 11ft 6 in., but very few of these were sold; problems of starting the sleeve valve engine from cold did not really appeal to the owner-driver, so, though the Daimler Company had tried unsuccessfully to enter this market time and time again, their cars were really chauffeur driven carriages. The highly successful 35/120 went out of production in 1932.

Rolls-Royce Ltd had really nothing to fear from Continental producers, but America was a different story. The vast resources and gigantic output of American motor manufacturers, particularly General Motors, made competition with them very difficult. The Cadillac V12 and V16, I am given to understand, were actually selling at a loss, but they had so many cheaper lines on which to rely, Chevrolet, Pontiac, Oldsmobile and Buick, that what they lost over their prestige car, the Cadillac, they made up for with the sales of Chevrolet alone. The output was enormous for one maker and far greater than any of the more popular British Manufacturers, such as Morris, Austin, Hillman or Standard.

At the same time Packard, which has been called the 'Rolls-Royce' of America, offered some very fine Straight-Eights, and later a V12; so highly was the Packard regarded that in Robert E Turnquiste's book *The Packard Story* he says that Packard were outselling all other luxury makes at a ratio of 4 to 1.

In 1932 and the next few succeeding years multi-cylinders were in vogue; the public clamoured for smoothness, with the result that in the family saloon market a number of makers came out with a model of not more than 1½ litres, but having a 6-cylinder engine; none of these was a success for though the engines were smooth, they were utterly 'gutless', and having small pistons relying on high revolutions, the pistons and cylinder bores wore out extremely rapidly.

At the other end of the scale the V12 was beginning to enjoy a tremendous popularity in America and besides the three biggest manufacturers, General Motors with their Cadillac, Ford with their Lincoln, and Packard, such manufacturers as Stutz, Marmon, Pierce-Arrow, etc., all brought out a V12; so it naturally followed that with the great experience which Rolls-Royce had in building V12 aero-engines, they would turn to this type of engine for a new model. So Royce and his design team began to think in these terms for a new 40/50 to replace the Phantom II.

The Phantom III is probably the most controversial model which Rolls-Royce Ltd have ever made; it has been called 'Best of the Best' by some owners who possess and love the marque, it has also been described as the most diabolical car that has ever been made! Neither of these extreme views is quite right. Although it is a fabulous car in every way, there are also two serious drawbacks for the ordinary owner-driver, the corrosion problems and the terrifying cost of repairs.

The model was only in its embryo-form when Royce had a hand in it, in that Summer of 1932. He was very tired and his old trouble of 1912 had returned, in many ways he had worn himself out with his work on the Schneider Trophy races of 1929 and 1931. He had been awarded a Baronetcy in the 1930 New Year's Honours List for his work for the 1929 race.

Following his normal routine he went to Le Canadel for the last time in December 1931 returning to West Wittering in April 1932, leaving the majority of his design team at 'Camacha', the drawing office at West Wittering.

Whilst Royce was in the South of France, Elliott, who had been Royce's right hand man for many years, departed without the 'Old Man's' knowledge, to Derby, where he proceeded to form a design team of his own; his last design under a Le Canadel number was drawing number 2979 Le C Phantom II - Diamond Mounting modification to facilitate Assembly, this is dated 30 November 1931.

Following the acquisition of the Bentley Company, Royce was working on designs for a new Bentley car using the Peregrine engine, which Sidgreaves in the Sales Department thought would be acceptable to former Bentley clientele, but this project posed many problems, the Peregrine engine objected strongly to its super-charger and was continually blowing its head gasket. Royce had used a super-charger because he wished to differentiate between the Bentley type sports car and the Rolls-Royce silent luxury model, in order to avoid competition between the two marques.

Finally it was Robotham who said 'why not get the same h p with a naturally aspirated engine, which we already have'. The result was

that a 20/25 engine, suitably modified was installed into the Peregrine chassis and so 'The Silent Sports Car' was born.*

When Royce returned to West Wittering and received the bombshell that Elliott had departed to Derby, taking Jenner with him, he was very upset. He called the rest of his design team together and gave them the choice of also going to Derby if they wished; but they preferred to remain with him.

During the summer of 1932, work started on designs for a replacement car to the Phantom II, which finally emerged as the V12 Phantom III, but months before Royce died he said sadly to a colleague, 'I shall never live to see this new car'.

For the last two months before he died, Royce was working on the designs for a cottage for one of his farm workers. He farmed 70 acres and this cottage was to be built at Well's Farm, Ivan Evernden actually drew the scale drawings for the plans which Royce worked on in great detail, whilst lying in bed. As usual Royce was absolutely insistent on having exactly what he wanted and had to overcome considerable opposition from the County Council. For almost the whole of this period Royce was bedridden and, on 16 March 1933, he was visited for the last time by Hives (Hs), Robotham (Rm) and Rowledge (RG), who had driven down in a prototype 3½-litre Bentley.

On 13 April 1933 Dr Campbell Thompson (a neurologist and an old friend of both Royce and Claude Johnson), came down from London to see Royce, and Ivan Evernden and the design team were told that the end was not far off.

The plans for the cottage were completed and Ivan Evernden had been sent to London by Royce to have copies reproduced, as there was no one in Chichester who could do this. He was still in London when he received a telegram from Nurse Aubin asking him to return to West Wittering immediately, he caught the first available train, but unfortunately arrived too late. Royce died peacefully at 7 a m on Saturday 22 April.

True to his unassuming nature, not long before he died, he said to Nurse Aubin 'I have but a little while to live - I know that I am dying, but please let there be no trouble about it for anybody'.

*Code name for the ex-chassis Bentley models was Bensport

The Company's Solicitors Messrs Claremont, Haynes were in charge of the funeral arrangements and they gave instructions to Messrs Leverton & Sons Ltd, Funeral Furnishers, who had premises near Euston Station in London, to go to West Wittering and convey Royce's body to Golders Green for the cremation service.

Messrs Leverton had just had an old Rolls-Royce of the Silver Ghost type converted into their first motor-driven hearse, it was fitting that the first occasion this car was used was for the last journey of its designer. (Incidentally this firm is still in existence and they now run a fleet of Phantom III limousines, unfortunately though, due to overheating problems, these beautifully kept cars have been converted to Rolls-Royce B60 engines).

There was difficulty in getting Royce's coffin down the narrow stairs of 'Elmstead', and during this waiting time the old Rolls-Royce stood outside in the lane with the engine ticking over very slowly and silently, Ivan Evernden who was much moved by the occasion could not help remarking 'what a wonderful tribute to the "Old Man" '.

By Royce's express wish no one attended the cremation service except Mr Claremont, who was the brother of his original partner and Mr Tildesley who was a partner in the firm of Messrs Claremont Haynes, and who later married Ethel Aubin who had looked after Royce so devotedly for so long.

Royce's ashes were then sent to Derby where they were placed in No. 1 shop, where they remained until the outbreak of War when Nurse Aubin and her husband made the necessary arrangements for them to be removed to Alwalton Church, the little village where Royce was born, there they attended the interment service.

With his death, his place as head of the design staff was taken by his colleague for many years, A G Elliott, a brilliant designer who had always worked, to use his own words to me 'with Royce looking over my shoulder and approving everything I did'.

Suddenly, Royce, who was not only designer but also a practical engineer, was not there anymore. For the first time decisions had to be made by Elliott, who, brilliant designer though he was, was not a practical man, and where the Phantom III is to be criticized in its design, is that no real thought was ever given to the time when an overhaul would have to be done and the question arose of having to dismantle and re-assemble it.

For this new model, a change in the shape of the famous radiator was contemplated, at this period the fashion was to have a V shaped radiator which swept outwards and forwards towards the bottom after the style of the big Humber of the period and Elliott was rather in favour of this. So, much against his will, Ivan Evernden worked on a design which I have seen and which personally I think is terrible. Fortunately, so did everybody else, including Evernden, so Elliott agreed to leave the familiar radiator unchanged.

The new and untried design was given the code-name 'Spectre', the first example of which, chassis No. 30 EX, was running on the road early in 1934. Ian Rimmer says the original chassis No. was 3-S-1. The Index number of this car was RC 3054, and the coachwork was an enclosed limousine by Park Ward finished in all black which was, in fact, a standard Phantom II body, modified to fit the new chassis, the complete vehicle weighed 47 cwt 3 qrs 21 lb.

It would appear that this prototype chassis presented so many problems that, by 9 October 1937, when it had only run 25,217 miles, the body was removed from the chassis and was prepared for a dynamometer test. The last recorded entry in the log book reads that the chassis was still on test on 15 April 1939. Apparently the second chassis, 31 EX, was also an enclosed limousine by Park Ward, finished in blue and black having an unladen weight of 49 cwt 14 lb, and bearing the registration number RC 2406. This was also a Phantom II body but it incorporated modified Bentley body sections. On 19 November 1935, whilst on test at Chateauroux it was involved in a bad accident. When Hancock reported the accident to Hives, he explained the condition of the car as follows:

'So badly damaged as to be beyond repair, a cyclist, Mr Nivet, aged 48 years, was killed instantly, but John Barrie English, who was driving, escaped uninjured. R Patterson in charge of the car had a fractured left arm above the elbow'.

However, this car must have been rebuilt as Ron Haynes has told me that 31 EX, was a Company car from November 1944 until October 1945. It was then sold to a Mr F F Thompson, 135 County Road, Liverpool, who had the cut-out on the electrical circuit repaired in November 1945.

It would seem that the basis for the production Phantom III was the third chassis to be erected, 32 EX. This was a Continental touring saloon by Park Ward, finished in dark grey with an unladen weight of 51 cwt; the body was of aluminium and wood construction, as recommended by Ivan Evernden and the car bore the registration number RC 2545.

On its initial 10,000 mile test at Chateauroux 32 EX proved to be most unsatisfactory. The front suspension collapsed and a valve broke in the engine damaging a piston and cracking a cylinder sleeve. The back tyres were completely worn out at 2,963 miles and leather covers to the front half of the rear springs were torn away; also the exhaust tail pipe was so battered from stones on the road that it was leaking very badly.

However, it is unfair to condemn the car, as it can be seen from what happened to the tail pipe of the exhaust and the leather gaiters covering the rear springs, the car had taken a tremendous battering. It must also be remembered that it was a completely new and untried design, which was really being driven to destruction. Naturally, faults in the design manifested themselves, which is exactly what was intended.

The Spectre was producing so many problems that on 12 February 1935 Sidgreaves wrote to Wormald, copies of which were sent to Hives and Elliott. He proceeds:

Secret - Car Programme

Referring to my note re. the question of whether we build more Phantoms or not, a suggestion has been made which seems worthy of consideration, and that is as follows: Could we introduce the Spectre engine in the Phantom chassis and so have the car available fairly early?

The worst feature of the Phantom is its large 6-cylinder engine - the rest of the chassis is pretty good.

If we did this it would be following much the same procedure as when we changed from the Silver Ghost to Phantom I and then later came the Phantom II.

Apart from the fact that it would apparently - so far as I can see - enable us to have something new to sell fairly quickly, it would also limit our risk to the engine, whereas the complete Spectre chassis has so much new in it that one feels nervous of its being introduced in any sort of a hurry.

Signed: Sg

Ernest Hives must have been a remarkable man to endure the pressures that were brought upon him from all sides. The Sales Department under Arthur Sidgreaves, always eager for something new to offer the public; the design staff under Elliott demanding more time for development and modifications and the production side of the Derby Works, under Wormald, never wanted anything changed at all! But Hives was never ruffled, always kept his equanimity, but at the same time was never satisfied with the work in his department, striving all the time to produce a better finished product. Early in 1935 Hives and Robotham took 32 EX on a tour of the mountain passes; Robotham describes how they attempted to climb the Stelvio on pages 102 - 103 in his excellent book *Silver Ghost to Silver Dawn*.

It was 3 months after Sidgreaves wrote the above letter that the decision was made to cease production of the Phantom II on 23rd May 1935, a great deal of progress had been made in the Experimental Department with the 'Spectre' and the Company now felt sufficient confidence in the new model to arrange for its production, as the following letter shows:

23.5.1935. **Private and very urgent.** 40/50 h p chassis. Will you please arrange to stop all work at once on the last 83 Phantom chassis of U 2 series. The parts should be collected and put into store together. This means we shall only build another 20 chassis and we should only use that material which is nearest the finishing stage. This will give us 42 chassis in the U 2 series only.

Sidgreaves was still pushing for the new model and on 24 July 1935 he wrote to Hives in reference to 31 EX as follows:

Spectre: Would you please let me know when the next Spectre is going to France.

I am anxious that when the next car goes, instead of just going to Chateauroux for the usual routine test round and round the standard course, it should definitely go over the Alpine passes. These passes get closed about the latter part of September and if we miss the opportunity of the passes then we are unable to do so until next Summer, which might be too late for some important points.

I should like you therefore to put someone on to the job of making out a definite trip which should include the highest passes such as Stelvio, Galibier, Furka, D'Iseran, Julier and Grimsel.

There is a new pass just opened over the Austrian Alps, *i.e.* Grossglockner full particulars are in the Autocar 31 May.

Please let me know before the end of next week when the car will go and what course it will follow.

Signed Sg.

Hives replied two days later sending copies of his letter to Sidgreaves, to Wormald, Elliott and Cox.

At least three weeks before the next Spectre goes to France. We took the Spectre to Austria, Italy, *etc* and went up numerous mountain passes and although we failed to get to the top of the Stelvio because of snow, we obtained sufficient information for us to be able to anticipate what difficulties would occur. Since then Hancock has been able to reproduce the troubles at Chateauroux.

There is no need to send a Spectre to the mountains to confirm the faults we already know. The next time we send a Spectre there, we want to know it is for the purpose of confirmation that the modifications which have been made have made it satisfactory.

We get infinitely more information from running a car at Chateauroux than any other form of road test.

We know quite well the worst that can happen on mountain passes.

1 Is the failure of the petrol system.
2 Water boiling.

We have so many other problems with the Spectre car that we think it would be unwise to lay down a particular programme for the next car to go to France until a later date.

It may be more convenient for us to send the present car, 32 EX, that is in France after it has completed 20,000 miles and before it returns to England, over some of the passes.

Signed: Hs

PART III   CHAPTER 2

The Reports of 32 EX on test at Chateauroux; this car was to form the basis for the production Phantom III

By 1935 the 10,000 miles test at Chateauroux had been increased to 12,000 miles and on 31 July of that year Hancock sent in his reports on the 12,000 mile test of chassis No. 32 EX. Speaking generally, he was quite impressed with the handling of the car which he was able to compare very closely with a Cadillac that the Company had purchased and which was undergoing the same tests at the same time. Part of Hancock's report on 32 EX reads as follows:

The general impression of the car is that with minor alterations, there is every possibility of producing a car superior in every respect to the Phantom [meaning the current production Phantom II]. In comparison with the Cadillac the car feels at all speeds more under control.

The acceleration exceeds that of the Phantom, up to speeds of 70 mph it is accomplished with smoothness and silence. With maximum speeds on the long stretches of the Continental roads, there is no sign of the engine power failing, so frequently met with on other makes of cars. Slow running is not as yet a good feature [As originally designed the Experimental Phantom III was fitted with 4 carburetters which it was quite impossible to keep in tune for slow running; at the same time once these carburetters were fitted on to the engine it was impossible to remove the sparking plugs without first removing the carburetters, this extremely awkward arrangement did not appear on production model Phantom IIIs as the carburration system was completely re-designed and the car fitted with one downdraft carburettor].

Springing

The springing of the car is ideal for the Continental roads. The riding in the rear seats is very good. In many respects it is superior to that of the Cadillac we tried over here. At low and medium speeds, very little of the undulating road surface can be felt. On good surfaced roads it is ideal. In the front seats, the ride is not quite so good. The front of the car hits the buffers too frequently. In our opinion a torsion bar would improve it, with softer tyres such as the latest Michelin which we tried, adds further to the riding qualities.

Steering

The steering is the most improved unit of the car. It is free from the usual Phantom violent reactions of the road wheels.

The period of slight reactions, between 40 and 60 mph can be easily checked by a firmer grip of the wheel, without any undue distress.

The steering is stable and selective, choose what speed the car is driven. The ratio is right for cornering, manoeuvring and control ability at high speeds. The self-centring is positive, at medium speeds, it has a tendency to self-centre too readily.

Brakes

The braking is good with the increased front braking. It is progressive with the load applied to the foot pedal. No undue pressure is required. There has been no undue failing of the brakes with continual use. Wear of the linings is normal for Continental use.

Hydraulic Dampers

The initial loading gives a soft ride. The maximum loading with the hand control does not spoil the riding at high speeds, and is sufficient to keep the car well under control.

During a tour one meets the inevitable hump on the road surface which looks harmless. Upon going over it at even medium speeds the result is, the rear passengers are lifted off their seats. The dampers under these conditions are ineffective and buffers have insufficient length to soften out the rebound or lump.

Rear Axle

Under certain conditions of road surfaces, the rear axle jaggers over badly, and gives a bad impression to those riding in the rear.

Servicing the Car

We have never had a car on Test which was so inaccessible, and so much time taken up in removing unnecessary parts to carry out adjustments and replacements.

ENGINE

Carburetters

To remove these takes on an average half-hour each. To replace, one hour can easily be taken, and two hours occupied to get the petrol unions connected when the alignment is not exactly correct. The Tee junctions are too rigid. Spanners have to be bent and made special to get at the nuts.

Ignition Plugs

The plugs situated on the inside of the Vee, require a special box spanner to get at them. They are most inaccessible. The high tension leads should not be fastened on with nuts, but should be clipped on. It was intended to use clips on Terminals, but the present design is unsatisfactory.

Oil Pipes for filters, Release Valve

We have found the union connections have to be over-tightened to prevent leaks.

Lower Half

To remove the lower half, it is first necessary to remove the side trays, the exhaust pipe has to be uncoupled from the front silencer, also the intermediate pipe.

The front silencer has to be removed also the Clutch under-pan.

On the Cadillac nothing had to be removed.

To dismantle the pistons, the cylinder head, carburetters, air silencer, ignition wires, controls, all have to be dismantled.

On the Cadillac, the 16 pistons and rods could be removed with dismantling the lower half only.

Clutch

To dismantle the clutch case, is one of the most inaccessible problems one could meet. Between two and four hours is needed to dismantle the cases. It is necessary to withdraw six studs.

The rear of the engine has to be lifted a certain height to clear the operating shafts. The trunion operating levers can be got out of position by removing the end bush and locking rings and by judicious wangling the lower half case, it will just come off. The top half has to be threaded round to the lower half position before it can be removed. To re-assemble the same routine has to be adopted.

FAILURES WHICH HAVE OCCURRED DURING THE MILEAGE

Engine

1 Petrol supply failed due to vapour lock with heat. Filter had to be removed under bonnet. Carburation too strong after standing. Petrol pump failed.
2 Bonnet difficult to fasten up and open, due to flexibility of sides, not allowing lock to line up, catches would not clear slots when released.
3 At 6,000 miles, the oil radiator cracked at bottom seam and allowed water to escape into oil system.
4 At 6,400 miles, No. 5 cylinder, the head of the exhaust valve broke off. This caused a cracked piston and cylinder sleeve.
5 Trouble with water boiling at atmospheric temperature of 31º C.
6 Crankshaft damper load not remaining consistent.
7 Very bad oil leak from rear engine bearing.
8 No. 1 A Block exhaust push rod broken. No. 1 B Block inlet push rod broken. These broke at 10,700 and 13,000 miles.

Front Dampers

9 Bad oil leak from Spring pot joints to sleeve on frame.
10 Oil leak from Behours joint.
11 Top screws for bleeding pipe fouled the top suspension lever.
12 Bottom lever hit the underside of frame on rebound.
13 Front rubber buffers cut to pieces through hitting sharp edge of stop.
14 White metal linings have picked up slightly. Flakes of white metal were found floating in oil. On one damper the high and low pressure valves were sticking, owing to white metal flakes having got into the sleeve. The steel sleeves were in good condition. The Road Springs are in good condition.

Front Suspension

17 Bad oil leak from oil seal glands of top anchorage of pivot yoke.
18 No oil getting to cross steering tube spherical joints of steering arm.
19 Insufficient supply of oil to steering pivots and steering arms.
20 Springs fouled on inner side of spring pots, causing a grunting noise.

Steering

21 Oil leaking out of box into bijur pipeline.

Gearbox

22 Noise continuous gears. Bad loss of oil from box. Synchromesh of 3rd and top gears has not functioned properly.
23 Floating bush of 1st and 3rd motion shaft seized.
24 2nd motion shaft floating bushes seized. No oil supply.

Clutch

25 Slipped very badly, smothered in oil from rear engine bearing. Clutch spigot shaft not getting any lubrication was found rusty on serrations and bearing length. Trunion ball race became dry and noisy.

Rear Dampers

26 No lubrication to link spherical joints became worn and chattered, link tubes too thin, bent and dented by stones. Coiled springs for retaining dust shields became unwound and lost. Dust shields eaten away by stones and grit.

Rear Tension Rod

27 Spherical bearings insufficient lubrication, became worn in spherical bearings and floating bearings, rattled.

28 Connecting links for Tension Rod. No lubrication to top spherical joints, very badly worn.

Rear Road Springs

29 Lubrication ceased to supply spring leaves, oil holes and grooves filled up with swarf at front and rear anchorage. Riding of car became very hard.

Rear Axle

30 Bad oil leak developed from pinion bearing housing. Hand brake rope on axle chafed on nuts of pinion housing and frayed through.

31 Oil leak down offside Axle Tube worked its way through cap of hub on to road wheel.

Exhaust

32 Whistle developed from snout.

33 Joint washers of Exhaust Manifold burnt out. Joint washers of down-take pipe to front silencer burnt out.

34 Stay from Intermediate Pipe to clutch housing broke.

THE FOLLOWING ITEMS HAVE BEEN MODIFIED, OR ARE BEING ATTENDED TO

Engine

1 Petrol supply has not failed during running after removal of filter to underside of frame.

4 Undrilled type of Exhaust Valves fitted, no further failures.

5 With radiator grille removed only occasional boiling takes place. This should apply with radiator shutters.

7 Oil leak from rear of Engine, by air pressure supplied to flywheel.

Front Dampers

10 & 11 Behours unit turned round and screws for bleeding system made flush with case. No further trouble.

12 Fitting of extra plate on buffers stop has prevented lever fouling.

13 Larger diameter stop plate has prevented cutting of buffers.

Front Suspension

17 Cured by extra asbestos packing, should be cured by correct perfect seal packings.

18 A Bijur giving 6 times the amount of a No. 3 Bijur has given sufficient lubrication.

19 Cured by attention to No. 17.

Gearbox

22 Cause of loss of excess oil was due to a pressing inadvertently being left out of swinging arm bracket. Improved drain schemes from bearings of Servo drive shaft cured other leaks.

23 An improvement in the oiling of the 1st to 3rd motion shafts has been made, but was not good enough. A further modification was made, results at present unknown.

24 The second motion shaft bushes were well oiled with the modifications made.

Clutch

25 Slipping of clutch through oil getting on to fabrics 100% cured by scheme to rear Engine bearing. The clutch has been examined and not a drop of oil was found inside the clutch. A Hand oiling scheme has been fitted to lubricate the Clutch spigot. A No. 1 Bijur was fitted to the Trunion ball race deleting a No. 0 Bijur.

Rear Road Springs

29 Lubrication increased by fitting unrestricted Bijurs, test not completed to give results.

Engine Mounting

The rubber mounting at this mileage does not show any defects. With the lining-up of the Engine to the coupling of the Gearbox, the transmission period was cured.

Quiet Tappets

The Tappets have not remained quiet. No particular one has given trouble. They have been inconsistent. The trouble has been through two causes - oil supply ceasing part restricted jet, and poppet valves in plungers leaking. At times a tappet has remained noisy throughout a run, at other times it has become quiet after a short run.

There is too much oil in the rocker cover casing, the angle of the cylinder head causes a well of oil, which reaches above the joint covers, while the Engine is running. It will have to be more efficiently drained, as it not only submerges the valve springs, but leaks out of the joint. A considerable amount of this oil is sucked out by the breather tubes. The air silencer is saturated, the carburetter air cylinders have been found with a quantity of oil in. The intakes of the carburetters were free of oil when dismantled.

Radiator

The radiator mounting is satisfactory. The water level (½ in. in header tank) was maintained when no trouble with water boiling occurred.

The two front wing stays which were held to the radiator shell by setscrews were continuously working loose. It was not thought possible to use studs or nuts because of the clearance of the fitting. By a slight alteration to the inner bottom flanges of the stays we have been able to fit studs and use a pin nut and spring washers. The two wing stays have remained firm by this method.

Distributors for Ignition

We should like to criticise the Cam of the distribution and the drive. With the amount of backlash in the drive, timing of the contacts is very uncertain, the lag has to be allowed for.

It is very easy to get 10° advance or retard of the Ignition. Another disadvantage in the cam being small in size brings the make and break of A and B side very close together. It is easy [to make] a mis-reading of which set of contact points are making or breaking.

A slightly larger cam would increase the time limit of breaking of the two contacts (checking timing electrically).

We are of the opinion that the two switches A Block and B Block will give rise to complaints when actually there would not be sufficient cause. In this respect we have found that A or B singly were misfiring, but when both ignitions were in use there was no misfire. On other occasions for no apparent reason, the speed of the car would be slowed when running on B or A singly.

The two firing together, normal speed was obtained. One plug not firing would not materially affect the running of the car, and most probably would begin to fire again, but the owner having found one plug out would not be satisfied until it was made right.

Carburetters

The carburation has been affected by the heat of the Engine. The fitting of the carburetters in the Vee, and the petrol pipe lying on top of the tappet cover case, has caused a very strong mixture to be drawn into the Engine, when starting after the Engine has been stood for over 10 mins.

The heat from under the bonnet and engine has been absorbed by the carburetters. Taking cool air to the carburetters does not overcome this trouble.

We have since obtained good slow running.

Front Suspension

Apart from the lubrication faults of the front suspension and the fouling which has occurred, the condition of the front suspension is good. The springs have not collapsed. No wear can be detected in the pivot bearings or the bearing pins of the levers.

Steering

The cross steering tube ball joints show chattering of the Behours cups. These cups should be a press fit in the recess of the tube. It is not a question of lack of lubrication. The chattering is exactly the same as experienced on the crankshaft, where the damper cone used to chatter.

Starter Motor

The starter motor has not given the slightest trouble throughout the mileage.

Dynamo

The output has been satisfactory. No undue evaporation of the water from the battery has taken place.

Full lighting has not been in use.

Petrol Gauge

This failed at the beginning through a fuse blowing in the instrument. The cause was due to a small blob of solder having dropped on the resistance of the Unit in the Tank, when making the connections. No further trouble has occurred.

Petrol Tank

The tank has not given any trouble, a peculiar feature is that although the connecting links of the damper, spring gaiters, and dampers have suffered by stones, the tank has not received any damage.

There has been a strong smell of petrol in the rear seats when the tank was full.

Speedometer

The trip reading failed early in the test. It would not read over 10 miles, then it stopped at 100, finally ceasing to work. The Speed Indicator has at times stuck at 30 mph mark.

The lighting of the instruments is good. One can read the miles at the end of a run with the illumination.

The lighting under the Bonnet is a decided advantage.

Side Spare Wheels

These rode very steady. No failure of the brackets has arisen.

Servo

The Servo has been efficient, and when examined was in a good condition.

Damper Control Unit

We had during the first part of the mileage a leak from the drive. Upon dismantling the acme thread to retain the oil leaking along the spindle, had seized and torn off.

This was replaced by a complete new spindle. No further trouble has occurred.

The pressure to the dampers has been maintained.

Body Work

The body has remained in a very good condition. No serious rattles have developed. The doors have not dropped. No cracks have developed in the wings or body work.

The faults that are noticeable are the poor fastening of the locks and levers of the rear luggage parallel. The levers made of brass have worn on the cam, and over-locks. The steel lever worked by the cam is finished off very roughly.

The O S front door handle goes over centre, wear has taken place in the lock. The door catches are poor, the second catch is too small and not reliable. A slight rattle has developed in the front doors, windows, when half open, and rear of ventilated roof when closed.

The front compartment becomes stifling with the scheme of ventilation.

The windscreen opens too far for comfort with the mechanism provided.

In the rear seats the floor at the N S becomes too hot and uncomfortable.

The body is free from booms.

```
Weight of Car .................... 48 cwt 1 qtr.
Average petrol consumption ............7.8 mpg.
Average oil consumption ............. 430 mpg.
Average speed .......................46.1 mph.
Petrol used ............. Esso - Azure - Standard.
Oil used:
Engine ...................Mobiloil 'D' Special.
Gearbox .............Wakefield's Hi-Press Light.
Rear Axle ............Wakefield's Hi-Press Heavy.
Tyres used: 7.00 x 18. Front:
    Goodyear 'Heavy Duty' 7.202
    Dunlop '90'           6.852
    Michelin 'Stop' Not worn out

            Rear:
    Goodyear 'Heavy Duty' 2.299
    Dunlop '90'           2.953
    Michelin 'Stop'       2.764
```

                                    G W H

Headlamps

The N S headlamp has given considerable trouble. The earth wire has broken off the dipping unit. It is not supported and vibrates. The earthing of the bulb by a plunger in the spider support burnt the contact away, the plunger not being robust enough to maintain the connection. The wire inside the tube broke away and is a difficult wire to replace as no provision is made for renewals.

The headlamp pillars have given no trouble and ride steadily.

Windscreen Wiper Motor

As reported at 3,000 miles the fixing of this unit is not satisfactory. It has broken off several times during the latter mileage.

The wiper unit fitted under the panelling at the bottom of the windscreen failed through a screw working loose and jamming in the teeth of the mechanism.

Body Work

The body work has remained generally in a good condition. The weaknesses shown up have been, the loss of the friction drive to the ventilating windows at the front, a slight rattle from the front N S door. The

front wings have cracked, the nearside at the outside edge where attached to the running board, and brim of the spare wheel well to outer edge of wing, also at the side on the front bend. The off-side wing cracked on the brim of the spare wheel across to the outer edge of the wing, rear end.

Rear number plate illuminated unit

The fitting of the bulb holder in this unit was the worst fitting I have ever come across. It consisted of a half filed down ordinary bulb holder and relied on being held in position by its fit and in a bit of tube half soldered on to the rear of the number plate back plate, a screw preventing it from dropping out. The earthing was poor. We had to fit a collar on to make an earth, and hold it in position. The red light is not large enough to be readily seen at a distance. The screws holding the number plate in position were too long and were forcing the back plate off. Park Ward's should be informed of this poor class of work.

The luggage grid chatters when folded up.

The stop lamp and reversing lamp both give trouble owing to poor earthing of the units.

Facia Board

The petrol gauge has at times been sluggish in action, and has not read correctly, the unit in the tank being at fault. The remaining instruments have given no trouble.

Side Spare Wheel Carriers LOP.D.73947

The spare wheels have been steady, and the wheels steady the front of the car. Without the wheels fitted there is flapping of the wings.

Wing Stays LOP.F.80678

The wing stays have been satisfactory.

The aluminium tube carrying the wire for the O S wing lamp broke away from the clip on the wing stay and fouled the road wheel.

```
Weight of Car:              2 tons 11 cwt.
Average speed:              46.2 mph.
Mobiloil D. Special used in engine.
```
Special Dunlop 7.00 x 19 type ('90' silent tread tyres used. Rear tyres worn out at a mileage of 5,914. Front tyres taken off at a mileage of 8,413.

                                    Signed: G W Hancock

When Arthur Sidgreaves received a copy of this report, which he read with interest, he wrote to Wormald, sending copies to both Elliott and Hives. He says that the remarks on page 1 are gratifying. He was particularly interested in the contents of page 1 as he says 'I see it says that on going over a bump in the road which looks harmless, even at medium speeds, the rear passengers are lifted off their seats. I am surprised to see this because it is what we found just over a year ago when we first tried the "Spectre" and when I was driving, I threw Hs and C up on the roof'.

Sidgreaves wanted to know how this characteristic could be overcome, then he raised the question of coachwork, and ventilation to the front compartment. Particularly what was being done to obviate the excessive heat, as he says 'I know from experience on some of the earlier Phantoms how objectionable this can be'.

This is one of the most difficult problems to overcome with a very big engine, especially when driving on a hot day when the air which the fan draws through the radiator is already hot, and is then forced back against what the Americans call 'the fire wall'. In this respect the 'Spectre', which later in production became known as the Phantom III is very much better than the Phantom II and all earlier 40/50 models, because the exhaust pipes are brought out right in the front of the engine and then sweep down behind the radiator, whereas on the earlier 40/50 the main exhaust down-take pipe comes out from the side of the engine, so is far more likely to 'roast' the feet of the front seat passenger. This problem was not really overcome until full refrigeration and air-conditioning came into existence with the Silver Cloud type of car, when it was only fitted as an expensive extra; but now with the current Silver Shadow series, it is a standard fitting.

The question of heat in the front compartment was not confined only to Rolls-Royce cars, it was a problem which faced every designer of a model with a large engine; the old Lanchester Motor Company tried to solve this 'roasting' problem, by fitting two miniature ship's ventilators on to the scuttle, which were a feature of all Lanchester 40s.

After spending the summer on these routine tests, production of the Phantom III was definitely under way, but meanwhile 32 EX was to be subjected to still more rigorous testing at Brooklands as well as at Chateauroux and modifications would be made to the chassis when and where the Experimental Department thought fit.

PART III CHAPTER 3

The decision is taken to replace the Phantom II with the 'Spectre' which will be known as the Phantom III, the first production cars in the AZ series. The problems that were encountered with the production cars once they got into the hands of their owners. Rolls-Royce Ltd issue their famous warning about 'motor-way driving'. The disposal of 32 EX and the subsequent story of this car as 3-DEX-202

The first series production Phantom IIIs were designated the chassis numbers 3-AZ-20 to 3-AZ-238 theoretically only even numbers were used in this series, but for some unknown reason the odd number 43 and 47 were also used. 3-AZ-43 was supplied to his Royal Highness the Duke of Kent and 3-AZ-47 to the Viceroy of India, who at the time was Lord Linlithgow.

The first announcement of the new Phantom III was published in the edition of *The Autocar* dated 4 October 1935, and on 8 October 1935, *The Motor* published a further announcement including two drawings of the new model, one depicted a Continental touring limousine and the other a full 7 passenger enclosed drive limousine. There was also a photograph of a Park Ward Sedanca de Ville on the Phantom III chassis which was quite clearly 37 EX, proving that the ten experimental Spectres were all built at about the same time; the latter ones incorporating improvements and modifications developed from experience gained from running the cars at Chateauroux.

What is interesting is that both *The Autocar* and *The Motor* published pictures of the engines for the first time. In both magazines, the engines are shown with four thumb screws to the rocker cover on the over-head valve mechanism (as on a Phantom II). In the text the engines are described as having four carburetters.

At a very early stage in the testing of the 'Spectre', the four carburetters were dispensed with and the air cleaner altered to the design which became standard on the production

Phantom III chassis. Also the four thumb screws fitted to the 6-cylinder Phantom II engine were replaced by small 'holding-down studs', all round the rocker cover; this was because as the rocker cover was set at an angle it was discovered that, with the thumb screw arrangement, oil leaks were inevitable.

In those days the Motor Show was held annually at Olympia and in 1935 was opened on 10 October. Of course one of THE cars which everyone wanted to see was the new Rolls-Royce Phantom III. The coachbuilders had taken full advantage of the new model and there were nine exhibits in all.

Orders for the new model came in fast, and a number of people who had Phantom IIs on order took delivery of the new Phantom III instead.

However well tested a new design is, once it reaches the hands of the general public it is quite extraordinary what troubles, abuse and mis-use will cause. As originally built, the Phantom III was fitted with hydraulically operated tappets, it was essential to clean the filters regularly, in order to keep them quiet. This was often neglected, also oils were nothing like as good as they are today and produced a great deal more carbon and sludge; as the pipe-lines to the tappets were very fine it only required a small particle of carbon to block the line with the result that the pressure was lost and the tappets became noisy. A conscientious chauffeur, who had been through the Rolls-Royce School of

Instruction and received a course on the maintenance of the Phantom III, would keep the filters clean and there would be less likelihood of this occurring. Rolls-Royce Ltd therefore urged new Phantom III owners to let their chauffeurs attend the School of Instruction and go through a course on the new model; but many employers were loathe to do this. They said that their chauffeur had already attended the School on one of the older models and they could see no point whatsoever in sending him on another course, mainly because they did not want to have to manage without him whilst he was at the School.

Due to this attitude, the Phantom III acquired a bad reputation in its earliest days, which was unfair to the car; so it was not very long before Rolls-Royce Ltd decided that drastic measures were necessary. Early in 1937, 32 EX was stripped in the Experimental Department at Derby, and re-built with solid tappets in place of the hydraulically operated ones and at the same time a different gearbox was fitted, which had an overdrive top gear. It had been found that owners were taking Phantom IIIs on the Continent and driving them mercilessly on the new German Autobahns, almost as if they were on the dodgem cars in a fairground; holding their foot to the board on the accelerator pedal from the moment they reached the Autobahn until the time they came off it (Major Lionel Beaumont Thomas, MC, JP, the first owner of 3-BT-79, a Park Ward Touring Limousine, told me that he covered 112 miles in 90 minutes with this car on the Continent in 1937, needless to say he had a great deal of trouble with this chassis). No engine with reciprocating parts would put up with this sort of treatment, every engine has a safe natural cruising speed and this is the speed at which it should be driven continuously. The drivers of locomotives, or the chief engineer on a ship, do not drive the engine or engines 'flat out' for hour after hour, or they would soon be in trouble. To try and emphasise this Rolls-Royce Ltd issued their famous warning:

When one escapes from the twisty, constricted· roads of the British Isles to the long straight motor roads which are being introduced all over the Continent, there is a very strong temptation to take advantage of the possibilities of continuous high speed which open before one. To do so is to court trouble. It is obviously in the interests of our customers that we draw attention to the danger of excessive engine wear introduced by the specialised motor roads, and such a warning would not be complete without indicating clearly the maximum speed at which our cars can be run continuously under such conditions. The speeds in question are:-

Phantom III - 75/80 miles per hour
Phantom II - 70/75 miles per hour
25/30 - 65/70 miles per hour
20/25 - 60/65 miles per hour

Speeds of this nature will not cause unnecessary wear and tear, but if higher speeds than these are maintained then the engine must invariably suffer, however well designed or constructed it may be.

Of course, there have always been people who like to decry Rolls-Royce cars, and the moment this warning was issued they started, 'There we are, what did we tell you, we always knew Rolls-Royce cars were fragile, etc., etc.,'. This was a most unfair criticism of a Company which was taking endless trouble to ensure that their customers were fully satisfied with their products. It can only be surmised that other Companies which did not issue such a warning did not do so in the hopes that perhaps their clients' cars would 'blow up' and they would then buy a new one.

When 32 EX was rebuilt with solid tappets and an overdrive gearbox, the car was back on the road for further testing. From his office in Conduit Street, Sidgreaves wrote to Robotham in the Experimental Department at Derby, a letter which reads as follows:-

'4 June 1937. If you want to get some real traffic running whilst 32 EX is up here, I suggest you instruct the driver to join the Ascot Throng at the height of the crush. It ought to be a good test for overheating in traffic as well as for the clutch. Signed: Sg'.

By this time overheating problems on the Phantom III were being overcome with an improved and slightly larger radiator matrix, at the same time a modification had been made to the clutch by fitting an improved type of clutch-plate. The new clutch was a great improvement on the older pattern but, frankly, I consider the clutch on a Phantom III is one of its worst features; it has nothing like the sweetness of action of the clutch on a Phantom II. The clutch on a Phantom III presented serious problems from the start and my own car, chassis No. 3-AZ-146, was returned to Hythe Road in March 1937 when it had covered a total mileage of 3,881 miles, to be fitted with the latest type of clutch-plate. It seems that the reasons for the clutch on a Phantom III being inferior to that fitted on the previous Phantom II are as follows:-

1 The engine of the Phantom III produces a very great deal more power than the previous model.
2 The gearbox on the Phantom III is mounted separately to the engine, there being a huge X-bracing on the chassis frame between the engine and the gearbox. This keeps the chassis most beautifully rigid over even the most terrible road surfaces, a feature which had produced a great many problems of 'jellying' with the Phantom II is completely eliminated.
3 Having the engine in the Phantom III rubber mounted and separate from the gearbox and the gearbox having independent rubber mountings, there is unavoidably a certain amount of movement between the two when the drive is first taken up.
4 Added to this I find that on 3-AZ-146 provided the clutch thrust has plenty of oil no 'juddering' takes place and the clutch works smoothly, but if the thrust bearing is allowed to run dry, the 'juddering' is terrible.

Not very long after 32 EX had 'joined the Ascot Throng', with no ill-effects at all, the gearbox seized up on the road. This was found to be due to the fact that the oil being used was unsuitable. So, prior to being sent for further testing at Chateauroux, a thermometer was fitted to the gearbox (which was filled with Price oil) and the car was taken to Brooklands and given a thorough speed trial. On 16 August 1937, the Experimental Department received a letter from Chateauroux which read as follows:-

'32 EX Phantom III. This car has covered 15,000 miles in all, 12,000 in France. At this mileage all previous Phantom III have broken up their big-end bearings. There is no sign whatever that the bearings are beginning to go on 32 EX'.

Just a week previously Robotham had written as follows: 'The deletion of hydraulic tappets seems to be a great success. No deterioration in silence and very little adjustment is required'.

From the above it can be seen that the original faults with the Phantom III were gradually being ironed out with continual testing and experimenting, but unfortunately a fortnight later Robotham was writing again:

Sg. from Rm/Gry, Copy to Hs., By, Da, Hdy. Rm/Gry 7RP, 28.8.37.
32 EX Rear Axle. Replying to Sg 9/e. 27.8.1937 we have arrived at the conclusion that the failure of the gear teeth in France was due to the inadequate lubricating properties of the oil at high temperatures.
Our reasons for this are confirmatory tests carried out at Derby on our chassis dynamometer.
We have always complained to Wakefields on the amount of sludging in their Hi-Press axle oil. They therefore evolved a new oil temporarily designated R-R E D oil, having thio-ether instead of sulphur chloride in solution. This oil is very free from sludging and has already run two 10,000 miles French Tests on 35 EX and 6 BN.
At high speeds in the hot weather the axle temperature of 32 EX reached 130°, we therefore ran our dynamometer axle at this temperature and then did several changes at high speed into 3rd gear, letting in the clutch with a jerk, at too low a speed, very shortly the gears had picked up. The test was then repeated on new gears on an American oil imported by the Vacuum Co, called Vacuum "Hypoid Gear Lubricant". No damage after considerable abuse was done to the gears. On changing the oil to R-R E.P. the gears very soon failed.
A 3rd pair of gears was then tested on our present Standard Hi-Press Oil. They survived the test.
We have therefore told Wakefields we will not use their new oil and they have guaranteed that it will be impossible for an R-R customer to obtain it from his garage, although they were in the process of standardizing it throughout England under the old name of Hi-Press. Rm/Gry.

It was as the result of the above failure that Castrol Hi-Press S C was evolved, for use in the back axles on both Phantom II and Phantom III models in addition to other Rolls-Royce cars which have Hypoid gears in the rear axle as this oil contains a sulphur base.
Late in 1937, 32 EX was returned to the Ex-

(*Top*) The 'Honeymoon Coupe', a Barker Drop Head Foursome Coupe designed by Ivan Evernden, on chassis 16-G-V, an experimental 20/25. Here, Sir Henry Royce is at the wheel, Nurse Aubin is seated behind with the 'light coloured' hat, with Rajah R's dog between her and Mrs Fell, outside his home at West Wittering (*photo M. H. Evans*)

(*Bottom*) 1930 Lanchester Straight Eight '30', a Barker Laudaulette de Ville on chassis number 8096 (*photo Francis W. H. Hutton-Scott*)

(See the 1928 New Phantom Barker Laudaulette and Daimler 35/120 Barker Enclosed Drive Laudaulette in the fourth and fifth sections of photographs, for comparison)

(Top) B-167-EJ, a Bentley 3½ litre with coachwork by James Young. It was built for the JY stand at the 1936 Motor Show in Olympia. It was used by the owner during the war on Government business. Mrs Wilcock stands by the parallel opening nearside door

(Bottom) Ivan Evernden stands beside B-167-EJ. The chassis was purchased after the war by the son of the original owner who restored it with this Park Ward body formerly mounted on a 4½ litre chassis *(photo F. M. Wilcock)*

(Top) A 25/30 with Salmon's Sedanca Coupe Drop Head on chassis number GXM5 belonging to Lawrence Dalton (photo L. Dalton)
(Bottom) 'Honeysuckle', Johnnie Green's 4¼ litre Bentley Vanden Plas Sports Tourer on chassis number B-154-MR (photo J. Green)

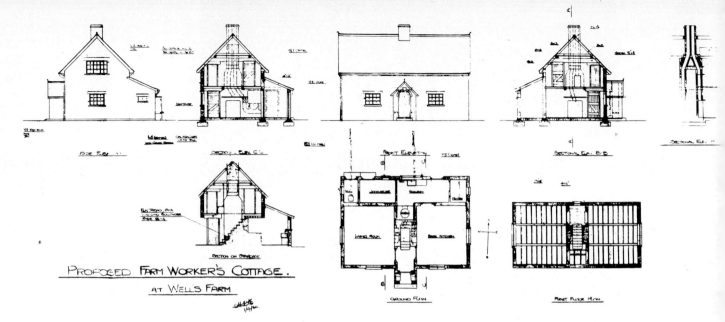

PROPOSED FARM WORKER'S COTTAGE.

AT WELL'S FARM

SCALE ¼ INS TO 1 FT

(Top) The drawing for a Farm Worker's Cottage executed by Ivan Evernden to Royce's design, which was his last work. See Part III, Chapter 1 *(photo Ivan Evernden)*
(Bottom) 1936 Packard V12 Sedanca de Ville by Le Baron imported into England by R. Beaumont-Thomas together with another, a Victoria Convertible. This photograph shows the car as it is today in the collection of J. C. Denne *(photo J. C. Denne)*

(Top) A Thrupp and Maberly Limousine 8 litre Bentley on chassis number YR5086 supplied to A. U. Bustard of Ulster, Northern Ireland. It has a 13 foot wheelbase. The car is now an Open Tourer with the chassis shortened and re-built by W. D. Lake. It is now in America (photo Miss V. Bustard)

(Middle) A Short Chassis example of an 8 litre Bentley fitted with Sports Saloon coachwork by Freestone & Webb on chassis number YR5089, it was built for R. Beaumont-Thomas, who won several prizes with it at the 1931 Eastbourne Concours d'Elegance held in September. The car was built for the 1931 London Motor Show to be exhibited on the Freestone & Webb Stand, but owing to the liquidation of Bentley Motors, it could not be shown. It was reputed to have been destroyed in the Blitz on Coventry in 1940, but has recently come to light in America with it's original index number MY9693 changed to that from another 8 litre Bentley also with coachwork by Freestone & Webb; this car which bore the index number GO4010 carried a Limousine and it is now thought that it was this car which was destroyed in the Coventry Blitz and that the number plates had been changed over some time before the Blitz on Coventry took place

(Bottom) A 'Wraith' of 1939. It is really a Hooper design but must in this case have been built by Barker after the firms merged. It is taken in the usual Hooper setting for such photographs

(Top and bottom) A Phantom III engine on test

(*Top*) This photograph shows the unusual radiator design of 30EX (*photo Ivan Evernden*)

(*Middle*) 30EX on first Road Trial. See Part III, Chapter 1 (*photo Ivan Evernden*)

(*Bottom*) Chassis number 30EX, the first 'Spectre' being prepared for the road in the Experimental Garage at Derby. See Part III, Chapter 1 (*photo Ivan Evernden*)

(*Top*) RC2406 is 31EX and RC2545 is 32EX. Note the difference in radiators (*photo Ivan Evernden*)

(*Bottom*) 31EX in France after its accident. See Part III, Chapter 1 (*photo H. F. Hamilton*)

perimental Department at Derby, and by 9 April 1938, when the Experimental Department had finished using the car, the total mileage it had run was 67,360 miles.

When the Experimental Department finished with 32 EX, its history becomes obscure. My conjecture is that it was used as a Company Car, for the transport of Directors of Rolls-Royce Ltd, then handed over to the Sales Department, where it would be gone over with a fine-tooth comb to make certain it was as good as it could possibly be. The registration number RC 2545 was then removed and in its place the car was re-registered as DMJ 600 (Bedfordshire County Council), when it was purchased by a Mr Messinger of Bedford, as a car in used condition. The speedometer had been put back to zero before Mr Messinger bought it, and in accordance with the Company's usual policy on selling experimental model Phantom IIIs, the chassis number was changed to 3-DEX-202.

The car was laid up during the War, and put back on to the road in 1946, but Mr Messinger's chauffeur found it too large to handle and it was laid up again in the mid-1950s.

In October 1965 an Australian Mr John Griffiths, who was a great Rolls-Royce enthusiast came to England on business and whilst in Britain he was determined to find a really good Phantom III. As he already possessed one he had some idea as to what sort of car he was seeking, finally, in answer to an advertisement he went to see 3-DEX-202, which he decided to purchase.

It should be noted here that when the Experimental Model Phantom IIIs were sold by the Company, some had their chassis numbers changed to AEX, which means that the car conformed to the 'A' series Phantom III, which were in the ordinary way given the AZ or AX prefix in their chassis number; but two chassis were designated DEX, which means that these were sold incorporating all the latest modifications which were fitted to the DL and DH series cars.

John Griffiths wrote an article on chassis No. 3-DEX-202 which was published in *Praeclarvn*, the quarterly magazine of the Rolls-Royce Owners' Club of Australia, which he has kindly given me permission to include in this book. So I cannot do better than allow the present owner of 3-DEX-202 to tell the rest of the story in his own words of the circumstances in which he purchased the car from Mr J H C Preen of Horndean, nr Portsmouth.

It would seem that Mr Preen had the car licensed for use on the road for only four months; it was not licensed between September 1964 and October 1965 when I purchased the car. It thus seems quite certain that the present mileage of 81,600 is genuine.

'Of course, anyone can see it's not immaculate', he said. He was right.

The water pump throws water everywhere, the shutters don't work, the valve gear is incredibly noisy, in fact, the whole engine looks as if it has had a hard life (as no doubt it has). There are chips in the windscreen and headlamp glasses, the plating is crazed, and inside, the carpets have been poorly renewed, the interior trim generally is far from perfect, and a heater has been fitted necessitating the repositioning of the instrument panel, and minor desecration of the woodwork and cooling system. However, to keep matters in perspective, the body was obviously very sound, as was the chassis underneath. All six tyres were practically new.

I wondered whether it was really possible that the overdrive gearbox was still there. I had always imagined that this item, mentioned in books almost with reverence, must be a separate overdrive unit or at least a fifth overdrive ratio. But there was no sign of either, and, undoing the leather stocking around the gear lever, I found a gate for four gears only. It was a bitter disappointment. However, taking the car for a drive it was soon obvious that second was a much higher gear than normal and I slowly realized that the magic overdrive gearbox was no more than a direct third ratio and an overdrive fourth, a system used by the Company so many years before. Setting aside this disappointment, and trying to ignore the dreadful noise coming from the engine, especially when changing down at speed, there was no doubt the car was indeed a delight to drive.

I stood at a distance and looked at it. I could not then, and still cannot, convince myself that its body style is outstanding. It does not possess the classic proportions I was seeking, but probably only a few Phantom IIIs do so in full measure. Clearly, I could expect to find no better. Reluctantly I rejected the thought of making an offer (as the car would certainly go if word got around), and paid up. With freight, duty, sales tax, insurance and landing charges, it has ended up being a rather expensive exercise, but perhaps the test is that I have not yet regretted the decision.

This is virtually the whole story of 32 EX or 3-DEX-202 as this chassis is now known and it has obviously found a good home and is being well cared for in Australia.

PART III CHAPTER 4

The Experimental chassis numbers 33 EX and 34 EX, Humfrey Symons approaches Rolls-Royce Ltd, with the suggestion that he uses a Phantom III to drive across the Sahara to Nairobi and back as a publicity stunt, the preparation of 34 EX for this trip in the Experimental Garage at Derby

Ivan Evernden was kind enough to give me the following information on 33 EX:

'Continental touring saloon. Park Ward. Maroon. Unladen weight: 50 cwt 2 qrs 0 lb. Body weight: 13 cwt 1 qr 2 lb. Wood and aluminium construction, but with steel panel and wings. Registration number RC 3168'.

It was first used on the road on 3 September 1935, unfortunately I have no details of this chassis when it was going through its tests at Chateauroux but on 8 June 1938, the car was sold for £1,500 after the chassis number had been changed to 3-AEX-33. It was sold as a used vehicle to George Heath & Co Ltd, of John Bright Street, Birmingham for their customer, James Cadman, Esq, DSC, JP, of Walton Hall, Eccleshall, Staffs. There is a note on the file that it was delivered on 25 June 1938, to George Heath Ltd, by Lillie Hall. It was sold with no guarantee, but as it stood, in used condition. The worn tyres had been changed and Barker & Co had buffed-up the radiator and replated the headlamps. The car had been repainted in black, lined in red, with red leather upholstery.

Later, 33 EX or 3-AEX-33 was owned by Jack Mackinlay of Simonstone Hall, Hawes, in Yorkshire, who called the car 'Jumbo'. I only discovered this quite by chance as it so happens that Jack Mackinlay is the present owner of Sir Julian Cahn's Phantom II open tourer, chassis No. 23 GN (see Part II, Chapter 8). Jack Mackiniay has owned many Rolls-Royce cars and it is interesting to note that when, in 1963, he was considering purchasing a Bentley S III Series Continental 'Flying Spur', he pointed out that in pre-War days, it was the Rolls-Royce Phantom II Continental which reigned supreme

and he felt quite certain that if Rolls-Royce Ltd, and H J Mulliner/Park Ward would produce a Rolls-Royce Silver Cloud III with the 'Flying Spur' coachwork there would be a very ready market for it; this they subsequently agreed to do and Jack Mackinlay is the owner of the first one of these extremely desirable and somewhat rare models as they were only produced at the very end of the period during which the Silver Cloud III was being built. Shortly afterwards the 'Shadow' was announced as a new model.

When Jack Mackinlay sold 33 EX, he retained the registration number, which is now on his Derby Bentley. The last known owner of 33 EX according to the files at Hythe Road was Sir Leonard Ropner, in October 1956.

34 EX is undoubtedly one of the most interesting of the experimental Phantom III chassis. The details which Ivan Evernden was kind enough to provide are as follows:

'Enclosed limousine. Park Ward. Fawn and black. Weight: 51 cwt 1 qr 7 lb. Wood and aluminium construction. Registration No. RC 3169.

This chassis was so satisfactory that it was retained at Derby and used principally as a V I P car. It was used for the opening of the Derby Assizes, which attracted a great deal of publicity, as it was the first time that a motor vehicle had been used for this purpose and photographs were taken showing Mr Justice Hawk and Col Handley, who was High Sheriff of Derby, alighting from the car. The car was also used by H.R.H. the Duchess of Gloucester for the opening of the Red Triangle Playing Fields at Winchester and photographs of both ceremonies appear in the Rolls-Royce Company's quarterly magazine *The Bulletin,*

September 1936. This superb magazine was sent to all owners of R-R cars and shareholders in the Company every quarter free of charge, but unfortunately, owing to production costs, this ceased in July 1957.

On 2 October 1936, *The Autocar* published a road test report of two Phantom III chassis, the one which was subjected to the most lengthy trials was 34 EX, but they also tested 3-AZ-38, (a 'Trials Car') which was used principally in the Alps and later sold to that great connoisseur Stanley Sears. This road test is included in the publication *Rolls-Royce in the Thirties*.

One of the exploits which holds even the most intrepid driver in awe, is the crossing of the great Sahara Desert in North Africa. It has been crossed many times by motor car and even before the 1914 - 18 War, daring motorists were venturing into it. On 5 February 1937, *The Autocar* published the following, which appears under 'Notes and News' and headed 'Twice Across the Sahara'.

On Monday of this week Mr H E Symons, motoring correspondent of the *Sunday Times*, gave an interesting lecture on his two journeys across the Sahara, at the Royal Geographical Society, before a distinguished audience. His lecture was illustrated by lantern slides and extracts from the well-known Morris films. It will be recalled that Symons made the journey to Timbucktu in seven days on a Morris 10 in 1935, and last year took a larger Morris by another route across the great Desert to Nigeria, which, in spite of a 23 hours hold-up in soft sand, he reached in a week from England.

It may be said that, graphically, as Symons writes and talks, no-one can possibly conceive the rough treatment these two cars had to submit to in order to do these journeys, unless he sees the films, which, by the way, are now being shown all over the country by Morris dealers.

Symons' lecture was most interesting and informative, and was much appreciated by the large audience. The Chairman announced that the lecturer was now preparing for a similar, yet even longer trip; but *The Autocar* is informed, not on a Morris car.

From the above it can be seen that H E Symons was well acquainted with driving conditions across the Sahara Desert and it seems that after reading the road test of R-R's latest model, his imagination was fired and he wrote to Arthur Sidgreaves putting forward his proposition:

To drive a Phantom III to Nairobi and back. February 1937

Object | To obtain for Rolls-Royce cars the maximum possible Press, Radio and Film publicity both at Home and Overseas, particularly in parts of the British Empire on the African Continent.

Method | Press and other publicity of the right kind is always obtained if a good News Story is provided.

My intention is to make the journey from London to Nigeria in one week to Kenya in two weeks, and thus show *how effortless,* how *comfortable* and how *short* a journey of such magnitude is, if effected in a Rolls-Royce car.

Incidentally, we shall travel to Nigeria, and also to Kenya, (Nairobi) in Rolls-Royce comfort and safety at *half the cost* and in *half the time* of first class (Union Castle Line) steamer and express train, showing that on such a journey the Phantom III provides a really economical as well as luxurious mode of travel. There will, of course, be no suggestion that we are out to break records, or do anything not in keeping with Rolls-Royce dignity and traditions. The impression we shall spread about is that to a Rolls-Royce such a journey is 'all in the day's work' and that a luxurious saloon car of this make does easily, rapidly and comfortably that which has hither to only been attempted by specially equipped cars.

Incidentally, this *will* be far and away the quickest 'through' motor journey ever accomplished and should thus arouse a considerable amount of enthusiasm. But the whole atmosphere surrounding the run is just that the Rolls-Royce provides the most *luxurious* way of 'getting there' and that the excellent time made is quite normal for such a car.

The run will also show convincingly that a Rolls-Royce is *not* only built for good roads but goes equally well on bad roads or desert tracks, and is thus suitable for ceremonial use for Governors of Provinces, etc.

No part of the route, however, is of a 'chassis breaking' character. Given ordinary care, no trouble whatever should be experienced.

Route: Passes through France, Algeria, Sahara, Nigeria, French Equatorial Africa, Belgian Congo, Uganda and Kenya Colony.

Publicity:

Passing through a good deal of British territory, the run would have considerable Imperial interest and should thus be good 'news' for London and Provincial papers, and, for instance, India and Australia and New Zealand newspapers.

I write for the five leading South African newspapers, to whom I have already mentioned the project without referring to any specified make of car. They are *most interested* and will publish a *Full Story* of the run in several successive issues.

The London *Sunday Times* and *The Sketch* will of course take a full story from me *weekly*, and *The Autocar* and *The Motor* will obviously do so. I can also arrange for the leading Daily and Provincial papers to deal with the run in England.

I am on excellent terms with the Algiers press and write also for the *Nigerian Daily Times*, and of course the British Colonies listed above have daily papers published in English and would be glad to make use of such a story.

Mr Buckley would issue to the Home press stories compiled from cables received from me, and Reuters and the Press Association would also very likely send out news paragraphs dealing with the run.

The B B C is also very keen on this sort of news story and is not averse to mentioning the name of the car in Empire broadcasts. The newsreel people also would be interested at the completion of the run.

I also propose to make a really good travel film on the return journey showing the Phantom III among pygmies, in the jungle, in the Sahara, etc. with a view of showing it before a distinguished gathering of the Royal Geographical Society, of which I am a Fellow.

I would, of course, take the opportunity of showing the car to the Governors of colonies passed through, as well as to Residents and other influential people.

Cost:

The cost of three people and the car (a Phantom III, which is the most suitable on account of the independent wheel springing) would be *under £400*, and I suggest that I be paid a fee of £250 for organizing the trip and undertaking all publicity in connection with it.

Preparation of the car:

The Phantom III is well suited for the conditions to be encountered and little extra preparation would be called for.

Unless the brake drums interfere with the fitting of wheels with 16 in. rims, tyres of 9.00 x 16 section should be fitted. In any case the very largest tyres which possibly can be fitted. These will prevent the car sinking in soft sand and will give 1 in. extra ground clearance.

When he had digested these proposals Sidgreaves became most enthusiastic about the idea. The first thing that had to be decided was to find a suitable car to undertake this arduous adventure; there was not a great deal of time left if the trip was to be undertaken that year (1937), as the weather conditions in North Africa were so changeable that virtually the only months suitable were February and March. It was then January and keeping to a tight schedule the car would have to be back in Algiers by the end of March at the very latest. It quickly became apparent that 34 EX was the most suitable car to use, it was in very good running order, the coachwork was a full 7-passenger enclosed drive limousine, which would allow someone to lie out at full length in the rear and sleep whilst the car was being driven by a co-driver. Mr Symons also thought it essential that the third passenger should be a fully qualified Rolls-Royce mechanic.

In April 1970 I spent a most pleasant day with W A Robotham and his family at his home in Kent and we discussed the Phantom III and the Nairobi trip. He was in charge of the Experimental Department at Derby at the time and he remembers very clearly his astonishment when he heard from Sidgreaves that a car was to be prepared to make this overland trip; he was very amusing about it, he told me, 'I cannot think of a more unsuitable car to use'.

Robotham had the entire Experimental Department to run, he was extremely busy and held a post of great responsibility and he therefore felt that it would be much better to hand the car over to one of his subordinates in the Experimental Department and to put him in charge of the whole operation. He thought that the same person should prepare 34 EX, then accompany the car on its trip to Nairobi, which was an extremely sensible way of dealing with the problem. He felt that the most capable person for this venture was H F Hamilton, who was in charge of the Experimental Garage at Chateauroux; so a telegram was sent which read as follows:-

27.1.37. Hamilton Francobrit Levallois-Perret France. Please return Derby by Saturday morning letter following. Robotham'.

The letter read:
Rm/HFH (Cos. to Rm/GWH - Rm/IMW). Rm 3/r. 27.1.37.
We have today wired you as follows: 'Please return to Derby by Saturday morning - letter following'.

There is a projected press trip on the P III and we have recommended you as the Technical Representative to accompany the car. Preparation of the chassis will commence on Monday next.

We should, therefore, like you to be back at the Works on Saturday morning, before they close, to discuss the project.

Rm.

In the meanwhile, the question of fitting over-size tyres to cope with driving through sand was being thoroughly explored with the Dunlop Rubber Co. On each of Humfrey Symons previous trips, the car he used had been fitted with a very much larger section tyre than was customary on a standard production model, and he felt that, in the case of 34 EX, (which was a very much larger and heavier vehicle than either of the previous ones in which he had crossed the Sahara), it was absolutely essential. No doubt he visualized being stuck and, owing to the great weight of the car, finding it absolutely impossible to extricate themselves from the sand.

Originally twin tyres to the rear wheels were contemplated, but this idea was soon abandoned as it meant major alterations to the rear axle and there was not time to do this. Also it was quickly realized that twin wheels at the rear would make the car look very ungainly and completely spoil the appearance of it.

Symons had written personally to the Dunlop Rubber Co asking for their advice and on 29 January 1937, he received the following reply:

Dear Humfrey,
With further reference to your letter of January 11th, I now have pleasure in passing on to you the information received from the Technical Department, for your talk before the Royal Geographical Society.

In general our recommendations for tyres when used on sand are based on the following considerations:

1 For fairly hard sand inflation pressures of 20 lb/sq in. seem satisfactory.
2 For soft sand inflation pressures of 15 lb/sq in. seem necessary.
3 For very soft sand inflation pressures as low as 10 lb/sq in. are necessary.
In each case a tyre size is chosen which will carry the maximum load at a reasonable deflection (22% deflection above the flange seems satisfactory for sand work. 18% is used for main road work).
On this basis the average contact pressure works out at about:

33 lb/sq in. - for class 1 above - fairly hard sand.
25 lb/sq in. - for class 2 above - soft sand.
20 lb/sq in. - for class 3 above - very soft sand.

It should be noted that this contact pressure is based on the ellipse area, since any pattern is quickly filled with sand. The ellipse areas quoted have been obtained on a hard surface and in practice on sand there will be some variation from these areas, depending on the type of sand and the way in which it packs.

The large increase in tyre size required when a vehicle operates in sand results in considerably increased power consumption, and to minimise this difficulty the following procedure can be adopted. When running on hard sand inflation pressures of 20 - 25 lb/sq in. may be used, when soft sand is encountered inflation pressures may be dropped to say 10 lb/sq in., when the soft sand has been negotiated the pressures can be increased again, lowered again for soft sand, and so on. In this way the minimum amount of running is done at low inflation pressures with consequent reduction in power consumption for long stretches of a journey.
Kind regards,
Yours sincerely,

A copy of this letter was sent to R-R Ltd together with the following tables.

TABLE I

Various Tyres carrying maximum tyre load of 4.75/16 (6½ cwts).

Tyre Size	Inflation pressures lb/sq in	Use	Ellipse area sq in	Contact pressure lb/sq in
4.75/16	28	Roads	20.2	36
4.75/16	24	Hard sand	21.9	33
6.50/16	8	Very soft sand	37.5	20

TABLE II

Various tyres carrying maximum tyre load of 6.50/16 (11¼ cwt).

6.50/16	30	Roads	30.7	41
6.50/16	22	Hard sand	37.7	33
7.00/16	18	Hard sand	41.6	30
9.00/16	13	Soft sand	58.5	21

TABLE III

Various tyres at 10 lb/sq in. Inflation Pressure

Size	Load (Cwts)	Use	Ellipse area	Average Contact pressure
4.75/16	3½	Very soft sand	21.2	19
6.50/16	7	Very soft sand	36.5	21
7.00/16	8	Very soft sand	41.6	21
9.00/16	9½	Very soft sand	60.	18

TABLE IV

Tyres with approximate load used in Mr Symon Desert Tours

Size	Load	Inflation Pressure	Ellipse area	Average Contact Pressure
6.50/16	10	20	36.7	31
6.50/16	10	26	30.9	36
7.00/16	16**	20	54.0	33
7.00/16	16	35	39.0	46

**This is a greater load than we would normally recommend at this pressure

Whilst the above correspondence was taking place between Humfrey Symons and the Dunlop Rubber Co, W A Robotham had made some calculations of his own by increasing the tyre section from 7.00 to 7.50 and below is the table which he worked out.

22.1.37.

Standard Dunlop 7 x 18 96 in. effective circumference.
Width unloaded - 6.9375 in.
Rim 4.000 in.
Road Wheel - Revs/mile - 660.

7.50 x 18 - 98.5 in. effective circumference.
Width unloaded - 7.8125 ins.
Rim 5.00 in.
Road Wheel - Revs/mile - 643.

After further discussions it was decided to adopt Robotham's idea as being the simplest one to secure the additional traction required whilst running through sand, and a set of 6 wheels were despatched to the Dunlop Rubber Co in Birmingham to have their rims knurled to take the larger section tyres.

On Monday, 1 February 1937, 34 EX went into the Experimental Department. Hamilton had arrived from Chateauroux and was there to supervise the preparation of the car for its ordeal and the following work was carried out to the chassis.

1 A new steam valve was fitted to the top of the radiator.

2 The engine, which was number 7; had the following modifications carried out to it:
(a) 4 felts were fitted in the valve end of each rocker.
(b) A .015 hole was drilled in the annulus of each rocker bush.
(c) The existing tappets adjusting screws were replaced by new ones incorporating the oil grooves, likewise the bottom ball ends of the push rods.
(d) Up to date gauze tappet and main oil filters were fitted.

3 A pair of much stiffer rear springs were fitted, this was partly to give greater ground clearance and at the same time to deal with the load which it was intended that the car should carry.

4 New halfshafts were fitted to the rear axle.

5 The rear brakes were re-lined.

6 The nearside front wing was altered, so that it had a well in it and an additional spare wheel carrier was mounted, so that the car had two spare wheels.

7 The wheels were altered by Dunlop to take the larger sectional tyres as has already been mentioned.

8 The clutch was re-lined with a more durable material.

In addition to the work which was carried out above, the following modifications were made:

1 A 4 gallon fresh water tank was mounted underneath each front wing between the chassis frame and the well of the spare wheel carriers.

2 The occasional seats of the 7-passenger limousine were removed from the rear compartment and in their place an additional 20 gallon petrol tank was fitted.

3 The rear compartment of the car was divided longitudinally down the centre, so that the nearside of the rear compartment became a stores and travelling workshop, the offside of the rear compartment was kept clear so that the third passenger had ample room to stretch out and rest whilst the car was travelling. (All food and provisions were supplied by Fortnum and Mason, most beautifully packed in special containers.)

4 The doors on the sides of the bonnet which are usually fitted on a Phantom III were dispensed with and the bonnet was louvred right the way along in order to give the maximum air flow through the radiator, at the same time a special fan of a high speed type working on two pulleys was fitted and additional petrol pumps were fitted to the frame.

5 A GB plate was fixed to the nearside at the rear of the car with a red tail-lamp over it, this is a regulation which no longer exists but in those days all cars carrying an international circulation plate had to have a means of illuminating it at night.

The fact that the car was in London on Tuesday. 16 February, and all this work had been carried out so rapidly, is a great credit to all those responsible.

As a guide to what would be required, Humfrey Symons furnished the Experimental Department at Derby with a most comprehensive list of spare parts which he had taken on the two Morrises during his previous trips.

This was followed by another letter:

The Cutting,
Grivons Grove,
Leatherhead.

- Robotham Esq.,
Experimental Department,
Rolls-Royce Ltd, Derby.   30 January 1937.

Dear Sir,

Nairobi Run
I did not raise the question of instruments in my letter yesterday.

In order that we may get the fullest possible data on this trip, I think we should fit temporarily, below the instrument board, the following additional thermometers for measuring:-

*1 Temperature at bottom of radiator
 2 Temperature under bonnet
 3 Temperature of oil

In addition, I always have a cheap 'Rototherm' thermometer mounted inside the car (above the windscreen or on a door-pillar) to give the air temperature inside the car. It would be interesting to have a similar instrument - an 'outdoor' model is made - fitted outside the body where it can be seen from the front seat, to give us the temperature in the sun.

These can be obtained at any chemist for 4.6d. retail, but they need checking for accuracy, being cheap, they may vary a great deal!

The two other instruments which are necessary are a Hughes motor compass (£2.10s. less 10 per cent) obtainable from S Smith & Sons (M A) Ltd or direct from Henry Hughes & Sons Ltd, 59 Fenchurch Street, E C 3, and a motor Aneroid, calibrated up to 9,000 ft - I think Smiths can supply this.

A Tapley gradient meter would also enable us to make interesting observations in the mountainous country in Kenya. Our road goes up to 9,000 ft - as high as the Stelvio Pass in Italy.

Will you therefore obtain and fit these instruments?

Turning to another matter, the carburetter setting should be on the *weak* side, or capable of being weakened below normal, preferably without having to stop and change jets.

Once we leave Algiers we shall be driving all the time at 1,300 to 2,000 ft above sea level. On the Col des Caravanes and Atlas Mountains we reach 4,500 ft and in Kenya even greater altitudes. Only ordinary petrol, with a rather poor octane value, is generally obtainable.

Economy on a run of this sort obviously matters much more than power.

Yours faithfully,
Sgn: H E Symons.
*Useful in case we appear to be boiling.

Robotham, thorough and conscientious as always, immediately wrote to Smiths of Cricklewood for a Hughes Motor Compass and also a Hughes Motor Aneroid, calibrated up to 9,000 ft, and he made arrangements that thermometers made by the well-known firm of Negretti and Zambra (the finest obtainable) should be fitted to the inlet pipe to the cooler and the second one to measure the under-bonnet temperature in the vicinity of the petrol pumps.

Humfrey Symons also made the suggestion that the inner tubes of the tyres should be filled with a special liquid rubber solution which he claimed would make them less liable to punctures or to bursts. This was one of his pet theories, but as it turned out, this idea was to prove a grave mistake.

The following is the list of spares, etc. which it was finally arranged would be taken in 34 EX:-

4 Inner tubes
Jack
Jack Fluid
Distilled Water
Fire Extinguishers
Soldering Iron
Solder
Spirits, Soldering
Files
Emery
Tyre covers (3)
Hack saw blades
Hammer
Holdite
Lapping paste
Copper wire - thick
Copper wire - thin
Iron wire
Repair outfit (Dunlops)
Insulation tape
Funnels (2)

Planks 5 ft 9 in. x 1 ft 1 in.
Lead Lamp
Bijur piping
Propeller shaft - Duckhams grease
Water pump
Soap
Rubber hose ½ in. dia. outside, 3 ft
Sheet - Alum:
Sheet - Iron
Parsons chains - 2 sets
Sparking plugs (24)
Petrol pump diaphragms, long and short spindle
1 petrolflex
High tension wire
Tail lamp wire
Fan belts (6)
Carburetter jets
Valve springs - 8 sets
Complete with grummets, wedges etc.
Piston and con rod, complete
Cylinder head gasket
Exhaust manifold washers
Front coil spring
Radiator, top hose and clips
Carburetter float
Oil filter element
Wiring diagram
Complete kit of hand tools other than those already on car
Hub extractor
Fan pulley extractor
Special stud for changing front spring
Schrader valves
Taps and dies
Hand brace
Tin shears
Drills (assorted)
Nuts and Bolts assorted
Split pins assorted
Large adjust. dipstick
Pinion ball race.

In addition the following electrical equipment was taken in 34 EX for this run to Nairobi:

Spares for make and break and distributors
1 make and break rocker arm and spring
1 condenser
1 coil
Dynamo brushes

12 side lamp bulbs
12 fuses
Coil of fuse wire
1 dynamo
1 voltage control complete
4 yds tail lamp wire (armoured)
12 ft high tension cable

1 Hughes motor compass (£2.10s.0d. less 20%) from S Smith & Son (M A) Ltd, and a motor Aneroid calibrated up to 9,000 ft, also from Smiths

And the following spares were obtained by Humfrey Symons:

First Aid outfit
Axe in case
Sand ladders
Canvas bucket
2 entrenching tools
100 yds lead line cord
2 tins of Never-leak
Hack saw frame

Tapley gradient meter
Aneroid (Smith)
Special Jack from Sessions.

Finally everything that could be done to 34 EX in the time allowed was completed. The speedometer was put back to zero but unfortunately no record was kept of the previous mileage, but when the car left for London, driven by Hamilton, the reading showed 820 miles. The choice of sending Hamilton (or 'Hoppy', as he was always called by his colleagues) was a wise one, as not only was he thoroughly capable but he had an extremely likeable disposition and would be thoroughly prepared to 'rough it' and take any adversity in his stride. When the car reached London it was photographed with Humfrey Symons, Hamilton and the photographer, Mr H B Browning, who was to accompany them, standing beside it, just before they set off on their adventure. There only remained one more thing to be done which was for the whole party to have the necessary inoculations required before going to this part of the world.

PART III CHAPTER 5

Chassis No. 34 EX sets out on 'THE NAIROBI RUN', an account of the journey across France, the tyre trouble in North Africa, Arthur Sidgreaves reaction to this, the return run from Nairobi

On Saturday, 20 February, with the speedometer reading 1,111 miles 34 EX was officially handed over to Humfrey Symons for his 'Propaganda Tour' as he called it.

He spent the weekend familiarizing himself with 34 EX, and on the Monday morning they drove to Folkestone, crossed to Boulogne and set off on the first leg of their journey, arriving in time for dinner at the Hotel de la Poste at Saulieu, having travelled 326 miles.

Humfrey Symons wrote a most interesting article on the whole trip entitled 'Half way round the world in seven weeks', which was published in two parts in *The Autocar* 28 May 1937 and 4 June 1937.

He shows clearly how appalling the roads were and what tremendous punishment the Phantom III had to endure. However, I do feel that he did not give due credit to 'Hoppy' Hamilton, who was largely responsible for the success of the enterprise.

After staying the night at Saulieu they set off for Marseilles, a distance of 380 miles. This run was accomplished so easily that they stopped just outside Marseilles at Aix-en-Provence, where they bathed and rested for 2½ hours, before arriving at the quayside in Marseilles for embarkation in the Compagnie Generale Transatlantique's *Ville d'Oran*. She and her sister ship *Ville d'Alger* were magnificent vessels of just over 10,000 tons and had only come into service the previous year. They were twin-screw ships with steam turbines, burning oil fuel and capable of 21 - 23 knots, and had been expressly built for the Mediterranean service and were the fastest vessels sailing between Marseilles and Algiers.

Describing the run across France, Symons gave the highest possible praise to the Phantom III, which he says was a relevation in comfort and silence. They never exceeded 70 mph but frequently averaged over 60 miles in one hour which, to the passenger dozing in the enormous rear compartment, seemed more like 30 mph and which they said was due to the dead silence and superb springing. This is still true today, 30 years after the Phantom III was first built; in its day it must have been absolutely fabulous, especially to Symons, who had not experienced a long run in one of these cars before.

When they arrived at Algiers, everyone was extremely helpful and they were soon clear of the city and on their way. The weather was perfect, darkness had fallen but they were all so enthusiastic that they decided to drive through the night, taking it in turns to drive for 2 hours at a time, one sleeping in the back, one driving and the other navigating. Browning was the oldest of the party; he was inclined to fall asleep at the wheel so a constant watch had to be kept while he was driving to keep him awake.

They arrived at Ghardaia the following morning, having travelled 395 miles in 9½ hours since leaving Algiers; during this time they had climbed over the Atlas Mountains and driven across desolate plains. To cover 395 miles in 9½ hours means an average speed of over 40 miles per hour, which was no mean feat; but from Laghouat it was a different story. Symons says that he had used this track on previous trans-Sahara journeys but he had never seen it is such a bad state, there were huge rocks sticking out of the ground and drifts of soft sand in all the cuttings. This was where the benefit of the independent front wheel suspension was really appreciated, they simply had to keep going otherwise the car would have stuck in the sand; as it was, the rear springs frequently went right to the rubber buffer stops and it would appear that they had to put up with this sort of motoring all the way to Ghardaia. Here they made quite a long stop at the Hotel Transatlantique, before climbing the zig-zag road on to the plateau above and it was clear moonlight as they made the oasis El Golea.

It was now that they encountered one of the hazards of driving a motor vehicle across the Sahara; the route consisted of wave upon wave of concrete-hard corrugations in the sand, which struck terror into the hearts of all drivers for fear of breaking springs and in fact totally wrecking the car. However, the superb independent suspension on the front of the Phantom III rode over these at speeds of up to 50 mph and shortly after 1.0 a m they pulled unscathed into the S A T T Hotel at El Golea, which had once been a Governor's Palace. Here the proprietor produced omelettes for them and his native boys refuelled 34 EX with petrol, and shortly afterwards they were climbing on to the Plateau known as Tademait. This next section was approximately 140 miles and it looked very desolate on this moonlight night.

As dawn broke they were still speeding across the Plateau, until they came across a cairn of stones which marked a change of direction where the track became a mountain road which took them down a 700 ft drop with many hair-pin bends. Once clear of this they were on another sandy track, but, though Symons had followed this route two years before, he now saw that there must have been some very big sand storms, as the old route which he had followed in 1935 was partially covered with huge sand dunes. They deflated their tyres slightly and, keeping the car in low gear, zig-zaged at speed through the dunes, fearful of getting stuck in one; they had nothing to guide them but their compass but at last they came to the gate of Ain Salah, where they had breakfast at the Hotel. They set off again immediately afterwards along a track which was so rutted that the petrol tank scraped on boulders and the rear springs were continually touching bottom.

The next stage of the journey took them to Arak, it was only about 100 miles, but with all the gorges they continually encountered this section seemed very tedious and took twice their average time before they reached the next S A T T Hotel; built like a fort 1,042 miles south of Algiers, right in the centre of the Sahara. The Frenchman and his wife who ran the establishment prepared them a very good dinner and, fortified and refreshed, they set out again on the 25 mile journey through gorges. Symons says that the cool of the night was very pleasant after the tremendous heat of the day and that the moon was so bright it was unnecessary to use the headlights; at 3.45 in the morning they entered Tamanrasset right in the heart of the Black Hoggar mountains.

On reaching Tamanrasset they were much surprised to find the petrol pump attendant lying asleep on the sand beside the pump, he was instantly awake and refuelled 34 EX with great speed. They could not quite understand this, until it was made clear to them that the Shell agents at Algiers had sent a telegram informing their agent in Tamanrasset that 34 EX was approaching and might need to be refuelled, hence the petrol pump attendant being in readiness to meet her.

The next stage of their journey to In Guezzam was to be the most difficult going of all; Humfrey Symons was quite aware of this, the last time he had made this trip it had taken him 26 hours as this area was riddled with pools of soft sand which were very difficult to see and usually the driver was completely unaware of them until the car was actually stuck.

As dawn broke they found themselves in the middle of a vast sandy plain, the track appeared to be quite smooth and Hamilton, who was driving, 'put his foot down' and the speedometer showed 70 mph. Before long they went over an enormous bump which brought forth curses from Browning, who was occupying the rear seat, and after this they did not exceed 50 mph! As they approached the worst section, Humfrey Symons took over; keeping the car in second gear he swung this way and that to avoid the horrible boulders and this time the tremendous torque of the Phantom III power unit and the 7.50 x 18 tyres kept them out of trouble. As it was, it was essential to keep going and the bumping was terrible, so much so that poor Browning was continually hitting his head against the roof in the rear compartment. They accomplished this part of the journey in 6¾ hours, which was very different from the previous trip; here they again refuelled and set out on their next stage to Agades. Symons says that he hoped to average 50 - 60 mph for the next section of 124 miles over a road of plain grey gravel, but winds had made sand dunes across the track and so once again it was a question of keeping in one of the lower gears and ploughing their way through.

From In Abbengrit the heat of the sun had cracked the earth into great fissures where on previous trips it had been very smooth going and the surface was very bad, but eventually they arrived in Agades at midnight, where they re-fuelled and drove straight on through Gangara to Nigeria with no further trouble. They crossed the border into the British Protectorate 5 days and 2 hours after leaving England and 2½ hours later they entered the City of Kano, having travelled 3,519 miles in 125 hours.

They were all in high spirits when Symons told them they had reached Kano in less time than it took to travel by air, in less than one-third of the time taken by a fast mail ship and express train and at considerably less cost per head. The time was 3 days, 7½ hours from Algiers to Kano, 2,327 miles. This was a record run, which has never been equalled since. The average running time across the Sahara worked out to 34.5 miles per hour; the Phantom III performed magnificently, the radiator had never been topped up, the car was giving 10 miles per gallon of petrol and 1,000 miles to the gallon of oil.

Symons ends his article with this paragraph:
'So at last, crossing the Sahara once again, we drove down from the Atlas mountains into Algiers, with every nut and bolt in the chassis tight and every wheel true. The Park Ward body was as silent, as dustproof and watertight as at the start of this great journey. And the radiator *still* required no water since the car left Derby 12,000 miles back!'

Actually, this trip to Nairobi was nothing like as trouble free as Humfrey Symons professed. It is true that 34 EX performed magnificently in spite of the tremendous punishment that was inflicted upon it; but they had enormous trouble with the tyres on the outward journey simply because Symons insisted on reducing the pressure in the tyres to a mere 20 lb, which caused continual flexing due to the tremendous weight of 34 EX and the speeds which the car was capable of attaining, with the inevitable result that the walls of the tyres collapsed.

On Symons' previous trips with the two Morrises, both cars had been considerably lighter than 34 EX and their engines did not produce anything like the amount of power that the Rolls-Royce V12 did, and so on several occasions they had become stuck in the sand and had reduced the tyre pressures to assist in extricating the car. It can only be surmised that he was terrified of being stuck with 34 EX as he could visualise that, owing to the tremendous weight, it would be well nigh impossible to extricate themselves, so he let down the tyres for certain sections of the route, hoping to avoid this catastrophe. But, having reduced the pressures, he did not bother to pump the tyres up again, with the result that they only just managed to limp into Fort Lamy, where they had to wait for new tyres to be flown out by Imperial Airways. On 1 March 1937, Symons sent a cable which reads as follows:

AHCS BM5 KANO 34 28 1058 - NLT GRILLS ROYCAR DERBY ENGLAND. Please send voltage control and four tyres and tubes Imperial Airways leaving London Tuesday addressed to me at Nairobi All Well Stop Have also wired Buckly about tyres - Symons.

And on the 4 March 1937, Sidgreaves was writing as follows:

Re 34 EX - Nairobi Run. Sg/5 E4.3.37.
I am very sorry to hear that the success of this trip has been ruined by failure of tyres. I do not understand the reason.
In Mr Symons' cable received 2 March he said '... decided to prolong stay Kano to attend shock absorbers and tyres stop Urgent please tell Dunlop dispatch four new tyres 7.50 x 18 by Imperial

Airways leaving Croydon Tuesday without fail addressed to me at Nairobi ...'

In Mr Symons' cable received this morning he says 'Every tyre burst unable move unless six covers and tubes sent immediately special aeroplane to Fort Lamy stop Car running splendidly great pity if unable achieve object owing inexcusably tyre failures stop Arrived Bongor to schedule but obliged return two hundred miles to nearest telegraph, repairing tyres every twenty miles stop No regular airmail calling here for 8 days leaving insufficient time for return trip stop Also send offside rear bottom spring pad with damper and stabilizer link ball ends complete communicate grills and radio reply to Symons Faugere Fort Lamy'.

This seems amazing because in these days one expects to be fairly free from tyre trouble.

What I do not know is what was done. The last I can find in the file is Mr Symons' letter of 4 February, in which he says '... all outstanding points except the question of tyre equipment have been settled. Mr Price of Dunlops was expected during the afternoon to advise on this'.

He goes on to say that Rm showed him a very fine tyre which seemed ideal for their requirements and would guarantee them a no-trouble run across the Sahara, thus enabling him to put up a much better performance.

He said that the wings would have to be altered to accommodate the larger tyres and he urged that this should be done, but I do not know if this was done. There is also something, I see, about liquid filling in the tyres which he had used on a previous occasion with great success.

What I really want to get to know is why we have had this tyre disaster which has ruined the trip.

Sgn. Sg.

Naturally Arthur Sidgreaves who had been so in favour of the trip was furious as not only had all his plans gone wrong, but it cost the Company a lot of money too; actually Robotham, when he heard the news, was in his own way quietly amused at it, as right from the outset he had said he thought the whole idea quite crazy.

'Hoppy' Hamilton tells me that he was paid £5 per week by the Company for going on this trip and a bonus of £30 and that he has had malaria annually ever since!

At Fort Lamy they settled down to wait until the new tyres arrived, they amused themselves stalking crocodiles in canoes, armed with the cine-camera, and spent a lot of time in the native market. Finally the Imperial Airways airliner arrived with six new tyres, the freight cost of which was £63. Shortly afterwards 'Hoppy', stripped to the waist in a temperature of 115° in the shade, was changing them single-handed; and in under an hour he had removed the old casings and fitted new ones, Browning and Symons taking turns to pump them up.

Shortly afterwards they departed on the final leg of about 3,000 miles to Nairobi. They had no more trouble with the tyres as, from Fort Lamy on, they did not reduce the tyre pressures at all and never once did 34 EX become stuck, either on the outward or the return journey.

At Nairobi 'Hoppy' Hamilton changed all the oil in 34 EX and gave her a complete service, and for the return run home he had to attend to the independent front wheel suspension, which he did completely unaided, he says it was quite easy as he had the necessary equipment to deal with it.

On the return journey to Algiers they motored slowly, taking a great deal of cine-film, which, at a later date, Humfrey Symons was to show before an audience of the National Geographical Society.

On the way back Browning contracted black water fever and had to be carried into the various forts where they spent the nights. The heat was terrible and sometimes the temperature inside the car was over 104° F. However, in spite of all tribulations they averaged 375 miles per day, which included stops for lunch and cinematography. When they reached Algiers Humfrey Symons, who was by now a little 'fed-up' with the whole trip, flew home with Browning, who was very ill, from Algiers, leaving Hamilton to bring 34 EX home across France from Marseilles single-handed.

On 21 April 1937, the car was back in the Experimental Department at Derby, with the speedometer showing 13,962 miles.

PART III CHAPTER 6

The report made on 34 EX by the Experimental Garage at Derby and the subsequent career of the car after it was sold by Rolls-Royce Ltd

When 34 EX returned to the Experimental Garage at Derby, the car was thoroughly examined, the coachwork removed and on 5 May 1937, 'Hoppy' Hamilton and W A Robotham gave their report on the car which reads as follows:

34 EX PHANTOM III - NAIROBI CAR

We give below report on the running and general behaviour of the above car during its outward and return runs from London to Nairobi in East Africa.

The *total distance covered* was *13,000 miles at an average speed of 32 mph*, under conditions which proved to be considerably harder and more hazardous than anything encountered during a 10,000 miles test in France. It should be pointed out, however, that although the suspension, steering, transmission and chassis in general suffered tremendous strain, the engine unit itself had a comparatively easy time, due to the low speed at which it continually ran, and apart from an occasional burst of power required for manoeuvring bad patches of sand, full throttle was very rarely required.

ENGINE

Starting up from cold was always good and instantaneous, and there were no traces of 'piston knock' at any time.

The engine ran well and was entirely free from major troubles of any sort. So as to avoid any possible failure on the return run, a new set of Lodge RL 14 plugs were fitted at Nairobi, although the old set appeared to be in very good condition.

Due to sand and dust, the torque reaction dampers became slack and lost their poundage at an early stage, consequently, the transverse engine movement became excessive and while ticking over or when accelerating from low speeds the reaction period became distinctly noticeable in the front seats.

The front engine rubber mountings were too soft for African conditions, as on bad one-sided bumps, it was found that the engine would be thrown over to one side, and ultimately caused the ignition control tube which is mounted between the engine and frame, to become bent and so put the hand control out of action.

The quality of petrol obtainable in the Sahara and Central Africa is poor and caused the engine to detonate to a considerable extent, and resulted in loss of power and acceleration at full throttle but did not appreciably affect the car's performance in sand.

The self-adjusting tappets behaved well, but on one occasion a tappet became noisy. This was due to oil sludge having collected on the tappet filter and so restricting the feed. After this had been cleaned, no further trouble occurred.

On five occasions the starter motor failed to mesh with the flywheel ring. It was evident that the armature had moved and had just touched the flywheel, but although it continued to spin, it would not go right home and properly mesh. On these occasions the car was pushed by natives, and the engine started by that means. Apart from these few times it gave no trouble, and during the last four thousand miles worked without fail.

During the run through Uganda the car reached a height of 9,000 ft but owing to having fitted weaker jets before the car started, the carburation was fairly good and did not run excessively rich, and at the same time gave us a consumption varying between 10 - 11 mpg at lower altitudes of 1,500 ft. The consumption on high ground varied between 8 - 9 mpg. The higher ground had more effect on the slow running bleed which required continued adjustment and again required adjusting when the car reached a lower level.

CLUTCH AND GEARBOX

The clutch gave no troubles and was smooth and free from slip. Although at times, more especially when driving off a ferry on to a steep bank it was necessary to make a very slow take-off with the engine running fairly fast, which naturally heated up the clutch linings considerably, but they did not seem to suffer to any extent and the clutch maintained its effectiveness throughout the run.

The gearbox was also free from troubles. The 2nd and 3rd synchromesh mechanism worked well but required careful handling. A very quick change, as was sometimes necessary when the car ran on to an unexpected piece of soft sand, would occasionally result in a crash, but on the average it was light and easy to operate. No oil was added during the whole mileage.

TRANSMISSION PROPELLER SHAFT

For the first 3,000 miles no trouble was experienced, although tremendous strain was frequently thrown on this unit. The fact that on two occasions the engine was actually knocking in 1st gear, gives some idea of the power that the propeller shaft had to transmit. After 3,000 miles it was found that the Enots lubricating nipple on the rear mechanics joint had broken off due to the shaft having hit the body floorboards on full bump. This allowed oil to escape under centrifugal force. Later the Enots nipple on the forward mechanical joint also broke off allowing the same thing to occur. At approximately 5,000 miles, when driving the car off a ferry on to a very steep gradient, the forward sweated sleeve joint sheared together with the taper pins which assist the sweating to secure the joint. With the assistance of many natives and much noise the car was pushed on to level ground, and a temporary repair was affected, by using primus stoves for sweating the joint, and screwdriver shafts and tommy bars for the manufacture of taper pins. Later at Nairobi the joint was re-made and gave no further trouble throughout the run.

On the return run across the Sahara desert, the forward mechanics joint started to show signs of wear and subsequently developed a loud knock on taking up the drive and on overrun. Within a mile from the Works at Derby the yoke pins in the forward mechanics joint broke right through and put the transmission out of action. The car was, however, towed back to the Works.

REAR AXLE

The rear axle remained free from major troubles throughout the run. No oil was added during the mileage. A very slight oil leak developed from the pinion housing joint and also from the differential box side plate joints, but both these were cured by tightening up the nuts and long bolts that pass right through the casing.

SHOCK DAMPERS

Considerable trouble was experienced due to loss of oil from both front and rear dampers. Altogether one gallon of oil was added to the system. It appeared that the chief cause of failure was due to ineffectiveness of the oil retaining glands on the rear dampers. Due to the intense heat the tallow in the packing melted and ran out in the form of thin oil, and left behind the string which of course served no effective purpose. Continual replenishment was necessary to maintain good damping. The oil level in the pressure pump remained constant, and maintained its pressure and effectiveness throughout

the run. It was found that the front spring boxes were also losing considerable quantities of oil, through the breather hole at the top of the boxes. This appears to be due to frothings of the oil in the inside of the boxes, which results in an emulsion of oil and air being forced through the breather holes. The oil level did not, however, get low enough to affect the working of the dampers.

After approximately 2,000 miles, a clattering developed under the car and was traced to the damper ball connections having worked loose in their mountings. This was apparently due to the 5/16 in. pinch bolts having stretched and broken under the violent action imposed by the exceptionally hard conditions. Following this failure, the new bolts were continually examined and nuts tightened so as to prevent further delay. Later new parts were sent out and fitted.

BRAKES

On leaving the works, the brakes on this car were good, and effective, but it was found that they quickly deteriorated and before reaching Marseilles the car was diving to the left and extraordinary pedal pressure was necessary. This was later traced to grease having got onto the O S F brake linings, which both caused the front brakes to pull to the left and accounted for the extra pedal pressure required to obtain adequate braking. The diving could be rectified to some extent by careful adjustment of the hand butterfly nuts, but these became increasingly hard to move due to sand and dust, and no amount of lubrication would satisfactorily keep them easy to operate. It appears that when these adjustments are in constant use under such conditions a gaiter or some form of protection is essential.

When 5,000 to 6,000 miles had been completed the brake ropes had considerably stretched, causing excessive pedal movement, the rear ropes were shortened as much as possible, but only reduced the pedal movement by a small amount. The remaining excess of pedal movement remained until the end of the run.

SUSPENSION

It was evident as soon as the car reached exceptional conditions, that the rear springing was too soft. The car when fully loaded weighed 3 tons 18 cwt. Under this weight the springs were continually hitting the rubber buffers, although the rear springs were considerably stronger than those fitted on a standard chassis. This continued banging did not harm the springs in any way, and the buffer clearances were only reduced by 1 in. during the whole 13,000 miles.

The front coil springs although new, were packed up with washers so as to obtain the maximum amount of buffer clearance before starting. Owing to the somewhat excessive weight the front wheels took on the 'knock-knee' aspect from the beginning of the run, and had 1½ in. to 2 in. bottom buffer clearance.

At Nairobi this had become reduced to 1 in. on the N S and 1¼ in. on the O S. The spring boxes were therefore dismantled and more washers making a total of 3 under each spring were added. The riding at the front of the car was remarkable throughout, over the very worst surfaces the front of the car remained steady and only hit the rubber buffers on a few occasions. On the other hand the ride in the rear of the car was poor, partly due to the fact that the rear damping had to be increased to compensate for the too soft rear springing. Over bad rocks and low lying sand dunes, the rear passenger was frequently thrown right off the seat and more than once was knocked out by hitting his head on the roof frame bars. The rear ride was also impaired due to the high tyre pressures. If the tyres were blown up to the instructed pressures *i.e.* 35 lb/sq in. they invariably increased to 42 - 45 lb/sq in. during the mid-day heat which averaged about 107º F, but on many occasions rose to 112º and 117º F.

The leather gaiters fitted to the rear springs were very soon torn away by stones and gravel and ultimately the aluminium guards round the front shackles of the rear springs were worn through and served no useful purpose as stone protectors.

STEERING

For the first 5,000 miles the steering was good, free from joggles and light to operate. The self centring qualities were good and it was pleasant to handle in every respect. No good tarmac roads were encountered until the car arrived at Nairobi, and not till then did the steering show any signs of low speed wobble. The wobble would start at 30 mph and come out of the period again at 40 mph. The cross steering tube poundages were checked and were found to be adequate. It was also found that there was considerable side play in the O S F pivot pin. This was therefore dismantled and the slack taken out. This in itself appeared to cure the wobble as no further trouble was experienced till Nigeria was again reached, another 5,000 miles. Later, the cross steering tubes were dismantled and the poundage on the ball ends was raised by packing up the springs with .10 in. thick washers, this sufficiently raised the poundage to stop all signs of wobble throughout the remainder of the run.

PETROL TANK AND SYSTEM

In addition to the 36 gallon tank at the rear, an extra tank was fitted holding 20 gallons. This was fitted inside the car. This quantity of petrol proved to be sufficient, as fuel was obtainable at approximately every 400 miles.

The petrol pipe line connecting the interior 20 gallon tank to the main system was broken by fatigue after 8,000 miles. The movement of the body in relation to the frame was found to be considerable over the tracks encountered, and on account of this movement the pipe line broke. A rubber connection was inserted and no further trouble ensued.

The petrol pump mounted on the frame side under the driver's seat continued to supply petrol without fail throughout the run, although the outside heat was at times nearly 50º C and naturally considerably more along the frame side due to the blast of hot air from under the bonnet.

At 10,000 miles one diaphragm showed a slight leak, and this was changed so as to avoid any trouble during the return Sahara crossing.

Considerable trouble and delay was experienced due to the fuel pipe from the main tank having been chafed through by a body bolt resulting in an air leak. This was satisfactorily repaired by connecting up with a piece of rubber tube.

COOLING SYSTEM

No water was added to the cooling system from the time the car left and returned to Derby after a journey of 13,000 miles in the most arduous condition. This in itself constitutes a record for the Sahara crossing.

SILENCING SYSTEM

No trouble was encountered with the system until 12,000 miles had been completed. On the return run across the Sahara, the pipe broke where it enters the main silencer, and had to be temporarily supported by wire until the necessary facilities for welding could be obtained. It appears that this failure was due to the lack of support in the correct place. As the design now stands too much supporting strain is thrown on to the piping itself. To avoid this trouble the silencers should be independently supported, quite apart from connecting tubes between them.

On bad dips and when coming off ferries on to steep banks the tail pipe would frequently touch down, and on more than one occasion the rear bumper bar itself scraped on the ground.

ELECTRICAL SYSTEM

After 1,500 miles running, the voltage control failed, and was replaced by a new one which lasted out for the remaining mileage. The dynamo failed to charge on two occasions due to dirt on the commutator. Both head lamp bulbs failed within half an hour of each other, due to vibration and general fatigue. By the time the Sahara had been crossed, the brake light and rear lights had been put out of action. The wires had been broken away from the junction box under the tail valance by flying stones and debris.

The starter motor jammed on four occasions and failed to mesh with the flywheel. This, however, righted itself and gave no trouble for the last part of the run.

The Lucas wind-tone horns worked effectively, but failed to blow on 'soft' due to sand and dust between the internal contacts. The current on 'loud' appeared to be sufficient to overcome the effect of the sand. The nature of the roads for the first part of the crossing was so rough, that both horns fell off. The brackets having broken through, where the two small screws secure the wiring clips to the brackets.

BIJUR PIPING

Considerable trouble was experienced due to Bijur piping breaking, either due to flying stones or fatigue and general movement. The chief troubles were pipes lubricating the rear springs and front suspension knuckle joints.

The main feed pipe to the axle and rear springs broke on three occasions and was repaired by sweating on an outer sleeve, but it was evident that the pipe had become hard due to continual flexing with the spring, although the existing coil inside the forward shackles was working correctly. A piece of high pressure air piping was substituted and gave no further trouble. The main feed pipe to the O S F pivot broke despite the coil, which is provided to prevent this happening.

HYDRAULIC JACKS

These worked very effectively until the pipe to the rear jack was swept away by a rock. A temporary repair was effected which enabled the jacks to be used with care.

It was also found that due to flying stones the edge of the barrels had become dented, and prevented the inner sleeves from returning when the release taps were opened. Consequently the sliding sleeve had to be forced back into place by hand.

BODY MOUNTINGS

For the first 8,000 miles the body mountings remained firm, but owing to the exceptional bumps and hollows that had to be negotiated, which exerted extraordinary strain on the body bolts, the securing bolts at the rear broke off throwing all the strain on the next two further up the chassis. The fact that these broke allowed the body to move about, and the aluminium round the rear bumper bar supports was considerably damaged.

The body itself remained in good condition, apart from the veneered woodwork, which cracked due to heat. The O S F door guiders broke off allowing the door to rattle. The outside coachwork was undamaged throughout the run and the paint remained in good condition.

The above report covers all serious troubles during the run. Many minor attentions were necessary but did not actually delay the run or cause any repair work. The petrol tank was frequently touching the ground and sustained many bad dents and knocks from rocks etc. but did not leak.

On future runs of this nature a strong guard of 1/10 in. steel should be made to cover the whole under surface of the tank.

It is also essential that the shock dampers be adequately protected as on one occasion during the run a stone hit the O S R damper and loosened the end plug, resulting in a small loss of oil. Also small Bijur pipes and fuel pipes should be adequately protected from flying stones.

It is preferable to have two fog lamps on the Sahara crossing, so as to cast a beam each side leaving the head lamp beams to deal with the middle of the track.

For the driver's own personal comfort it is absolutely necessary to have some sort of perforated seat cover to allow air to circulate behind the back. The Transport Tropiceau bus drivers have basket seats which seem to fulfil the purpose.

Rm/HFH

It is sad to think that having done such an epic journey 34 EX had to be towed the last mile to the Derby Works.

Exactly what happened to the car after this report was written is not known except to say that later the chassis was given an overhaul and re-numbered 3-AEX-34, and a new Hooper saloon body with division was fitted, finished in all black and upholstered in fawn leather. It was sold on 23 May 1938 to L A Nelson, Esq, of 36, Hanover Gate Mansions, Regents Park, London, NW1. It was delivered to him on 28 May 1938 by Lillie Hall, Mr Nelson having paid a deposit of £1,476.15.6d. on it, and Rolls-Royce Ltd, made Mr Nelson an allowance of £400 on chassis No. GSR 75, which was a 1930 model 20/25.

He was given a guarantee for 34 EX, now known as 3-AEX-34, dated from 3 September 1935, which is the actual date that 34 EX was first licenced as RC 3169. There is an interesting point here in that this particular chassis has retained its original registration number, whereas nearly always when a chassis was handed over to Sales and rebuilt with new coachwork, it did not retain its original registration number, but was issued with a new one, which in most cases was a London registration.

From 1938 until 16 April 1946, the history of this chassis is blank, but on this date it was registered in the name of Harold Radford & Co Ltd, Melton Court, London, SW1. This is a firm engaged in the buying and selling of motor cars, who later made a name for themselves with their Harold Radford conversions. They sold the car the following day on 17 April 1946, to Derek Curtis Bennett, KC, 1, Garden Court, Temple, London, EC4, who was followed by a further change of owners, as given below:

Selbourne (Mayfair) Ltd, 82, Park Street, London, W1 - London, November 1949.

Oslo Motors Ltd, Oslo Court, London, NW8 - London, 21 January 1950.

G G Ireland, Windsor House, Lyndhurst Road, London, NW3 - London 1950.

Oslo Motors Ltd, Oslo Court, London, NW8 - London 5 June 1951.

Richard Curtis Crampton, Hq Sq 10th TRW 9, R A F. Alconbury, Huntingdon, Hunts. - Huntingdon, 15 May 1961.

John Edward Little, Holly Lodge, Danesbury Park Road, Welwyn, Herts. - Change not acknowledged - no date stamp shown.

In April, 1971, I called in with 74 GN at Adams & Oliver's depot at Great Gidding. I was staying with Kenneth Hunnisett (74 GN's old chauffeur) at Haselbech, and we were having a day out together, when I decided to visit Great Gidding. Adams & Oliver have an excellent practice of painting the chassis number in white paint on each car, so you can imagine my surprise and delight when I walked in and saw a black Phantom III facing me with the number 3-AEX-34 painted on it. The engine was out of the frame and it appeared to me that the car, which was in a very sorry state, was awaiting its turn to be broken up. I immediately contacted Mr Adams by telephone at his other branch at Warboys in Huntingdonshire and I found him most helpful. A few days later I went to see him at Warboys and he put me in touch with the present owner of the car, Mr John Little, who had purchased 3-AEX-34 some twelve months previously and who is now in the process of restoring her.

I am most grateful to Mr Little for providing me with a list of the owners of 3-AEX-34 from 1946.

On Sunday 22 July 1973, I had a most interesting telephone conversation with Mr Little at his home in Welwyn, Herts. He assured me that he does fully intend to completely restore 3-AEX-34, but he has been so busy working on other Phantom III chassis that so far he has not had time to really deal with 3-AEX-34; but he has joined the Rolls-Royce Phantom III Technical Society of America and has gained the most valuable experience, which he will use in restoring 3-AEX-34, so we may hope to see this car on the roads once more.

PART III CHAPTER 7

The Experimental chassis Nos. 35 EX, 36 EX, 37 EX, 38 EX and 39 EX, (the last of these is the one and only Continental Phantom III ever to be built), the coachwork was transferred onto chassis No. 3-DL-152, the story of this car, used by the British Foreign Office, finally abandoned in Rangoon and fully restored by Henry Byroade

As with all the Experimental 40/50 chassis, I am indebted to Ivan Evernden for the details of the next Phantom III, 35 EX, Continental touring limousine: Park Ward, pale green. Unladen weight 51 cwt. Body weight 13 cwt 1 lb. Wood and aluminium construction. Registration number RC 3170.

I have no details of the testing of this chassis, all I know is that on 26 June 1939, with a speedometer reading of 93,833, the car was handed over by the Experimental Department to Repairs and in turn to Sales.

When and to whom this chassis was sold I have been unable to discover; the number 35 EX was changed to 3-DEX-204 before it was sold and if it had not been for my visit to Mr Adams at Warboys in reference to 3-AEX-34 (34 EX), I doubt whether I would have been able to have discovered anything about this chassis at all. Quite by chance when talking about Experimental Phantom III chassis, Mr Adams told me that he had had another Phantom III with a curious chassis number through his hands, he looked it up for me and by great good luck was able to find a photograph of the car, which he kindly let me have, thus providing me with photographs of the car when it was new and again at a very much later date.

He also gave me the address of a Mr Carter, of the Buckden Marina, in Huntingdonshire, who had at one time owned 35 EX, to whom I wrote and who replied as follows:

27 May 1971.

Dear Mr Oldham,

Thank you for your letter, I am afraid that I did dispose of the Phantom III two years after I purchased it, and have been full of remorse and sadness ever since. I did find this car in a stable, where it had lain unused for many years, and found it surrounded by tractors, pigs, chickens and all sorts of other objects. The car went extremely well and was sold to Mr Simmons, of Mayfair, who used to run a second-hand car business and I heard afterwards that he did remove the over-drive gearbox and replace it with an ordinary one, before selling it and I believe the car went to North Africa.

It must be at least 10 years since I owned the car, and the photographs Mr Adams gave you cannot be very recent. I have, however, nothing in that line which would be up to reproduction standard.

Perhaps someone will throw some more light on 3-DEX-204 when they read these lines and bring the story up to date.

The next Phantom III, 36 EX, was an enclosed limousine by Hooper, fawn and black. Unladen weight 52 cwt 3 qrs 14 lb. Wood and aluminium construction. Registration number RC 3695.

The only details I have of this chassis are as follows:-

Chassis No. 36 EX became 3-AEX-36. Tyres as fitted. Body enclosed limousine. Maker - Hooper & Co Ltd. Colour - black. Sale Price £1,500.
Date of Sale - 20 July 1938. Sold to E C Eliot-Cohen, Esq, Hollington House, Newbury, Berkshire. Deposit paid £150 on 21 July 1938. Balance of Price paid £1,350 on 25 July 1938. Car delivered 25 July 1938 to customer at Paddington Station by Hives.
Invoice No. 8503. Date 21 July 1938 - £1,516.14.9d. Instruction Book issued 25 July 1938, to customer. No. XI. Guarantee to apply from 25 March 1936.
Used car sold as it stands, the whole in second-hand condition, for the sum of £1,500.
One oblong plate - No. RC 3695.
One pair of wing lamps.
Two wiper blades.
Chromium-plated end piece for exhaust.

Refit bonnet 'N'.
Fog lamp and bracket. Lucas to Repair and replate lamp and replace glass.
Cost of licence from 1 August - 31 December 1938 - £16.14.9d.
Late Experimental Department.

This chassis is now in the collection of Tom Mason in Kent, at one time it was used as a private hire car and owned by the firm in London in which Anthony Bird, the well-known motoring historian, was a partner.
From Ivan Evernden:

37 EX - Sedanca de Ville. Park Ward. Pale Grey. Unladen weight 52 cwt 2 qrs 14 lb. Body weight 14 cwt 1 qr 10 lb. Wood and aluminium construction. Registration number RC 4090.

From Body Card at Conduit Street. No. 1 Card:

Chassis No. 37 EX became 3-AEX-37. Engine No. 9. H P 40/50.
Body - Sedanca. Maker - Park Ward. Colour - Grey, blue moulding.
Upholstery - blue leather. Car Price - £1,425 less 20%.
Sold to J S Inskip Inc, 32 East 75th Street, New York, U S A on consignment to Mrs Clare S Guilner, Valentine's Lane, Greenvale, Long Island, U S A.
Balance of deposit $15,817.04 on 19 August 1946.
Shipping Particulars: to Claridge, Hold & Co Ltd. Shipped per *S S Kainata*, from Liverpool, 22 February 1942.
Instruction Book issued to 'N' 30 January 1941.
Complete car sold as it stands, the whole in used condition for the sum of £1,425 less 20% discount.
Made in England Plate. Petrol gauge in U S gallons.
Freight charges - Liverpool - New York. C Holt & Co £88.
Carriage London - Liverpool - £10.15.0d.
Marine Insurance to value of £1,300 @ 10.6d.% - £6.16.6d.
War risks Insurance to value of £1,300 @ 50.0d.% - £32.10.0d.
Policy with stamp - 3.0d.
Removing charged plates from battery.
And fitting new dry plates.

Non-standard fittings.
Silencer system.
Roll bar and damper limbs.
Special mechanism for clutch withdrawal.
Starting handle.
U S duty and Landing charges $669.10 on consignment 5 May 1941.
N. Supplied 2 box spanners.
Set of spanners.
Valve spring.

Body Card No. 2.
Chassis No. 37 EX became 3-AEX-37.

Body Sedanca. Maker: Park Ward.
Four tyres to replace worn ones.
Front oblong plate - RC 4090. Registration No. RC 4090.
Tools and spares from 'W'.
One offside wing lamp.
Replate bumpers and headlamps.
Repair electric clock.
Barkers to buff up radiator.
Late Experimental Department. Repairs completed January 1938, passed by J L E 1st Test.

This car is now owned by Mark T McKee, Jnr, 64 Riverside Drive, P O Box 707, Mount Clements, Michigan, U S A and is in the Rolls-Royce Owners' Club of America.
From Ivan Evernden:

38 EX. Enclosed limousine, long wheel base. Park Ward. Maroon and black. Unladen weight 53 cwt 2 qrs 2 lb. Body weight 14 cwt 2 qrs 16 lb. All Steel body framework to Park Ward system and aluminium panels.

From Body Card at Conduit Street:

Chassis No. 38 EX became 3-AEX-38. Body All Steel. Enclosed limousine. Drawing No. LEC 4988.
Makers: Park Ward & Co. Order No. R 4529. Date: 5 January 1936.
Colour: dark maroon and black.
Upholstery: Maroon vaumol leather. Headlining - fawn cloth.
Coachbuilders instructed P W & Co letter 21 October 1936.
Tyres 7 in. section. 32.8 in. outside diameter.
Steering column: 'E'. Wheelbase: Long.
Offside wheel carrier: Yes. Type of bonnet: 15º slope back, standard shutters.
Luggage grid. R-R Mascot.
2 x P.100 R E D Headlamps.
2 wing lamps. One licence holder. Klaxon wiper.
One pair of 20 gauge steel front wings (Potts Bros).
Twinflow car heater (Delco Remy & Hyats).
Registration No. DGT 367.

Body Card No. 2. 3-AEX-38. Late 38 EX.
Engine No. 15. Body enclosed limousine. Park Ward. Black, fine lined white, maroon leather.
Index No. DGT 367.
Car sold to J S Inskip Inc, 32 East 57th Street, New York for £1,425, less 20% discount.
Car shipped to New York from London 'Pacific Grove' about 9 April 1940.
Late School Instruction Car. Duty and Landing charges £122.9.5d.

Body Card No. 3. 3-AEX-38. Engine No. 15.
Date of Sale: 12 November 1948 for £1,350, complete car as it stands in used condition. To George Newman & Co Ltd, 369 Euston Road, London, NW1.
Enclosed limousine by Park Ward Ltd.
Black, fine lined white - maroon leather.

From the above it can be seen that this chassis came back from America in 1948 and was re-sold by Rolls-Royce Ltd and here the trail ends.

The next chassis, 39 EX, is a particularly interesting one as, apart from being the very last Experimental Phantom III chassis to be made, it is also the one and only Phantom III Continental; unlike Phantom II Continentals the chassis length of 11 ft 10 in. was the standard Phantom III chassis and below are the details as given to me by Ivan Evernden.

39 EX. Continental touring limousine. Barker. Two shades of grey. Unladen weight 47 cwt. No further details except that the body was said to be of special all metal construction.

As the chassis of 39 EX was the prototype Continental it had a specially lightened frame, the rear axle ratio was 7% higher than that fitted to the standard model, 8 x 33 instead of 8 x 34. The compression ratio in the engine was raised to 6.5 to 1. The engine would run up to 4,600 rev/min and was fitted with tinned aluminium bearings and the weight reduction was 10%. Early in 1938 it was decided that a 15,000 mile test at Chateauroux for 39 EX was so costly that, unless the model was to be put in production they would not send this chassis to France. By 12 May 1938, when this chassis had only run 4,627 miles and had never been abroad at all, it was decided that no further work was to be continued on it. Its weight is given as 48 cwt, against 54 cwt for the standard model, the engine gave 20% more brake horsepower and the acceleration was 15% better. At first it was decided that the car should be sold to Mr Fairey of Fairey Aviation with no guarantee, as it stood, but by 20 December 1938, it had finally been decided what should be done with it, and it was handed over to the repair depot, where the chassis was stripped and one month later in January 1939 the body had been removed and was at Lillie Hall to be sold separately. Index number RC 4922.

*Short for All-Weather Motor Bodies

No doubt the enormous cost of Experimental and Research work on the Phantom III, coupled with the grave European situation in 1938 and 1939 stemming from Nazi Germany, were primarily responsible for the Company reviewing the whole situation. It was decided to bring the production of the Phantom III to an end and to revert to Royce's original idea of 1905, that of building one engine, using the same components, *i.e.* pistons, connecting rods, valves, cylinders, *etc.*, and simply increasing, or decreasing, the number of cylinders as was needed, instead of building three entirely separate very costly motor cars, such as Phantom III, Wraith and Bentley 4¼ litre. The man behind this move was W A Robotham, who envisaged a Straight-8 cylinder engine as the replacement for the Phantom III. The prototype for this, which ran with great satisfaction, was known as 'Big Bertha', a full 7 passenger enclosed drive limousine. The same engine with 6 cylinders was also tried with great success in a prototype Bentley chassis; but in the meantime, whilst these experiments were going on at Derby, the coachwork from 39 EX was mounted on to a new production Phantom III chassis, number 3-DL-152.

Stock - U S A Propaganda
Chassis No. 3-DL-152. Body: For completion with the Barker Touring Limousine.
H P: 40/50 Eng. No. E18.A. Body 39 EX.
Battery: P & R. Drawing No. to be mounted by All Weather Bodies.
Off Test: 24.3.39.
D.I. Issued: 15.3.39.
Axle Ratio: 8 x 34. Despatched: 23.3.39.
Tyres Standard Dunlop.

Trimming and Painting
Two shades grey.
Upholstery: Blue leather.
Chassis drawing advice sent: Hn 15.3.39.
Guarantee slip issued: 3.4.39.
Fittings: Standard. Column: 'E'.
Alteration to scuttle dash (A W M B)*
Offside wheel carrier: Yes
Type of bonnet: standard
R-R Mascot: Upright (Bch 13.6.39)
Brackets for rear bumper
Springs for 5-seater body, ex 39 EX, average 2/3 passengers, maximum luggage
2 cwt and usual - 1 cwt
Registration No.: FLX 886
Number plates to front and inserts to rear
Licence Holder: Yes

Windscreen wiper: Klaxon
To be fitted by A W M B
Case spare bulbs and dash lamps
Metal cover for spare wheel
Fog lamp: Lucas
Wiring by: Sangear
Driving Mirror: to spare wheel cover
Inside electric lights and switches
Tool accommodation of approved type
Fit lamps with double filament bulbs ex Amsterdam Show
Sangear to alter wiring to suit double filament bulbs
Ventilators: to top of scuttle
G B and A T 201 Lucas lamp. A W M B to fit and Sangear to complete wiring
Case spare bulbs to container
R-R Mascot
Bumpers - rear: full length
To be fitted by J R Eng. Co
R-R badge to rear bumper
Five black wheel discs with C P ribs. A W M B to fit
4 suitcases from T H Fuller.
Order large type motor-arms and blades for Klaxon wiper
Work as estimate of 7.2.39 from A W M B
Work as estimate of 30.3.39 from A W M B
One set upholstery covers for front and rear seat cushions and squabs only

As can be seen from the details on the preceding body card, 3-DL-152 was completed originally as a car for stock, to be offered for sale in the ordinary way. Another interesting point is that the body was mounted by All Weather Motor Bodies Ltd, Canterbury Works, Canterbury Road, Kilburn, London, which was one of the smaller and lesser known coachbuilders. They were, however, already familiar with the Phantom III chassis as they had built coachwork on chassis numbers 3-AZ-64 and 3-AZ-76. The latter car was built for the Duke of Sutherland and is now very well known in the 20 Ghost Club, having been owned by Capt R B Honnywill for many years and brought to numerous meetings.

It must have been shortly after 3-DL-152 was completed, carrying the coachwork formerly on 39 EX that it was decided to let Humfrey Symons take the car out to America for exhibition at the New York World Fair, which opened in May 1939. The exhibition's theme was the 'World of Tomorrow', its emphasis was on industry, commerce and transportation, and some 62 foreign nations had buildings and exhibits at this event. When the New York World Fair, closed the total number of people who had visited it was 25,817,265.

Since his epic trip across the Sahara with 34 EX in 1937, Humfrey Symons had taken part in a number of rallies in England and tested and written reports on many different makes of car. Perhaps his two most interesting exploits were in April 1938 when he took delivery of a brand new Austin 18 Norfolk saloon from Lord Austin, for a trip across the Libyan and Sahara Deserts to Djanet, a place which no British motorist had ever visited before, and later on in the year when he set off on another 'publicity stunt' which was to drive one of the latest Wolseley 18/85 saloons from London to Capetown, accompanied by his friend, H B Browning. Unfortunately, whilst crossing a native bridge near Naingaia in the Belgium Congo, the structure collapsed and the Wolseley crashed, falling on its side into the river below; it was very severely damaged and Symons and Browning, who were both in the car, were very lucky to escape with only minor cuts and a very bad shaking up, especially as they had to walk 4 miles to a 'Mission Station' to have their injuries treated. The car was retrieved from the river bed and repairs were effected to enable them to continue in the Wolseley to Capetown. In spite of this set back he made the fastest journey between London and Capetown that had been accomplished up to that time.

He returned from the World Fair in New York to take part in the Scottish Rally at Glasgow on 28 May until 2 June 1939 - so he must have left 3-DL-152 on exhibition there as the Fair did not close until the end of May. How and when the car was brought back to Great Britain is not known but it must have been put in store soon after the outbreak of War, as the headlamps were removed and transferred on to chassis No. 3-CM-203. This was a Park Ward touring limousine which had been built for stock, and bore the London registration number FLD 96, and engine number E 68 Y; this car had been sold on 27 May 1940 to J S Inskip Inc of New York, for the use of A L Humes Esq, 960 5th Avenue, New York City, and was shipped from London to New York aboard Messrs Furness Withy's Motor Vessel *Pacific Grove*. Incidentally, 3-CM-203 is now owned by William

K Barton, 861 6th Avenue South, St Petersburg, Florida, U S A who is a member of the Rolls-Royce Owners' Club of America.

In 1941 3-DL-152 was taken out of store and sold to the Under Secretary of State. The Foreign Office, London, SW1, for the use of Sir Noel Charles, CMG. MC, British Ambassador in Rio de Janeiro, Brazil. It went in to Park Ward for a few minor jobs to be done, including re-cellulosing the running boards and fitting P 100 headlamps to replace those which had been removed earlier.

I discovered the history of 3-DL-152 after 1941 in the following way: I had already discovered that 39 EX was the only Continental Phantom III ever built, and that the body from 39 EX had been mounted on to 3-DL-152. During a conversation with Ron Haynes I casually mentioned this fact to him; he was immediately most interested and said, '3-DL-152, why that is the Henry Byroade car'. He then proceeded to tell me the fascinating story of how this car was discovered in the East of Asia, completely restored and shipped back to America in a teak crate!

I wrote to Henry Byroade in America, giving him what details I had of his car, and in reply I received a most interesting letter which is reproduced below:-

Embassy of the United States of America,
Manila, Philippines
8th September 1970

To: W J Oldham Esq,
Le Canadel,
Rue Jutize,
Grouville, Jersey. C I

Dear Mr Oldham,

As you probably would guess, I was quite fascinated with your letter of August 23rd and very glad to receive it. It was forwarded to me here in Manila where I have been the American Ambassador for about a year as of now. Any further correspondence should therefore be addressed to me at the American Embassy, Manila, Republic of the Philippines.

You will find enclosed two notes from Ronald Belcher, a friend of mine who was formerly in the British Foreign Service. Through his help, and with the kind assistance of Mr Haynes in London, and from my own knowledge, it would seem that the history of this car (3-DL-152) would be as follows:-

January 1939 - First registered in London with Body of Barker, which had been taken from experimental chassis No. 39 EX.

1939 - Promotional tour of the U S ending at the World's Fair (San Francisco, I think).
1941 - Sold to Foreign Office and sent to the British Embassy in Rio de Janeiro, Brazil. The British Ambassador at that time was Sir Noel Charles and you will find enclosed a photograph, of a photograph, which contains his signature, which shows the car as it appeared at that time.
1949 - Shipped to Cairo, apparently for use of the Ambassador or the Treasury representative.
1952 - Returned to London for overhaul.
1953 - Sent to Rangoon for use by British Ambassador.
1956 - Sold to U Law Yone, Burmese citizen, editor of a newspaper called 'The Nation'.
1964 (Sept.) - Obtained by Henry A Byroade, U S Ambassador to Burma. Complete renovation started.
1967 (March) - Renovation completed (Is it ever?).
1968 (July) - Shipped to Washington, D C and used by the owner there for about one year.
1969 (July) - Driven by owner to place in storage at residence of Mr Ted Wilkinson 2217 Middleton Road, Hudson, Ohio.

As you can see from the above, this particular Old Lady is quite well-travelled. A Burmese lawyer friend of mine thought he could prove that this car was used by Sir Winston Churchill to tour the battle area in North Africa during the War. I thought for a time that this might be proven, but have since come to the conclusion that this couldn't possibly be true. I also heard, from a source I can't recall anymore, that a tree fell on this car while it was in Cairo. This one I believe, as I had lots of trouble with the left forward part of the body.

I discovered this car in an alley-way in Rangoon, for all practical purposes, abandoned. The owner was a political prisoner by that time, and the car had sat there for several years, through the Monsoons, with no attention at all! Being a complete perfectionist about things mechanical, I could hardly sleep until I could obtain and start restoring this beautiful piece of machinery. The story is a long one, far too long for this letter, but I finally got it in my physical possession (even though I couldn't get the title for about two years) and started rehabilitation.

The car had been abandoned for so long that I did not even try to start the motor. Rather I took the body off, the motor out, and then stripped the running gear down to the frame itself. I then scraped and painted the frame and started rebuilding. It was a long and arduous task which took all of my free time over a period of approximately 2½ years. If the part was not perfect it did not go back on the car. I ended up getting, I believe, about 106 major items through Mr Haynes.

We machined rather countless other items in Rangoon (if the part was not important for perfect operation). The Chinese machinists were very good in Rangoon, but they had virtually no sources of supply. The big problem was therefore getting the right steel, the right bronze, etc. In fact about the only thing I could get in Burma was teak wood and almost all of the original wood, even inside the doors, is now Burmese teak. Otherwise I had to shop all over the Far East. I got the upholstery in Singapore, the paints from ICI in Kuala Lumpur, batteries, glass and heavy parts in Bangkok, and dozens of little items every time I went on a trip outside Burma.

I had an amusing time with Rolls-Royce in the beginning of this project as they kept writing to me, in very reserved British language, urging that in effect I should not attempt the project. They told me that this was the most complicated car they ever built, had never even made up a Service Manual for it, etc. etc. Looking back on it all now I don't blame them one bit for this attitude, as I can imagine how they would feel if some American Ambassador somewhere decided to do this work himself! I finally convinced Haynes that I was serious when I sent him a polaroid picture of the frame. After that he was of tremendous assistance and I never could have completed the project without his help. It was with great pleasure later on that I was able to visit him at Willesden.

When I finally got the chassis running again I could hardly believe the performance of the car. I drove it some 500 miles prior to re-installing the body in order to test all parts of the chassis while it was still readily accessible. You will note that one of the pictures enclosed shows the car in this testing condition. The silver coloured weights mounted on the frame are two links from a chain that the British put across the Rangoon River during the War, which together almost exactly matched the body weight.

While all this was going on, the body was stored under a bridge on our Residence grounds, and I would work on it from time to time while waiting for parts for the chassis. Almost all of the wood had to be replaced as I have noted before. I had in fact quite a job on my hands in fixing up the body and at one point I had merely an aluminium shell. It is not a particularly pretty body, and is smaller inside than most. It is quite a light body, and I now understand why from your letter. We were able to take the body off and put it back on by the use of manpower alone.

The one major mistake that I think I made in rebuilding this car was in the paint job itself. I obtained the proper undercoat from ICI, but did not know that aluminium should be pretreated with an etching chemical. As a result the paint is beginning to peel off and when I get home again it will have to be completely redone.

Unfortunately, I have never taken any pictures of the interior, but it is now quite beautiful, and in design, at least, it is as it was originally. The upholstery is now a light ivory of a very good grade plastic. Perhaps this was a mistake, but Rolls-Royce people in Singapore advised me against the use of leather, particularly in moist climates. The arm rests are of lizard skin, the backs of the tea trays are python, and the trimming under the seats is real leopard skin. The floor is a very heavy good grade tan carpet. This may sound a bit gaudy to you but all these colours blend together very well indeed.

Rolls-Royce would indeed frown, but I have attempted to make it a thoroughly useable automobile under today's conditions. It is equipped, for instance, with AM-FM radio, with a stereo tape recorder, and with a refrigeration unit. The ignition system is now equipped with electronic magnetos which are just terrific.

Also the PIII is vastly overpowered for today's roads and driving conditions. I therefore changed the gear ratio in the rear end to 9 x 35 (Silver Wraith gears) instead of the original 8 x 34 gears. This actually is not quite enough of a change, and I may sometime in the future attempt to change it a bit more. It makes a great difference for long trips on good roads.

I may of course be prejudiced, but I think the Experimental PIII in which everything from the clock on up is in excellent condition. I have never been able to place it in competition where performance seemed to be much of a factor. In fact in the meets that I have been to, the judges never looked under the hood or started the motor! I am sure this car will go at least 100 mph and I honestly believe more. I had it once up to 90 mph and later on up to 93 mph on the Pennsylvania Turnpike when I drove it to the Cleveland area for storage. I could feel that if I had had more space that it would have gone quite a few miles faster. What held me back, I guess, was my own lack of nerve, as with some traffic on the road (and trying to watch out for the police) I slacked off both times before it had reached full performance.

I do not believe I could have obtained such a good end product had I attempted this job in America. In the Far East it is easy to have little things made to perfection, and it is very hard in America to get anyone to do this type of thing at all. If I had hired the work done in America it would, needless to say, have cost a fortune. As it was I did almost all of the work myself - from taking out the cylinder sleeves, steam cleaning the bloc, and all the rest. My Indian driver was my mechanic's helper, a Chinese carpenter from our Embassy helped me at weekends, and an Indian Muslim (who spoke no English) helped me with the upholstery.

The car today is on blocks until I leave this part and can come home to live. You will note one of the pictures shows 3-DL-152 in the process of being crated for shipment to America. I designed and made this frame myself and it is all of the best teak. As I foresaw the need for some teak later on in the States, I used extremely heavy timbers - in fact the wood in the crate weighs two tons. I would guess this is the only PIII that ever moved around the world in a teak crate!

(Top) 32EX on test. From left to right: Hoppy Hamilton, Ivan Waller, George Hancock and Joc Beanan on Mount Ventoux. See Part III, Chapter 1 (photo H. F. Hamilton)

(Middle) Originally 'Spectre' chassis number 32EX with a Continental Touring Saloon body by Park Ward. This is a very important car as it is the one on which production Phantom IIIs were based. When sold the chassis number was changed to 3-DEX-202. The car is now in Australia. See Part III, Chapter 3

(Bottom) 33EX, later when chassis number 3-AEX-33. See Part III, Chapter 4 (photo Jack Mackinlay)

(Top) 34EX with Humfrey Symons and Hoppy Hamilton before leaving for Niarobi *(photo H. F. Hamilton)*

(Middle) This photograph shows 34EX, a Park Ward Limousine, after modifications had been made for its run to Niarobi before it set out. The four gallon water tank can be clearly seen beneath the spare wheel mounting and the top half of the plywood partition in the rear of the car dividing the mobile workshop from the sleeping compartment provided in the rear. Compare this with the next photograph *(photo M. H. Evans)*

(Bottom left) An example of the terrain crossed by 34EX. This is the corrugated track on the Tademait plateau *(photo H. F. Hamilton)*

(Bottom right) The interior of 34EX after preparation for the Niarobi trip *(photo H.F. Hamilton)*

(*Top Left*) The 'Niarobi Car' in the market place of the walled 'Secret City' of Ghardoia. Note the roof of 34EX which has been painted white to deflect the sun (*photo H. F. Hamilton*)
(*Top right*) 34EX's home coming from Algiers (*photo H.F. Hamilton*)
(*Bottom left*) Hoppy Hamilton and Humfrey Symons at Fort Lamap waiting for new tyres (*photo H.F. Hamilton*)
(*Bottom right*) 34EX at Algiers with Hoppy Hamilton and the photographer Browning, this photograph was taken just prior to shipping the car home and shows some of the punishment that it took during its run to Niarobi. See Part III, Chapter 5 (*photo H. F. Hamilton*)

(Top) 35EX as delivered (photo H.J. Mulliner/Park Ward)

(Middle) The result of the accident to 35EX in Paris (photo Ian Dimmer)

(Bottom) 35EX Continental Touring Limousine by Park Ward. 35EX or 3-DEX-204 showing later changes made in the wings to try to 'improve' the car, the date of this photograph is not known (photo J.B.M. Adams)

(Top) 37EX as delivered *(photo H. J. Mulliner/Park Ward)*

(Middle) 39EX. The one and only Phantom III Continental fitted with Baker Touring Limousine coachwork had 'E' type steering. In 1938 its chassis was dismantled and the body transferred to chassis number 3-DL-152 *(photo S. J. Skinner)*

(Bottom) 3-DL-152. See over

(Top left and right, middle left and right and bottom) 3-DL-152 being used by the Foreign Office. Carrying coachwork from 39EX this was the only Continental Phantom III ever made. The sequence of photographs show the original car, and then it being stripped and restored to an all time high. The car is then being crated to return to England from Singapore (photos Henry Byroade)

(*Top*) A dummy Hooper Limousine built for the Olympia Motor Show in 1935. The body was later mounted on chassis number 3-BT-91

(*Upper middle*) Another Hooper Limousine dummy but this time for the Hooper & Co stand at the 1935 Olympia Motor Show. The body number is 8476

(*Lower middle*) The second Phantom III to be built. 3-AZ-22 is a Hooper Enclosed Limousine 'Trials' car of 1936. The engine number is Z14A, 'E' type steering, index number CYP921, body number 8534. The car was not sold until 1938

(*Bottom*) 3-AZ-38 was a Rolls-Royce 'Trials' car later sold to S. E. Sears. It carries a Barker Touring Limousine body with 'E' type steering (*photo S.J. Skinner*)

(Top) 3-AZ-43 carries a Barker Enclosed Limousine body with special 'F' type steering. The car was specially built for HRH The Duke of Kent

(Upper middle) A Barker Allweather body on chassis number 3-AZ-74 was built for Miss E.W. Thompson of Glasgow with 'E' type steering. She requested no mascot and a rear mounted spare wheel

(Lower middle) 3-AZ-86 carries a Coupe Cabriolet body by Arthur Mulliner of Northampton, built to order of The Hon A. C. Nivison, who requested a special steering position, no mascot and black P100 headlamps with special sidelights of the old pattern

(Bottom) 3-AZ-92, a Barker Sedanca de Ville with 'E' type steering. It was supplied to Earl Beatty *(photo S.J. Skinner)*

I have asked my staff to photograph some of my photographs for you, so they will not be as good as the originals, and unfortunately some of those were polaroids that have faded. I am attaching an extra page to this letter describing these photos.

Best wishes for your book. I often wish I could get away from some of the things I am constantly involved in, and pursue a subject as interesting as the one you are now working on.

Sincerely,

Sgn. Henry A Byroade,
American Ambassador

With Henry Byroade's wonderful description of his fantastic restoration of 3-DL-152 there remains little more to be said.

The story of the Experimental chassis which were built for all post-1914 War 40/50s has now been told as far as the information is available, but for readers who are requiring more information on 3-DL-152, Henry Byroade wrote an article which appears in January 1966, No. 66/1, pages 854-855, in *The Flying Lady*.

PART III CHAPTER 8

Chassis No. 3-AZ-146, a Hooper Pullman enclosed drive limousine, the story of this car and the present owner's personal experiences of running and owning a Phantom III over a period of 9 years and a mileage of just over 20,000

How I first made my acquaintance with 3-AZ-146 has already been described (see Part II, Chapter 8), so there is no need to dwell on this part of the story again, but simply to say that though I first saw the car standing in the garage at Haselbech as long ago as March 1958, it was only on one occasion that I saw her actually in use on the road. This was on 15 October 1960, when a member of the Ismay family was married and a reception was held at the Basil Street Hotel, Knightsbridge. It was dark when we came out of the Hotel and there stood 3-AZ-146, right outside the Hotel entrance with Hunnisett in attendance; the side lights and tail lamp were on and the interior of the car was a blaze of light, as she waited to take Mrs Bower Ismay back to her flat, Eyre Court, St Johns Wood. The car was a wonderfully nostalgic sight, recalling the days long before the War, when similar cars queued in the Mall, taking debutantes to be presented at Court.

When we bought the Phantom II 74 GN, I was not particularly interested in the Phantom III, that it was a magnificent example of a motor carriage I would be the first to admit, but I really did not want an enormous chauffeur-driven limousine, even if it was in quite outstanding condition. Apart from this I had been somewhat prejudiced against the Phantom III as a car to own; I had heard the most hair-raising stories about endless boiling troubles and bills of such magnitude when things went wrong, that the owner almost went bankrupt! I had also heard that the hydraulically operated tappets were a continual source of bother and that the cost of modifying a Phantom III engine was fantastically expensive, so I regarded the Phantom III generally as being a car that was completely beyond my means. However, on the 20 September 1964, after a delightful tour of

Scotland in 74 GN, on our way home to Cornwall we called in on Hunnisett at Haselbech. He still had the Phantom III and this time I had a very good look at her; he had maintained this car so superbly that she was almost like a brand new vehicle, the speedometer was reading just over 69,000 miles. I asked him if the engine had been modified from hydraulic to solid tappets and he told me that it had not, and this seemed to be one of the reasons why he was not able to sell the car.

We had a very long talk about it, then I telephoned Jack Compton and told him all about it. Jack said that the Phantom III was the most fabulous piece of machinery, that if the car was in as good a condition as I described and that if I could purchase it for a reasonable figure and then bring it straight to him, he would modify the engine from hydraulic to solid tappets at a cost of £250. He said he would require the car for approximately eight to ten weeks, but he warned me it was most important that, before finally deciding whether to buy or not, I should have an extended road trial on the car in order to see whether it overheated, and that if there was the slightest sign of overheating to drop all thought of having it.

This was arranged for mid-December and, accompanied by Hunnisett, I covered 35 miles at various speeds. The water temperature never rose over 80⁰ once the shutters had opened. The upshot of the trial was that I bought the car and set off on the 75 mile run south to Jack Compton.

As soon as Jack Compton saw her and the outstanding condition she was in, he wanted to buy her there and then; but I was very pleased with the way she had run down from Haselbech and said I would like him to carry out the modification to the tappets first, but that I might consider selling the car at a later date. By the time we reached Woldingham, the engine was thoroughly hot right through and was ticking over extremely quietly, except for one persistent steady tap. Compton listened to this and said that the tappets were working well, that they were scarcely audible, and that the tap was coming from one of the cam followers (shades of Phantom II trouble with cam followers) and that this would only disappear when the engine was modified and the new camshaft fitted.

On 3 February 1965, I collected 3-AZ-146 from Compton. In addition to modifying the tappets he had made up and fitted two small conical gauze filters which had been inserted into the hoses between the cylinder blocks and the radiator uptakes. These filters are sometimes referred to as 'Witches Hats', as this is exactly what they look like. Compton said that it was essential that some form of filtration was fitted to the cooling system as, though it was completely clear now and the engine remained cool, there was no doubt that during its last period of idleness of about 18 months, silt, etc. had probably accumulated in the cylinder blocks, which on a long run at high speed, would eventually be thrown into the matrix, with the result that the radiator would choke, producing boiling troubles. Though it was February when I collected the car I was strongly urged on all sides not to use any sort of anti-freeze in the radiator, but to drain the system at night if the car had to stand in exposed places or in an unheated garage, and refill with fresh water in the morning. Once I had the car in Cornwall it would go into a heated garage and frosts are so rare in the West Country that the problem of anti-freeze did not arise.

Compton had told me when I brought the car away from Woldingham that she needed to be used, and 'the more she was used the better, before I took her over to Jersey where the mileage would naturally be very restricted. As I had started researches for my book *The Hyphen in Rolls-Royce* I decided that I would use her for all the travelling about the country which this would entail.

As soon as I had the car home, with the speedometer showing 70,230 miles, I had wing mirrors, an additional reversing light and a windscreen washer fitted; the first two items presented no problems at all, but the screen washer was difficult; there was absolutely no room under the bonnet to fit a Lucas electric screen washer, such as I had fitted on both 101 SK and GGP 28 a long while before. It was finally decided that the only type which could be fitted would be a hand operated Trico made for a modern Ford! This pattern had a plastic water container rather like a hot water bottle which would just fit on to the nearside of the front compartment out of the way of anyone's feet. It seems a strange and rather primitive thing to fit on to a Rolls-Royce car of any sort, let alone a Phantom III, but hardly anyone has been aware of its presence during the years it has been on the car and is most efficient and invaluable on long runs.

What Jack Compton had forecast about the filters on the cooling system was absolutely correct, as I soon noticed that, once a mileage in excess of 350 was covered, the water temperature rose quite rapidly and the thermometer showed a reading of 85°, or even on occasions 90°, but by draining some of the water out and cleaning the filters, the engine remained cool again. With practice, it became easy to clean both filters in less than 10 minutes; whenever they were dismantled they looked exactly the same, choked with a greyish-white sort of slime in which some small crystals about the size of a piece of lead pencil would be found. Once cleaned the car would run 300 miles with no bother at all, so I began cleaning them regularly.

In February I had made arrangements to travel to London to start work on research, staying the night at Newbury on the way. On 4 March I left the Lizard Peninsular in Cornwall for Newbury and had an excellent run as far as Wincanton, when I ran into very heavy snow, unbeknown to me there had been a blizzard raging over Wiltshire most of the morning and the A303 was blocked from Wincanton to Amesbury. The Police at Wincanton were extremely helpful and advised me to make a large detour through Castle Cary to Chippenham and so on to the Bath road. It was about 3 p m when I left Wincanton, the wind was blowing strongly causing the snow to drift all over the road, but the Phantom III behaved superbly, never once was there a trace of wheel spin or skidding; the road was littered with abandoned cars, but the Phantom III just motored on as if it was being driven under normal conditions. I quickly began to realize how 34 EX must have performed when negotiating sand on its run to Nairobi. This performance was in a large part due to the tremendous torque of the V12 engine, coupled with the great weight of 3-AZ-146 (unladen the car goes 2 tons 16 cwt with a full tank of petrol on the Public Weighbridge in Guildford).

When I arrived at Newbury, the snow in the drive at Speen Place was above the running boards on the car and Francis Hutton-Stott greeted me like someone from outer space! The telephone wires were down and Francis and Joan had quite decided that I was still down in Cornwall, thinking conditions were so bad that I had never left home at all.

The rest of the trip was completely uneventful, the car ran absolutely perfectly and I returned with it to Cornwall during the following week.

Before I finally took the car over to Jersey I had run 6,658 miles since Jack Compton had modified the engine.

Like any other enthusiast who buys an old car which he intends to keep, I wanted to know its previous history. At this time all I knew was that Mrs Bower Ismay had bought it second-hand from Jack Barclay Ltd, George Street, Hanover Square, in April 1939, that the mileage was very low indeed and that Hunnisett thought the car had originally been built for an invalid.

In tracing the early history of 3-AZ-146 I first went to the Cornwall County Council, Licensing Dept, and asked to see the file on the car. From this I learned that the car had originally been supplied to a Miss Harriet Maconochie of 18, Glenferness Avenue, Bournemouth, on 23 October 1936, by Messrs Edwards & Co, of Christchurch Road, Bournemouth, who were the Rolls-Royce retailers; but I was surprised to learn that the car was originally finished in black and grey. I wrote to Edwards & Co, asking them if they had details of the car and received a reply saying that their records had been destroyed but that the writer could

*Lillie Hall

remember the car which he thought had cost something in the region of £4,000 and that it was a special order for Miss Harriet Maconochie.

Later, from the files in Conduit Street I was able to find the Body Card, details of which are as follows:-

Chassis No. 3-AZ-146
Engine No. P.14.K.
HP 40/50 - PIII
Type 'A'
Off Test: 31.8.36.
Axle ratio: 8 x 34
Despatched: 1.9.36.
Battery: Peto and Radford.
D.I. Issued: 9.5.36.
Sold to: Edwards & Co., (Bournemouth) Ltd, 189-193, Old Christchurch Road, Bournemouth.
For: Miss H R Maconochie, 18, Glenferness Avenue, Bournemouth. Tyres: Dunlop.
Size: 18 x 7. Date of Order: 9.5.36. No T A 18.
Ordered from: 'W'
Coachbuilders: Hooper
Delivery: Quoted' 1st week of August.
Balance of chassis price paid: Date 2.9.36. £1,482.8.9d.
Invoice No: 6671. Date: 31.8.36. Amount £1,482.8.9d.
Chassis delivered on: 2.9.36. To: Hooper & Co. By: L H.*
Instruction Book No: 10. Sent to: Edwards & Co. On: 21.9.36.
Erection particulars dated 23.3.36. From: Edwards.
Wheelbase: Standard. Steering Column: 'C'.
Springs for: Body: Enclosed limousine. Weight: 14½ cwt.
Seating: 7 usually: 3-4. Luggage: Max. 2 cwt, average - cwt.
Allowance for accessories - Standard 40 lb. Special rear bumper.
Car for use in: U K - town work - speed practically never exceeds 50 mph.
Bonnet hinge mouldings to be: Painted.
Chassis price - £1,850.
Bonnet with flap shutters and rear end shaped at 7⁰.
Locks to bonnet: Yes.
Mascot to radiator cap: Yes (Charge Hoopers).
Wheel carrier: To offside.
Necessary fittings for Clayton Heater - charge Hoopers.

On another occasion whilst staying with Jimmy Skinner and looking through his vast collection of coachbuilder's photographs, I was delighted to find that amongst these was an original Hooper photograph of the car, taken when it was brand new, before delivery to Miss Maconochie, added to this I was lucky to obtain from the Science Museum in London a copy of the original Hooper Coach-builders' drawings. It is interesting to note that these are captioned 'Specially designed for Miss Maconochie - Hooper enclosed limousine 40/50 h p Rolls-Royce, 'C' steering, Phantom III and that no chassis number is given; this is probably because when the car was ordered, early in May 1936, it had not been decided which chassis should be allocated to Miss Machonochie.

From the chassis erection card, which is held at Crewe, the following information was obtained:-

3-AZ-146
Date despatched: 1.9.36.
Guarantee: 24.10.1936.
Finish No. 8. Untarnishable.
Dynamometer Test:

1000 rpm	2000 rpm	3000 rpm	4000 rpm
49	92	125	226

Date of Test: 10.8.36.
Engine Freedom Good.

Miss Maconochie was a regular client of Rolls-Royce Ltd. Late in 1926 she had taken delivery of a 'New Phantom' chassis No. 72 YC, fitted with a Connaught enclosed drive limousine; then in March 1932 she took delivery of a Phantom II, chassis No. 52 JS, this was an enclosed drive limousine by Park Ward, fitted with specially low-rated springs which was also supplied by Edwards & Co, of Bournemouth.

I saw Hunnisett later in 1965 when I was using the car regularly, and took it to Haselbech with me, and naturally I questioned him closely about it. He told me that in 1939 Mrs Bower Ismay was thinking of replacing 74 GN which had then run 125,000 miles, and she heard about 3-AZ-146 at Jack Barclay's. When it was brought round for a trial run it was painted the most 'horrible shade of duck-egg green'. However she bought it and he did not see it again until it had had the lower panels repainted dark blue with a gold line round the waist and Mrs Ismay's initials, *MCI, on the two rear doors; also a luggage rail had been fitted to the roof with slats reinforcing the roof of the car, so that it was possible to walk on it when loading the mountains of luggage they always took everywhere with them.

When I bought the car, it only had one spare wheel, but I felt that as it would be used in the future far more on the Continent than in the U K it was essential to mount a second spare wheel on the near side and for this work to be done I took the car to Hooper Motor Services Ltd, at their works in Kimberly Road, North London, in July 1965. Jack Compton supplied some of the necessary parts, wheel, discs, etc, and by great good fortune it was discovered that Hooper Motor Services had in stock a brand new carrier bracket, to mount on the chassis. They made a superb job of it and charged me £136.10.0d.

They had the car for about a fortnight and I collected it about 10.0 a m on Saturday 17 July 1965, with the intention of driving north to Haselbech. At that time, at weekends, during the summer months, there was a maximum speed limit of 50 mph on many roads. The traffic was very heavy, most of it frustratingly slow moving; I was travelling on the outer lane dead on 50 mph, overtaking as many vehicles as possible, when suddenly I was overtaken by a policeman on a motor cycle, who waved me in to the nearside of the road. I looked in my mirror to see what was coming behind and saw a motorcade, consisting of three or four Rolls-Royce cars, all with their headlights full on; the first one was a Phantom V, with a huge flag flying from each front mudguard. I had seen this car a few days before in London and realized that it was the President of one of the South American Countries who was over here on a State Visit. As the last of the motorcade of Rolls-Royce cars swept past I suddenly had an inspiration - I too was driving a big Rolls-Royce limousine painted in dark colour, it was an opportunity too good to miss, so I too switched my headlights full on, drew out into the centre lane and joined on behind; I was now part of the procession.

We swept along at speeds of up to 60 mph overtaking everything on the road, at all cross roads, traffic lights, etc., there was a policeman on point duty, these all waved me on and saluted as I sailed past, it was quite wonderful! We travelled all the way to St Albans like this until they turned off into the town and I regretfully turned off on to the Motorway, the M1, to Northampton.

In October 1965 3-AZ-146 came over to

*Matilda Constance Ismay

Jersey, my last long run in her was from Perth to Bournemouth where we were to board the Air Ferry at Hurn Airport. On arrival in Jersey the number plates were changed from CLJ 600 to the present number, J376, and not very long after the car came to the Island I had the lower panels repainted grey to match 101 SK and my 20/25, GGP 28, which improved the appearance considerably.

In addition, the headlamps were converted to take double filament bulbs, so that they both dipped together and complied with the Laws for motoring on the Continent, also a pair of Lucas fog-lights, as fitted to the Silver Cloud I and II incorporating flashing indicators were added, and a pair of stop-tail and flashing indicators made by Lucas, of the type usually fitted to Rover cars, were mounted on the rear wings. This meant that 3-AZ-146 was now suitable for world-wide use.

The car returned to England for the final researches for *The Hyphen in Rolls-Royce* and I decided to take it to the Rolls-Royce and Bentley Pageant at Goodwood on 20 May 1967, and was pleased when we shared first prize in the multi-stable competition with John Hampton's 120 EU and his Continental R-type Bentley.

In view of the fact that Ron Haynes had recommended me to use an anti-freeze which contained an inhibitor for aluminium engines, in place of ordinary water as a coolant, and as the car had not originally been capable of running much more than 300 miles without cleaning out the 'Witches Hats' filters, I felt that it was essential to fit larger filters. I telephoned Jack Compton and asked him to have a pair all prepared and ready to fit as soon as the car arrived in England. These new filters are a tremendous success, they are filled with nylon pot-scourers from Woolworths, packed tightly. I open and clean them once a year and it is quite surprising how little sediment they collect. I do not think that there is any doubt that the 'Witches Hats' disposed of the original accumulation of filth which had been deposited in the engine over the years and it is now quite clean inside; it runs extremely cool for a Phantom III, the radiator shutters open at 85° and then the temperature drops back and runs between 70° to 75°.

A postscript can be added to this, as when we were in France for a few days last year, I was alarmed to discover on one days motoring that the water temperature went up to just over 90°. I put this down to the heatwave at the time; however, when we stopped at our Hotel for the night, I decided to investigate and discovered that some of the pot-scourers on the near side filter had entered the water uptake to the radiator itself and were thus partly restricting the flow. I removed them and though they contained very little sediment washed and replaced them, in spite of the heatwave the car ran beautifully afterwards at whatever speeds I cared to drive it. Later, I spoke to Ron Haynes on the telephone about this incident and he said, 'Oh yes, I have heard of this happening before'.

The hydraulic jacking system has given some trouble in the past and the rubbers on all the jacks have been renewed, I now change the fluid in the system every two years, washing the system through with methylated spirit before refilling. Also I raise and lower the jacks fairly frequently, but frankly I do not think that they can be relied upon; in theory they are a wonderful idea, which, on a lighter car would probably give no trouble at all, but the Phantom III is such a heavy car that to be on the safe side I always carry two ordinary hydraulic bottle-jacks with me, and would never go under the car without these or axle stands in place.

When I started to write this book I asked Ron Haynes if I could see the service file of the car, I wanted to give a complete picture of the life story of a Phantom III from when it was built, in the hope that this would end some of the ill-founded criticisms to which this model is subjected, either by people who have once owned a Phantom III and not looked after it properly, or by others who know nothing of the model at all, but simply pass on disparaging stories about what is an exceedingly fine motor car.

The Service File on 3-AZ-146 bears out exactly what I have always felt about the Phantom III, which is that the Sales Dept at Rolls-Royce were pushing the Design Dept too hard, consequently the model was put on the market before all the teething troubles were overcome; added to which it appears to me that Miss Maconochie's chauffeur was not a particularly good one, as the car was returned to Hythe Road from Bournemouth with a total mileage of 15,917 for brakes to be relined, at the same time a modified long type clutch plate was fitted and the radiator matrix altered to combat over heating problems.

When Miss Maconochie died her executor instructed Jack Barclay Ltd to sell the car when the total mileage was 19,334 and there is a note on the file to say 'Carry out all work necessary to put chassis in good running order for re-sale'.

Notes dated 28 February 1939, total mileage 19,412. Car to be ready by 4.0 p m 3 March 1939. Carry out following modification; long type clutch plate, remove oil cooler, cross steering tubes, adjust all brakes, test out one-shot lubrication system, remove rattle from clutch trunion, dismantle and re-erect Clayton pipes, dismantle and re-erect starter motor.

All this work was carried out before delivery to Mrs Ismay.

When War was declared in September 1939, the car was laid up in the garages at Haselbech Hall, where it was to remain until the latter part of 1952.

Petrol rationing finally came to an end in 1950 and in 1952 it was announced that, commencing 1 January 1953, the horse-power tax would be dispensed with and a new type of flat-rate duty of £12.10.0d. per vehicle would come into force so, in the Autumn of 1952, Mrs Bower Ismay decided to put 3-AZ-146 back on the road from 1 January of the following year.

As neither 74 GN nor 3-AZ-146 had been used since 1939, she very wisely decided that the car should be thoroughly inspected by Rolls-Royce Ltd, before she attempted to use it, so the following telegram was despatched from Haselbech Hall to Hythe Road on 23 September 1952.

'Silvagost Wesphone London - Can you send Inspector this week to advise about two 40/50 Rolls-Royce laid up since 1940 could meet your man Northampton Ten Forty Leave Euston Nine Five - Ismay Maidwell 235'.

This telegram was reply-paid and Hythe Road sent the following:

'Ismay - Maidwell 235 - If cars are drivable recommend arrangements drive them here.

Considerable work possibly required. Beyond capacity visiting engineer. Silvagost'.

To this Mrs Bower Ismay replied as follows: 'Rolls-Royce Ladbroke 2444 London - Cars undrivable need inspection and advice before ordering work please send competent inspector and adviser - Ismay Maidwell 235'.

In view of Mrs Bower Ismay's telegram, arrangements were made for a 'Competent' mechanic from Hythe Road to go up to Haselbech, put 3-AZ-146 into running order, then take the car to Hythe Road for a complete check-over. On 28 October 1952, Mrs Ismay wrote as follows:

Dear Sir,
Thank you for your letter of October 3rd. Please arrange to send a man for the limousine, any day up to and including Monday, 3rd November, if after that any Saturday or Monday. Will you be taking it back with a trade plate as it is not licenced? We will comprehensively insure it. With regard to the Brake (74 GN) our man has removed the Autovac; he thinks he can remove the petrol tank and he would like to know if he should remove the carburetter as a complete unit. He thinks in this case all three parts would go to you, with the limousine. They could come back in good order in the limousine, be fitted and then your man could bring the Brake (74 GN up to you for testing, etc. He prefers this to using a local garage. M C Ismay.

On 3 November 1952, a mechanic from Hythe Road arrived at Haselbech and proceeded to prepare the car for the road in order to take it back to London with him, where Hythe Road mechanics would go right through it and see that it was in perfect running order, the cost of this work was £41.18.5d.

When 3-AZ-146 reached Hythe Road, the engine was checked over, the water pump stripped and re-erected, the petrol tank removed and thoroughly cleaned out, also the hydraulic jacks were completely overhauled and two were replaced. The car was completely serviced and the one-shot lubrication system was tested to see that oil was reaching all parts. The dynamo was dismantled, stripped, cleaned and re-erected. The horns were re-wired to by-pass the ammeter. Two new petrol pumps were fitted to the bulkhead and a new petrol gauge together with tank unit were put on the car. The total account for all this work was £160.10.4d.

From January 1953 until her death in February 1963 Mrs Bower Ismay used 3-AZ-146 as her principal car, most of the journeys were between Haselbech and her London flat at Eyre Court, St Johns Wood, North London; the car ran backwards and forwards between Haselbech and London in all weathers with the regularity of an express train; it was always heavily loaded with six suitcases on the luggage carrier at the rear and the luggage rail on the roof would also be fully loaded with hampers of fresh vegetables, etc., the whole being sheeted down underneath black tarpaulins. Once the M1 was opened this was the route which they nearly always used, and the car must have looked a splendid sight, travelling down the middle lane at a steady 60 - 65 mph, loaded in this way, with Mrs Ismay comfortably seated in the back reading her book. It only failed once, and that was on the way to Haselbech on the M1 when the fibre wheel in the timing sheared and the car had to be towed in to Coupers, the R-R Agents in St Albans, for repairs. The brakes were re-lined at just over 37,000 miles in 1956 and apart from adjustment they have never been touched until July 1973, when Jack Compton roughed up the linings for me.

In April 1967, when I had the car in London, I spent an extremely pleasant afternoon with Mr Osmond Rivers, who was Chief Designer at Messrs Hooper & Co, for so many years, and who was actually entirely responsible for the coachwork on 3-AZ-146. He was most interested to see the car again and to see how well it had stood up to the passage of years and he pointed out to me many of the little features which had been specially incorporated for Miss Machonochie, the upholstery was a special weave which cost £14 per yd, pre War!

On 25 May 1967, 3-AZ-146 returned to Jersey by Air Ferry from Southampton, having been in the U K for 6 weeks, during which time the car ran just over 3,600 miles, which were completely trouble free. Back in Jersey the car was in regular use, but covering a very small mileage annually, until 30 June 1973, when advantage was taken of using the new drive-on ferry to St Malo. We motored across France to Boulogne and so crossed to Folkestone and from there to Jack Compton at Woldingham in Surrey, so that he could give 3-AZ-146 a thorough check over, he had not done any mechanical work on the car for almost 9 years and I felt that it was time that an expert had a good look at it.

A Phantom III in France is an unforgettable experience, the car really comes into its own, the model has been described as the nearest equivalent to riding on a 'Magic Carpet'.

Jack Compton gave me an excellent report on 3-AZ-146 and had carried out the following work. - The brakes had been roughed up, they did not require re-lining, even though the car had run almost 50,000 miles since this was last done. The servo, however, was re-lined as it was oily. A new water-pump was fitted. New points in the ignition, the plugs were cleaned and re-gapped and the tappets adjusted. The shock dampers had their poundage increased by 7 lbs in order to make the car ride better at speed on the Continent, (it was designed for Town Work in the U K), now it rides superbly. The sump was removed owing to a leaking gasket. The trumpets of the Lucas Mellotone Horns were re-chromed. The one shot lubrication system was checked over to make sure that oil was reaching all parts.

Finally, the matrix to the radiator was renewed, there was a small leak from the offside top corner when the car stood for a period, so as the car lives permanently abroad, it was decided to fit a new matrix, this carries a guarantee of 3 years and the total cost for all the work was £665.

I collected the car from Jack Compton on 25 September 1973, the speedometer showed a reading of 86,496 miles and before returning with the car to Jersey on 18th October, I used it every day and it ran 2,401 miles completely trouble free during this time.

On 22 May 1974, 3-AZ-146 was down on the Albert Quay, St Helier at 6.15 a m to embark in *Falaise* to Weymouth, I was taking all the photographs for this Book to the publishers. Again whilst in England the car was used as everyday transport and returned to Jersey on 6th June, between these dates the car ran 1,428 miles and used 140 gallons of petrol and 2 gallons of Castrol GTX in the engine and never gave one moment's trouble. The speedometer now reads 91,225 miles and the engine has never had an overhaul, apart from the work described in this Chapter.

This completes the story of a most satisfactory Phantom III, which has given me almost 9 years and over 20,000 miles of the most enjoyable motoring it is possible to have.

PART III CHAPTER 9

The details of various production model Phantom IIIs that were purchased by very important people. Together with chassis No. 3-DL-94 with centre gear-change. The first 10 production cars which were for 'Trials'. Stanley Sears chassis No. 3-AZ-38, 3-BU-118 and 3-DL-76. Frederick Wilcock chassis No. 3-AZ-186 which was used by Field Marshall Montgomery for a time during the 1939-45 War

Out of the 717 production Phantom III chassis built, 131 were purchased by titled people ranging from Reigning Monarchs and Royal Dukes to Baronets and Knights, taking in Indian Princes and other foreign potentates on the way.

Chassis No. 3-AZ-50, fitted with a 2-door Sedanca drop-head coupé body by Gurney Nutting was supplied to King Carol of Rumania on 1 April 1936. He was obviously pleased with it as in the following July he took delivery of a second one, chassis No. 3-CP-34, a Park Ward sports limousine which had been used as a 'Trials Car' by Jack Barclay.

The other two Phantom IIIs supplied to foreign royalty were both for King Farouk of Egypt; the first was 3-CM-63, a Hooper Enclosed Limousine specially built for the King and shipped out to Egypt on 20 January 1938. The second was 3-DL-182, which in fact was supplied in April 1940; rather surprising considering the state of emergency which existed at the time.

Our own Royal Family purchased two Phantom III chassis, both of which were specially built. The first was 3-AZ-43 with Barker Touring Limousine coachwork supplied to H M King George V's youngest surviving son, His Royal Highness the Duke of Kent, who had formally been a great Bentley enthusiast, having had a 3 litre, 6½ litre and 8 litre, all built by the old Bentley Company.

For his Phantom III the Duke of Kent had several special features incorporated, the first was a special 'F' type of steering, 2 in. longer than standard, then he asked for Marchal headlamps in place of Lucas, and two Bosch horns under the bonnet operated by a horn ring on the steering wheel; the usual Lucas Mellotone horns were not fitted, but he had an American police-siren instead! He also asked for the instruments to be sent separately to Barkers, who were building the body, (a touring limousine with one rear mounted spare wheel), as he wished to design his own instrument panel and for some reason the arrangement he finally chose did not include a clock. The AZ Phantom series are usually all even numbers but there were two cars in this series which had odd numbers; one was the Duke of Kent's, and the other was 3-AZ-47, a Hooper Limousine supplied to Lord Linlithgow, Viceroy of India, for his use in that country.

It will be recalled that the Duchess of Gloucester had used 34-EX to open the Winchester Playing Fields before this car did its epic run to Nairobi, and it is possible that it was after using 34 EX and also hearing his younger brother's satisfaction with 3-AZ-43, that the Duke of Gloucester, who had previously owned Sunbeams, also decided to order a Phantom III. This chassis No. 3-AX-195 also had Barker coachwork, but this time it was an Enclosed Limousine, painted all black with a dull matt finish, but with wings in a bright finish; there is a note on the Body Card stipulating brown leather upholstery 'as in the Sunbeam car'. The steering position was again 'F' and the same Eural horn-operating ring was fitted, also a Klaxon horn from the Sunbeam was mounted and the main headlamps and Mellotone Horns were made to swivel in any direction. Finally there was a special mascot for the radiator cap. The registration number XH 8888 was transferred from the Sunbeam on to 3-AX-195.

HRH the Duke of Gloucester was undoubtedly a man who knew his own mind as the body card for this chassis covers no less than four pages, which give details of exactly what was required, including a Philco wireless with two speakers which could be operated from the front or rear seats, silk blinds to the rear doors and on the partition window. The quarter lights, which were fixed, did not have blinds but it was possible to screen these off with double glazing in the form of Purdah blue glass; there was a special aluminium carrier bag as a receptacle for umbrellas in the front compartment, and the gear lever was connected so that the moment reverse was engaged the reversing light came on automatically, which was an innovation in those days. The car was fitted with two batteries, and Lucas was specified; also a Lucas 'Screen-Spray', which again must have been one of the earliest forms of Lucas wind-shield washers. The date of sale of the chassis is not recorded but Barkers delivered the finished car to the Duke of Gloucester's chauffeur on 1 May 1937.

This car is now in the Rolls-Royce Enthusiasts' Club and belongs to R A Benge, 10a, Avondale Road, St Leonards-on-Sea, Sussex, but the registration number has been changed and is now LGY 408.

One of Rolls-Royce Ltd chief selling points was always to try and provide what the customer wanted, chassis No. 3-DL-94 is a most interesting vehicle in this respect as this is the one and only Phantom III ever to be made which has the gear lever in the centre position, it was supplied by special request to a Mr H L Bilbrough, of Winton, Chislehurst, Kent, who was a wealthy stockbroker and had been a Packard owner for many years; but when that Company started to produce their famous '120' model he felt that the Packard image had been cheapened so he no longer wished to be associated with them. He had been used to a centre gear change and when he decided on a Phantom III as his new car he stipulated that it must have the same arrangement. He liked open motoring, was somewhat old-fashioned in his ideas and asked Freestone and Webb to build him an All Weather Tourer with a four piece wind-screen. He also arranged 'no mascot to the radiator, two spare wheels and all the instru-ments to have white dials and black figures' which is exactly the opposite to the standard arrangement on the Phantom III; there was to be no clock and the car was built for U K - town use and touring.

It is at present owned by Dr John R Fischer of 18, Cricklewood Place, Frontenac, No. 63131, who is a member of the Rolls-Royce Owners' Club of America, Inc, and to whom I am extremely grateful for the information which he has given me about this car, which he discovered for sale in a garage in Swindon.

Dr Fischer and his wife were coming to Europe on a visit and he had inserted an adver-tisement in *The Autocar* stating that he wanted a Pre-War open-bodied Rolls-Royce car. In reply to his advertisement he heard that the Victoria Garage (Swindon) Ltd, Victoria Road, Swindon, had an open touring Phantom III which they were offering for sale with a total mileage of 33,840 on the speedometer; naturally Dr Fischer was most interested and wrote to the late Mr Cyril Reed, requesting him to give the car a thorough inspection and to report on it for him. He received a most lengthy report part of which reads as follows:-

I think if you buy this car the following mechanical repairs should be carried out before you take it back to America.

Attend to slipper drive to improve vibration in engine.
S & F new camshaft wheel.
Carry out Schedule B, lubrication and adjustments.
Supply and fit chrome extension to exhaust swan neck.
Make centralised lubrication pump work correctly.
S & F new fanbelt
Remedy leaks from tappet rocker cover joints. Approx. £140.

It is to be noted that this report has been compiled in good faith from a road test, a jack test and a superficial examination on 5 April 1962. *Absolutely no dismantling* has taken place and responsibility cannot be accepted for any defects found upon subsequent dismantling.

Incidentally Dr Fischer is also the owner of another Phantom III, chassis No. 3-CM-67 an H J Mulliner Sedanca de ville, the chassis of which was purchased new on 20 July 1937 by Jack Barclay, who ordered the coachwork. The car, ordered for stock purposes was sold on 13 November 1937 to Mrs S W Tanfield, White Place, Taplow, Bucks. Dr Fischer purchased this car unseen from Sanderson & Holmes, the Rolls-Royce retailers of Leicester, when it had done less than 30,000 miles. He also told me of another interesting car, chassis No. 3-DL-86, owned by Norris Allen, an Attorney-at-Law, in St Louis, Missouri, who is a great enthusiast and has several Rolls-Royce cars.

This is a 2-door 4-light sports saloon Coupé built by James Young of Bromley, to their design number 4531 R, for Jack Barclay; it was exhibited on the James Young stand at the last Earls Court, London Motor Show to be held prior to the outbreak of World War II, in October 1938. The car is particularly interesting because there was a departure from James Young's standard design for this coachwork, in that the doors were parallel opening; James Young had already built one or two cars with this arrangement. The idea was that two large doors required a good deal of room to open wide, whilst a parallel opening door only came out just beyond the width of the running board, then slid back, making access to the interior very easy in a confined space. Another point about this car which interested me is that Norris Allen, like myself, felt that the Phantom III is too low geared for long distance travel and he fitted an overdrive, about which he wrote as follows:

> You enquired about the overdrive. The P-III has an engine-to-rear-axle ratio of 4.25 to 1. This is fine for the Alps. I abhor driving the car with the engine working its head off. I looked around and found that in about 1934 a man named Anderson designed a very large epicyclic overdrive unit, which in various forms was constructed and appended at the rear of the transmission of Chrysler Airflows, Ambassador Nashes and a few others. This unit had 5 rather large gears inside the external gear instead of three smaller ones. Since the thing was made with no front end on it, it having been appended directly to the rear of the transmission on these cars, I fashioned a front end for it and had the main shaft out of the transmission machined off and splined and a bearing case made for the front end. I suspended it behind the cross member, which is behind the transmission or gear box on a PIII. The ratio of this overdrive is .7, which meant that in overdrive the engine to rear wheel ratio is 2.975 to 1., slightly under the 3 to 1.
>
> Four cars started out for the Montreal Rolls-Royce Owners Club meet - 2 PIIIs, 1 PI, and 1 PII. The results were interesting. The PIII which had been completely overhauled in England, the Freestone and Webb one, picture of which is enclosed, by the time

we got to Canada, used 6 quarts of oil. I had overhauled mine and was driving in overdrive. I added no oil. By the time we got to Montreal, the Freestone & Webb had used 10 quarts of oil. Mine had used none. I pulled into every other filling station and waited for the other 3 cars to fill up. They got about 9 miles to the American gallon and I got 12½. Mind you, this is an American gallon and not an Imperial gallon. This means over 15 miles to the Imperial gallon. I stopped looking at the oil and drove 3,500 miles at highway speeds, 60 to 70 miles an hour, and when I got home I drained the oil and I had used 1 quart. So you can see what the overdrive does. Thereafter, I fitted one of these to an 8 litre Bentley I own, and this thing fairly floats.

The first 10 Phantom III chassis to be built were all originally 'Trials Cars' as follows:-

3-AZ-20 - H J Mulliner 4 door saloon with division - 'Paris Trials Car'.

3-AZ-22 - Index number CYP 921 - Hooper enclosed drive limousine - Conduit Street 'Trials Car'.

3-AZ-24 - Barker sports Sedanca de ville - 'Trials Car' - Barker & Co.

3-AZ-26 - Thrupp & Maberly sports limousine - Rootes Ltd, 'Trials Car', Devonshire House, Piccadilly, London.

3-AZ-28 - H J Mulliner sports limousine - Jack Barclay 'Trials Car'.

3-AZ-30 - James Young sports Sedanca de ville - Jack Barclay 'Trials Car'.

3-AZ-32 - Gurney Nutting sports Sedanca de ville - H R Owen Ltd, 'Trials Car'.

3-AZ-34 - H J Mulliner sports saloon with division Car Mart 'Trials Car'.

3-AZ-36 - Hooper Touring limousine - Index number CYY 2 - Hooper & Co 'Trials Car'.

3-AZ-38 - Barker Touring limousine - Conduit Street 'Trials Car' - Index number CXU 976

After a while all these 'Trials Cars' were sold and replaced by one of a later design, but before it was sold, the last of these, 3-AZ-38, had been used by Conduit Street and had toured the Continent very extensively whilst still a Company car; there was a lengthy article on touring the Alps with this chassis in *The Autocar*, 13 August 1937, entitled 'Col de L'Iseran'.

By the early part of 1938 it had been decided that 3-AZ-38 should be sold. At the time Stanley Sears had just had an unfortunate accident with his Bentley. He had been proceeding up the Brighton Road on his way home to Bolney and was just about to overtake a lorry when it suddenly veered across in front of him to avoid a cyclist and the inevitable collision took place. So the Bentley was in the London Service Station for repairs and Major Cox of the Sales Department offered to lend Stanley 3-AZ-38 until his own car was ready.

Of course Stanley was completely delighted with 3-AZ-38, indeed, on 24 February 1938 he bought the car, part-exchanging the Bentley. Immediately it became his property he attended the Rolls-Royce School of Instruction for the second time, taking the complete course on care and maintenance of a Phantom III.

During the period prior to the outbreak of War, the car covered an enormous mileage; he entered many long distance rallies and trials with it and it never gave a moment's trouble, not even with the hydraulic tappets as, needless to say, he always kept the filters scrupulously clean, and changed the engine oil every 2,000 miles.

His mother, who spent most of her time living in the old family home at Collingtree, just outside Northampton, also had another house, 'Pedn Billy', on the Helford River in Cornwall, which she visited several times a year, travelling to and fro in her Phantom II, chassis No. 41 JS which was fitted with an Arthur Mulliner sports limousine body.

By 1938 she was thinking of replacing this car with a later model Rolls-Royce and as the Motor Show of that year approached the new model 'Wraith' was announced and she felt that one of these would suit her requirements perfectly. However, Stanley did not agree, he felt certain that for the very long journey between Northampton and Cornwall, which she always insisted on doing in one day's travel, and also taking into consideration the amount of luggage she took with her, a Wraith would be underpowered. So, when he accompanied his mother to the London Motor Show, he convinced her that the replacement car should be a Phantom III, which they decided to buy direct from the Motor Show. There were eight exhibits in all on Phantom III chassis (see Part III, of Appendix, 'A' for details of Phantom IIIs exhibited). The one they both preferred was chassis No. 3-DL-76, a

Thrupp & Maberly touring limousine, finished in a deep maroon. Mrs Sears bought it on the spot and it was delivered to her Northamptonshire home after the Show, bearing the Index number ANV 688.

When War was declared 3-DL-76 and 3-AZ-38 both went down to Cornwall to Mrs Sear's home and were laid up there. 3-DL-76 had only run 6,135 miles. It was virtually a new car. After the war, whilst petrol was still rationed, Stanley could see no hope of ever being able to run 3-AZ-38 again, so he sold the car to a Squadron Leader in the R A F and all trace of this car has been lost. Later he very much regretted selling it and looked around for another Phantom III, which he bought in 1947/8, chassis No. 3-BU-118. It was fitted with a touring limousine body by Arthur Mulliner of Northampton.

In 1952 Mrs Sears died and Stanley sold 3-BU-118 and bought 3-DL-76 from her executors. He had it re-painted in his favourite colour, green, and the car has now done something in the region of 25,000 miles from new. As with all his cars, it is most meticulously maintained and in immaculate condition.

I am indebted to Michael Wilcock for an account of chassis No. 3-AZ-186, a Phantom III which has had a most eventful career. This car carries Touring Limousine coachwork by Freestone & Webb, is finished in green and black with green leather upholstery, and was built to the special order of his father Frederick Wilcock, a Chartered Accountant by profession. In the early 1920s he became a Director of the English Talbot Motor Company, which had premises at Barlby Road, Ladbroke Grove, in North London. After owning many Talbots and taking an active interest in the Company, Mr Wilcock, who had always liked cars of quality and performance, purchased second-hand in 1933 an 8 litre Bentley with Freestone & Webb coachwork.

Amongst his various friends in the motoring world were the well known partners, Mr Pass and Mr Joyce, who traded as Pass & Joyce, Ltd, of 373-75, Euston Road, London, NW1. They were Rolls-Royce retailers, so, when Mr Wilcock decided to replace his existing 8 litre Bentley with a more up-to-date car in the form of a Rolls-Royce Phantom III, he ordered the chassis through them. As he had liked and been so satisfied with the Freestone & Webb body on his Bentley, he decided to have the coachwork for the Phantom III built by them also.

When 3-AZ-186 was delivered, the Wilcocks were living at Beckenham, Kent; but they also had a house at Angmering-on-Sea in Sussex, where they went nearly every weekend. Sometime after 30 November 1936, the day the car was delivered (and the day from which the Guarantee was effective), they all set off in it for the weekend by the sea. The car was heavily loaded and the entrance drive to Ham Manor was steep, with not sufficient room to turn a big car in front of the house, so Michael's father usually reversed his 8 litre Bentley up the drive, but when he attempted this with the Phantom III the clutch judder in reverse gear was appalling. He was very disappointed with his brand new car and on Monday morning it went into the Rolls-Royce service station to have this trouble rectified, but the following weekend the same thing happened, there was no improvement at all. Mr Wilcock was so furious that in his annoyance he pulled the hand-brake on so tightly it would not come off, not even the local garage could move it. It was eventually released by his hefty gamekeeper!

Michael's father enjoyed fast driving and on the run down to Angmering there was a long straight stretch just beyond Horsham where he invariably exceeded 90 mph and just as invariably burst a back tyre. Curiously, although they came home on the Sunday night at exactly the same speed on the same road, they never had any tyre troubles on the return journey despite a heavy load; so the bursting of tyres must have had something to do with the temperature during the day. Another of his pleasures was to spend his holidays touring the mountain passes of Switzerland and Austria and always drove himself, driving single-handed all the way. Over the years he had taken his 8 litre Bentley abroad many times, now in July 1937 he looked forward to his first Continental tour in 3-AZ-186. On the outward journey across France, making for Paris, he was surprised to find that the engine boiled if a speed of 65 mph was exceeded; so he took the car in to the Talbot

Works in Paris for them to examine it. They looked at it closely, made some calculations, and came to the conclusion that the radiator was much too small and there was nothing could be done. The only thing to do was to buy a collapsible leather bucket which could be kept under the front seat, so that if the engine did boil when they reached the Alps they could re-fill from mountain streams. One of the Passes they went over the famous Grossglockner. In the latest edition of the A A Continental Handbook it says that 'this Pass is open from May until October - it has numerous well engineered hairpin bends with moderate gradients but very long descents. The actual height of the Pass is 8,212 ft and the maximum gradient is 1 in 8'. On the way up the Pass they overtook an Austin 7 of the 1931 - 32 period, but when they reached the top the PIII's engine was boiling. So they stopped the car and opened the bonnet to allow it to cool down before re-filling with water. Presently the Austin 7 arrived on the scene, giving no trouble at all, and the driver stopped and asked Mr Wilcock if he could do anything to assist him. He was a little surprised at this, if not somewhat mortified, but it transpired that the Austin 7's owner was on holiday from Derby where his job was building Phantom IIIs!

When the car returned to England the matrix was modified and the boiling trouble finally overcome.

In September 1939 3-AZ-186 was laid up for the duration of the War at Ham Manor, but later the Government started a scheme to requisition large cars for the use of senior members of the War Department. On the staff of this body, known as 'The Vehicle Acquisition Control Board', was a personal friend of Frederick Wilcock, and it was he who approached him and asked him if he would lend 3-AZ-186 to Field Marshal Montgomery, rather than make out a formal requisition order for the car. Michael, by then aged 16, remembers putting the car in running order again himself. On 2 December 1943, he travelled with his mother and father in the car to London as far as Oxford Circus, from where it was taken on to Hythe Road. Early in the New Year, preparations were being made for D-Day and the Government asked if they could buy the car as it was already booked to accompany the Field Marshal overseas. However, this proposition was turned down flat. Mr Wilcock said that he did not mind the car being used on essential Government work as he knew that it was being properly maintained, but it was his intention to use it again himself when hostilities ceased, and things became normal. His attitude is completely understandable. Freestone & Webb had built the coachwork especially to his own requirements and the body had all sorts of features incorporated at his special request. For instance as both he and his wife were very keen golfers, the top portion of the luggage boot opened and was specially designed to carry their golf clubs.

As he was adamant over having his car returned to him eventually, another one was allocated to Field Marshal Montgomery for his use overseas, so 3-AZ-186 was transferred to the Americans and for a time was used by General Carl Spaatz, of the American Air Force.

Unfortunately, on one occasion when it was parked in the American Air Force Base's garage in North London, a tanker backed into it and damaged it. The U S Air Force hastily repaired it, but did not do a very good job. Shortly afterwards they decided to return the car to the owner, so Michael and his father went to Rolls-Royce Ltd, at Hythe Road, where the car had been left for collection. This was in the Autumn of 1944 just when the V1 Flying Bombs (Doodle-Bugs) were being sent over London. In consequence they had an exciting journey taking the car back to Angermering for it to be laid up for the rest of the War.

Sadly, this was the last time that Mr Wilcock drove 3-AZ-186 as the following year he died quite suddenly at the tragically early age of 47.

Later, in 1945, after the end of the War in Europe, his widow decided to sell the car and it became the property of John Steel of Bingley Hall, Bingley, Yorkshire. It is not known how long John Steel owned 3-AZ-186 but in February 1947, the car was in Rippon's of Huddersfield, for overhaul. The engine was removed from the chassis, sent to Crewe and was converted from hydraulic tappets to solid.

By 1956 3-AZ-186 was in the hands of its 5th owner William Henry Downes, a business man home on leave from Malaya. He bought the car from H R Owen Ltd and in October 1956 drove down to Lydd, put it aboard the Air Ferry to Le Touquet, then proceeded to Geneva via Paris, Zurich, Innsbruck, over the Bremmer Pass, through Austria, Venice and Milan. At the end of October he shipped the car to Malaya in the *Asia* but, between Genoa and Naples, the 'Suez Affair' blew up, the Italians became extremely worried about this and put Mr Downes and 3-AZ-186 ashore at Naples. After a great deal of trouble he arranged to ship the car to Malaya via the Adriatic and the Cape, whilst he flew to his home in Malaya.

3-AZ-186 arrived in Singapore in February 1957 and Mr Downes went down to collect her from the Rolls-Royce Agent. Unfortunately, when they serviced her, they forgot to refill the sump with oil so that on the run up to Penang, the engine overheated. The only oil obtainable was olive oil, so this was used to fill up the crankcase, after which she ran beautifully to Penang! Later he part-exchanged the Phantom III for a 220 Mercedes, through Lowe Motors, Penang.

This firm used the car on special occasions, such as the Coronation of the Sultan of Kedah in 1961, weddings and other celebrations, and sometimes as transport for various Malayan Potentates.

When Mr Downes exported the car to Malaya he wrote to the London County Council and returned the registration book stating that the car had been shipped permanently overseas, so the registration number DGY I was removed and replaced by the Malayan registration number PA 8282.

In 1963 the car changed hands for the seventh time and was bought by Mr H R Davis of Kuala Lumpur in February 1963. He saw it quite by chance, he had called in at Lowe Motors in Penang for them to repair a broken fan belt on his Jaguar. When he saw 3-AZ-186 at the back of the garage, looking very forlorn, he felt he must have her; the works foreman said the car took up a lot of space and helped to persuade the proprietor of the garage, who in fact owned 3-AZ-186, to part with it for £300. Mr Davis came home to Yorkshire in April 1963 and brought the car back with him to have it put in proper order whilst he was on leave. He felt that apart from a complete rewire, the other work he had had done on the car whilst out East was unsatisfactory. However, he did not go abroad again after all and decided it was too extravagant for him to run in England, so he sold it to a well known dealer in pre-war Rolls-Royce cars, who intended to sell it to a prospective purchaser coming on leave from the Persian Gulf.

Meanwhile Michael Wilcock, who had joined the Veteran Car Club of Great Britain when he was 17, having acquired a 1912 Talbot, had decided that he would try and find some of the cars which had formerly been owned by his father. In this he was very fortunate, first of all he was able to trace his father's 3½ litre Bentley, later he purchased his 8 litre Bentley and having regained these, he set about seeing what he could do in regard to 3-AZ-186.

He first wrote to Mr Downes at an address in Windsor and this started him on a chain of letters, each time he traced the owner the car had just been sold and he had to start again. He gave each one to whom he wrote a little of the car's previous history and, during all this correspondence, the various owners became, in Michael's own words, 'very matey with one another'. Eventually he caught up with it just after Mr Davis had sold it. He wrote at once to the dealer who had it, explaining his sentimental interest in the car, that his father had had the car built originally, had owned it when he died and that therefore he, Michael, would very much like to buy it back. However, he received only a curt note in reply, saying the car had been sold and was going abroad again, but would not divulge the name of the new owner.

However, by a lucky chance Michael discovered that the registration number was 5545 RH and from this was able to trace the owner, Mr Royston Tookey of Yorkshire. He replied to Michael's letter saying that he had bought the car to use whilst on leave, but that he had had trouble with the gearbox and had put it into Ristes Motors of Nottingham, who had removed the gearbox and sent it to Crewe for overhaul. When Mr Tookey heard the whole story he agreed to sell it back to Michael, who finally was able to bring his father's car home to Sussex.

In spite of the fact that it had had so many owners and such a varied life, the mileage was still only 120,000 and the Freestone & Webb body had stood up to the exacting conditions in Asia extremely well. The worst feature was the upholstery, so Michael had the entire car re-upholstered throughout in the same green hide as the original, he also re-united the car with the tools which he had removed from the boot when he heard that his mother was selling the car. She had been annoyed when she had discovered what she had done and Michael had difficulty in preventing her sending them on to the new owner but Michael pointed out that the car had been seen and bought without them, so she was persuaded to let him keep them.

He wanted the car exactly as it had been when his father had it including its original number, DGY 1, so he wrote to the London County Council explaining the situation, he had a reply saying it was a 'void' number and could not be re-issued. However, Michael was not going to be easily put off after his long and determined efforts. He wrote again to the London County Council and informed them that he had bought the car, not only out of sentiment, but also for historical reasons, as the car had been used by Field Marshal Montgomery during the War, when it had born the number DGY 1. Therefore unless it could have its original number, half the authenticity was lost. In the circumstances the County Council agreed to re-issue DGY 1, which number the car now bears.

Michael does not use the car a great deal but he did take it on one rally to Sweden, when it went extremely well. At the time of writing 3-AZ-186 is in Jersey and forms the central exhibit in the Jersey Motor Museum, which Michael opened last year and which is proving an enormous success.

As a quick reference the various owners of 3-AZ-186 are tabulated below:

1936 - 45 - F Wilcock	1956 - Lowe Motors
1945 - John Steel	1963 - H R Davis
1945 - Alfred Beaumont	1963 - Rolls-Royce Specialist
1945 - J A Green of Chelsea	1963 - Roystone Tookey
1945 - H R Owen	May 1964 - F M Wilcock
1956 - William Downes	

PART III CHAPTER 10

Plans are formulated, acting on Robotham's ideas of a rationalized range, 'Big Bertha' the intended replacement car for the Phantom III if War had not broken out in September 1939. Messrs Barker & Co, being taken over by Messrs Hooper & Co. The sale of various Phantom III chassis after War had been declared. The Phantom III Technical Society is formed in America with the object of preserving these wonderful cars

By 1937 it was quite obvious that some drastic alterations needed to be made in the Company's policy. In 1907, when Claude Johnson had put the 40/50 h p model on the map by his exploits in 'The Silver Ghost', his theory of having only one model in production had paid off and up until the outbreak of the Great War 1914 - 1918 the 40/50 h p car had shown a profit. However, gradually this policy had been abandoned until now, in 1937, the Company was building three different and very expensive chassis, the Phantom III, a 25/30 h p car and the Bentley 4¼ litre, the total sales of which were very small and the profits even less.

The Phantom III was in a class on its own, there was nothing made in Britain to equal it for smoothness, silence, top-gear performance and acceleration, but as far as the Company were concerned it was the most disastrous model financially which they had ever made; in fact it was losing money owing to the troubles encountered when it passed into the hands of private individuals.

The Daimler Company had also completely changed; their largest car was a 32 h p, overhead valve, push-rod operated Straight 8; the sleeve valve engine had completely disappeared and the big Straight 8 Daimler was offered in one length of wheelbase only; it was an exceedingly large car with dimensions almost identical to those of the Phantom III, but costing about £1,000 less when fitted with identical Hooper enclosed coachwork. However, it had a maximum speed of only 72 mph and, in spite of the fluid flywheel and self-changing gearbox, it did not really hold a candle to the Phantom III.

In the Experimental Department at Derby Robotham, who was most concerned about the future of the Company, suggested reverting to Royce's original practical policy before the 40/50 hp was built, that of saving production costs by designing different models which all used identical parts.

Using this principle, it was decided to build two prototype models, the first a big 7 passenger enclosed drive limousine, having a Straight 8 engine, which utilised all the same parts as a 6 cylinder engine which could be installed in the smaller chassis, leaving only the crankshaft, cylinder block and cylinder head to be made independently.

For the larger car the frame would be lengthened to accommodate five persons in the rear compartment, but axles, steering, etc. would be identical in both types; only the rear springing on the Straight 8 would have a greater poundage to carry the increased load.

Another innovation was also made, it was decided that a great many of the components would now be 'bought out' to save expense.

It was not until mid-1939, that both prototype cars were on the road, during which time the political situation in Europe had deteriorated very badly indeed; the Munich Crisis had come and gone and everyone knew that it was only a question of time before another major European War took place. For some time Hives had seen 'the writing on the wall' and, with his usual vision and foresight, had concentrated all his energies on winning contracts for aero-engine production and had left the matter of future car policy entirely in Robotham's extremely capable hands.

The Straight 8 was given the name 'Big Bertha' and there was an owner-driver Bentley version. In *Silver Ghost to Silver Dawn* Robotham tells the story of how he decided to take the two cars on to the Continent for extended testing, first on the German Autobahns for high speed and later into the Alps for manouevrability and hill climbing.

On the Autobahns 'Big Bertha' sailed along at a steady 90 mph, presenting no problems, the Bentley was very much faster and capable of cruising at well over the 100 mph mark, but the tyres of that time were not up to this sort of stress and about every 15 miles there was trouble.

Although private motoring ceased not long after the beginning of the War, Robotham, in charge of the car division, was determined that Rolls-Royce should not be caught out again as they were at the end of the 1914 War, with no new model to offer the public. As there was no means of telling what the situation would be after a world war of this magnitude a whole range of models were on the drawing board, ranging from an 8 h p 4 cylinder, 12 h p 4 cylinder, up to a large Straight 8 of over 30 h p; the names that some of these models were given were 'Ripple', 'Ripplet', etc., and the big car was 'Silver Phantom'. They felt that by having a wide variety of models they would be ready for anything and could meet whatever demand there was.

The outline drawing of all these models was based on that of the 1939 'Wraith' sports saloon with coachwork by Park Ward, built for the owner-driver, which incidentally is the bodywork upon which the first post-war Mark VI Bentley and Rolls-Royce 'Silver Dawn' is based.

Production of the Phantom III continued until 1939, but there was never any intention of continuing to build it after this. As can be seen from previous chapters the EX chassis were being disposed of in 1938, even after the outbreak of War there were still quite a number of brand new unused Phantom III chassis, complete with coachwork, standing unsold in a number of retailers showrooms. Most of these were shipped out to America to J S Inskip, Inc of New York, after the War in Europe had begun.

It is interesting to note that chassis No. 3-DL-186 and 3-DL-190 were originally intended intended for the Show Stand of the 1939 Earls Court Motor Show, which never took place.

3-DL-186 was a touring limousine with coachwork by Thrupp and Maberly, finished in pastel green with red lines and green leather interior with matching headcloth; the coachbuilders were instructed to prepare this car for the Rolls-Royce Company's Stand at Earls Court on 2 August 1939, but instead, on the 15 December 1939, the car was shipped out to New York to J S Inskip Inc aboard the Cunard White Star Liner *Lancastria*. On arrival, Inskip's sold the car to W Wallace Potter, Newport Avenue, Pawteket, Rhode Island.

3-DL-188 carried a Sedanca quarter light body by Hooper & Co, the car was finished in ivory and black with plain cloth to rear and fawn leather to front and was sold for £2,980 to J S Inskip Inc for the use of David H Marx, 990, Fifth Avenue, New York City. The car was shipped from London to New York aboard the S S *American Banker* on 24 October 1939.

3-DL-190 was sold on 25 June 1939 to Hooper & Co, for exhibition on their stand at the Earls Court Show of 1939; it also was to be a Sedanca quarter light, but having 'E' type steering in the place of 'C' type as on 3-DL-188. However, the coachwork for this car was never built and the chassis was re-sold with a price increase of £100 to Jack Barclay, who instructed James Young of Bromley to build a sports limousine on to it. However, owing to the all-out war effort, work on this chassis ceased and the car was not completed until 1945, the body price was £1,075. The completed vehicle was sent out to America to J S Inskip Inc as a stock car on sale or return; it was finished in metallic grey cellulose with chromium mouldings and dark pigskin upholstery. However, it was successfully sold to Dr Dennistoun M Bell, Broadview, Amagansett, Long Island, New York. Incidentally, both chassis Nos. 3-DL-188 and 3-DL-190 are now in the Rolls-Royce Owners' Club of America.

Chassis No. 3-CM-25 was bought by Windovers on 5 July 1937 for stock and they built a limousine de ville body on to this chassis, which remained unsold when War broke out. It was stored throughout the whole of the War and when hostilities ceased arrangements were made principally through the late Sir Winston Churchill, to make a presentation to King Ibn Saud of Arabia for all the help he had given in supporting the allied cause; it was decided that the presentation should take the form of a new Rolls-Royce car. When it was discovered that chassis No. 3-CM-25 was still unsold, the Windover limousine de ville coachwork was removed and the chassis was sent to Hooper & Co, who built a 4 door All Weather tourer with wind-down windows and concealed hood. It was most elaborately fitted with an electric fan, a built-in radio and a solid silver wash basin and hair brushes etc built in to the back of the front seat. It was the first body which Hooper & Co, built after the War.

A great change had taken place with Hooper & Co. Prior to the outbreak of War the principal shareholder in the old established business of Barker & Co, had wished to dispose of her shares. When this became known Rolls-Royce Ltd had been interested in acquiring Barker & Co, so that they had a coachbuilding business of their own, but they had not the necessary funds to carry out this transaction; instead Hooper & Co, who had a fine new factory at Park Royal on the Western Avenue, took over Barker & Co.

However in 1940, Hooper & Co, (now incorporating Barker & Co), were in turn taken over by the Daimler Co, whose chairman at the time was Sir Bernard Docker, who was principally responsible for arranging this transaction.

After this a few more Barker bodies were produced mounted only on Daimler chassis; they were made by some of Barker's old employees working in the Daimler Company's works at Coventry, principally for the D E 27 chassis during the late 1940s. Eventually the name Barker completely disappeared, but Hooper & Co, survived as part of the B S A Group still with their factory at Park Royal and exhibited at the Earls Court London Motor Show for the last time in 1959.

During the late 1940s and early 50s Britain was struggling to recover from the War economically. It was an austere and difficult time with a Labour Government in power. Sir Bernard Docker's wife, Norah, was on the Board of Daimler Company and took a great interest in the Company's affairs. She had the brilliant idea that what the public needed was a bit of glamour and excitement to lighten the load a little; she felt that a really eye-catching car at the Motor Show would be wonderful publicity for both Daimler and Hoopers. So she designed the series of 'Docker Daimlers' which became famous. One had gold plated fittings and gold stars on the coachwork with crocodile hide suitcases.* They made a terrific impact and Daimler sales received a boost. In fact, for the first time in history, the target of 10,000 cars sold in the year was reached - the Company was actually paying. Unfortunately, as so often happens, success breeds jealousy and there were forces in the Company working against them and eventually Sir Bernard was forced to resign, after which the Daimler Co, began to go downhill again and was finally taken over by Jaguars.

Since completing my original research, further information has come light which I included briefly here.

Quite recently two cars (unfortunately the chassis numbers are unknown) were found in a cellar in East Berlin, where they had been bricked-up; it would appear that they had been sent out to Germany before the War, probably to the coachbuilders Erdmann & Rossi, who never had an opportunity to mount coachwork on them. One is believed to have been airlifted from the Russian Sector and returned to England, it is not known what has happened to the other.

At the time of writing, most of the Phantom IIIs that survive in good order are in the United States, the owners are Members of the Rolls-Royce Owners' Club of America Inc. The cars will be preserved carefully for posterity as they have a tremendous following amongst those who appreciate really fine machinery. For this purpose a new Society was formed in 1971 within the Rolls-Royce Owners' Club of America. The prime movers behind this Society, which is known as the 'Phantom III Technical Society', are Dr Ned Estridge, a neuro-surgeon of California and Bob Schaffner of Mechanicsburg, Pennsylvania.

It was felt that the Phantom III will soon be

*Another was finished in grey and blue with four leaf clovers on the lower panels and was finished in lizard skin in place of the usual wood fillets

227

40 years old and most of the men who originally worked on these cars had either died or were living in retirement, whilst a new generation of enthusiasts had grown up who knew little or nothing about the inner workings of this model; so it was becoming more and more difficult to maintain the cars to the standard in which they were kept when new. It was therefore decided that a workshop manual to assist owners with their cars should be put together and this is now being done.

It will be the very first workshop manual ever produced for a pre-war Rolls-Royce, there has never been need of one before; in fact very few makes of cars had a workshop manual in pre-war days. As far as Rolls-Royce cars were concerned, any customer who wished to have work done on his or her chassis (which was beyond the power of a chauffeur who had been through the Rolls-Royce School of Instruction), returned the car to the London Service Station which was thoroughly familiar with the different models.

However, nowadays there are few people left who understand the pre-war cars, so Rolls-Royce Ltd, have co-operated to the full with Ned Estridge and Bob Schaffner by letting them have drawings and diagrams to illustrate this new workshop manual which will be of inestimable value to owners of Rolls-Royce Phantom IIIs.

The Phantom III is still a most wonderful car, every now and again one is tested by some motoring correspondent, in whose report it is sometimes possible to detect a slight disappointment in the model; but I cannot help feeling that those people are unfamiliar with the car, they forget how old it is now and they expect too much from it by comparing it with modern V12 engines, which, though smaller, give off considerably more brake horse power, while pulling far, far less weight.

There is no doubt about it, that in its day it was and in fact still is one of the most fabulous cars ever made.

APPENDIX A PART I
'Silver Ghost' & 'New Phantom'

The known cars which were named by Claude Johnson:

Chassis No. 24263 - 'Grey Ghost'. 4 cylinder 20 h p, 1905. This car was used by the Hon C S Rolls in April 1905 to practise for the Isle of Man T T.

Chassis No. 60542 - 'Prior's Pride'. The First named 40/50 h p, Index number R559. Short Chassis, Limousine by Barker.

Chassis No. 60551 - 'The Silver Ghost'. Index number AX 201. 'Trials Car'. Sold 14 July 1908 for £750. Returned to Rolls-Royce Ltd 1949.

Chassis No. 60583 - 'The Dreadnought'. Barker Limousine Landaulette sold to Miss Dodge, 25, St James Place, SW1 on 15 October 1907 and delivered to her on 17 March 1908 at Conduit Street, finished in black and green striping, light tan cloth, Index number AX 208. It would appear that later this became a Company car called 'The Dreadnought' and the Index number was changed to R 540. It was sold to Lord Devonport on 30 January 1914 when the Index number became R 1066.

Chassis no. 60726 'White Knave'. Index number R521. Roi-des-Belges by Barker finished in white with green leather and nickel fittings. Driven by Claude Johnson in 1908 Scottish Reliability Trials and retired with a seized piston. Sold 30 May 1911 for £650 to Frank Green Esq, Treasurers House, York. This chassis seems to have been a very temperamental one as not only did it 'play up' with CJ, but later the differential case in the rear axle had to be changed owing to leaking oil.

Chassis No. 60737 - 'Silver Rogue'. Index number R 522. Driven by Percy Northey to first place in 1908 Scottish Reliability Trial. Sold 10 April 1909 at Conduit Street, sale price £1,150. The Rudge Whitworth wire wheels were changed for wooden spoked artillery before the sale.

Chassis No. 60779 - 'Silver Silence'. Index number R 577. 'Trials Car'. Roi-des-Belges finished in Silver with green leather. Sold 26 July 1909 for £900 to John P Dixon, The Mount, Great Marton, Lancashire.

Chassis No. 60785 - 'The Cookie'. Index number R 535. This was the Hon C S Rolls famous Balloon Car. Car delivered to C S R of South Lodge, Knightsbridge, London SW1 on 28 October 1908 at Derby. The Rudge Whitworth wire wheels came from Chassis No. 60707 and when C S R sold this car before his death, it was converted to wooden artillery wheels.

Chassis No. 1100 - 'The Silver Phantom'. Index number R 567. 'Trials Car' used by Claude Johnson all over the Highlands of Scotland. Barker Roi-des-Belges finished in silver with green leather. It was sold for £600 on 30 January 1914, having been re-painted dark green and fitted with Frankonia curved wings, to a gentleman named Warre.

Chassis No. 1106. 'Silver Phantom'. Index number R 724. 'Trials Car'. Used by Claude Johnson. Special Barker Roi-des-Belges finished in aluminium with dark green morocco leather. Sold 12 November 1910 for £900 to H L Pickles Esq, Rooks Mount, Nr Halifax for delivery 15 November 1910. Car delivered 26 November 1910 at Conduit Street - driven away by Mr Pickles.

Chassis No. 1162. - 'The Charmer'. Index number R 568. Barker double enclosed Pullman Limousine formerly used by Percy Northey as a 'Trials Car', but later used by Claude Johnson as personal transport. Took Royce to Le Canadel for first time.

Chassis No. 1423. - 'The Whisperer'. Index number R 1050. Formerly Mr Hanbury's 'Trials Car' later 'French Trials'. Double Coupe (inside driving) coachwork by Labourdette, finished in green, lined in yellow and black. Fitted with Vinet detachable rims and two spare wheels.

Chassis No. 1601. - 'Silver Spectre'. Index number R 859. Claude Johnson 'Trials Car'. Double Coupe inside driving coachwork by Labourdette, finished in silver, upholstered in green leather. Vinet detachable rims and two spare wheels. Sold for £1,073.3.5d on 7 April 1915 to the War Office after the original body had been removed and a Barker Pullman Limousine finished in grey throughout had been fitted and the wheels had been changed to Rudge Whitworth wires with two spare wheels and a Lucas electric nickel plated lighting set had been fitted.

Chassis No. 1826E - 'The Mystery'. Index number R 1265. 'Trials Car' used by Claude Johnson, open tourer London/Edinburgh type. Coachwork by Holmes of Derby finished in grey. Sold 7 July 1915 for £950 to Lieutenant Beardmore, Hotel Cecil, London.

The naming of certain motor cars goes back to long before Rolls-Royce Ltd came into being, when Claude Johnson was the first Secretary of the Automobile Club of Great Britain and Ireland, he had a 7 h p New Orleans which he named 'The Sluggard'. A number of other Rolls-Royce owners gave their cars a name, one of the best known being owned by the first Lord Montagu of Beaulieu which was an open touring 40/50 named 'The Dragonfly' Index number AA 19.

The first known chassis numbers of the 40/50 h p car are given in Part I, Chapter 2, so there is no need to record them here, but the last six of the 'Silver Ghost' type to be built are as follows:

120 EU - Index numberXY 6932. Barker 7-seater open tourer. 'D' type steering. Chassis sold 19.12.24 to John Henry Thomas; now owned by John Hampton of the R.R.E.C.

121 EU - Long chassis open tourer Australian body, sold to Dalgety & Co for Sir George Tallis. Chassis shipped Melbourne 31.1.25 by *Port Porie*.

122 EU - Index number XY 4893. Long chassis, Windover enclosed drive limousine. Sold 11.8.24 to W S Robinson, Esq, 3 Mansfield Street, London, W1.

123 EU - Index number PM 7921. Long chassis, enclosed drive cabriolet by Hooper. 'C' type steering. Grey and black. Sold on 7.11.23 T H C Mackenzie Esq, Beacon Hotel, Crowborough. Car delivered 6.5.25.

124 EU - Long chassis enclosed drive limousine. American coachwork. R-R Inc 'C' type steering. For Mrs F E Lewis, sold 20.11.24. Chassis shipped 2.5.25. Liverpool/New York aboard *Celtic*.

125 EU - Short chassis, sold 18.12.25 to R-R Inc for J F Carlisle. Enclosed drive limousine American coachwork. Chassis shipped Liverpool/New York aboard *Laconia*.

126 EU - 28.3.25. Park Ward limousine. Sold to Mr Gill, 30 Victoria Park Road, Kensington, London, W8 and 23 Austin Friars, London, EC2.

First six 'New Phantom' Chassis

1 MC - Sold 16.12.24 to Car Mart Ltd for Mrs Waldock, Imperial Hotel, London, WC. 'D' type steering. Barker ¾ coupe with dickey.

2 MC - Sold 28.12.24. Long chassis, 'C' type steering. Limousine by Jonexon of Paris. For Pascudol S de Vieuna, Madrid.

3 MC - Long chassis, 'A' type steering. Enclosed cabriolet by Hooper. For Mlle Luz Bringas, Paris.

4 MC - Sold 10.9.24 to William Gibbs, Esq, 5 Marine Parade, Penarth, Glam. Long chassis, 'B' type steering. Enclosed drive limousine by Hooper.

5 MC - Sold 18.11.24 to Barker & Co. Long chassis, 'D' type steering. Brougham cabriolet. Demonstration.

6 MC - Sold 22.1.25. Barker cabriolet de ville. Long chassis, 'D' type steering. For Mr W Whitworth, The Homestead, Disley.

It is interesting to note that all these chassis were sold some six months before the 'New Phantom' was announced, they were obviously orders that had been taken in the ordinary way and the owners did not know exactly what sort of model they would receive when delivery took place. Ron Haynes says that a number of the early 'New Phantoms' started life in the erection shop with the old 'Silver Ghost' type of engine, but these were removed and the later 'New Phantom' engine was installed. Almost every single one of the above chassis was delivered to the coachbuilders in mid-June 1925 from Lillie Hall, with the exception of 6 MC which was delivered to Barker's by road from Lillie Hall on the 29.5.25.

Last six 'New Phantom' chassis

86 OR - Sold to Thos. Wolfe & Son, London, WC1. Long chassis, 'C' type steering. To Gill 27.8.29. Saloon landaulette by Gill.

87 OR - Sold 17.5.29 for Jose Arnat, Barcelona, Spain. Long chassis, 'E' type steering. Spanish body, fixed head cabriolet de ville, Baltoser Fiol.

88 OR - Sold 12.6.29. Windover, but cancelled.

89 OR - Long chassis, 'C' type steering. Sold 1.3.30 to Aros Ltd, Bush House, London, WC2. Enclosed limousine by Park Ward.

90 OR - Sold 12.6.29. Windover Ltd. Sedanca body. Long chassis, 'E' type steering. But order withdrawn. Sold 16.7.29 to Car Mart for Frank C Minoprin, Avening Court, Avening, Gloucester. Weymann saloon by H J Mulliner, 4-light.

91 OR - Sold 27.9.29 to Franz Norstrand, Copenhagen. Long chassis, 'E' type steering. Sedanca by Letouraeur & Marchand.

'New Phantoms' exhibited at the Olympia Motor Show
9-17 October 1925.

Rolls-Royce (Stand 183)	One Chassis. One Limousine.
Barker & Co Ltd (153)	Cabriolet de Ville in polished grey walnut exterior, Grey suede calfskin hide to rear interior compartment. Open Torpedo Tourer in polished aluminium.
Joseph Cockshoot (154)	Saloon limousine finished in brownish carmine with leather interior to match.
Hooper & Co Ltd (115)	Saloon limousine in grey and black, dark grey leather to front, suede velvet calfskin to rear.
Arthur Mulliner Ltd (134)	Limousine in all black, fine lined in white. Curved sliding division with grey cloth interior to rear.
Rippon Bros Ltd (194)	Limousine in royal blue; silver-plated fittings leather to front, cloth to rear disappearing occasional seats with an oval table and built-in toilet requisites.
Thrupp & Maberly (151)	Limousine in fancy patterned cloth with silver and ivory fittings.
Windovers Ltd (132)	Enclosed limousine of angular lines of the Brougham pattern, painted black with straw line and upholstered in fawn plain cloth. Chassis No 33RC.

Eight exhibits in all, plus one chassis.

The ROLLS-ROYCE 40/50 hp

Olympia Motor Show, 22-30 October 1926

Rolls-Royce (Stand 105)	Enclosed drive limousine by Hooper & Co in dove and black - £2,957.
	Barker enclosed cabriolet de ville in dark blue and black - £3,018.
Barker & Co Ltd (74)	Sedanca limousine de ville, quarters in black leather, finished in oak graining, brown leather to front, suede calf interior to rear.
Carroserie Kellner (150)	Cabriolet de ville, 4-door 6-light, described as Coupe de ville, folding quarter lights on account of wheel arches. Maccassar wood work, cloth upholstery.
Joseph Cockshoot (125)	Enclosed limousine in primrose and black. West of England cloth to rear, mahogany woodwork.
Hooper & Co Ltd (88)	Enclosed cabriolet de ville with interior exhaust heater.
Arthur Mulliner (72)	Vee fronted limousine in two shades of blue, interior in silk tapestry and burr walnut. Chassis No 30YC.
Rippon Bros (121)	Enclosed limousine.
Thrupp & Maberly (55)	Enclosed limousine in black with fine white lines.
Windovers Ltd (90)	Enclosed limousine with gold interior fittings.

Ten Exhibits in all.

Olympia Motor Show, 13-22 October 1927

Rolls-Royce (Stand 68)	Barker sedanca landaulet de ville - £3,301. Chassis number 34 RF.
	Hooper limousine with drop partition - £2,906.
Barker & Co Ltd (110)	An open sporting boat-tailed tourer, finished in black with flared wings lined in red with red leather upholstery and polished aluminium top deck. Chassis No. 35 RF.
	Sedanca limousine de ville, specially built for the Prince of Wales.
Joseph Cockshoot (122)	Enclosed drive limousine finished in dark blue. Chassis No. 39 RF.
Hooper & Co Ltd (54)	Sedanca cabriolet de ville. Chassis No. 33 RF.
Arthur Mulliner (72)	Cabriolet coupe de ville finished in two shades of blue, the interior door handles are in silver gilt and the upholstery in blue tapestry. Chassis No. 41 RF.
Rippon Bros (87)	Enclosed drive limousine finished in dark blue and black with silver-plated interior fittings. Chassis No. 40 RF.
Thrupp & Maberly (111)	Enclosed drive landaulet in all black with soft fawn cloth upholstery. Chassis No. 52 RF.
Windovers Ltd (73)	Landaulet all weather coupe de ville style. Enclosed drive limousine painted black with fine yellow lines, upholstered in plain fawn cloth. Chassis No. 38 RF.

Note: Park Ward & Co were unsuccessful in the Ballot for a stand at Olympia; the only representative example of their coachwork appeared on Stand No. 8, on which a 6-cylinder 31 h p Excelsior, a Belgian car, was displayed.

Eleven 'New Phantoms' in all

(Top) 3-AZ-100, a Hooper Enclosed Drive Landaulette supplied to the Earl of Derby
(Middle) 3-AZ-132, a Two Seater Coupe built to the order of Vincent Hemery Esq, by H. J. Mulliner (photo R. D. Shaffner)
(Bottom) 3-AZ-134, an Arthur Mulliner Enclosed Drive Limousine supplied to the order of Miss V. E. Wills, who ordered two spare wheels and no mascot. This car was the first Phantom III in which the author rode with six other passengers ; the car exceeded 98 mph across Ditchling Common in Sussex (photo R. D. Shaffner)

(Top) A 6/7 passenger
Hooper Enclosed Limousine,
chassis number 3-AZ-144 supplied
to Martin H. Benson Esq
(Middle) Osmond Rivers, who was
Hooper and Company Limited's
chief designer, made these drawings
of an Enclosed Limousine to the
order of Miss Harriet Maconochie
and the completed coachwork was
mounted on Phantom III chassis
number 3-AZ-146. See Part III,
Chapter 8
(Bottom) Hooper photograph of
the completed car 3-AZ-146 taken
before delivery to its owner. See
Part III, Chapter 8

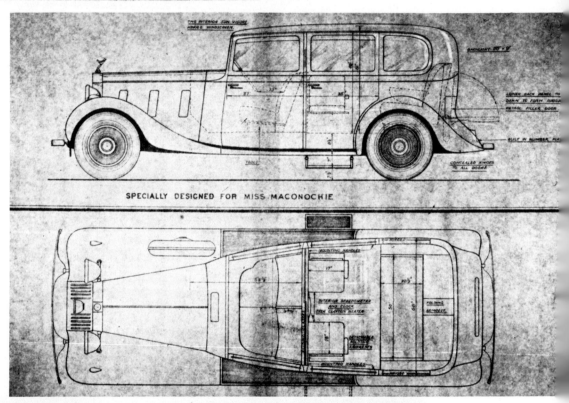

SPECIALLY DESIGNED FOR MISS MACONOCHIE

(*Top left and right*) The interior of 3-AZ-146. See Part III, Chapter 8

(*Middle*) Chassis number 3-AZ-146 outside the Head Office of Rolls-Royce Limited in Moor Lane, Derby in July 1965. The car is finished in dark navy blue with black top and wings and gold line around the coachwork, as it had been repainted for Mrs Bower Ismay in April 1939. See Part III, Chapter 8

(*Bottom*) 3-AZ-148, a Barker Enclosed Limousine with 'E' type steering as supplied to Sir Pomeroy Burton (*photo S. J. Skinner*)

Top) A Freestone and Webb Drophead Sedanca Foursome Coupe on chassis number 3-AZ-174 *(photo Norris Allen)*

Middle left) At the age of 9 Michael Wilcock photographed his father's car at the summit of the Glossglockner, 8,212 feet, in August 1937. The picture shows 3-AZ-186 with the engine boiling. See Part III, Chapter 9 *(photo M. Wilcock)*

Middle right) Chassis number 3-AZ-186 fitted with Freestone & Webb Touring Limousine coachwork, photographed in Jersey, having passed through the hands of numerous owners. It is now owned by F. M. Wilcock, the son of the original owner, who has the car on display in his Jersey Motor Museum. See Part III, Chapter 9

Bottom) 3-AZ-120, a Barker Enclosed Limousine with 'F' type steering built for Commodore Louis Beaumont of Paris *(photo S. J. Skinner)*

(Top) 3-AZ-218, a Barker Sedancalette
de Ville with 'E' type steering built
for Mrs E. C. Snagge, the mother of
John Snagge, the well-known BBC
commentator

(Upper middle) 3-AZ-232 Hooper
Limousine with 'C' type steering
built to the order of the Duke of
Devonshire

(Lower middle) 3-AX-45, a Barker
Enclosed Limousine with 'E' type
steering and extra forward facing
seats. It was sold to Major Sidney
Griffiths of Park Lane, W1 (photo
S. J. Skinner)

(Bottom) An H. J. Mulliner Sports
Limousine on chassis number
3-AX-79 was ordered by S. A.
Butler of Hyde Park Garden, W2.
It was used by Lord Gart as a Staff
car at the beginning of the war
in September 1939. It was later
used by General Montgomery
and became his own property. The
car is now in America

(Top) 3-AX-87 is a Barker Saloon with
'F' type steering raised 1 inch above
normal for HH The Nawab of Bahawalpur
(photo S. J. Skinner)

(Upper middle) 3-AX-97 Barker Enclosed
Laudaulette was built to the special
requirements of Sir John Latta, Chairman
of the Lawther, Latta Steamship Company,
who thought that Captain Stanley Lord of
the SS Californian, belonging to the Leyland
Line was very unfairly treated when he was
dismissed after the sinking of the Titanic;
later Sir John Latta made Stanley Lord
Commodore of his fleet

(Lower middle) A Barker Enclosed
Limousine on chassis number 3-AX-121
(photo S. J. Skinner)

(Bottom) Major J. O. K. Delap of Kenya
purchased this Hooper Owner Driver
Sports Saloon on chassis number 3-AX-199.
It was delivered in February 1937

(Top) The Major J. O. K. Delap car
3-AX-199 (photo S. J. Skinner)
(Upper middle) 3-AX-201 is a Hooper
Enclosed Limousine with a sun-roof
ordered by HH The Maharajah
Gackwar of Baroda
(Lower middle) 3-BU-18 is a Hooper
Sports Enclosed Limousine for 4/5
passengers sold to J. Craig Murray of
Queen Anne's Gate, SW1
(Bottom) Built for HH the Aga Khan
on chassis 3-BU-68 was this Hooper
Sedanca de Ville

(Top) 3-BU-124 Barker Enclosed Laudaulette with 'C' type steering built to the order of E. R. Makower Esq of 75, Brook Street, London W1

(Upper middle) This Barker Tourer was ordered by HH The Maharajah of Kolhapur on chassis number 3-BU-134. Finished in cream with a fawn hood, it had 'E' type steering and extra forward facing seats

(Lower middle) This Barker Sedancalette on chassis number 3-BU-168 had black finish bumpers and lamps and was supplied to Lord Fairhaven

(Bottom) 3-BU-168 with a new body in America. This car was used in the James Bond film Goldfinger (photo R. D. Shaffner)

Olympia Motor Show, 11-20 October 1928

Rolls-Royce (Stand 128)	No 'New Phantoms' are described in this stand in *The Autocar*, but the report reads that two cars were exhibited with improvements in the form of a new type of cylinder head. Shutters re-set into the radiator. A new patent type of Rolls-Royce shock damper is now fitted.
	Hooper Sedanca, Chassis No. 14 CL
	Barker Limousine, Chassis No. 15 CL.
Barker & Co Ltd (54)	Sedanca de ville in yellow and black. Chassis No. 20 CL.
	Pullman Limousine de ville in yellow and black. Chassis No. 25 CL.
Joseph Cockshoot (110)	An enclosed limousine in brown and black. Chassis No. 18 CL.
Connaught Motor & Carriage Co (109)	An enclosed drive limousine in blue cellulose with exterior fittings in Firth's Stainless Steel. Chassis No. 46 FH.
Hooper & Co Ltd (108)	Sedanca de ville in green and black. Upholstered in brown woven leather to rear seats with ebony woodwork and front seats in brown lizard skin. Chassis No. 21 CL.
Mann, Egerton (141)	Coupe de ville in amaranth red and black with blue and gold tapestry and silver-plated fittings to rear compartment. Chassis No. 23 CL.
Arthur Mulliner (70)	Enclosed drive limousine with staggered V–screen, the exterior finish in blue and black with silver-plated fittings, while the interior is upholstered in tapestry with dull gold fittings. Chassis No. 22 CL.
Rippon Bros (119)	Enclosed drive landaulet finished in black lined in white. The interior is fawn cloth, all interior fittings are silver-plated. Chassis No. 17 CL.
Thrupp & Maberly (122)	Enclosed drive limousine de ville finished in black and trimmed in Box Cloth with silver-plated fittings.
Windovers Ltd (121)	Enclosed drive limousine finished in black and lined in white. Chassis No. 16 CL.

Twelve 'New Phantoms' in all.

Production List of 'New Phantoms' chassis showing years produced
and modifications made during production run, May 1925 - September 1929

1925	MC	1–122	except 12 UMC, 45 MC (Ex 73 MC), 55 MC (Ex 81 MC); 12 UMC was formerly 46 PK. Additional chassis MC 145.
1925	RC	1–125	
1925	HC	1–109	All above Chassis are V series.
1925	HC	110–122	Radiator 1 in. higher.
1925/6	LC	1–131	
1926	SC	1–7	This series and from HC 110 are W.
1926	SC	8–121	SC 38 erected as 121 SC.
1926	DC	1–87	X series.
1926	DC	88–121	Y series. .720 Lead Steering 38 TC.
1926	TC	1–70	
1926	TC	71–121	AZA Tubular Luggage Grid. 106 TC re-numbered 122 YC.
1926	YC	1–50	AZA Tubular Luggage Grid.
1926	YC	51–123	AZB Servo Damping ring. 59 YC. YC 95 re-numbered 119 NC.
1926	NC	1–30	

233

1926	NC	31–131	B2 Autovac Restriction Valve. Front hydraulics S/D. Light clutch.
1927	EF	1–101	C2A Right Brg. throttle. light front axle; 3-gallon reserve; SL x stg. tube; well base wheels 7.00 x 21 tyres.
1927	LF	1–101	C2B Servo friction device; tappet lub.; 65 LF. 10 LF re-numbered 102 LF,
1927	RF	1–101	D2A Rear hydraulics. New side levers.
1927	UF	1–101	D2B Silencer heat shield, 79 UF, UF 77 re-numbered 102 EH.
1927	EH	1–101	E2A Tungsten, 37 EH; strutted cylinders, 73 EH.
1928	FH	1–101	E2B.
1928	AL	1–101	F2A Axle control dampers; stiffer crankshaft; semi-rigid dist. cont.; choke valve lub. Note: AL 23 Company car for Lord Wargrave, No Guarantee. AL 100 for Cox's use, no guarantee.
1928	CL	1–101	F2B Aluminium cylinder head; rear spare wheel carrier; chassis frame extended at rear, see drawing. 20 in. pendulum lever.
1928	WR	1–101	G2A Flexible engine suspension.
1928	WR	102–131	G2B Cast dash; side by side brakes; Zenith petrol filter; radiator 1 in. higher; battery in frame; felt pads. 1 KR.
1929	KR	1–71	As above.
1929	KR	72–131	H2 Cadnium plated springs. 19 OR.
1929	OR	1–90	As above. 31 OR not erected.

Number of 'Ne wPhantoms' actually built: 2,257.

The figure '13' not used in any series.

In addition, there were 10 Experimental chassis built, these were numbered 7-17 EX inclusive, but excluding 13; they were known as E A C, which stands for Eastern Armoured Car.

The following information is taken from the Rolls-Royce Owners' Club of America's Magazine *The Flying Lady*, the full text of which appears on pages 227, 228 and 229 of that magazine:-

Springfield 'New Phantom' Chassis

1926	S	400–465	FL	Ohv iron cylinder head. Central lubrication. Autovac. Four wheel brakes.
1927	S	66–200	PM	Four wheel brakes. Servo operated.
1927	S	201–300	RM	
1927	S	301–400	FM	De Jon Ignition from S 336 FM.
1928	S	101–200	RP	
1928	S	201–300	FP	
1928	S	301–400	KP	7.00 x 20 tyres. External valances.
1929	S	101–200	FR	Aluminium cylinder head. Chromium plating.
1929	S	201–300	KR	Conical lamps, flat bumpers, automatic shutters, swinging trunk rack.
1929	S	301–400	LR	
1930	S	401–500	MR	
1930/1	S	191–241	PR	

Number produced: 1,240 at Springfield.

The 'New Phantom' went into production at Springfield in September 1926, just 16 months after production of the model started at Derby.

The first 66 cars delivered did not have 4-wheel brakes, most were recalled and modified later. A centralized chassis lubrication system was fitted from the beginning. Most Springfield built 'New Phantoms' carried coachwork built by Brewster, an old established body builder whom Rolls-Royce purchased in 1926. Like the Derby-built car the early 'New Phantoms' were fitted with iron cylinder heads; in July 1928 the Derby-built 'New Phantom' was fitted with an aluminium cylinder head and the Springfield one followed suit in December 1929.

The best production year for the Springfield 'New Phantom' was 1928, when 400 units were sold, this dropped in 1929 to 200 units owing to the Slump, then with the introduction at Derby of the Phantom II in September 1929 most people preferred the Derby-built Phantom II and production of the Springfield 'New Phantom' finally ceased in January 1931. Later, a specially built Phantom II with centre change and left-hand drive was built at the Derby works for the American market.

Not withstanding this, in my opinion a late type Springfield 'New Phantom' is a most desirable car to own and one of the best in the whole range, although little known to most English enthusiasts for the 'New Phantom'.

APPENDIX A PART II
Phantom II

First six 'Phantom II' chassis

1 WJ - 'Trials Car'. Close coupled saloon by Barker. Long chassis, 'E' type steering. Duplicate of 18 EX, 19 EX, 24 EX and 14 WJ. Laid down as 24 EX.

2 WJ - 'Trials Car'. Enclosed drive limousine by Hooper. Long chassis, 'C' type steering. Body laid down for 26 EX.

3 WJ - 'Trials Car'. Open touring by Barker. Long chassis, 'E' type steering.

4 WJ - Paris Show, R-R Stand. Saloon limousine by Hooper. Long chassis, 'E' type steering.

5 WJ - Paris Show R-R Stand. Sedanca de ville by Barker. Long chassis, 'D' type steering.

6 WJ - Paris Show (Olympia Erased). Date of Sale: 22.5.29, to Barker & Co for Mrs Kruse, Sunningdale. Sports sedanca by Barker. Standard chassis? 'E' type steering.

Last six 'Phantom II' chassis

76 UK - Sold 13.7.35 to Springfield Corp for A L Humer, Lake End, Rhode Island, New York. U S coachwork. Shipped as chassis Liverpool/New York aboard *Laconia*. Long wheelbase. 'E' type steering. Now in R R O C Inc. Brewster Town Car.

78 UK - Sold 12.7.35 to Hooper & Co for The Earl of Inchcape. Long chassis, 'E' type steering. Enclosed limousine de ville.

80 UK - Sold 20.8.35 to Maharajah of Jodhpur. Long chassis, 'E' type steering. Coupe body by Windover.

82 UK - Sold 16.7.35 to Lancefield Coachwork for Sir A Lindsay Parkinson, JP, Royal Bank, Blackpool. Long chassis, 'D' type steering. Enclosed drive limousine by Lancefield Coachworks.

84 UK - Sold 18.6.36 Barker & Co for The Dowager Lady Fox, Greys, Puttenham, Guildford. Long chassis, 'C' type steering. Enclosed limousine, now owned by T Mason, Esq.

Note: 84 UK was a very special order, production of the Phantom II ceased in June 1935 and this chassis was not ordered by Lady Fox until the date that it was sold. It came off test on 15 October 1936, and was delivered by road to Barker & Co from Lillie Hall the following day. There is a note on the Body Card which reads: *N.B.* Chassis will be similar to the 'U' series type.

Cars Exhibited at the Olympia Motor Show, 17-26 October 1929

Rolls-Royce (Stand 53)

No actual details of the two cars exhibited are given, the whole description in *The Autocar* centres on the announcement of the new model, the Phantom II, which it says has been radically altered and is one of the outstanding exhibits of the show.
Barker Saloon. Chassis No. 14 WJ.
Hooper Limousine. Chassis No. 15 WJ.

Barker & Co Ltd (113)

A Pullman limousine de ville finished in ivory and blue, all bright fittings in silver-plate and upholstered in Sandstone cloth. Chassis No. 16 WJ.

Sports torpedo cabriolet with concealed hood, which when lowered forms an attractice sports torpedo, the colour scheme is ivory, white and blue. Chassis No. 23 WJ.

Note: All the cars on the Barker stand were finished in ivory, white and blue this year, which made a fine splash of colour; the third car was a 35/120 Daimler enclosed drive pullman limousine with sunshine roo f to the rear compartment, trimmed in Sandstone cloth.

Joseph Cockshoot (132)

Enclosed drive limousine finished in blue and black. Chassis No. 19 WJ.

Hooper & Co Ltd (85)

Sedanca de ville, sunshine roof to rear compartment. This is coach-painted pastel blue on the body panels, the remainder in black cellulose. Woodwork is Ebony veneer, fittings silver and ivory. Chassis No 17 WJ.

Arthur Mulliner (65)

Enclosed drive limousine painted blue and black, trimmed in tapestry with dull gold fittings. Chassis No. 21 WJ.

Park Ward (77)

Enclosed limousine de ville finished in ivory and black, upholstered in plain cloth. Chassis No. 24 WJ.

Rippon Bros (68)

Enclosed drive limousine finished in ivory and black with Vee windscreen, upholstered in West of England cloth. Chassis No. 20 WJ.

Thrupp & Maberly (101)

Limousine de ville enclosed drive with adjustable driving seat. Chassis No. 18 WJ.

Windovers Ltd (67)

Enclosed drive limousine finished in black, front seat in brown leather, rear in fawn cloth, silver and ivory fittings. Chassis No. 22 WJ.

Eleven cars in all.

Olympia Motor Show, 16-25 October 1930

Rolls-Royce (Stand 58)

Hooper sedanca de ville, £3,054. Chassis No. 90 GY.

Barker enclosed limousine, £3,018. Chassis No. 83 GY.

Thrupp & Maberly convertible, £2,952. Chassis No. 91 GY.

Barker & Co Ltd (123)	Semi-sports torpedo cabriolet painted blue (Ulster) with polished aluminium top deck and top scuttle panels and bonnet. Concealed hood. Chassis No. 92 GY.
Hooper & Co Ltd (104)	Enclosed drive Pullman limousine de ville finished in blue and black and upholstered in woven brown leather with silver-plated interior fittings and ebony woodwork. Chassis No. 95 GY.
Arthur Mulliner (61)	Enclosed drive limousine finished in blue and black, upholstered in tapestry. Chassis No. 101 GY.
H J Mulliner (105)	Weymann semi-panelled touring limousine with a partially sliding roof over the front compartment.
Park Ward (71)	Limousine de ville finished in Suffolk green and black mouldings and wings, front seat in green crushed grain leather, rear compartment in West of England cloth. Chassis No. 105 GY.
Rippon Bros (101)	Enclosed limousine with revolving armchair seats. Chassis No. 71 GY.
Thrupp & Maberly (77)	Enclosed limousine finished in black, fine lined in red, upholstered in West of England cloth. Chassis No. 100 GY.
Windovers Ltd (63)	Sedanca de ville finished in black and white. Chassis No. 96 GY.

Eleven cars in all.

Olympia Motor Show, 15-24 October 1931

Rolls-Royce (Stand 132)	Continental touring saloon, £2,675. Chassis No. 11 JS.
	Pullman limousine, £2,825. Chassis No. 10 JS.
Barker & Co Ltd (142)	Continental type sports saloon. The lower panels were finished in black. the upper ones in ivory. The car had a swept tail with two spare wheels recessed upright in the sloping tail, which makes it appear incredibly ugly. Chassis No. 12 JS.
Hooper & Co. Ltd (103)	Enclosed drive limousine de ville finished in black, lined in green, upholstered in brown cloth.
Arthur Mulliner (92)	Enclosed drive limousine finished in blue and black, with blue woven cloth interior.
Rippon Bros (125)	Enclosed drive limousine finished in ivory and black with revolving armchair seats, upholstered in fawn cloth with an oval rear window.
Thrupp & Maberly (93)	Continental sports saloon finished in green and cream, upholstered in green leather with light beige headcloth and woodwork in Italian laurel. (This is a very handsome car).
Windovers Ltd (116)	Enclosed drive limousine finished in claret and black, upholstered in cloth.

Eight cars in all.

Note: There were only 8 Phantom IIs exhibited. This was no doubt due to the world economic depression

Olympia Motor Show, 14-22 October 1932

Rolls-Royce (Stand 41)	Continental touring saloon by Barker, finished in blue with chromium plated disc wheels.
	Enclosed drive limousine.
Barker & Co. Ltd (191)	Sedanca de ville in black lined in white with built-in luggage container.
Hooper & Co. Ltd (192)	Continental touring saloon in two shades of blue. Telescopic direction indicators, well shaped boot, illuminated rear number plate.
Park Ward (178)	Continental touring saloon, rear wings in form of outside halves only. Boot with rear mounted spare wheel. Four suitcases. Two sets of golf clubs withdrawn through opening in side of boot. Finished in black with blue leather.
Rippon Bros (189)	Enclosed limousine in black lined in white, dark blue leather to front and cloth to rear. Armchair revolving occasional seats.
Windovers Ltd (206)	Sedanca de ville with streamline wings and platforms finished in two shades of grey with blue wings and chassis. Trimmed in Vaumol leather.
	Seven cars exhibited in all

Note: The number of Continental chassis now predominate, but there are only 7 exhibits, the lowest number of 40/50 chassis shown since the 'New Phantom' example came into being in 1925.

Olympia Motor Show, 12-21 October 1933

Rolls-Royce (Stand 127)	Barker Continental touring saloon, £2,471.
	Hooper Pullman limousine, £2,490. Chassis No. 8 PY.
	(Improvements for new models: built-in jacking system. New type carburettor. Complete chassis lubrication. Higher compression).
Barker & Co. Ltd (25)	Sedanca de ville in black with chrome strip to waist. Chassis No. 18 PY.
Hooper & Co. Ltd (18)	Enclosed limousine finished in blue and black with new type telescopic direction indicators and concealed luggage grid. Chassis No. 20 PY.
Arthur Mulliner (17)	Sports limousine, 4-light, with dummy hood irons. Tapestry upholstery. Finished in blue and black. Chassis No. 12 PY.
H J Mulliner (12)	Sedanca de ville with new type of sliding sedanca front and cant rails finished in black. Chassis No. 14 PY.
Park Ward & Co. (15)	Continental touring saloon with division. Chassis No. 24 PY. Note: This was Laurie Dalton's car; it is now in Eire.
Rippon Bros (27)	Enclosed limousine in black with fine white lines, sliding roof to the front compartment. Chassis No. 10 PY.
Thrupp & Maberly (24)	Continental touring saloon in two shades of grey. Rear mounted spare wheel with Ace cover. Chassis No. 22 PY. *Note:* This car was at Wilkinsons in Derby when 74 GN was there having her present Victoria 5-seat coupe body built in 1968. It was a complete wreck being re-built.
Windovers Ltd (26)	Sedanca de ville in two shades of blue. Pullman-type arm-rests, two spare wheels with Ace covers and built-in luggage trunk at rear with its own cases. Chassis No. 16 PY.

Note: It will be noticed that the number of exhibits had gone up again to 10.

Olympia Motor Show, 11-20 October 1934
The last Show at which the Phantom II appeared

Rolls-Royce (Stand 116)	Pullman limousine by Hooper. Chassis No. 72 SK.
	Continental touring saloon by Barker. Chassis No. 70 SK.
Barker & Co. Ltd (21)	Sedanca de ville with cloth interior. Chassis No. 74 SK.
Hooper & Co. Ltd (20)	Sedanca de ville to seat seven, finished in black. Chassis No. 76 SK.
Arthur Mulliner (19)	Sports limousine finished in light blue and silver. Chassis No. 80 SK.
H J Mulliner (27)	Sports touring limousine. Chassis No. 84 SK.
Park Ward (24)	Streamlined 6-light saloon finished in black with coronation red mouldings and red upholstery. Chassis No. 86 SK.
Rippon Bros (33)	Enclosed drive limousine finished in black with plain white lines. Chassis No. 82 SK.
Thrupp & Maberly (22)	Continental sports saloon finished in two shades of grey. Chassis No. 88 SK.
Windovers Ltd (26)	Touring limousine in pastel blue with inset stainless steel mouldings with fine red line, upholstered throughout in soft hide. Chassis No. 66 SK.

Ten cars in all.

The Phantom II Continentals

The following Phantom II chassis numbers were despatched as Continentals. All are on the short chassis of 12 ft wheelbase, except the 4 marked with an asterisk which were to special order on the long 12 ft 6 in. wheelbase.

A Continental Phantom II is one which has the special five thick leaves to the springs, 'F'-type steering in practically every case, and the axle ratio of 12 x 41, instead of the standard ratio of 11 x 41.

This list is taken from details supplied by Rolls-Royce Ltd many years ago, and ties in with the list supplied by the Rolls-Royce Owners' Club of America, Inc.

1930	26 EX (prototype)	1931	51 GX		1931	256 AJS	
1930	82 GY	1931	52 GX		1932	286 AJS	
1930	104 GY	1931	53 GX				
		1930	54 GX		1932	207 AMS	
1930	6 GX	1931	55 GX		1932	208 AMS	
1930	28 GX	1931	56 GX		1932	209 AMS	
1930	31 GX	1931	57 GX				
1931	40 GX	1931	58 GX		1931	1 JS	
1930	41 GX	1931	59 GX		1931	4 JS	
1930	42 GX	1931	60 GX		1931	8 JS	
1930	43 GX	1931	61 GX		1931	11 JS	
1930	44 GX	1931	62 GX		1931	12 JS	
1930	45 GX	1931	63 GX		1931	20 JS	
1930	46 GX	1931	64 GX		1931	24 JS	
1931	47 GX	1931	65 GX		1931	33 JS	
1931	48 GX	1931	66 GX		1931	34 JS	
1931	49 GX	1931	67 GX		1932	35 JS	
1931	50 GX	1931	68 GX		1932	39 JS	

1932	60 JS	1933	62 MY	1933	66 PY
1932	63 JS	1933	64 MY	1933	70 PY
1932	64 JS	1933	72 MY	1933	72 PY
1932	65 JS	1933	74 MY	1933	74 PY
1932	72 JS	1933	80 MY	1933	82 PY
1932	73 JS	1933	82 MY	1933	84 PY
1932	74 JS	1933	90 MY	1933	86 PY
1932	80 JS	1933	92 MY	1933	90 PY
1932	81 JS	1933	94 MY	1933	92 PY
1932	82 JS	1933	106 MY	1933	94 PY
1932	83 JS	1933	116 MY	1933	98 PY
1932	84 JS	1933	118 MY	1933	104 PY
1932	85 JS	1933	124 MY	1933	106 PY
		1933	126 MY	1933	118 PY
1932	2 MS	1933	128 MY	1933	136 PY
1932	4 MS	1933	130 MY	1933	142 PY
1932	20 MS	1933	134 MY	1933	144 PY
1932	24 MS	1933	140 MY	1933	154 PY
1932	28 MS	1933	142 MY	1933	156 PY
1932	32 MS	1933	156 MY	1933	158 PY
1932	36 MS	1933	166 MY	1933	160 PY
1932	48 MS	1933	170 MY	1933	162 PY
1932	50 MS	1933	172 MY	1933	164 PY
1932	54 MS	1933	176 MY	1934	180 PY
1932	58 MS	1933	182 MY	1934	204 PY
1932	60 MS	1933	186 MY		
1932	64 MS			1934	7 RY
1932	66 MS	1933	3 MW	1934	9 RY
1932	70 MS	1933	7 MW	1934	15 RY
1932	72 MS	1933	15 MW	1934	23 RY
1932	74 MS	1933	19 MW	1934	37 RY
1932	76 MS	1933	25 MW	1934	47 RY
1932	80 MS	1933	31 MW	1934	49 RY
1932	86 MS	1933	33 MW	1934	55 RY
1932	88 MS	1933	39 MW	1934	57 RY
1932	90 MS	1933	41 MW	1934	59 RY
1932	98 MS	1933	45 MW	1934	71 RY
1932	100 MS	1933	47 MW	1934	77 RY
1932	104 MS	1933	55 MW	1934	79 RY
1932	106 MS	1933	67 MW	1934	83 RY
1932	114 MS	1933	69 MW	1934	85 RY
1932	116 MS	1933	71 MW	1934	89 RY**
1932	118 MS	1933	73 MW	1934	91 RY
1932	122 MS	1933	99 MW	1934	97 RY
1932	124 MS	1933	101 MW	1934	99 RY
1932	132 MS	1933	103 MW	1934	101 RY
1932	148 MS			1934	109 RY
1932	150 MS	1933	2 PY	1934	117 RY
1932	158 MS	1933	4 PY	1934	119 RY
		1933	8 PY	1934	121 RY
1933	2 MY	1933	22 PY	1934	125 RY
1932	8 MY	1933	24 PY	1934	127 RY
1933	10 MY	1933	30 PY	1934	139 RY
1933	14 MY	1933	32 PY	1934	143 RY
1933	16 MY	1933	36 PY	1934	147 RY
1933	20 MY	1933	42 PY	1934	149 RY
1933	24 MY	1933	44 PY	1934	153 RY
1933	26 MY	1933	52 PY	1934	155 RY
1933	32 MY	1933	54 PY	1934	157 RY
1933	56 MY	1933	62 PY	1934	159 RY
1933	58 MY	1933	64 PY	1934	165 RY

1934	169 RY		1934	99 SK		1935	149 TA
1934	175 RY		1934	101 SK		1935	161 TA
1934	185 RY		1934	103 SK		1935	179 TA
1934	189 RY		1934	109 SK		1935	187 TA
1934	191 RY		1934	119 SK			
1934	197 RY		1934	120 SK		1935	5 UK
1934	201 RY		1934	128 SK**		1935	42 UK
1934	203 RY		1934	138 SK		1935	62 UK
			1934	154 SK			
1934	2 SK		1934	170 SK			
1934	4 SK		1934	188 SK			
1934	6 SK		1934	190 SK**			
1934	8 SK						
1934	14 SK		1934	17 TA			
1934	18 SK		1934	21 TA			
1934	24 SK		1934	25 TA			
1934	60 SK		1934	27 TA			
1934	68 SK		1934	29 TA			
1934	70 SK		1935	45 TA			
1934	86 SK		1935	53 TA			
1934	88 SK		1935	97 TA**			
1934	90 SK		1935	103 TA			
1934	92 SK		1935	109 TA			
1934	94 SK		1935	123 TA			
1934	96 SK		1935	131 TA			

The following are the order of chassis built in the Phantom II Series

1	—	133 WJ	1929/30	
1	—	204 XJ	1929/30	
1	—	202 GN	1930	7.00 x 20 tyres from 169 GN
1	—	207 GY	1930	
1	—	68 GX	1930/31	Thermostatic radiator shutters
201	—	303 AJS	1931/32/33	(Left hand drive)
2	—	170 MS	1932	
201	—	224 AMS	1932/33/34	(Left hand drive)
2	—	190 MY	1933	7.00 x 19 tyres
3	—	115 MW	1933	
2	—	206 PY	1933/34	Controllable dampers from 160 PY
3	—	211 RY	1934	
2	—	196 SK	1934	
1	—	201 TA	1934/35	
2	—	82 UK	1935	
		84 UK	1936	

For American and Overseas Markets requiring left hand drive

201 AMS		1932
202 AMS	— 206 AMS	1933
207 AMS	— 209 AMS	1932
210 AMS	— 220 AMS	1933
221 AMS	— 222 AMS	1934
223 AMS	— 224 AMS	1932

As with all other 40/50 models, Phantom II chassis did not run straight through a series; for an explanation see Part III of this Appendix.

76 WJ space left blank.
123 WJ was taken back in part-exchange, and after overhaul and repairs re-erected as 134 WJ-EX.
16 WJ was not erected.
92 XJ was erected as 207 GY.
113 XJ not erected.
58 GN not erected.
112 GN space left blank.
125 GN space left blank.
118 GN erected as 205 GY.
145 GN space left blank.
152 GN not erected, re-numbered as 204 GY.
184 GN space left blank.
EX-203 GN chassis sold to Arthur Mulliner 4.5.1931.
23 GX re-numbered as 25 JS
26 GX re-numbered as 27 JS
29 GX re-numbered as 29 JS
30 GX re-numbered as 30 JS
33 GX re-numbered as 41 JS
34 GX re-numbered as 42 JS
36 GX re-numbered as 31 JS
37 GX re-numbered as 43 JS
16 JS re-numbered as 86 JS
44 JS re-numbered as 76 JS
45 JS re-numbered as 77 JS
48 JS re-numbered as 78 JS
57 JS re-numbered as 82 JS
58 JS re-numbered as 83 JS
59 JS re-numbered as 84 JS
85 JS space left blank
MS. No odd numbers in this series.
2-190 MY even numbers only.
3-107 MW odd numbers only.
65 MW space blank.
2-206 PY even numbers only.
190 PY re-numbered as 43 RY
192 PY re-numbered as 55 RY
202 PY re-numbered as 79 RY
3-211 RY odd numbers only.
2 SK-196 SK Series.
28 SK not built.
36 SK   "   "
38 SK   "   "
46 SK   "   "
52 SK re-numbered 119 SK
56 SK not built.
Odd numbers in SK Series:-
101 SK
103 SK
107 SK
109 SK
111 SK
115 SK
117 SK
119 SK
TA Series - odd numbers only. (1-201)
UK Series - even numbers only; last series of Phantom II reverted to low lift camshaft commencing 101 TA. Synchromesh on 2nd gear and flexible engine mounting.

Note: 84 UK was a special order after Phantom II ceased production. This chassis was erected late 1936.

APPENDIX A PART III
Phantom III 40/50

Cars Exhibited at the Olympia Motor Show 17-26 October 1935

Rolls-Royce (Stand 107)	Hooper Pullman limousine, finished in grey and black.
	Barker touring limousine, £2,540.
Barker & Co. Ltd (26)	Barker enclosed limousine in black with chrome metal moulding, upholstered in calf skin, burr walnut with gold inlay, wireless in cabinet and built-in luggage container.
Hooper & Co. Ltd (27)	Enclosed limousine finished in black with plain cloth to rear and ebony veneer woodwork.
Arthur Mulliner (28)	Sports limousine finished in red and cream, trimmed in red morocco with sunshine roof over driver and chrome moulding to waist.
Park Ward & Co. (35)	Sedanca de ville of a new type with sloping rear panel and concealed luggage panel. Chassis No. 37 EX.
Rippon Bros (22)	Enclosed limousine with sliding roofs to both front and rear compartments finished in black with white line. Rear in plain fawn cloth, folding tables and revolving armchair occasional seats.
Thrupp & Maberly (20)	Continental saloon finished in bronze maroon with built-in luggage locker, a heater is installed in rear compartment and wireless set with two speakers.
Windovers Ltd (21)	Sedanca de ville in cream and brown finish with interior upholstered in brown satin with rosewood and coromandel cabinet work. Both a wireless and heater are fitted.

Nine cars in all, but it is understood that the only one completed with engine and gearbox was 37 EX, the others were all Dummies as the Phantom III was not in full production.

Olympia Motor Show, 15-24 October 1936

Rolls-Royce (Stand 113)	Hooper enclosed limousine in black, £2,605. Chassis No. 3-AZ-104.
	Barker touring limousine, £2,650.
Barker & Co. Ltd (26)	Barker touring limousine finished in black and with both compartments upholstered in soft nut brown leather, the windscreen wiper operated on both sides of the glass. 3-AZ-148.
Hooper & Co. Ltd (25)	Sedanca de ville with sliding roof over front and finished in black and cream cellulose. 3-AZ-164.

Arthur Mulliner (27)	Enclosed limousine finished in all black. Chassis No. 3-AZ-180.
H J Mulliner (20)	Sedanca de ville on sporting lines with luggage boot at rear, finished in blue with grey cloth interior.
Park Ward (22)	Touring saloon finished in maroon and black. Chassis No. 3-AZ-70.
Rippon Bros (10)	Enclosed limousine finished in all black with chrome moulding to waist, built-in luggage container and concealed grid. The interior is in cloth to the rear with folding tables and revolving armchair occasional seats.
Thrupp & Maberly (19)	Enclosed drive limousine, the interior is in Circassian walnut and the rear seat adjusts to three positions. Chassis No. 3-AZ-118.
Windovers Ltd (24)	Limousine de ville finished in Mulberry and black.

Ten cars in all.

Earl's Court Motor Show, 14-23 October 1937

Rolls-Royce (Stand 83)	Hooper Pullman limousine, Chassis No. 3-CP-188.
	Barker sedanca de ville, £3,040. Chassis No. 3-CP-186.
Barker & Co. Ltd (23)	Enclosed limousine de ville, which is finished in Charrington blue throughout with sandstone cloth upholstery. Blue leather for the front seats. Chassis No. 3-CP-184.
Hooper & Co. Ltd (45)	Sedanca de ville. Chassis No. 3-CP-130.
Arthur Mulliner (36)	Enclosed limousine trimmed in fawn cloth and with black walnut woodwork, the exterior is cellulosed in black throughout. Chassis No. 3-CP-72.
H J Mulliner (46)	Sedanca de ville with latest type 'Square' lines. Chassis No. 3-CP-172.
Park Ward (37)	Sedanca de ville with unusual lines finished in black and ivory with electrically operated division and rear blind.
Rippon Bros (27)	Pullman limousine finished in black with sliding roofs over both compartments, revolving armchair occasional seats. Chassis No. 3-CP-160.
Thrupp & Maberly (19)	Touring limousine with the latest fashionable angular lines, finished in a new type known as 'black pearl'. Chassis No. 3-CP-150.
Windovers Ltd (44)	Enclosed limousine finished in black and cream with stainless steel moulding, interior woodwork in two shades of walnut, in rear light fawn fabric piped with brown leather. Chassis No. 3-CP-16.

10 cars in all.

Earl's Court Motor Show, 13-22 October 1938

The last before the War and the last at which the Phantom III was to appear

| Rolls-Royce (Stand 149) | Hooper sedanca de ville finished in silver. Chassis No. 3-DL-74. £2,970. |
| | Thrupp & Maberly touring limousine in maroon. £2,960. Chassis No. 3-DL-76. |

Hooper & Co. Ltd (93)	Hooper sedanca de ville. Chassis No. 3-DL-62.
H J Mulliner (94)	Sedanca de ville. Chassis No. 3-DL-88.
James Young (82)	Saloon coupe 2-door 5-seater with perspex roof and parallel opening doors and electrically operated sliding roof. Chassis No. 3-DL-86.
Park Ward (104)	Touring limousine with no rear mudguards, the body being built right out to the full width of the vehicle. Finished in black with fan type blinds fitted to the rear quarter lights. Sliding drawers beneath the rear seat accommodate a picnic set. Chassis No. 3-DL-84.
Rippon Bros (100)	Touring limousine with full view vision by using very narrow pillars finished in black lined in blue with sliding glass panel to roof and revolving armchair occasion seats. Chassis No. 3-DL-78.
Windovers Ltd (102)	Enclosed limousine de ville with streamlined wings and running boards. Finished in golden brown and beige with dark brown leather for front seats and two shades of straw for the rear compartment.

8 Cars in all.

Note: Barker & Co have disappeared from the Motor Show, and so have Arthur Mulliner of Northampton, the former have gone out of business.

1939

Owing to the outbreak of War in September 1939, there was no annual Motor Show held in London until October 1948, but as was the usual practice every year about April-time, the leading coachbuilders were beginning to think of what they would be exhibiting at the Show and laying their plans for this Event. The following chassis were purchased from Rolls-Royce Ltd and bodies were built on to these for the 1939 Show, which never took place.

Chassis No. 3—DL—186	Thrupp & Maberly touring limousine for the Rolls-Royce Show Stand.
Chassis No. 3—DL—188	Hooper sedanca de ville, quarter light sedanca, Rolls-Royce Show Stand.
Chassis No. 3—DL—190	This was to be a Hooper Quarter Light sedanca de ville, but it appears that this chassis was later sold to James Young of Bromley, who completed it as a sports saloon or limousine, and it was sold to J S Inskip of New York for a Dr Dennistoun. M. Bell of Long Island. New York, and the car was delivered to New York on 28 June 1940 by the Cunard White Star Liner *Samaria*, sailing from Liverpool.

It would appear that right from the outset people have been changing bodies on Phantom III chassis and this is still going on to this day, both here in the UK and in the United States. This is something which shows the very high esteem in which the Phantom III is held.

To give some examples of the body changing that has taken place over the years:

Chassis No. 3-AZ-178 was originally a Barker limousine of a very old fashioned type. It was specially built for a Mr A J Coppinger, of 57 Eaton Place, Belgravia, London, SW1. (I knew this car well as we lived in Eaton Place from 1929 - 1939). When the car was sold, it was purchased for use in India and rebodied as a 4-seater sports coupe by Thrupp & Maberly; it has not long returned from India and is now in Kent, the owner has joined the Rolls-Royce Enthusiasts' Club.

Chassis No. 3-DH-7 is now in chassis form only in the Le Mans Motor Museum in France. This chassis was shipped out to New York in the Elder Dempster steamer *Biafra* on 21 November 1940, carrying a Hooper limousine body; later the body was transferred on to Chassis No. 3-AX-57, which had been shipped out to New York as a chassis only, sailing from Liverpool on 5 November 1936 destined for a Dr Seth Gregory, who had a Keswick limousine body built on to the chassis by J S Inskip, Inc of New York. 3-AX-57 was later fitted with the Hooper limousine body from 3-DH-7 and returned to Great Britain carrying this body and was sold by Rolls-Royce Ltd in September 1949 for £1,025 to George Newnham as a used car.

There is a third car involved in this curious story, it is chassis No. 3-BT-53, which was shipped out to America as a chassis only on 10 April 1937 aboard the Cunard White Star liner *Scythia*, sailing Liverpool/New York. This chassis had been ordered through the R-R American Retailers, J S Inskip Inc, for delivery to a Mr F B Rentschler of Hertford, Connecticut. It was fitted with an enclosed sports saloon body seating 5 persons and built in America. Later the body from this chassis was removed and fitted on to 3-DH-7 and in its place was mounted another body. This is described as a Barker club saloon by the present owner of the car, who is a member of the Rolls-Royce Owners' Club of America, Inc. Where the present Barker body came from, fitted on to 3-BT-53, I have been unable to discover, nor have I been able to find out how 3-DH-7 arrived at the Le Mans Motor Museum in chassis form only, except to say that it arrived at the Museum at Le Mans via Switzerland and it is on permanent loan. As for the present whereabouts of 3-AX-57, this too I have been unable to discover.

In America the Phantom III has a very great following indeed, and totalling up the number of cars listed in the Rolls-Royce Owners Club list, the number comes to 36 cars in the AZ series, 30 cars in the AX series (including one AEX, which is an experimental chassis), 37 cars in the BU series, 35 cars in the BT series, 37 in the CP series, 39 in the CM series, 44 in the DL series, which again includes one DEX chassis, which is another ex-experimental one, and finally 3 chassis in the DH series. This makes a total of 259 cars, excluding the two experimental chassis, out of a total production figure of 717 Phantom III that were originally built. It must be added that most but not all the 259 cars quoted above are in America, the membership of the Rolls-Royce Owners' Club of America, Inc. is world-wide.

It is not known what has happened to the remainder, more than likely some have been broken up and I feel sure that some are still tucked away, possibly out of use, in the hands of their original owners, who are now elderly and who owing to the fact that these cars are not exactly cheap to keep in commission with present-day taxation, have turned to a lighter and more economical car.

In the most up-to-date List of the Rolls-Royce Enthusiasts' Club there are 71 Phantom III chassis in the list of cars in the back of the Membership List, and in the 20 Ghost Club List there are another 21, but it must be added that some of these cars are in all three Club Membership Lists. My own 3-AZ-146 is listed in each Club List, and there are several other cars which come into this category besides mine.

Unfortunately, an engine overhaul for a Phantom III is an extremely expensive exercise and a number of cars in England have had their engines removed and either been fitted with one of another make or else with the same type of 8-cylinder-in-line engine as was fitted into the Phantom IV. To my mind the fitting of a Straight-8 Rolls-Royce engine is the lesser evil of the two, but it is still a tragedy - the whole beauty of the Phantom III is that wonderful V12 engine.

In the Smithonian Institute there is a Phantom III engine on view; this is engine No. K 14 P. It was once installed in chassis No. 3-AZ-88, which carried a H J Mulliner sports limousine body with a special sprung steering wheel, the car was supplied by Jack Barclay to Capt Woolf Barnato of Bentley Racing Driver fame.

When the Phantom III was a current production model, it was purchased by all sorts of people to be used under entirely different conditions and below is a sample of chassis orders and the special requirements of each customer:

3—AZ—66   Hooper sports limousine. Special attention to springs. Customer does not want harsh springing.

3—AZ—106   Park Ward limousine. U K & Continent Touring at comparatively high speed.

3—AZ—146   Hooper Pullman enclosed limousine. U K use, town work. Speed practically never exceeds 50 mph.

3—AZ—216   Vesters & Neirinck saloon for use in Belgium. If not satisfactory may cancel order.

3—BU—28   Barker sports saloon. Customer requires light springing, usually travels at 45 mph.

3—BU—106   Kellner enclosed drive. Car to be used in Europe-India-Town work-Touring purposes.

3—BT—27   Mann Egerton limousine. UK, mainly town work, but occasionally slow touring.

3—BT—143   Barker touring limousine. Special attention to be given to chassis to avoid experience with GBJ 65.

3—CP—88   Binder saloon. For use in France, Germany, Austria, Switzerland, Italy and England also U S A, for both town work and touring at moderate speeds.

3—CP—94   Barker touring limousine. Special attention to chassis to avoid repetition of complaints experienced with 25/30 GUL 22.

3—CP—196   Mayfair limousine de ville. U K use - mainly long fast runs. Owner keen on high average speeds.

3—CM—57   Hooper sports limousine. Car for use in U K and on the Continent. Normally used by two persons at speeds of 50 - 55 mph but for six weeks at much higher speeds on Continental roads with 4/5 passengers. passengers.

3—CM—71   Hooper limousine. Customer is a confirmed invalid. Speed only 35 mph for U K, town work and touring. Special attention to springing.

3—CM—73   Chapron saloon. U K and France, touring and town work, at speeds of 70/85 mph.

3—CM—189   Hooper enclosed limousine. Car to be used in Switzerland and on Continent at low speeds. Springing most important. The owner is aged 77. Maximum speed 100 km per hour.

3—DL—18   Hooper enclosed limousine. U K, for touring at speeds of 45 mph, fit rear speedometer.

3—DL—98   Hooper sports limousine. Car to be used in France, based in Paris. For both town work and touring at high speeds, special attention to springing.

3—DL—144   Binder sedanca de ville. France and Switzerland - mainly touring. Special adjustments to be made to prevent car from exceeding 120 kms per hour (75 mph).

As can be seen from the wide assortment above, it was not an easy position which Rolls-Royce Ltd had to fill to keep such a wide variety of clients happy, and naturally there were some who were very difficult to satisfy, but the Company, as always, did their best to meet individual requirements.

The succeeding sheets give a complete list of coachbuilders who mounted their bodies on Phantom III chassis; this list is compiled from the Body Cards held at Conduit Street. It is not always quite correct, as on rare occasions a Body Card was completed and then a client cancelled his or her order, or changed their mind about a type of body, and the record was not amended.

This list is in columns of chassis series and gives the number of bodies that each individual coachbuilder mounted on Phantom III chassis; this is followed by the various types of bodies mounted, which in turn is followed by the Countries to which Phantom III were exported when they were new.

COACHBUILDING

Name of English Coachbuilder	AZ	AX	BU	BT	CP	CM	DL	DH
				Chassis Series				
E D Abbott Ltd, Farnham, Surrey	1	1	—	1	—	—	—	—
All-Weather Motor Bodies Ltd	2	—	—	—	—	—	—	—
Atcherley of Birmingham	—	—	—	—	1	—	—	—
William Arnold of Manchester	—	—	1	—	—	—	—	—
Barker & Co Ltd	17	18	25	16	18	13	1	—
Cooper Motor Bodies, Putney	—	1	—	—	—	—	—	—
Joseph Cockshoot	—	—	1	—	—	—	—	—
Crosbie & Dunn	1	—	—	—	—	—	—	—
Freestone & Webb	3	4	2	2	1	—	2	—
Gurney Nutting	12	7	1	1	4	3	2	—
Hooper & Co Ltd	19	17	19	28	22	25	31	4
Lancefield Coachworks	1	1	—	—	—	—	—	—
Mann, Egerton Ltd, Norwich	1	—	—	1	1	1	—	—
Mayfair Carriage Co	—	—	—	1	1	—	—	—

The ROLLS ROYCE 40/50 hp

Arthur Mulliner, Northampton	3	2	5	4	3	4	3	—
H J Mulliner, Chiswick	16	11	9	7	7	21	16	—
H R Owen	—	—	1	—	—	—	—	—
Park Ward & Co	6	11	10	7	8	14	13	1
Rippon Bros.	2	2	2	1	3	3	3	—
Thrupp & Maberly	6	6	6	3	5	4	4	—
Vanden Plas Ltd	—	1	—	1	1	1	—	—
Windovers Ltd	8	4	10	11	6	8	2	1
Woolley of Nottingham	—	2	—	—	—	—	—	—
James Young Ltd	2	1	—	3	1	1	2	—

American Coachbuilders

Brewster	1	1	—	1	—	—	—	—
J S Inskip, Inc.	—	3	2	4	5	—	3	—

* * * * *

Australian Coachbuilder	1	—	—	—	—	—	—	—

* * * * *

Continental Coachbuilders

Binder	1	—	1	2	2	—	4	—
Chapron	—	—	—	—	—	1	—	—
Doll & Ruhrbeck	—	—	—	1	—	—	—	—
Erdmann & Rossi	—	1	1	—	1	1	2	—
Fernandez & Darrin	—	—	—	—	1	—	—	—
Franay	—	—	—	—	1	1	—	—
Kellner	4	—	1	1	—	1	—	—
Labourdette	—	—	—	—	—	—	1	—
Schutter van Bakel	—	—	1	—	—	—	1	—
Vanvooren	—	—	1	—	1	1	—	—
Vester & Neirinck	1	1	1	1	1	—	1	—
Wiklunds	—	—	—	—	—	—	1	—

Note: This is about the closest it is possible to get to the number of bodies each coachbuilder mounted on a Phantom III Chassis as some of the Cards are missing and no information is available. Some cars had body changes viz; 3-DL-120 was originally a Hooper Sedanca de ville later an open 2 seater by Henri Labourette of Paris. 3-DL-152 carried Barker Coachwork originally mounted on 39 EX.

Every conceivable type of body was fitted to Phantom III chassis, from a 2-seater with a dickey, coupe cabriolet (often now called a Doctor's coupe) to an enclosed drive landaulette, Brougham de ville; in fact it is quite impossible to give a complete run down of all the coachwork, as the different makers had different names for the same type of body. Arthur Mulliner had one they called a 'sports limousine'; I rather think this is the same as the one Hooper called a 'touring limousine', but I cannot be quite sure. Barker & Co Ltd had one name peculiar to themselves, a 'sedancalette de ville, this was in reality a sedanca de ville, but the rear quarter of the hood opened as on a landaulette, but there was no rear quarter window, hence the name 'sedancalette de ville'. In several instances a cabriolet refers to an open tourer, but the body has wind-up windows; when the head is lowered the car becomes what is virtually an open tourer and is quite unlike the old cabriolet of the days of the 'Silver Ghost' type and the 'New Phantom'.

Below is the list of the Countries to which the Phantom III was exported with the number of cars in each case. It will be seen that the United States ranks high on this list.

Australia	1
Austria	1
Beirut	1
Belgium	6
Canada	4
Czecho-Slovakia	2
Egypt	2
Eire	1
France	27

Germany	5
Holland	3
India	19
Iran	1
Kenya	1
Northern Ireland	1
Portugal	1
Rumania	2
Siam	1
South Africa	2
Sweden	1
Switzerland	5
United States of America	35

It is usually imagined that with each series the chassis numbers go alternatively even and then odd numbers; this is so basically, but in practice both even and odd numbers were used in certain series and some numbers not used at all, as with the 'New Phantom' and the Phantom II.

The correct chassis list of Phantom III is as follows:-

AZ Series - even numbers only, commencing 20 to 238, but in addition two chassis were erected in this series having odd numbers -

3-AZ-43 was for the Duke of Kent.

3-AZ-47 was for the Viceroy of India.

AX Series - odd numbers right through, commencing 3-AX-1 and finishing 3-AX-201, 3-AX-203 became 3-CM-92.

BU Series - even numbers only, commencing with 3-BU-2 and finishing with 3-BU-200.

BT Series - started with 3-BT-1, odd numbers only, finishing 3-BT-203.

CP Series - even numbers only, starting with 3-CP-2, but chassis No. 3-CP-152 had its number changed to 3-CM-104 whilst it was being erected and likewise 3-CP-156 - this chassis was sold as 3-CM-106. There could be several reasons for this change, one of them being that the chassis was not actually allocated to a customer and it was what was known at Derby as a 'Rogue Chassis' and the testers would not pass it out: in the meantime some more up to date features had been incorporated in other chassis, so it was decided to embody these and up-date it, so the original number was not used.

CM Series - odd numbers only, starting with 3-CM-1, but 3-CM-11 was re-numbered as 3-CM-112, and 3-CM-27 passed out as 3-CM-110. 3-CM-59 left the Derby works as 3-CM-108. In addition to these changes in this series, there is a 3-CM-92, 3-CM-104 and 3-CM-106; in addition to the even numbers mentioned at the beginning of this paragraph (3-CM-112, 3-CM-110, 3-CM-108) there is a 3-CM-114. After this the numbers revert to odd ones only until 3-CM-203, which is the last of the series.

DL Series - all even numbers from 3-DL-2 up to 3-DL-200, but 3-DL-80 was re-numbered 3-DH-9, after this only one more Phantom III chassis was built.

The last Series of odd numbers contains only the following chassis: 3-DH-1, 3-DH-3, 3-DH-5, 3-DH-7, 3-DH-9 and 3-DH-11. It was the end of an era of one of the finest motor cars that has ever taken to the roads.

And finally a List of Titled Owners who were supplied with Phantom III Chassis when they were new.

3−AZ−26	Ex-Trials, Earl of Carnavon	Thrupp & Maberly sports limousine
3−AZ−32	Viscountess Castlerosse	Gurney Nutting Sports saloon
3−AZ−43	H.R.H. Duke of Kent	Barker touring limousine
3−AZ−44	The Hon. Lloyd George	Enclosed limousine by Abbott Ltd.
3−AZ−46	Lord Doverdale	H J Mulliner Sedanca de Ville
3−AZ−47	Lord Linlithgow, Viceroy of India	Hooper enclosed limousine
3−AZ−50	H.M. The King of Roumania	Gurney Nutting Sedanca 2 door Drop-Head Coupe
3−AZ−58	Sir Edward Hammer, Bart.	H J Mulliner 6-light saloon
3−AZ−62	The Hon. Seymour Berry	Gurney Nutting sedanca de ville
3−AZ−68	Sir John Leigh	Freestone & Webb sports saloon
3−AZ−76	Duke of Sutherland	All Weather Bodies cabriolet
3−AZ−86	The Hon. A C Nivison	Arthur Mulliner coupe cabriolet
3−AZ−92	Earl Beatty	Barker limousine de ville
3−AZ−94	Viscount Bearsted	H J Mulliner sports saloon with division
3−AZ−96	Count C Haugwitz Reventlow	Thrupp & Maberly sports saloon
3−AZ−100	Earl of Derby	Hooper enclosed drive landaulette
3−AZ−116	Sir William Firth	Barker limousine

3—AZ—118	Sir Edmund Davis	Thrupp & Maberly limousine
3—AZ—136	The Hon. P Henderson	H J Mulliner sports saloon
3—AZ—142	Lord Brocket	Barker enclosed drive limousine
3—AZ—148	Sir Pomeroy Burton	Barker enclosed drive limousine
3—AZ—152	Sir Adrian Baillie	H J Mulliner sports saloon
3—AZ—154	The Hon. M R Samuel	Gurney Nutting sedanca de ville
3—AZ—156	Lord Glendyne	Park Ward sedanca de ville
3—AZ—158	Lord Roseberry	Gurney Nutting drop head sedanca 4-some coupe
3—AZ—168	Sir H Smith, Bart.	Gurney Nutting sedanca de ville
3—AZ—172	Sir Norman Watson, Bart.	Thrupp & Maberly All Weather open tourer
3—AZ—176	Lady Buckland	H J Mulliner sedanca de ville
3—AZ—206	Princesse de Fancigny-Lucingo	Kellner Town Car
3—AZ—208	Contessa Freda Constantine	Kellner sedanca de ville
3—AZ—226	Sir Walter Rea	Hooper enclosed drive limousine
3—AZ—228	Sir Charles Craven	Gurney Nutting sports saloon
3—AZ—230	Sir Walter Forest	Park Ward sedanca de ville
3—AZ—232	The Duke of Devonshire	Hooper enclosed drive limousine
3—AZ—234	Lord Milton	Gurney Nutting sedanca de ville
3—AX—5	Sir H White	Hooper sports saloon
3—AX—15	Sir Julian Cahn, Bart	Sports saloon limousine by J S Woolley
3—AX—37	Sir Julian Cahn, Bart	Enclosed drive limousine by J S Woolley
3—AX—49	The Duchess of Marlborough	Hooper sedanca de ville
3—AX—55	The Hon. Mrs Brindsley-Plunkett	Gurney Nutting sedanca de ville
3—AX—83	Sir George Mellor	Park Ward limousine
3—AX—87	Ruler of Bahawlpur	Barker saloon limousine
3—AX—97	Sir John Latta	Barker landaulette
3—AX—99	Lt Col. Sir J Humphreys	Park Ward enclosed limousine
3—AX—107	Baron Hirst of Wilton	Park Ward limousine
3—AX—109	The Marquess of Queensbury	Gurney Nutting sedanca de ville
3—AX—111	Lord Moyne	Lancefield limousine
3—AX—123	Lord Aberconway	Open Phaeton by Cooper Motor Bodies, of Putney
3—AX—147	Maharajah Holker of Indore	Gurney Nutting enclosed drive limousine
3—AX—149	Sir David Milne Watson	Thrupp & Maberly enclosed limousine
3—AX—161	Sir Eric Geddes	Barker enclosed limousine
3—AX—173	Lord Portal	Windovers enclosed limousine
3—AX—181	Sir Edmund Crane	Windovers saloon
3—AX—195	H.R.H. Duke of Gloucester	Enclosed limousine by Barker
3—AX—201	Maharajah of Baroda	Hooper enclosed limousine with sun roof
3—BU—14	Sir R Milbourne	Hooper enclosed drive limousine
3—BU—16	Sir George Martin	Park Ward Sedanca de ville
3—BU—34	Sir Albert Bingham	Hooper sports saloon
3—BU—46	Sir Alfred Butt, Bart.	Hooper limousine
3—BU—52	The Lady King	Barker enclosed limousine
3—BU—68	The Aga Khan	Hooper sedanca de ville
3—BU—74	Lord Bradford	Windovers saloon with division
3—BU—76	Maharajah Jaipur	Barker sedanca de ville
3—BU—82	Maharanee of Nabba	Hooper sedanca de ville
3—BU—86	Ruler of Bhopal	Thrupp & Maberly sports saloon
3—BU—92	The Lady Buckland	Hooper enclosed limousine
3—BU—102	Maharajah of Jodhpur	Hooper enclosed limousine
3—BU—106	Maharanee of Baroda	Kellner enclosed drive
3—BU—128	Sir Edgar Horne, Bart.	H J Mulliner sedanca de ville
3—BU—132	Lord Glanelly	Hooper enclosed drive limousine
3—BU—134	Maharajah of Kolhapur	Barker open tourer
3—BU—136	Sir John Leigh	Freestone & Webb drop head coupe
3—BU—144	Lord Somers	Barker enclosed limousine
3—BU—162	Lord Roseberry	Gurney Nutting sports sedanca de ville (cancelled)
3—BU—168	Lord Fairhaven	Barker sedanca
3—BU—172	Sir Abe Bailey, Bart.	Hooper enclosed limousine
3—BU—174	Sir Montagu Burton	Barker landaulette
3—BU—176	The Lady Foley	Barker sedanca de ville

3—BU—196	Lord Plunket	Owen sedanca de ville. Originally for Marquis of Queensbury
3—BU—198	Maharajah Rajppla	Windovers sedanca de ville
3—BU—200	Countess Haugwitz Reventlow	Thrupp & Maberly saloon with division
3—BT—5	Duke of Alba	Hooper sports saloon
3—BT—11	Lord Portalington	Windovers limousine
3—BT—15	Lady Ward	Windovers enclosed drive limousine
3—BT—19	Lord Illiffe	Hooper enclosed drive limousine
3—BT—25	Sir Patrick Duncan, Bart. Governor SA	Hooper landaulette
3—BT—41	Lord Camrose	Hooper enclosed drive limousine
3—BT—43	Lady Grace Dance	Windovers enclosed limousine
3—BT—57	Sir A Kay Muir	Windovers enclosed limousine
3—BT—61	Sir William Jeffrey	Windovers sports saloon
3—BT—63	Sir Robert Hadfield	Windovers enclosed limousine
3—BT—69	Sir Hugh Bray	James Young saloon with partition
3—BT—75	The Hon. Charles Fitzroy	Windovers 7 passenger saloon
3—BT—87	Lord Vesty	Hooper enclosed limousine
3—BT—95	Lord Ebbisham	Barker limousine
3—BT—99	Sir John Leigh	Freestone & Webb sports saloon
3—BT—167	Lord Londonderry	Barker enclosed limousine
3—BT—171	Sir H Wernher	Barker enclosed limousine
3—BT—177	Lady Charles Montague	Hooper sedanca de ville
3—BT—179	The Hon. William Bithell	H J Mulliner sedanca de ville
3—BT—181	Ruling Chief of Keonjhar State	Barker sports torpedo cabriolet
3—BT—193	Sir John Jervis	Hooper limousine
3—CP—2	Baroness von Einser	Freestone & Webb saloon with division
3—CP—6	Sir Cecil Rolls	Ex-stock Hooper standard enclosed limousine.
3—CP—12	Hon. S Vesty	Hooper enclosed landaulette
3—CP—22	Sir Emsley Carr	H J Mulliner limousine de ville
3—CP—26	Mme La Duchess de Talleyrand	Barker standard touring limousine
3—CP—34	King of Roumania	Park Ward sports limousine
3—CP—54	Sir Charles Craven	Gurney Nutting sedanca de ville
3—CP—86	Sir Philip Sassoon	Barker cabriolet sedanca de ville
3—CP—90	Count Maurice de Bosdari	Sedanca de ville by Fernandez & Darrin
3—CP—94	Sir Frederick Minter	Barker touring limousine
3—CP—100	Governor of Bombay	Hooper enclosed limousine
3—CP—108	Sir Francis Peel	Ex-stock H J Mulliner sports limousine
3—CP—110	Sir John Latta	Barker landaulette
3—CP—112	Prince of Baroda	Windovers saloon
3—CP—116	Prince Berar	Windovers cabriolet
3—CP—180	Countess of Inchcape	Hooper enclosed landaulette
3—CP—182	Sir Frederick Richmond	Windovers sedanca de ville
3—CP—190	Lord Portalington	Windovers enclosed limousine
3—CM—19	Lord Craigmyle	H J Mulliner limousine
3—CM—23	Sir H Harmsworth	Park Ward sports saloon
3—CM—31	Sir Herbert Smith, Bart.	Gurney Nutting sedanca de ville
3—CM—37	The Rajah Baliadur of Panchakota	Park Ward Continental touring saloon
3—CM—51	Sir Richard Sykes	H J Mulliner touring limousine
3—CM—55	Lady Cora Fairhaven	Barker landaulette
3—CM—63	H.M. King of Egypt	Hooper enclosed limousine
3—CM—71	Lady Brumner	Barker landaulette
3—CM—85	Sir James Roberts	Hooper standard enclosed limousine
3—CM—92	Sir George Grant	Barker touring saloon
3—CM—97	Sir Hardman Lever	H J Mulliner enclosed limousine
3—CM—99	Earl of Dudley	Barker saloon with division
3—CM—115	Sir Ernest Cain	Gurney Nutting sports saloon
3—CM—121	Lady Ludlow	Barker enclosed limousine
3—CM—137	Lady Llewellyn	Hooper limousine
3—CM—139	Sir Robert Mc Alpine	Thrupp & Maberly enclosed limousine
3—CM—167	The Hon. Philip Henderson	James Young sports saloon
3—CM—171	Lord Cowdray	Park Ward enclosed limousine

3—CM—187	Princess Fancigney-Lucinge	Kellner sedanca de ville
3—CM—193	Viscountess Wimborne	Hooper sports saloon
3—DL—18	Sir John Lorden	Hooper limousine
3—DL—26	Maharajah Sadret of Barlakinadi	Thrupp & Maberly 4-door All Weather
3—DL—34	Sir Ernest Oppenheimer	Ex-stock H J Mulliner sedanca de ville
3—DL—52	Lord Craigmyle	Hooper standard enclosed drive limousine
3—DL—68	Lord Rothermere	Hooper enclosed drive limousine
3—DL—82	Lady Lindsay	H J Mulliner sports saloon
3—DL—84	Sir George Sutton, Bart.	Park Ward touring limousine
3—DL—92	Baron Brigman de Walzin	Vester & Neirinck interior drive with division
3—DL—96	Maharajah Shabeb of Moroi	Park Ward Phaeton
3—DL—104	Sir Herbert Smith	Ex-stock. H J Mulliner sedanca de ville
3—DL—106	Lady Patricia Guiness	Hooper sedanca de ville
3—DL—118	The Hon. Peter Beatty	Park Ward convertible sedan
3—DL—130	Sir Edmund Crane	H J Mulliner 4-light touring saloon
3—DL—138	The Imperial Court of Iran	Park Ward touring limousine
3—DL—148	Lord Glanelly	Hooper touring limousine
3—DL—154	Sir John Leigh	Freestone & Webb touring limousine
3—DL—158	Prince Aditya of Siam	H J Mulliner limousine de ville
3—DL—166	Lord Inverforth	Windovers enclosed limousine
3—DL—182	H.M. King of Egypt	Body Card missing. Hooper limousine
3—DL—200	High Commissioner for India	Park Ward coupe cabriolet
3—DH—1	Marquise Marie Suzanne de Villory	Hooper sedanca de ville

NOTE: The description of body style in each case is taken direct from the Body Card, but it should be noted that the Body Cards of the following chassis numbers are missing from the tin boxes originally held in Conduit Street, so no information is available.

3—AZ—122	3—BT—193	3—CP—142	3—DL—4	3—DL—32
3—DL—40	3—DL—44	3—DL—74	3—DL—76	3—DL—96
3—DL—104	3—DL—114	3—DL—116	3—DL—118	3—DL—122
3—DL—124	3—DL—136	3—DL—146	3—DL—156	3—DL—174
3—DL—178	3—DL—182	3—DL—184	3—DL—192	3—DL—194
3—DL—196	3—DH—11			

APPENDIX B

A legend has grown up over the years that Henry Royce, though a brilliant engineer and designer, was a somewhat eccentric character, practically a recluse, who lived in a world of his own at West Wittering in Sussex and Le Canadel in the South of France remote from the cares and commercial values of everyday life. This was an image largely created and carefully preserved by Claude Johnson, who had a keen sense of publicity and a flair for establishing his favourite ideas in the public mind. He wished Royce to be regarded with a certain awe, as the genius who was responsible for 'The Best Car in the World' and the finest aero engines.

At the same time it was his policy to keep Royce away from the Derby Works where Royce's insistance on perfection led to difficulties! However, in fact, this picture of Royce is not at all a correct one. He had after all run a successful business long before he met Charlie Rolls or Claude Johnson. It must be remembered he was over forty when he went into partnership with them and had far more business acumen than is generally supposed and was also far seeing and practical in commercial matters. To illustrate this side of his character, which has never been properly realized before, some of his own comments and minutes have been included in this Appendix and from these it can be clearly seen how, very often, it was Royce who put his finger on the crux of the matter and saw the financial possibilities or otherwise of various problems.

Again, contrary to the general opinion, engendered by the fact that they produced a luxury product, that Rolls-Royce was a wealthy firm. Indeed they were nothing of the kind and often were prevented from carrying out some design or development they wished to undertake, purely from lack of funds.

It is greatly to the credit of both Claude Johnson and Henry Royce that the Company was steered through these troubled waters and gained the public acclaim and esteem it has so richly deserved.

Royce himself never attended a Board Meeting, as he considered he had more important work with which to occupy his time; but he was always kept most fully informed as to what went on and it is from his comments on current events, either in the form of a letter or a brief minute, that the following extracts have been taken:-

At the end of the 1914 - 1918 War when Claude Johnson saw that the future sales of the 40/50 were going to be limited, he suggested to Royce that a smaller car was essential, in November 1920 Royce wrote as follows:-

> It seems manifest to me that a small output at Derby will not allow the Rolls-Royce Company to exist. So that supposing there is not sufficient market for the big car, or that we shall be spoiling our markets by flooding the big car markets, the prospects of aero work being limited, our best field appears to be in the smaller car market. Owing to our reputation we ought to be able to sell a high quality small article at a figure above what it costs. It would be dealt with in the same Sales, Design and Test organisations and so contribute towards the standing charges, which would otherwise on a small output ultimately become too large.
>
> I would like it clearly understood, that I should not for a moment recommend a smaller model if we could fill the Derby factory with the large model.

Royce had always liked a car with, to use Elliott's own words to me (see page 108 'The Hyphen in Rolls-Royce'), 'an engine with plenty of fizz in it'. By 1925, the Bentley car had made a tremendous reputation for itself both as a sports car and in competitive events and in October from West Wittering, Royce sent the following:-

Regarding the Bentley*, the makers are evidently out to capture some of our trade, but we do not think we can learn much by buying a car because we can see in which way it can be better than we are - that is - for high-speed performance, because it has four valves per cylinder. It would appear more costly than ours to produce for equal silence. We have the advantage of better machinery, staff and plant: they get much of their work done outside, but at the same time we are under heavy expenses.

And the following year from Le Canadel he wrote:-

I would like to design a high-speed sports car, not expecting much in the way of sales but for the good or ordinary sales.

These chassis were of course 15, 16 and 17 EX. In February 1927 Royce continued

I am very keen on seeing a very smart sports car of some kind on our stand at Olympia.

During 1928 the designs for a replacement 40/50 to the 'New Phantom' took up practically all Royce's time and in designing the new model he gave the following opinion:

I have long considered our present chassis out-of-date. The back axle, gearbox, frame, springs, have not been seriously altered since 1912.

Now we all know it is easier to go on the old way, but I so fear disaster by being out-of-date, and having a lot of old stock left, and by the sales falling off by secrets leaking out, that I must refuse all responsibility for a fatal position unless these improvements in our chassis are arranged to be shown next autumn, and to do this they must be in production soon after Midsummer 1929. I will take moral responsibility for the risk, and think it is far less than having old stock (to wit the aero engine position two years ago) and other risks of our present situation.

Royce had never liked American cars but was slowly accepting some of their ideas, so he wrote:

'Bumpers I hate but I suppose they are needed to justify fashion. In the case of accident or even small collisions the usual Bumpers are almost valueless, and suggest horrible manners'.

In Part II, Chapter 1 of this book, which tells the story of 18 EX, the following Minute from Royce, which he wrote from Le Canadel in April 1928 on the subject of instrument panels, should be noted and certainly shows evidence of his sound good sense and honesty.

* New 6½ litre model.

It is astounding that we, charging the *very top prices* cannot give as good a scheme as Citroen and Chrysler, and I am looking upon it as my duty to make our scheme so attractive in appearance and price that our Sales cannot do otherwise than adopt it. It should be realised that it is the first principle of good trading *to give good value for money,* and if you are posing as making the best, see that your buyers get it, and do your very utmost that the customers, for your good, are not overcharged by the retailers. We must knock over any conditions that get in our way. When you are sure that the scheme is as good as can be made - I mean all round, appearance practical, and minimum cost - we should next decide if it is *desirable at this cost to the customer.*

Two years later, when the Phantom II was in production Hives went to America, taking 25 EX with him (see Part II, Chapter 4) and visited the New York Show. He later said 'when a Cadillac, Packard or Lincoln has a custom built body, as regards general lines, and finish, we can show them nothing very much better. As regards price, one almost hesitates to make a comparison'. Hives concluded his report with the comment that there must be some solution whereby Rolls-Royce could sell their products in such a huge market.

This report produced the following from Royce:-

I thank Mr Hs for his very able and complete report. To make cars at Derby and to sell them in the United States (by RRAL) and enable them to make a profit is very difficult, and perhaps impossible (something like a single firm against a nation). I am quite in agreement with Mr Hives that the time has come when we must study cost with the greatest possible vigour, and we are all agreed that it is possible to make great economies without loss of perfection, which as before must be our very first requirement; but we might sacrifice 1% of perfection for 10% in cost. There is no doubt that many people are, and have been. watching Rolls-Royce very closely as a standard of perfection etc., and are often trying to make a cheap edition of our work. Naturally they are taking parts from others also: we are not vain enough to think that we are the only good pebble on the beach. We also know that after we have achieved a certain degree of perfection it is very often possible to re-design for economical production without losing much in efficiency, but through want of capacity and the difficulty of changing we do not do so. Generally also we do not get the final requirements until we are well on with production - (also for the reason of having too much in hand). It must be remembered that we have a great deal of work of a very highly technical character and it must be realised that while we must economise to reduce our establishment charges from their very high ratio to output, we must not reduce our technical capacity. We know that it is possible to do more with the same expenditure, but that is not the wasteful part of our expenditure.

We are thankful that the aero-engine prospects are bright but while these are promising us support we ought to set about trying to make the Company's operations more efficient - *i.e.* while there is time, and we can, because if we were to save all the direct labour cost our productions would still be too costly to compete with the U S A. Either we have to increase our productions or to decrease our establishment charges, *because no matter how good our work is technically we cannot expect to get the present prices.* So we must look forward to the fact that we must part with our production in the near future for considerably less money, so that to get the present turnover we must be doing 100% more productive work.

Materials in England are higher in price than in the U S A. This supports my statement that with us it falls more heavily upon our Company *because the whole country is less efficient.* We have always found this forced us into making many things that similar people in the U S A bought from specialists. This is still glaringly forced upon us.

To conclude, we must thank Mr Hives for his excellent report with which we thoroughly agree. I suggest strengthening our purely technical staff, which one thinks is far better than the average of British Companies, and shows that our apparent extravagance is really our strength, and that economies must be made in other directions, and by increasing the efficiency of the technical staff, which I am pleased to say I think far better than even a few years ago.

Not very long after this, whilst the design team was working on improving the 20/25, Royce wrote Sidgreaves a letter which clearly shows that he had no illusions about the future:

You know how terribly anxious I am to get this model right as quickly as possible, and put it into mass production so that we can sell at such a price as to be able to make enough in number to be profitable. MY GREAT MOTTO FOR GREAT BRITAIN AND OURSELVES IS MASS PRUDUCTION WITH QUALITY. UNLESS WE DO THIS WE ARE FATED SO LET US DO IT BEFORE IT IS TOO LATE, BECAUSE AT THE MOMENT ENGLAND CANNOT TRULY BOAST OF EITHER.

Unfortunately, excellent though Royce's ideas were, the cost of tooling and setting up for mass production methods was quite beyond the Company's finances.

Royce's final Minute is an interesting one and reads as follows:

It should be clear that I am not an obstructionist, but wish anything hopeful to be tried that can be bought both for test and special customers.

I have preached for many years the practice of - 'when in trouble find out what others are doing, and that we have enough well educated and inexpensive young men to take a personal interest in any special subject, and give them a chance of showing their ability and ingenuity. We older engineers will use our experience to pick out that which we think is worth working on, and it must be remembered that time and money will not allow us to try or make everything and someone knowing most of our history is best able to make the choice. We want to avoid the resources of the Experimental Department being crowded by ill-considered, half thought out schemes, so that things which have had much time and thought are never made, or are pushed aside before they are tested to a finish.

I have no desire to spend the small hours of the morning seeking solutions of our difficulties, and features of design, etc., because this practice (forced upon me) has done much to make my life - through ill-health nearly unbearable.

R.
At Le Canadel. 5.3.32.

Sadly it was not until after Royce's death that his ideas were gradually put into practice. A great deal of the credit for the change over is due to Hives, Harvey-Bailey and those in the Experimental Department at Derby, especially W A Robotham, who had a very clear insight into the future and production costs. It was he who instigated the policy of purchasing in bulk, components which could be manufactured by specialist firms cheaper than Rolls-Royce could make the same article. It is for this reason too that the post-War Mark VI Bentley was fitted with standard pressed steel coachwork, unless a coachbuilt body was ordered specially.

BIBLIOGRAPHY

The following works have been consulted in preparing this book, and to the authors of same I must give acknowledgement:

The Magic of a Name by Harold Nockolds
At the Wheel, Ashore and Afloat by Montague Grahame-White
The Life of Sir Henry Royce by Sir Max Pemberton
Two Brave Brothers by H. F. Morriss
The Rolls-Royce Motor-Car by Anthony Bird and Ian Hallows
Rolls-Royce, The Living Legend Anon
The Badminton Library: Motors by Lord Northcliffe and others
Northcliffe by R. Pound and G. Harmsworth
The Antique Automobile by St John C. Nixon
The Book of the Silver Ghost by Kenneth Ullyet
The Book of the Phantoms by Kenneth Ullyet
Rolls-Royce Manual, 1925-1939 by J. H. Haynes
The Power of Grace by W. L. H. Allport
An Early History of Motoring by Claude Johnson
Roads Made Easy by Claude Johnson
Milestones of Music by Claude Johnson
The Little Knights and Jacko and Minnie by Claude Johnson
The Motor Book Edited by T. R. Nicholson
The Motor Car, 1765-1914 by Anthony Bird
Old Cars the World Over by Elizabeth Nagle
The Veterans of the Road by Elizabeth Nagle
The Book of Motors by F. J. Camm
The Vintage Motor-Car by Clutton and Stanford
Rasputin by Heinz Lupman
The Thoroughbred Motor-Car by David Scott-Moncrieff
Forty Years of Motoring by Edward Young
Cars of the Connoisseur by J. R. Buckley
A History of the World's Classic Cars by R. Hough and M. Frostick
The Wonder Book of Motors by G. Gibbard Jackson
The Motorists' Reference and Year Book, 1928 by G. Gibbard Jackson
The Romance of the Motor Car by G. Gibbard Jackson
Lost Causes of Motoring by Lord Montagu
Lanchester Motor Cars by Anthony Bird and Francis Hutton-Stott
A History of Coach-building by Geo. A. Oliver
W.O. by W. O. Bentley
The Cars in my Life by W. O. Bentley
Fifty Years with Motor-Cars by A. F. C. Hilstead
The Sports Car by John Stanford
Veteran and Edwardian Motor Cars by David Scott-Moncrieff
Floyd Clymer's Catalogues of 1924, 1927 and 1929 by Floyd Clymer
Motor Scrap Book, Ford by Floyd Clymer
Forty Years with Ford by Charles E. Sorensen
The Boys' Book of the Motor Car by J. Harrison
Automobile Engineering. Vols 1-6 Published by The American Technical Society
The Automobile in Three Volumes Edited by Paul N. Hasluck
Modern Motor-Cars General Editor: Arthur W. Judge
Veteran and Vintage Cars by Peter Roberts
The Boys' Book of Veteran Cars by Ernest F. Carter
True's Automobile Year Book published by *True* the Man's magazine
A Picture History of Motoring by L. T. C. Rolt
The Packard Story by R. E. Turnquiste
Daimler, 1896-1946 by St John C. Nixon
Forty Years' Progress by John Prioleau
My Life and My Work by Henry Ford
The Book of Sports Cars by Charles Markman and Mark Sherwin
The Automobile Book by Ralph Stein
Sixty Years a Queen by Sir Herbert Maxwell
Queen Victoria by Helmut and Alison Gernshem
Edward VII. His Life and Times Edited by Sir Richard Holmes
North Atlantic Seaway by N. R. P. Bonsor
Rolls-Royce Memories by Massac Buist
Victoria R.I. by Elizabeth Longford
King Edward VII by Sir Philip Magnus
Queen Mary by James Pope Hennessy
George VI by John W. Wheeler-Bennett
The Good Years by Walter Lord
Rolls of Rolls-Royce by Lord Montagu
The Kaiser by Joachim von Kurenberg
The Daimler Tradition by Brian E. Smith
Duesenberg, the Mightiest American Car by J. L. Elbert
Seventy Years of Buick by George H. Dammann
Fifty Years of Lincoln by George H. Dammann
The Custom Body Era by Hugo Pfau
Cadillac. Standard of the World by Maurice Hendry
The American Car since 1775 Published by The Automobile Quarterly
The Year Books of the R.A.C. of G.B. 1901 and 1906
The Year Book of the R.A.C. 1908, 1917, 1918, 1919
The Encyclopaedia Britannica
Coach Building, Past and Present (Hooper & Company) by Cecil Robertson
From Chariot to Car (Barker & Company) by Robert J. Priest
Rolls-Royce in the '20s A reprint from *Autocars* and *Motor*
Rolls-Royce in the '30s A reprint from *Autocars* and *Motor*
The Bulletin A periodical magazine published by Rolls-Royce Limited
Sundry Rolls-Royce Sale Catalogues and Instruction Books, for the various models
Sales Catalogues and Drivers' Manuals for the Daimler Company's Sleeve Valve Series
The Lanchester Company's Sales Catalogues
The back files of *The Autocar* and *The Motor*
The 20/Ghost Club Record
The Rolls-Royce Enthusiasts' Club *The Bulletin*
The Rolls-Royce Owners' Club Inc *The Flying Lady*

(Top and upper middle) 3-BT-67, this Hooper All Weather was supplied to R. A. Camenirce Esq of Liverpool, who specified two spare-wheels and no mascot
(Lower middle) 3-BT-119, Barker Sedanca de Ville with 'E' type steering and extra forward facing seats was supplied to Mrs R. Tritton
(Bottom) 3-BT-135, a Thrupp and Maberly Enclosed Drive Landaulette. The car was sold to R. Wemyss Honeyman of Kirkaldy, Scotland. Later the car was bought by Pitchers Taxis Ltd of St Helier, Jersey. The car is wearing the Royal Standard for HM Queen Elizabeth II on her visit to Alderney. At some time the original engine was removed and an Austin engine installed. Tom Mason of Kent, the present owner, has installed another Phantom II engine coming from chassis number 3-BT-51 *(photo Pitchers Taxis Ltd St Helier, Jersey)*

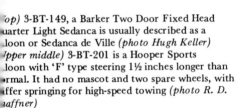

(Top) 3-BT-149, a Barker Two Door Fixed Head Quarter Light Sedanca is usually described as a Saloon or Sedanca de Ville (photo Hugh Keller)

(Upper middle) 3-BT-201 is a Hooper Sports Saloon with 'F' type steering 1½ inches longer than normal. It had no mascot and two spare wheels, with stiffer springing for high-speed towing (photo R. D. Shaffner)

(Lower middle) Barker Enclosed Limousine coachwork is shown on chassis number 3-CP-84. It has 'F' type steering and extra forward facing seats (photo S. J. Skinner)

(Bottom) Sir Philip Sassoon Bart PC, GBE, CMG, MP purchased this Barker Cabriolet de Ville on chassis number 3-CP-86

(Top) This Barker Enclosed Limousine de Ville on chassis number 3-CP-184 was on the Barker stand at the Earl's Court Motor Show of 1937 *(photo S. J. Skinner)*

(Upper and lower middle) The razor-edged 3-CP-186 Barker Sedanca de Ville was shown on the R-R stand at the 1937 London Motor Show. It was originally sold to British Ropes, at one time owned by Derek Randall, Editor of the R-REC Bulletin *(photo Mrs D. Randall)*

(Bottom) This James Young of Bromley Two Door Four Light Coupe, chassis number 3-DL-86, was shown on the Young stand at the London Motor Show of 1938. This car is now in America *(photo Norris Allen)*

(Top left) The James Young 1938 Motor Show car was fitted with a parallel opening car, which is not obvious in the other photograph (photo Norris Allen)
(Top right) 3-DL-94 with the hood down
(Middle) The central gearchange and the special white faced instruments fitted to 3-DL-94 (photo Dr Fischer)
(Bottom) 3-DL-94, a Freestone and Webb Cabriolet was the only Phantom III fitted with a centre gearchange (photo Dr Fischer)

(Top) The nearside of a Phantom III engine
(Bottom) The offside of a Phantom III engine

(Top) Phantom III chassis 3-DL-120, a Hooper Sedanca Quarterlight de Ville built for the Brussels and Geneva Motor Shows of 1939. The car was exhibited at the New York's World Fair in the same year

(Middle) Phantom III 3-DL-120 rebodied by Henri Labourdette as a Convertible Coupe with cowled radiator. All bright parts are gold-plated and the windows and hood are electrically operated. Unfortunately it is not known when this body change took place *(photo John McFarlane)*

(Bottom) Another view of 3-DL-120 showing the rear treatment of the coachwork *(photo John McFarlane)*

(Top) 3-DL-140, a Brougham de Ville specially built by Schutter van Bakel of Amsterdam for use by Dr Fritz Mannheimer as a town car in Amsterdam. This was always a very favoured type of body, especially in America ; probably more bodies of this type were mounted on Lincoln than any other chassis, most were built by Willoughby and they were still produced until 1941

(Middle) The replacement car for the Phantom III 'Big Bertha'

(Bottom) 'Big Bertha'

(*Top*) The interior of King Ibn Saud's Phantom III with the windows and partition down
(*Bottom*) Formerly a Windover Limousine de Ville built in July 1937, 3-CM-25 was re-bodied by Hooper & Co as an Open Tourer for Ibn Saud in 1946. It was the first body they built after the 1939/45 war

GENERAL INDEX

A

Adams & Oliver (RR Specialist). 202, 203
Agricultural Hall, Islington. 32
Allen, Norris. (Owner of 3-DL-86). 220
American Salons. 97-100
Aubin, Ethel. (R's nurse). 44, 91, 113, 172, 173
Austrian Alpine Trials. 29, 37
Autocar. 18, 45, 91, 102, 111, 149, 158, 163
182, 187, 194, 219, 220

B

Barnato, Woolf. 95, 96
Beaumont-Thomas. Lionel. (Owner of 3-BT-79)
183
Beaumont-Thomas. Nora C. (Mrs). (Owner of
167 GN). 148, 149
Beaumont-Thomas. Reginald. A. (Owner of 63
GN). 148, 149
Beaumont-Thomas. Richard. (Owner of 2445).
27, 28
Benge.R.A. (Owner of 3-AX-195). 219
Bentley.W.O. 167, 168
Berry.D. (Owner of 9 GX).
Brae Cottage, Knutsford. 9
Briggs.A.H. 11
British Motor Speedway. 95, 96
Buist.Massac.H. 9
Byroade.Henry. (Owner of 3-DL-152). 207,
209

C

Cahn.Sir Julian. (Bart). (Owner of 74 GN &
others). 150
Campbell.Colin. Lt-Commdr. (Owner of 7 EX &
101 SK). 75, 158
Campbell.Malcolm. 95, 96
Caswell, Florence. (Secretary to C.S.R. & C.J.).
91

Chateauroux. (RR French Testing Centre). 74,
81, 115-134, 142 143, 173-186, 205
Claremont, Ernest.A. (R's brother-in-law). 9, 11
31, 32
Claremont/Haynes. (R's Solicitors). 173
Compton, Jack, Ltd. 101, 157, 160, 161,
210-213
Conduit Street. (RR London Offices). 8, 14,
16, 19, 35, 40, 59, 63, 73, 75, 91, 124, 158,
203, 204, 212

D

Delhi Durbar. of 1911. 25, 26
Derby Works. (RR Ex-Garage). 23, 25, 27, 74,
99, 100, 113-115, 124, 125, 130, 146, 172-174,
182, 190, 198-201
Docker, Sir Bernard and Lady Norah. 227
Duke of Gloucester. HRH. (Owner of 3-AX-195).
218, 219
Duchess of Gloucester. HRH. 186
Duke of Kent. HRH. (Owner of 3-AZ-43). 218
Duke of York. HRH. (Later HM King George
VI). 93

E

Edmunds Henry. 9
Edward VII.H.M.The King. 20, 59
Elliott.A.G. (i/c Design Phantom III). 114,
172-175, 180
Elizabeth.H.M. The Queen. (now the Queen
Mother). 105
Emperor of Japan. H.I.M. 40, 41
Empress Marie of Russia. H.I.M. (The Dowager
Empress). 29
Evernden.Ivan.S. 34, 74-79, 80-84, 90, 95, 113,
124, 125, 130, 131, 136, 143, 157, 172-174, 186,
203, 205

257

Index to Rolls-Royce Cars

Springfield built chassis No. S-288-PL 68
40/50 hp Experimental Chassis of the 'Silver
Ghost' type Post 1914/18 War
Chassis No. 1 EX 35
Chassis No. 2 EX 35
Chassis No. 3 EX 36, 73
Chassis No. 4 EX 36, 37
Chassis No. 5 EX 37, 38
Chassis No. 6 EX 38
'New Phantom' 15, 29, 41, 44, 60, 69, 71, 89,
90, 97, 99, 100, 112, 113
Announcement of:- 73
Experimental Chassis 7 EX 74, 75, 113
E.A.C. or Eastern 8 EX 75

Armoured Car. (Code name). 9 EX 75
                            10 EX (CJ Special)
76-79
                 11 EX 80, 81
                 12 EX 81, 115
                 14 EX 81
                 15 EX 81, 83
                 16 EX 83-87
                 17 EX 87,88
Production Chassis 74 SC. 101-104
                    53 DC. 104-106
                    76 TC. 107, 108
                     1 OR. 108-110

Springfield built chassis No. 5154 FR. 110
Phantom II. 14, 29, 78, 79, 99-101, 111-172,
Experimental Chassis:- Code S.S. or 'Super
Sports'.   18 EX. 111-127
             19 EX. 127-129
             20 EX. 130
             21 EX. 130-131
             22 EX. 131-132
             23 EX. 132
             24 EX. 132-133
             25 EX. 133-135
             26 EX. 136-141
             27 EX. 142-143
             28 EX. 143-144
             29 EX. 144
             31 GX. 144-145

Production Chassis 1 WJ. 146-148
                    2 WJ. 146-148
                    3 WJ. 146-148
                    4 WJ. 146-148
                    5 WJ. 146-148
                   63 GN. 148, 149
                  167 GN. 148, 149
                   74 GN. 119, 150-157, 211
                    9 GX. 164-166
                  101 SK. 72, 141, 158-164,
                           211, 119
Phantom III. 14, 101, 104, 171-229
Experimental Chassis:- Code Name 'Spectre'.
30 EX. 173
31 EX. 173
32 EX. later became 3-DEX-202. 174-185
33 EX. later became 3-AEX-33. 185
34 EX. later became 3-AEX-34. 185-202
35 EX. later became 3-DEX-204. 203
36 EX. later became 3-AEX-36. 203, 204
37 EX. later became 3-AEX-37. 204
38 EX. later became 3-AEX-38. 204
39 EX. Body mounted on 3-DL-152. 205-209

Production Chassis 3-AZ-38. 220-221
                    3-AZ-43. 218
                    3-AZ-146. 68, 71, 119, 156,
                             210-217
                    3-AZ-186. 221-224
                    3-AX-195. 218
                    3-DL-76. 108, 221
                    3-DL-86. 221
                    3-DL-94. 219

The Model intended to replace the Phantom III:-
Code Name 'Big Bertha'. 205, 225, 226
20 hp. 29, 33, 37, 55, 70, 74, 81, 89, 95, 98,
101, 111, 119, 143, 164
20/25 hp. 29, 110, 119, 134, 143, 159, 164,
168, 172, 211, 214
25/30 hp. 29, 225
Wraith. 29
Peregrine. 168, 172
Bentley Mark VI. 226
R.R. type 'Flying Spur'. 186
'Silver Dawn'. 226

Index to Coachbuilders, whose Bodies were mounted on Rolls-Chassis mentioned in Text

Other Makes of Automobiles mentioned in the Text

Index to Ships mentioned in Text

Rolls-Royce Chassis Prints

Four drawings appear overleaf covering the Silver Ghost, 'New Phantom', Phantom II and Phantom III chassis. These are copies of the Rolls-Royce factory drawings which were supplied to the various coachbuilders which built bodies on their chassis

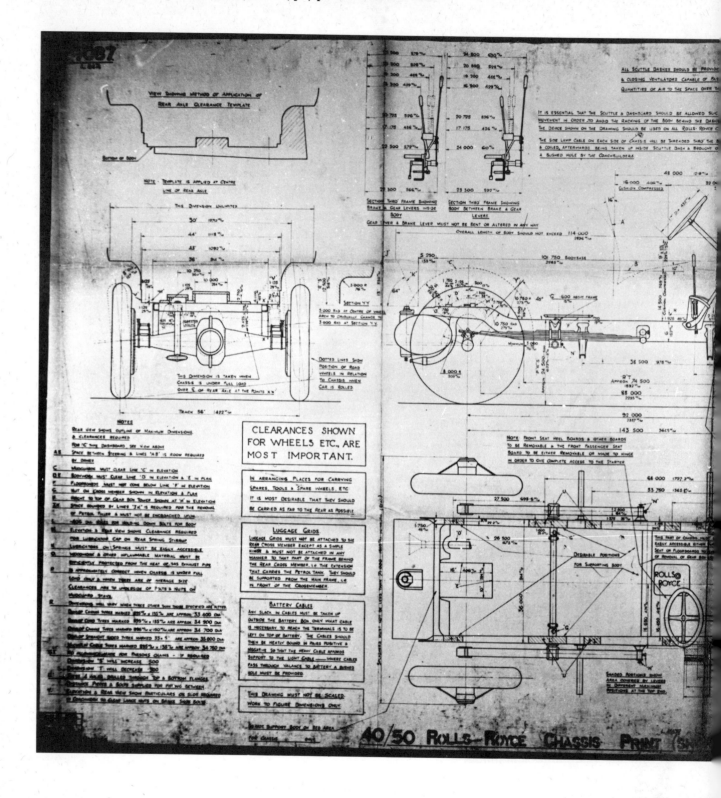

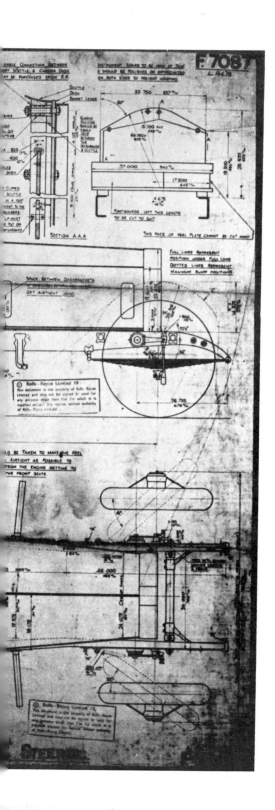

F.7087
L.1478

INSTRUMENT BOARD TO BE MADE OF TEAK
& SHOULD BE POLISHED OR IMPREGNATED
ON BOTH SIDES TO PREVENT WARPING

ENSIBLE CONNECTION BETWEEN
DY SCUTTLE & CARBON DASH
AY BE PURCHASED FROM R.R.

SCUTTLE
DASH
BONNET LEDGE

60°

33.750 857 %

15.750 RAD
388 %
60.750±
878 %

37.000 940 %

17.500
445 %

4.675
⅛

FOOTBOARDS LEFT THIS LENGTH
TO BE CUT TO SUIT

SECTION A.A.A

THIS FACE OF HEEL PLATE CANNOT BE CUT AWAY

FULL LINES REPRESENT
POSITION UNDER FULL LOAD
DOTTED LINES REPRESENT
MAXIMUM BUMP POSITIONS

SPACE BETWEEN DASHBRACKETS
GET AIRTIGHT JOINT

C

1.900
46 %
225°

76.725
879 %

Rolls - Royce Limited 19
This document is the property of Rolls-Royce
Limited and may not be copied or used for
any purpose other than that for which it is
supplied without the express written authority
of Rolls-Royce Limited.

LD BE TAKEN TO MAKE THE HEEL
AIRTIGHT AS POSSIBLE TO
FROM THE ENGINE GETTING TO
THE FRONT SEATS.

46.000
46 %

Rolls - Royce Limited 19
This document is the property of Rolls-Royce
Limited and may not be copied or used for
any purpose other than that for which it is
supplied without the express written authority
of Rolls-Royce Limited.

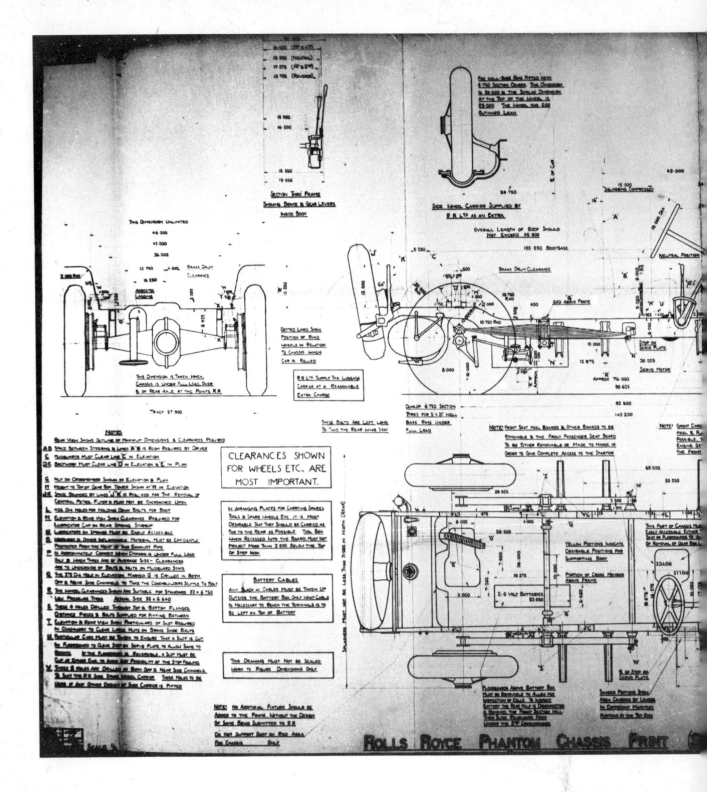

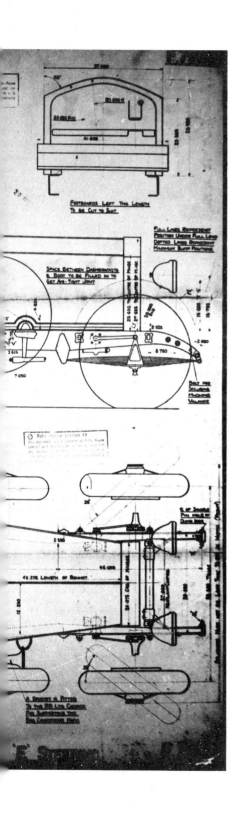

FOOTBOARDS LEFT THIS LENGTH
TO BE CUT TO SUIT

FULL LINES REPRESENT
POSITION UNDER FULL LOAD
DOTTED LINES REPRESENT
MAXIMUM BUMP POSITIONS

SPACE BETWEEN DASHBOARDS
& BODY TO BE FILLED IN TO
GET AIR-TIGHT JOINT

BOLT FOR
SECURING
MACHINED
VALANCE

LENGTH OF BONNET

A BRACKET IS FITTED
TO THE DASH LIKE CORNER
FOR SUPPORTING THE
END CONDENSER HEAD

'E' STEERING

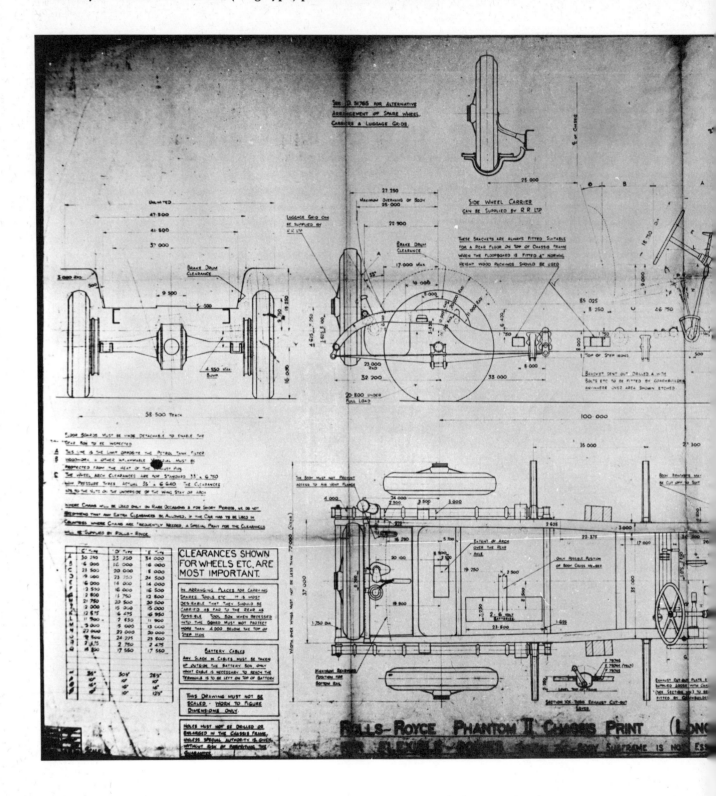

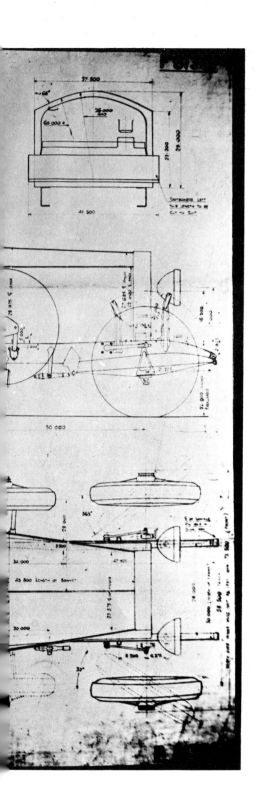

Rolls-Royce Phantom III Chassis print number F88227

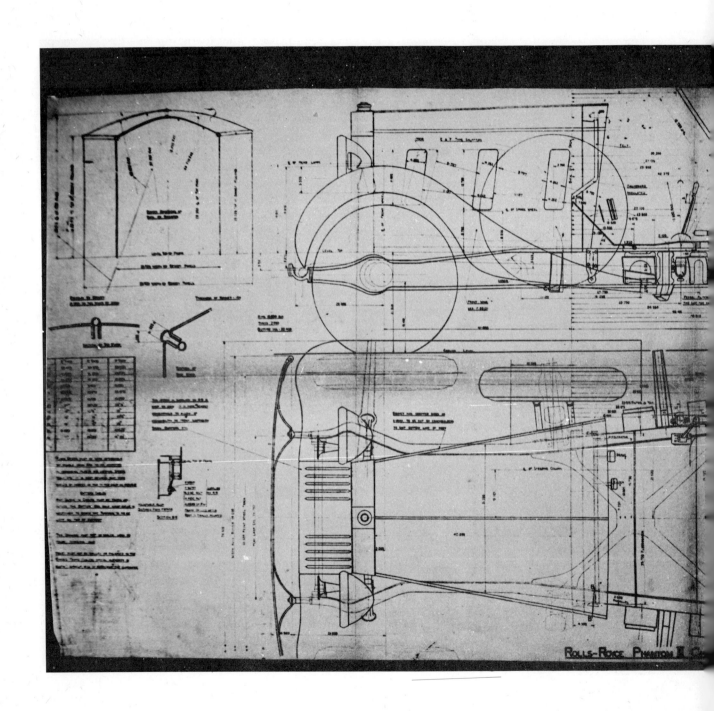

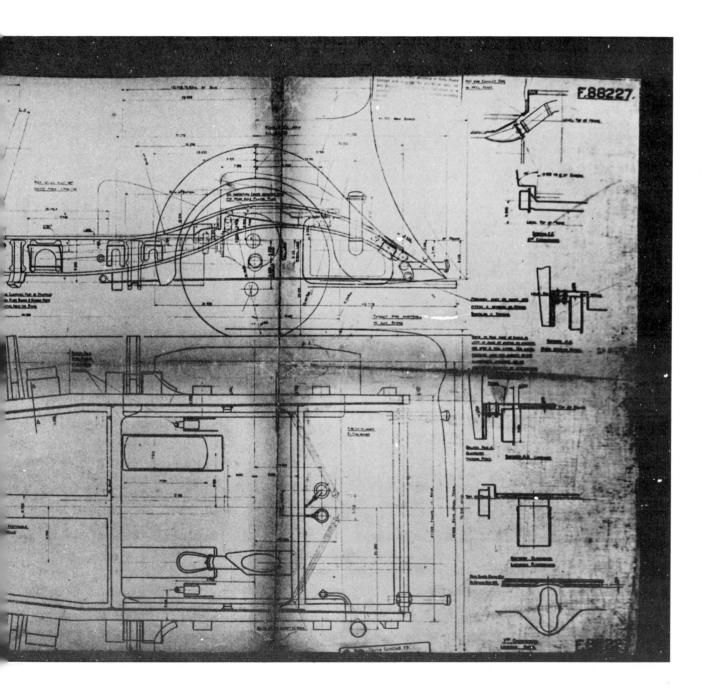

F.88227.